AF352653

Syntax-Prosody in Optimality Theory

# Syntax-Prosody in Optimality Theory

## Theory and Analyses

Edited by
Jennifer Bellik, Junko Ito,
Nick Kalivoda, and Armin Mester

SHEFFIELD UK    BRISTOL CT

Published by Equinox Publishing Ltd.

UK: Office 415, The Workstation, 15 Paternoster Row, Sheffield, South Yorkshire S1 2BX
USA: ISD, 70 Enterprise Drive, Bristol, CT 06010

www.equinoxpub.com

First published 2023



British Library Cataloguing-in-Publication Data

A catalogue record for this book is available from the British Library.

ISBN-13 978 1 80050 275 8 (hardback)
        978 1 80050 276 5 (ePDF)
        978 1 80050 358 8 (ePub)

Library of Congress Cataloging-in-Publication Data
Names: Bellik, Jennifer, editor. | Itō, Junko, editor. | Kalivoda, Nick
   (Researcher in linguistics), editor. | Mester, Armin, editor.
Title: Syntax-prosody in optimality theory : theory and analyses / edited
   by Jennifer Bellik, Junko Ito, Nick Kalivoda, and Armin Mester.
Description: Sheffield, South Yorkshire ; Bristol, CT : Equinox Publishing
   Ltd, 2023. | Series: Advances in optimality theory | Includes
   bibliographical references and index. | Summary: "This volume presents a
   series of complete analyses of the syntax-prosody interface, thanks to
   their use of the Syntax-Prosody in Optimality Theory (SPOT) application.
   This JavaScript application, developed by the editors of this volume,
   automates candidate generation and constraint evaluation, making a
   rigorous Optimality Theory analysis of syntax-prosody possible"--
   Provided by publisher.
Identifiers: LCCN 2022051981 (print) | LCCN 2022051982 (ebook) | ISBN
   9781800502758 (hardback) | ISBN 9781800502765 (ePDF) | ISBN
   9781800503588 (ePub)
Subjects: LCSH: Optimality theory (Linguistics) | Grammar, Comparative and
   general--Syntax. | Prosodic analysis (Linguistics) | LCGFT: Essays.
Classification: LCC P158.42 .S96 2023  (print) | LCC P158.42  (ebook) | DDC
   415--dc23/eng/20230310
LC record available at https://lccn.loc.gov/2022051981
LC ebook record available at https://lccn.loc.gov/2022051982

Typeset by Sparks – www.sparkspublishing.com

# Contents

# Acknowledgements

We would like to thank Richard Bibbs, Dan Brodkin, Benjamin Eischens, and especially Nicholas Van Handel for their contributions to ensuring the correctness and clarity of the chapters in this volume. Thanks are also due to Birgit Alber, Eirini Apostolopoulou, Ryan Bennett, Natalie Delbusso, Emily Elfner, Joachim Kokkelmans, Nazarré Merchant, Alan Prince, Tor Håvard Solhaug, and Natalie Weber, for their many helpful comments.

The research in this book was supported by NSF grant #1749368 to Junko Ito and Armin Mester.

# Chapter 1

# Syntax-Prosody in Optimality Theory (SPOT)

Jennifer Bellik, Junko Ito, Nick Kalivoda, and Armin Mester

## 1.1    Introduction

In syntax–prosody mapping, a syntactic tree S maps to a prosodic tree P, and the constituent structure of P defines the domains of phonological processes. While P is typically based on S, the two trees are not always isomorphic; mismatches can occur, and these are often attributable to purely phonological pressures like eurhythmy and length. Syntax–prosody mapping is therefore particularly amenable to analysis within Optimality Theory (OT; Prince and Smolensky 1993/2004), with mapping constraints (analogous to faithfulness constraints) favoring perfect syntax–prosody isomorphism, and prosodic markedness constraints that sometimes demand deviation from perfect matching. Syntactic trees serve as inputs, and are mapped to outputs in the form of prosodic trees. The study of syntax-prosody in OT has proved extremely fruitful, and this book continues in this research tradition.

As our understanding of Optimality Theory has advanced, increasing emphasis has been placed on the need to consider all candidates admitted by GEN, and to evaluate them against all constraints contained in CON (Prince 2017a,b among many others). In syntax–prosody mapping, achieving this level of rigor has long proved daunting, since the number of possible prosodic outputs for a given input can be immense. Depending on the details of GEN, there may be thousands of candidates for how to prosodify even a simple sentence.

The papers in this book rise to meet this challenge by using an open-source JavaScript application called SPOT ("Syntax-Prosody in Optimality

Theory"), developed as part of a collaborative research project with the same name in the Linguistics Department at the University of California, Santa Cruz, funded by National Science Foundation Grant #1749368. The SPOT application allows the user to rigorously investigate mapping from syntactic to prosodic structure by automating the generation of syntactic and prosodic trees according to customizable GEN specifications, and by automating constraint violation counting, given a customizable constraint set CON. SPOT news and information are available at the SPOT website (http://spot.sites.ucsc.edu), which links to the web application and codebase. SPOT produces violation tableaux which can be viewed in the browser or downloaded and imported into OTWorkplace (Prince, Merchant, and Tesar 2007–2020) or other OT tools for further analysis.

This chapter is structured as follows: §1.2 provides background information on syntax–prosody mapping; §1.3 introduces Optimality Theory; and §1.4 provides an overview of the book.

## 1.2    Syntax-prosody background

This section discusses the theoretical backdrop of syntax–prosody mapping, covering Prosodic Hierarchy Theory (§1.2.2) and Align and Match Theory (§1.2.2). It also introduces tree vocabulary and labeled diagrams in §1.2.3, and forms of syntax-prosody mismatches in §1.2.4.

### 1.2.1    Prosodic Hierarchy Theory

There are two major approaches to the syntax-phonology interface: direct and indirect reference theories (Inkelas 1990; see Elordieta 2008 for detailed summary and discussion). According to direct reference theories, phonological processes are directly sensitive to syntactic structure. Indirect reference theories, by contrast, maintain that the effect of syntax on phonology is mediated by purely prosodic structures derived from syntactic trees, but not necessarily isomorphic to them, and impoverished of much information such as lexical category and other purely syntactic features.

The papers in this book assume indirect reference, and in particular Prosodic Hierarchy Theory (Selkirk 1980 and subsequent work, see Elordieta 2008). The main claim of this theory is that phonological representations are organized in hierarchical tree structures built from a small set of prosodic categories. While the precise inventory of prosodic categories is a matter of debate, we follow Ito and Mester (2009a) in restricting them to the intonational phrase ($\iota$), the phonological phrase ($\varphi$), the prosodic word ($\omega$), the foot (ft), and the syllable ($\sigma$). The first three of these, $\iota$, $\varphi$, and $\omega$, are interface categories which reflect aspects of syntactic structure, while the foot and the syllable are sub-word rhythmic categories. The papers in this book focus almost exclusively on the interface categories.

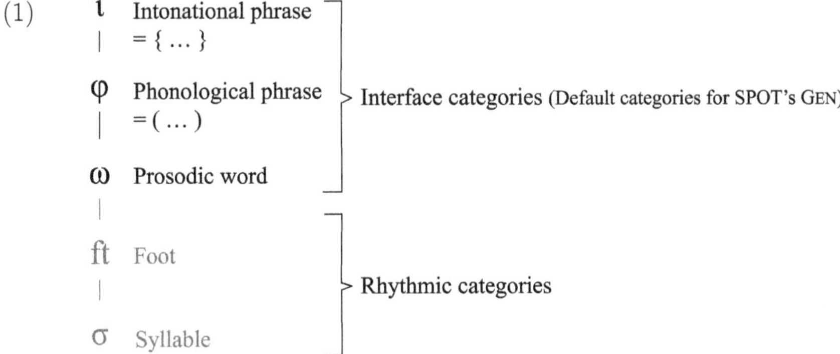


(1)

As its name implies, the prosodic hierarchy imposes a hierarchical structure on the inventory of prosodic categories: the intonational phrase ι is higher than the phonological phrase φ, which in turn is higher than the prosodic word ω. According to Layeredness, which we take to be an inviolable principle of phonological representation, a prosodic category cannot dominate a category that is higher on the prosodic hierarchy. This rules out structures in which an ω dominates a φ or ι, or a φ dominates an ι.

Layeredness is one component of what Selkirk (1984) dubbed the Strict Layer Hypothesis (SLH; also known as Strict Layering), which imposes additional requirements on prosodic trees. According to Strict Layering, the principle of Exhaustivity requires every node of level $i$ of the prosodic hierarchy to be dominated by a node of level $i + 1$ (unless $i$ is itself the highest level in the hierarchy, in which case a node of level $i$ is the root node of the tree). With a hierarchy ι $> φ > ω >$ ft $> σ$, Exhaustivity requires that every σ be contained in a ft; every ft in an ω; every ω in a φ; and every φ in an ι. A second component of the SLH is a ban on prosodic recursion, Non-recursivity. This principle demands that no node dominate another node of the same prosodic category; no φ may dominate a φ, etc.

While Layeredness is still broadly assumed, Exhaustivity and Non-recursivity have more recently been demoted from their status as inviolable conditions on representations, and have instead become violable constraints (Truckenbrodt 1999, Ito and Mester 2009a). In Optimality-Theoretic (OT) terms, they are no longer taken to be conditions on GEN, but constraints in CON, the universal constraint set. Thus, while a prosodic category of level $i$ is still unable to dominate one of a category greater than $i$ (Layeredness), it may immediately dominate one at a level less than $i - 1$ (violating Exhaustivity) or at level $i$ (violating Non-recursivity). For instance, an $\omega$ may be immediately dominated by an $\iota$ instead of a $\varphi$; a $\varphi$ may dominate another $\varphi$; etc. The proposal that such prosodic trees are admissible is known as the Weak Layer Hypothesis, or Weak Layering (Ito and Mester 2003).

Many papers in this volume adopt some form of Weak Layering when defining GEN for the OT systems they consider. Details of implementation vary, but are always stated precisely in the definition of GEN. Cao, Bibbs, and Bellik (Chapter 9) are a notable exception, as they explore several systems with Strict Layering in their analysis of Xiamen Chinese. Tarlov (Chapter 3) also studies two systems with Strict Layering, comparing them to minimally different systems with Weak Layering. Shingler and Bellik (Chapter 2) consider several gradations between Strict and Weak Layering, which are possible settings for GEN in the SPOT application (Bellik, Bellik, and Kalivoda 2015–2021).

While Prosodic Hierarchy Theory posits a universal hierarchy of prosodic categories (or at least *available* prosodic categories), these categories have different phonological reflexes in different languages. According to Selkirk (1980), prosodic constituents are domains for phonological processes, which can be classified as domain span rules, domain juncture rules, and domain limit rules. These are phonological processes which may occur throughout a domain, at the border between two domains of the same category, or simply at the left or right edge of a domain. Each category of the prosodic hierarchy has been identified as the domain for a wide range of phonological phenomena in diverse languages. For instance, Tarlov (Chapter 3) follows Bickmore (1989, 1990) in identifying the $\varphi$ as the domain of High Tone Deletion in Kinyambo, and Cao, Bibbs, and Bellik (Chapter 9) follow Chen (1987) in treating the $\varphi$ in Xiamen Chinese as the domain of tone sandhi. Sometimes prosodic structure is diagnosed not by an overt segmental or tonal process like these, but by the alignment of some element to a domain edge. This is exemplified by Bibbs' (Chapter 8) treatment of weak pronoun placement in Chamorro, based on work by Chung (2003).

The advent of Weak Layering, and in particular the loosening of the Non-recursivity requirement of Strict Layering, opened the door to analyses in terms of recursive prosodic domains. In a structure like $(_\varphi \, (_\varphi \, \omega_1 \, \omega_2) \, \omega_3)$, a phonological process that marks the left edge of a $\varphi$ will apply to $\omega_1$, while a process that marks the right edge of a $\varphi$ will apply both to $\omega_2$ and to $\omega_3$. With Strict Layering, such behavior would be deeply mysterious; in a strictly layered structure, $\omega_2$ and $\omega_3$ could not both be at right $\varphi$-edges without a left $\varphi$-edge between them as well. Strong evidence for such structures is rare, since for many languages, researchers have only identified evidence for one edge of a given prosodic constituent: left or right. However, several languages indicate that such structures are indeed necessary. On Truckenbrodt's (1995, 1999) reanalysis of Odden's (1987) data from Kimatuumbi, a φ-final ω is immune to vowel shortening, which applies elsewhere, and the left edge of every non-utterance-initial φ is preceeded by a high tone, which docks to the last word of the preceding φ. With this interpretation, Kimatuumbi displays phonological phrases of the form $(_\varphi (_\varphi \omega_1 \omega_2) \omega_3)$. Structures of this type are also proposed by Selkirk (2011) for Xitsonga (with data from Kisseberth 1994 as well as Cassimjee and Kisseberth 1998), with evidence from High Tone Spread within the φ.

Truckenbrodt's reanalysis of Kimatuumbi and Selkirk's reanalysis of Xitsonga are instances of the simplest assumption about the interpretation of recursive prosodic categories: every category of level $i$ has the same phonological consequences, regardless of whether it contains or is contained by another category of level $i$. But Ito and Mester (2007, 2009a, 2009b) have pointed out that we can differentiate prosodic categories based on their minimality and maximality. A minimal prosodic category π is one that does not dominate another π, and a maximal π is one that is not dominated by another π. Thus, in trees containing prosodic recursion, nodes may be identified not only by their prosodic category, but also by the features [±minimal] and [±maximal], which freely cross-classify. Ito and Mester observe that if phonological processes can be sensitive not only to prosodic category labels, but also to these features, then we can attribute divergent phonological phenomena to prosodic categories of the same level of the prosodic hierarchy, but at different levels in the tree. For instance, Ito and Mester (2009b) propose that in Japanese, the maximal φ is the domain of downstep, while the left edge of every φ is the locus of initial rise. Taking up this notion, Elfner (2012, 2015) proposes that the left edge of every non-minimal φ is marked by an LH tonal complex in Irish, while the right edge of every φ is marked by HL. Both of these analyses are discussed by Kalivoda, in Chapters 7 and 4, respectively.

Prosodic recursion, plus minimality and maximality features, allows Ito and Mester to propose a prosodic hierarchy with only three interface categories: $\iota > \varphi > \omega$. This is a significant reduction in the number of prosodic categories when compared to earlier proposals (Selkirk 1980, Nespor and Vogel 1986) assuming an utterance category above $\iota$ and a clitic group above ω. In Japanese, the domain of downstep has been identified with a Major Phrase and the domain of initial rise with a Minor Phrase (McCawley 1968, Haraguchi 1977, Poser 1984, Kubozono 1988, Pierrehumbert and Beckman 1988, Selkirk and Tateishi 1988, etc.). All of these categories can be reduced to $\iota$, φ, and ω with different values for minimality and maximality. The utterance can be reinterpreted as the maximal ι; the clitic group as the maximal ω; the Major Phrase as the maximal φ; and the Minor Phrase as the minimal φ. The papers in this book all employ Ito and Mester's prosodic hierarchy, though the main theoretical points of each chapter would remain intact if more prosodic categories turned out to indeed be needed, as argued for instance by Vogel (2009).

### 1.2.2    Align Theory and Match Theory

As mentioned above, prosody mirrors syntax imperfectly. Under Align Theory (Chen 1987, Selkirk 1986, Truckenbrodt 1999), the mapping process itself yields mismatches, and there is no pressure for prosody to be perfectly isomorphic to syntax. By contrast, under Match Theory (Selkirk 2011), the mapping process demands that the prosodic structure be isomorphic to the syntactic structure, and mismatches come from purely phonological factors. Align Theory and Match Theory are the dominant OT approaches to syntax–prosody mapping, and we introduce them here because they feature prominently in most of the chapters of this volume.

Align Theory grew out of Selkirk's (1986) pre-OT end-based theory, in which phonology is sensitive only to the ends of syntactic constituents. This edge-oriented approach to syntax–prosody mapping is implemented in Optimality Theory through constraints like AlignLeft($X_{Lex}$, ω) (WdCon in Selkirk 1996), AlignRight(XP, φ), and AlignRight(Focus, φ) (Truckenbrodt 1999), connecting to Generalized Alignment (McCarthy and Prince 1993). These constraints typically require the $d$ (direction: left or right) edge of a syntactic constituent $s$ to be mapped to a corresponding $d$ edge of a prosodic constituent $p$ of the correct category. Multiple syntactic edges can be mapped to a single prosodic edge. In this framework, languages are understood to typically prioritize mapping of one edge over the other. For example, in Zulu, right edges of CPs are generally mapped to right edges of ι, but left edges of CPs are not mapped to left edges of ι (Cheng and Downing 2007); this can be modeled with a constraint ranking AlignRight(CP, ι) ≫ X ≫ AlignLeft(CP, ι), where X is a constraint that conflicts with mapping both edges simultaneously, such as NonRecursivity. Other work in this edge-based framework (Truckenbrodt 1995, 1999) also introduced a cohesional constraint Wrap(XP), which demands that each XP be contained in a phonological phrase. It conflicts with Align(XP) when the syntactic input contains recursive XPs and the prosodic output does not. For example, Wrap(XP) objects to the non-recursive parse $[_{XP1}\ XP_2\ X_1] \rightarrow (XP_2)(X_1)$, which satisfies AlignRight(XP, φ), but not to the isomorphic recursive parse $[_{XP1}\ XP_2\ X_1] \rightarrow ((XP_2)\ X_1)$, which also satisfies AlignRight(XP, φ).

It is common for analyses employing Align Theory to consider only non-recursive and exhaustively parsed prosodic representations (Selkirk 2000, Cheng and Downing 2007)—that is, it is common for them to adopt Strict Layering, explicitly or implicitly. Strictly layered structures can fully satisfy both AlignLeft and AlignRight without being isomorphic to the syntax, as in (2), where every left XP edge has a corresponding left $\varphi$-edge, and likewise for right edges.

(2)    $[_{XP}\ [_{XP}\ A]\ [_{XP}\ [_{XP}\ B]\ C]]$
       (          ) (          ) (  )

Selkirk (2011) introduced a new indirect reference theory of the relationship between syntax and prosody: Match Theory. According to Match Theory, prosody is sensitive not only to syntactic edges, but to syntactic constituents. Therefore, constraints on syntax–prosody mapping are fully satisfied only when prosody is isomorphic to syntax. Selkirk's (2011) original formulation of Match constraints referred simultaneously to left and right edges, similar to a combination of AlignLeft and AlignRight. Elfner (2012) reformulated Match constraints to refer to the set of terminals contained in a constituent, rather than referring to edges. We adopt Elfner's definitions of Match throughout this volume; these versions of the Match constraints ensure that reordering terminals in prosody (see Bennett et al. 2016) does not alter the correspondence between a syntactic and prosodic constituent. In (3), for example, a Match(XP, $\varphi$) constraint that referred to both left and right edges would be violated for the vP, because there is no $\varphi$ that has *é* at its left edge and *scoile* at its right edge. But a terminal-based Match(XP, $\varphi$) implementation is satisfied for vP, because there is a $\varphi$ that contains all and only the set of terminals {*é, fhad, le, teach, na, scoile*}, even though they are not in the same order in the prosody as they are in the syntax.

(3)      $[_{\Sigma P}$ thug $[_{DP}$ mo mháthair] $[_{vP}\ [_{DP}$ é] $[_{PP}$ fhad le teach na scoile]]]
         (   thug     mo mháthair) (  (          fhad le teach na scoile)   é)
                          Bennett, Elfner, and McCloskey 2016 (70b)

Align Theory has been argued to have been superseded by Match Theory (Selkirk 2011), but has since been shown to still be needed in order to capture asymmetries in syntax–prosody mapping (Bellik et al. 2022).

Match Theoretic analyses normally include one syntax-to-prosody mapping constraint, and one prosody-to-syntax mapping constraint. Align Theoretic analyses, however, normally include two (or three, if Wrap is included) syntax-to-prosody mapping constraints and no prosody-to-syntax mapping constraints (though see Cheng and Downing 2016 for a counter-example). Since having more constraints inevitably increases the size of the predicted typology, Align systems tend to generate larger typologies than Match systems, as will be illustrated in Chapter 3.

### 1.2.3 *Tree vocabulary and labeled diagrams*

In the domain of syntax–prosody mapping, inputs are syntactic trees and outputs are prosodic trees. A candidate is a pair ⟨s-tree, p-tree⟩. This book frequently discusses trees and their structure, so we will briefly introduce several relevant terms that occur throughout the volume. The terms are illustrated below in (15). A tree, in the sense employed in linguistic representations, is a graph-theoretic object, consisting of labeled vertices (*nodes*) that are connected by edges (*branches*), in such a way that the structure contains no cycles. The trees we will be concerned with are rooted trees, in which the top node in the tree is designated as its *root*, and contains the rest of the tree. In the trees below, CP is the root of the syntactic tree on the left, and ι is the root of the prosodic tree on the right. Every branch in a rooted tree connects a *parent* node (closer to the root) with a *child* node (farther from the root). Parents will always be depicted above their children. Children in a tree that share an immediate parent are called *sisters*, as is standard in linguistics, though not in graph theory. No child node will have multiple parents, due to the requirement that a tree contain no cycles; there is only one path between any two nodes in the tree.

The trees we will be concerned with represent syntactic or prosodic structures. Nodes in syntactic trees are labeled with their syntactic category; the categories relevant to syntax–prosody mapping are CP, XP, and $X^0$. They may also be labeled with additional information, such as whether the projection is lexical or functional, or what type of syntactic phrase an XP is (noun, verb, adjective, etc.). Nodes in prosodic trees are labeled with a prosodic category drawn from the prosodic hierarchy in (1).

The *terminals* in a tree are the nodes that have no children, in this case, the $X^0$s and ωs. We sometimes also refer to the *terminal string*, as a way to reference all the segmental content of a tree or trees; the sample trees in (4) have the same terminal string, *that dog barks* (non-branching XPs are depicted here as $X^0$s for visual simplicity). Sometimes we extend the botanical analogy of the tree by calling the terminals in a prosodic tree *leaves*; this term is standard in graph theory, though not widely used in linguistics. Finally, we refer to a non-root node that is the sole child of the root as the tree's *stem*. Unlike the other terms introduced here, 'stem" is not standard vocabulary in either linguistics or graph theory.

(4)

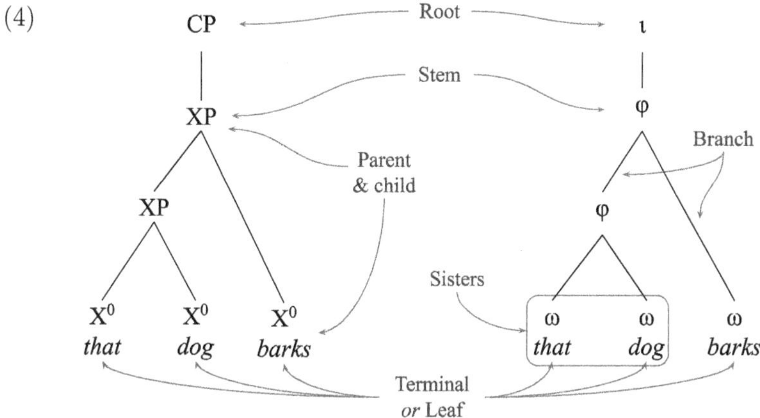

### 1.2.4    *Forms of syntax-prosody mismatches*

A key theme in this book is mismatches between syntactic and prosodic structure. There are numerous ways for the prosodic structure to diverge from the syntactic structure that it corresponds to. In (5) and (6), we list particular forms of syntax-prosody mismatch that recur throughout the book.

(5)     *Strong mismatch* (cf. Kalivoda 2018, p. 39), or *rebracketing*:

- A strong mismatch occurs when the syntactic tree contains two terminals $a$ and $b$ that belong to a syntactic constituent to the exclusion of some additional terminal $z$, while the corresponding prosodic tree instead contains a prosodic constituent containing $b$ and $z$ to the exclusion of $a$, or $a$ and $z$ to the exclusion of $b$.

- The prosodic tree in this scenario contains a correspondentless constituent whose brackets would cross those of the missing syntactic constituent.

For example, the mapping $[[[a\ b]\ c]\ d] \rightarrow ((a\ b)(c\ d))$, as in Japanese (Chapter 4), is an example of a strong mismatch, where we find crossing brackets: $[_{\text{XP}}\ a\ b\ (_{\varphi}\ c\ _{\text{XP}}]\ d\ _{\varphi})$. The syntax contains a constituent $[a\ b\ c]$, which excludes $d$, while the prosody instead contains the constituent $(c\ d)$, which parses $c$ and $d$ together while excluding $a$ and $b$.

We refer to mismatches that are not strong, or do not involve rebracketing, as weak mismatches. This term is employed descriptively in Kalivoda (2018, p. 39) without a formal definition. Weak mismatches typically come in three flavors, as in (6).

(6)       *Weak mismatches* (cf. Kalivoda 2018, p. 39)

      a.     *Category promotion* occurs when a syntactic constituent is mapped to a prosodic constituent that is too high in the PH to satisfy MATCH.

      b.     *Category demotion* occurs when a syntactic constituent is mapped to a prosodic constituent that is too low in the PH to satisfy MATCH. For example, when an XP is mapped to an ω.

      c.     *Flattening* occurs when the prosodic tree is shallower than the syntactic tree.

For example, in [[[a b] c] d] → (a b c d), the syntactic tree is three levels deep, but the prosodic tree has been flattened and has only one level. It lacks the substructure present in the syntactic tree. A less extreme version is the mapping [[[a b] c] d] → ((a b) c d), which we refer to as *partial flattening*, or sometimes *squishing*. These are all mismatches in which one or more syntactic constituent has no prosodic correspondent.


## 1.3     Optimality Theory

This section introduces OT systems and Property Theory in §1.3.1 and §1.3.2, respectively, and the computational tools SPOT and OTWorkplace in §1.3.3.


### 1.3.1    OT systems

The papers in this volume all deal with precisely defined Optimality-Theoretic *systems* in the sense of Alber et al. (2016) and Prince (2017a,b). An OT system S is a formal object ⟨S.GEN, S.CON⟩, in which S.GEN determines a set of candidate sets (csets) and S.CON is a constraint set (i.e., a set of functions from the candidates of S.GEN to the non-negative integers). Every system S gives rise to a factorial typology S.Typ, which can be viewed both extensionally as a set of languages and intensionally as the grammars associated with those languages. While S.CON is necessarily finite, S.GEN need not be; a system can admit finitely or infinitely many csets, and each cset may include finitely or infinitely many candidates.

Explicitly spelling out GEN and CON for an OT system is necessitated by the definition of optimality itself. As Prince (2017a) points out, for a candidate to be optimal according to a constraint hierarchy, it must win out against *all* of the competitors in its candidate set. To determine whether a candidate beats all of its competitors, we need to know exactly what all of its competitors are, i.e., we must have a fully explicit GEN function (or simply an exhaustive list of candidates). Further, as Prince (2017a) puts it, "Comparison polls the judgment of all constraints," meaning that every constraint in CON must be specified, and must assign a violation count to every candidate. Without these pieces in place, the concept of optimality in OT loses meaning. These assumptions are at least tacitly in the background of all work in OT, dating back to Prince and Smolensky (1993/2004), but only more recent work has embraced full explicitness. The papers in this book strive for perfect clarity in system definitions.

While the details of S.GEN and S.CON vary across systems, all of the systems in this book share certain characteristics. On the GEN side, all candidates are input–output mappings in which the input is a syntactic tree made up of syntactic clauses, phrases, and words, and the output is a prosodic tree made up of prosodic categories like intonational phrases, phonological phrases, and phonological words, as in (1) above.

In terms of CON, every system in this volume involves syntax-to-prosody and/or prosody-to-syntax *mapping constraints* (analogous to faithfulness constraints) as well as purely prosodic *markedness constraints.* Mapping constraints include MATCH constraints and ALIGN constraints that refer both to syntactic and prosodic categories. Markedness constraints include constraints like various versions of STRONGSTART, EQUALSISTERS, and BINARITY. Several chapters (Tarlov Chapter 3, Kalivoda Chapter 4, Bibbs Chapter 8, Cao et al. Chapter 9) compare the predictions of the two main approaches to syntax–prosody mapping in OT: Match Theory and Alignment Theory (see §1.2). The contrast between these two theories arises only in the realm of mapping constraints; both share basic assumptions about GEN and markedness constraints. Other chapters (Bellik and Van Handel Chapter 10, Bellik Chapter 11) explore systems that differ only in terms of the markedness constraints included in CON, while Van Handel et al. (Chapter 5) examine systems that employ different types of MATCH constraints.

In all chapters, the concept of the *factorial typology* is central, even when the authors have the narrower aim of accounting for the facts from one particular language. For each system S, the authors have calculated the typology S.Typ using OTWorkplace (Prince, Merchant, and Tesar 2007–2020), a software for OT calculations. Given the importance of factorial typologies in this book, it is worth elucidating the concept in more detail.

Following Prince (2017a), we define a *language* as the collection of candidates that emerge as optimal under a given constraint hierarchy. Extensionally speaking, S.Typ is the set of languages admitted by S. Which languages make up S.Typ is determined by considering all possible rankings of the constraints in S.CON. Each linear order of the constraints in S.CON selects a particular set of optima, selecting one or more optima from each cset given by S.GEN. Selection of optima according to a constraint hierarchy proceeds by the usual process of OT candidate filtration. For details, see Prince and Smolensky (1993/2004) and Prince (2017a).

Each language in a factorial typology has an associated *grammar*. OT grammars can be stated in two different ways (Merchant and Prince, to appear). On the one hand, grammars are sets of all constraint rankings that deliver the same language. Merchant and Prince call the individual rankings within a ranking grammar *linear extensions of the grammar*, or *legs*. Grammars stated as sets of legs are called *ranking grammars*. Alternatively, an OT grammar can be viewed as a collection of *elementary ranking conditions* (ERCs; Prince 2002a,b), i.e., as an *ERC grammar*. The ERCs of an ERC grammar delineate the exact criteria for a leg's membership in a language's ranking grammar. A system's factorial typology, at an intensional level, is its set of grammars, whether viewed as ranking grammars or ERC grammars.

### 1.3.2   Property Theory

In many chapters, the interest in calculating a system's factorial typology lies (at least partially) in proving that the typology contains or does not contain a pattern associated with a particular language, such as Kinyambo (Tarlov Chapter 3), Irish (Kalivoda Chapter 4), Japanese (Kalivoda Chapter 7), Chamorro (Bibbs Chapter 8), or Xiamen Chinese (Cao et al. Chapter 9). The authors then go on to analyze the language's grammar, discussing all of the crucial rankings involved by presenting elementary ranking conditions (or if the language is not present in the typology, they discuss why this is so).

Several chapters, however, treat factorial typologies as objects of study in themselves, using the tools of Property Theory (Alber et al. 2016; DelBusso 2018, Alber and Prince 2021), a theory of the structure of OT typologies. The authors that use Property Theory are Tarlov (Chapter 3), Kalivoda (Chapter 4, Chapter 7), Bellik and Van Handel (Chapter 10), and Bellik (Chapter 11).

The basic claim of Property Theory is that an OT typology can be analyzed using *properties*, which are ranking conditions of a certain narrowly defined type. The grammars of a typology can be characterized by the *values* they take for the properties, and ideally, these are then associated with extensional *traits* in the corresponding languages. A *property analysis* of a typology is a set of properties which, taken together, completely characterize the grammars of the typology.

The most basic form of a property is A<>B, where A and B are individual constraints. Call this property P.a/b, where 'a" and 'b" are the values of the property. A grammar has the value P.a if A dominates B in all of its legs, and P.b if B dominates A in all of its legs. If A dominates B in some of the grammar's legs, while B dominates A in others, the property P.a/b is *moot* for the grammar. As an example, consider the typology of Tarlov's (Chapter 3) system Match.Rec. The system's constraint set, Match.Rec.Con, contains three constraints: sp.Match, m.BinMin, and m.BinMax. (The constraint prefix "sp" stands for "syntax-to-prosody," and "m" stands for "markedness".) The system's typology, Match.Rec.Typ, contains two languages: one in which unary φs are permitted (L.1), and one in which every φ must be branching (L.2). Expressed as ERCs, the grammars of the two languages are presented in the following comparative tableaux.

(7)      Comparative tableau for L.1 of Tarlov's (Chapter 3) Match.Rec

| Input | Winner | Loser | sp.Match | m.BinMin | m.BinMax |
|-------|--------|-------|----------|----------|----------|
| [[a][b]] | ((a)(b)) | (a b) | W | L | e |

(8)      Comparative tableau for L.2 of Tarlov's (Chapter 3) Match.Rec

| Input | Winner | Loser | sp.Match | m.BinMin | m.BinMax |
|-------|--------|-------|----------|----------|----------|
| [[a][b]] | (a b) | ((a)(b)) | L | W | e |

The comparative tableau in (7) shows that in L.1 of Match.Rec, sp.Match dominates m.BinMin. The 'W' under sp.Match indicates that this constraint favors the L.1 winner, [[a][b]] → ((a)(b)) over the L.1 loser, [[a][b]] → (a b). The 'L' under m.BinMin indicates that this constraint favors the loser over the winner. The 'e' under m.BinMax indicates that this constraint does not favor either the winner or the loser. The comparative tableau in (8) indicates that the opposite ranking holds in L.2, i.e., that m.BinMin dominates sp.Match.

The two ERC grammars in (7) and (8) are equivalent to the following ranking grammars:

(9)      Ranking grammar for L.1 of Tarlov's Match.Rec
    {[sp.Match ≫ m.BinMin ≫ m.BinMax],
    [sp.Match ≫ m.BinMax ≫ m.BinMin],
    [m.BinMax ≫ sp.Match ≫ m.BinMin]}

(10)     Ranking grammar for L.2 of Tarlov's Match.Rec
    {[m.BinMin ≫ sp.Match ≫ m.BinMax]
    [m.BinMin ≫ m.BinMax ≫ sp.Match],
    [m.BinMax ≫ m.BinMin ≫ sp.Match]}

The legs in (9) are the three legs compatible with the ERC in (7), while those in (10) are the legs compatible with the ERC in (8). In every leg in (9), sp.MATCH dominates m.BINMIN, and in every leg in (10), the opposite holds. This fact allows Tarlov to establish the property p.MapUnary:

(11)      Property for Tarlov's Match.Rec
          p.MapUnary: sp.MATCH $<>$ m.BINMIN
          *Values*: unary.allowed / unary.banned

L.1 has the property value *unary.allowed*, because sp.MATCH dominates m.BINMIN in every leg of its ranking grammar, while L.2 has the property value *unary.banned*, because m.BINMIN dominates sp.MATCH in every leg of its ranking grammar. Tarlov associates each of the intensional property values with an extensional trait. In a language with the value *unary.allowed*, a $\varphi$ can contain a single word, while in a language with the value *unary.banned*, a $\varphi$ must be branching.

Tarlov's p.MapUnary is an example of an elementary property, consisting of two constraints in opposition to one another, but properties can also be more complex, with one or more side consisting of a constraint class suffixed with an operator. The two possible operators are '.dom' and '.sub'. Suppose K is a set of constraints $\{C_1, C_2, ..., C_n\}$. For an individual leg $\lambda$, K.dom returns the highest ranked element of K in $\lambda$, while K.sub returns the lowest-ranked element of K in $\lambda$. For example, take a leg $\lambda_1 = [A \gg B \gg C]$ and a constraint set $J = \{A, B\}$. J.dom$(\lambda_1) = A$, and J.sub$(\lambda_1) = B$. By allowing either side of a property to take the form of a constraint class with a suffixed operator, we generalize the notion of property to allow for more complex typological analysis.

### 1.3.2.1   The .dom operator

As a concrete example of the usefulness of the '.dom' operator, consider a property from Kalivoda's system $SB_4$ in Chapter 7. This system's constraint set includes four constraints, which we abbreviate here as sp.MATCH, sp.ALIGN-L, sp.ALIGN-R, and m.BINMAX. The system's typology consists of four languages called Iso, Bal, EP.L, and EP.R. The grammars of these languages are shown in the following *skeletal bases*, special comparative tableaux which condense ERC grammars into their bare essentials (Brasoveanu and Prince 2011). The *e*-values are omitted for clarity.

(12)      Skeletal basis for Iso in Kalivoda's $SB_4$

| sp.Match | sp.Align-L | sp.Align-R | m.BinMax |
|----------|------------|------------|----------|
| W        |            | W          | L        |
| W        | W          |            | L        |

(13)      Skeletal basis for EP.L in Kalivoda's $SB_4$

| sp.Align-L | m.BinMax | sp.Match | sp.Align-R |
|------------|----------|----------|------------|
| W          | L        |          |            |
|            | W        | L        | L          |

(14)      Skeletal basis for EP.R in Kalivoda's $SB_4$

| sp.Align-R | m.BinMax | sp.Match | sp.Align-L |
|------------|----------|----------|------------|
| W          | L        |          |            |
|            | W        | L        | L          |

(15)      Skeletal basis for Bal in Kalivoda's $SB_4$

| m.BinMax | sp.Match | sp.Align-L | sp.Align-R |
|----------|----------|------------|------------|
| W        | L        | L          | L          |

In the Iso language of $SB_4$, all syntactic inputs map to perfectly matching prosodic outputs, while the other three languages all exhibit some amount of syntax-prosody non-isomorphism. Among the three languages that display non-isomorphism, EP.L and EP.R always preserve what Kalivoda calls their *main edge*, mapping the main edge of every XP to the main edge of some φ. In EP.L, this is the left edge, while in EP.R it is the right edge. These *edge-preserving* languages differ from the fourth language Bal, in that Bal maps syntactic structures to wildly mismatching prosodic structures, sometimes failing to align both the left and right edges of XPs. To distinguish the edge-preserving EP.L and EP.R on the one hand from the non-edge-preserving Bal on the other, Kalivoda introduces a property p.MainEdge.pres/del.

(16)      p.MainEdge.pres/del
          {sp.Align-L, sp.Align-R}.dom <> m.BinMax

EP.L and EP.R both have the value p.MainEdge.pres. In both, the *dominant* alignment constraint of the class {sp.Align-L, sp.Align-R} outranks m.BinMax, but which alignment constraint is dominant depends on the language. In EP.L, {sp.Align-L, sp.Align-R}.dom = sp.Align-L, and in EP.R, {sp.Align-L, sp.Align-R}.dom = sp.Align-R.

The ranking grammar of Bal in $SB_4$ contains all legs in which m.BinMax dominates the other three constraints. In some of these legs, sp.Align-L outranks sp.Align-R, while in others, the reverse holds. Bal has the value p.MainEdge.del because regardless of which alignment constraint is dominant in any one of its legs, m.BinMax dominates that alignment constraint.

The constraint class {sp.Align-L, sp.Align-R} in the above property is not simply arbitrary; it consists of the system's two constraints from the sp.Align family. And in fact, in Kalivoda's property analysis of $SB_4$, there is an additional property p.Align.L/R, which has the form sp.Align-L <> sp.Align-R. Since the constraints in the class {sp.Align-L, sp.Align-R} are exactly those from the property p.Align.L/R, they are what Alber and Prince (2021) call a *public class*, and in the property definition of p.MainEdge.pres/ del we can write {sp.Align-L, sp.Align-R}.dom as c.Align.dom, underscoring the fact that these constraints face off in a separate property.

### *1.3.2.2   The .sub operator*

Finally, to demonstrate the use of the "'.sub" operator, consider the third property from Kalivoda's property analysis of $SB_4$: p.Match.iso/mis.

(17)    p.Match.iso/mis
        {sp.Match, c.Align.sub}.dom <> m.BinMax

This separates the language Iso, with the value p.Match.iso, from the other three languages, with the value p.Match.mis. The left side of the property is a complex class: the *dominant* constraint in the class containing sp.Match and the *subordinate* alignment constraint. In other words, in every leg of Iso's ranking grammar, either sp.Match or *both* alignment constraints dominate m.BinMax. Iso's ranking grammar contains fourteen legs, among them [sp. Match ≫ m.BinMax ≫ sp.Align-L ≫ sp.Align-R], in which {sp.Match, c.Align.sub}.dom = sp.Match, and [sp.Align-L ≫ sp.Align-R ≫ m.BinMax ≫ sp.Match ], in which {sp.Match, c.Align.sub}.dom = sp.Align-R.

Additional information about Property Theory is provided in the chapters that make use of it. For a complete introduction to the theory, the interested reader is referred to Alber and Prince (2021).

### 1.3.3   SPOT and OTWorkplace

Defining an OT system for an analysis of syntax–prosody mapping entails defining a candidate set consisting of pairs of trees. For the sake of illustration, let us consider the candidate sets of two very simple OT systems, SL for Strict Layering and WL for Weak Layering. Both SL and WL will have a single input syntactic tree, for presentational simplicity. Let this input be a uniformly left-branching, binary syntactic tree with four terminals, as in (16).

(18)    Input to GEN in SL and WL: $[_{XP}\ [_{XP}\ [_{XP}\ a\ b]\ c]\ d]$

In the interest of simplicity, we define GEN for SL and for WL to differ in the output structures that they admit. The first system, SL, will admit any prosodic tree that conforms to Strict Layering and does not add, remove, or reorder any terminals relative to the input syntactic tree.

(19)    GEN.SL$(s)$ = {All $\langle s,\ p \rangle$ pairs such that $p$ fulfills the conditions in (a-f)}
   a.    $p$ is a tree rooted in an intonational phrase (ι).
   b.    All non-root, non-terminal nodes in $p$ are phonological phrases (φ).
   c.    All terminal nodes in $p$ are prosodic words (ω).
   d.    Each terminal in $p$ corresponds to a unique terminal in $s$, and each terminal in $s$ corresponds to a unique terminal in $p$, with linear precedence relations between terminals being identical in both trees.
   e.    Exhaustivity: No child of ι is an ω or lower.
   f.    Non-Recursivity: No child of a φ is also a φ.

It is reasonably possible to build all the candidates in GEN.SL by hand. There are eight possible prosodic trees with four terminals that fit the conditions in (19); they are listed in (20). Curly braces { } stand for ι boundaries, and parentheses ( ) stand for φ boundaries. Each letter stands for a terminal ω. Despite the relatively small number of possible prosodic trees here, however, it would be easy to accidentally omit one or more of them when constructing the list by hand, particularly if the analyst doing the tree construction has not calculated how many such trees are possible.

(20)     All possible values of $p$ for GEN.SL, given that $s = [[[a\ b]\ c]\ d]$

| | | | |
|---|---|---|---|
| a. | {(a b c d)} | e. | {(a)(b c d)} |
| b. | {(a b c)(d)} | f. | {(a) (b c) (d)} |
| c. | {(a b)(c d)} | g. | {(a) (b) (c d)} |
| d. | {(a b) (c) (d)} | h. | {(a) (b) (c) (d)} |

The difficulty of constructing all the trees in the candidate set becomes much more acute when we consider a second system, WL. WL admits not only the strictly layered trees, but also prosodic trees that contain recursive phonological phrases (level-doubling) and/or prosodic words that are non-exhaustively parsed directly into the root intonational phrase (level-skipping).

(21)     GEN.WL($s$) = {All ⟨$s$, $p$⟩ pairs such that $p$ fulfills the conditions in (a–e)}

a.     $p$ is a tree rooted in an ι.

b.     All non-root, non-terminal nodes in $p$ are φs.

c.     All terminal nodes in $p$ are ωs.

d.     Each terminal in $p$ corresponds to a unique terminal in $s$, and each terminal in $s$ corresponds to a unique terminal in $p$, with linear precedence relations between terminals being identical in both trees.

e.     Headedness: Every ι contains at least one φ.

The cardinality of GEN.WL is dramatically larger than that of GEN.SL: There are 351 trees that satisfy the conditions in (4). For a discussion of how we can know that this is the correct number of trees, see Shingler and Bellik (Chapter 2)., 'Counting tree parses". A small subset of the prosodic trees admitted by GEN.WL is listed in (22); these are the first eight and last five trees in the list SPOT generates.

(22)     Some possible values of $p$ for GEN.WL($s$), given that $s = [[[a\ b]\ c]\ d]$

| | | |
|---|---|---|
| a. {(a b c d)} | | h. {(((((a) (b)) (c)) (d))} |
| b. {((a b c) (d))} | | i. ... |
| c. {((a b c) d)} | | j. {a (b) (c (d))} |
| d. {(((a b) (c)) (d))} | | k. {a (b) c d} |
| e. {(((a b) (c)) d)} | | l. {a (b) (c) (d)} |
| f. {(((a b) c) (d))} | | m. {a (b) (c) d} |
| g. {(((a b) c) d)} | | n. {a (b) c (d)} |

Generating the full candidate set for GEN.WL by hand would be difficult, time-consuming, and impractical. Instead, most syntax-prosody analyses manually generate a handful of prosodic structures that appear, to the analyst's intuition and reasoning, to be all the relevant possible optima. There is some justification to this approach, since most of the 351 candidates above will turn out to be harmonically bounded in many systems. For instance, if the constraint set consists of the four constraints on mapping and BINARITY in (23), only the two structures in (24) are possible optima; the other 349 are harmonically bounded.

(23)    CON1
    a.    MATCH(XP, φ): Assign a violation for every XP in the input that lacks a corresponding φ in the output.
    b.    MATCH(φ, XP): Assign a violation for every φ in the output that lacks a corresponding XP in the input.
    c.    BINMAX(φ, branches): Assign a violation for every φ that has more than two branches (children).
    d.    BINMAX(φ, ω): Assign a violation for every φ that dominates more than two ωs (at any level).

(24)    Possible optima in WL, where CON.WL = CON1
    a.    Isomorphic: {(((a b) c) d)}
    b.    Squished: {(a b) c d}

The problem with this intuitive approach, however, is that it is not at all easy to correctly identify which particular outputs are possible optima, when the full candidate set is not being considered. In fact, the squished candidate (24b) is not the competitor to the isomorphic parse (24a) that is considered in Selkirk (2011), which instead contrasts (24a) with a recursive balanced parse {((a b)(c d))}. Ishihara (2014) identifies another candidate that harmonically bounds the balanced parse, which is the non-recursive balanced parse: {(a b)(c d)}. The squished parse is not considered in either analysis, but Kalivoda (2018) shows that it harmonically bounds the balanced parse under both Selkirk's and Ishihara's constraint sets (see Bellik et al. 2022 for further details on the problem of candidate omission for this input).

The SPOT app (Bellik, Bellik, and Kalivoda 2015–2021) offers an alternative. All analyses in this book were developed using SPOT to generate the violation tableaux, and the Excel extension OTWorkplace (Prince, Merchant, and Tesar 2007–2020) to generate and analyze the resulting typologies. OTWorkplace can calculate the typology generated by a violation tableau (that is, a candidate set, or cset, and the violation profiles of each candidate), as well as provide constraint ranking information for each language in the typology. It also identifies which output structures are possible optima, and which are harmonically bounded, as well as identifying a support (a subset of the input structures that is sufficient to generate the entire typology). We have also used OTWorkplace in developing and validating the property analyses in this volume. The use of SPOT and OTWorkplace ensures that no candidates were accidentally omitted, and all possible optima were taken into account.

## 1.4    Overview of the book

We now turn to an overview of this volume, with a chapter-by-chapter summary in §1.4.1, and a discussion of recurring themes across chapters in §1.4.2.

### 1.4.1   Chapter-by-chapter summary

This book consists of four parts, dealing with GEN settings (Part I), Match Theory (Part II), Alignment (Part III), and prosodic well-formedness (Part IV), followed by a SPOT tutorial (Part V). We here give a brief description of each part to guide the reader regarding the theoretical and descriptive focus of individual chapters.

Part I contains two chapters focused on the GEN settings for syntax–prosody mapping. A key component of an OT system is the GEN(erator) function, which defines the candidate sets for that system. In the domain of syntax–prosody mapping, the candidates are ⟨syntactic tree, prosodic tree⟩ pairs. The goal of Chapter 2 (by Shingler and Bellik) is to develop a deeper understanding of how to construct the outputs in syntax–prosody mapping candidate sets, and of how the number of candidates grows with the addition of terminals. This chapter describes the options that the SPOT app makes available for defining GEN, and establishes through mathematical reasoning that SPOT's GEN functions are generating the correct number of candidates for each set of parameter values. Even though much of Optimality-Theoretic research is concerned with the interaction of constraints, OT analyses require a well-defined GEN in addition to a well-defined CON and EVAL. Chapter 3 (by Tarlov) shows how different definitions of GEN can interact with constraints in ways that are not immediately obvious. Different approaches are pursued in the analysis of phrasing issues arising in the Bantu language Kinyambo, and a property analysis of the resulting typologies yields interesting results.

Three chapters comprise Part II, which focuses on Match Theory, as seen from the perspective of SPOT. Chapter 4 (by Kalivoda) takes up Irish phonological phrasing, which has been the subject several influential analyses in recent years, in particular, by Elfner (2012, 2015) and Bennett, Elfner, and McCloskey (2016, 2019). However, a ranking paradox first noticed by Elfner (2012) remains unsolved in the context of standard OT with strict domination. The problem finds a solution by introducing a MATCH constraint sensitive only to overtly headed XPs, and by altering the definition of STRONGSTART to refer specifically to the left edge of the intonational phrase. The resulting analysis furthermore makes predictions for longer sentences of Irish. Chapter 5 (by Van Handel, Brodkin, and Eischens) examines MATCH constraints that are sensitive to subcategories, such as that of Ishihara's (2014) sp.MATCH($XP^{[+max]}$, $\varphi^{[+max]}$). Admitting subcategory-sensitive MATCH constraints leads to two theoretical problems: first, a proliferation of possible MATCH constraints, and second, the emergence of MATCH constraints which enforce syntax-prosody non-isomorphisms, e.g., sp.MATCH($XP^{[-max]}$, $\varphi^{[+max]}$). Chapter 5 presents the results of a SPOT investigation showing that two sets of subcategory-sensitive MATCH constraints drive non-isomorphism: (i) those in which only the second argument has a feature specification for its subcategory, e.g., sp.MATCH($XP$, $\varphi^{[+max]}$), and (ii) those in which the first and second arguments have conflicting specifications for subcategory, e.g. sp.MATCH($XP^{[+max]}$, $\varphi^{[-max]}$). A ban on the existence of these constraints is proposed, and it is argued that this ban follows from the integration of MATCH constraints into the theory of Faithfulness. Finally, Chapter 6 (by Van Handel) raises an important question in Match Theory concerning which syntactic constituents are visible to MATCH constraints. Based on data from Italian, Irish, and Xitsonga, and focusing on three proposals at the phrasal level: (i) MATCH($XP_{Lexical}$, $\varphi$), which sees only lexical XPs; (ii) MATCH($XP_{OvertlyHeaded}$, $\varphi$), which sees only XPs with phonologically overt heads; and (iii) MATCH($XP$, $\varphi$), which sees all XPs. It is argued that MATCH($XP_{OvertlyHeaded}$, $\varphi$) usually can and sometimes must be used instead of MATCH($XP_{Lexical}$, $\varphi$). This raises the question of whether the lexical/functional distinction is actually needed: although the lexical/functional distinction is a useful heuristic, because it often correlates with the silent/overt head distinction, it may not be necessary to capture the full range of phrasing data.

While Match Theory was intended to replace Align/Wrap Theory, Part III contains two chapters arguing that ALIGN is a necessary ingredient in the analyses of Japanese phrasing asymmetries (Chapter 7) and Chamorro clitic movement (Chapter 8). Bellik, Ito, Kalivoda, and Mester (2022) already showed (i) that MATCH and markedness alone cannot handle the left/right phrasing asymmetry in Japanese, while ALIGN can, whereas (ii) ALIGN cannot account for prosodic recursion of sufficient depth, and so MATCH is needed, as well. Chapter 7 (by Kalivoda) analyzes the resulting hybrid theory with MATCH, ALIGN, and BINARITY constraints, by defining an OT system with these constraints, generating its factorial typology, and elucidating the relation between intensional properties of its grammars and extensional traits of its languages in terms of Property Theory (Alber and Prince 2021). Clitic movement is usually considered to be syntactically driven, but previous work has shown that there are cases where this movement is prosodically motivated, e.g. by prosodic subcategorization (Chung 2003), or via constraints on prosodic well-formedness (Bennett, Elfner, and McCloskey 2016). Chapter 8 (by Bibbs) argues that for Chamorro, clitic movement does not require prosodic subcategorization, and instead can be motivated through the interaction of syntax–prosody mapping constraints and markedness constraints on prosodic well-formedness. Furthermore, detailed investigations with SPOT reveal that only ALIGN constraints on syntax-prosody relations can motivate clitic movement, while MATCH constraints are insufficient. Somewhat different conclusions are reached in Chapter 9 (by Cao, Bibbs, and Bellik), where tone sandhi in Xiamen Chinese can be properly accounted for by either MATCH or ALIGN constraints, so long as the mapping constraints are subcategorized to the non-minimal syntactic phrase.

Moving beyond the faithfulness aspects of syntax-prosody (MATCH and ALIGN) in the previous chapters, Part IV focuses on the markedness constraints that play a role in determining optimal prosodic form. Analyses of syntax–prosody mapping rely on notions of purely phonological well-formedness, and yet the constraints defining this well-formedness are not as clearly defined as the mapping constraints, in part because the space of possible prosodic mismatches has not been fully explored. Chapter 10 (by Bellik and Van Handel) provides a formal examination of the commonly used BINARITY constraints to capture size effects, that is, the tendency for longer strings to be parsed into more prosodic constituents. In some implementations, BINARITY is assessed locally by counting immediate children (= branch-counting); in others, BINARITY is assessed globally by counting all descendants of some category (= leaf-counting). Branch-counting BINARITY motivates size-driven prosodic recursion, and operates as a special case of MATCH(XP). In contrast, leaf-counting BINARITY motivates size-driven category promotion, and conflicts with MATCH(XP), leading to larger typology sizes. A constraint on UNIFORMITY is shown to be able to derive size-driven mismatches as well. Chapter 11 (by Bellik) examines several ways to define the prosodic well-formedness constraints EQUALSISTERS (Myrberg 2013) and STRONGSTART (Elfner 2012, Bennett, Elfner, and McCloskey 2016), and the consequences of these definitions for the predicted typology, with a focus on stringency interactions between them. Results are argued to support the use of categorical, parent-oriented definitions of both EQUALSISTERS and STRONGSTART.

The final chapter of this volume is the SPOT tutorial Chapter 12 (by Bellik and Kalivoda), which contains a step-by-step guide on how to use SPOT to build violation tableaux, as well as information on how to further analyze these tableaux in OTWorkplace and other OT software.

### 1.4.2   Recurring themes across chapters

Three major themes concerning constraint interactions recur in multiple chapters in this book. The first is the comparison and sometimes interaction of MATCH and ALIGN constraints; Chapters 3, 8, and 9 compare systems that differ only in their choice of mapping constraint, while Chapter 4 combines MATCH and ALIGN in the same system. Chapter 3 tries to derive subject-branchingness sensitivity (SBS) using either MATCH or ALIGN, and finds that either theory of mapping constraints can derive a less stringent version of SBS, but that only MATCH, used in a recursive system, can model a more stringent version of SBS. Furthermore, MATCH functions in a comprehensible way with a GEN function that permits prosodic recursion, while driving complex mismatch patterns under Strict Layering. ALIGN, in contrast, is compatible with either recursive or Strict Layering GEN. Similarly, Chapter 9 finds that either MATCH or ALIGN, when subcategorized appropriately, can account for the syntax–prosody mapping of Xiamen Chinese tone groups in a Strict Layering system. ALIGN predicts a larger typology due to the inclusion of five mapping constraints (WRAP plus four different ALIGN constraints); the equivalent MATCH system has only two constraints and two languages. In Chapter 8, in contrast, a similar comparison of MATCH and ALIGN systems finds that only ALIGN can yield the desired leftward clitic movement in Chamorro weak pronoun placement; MATCH does not work. Yet another situation obtains in Chapter 4, where MATCH and ALIGN must combine to yield asymmetric rebracketing that is still sensitive to depth of recursion, as observed in Japanese.

The second major theme is the interaction of mapping constraints (primarily MATCH but also ALIGN) with BINARITY. This issue is explored in the greatest depth in Chapter 10 (by Bellik and Van Handel), which defines branch-counting and leaf-counting BINARITY. Branch-counting BINARITY functions as a special case of MATCH, while leaf-counting BINARITY conflicts with MATCH. In Chapter 3, Tarlov includes both minimal and maximal BINARITY, which interact with both ALIGN and MATCH, in two different candidate sets. Minimal BINARITY conflicts with ALIGN and MATCH in all systems; the conflict is more complex in ALIGN systems, where it defines two separate properties. Maximal BINARITY, in contrast, only conflicts with mapping constraints in non-recursive systems; all optima satisfy BINMAX in the recursive systems. In fact, the non-recursive systems involve more complex interactions overall than the recursive systems, because they do not allow BinMax to be satisfied by building recursive prosodic structure, so that BinMax and BinMin are pitted against each other. Chapter 4 (by Kalivoda) takes up this theme from a different angle: only binary-branching candidates are considered, so this chapter examines the interaction of leaf-counting maximal Binarity with mapping constraints when branch-counting maximal Binarity is inviolable.

Limitations on Match's ability to promote isomorphism form a third theme in this volume. Under some circumstances, contrary to their originally envisioned purpose, Match constraints favor syntax-prosody mismatches—what we call Anti-Match effects. This is documented in Chapters 3, 5, and 9. In the non-recursive Match system in Chapter 3, strong mismatches are optimal for certain inputs. Match is surprisingly unable to distinguish between [a [b [c]]] → (a)(b c), a weak mismatch, and [a [b [c]]] → (a b)(c), a strong mismatch. These are optimal in some languages of this typology because the structures that better fulfill Match are excluded from Gen. Next, Chapter 5 reveals that some ways of subcategorizing Match constraints produce Anti-Match effects even when Gen is unrestricted. In particular, when the specifications on the first and second argument differ, or when only the second argument is subcategorized, then the subcategorized Match conflicts with the unrestricted Match. The authors suggest that Anti-Match effects can and should be avoided by restricting the range of possible subcategorizations. We see in Chapter 9, however, that the concept of an Anti-Match effect needs to be refined when other factors, such as a restricted candidate set, prevent Match from selecting an isomorphic output. When Gen is restricted to non-recursive candidates, as in Chapter 9, general Match prefers to match the greatest number of XPs, which means matching minimal XPs in preference to matching non-minimal ones. In the absence of any prosodic well-formedness constraints, this does not result in any rebracketed optima, but it does produce many weak mismatches with non-minimal XPs having no prosodic correspondent, when Match is undominated. General Match in this system conflicts directly with the subcategorized constraint Match-NonMin, which demands that non-minimal XPs be matched in the prosody, but ignores minimal XPs. This constraint does not have Anti-Match effects in Chapter 5, where recursive candidates are included and are optima, but does have Anti-Match effects in Chapter 9, where the candidate set is restricted to strictly layered structures. The term ''Anti-Match'' may actually be misleading in this context, however, since matching the non-minimal XPs actually produces a better category-blind Match—meaning it has fewer mismatches if we disregard category promotion and demotion, and focus on whether every syntactic constituent has some prosodic correspondent (of any category). Having MatchNonMin dominate the general Match produces a prosody that better reflects the overall constituency of the syntax.


# References


Alber, Birgit, Delbusso, Natalie, and Prince, Alan (2016). From intensional properties to universal support. *Language* 92: e88–e116.

Alber, Birgit and Prince, Alan (2021). *The Structure of OT Typologies.* Chapter 1: Introduction to Property Theory. Unpublished manuscript. ROA 1381, Rutgers Optimality Archive, http://roa.rutgers.edu.

Bellik, Jennifer, Bellik, Ozan, and Kalivoda, Nick (2015–2021). Syntax-Prosody in Optimality Theory (SPOT). Javascript application. http:// spot.sites.ucsc.edu. Codebase at https://github.com/syntax-prosody-ot.

Bellik, Jennifer, Ito, Junko, Kalivoda, Nick and Mester, Armin (2022). Matching and alignment. In Haruo Kubozono, Junko Ito, and Armin Mester (eds.) *Prosody and Prosodic Interfaces.* Oxford University Press. 457–481.

Bennett, Ryan, Elfner, Emily, and McCloskey, James (2016). Lightest to the right: An apparently anomalous displacement in Irish. *Linguistic Inquiry* 47: 169–234.

Bennett, Ryan, Elfner, Emily, and McCloskey, James (2019). Prosody, focus, and ellipsis in Irish. *Language* 95(1): 66–106.

Bickmore, Lee (1989). *Kinyambo Prosody.* PhD dissertation, University of California, Los Angeles.

Bickmore, Lee (1990). Branching nodes and prosodic categories: evidence from Kinyambo. In Sharon Inkelas and Draga Zec (eds.) *The Phonology-Syntax Connection* 1–18. Chicago: University of Chicago Press.

Brasoveanu, Adrian and Prince, Alan (2011). Ranking and necessity: The Fusional Reduction Algorithm. *Natural Language and Linguistic Theory* 29: 3–70.

Cassimjee, Farida and Kisseberth, Charles W. (1998). Optimal domains theory and Bantu tonology: A case study from IsiXhosa and Shingazidja, in Larry M. Hyman and Charles W. Kisseberth (eds) *Theoretical Aspects of Bantu Tone.* Stanford, CA: CSLI. 33–132.

Chen, Matthew (1987). The syntax of Xiamen tone sandhi. *Phonology Yearbook* 4: 109–149.

Cheng, Lisa Lai-Shen and Downing, Laura J. (2007). The phonology and syntax of relative clauses in Zulu. In Nancy C. Kula and Lutz Marten (eds.), *Bantu in Bloomsbury: Special Issues on Bantu Linguistics.* SOAS WPL 15: 51–63.

Cheng, Lisa Lai-Shen and Downing, Laura J. (2016). Phasal syntax = cyclic phonology? *Syntax* 19: 156–191.

Chung, Sandra (2003). The syntax and prosody of weak pronouns in Chamorro. *Linguistic Inquiry* 34: 547–599.

DelBusso, Natalie R. (2018). *Typological Structure and Properties of Property Theory.* PhD dissertation, Rutgers University.

Delbusso, Natalie (2020). The final-over-final condition, stringency, and typological structure. *Linguistic Inquiry* 51: 765–784.

Elfner, Emily (2012). *Syntax-Prosody Interactions in Irish.* PhD dissertation, University of Massachusetts Amherst.

Elfner, Emily (2015). Recursion in prosodic phrasing: Evidence from Connemara Irish. *Natural Language and Linguistic Theory* 33: 1169–1208.

Elordieta, Gorka (2008). An overview of theories of the syntax-phonology interface. *International Journal of Basque Linguistics and Philology* 42: 209–286.

Haraguchi, Shosuke (1977). *The Tone Pattern of Japanese: An Autosegmental Theory of Tonology.* Tokyo: Kaitakusha.

Inkelas, Sharon (1990). *Prosodic Constituency in the Lexicon.* New York: Garland.

Ishihara, Shinichiro (2014). Match theory and the recursivity problem. In Shigeto Kawahara and Mika Igarashi (eds.) *MIT Working Papers in Linguistics 73: Proceedings of Formal Approaches to Japanese linguistics 7* 69–88. Cambridge, MA.

Ito, Junko and Mester, Armin (1992/2003). Weak layering and word binarity. In Takeru Honma, Masao Okazaki, Toshiyuki Tabata and Shin-ichi Tanaka (eds.) *A New Century of Phonology and Phonological Theory: A Festschrift for Professor Shosuke Haraguchi on the Occasion of His Sixtieth Birthday* 26–65. Tokyo: Kaitakusha.

Ito, Junko and Mester, Armin (2007). Prosodic adjunction in Japanese compounds. In Yoichi Miyamoto and Masao Ochi (eds.) *MIT Working Papers in Linguistics 55: Proceedings of Formal Approaches to Japanese Linguistics 4* 97–111. Cambridge, MA.

Ito, Junko and Mester, Armin (2009a). The extended prosodic word. In Janet Grijzenhout and Barış Kabak (eds.) *Phonological Domains: Universals and Deviations* 135–194. Berlin: Mouton de Gruyter.

Ito, Junko and Mester, Armin (2009b). The onset of the prosodic word. In Steve Parker (ed.), *Phonological Argumentation: Essays on Evidence and Motivation* 227–260. London: Equinox.

Kalivoda, Nick (2018). *Syntax-Prosody Mismatches in Optimality Theory.* PhD dissertation, University of California, Santa Cruz.

Kisseberth, Charles W. (1994). On domains, in *Perspectives in Phonology*, ed. By Jennifer Cole and Charles Kisseberth, 133 – 166, Stanford, CA: CSLI.

Kubozono, Haruo (1988). The Organisation of Japanese Prosody. University of Edinburgh dissertation.

McCarthy, John J. and Prince, Alan (1993). Generalized alignment. In Geert Booij and Jaap van Marle (eds.) *Yearbook of Morphology* 79–153. Dordrecht: Kluwer.

McCawley, James D. (1968). *The Phonological Component of a Grammar of Japanese.* The Hague: Mouton.

Merchant, Nazarré and Prince, Alan (to appear). The Mother of All Tableaux: Order, Equivalence, and Geometry in the Large-scale Structure of Optimality Theory. Equinox Press.

Myrberg, Sara (2013). Sisterhood in prosodic branching. *Phonology* 30: 73–124.

Nespor, Marina and Vogel, Irene (1986). *Prosodic Phonology.* Dordrecht: Foris.

Odden, David (1987). Kimatuumbi phrasal phonology. *Phonology Yearbook* 4, 13 – 36.

Pierrehumbert, Janet and Beckman, Mary (1988). *Japanese Tone Structure.* Cambridge, MA: MIT Press.

Poser, William J. (1984). The Phonetics and Phonology of Tone and Intonation in Japanese. MIT, dissertation.

Prince, Alan (2002a). Arguing optimality. In Angela Carpenter, Andries Coetzee, and Paul de Lacy (eds.) *Papers in Optimality Theory II* (University of Massachusetts Occasional Papers in Linguistics 26) 269–304. Amherst, MA: GLSA.

Prince, Alan (2002b). Entailed ranking arguments. Unpublished manuscript. ROA 500, Rutgers Optimality Archive, http://roa.rutgers.edu.

Prince, Alan (2007). The pursuit of theory. In Paul de Lacy (ed.) *The Cambridge Handbook of Phonology* 33–60. Cambridge: Cambridge University Press.

Prince, Alan (2017a). What is OT? ROA 1271, Rutgers Optimality Archive, http://roa.rutgers.edu.

Prince, Alan (2017b). OT Checklist. ROA 1306, Rutgers Optimality Archive, http://roa.rutgers.edu.

Prince, Alan and Smolensky, Paul (1993/2004). *Optimality Theory: Constraint Interaction in Generative Grammar.* Malden, MA: Blackwell Publishing.

Prince, Alan, Merchant, Nazarré, and Tesar, Bruce (2007–2020). OTWorkplace. http://sites.google.com/site/otworkplace

Selkirk, Elisabeth (1980). Prosodic domains in phonology: Sanskrit revisited. In Mark Aronoff and Mary-Louise Kean (eds.) *Juncture 7* 107–129. Saratoga, CA: Anma Libri.

Selkirk, Elisabeth (1984). *Phonology and Syntax: the Relation between Sound and Structure.* Cambridge, MA: MIT Press.

Selkirk, Elisabeth (1986). On derived domains in sentence phonology. *Phonology Yearbook* 3: 371–405.

Selkirk, Elisabeth (1996). The prosodic structure of function words. In James L. Morgan and Katherine Demuth (eds.) *Signal to Syntax: Bootstrapping from Speech to Grammar in Early Acquisition* 187–213. Mahwah, NJ: Erlbaum.

Selkirk, Elisabeth (2000). The interaction of constraints on prosodic phrasing. In Merle Horne (ed.) *Prosody: Theory and Experiment. Studies Presented to Gösta Bruce* 231–261. Dordrecht: Kluwer.

Selkirk, Elisabeth (2011). The syntax–phonology interface. In John A. Goldsmith, Jason Riggle, and Alan C. L. Yu (eds.) *The Handbook of Phonological Theory* 435–484. Blackwell Publishing.

Selkirk, Elisabeth O. and Koichi Tateishi (1988). Constraints on minor phrase formation in Japanese, in Proceedings of the 24th Annual Meeting of the Chicago Linguistics Society, ed. by Gary Larson and Diane Brentari, 316 – 336, Chicago, IL: Chicago Linguistics Society.

Truckenbrodt, Hubert (1995). *Phonological Phrases: Their Relation to Syntax, Focus, and Prominence.* PhD dissertation, Massachusetts Institute of Technology.

Truckenbrodt, Hubert (1999). On the relation between syntactic phrases and phonological phrases. *Linguistic Inquiry* 30: 219–255.

Vogel, Irene (2009). Universals of Prosodic Structure. In Sergio Scalise, Elisabetta Magni, Antonietta Bisetto (eds.) *Universals of Language Today* 59–82. Amsterdam, Springer.


## About the authors


*Jennifer Bellik*

Postdoctoral researcher and lecturer, Department of Linguistics, UC Santa Cruz. Research interests: syntax-prosody interface, Optimality Theory, Articulatory Phonology, and Turkish phonology. Recent publications: "An acoustic study of vowel intrusion in Turkish onset clusters", *Laboratory Phonology* 2018; "Automated tableau generation with SPOT" with N.Kalivoda, *Linguistics Vanguard* 2019; and 'The effect of speech style and deaccentuation on vowel intrusion in Turkish complex onsets", *Proceedings of ICPhS* 2019.

*Junko Ito*

Research Professor, Department of Linguistics, UC Santa Cruz. Research interests: Phonology, Optimality Theory, syntax-prosody interface, the phonological lexicon, the prosodic morphology of Japanese. Recent publications: 'Match Theory and Prosodic Wellformedness Constraints" 2020 with A Mester in *Prosodic Studies. Challenges and Prospects*, Routledge; 'Kattobase: The linguistic structure of Japanese baseball chants," 2019 with H. Kubozono, A. Mester, and S. Tanaka. *Proceedings of AMP 2018*; 'Tonal alignment and preaccentuation" 2018 with A. Mester, *Journal of Japanese Linguistics* 34.

*Nick Kalivoda*

Postdoctoral researcher, Centre for Languages and Literature, Lund University. Research interests: syntax–prosody interface, syntax, phonology, and Optimality Theory. Recent publications: "Automated tableau generation using SPOT (Syntax Prosody in Optimality Theory)", with J. Bellik, *Linguistics Vanguard* 2019, 'XP- and $X^0$-movement in the Latin verb: Evidence from mirroring and anti-mirroring" with E. Zyman, *Glossa* 2020, and 'Match Theory: An overview", with S. Ishihara, Language and Linguistics Compass 2022.

*Armin Mester*

Research Professor, Department of Linguistics, UC Santa Cruz. Research interests: Prosodic phonology and morphology, syntax-prosody interface, phonology, Optimality Theory. Recent publications: 'Recursive prosody and the prosodic form of compounds" 2021 with J. Ito, *Languages* 6: 65; 'Match as Syntax-Prosody Max/Dep: Prosodic Enclisis in English" 2019 with J. Ito, *English Linguistics* 36; 'Pitch accent and tonal alignment in Kagoshima Japanese" 2019 with J. Ito, *The Linguistic Review* 36.

# Part I

# GEN settings

# Chapter 2

# Counting tree parses

Edward Shingler and Jennifer Bellik[*]

## 2.1    Introduction

A key component of a system in Optimality Theory (OT; Prince and Smo-lensky 1993/2004, Prince 2017) is the GEN function, which defines the system's candidate set. The Syntax-Prosody in Optimality Theory app (SPOT; Bellik, Bellik and Kalivoda 2015–2021) automates a number of possible GEN functions, each of which takes a string of terminals as its input, and produces a complete set of phonological trees with alternative groupings of words within a chosen prosodic category. The goal of this chapter is to do for tree parses of $n$ prosodic words what Prince (2018)'s 'Counting parses" does for metrical parses of $n$ syllables—namely, 'to gain knowledge not only of parsing numerics, but also of the entire range of structures implied by our structural assumptions" (Prince 2018, p.14). A secondary goal is to validate SPOT's functions for constructing the candidates, since SPOT began with a method of constructing parses, without addressing, until now, the question of how many tree parses there should be.

SPOT assumes the prosodic hierarchy shown in (1), which is widely used in the current syntax-prosody literature, particularly works employing

[*] The authors gratefully acknowledge the helpful and thorough comments from Nick Kalivoda and Nazarré Merchant, which improved the clarity and precision of this paper. In fact, we owe the genesis of this chapter to Nick Kalivoda, who has provided helpful discussion and suggestions through all stages of its development. Our thanks also to Peter Luschny for assistance with the mathematics of GEN[+Exhaustivity]; to Netta Ben-Meir for identifying all the possible GEN functions; and to Nick Van Handel for assistance in proofreading. All errors remain our own.

Match Theory (e.g., Selkirk 2011, Elfner 2012, Ito and Mester 2013, Bennett et al. 2016, Kalivoda 2018, *inter alia*), as well as all the other chapters of this volume. In its present incarnation, SPOT does not generate parses with other categories, such as the Major and Minor Phrase, clitic group, or utterance, which have been proposed elsewhere (e.g., Nespor and Vogel 1986, Pierrehumbert and Beckman 1988, Jun 1998). We restrict our attention in this chapter to the top three categories, which will be the only categories to feature in the prosodic structures considered here. The diagram in (1) also shows SPOT's convention for bracket representations of prosodic trees, in which curly braces { } stand for intonational phrase boundaries, while parentheses ( ) stand for phonological phrase boundaries.

(1)        Prosodic hierarchy

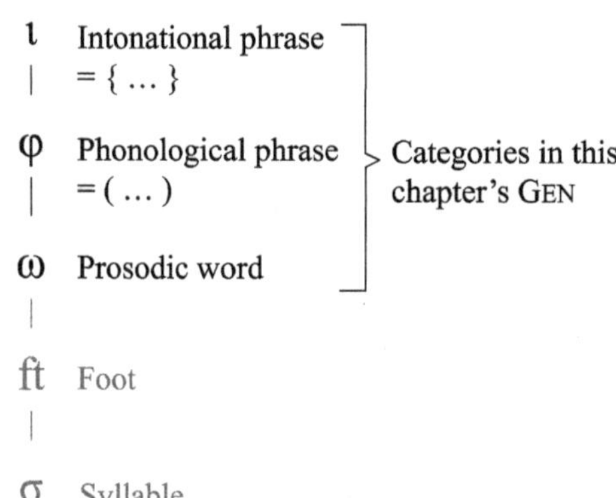


The GEN functions of interest in this chapter are SPOT's core GEN function, defined in (2), and various more restricted versions of it. A crucial characteristic of all GEN functions considered in this chapter is that a maximum of three prosodic categories are represented in each prosodic tree, and that each prosodic category is restricted to a particular position in the tree. The intonational phrase appears only as the root; phonological phrases are always non-root, non-terminals; and prosodic words are always terminals. We set aside from consideration three kinds of other extensions supported by SPOT. The first of these extensions allows multiple categories for non-root, non-terminals, contra (2b), i.e., phonological recursion at both the phrase and word levels. The second allows multiple categories for terminals, contra (2c), i.e., allowing some terminals to be labeled as clitics while others are prosodic words, as in Bibbs (Chapter 8). The third allows reordering of some or all terminals in the prosody, contra (2d), as with clitic movement in Chapter 8.

(2)    SPOT's core GEN function: GEN(s) = all pairs $<s, p>$ where $s$ is a syntactic tree whose terminals are $X^0$s, and $p$ is a prosodic tree such that

    a.    $p$ is rooted in an intonational phrase.

    b.    All non-root, non-terminal nodes in $p$ are phonological phrases.

    c.    All terminals in $p$ are prosodic words. Each word in $p$ corresponds to an $X^0$ in $s$, and every $X^0$ in $s$ corresponds to a word in $p$.

    d.    Linear order of terminals in $s$ is preserved in $p$.

Because the trees in the core GEN contain nodes of up to three categories (the intonational phrase, phonological phrase, and prosodic word), the findings here can be transferred to other sets of three hierarchically adjacent prosodic categories (e.g., the phonological phrase, prosodic word, and foot), so long as the same structure-based restrictions apply to those categories: that the root is the only node of the highest category in the set of three prosodic categories; all non-root, non-terminals are of the middle category; and all terminals are of the lowest prosodic category. For concreteness, however, we refer to the categories in (2) throughout the chapter.

The core GEN function in (2) defines prosodic structures that conform to Layering, but may violate the principles of Headedness, Exhaustivity, and Non-Recursivity. These parsing principles, defined in (3), are inviolable under the Strict Layer Hypothesis (Selkirk 1984). The Strict Layer Hypothesis defines a single GEN function, *modulo* variations in the value of $K$. Any Strict Layering GEN implemented in SPOT will create trees with three levels, since we are considering the possible groupings for a single prosodic category at a time, and Strict Layering will allow only one layer of that category per tree. That is, in SPOT, for every Strict Layering GEN, if terminals are of category $K$, their parents (the intermediate, non-root, non-terminal layer) will be of category $K + 1$, and the root will be of category $K + 2$.

(3)    Strict Layering

    a.    Layering: All children of a node of category $K$ are of category $\leq K$, i.e., $\forall$Parent, Child: $K_{\text{Child}} \leq K_{\text{Parent}}$.

    b.    Headedness: Every non-terminal node of level $K$ immediately dominates at least one node of level $\geq K - 1$, i.e., $\forall$Parent$_K$: $\exists$Child$_{\geq K - 1}$.

    c.    Exhaustivity: All children of a node of level $K$ are of category $\geq K - 1$, i.e., $\forall$Parent, Child: $K_{\text{Child}} \geq K_{\text{Parent}} - 1$.

    d.    Non-Recursivity: All children of a node of level $K$ are of category $< K$, i.e., $\forall$Parent, Child: $K_{\text{Child}} < K_{\text{Parent}}$.

However, under Weak Layering (Ito and Mester 2003/1992; see also prosodic recursion in Nespor and Vogel 1983 and Ladd 1986, 1988), the principles of Non-Recursivity, Exhaustivity, and possibly Headedness become violable constraints. These constraints, therefore, become three (or four, including Headedness) distinct requirements that may or may not be enforced as properties of GEN. Admitting prosodic recursion to the candidate set means that GEN can be further specified as to whether the root category can differ from the category of intermediate nodes, or must match it—another GEN parameter. In terms of the number of candidates produced, requiring the root's category to be the same as that of intermediate nodes is equivalent to requiring that the tree have a "stem" of the intermediate category—that is, a single child which contains the complete terminal string for the tree.

All of these parameters, and one more related to BINARITY rather than Layering, can be set independently for SPOT's core GEN algorithm. Thus, keeping the terminal and intermediate categories constant, the five parameters listed in (4) determine the prosodic tree structures produced by SPOT's core GEN function. For concreteness, the definitions in (4) refer to the categories specified in (2), which are assumed throughout this chapter.

(4)        GEN parameters in SPOT
- a.    Headedness
  - i.     [+Hd]: Every ι contains at least one φ, and every φ contains at least one ω.
  - ii.    [−Hd]: An ι may have only ω children, and contain no φ.
- b.    Exhaustivity
  - i.     [+Exh]: The parent of every ω is a φ.
  - ii.    [−Exh]: The parent of an ω may be a φ or an ι.
- c.    Non-Recursivity
  - i.     [+NonRec]: All children of a φ are ωs.
  - ii.    [−NonRec]: One or more children of a φ may be φs.
- d.    φ stem
  - i.     [+φ stem]: The root ι has a single φ child (a φ stem) that contains the rest of the tree.
  - ii.    [−φ stem]: The root ι can have more than one child.
- e.    Intermediate Branching
  - i.     [+Branching]: Every φ has at least two children.
  - ii.    [−Branching]: Minimal φs can be unary (non-branching).

An increase in the number of input words causes an approximately exponential increase in the cardinality of the GEN's candidate set. This increase can be described by recursive functions and depends on the parameters applied to GEN. The remainder of this chapter describes how these recursive functions arise from the various parameter combinations, and is organized as follows. Section 2.2 establishes scopal relationships among the GEN parameters, and lays out the sixteen non-redundant combinations of parameter settings, or sixteen GEN functions that this paper considers. Six of these functions are simple, and are fully characterized within §2.2. The remaining ten functions are more complex, and are discussed at length in the following sections. Section 2.3 describes four GEN functions that exclude prosodic recursion, and provides formulas that characterize the cardinality of the candidate sets they generate. Each of these formulas for candidate sets that exclude prosodic recursion are related either to the Fibonacci sequence, or to the powers of two. For each function, we also include a proof of why these recurrence relations appropriately express the relationship between the number of candidates with $n - 1$ terminals, and the number of candidates with $n$ terminals. Section 2.4 does the same for the remaining six GEN functions, which do allow prosodic recursion. The size of these candidate sets is related to the little Schröder numbers, and in some cases to the Big Schröder numbers as well. Section 2.5 summarizes and concludes.

## 2.2    Parameter scope

Keeping the prosodic categories constant, there are 32 logically possible combinations of the five GEN parameters ($2^5 = 32$). However, many of these combinations are redundant or define GEN functions whose cardinality is a constant, because some of the five parameters are not independent of each other (5).

(5)      Implicational relationships among GEN parameters
    a.    [+NonRec, +φ stem] → |GEN(n)| = 1
    b.    [+φ stem] → [+Exhaustivity]
    c.    [+Exhaustivity] → [+Headedness]

|GEN[+NonRec, +φ stem]| (5a) is a constant because the only way to parse $n$ ω terminals into a tree whose root is a φ, while conforming to both Layering and Non-Recursivity, is to parse all terminals directly into the stem φ, with no intermediate levels. Concerning (5b), the combination [+φ stem, −Exh] is redundant, because any tree with a φ stem and with words as its terminals will necessarily conform to Exhaustivity. When [+φ stem] is enforced, then [Exh] has no effect. Exhaustivity can therefore be thought of as scoping under [−φ stem]. Similarly, when [+Exh] is active, Headedness is necessarily satisfied (5c), such that [+Exh, ±Hd] are identical. Enforcing Exhaustivity entails that every non-root node of category $K$ is dominated by a parent of level $K$ or $K + 1$, so that the children of every non-terminal node are

necessarily of level $K$ or $K - 1$, excluding headless trees from the candidate set. Headedness, then, scopes under [–Exh]. The following diagram depicts the scopal relationships between the GEN parameters, and enumerates the non-redundant parameter combinations.

(6)      Scopal relationships among GEN parameters

     a.     Tree diagram

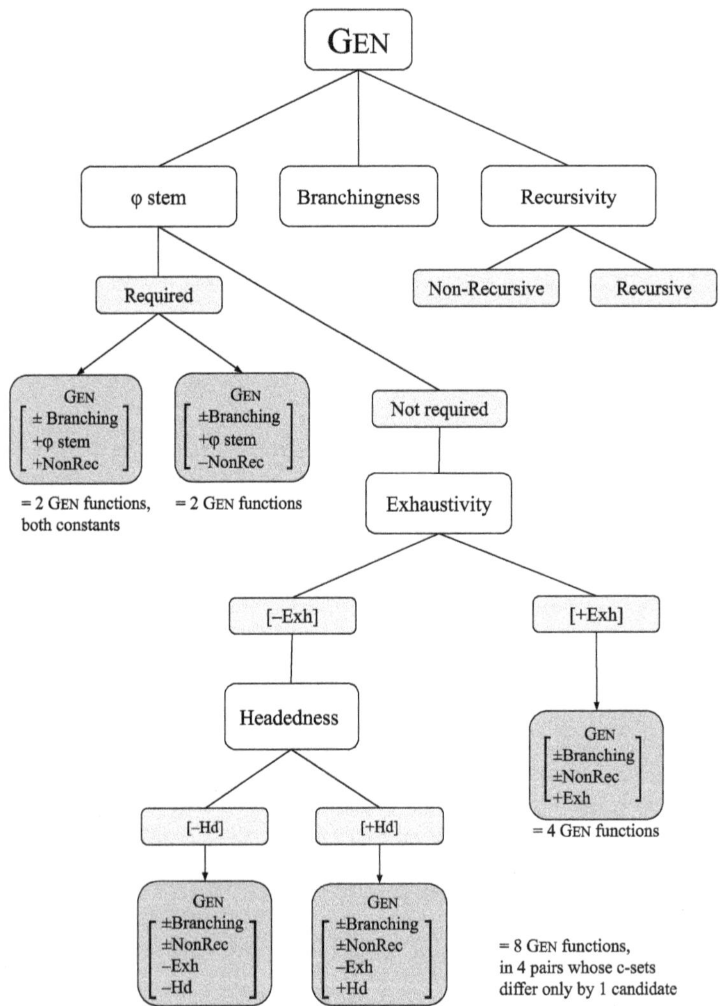

b.   Table of scopal relationships

| Branch | $\varphi$ stem | NonRec | Exh | Headed | Gen count |
|---|---|---|---|---|---|
| ± | + | + | moot | moot | 2 |
| ± | + | − | moot | moot | 2 |
| ± | − | ± | − | − | 4 |
| ± | − | ± | − | + | 4 |
| ± | − | ± | + | moot | 4 |
| | | | | Total: | 16 |

These parameters define sixteen meaningfully different GEN functions (7). The first six GEN functions, in the leftmost column, are either inherently simple, or can be simply derived from other GEN functions. The remaining ten, in the second and third columns of (7), are more interesting, and will be discussed in §§2.3 and 2.4. First, however, we address the six simple GEN functions.

(7)   Table of all GEN functions in this chapter, full parameter specifications, in order of appearance. NR = Non-Recursivity, Br = Branching, $\varphi$ st = $\varphi$ stem.

| Simple (§2.2.1) | More complex | |
|---|---|---|
| | [+NonRecursivity] (§2.3) | [−NonRecursivity] (§2.4) |
| 1. [+NR, −Br, +$\varphi$ stem] | 7. [+NR, +Br, −$\varphi$ stem, +Exh] | 11. [−NR, +Br, +$\varphi$ stem] |
| 2. [+NR, +Br, +$\varphi$ stem] | 8. [+NR, +Br, −$\varphi$ stem, −Exh, −Hd] | 12. [−NR, −Br, +$\varphi$ stem] |
| 3. [+NR, +Br, −$\varphi$ st, −Exh, +Hd] | 9. [+NR, −Br, −$\varphi$ stem, +Exh] | 13. [−NR, +Br, −$\varphi$ stem, −Exh, −Hd] |
| 4. [+NR, −Br, −$\varphi$ st, −Exh, +Hd] | 10. [+NR, −Br, −$\varphi$ stem, −Exh, −Hd] | 14. [−NR, −Br, −$\varphi$ stem, −Exh, −Hd] |
| 5. [−NR, +Br, −$\varphi$ st, −Exh, +Hd] | | 15. [−NR, +Br, −$\varphi$ stem, +Exh] |
| 6. [−NR, −Br, −$\varphi$ st, −Exh, +Hd] | | 16. [−NR, −Br, −$\varphi$ stem, +Exh] |

## 2.2.1 Simple GEN functions

The non-recursive but $\varphi$-rooted GEN functions are both effectively constant functions, and the four GEN functions that enforce Headedness can be very simply derived from their non-Headed equivalents. These six GEN functions are described here and then set aside.

### 2.2.1.1.  GEN[+NonRec, +φ stem]

When [+φ stem] and [+NonRec] are both enforced in GEN, the candidate set for any value of $n$ is a set of one non-empty tree (8a). Since recursive structure is prohibited, the φ must be the immediate parent of all words, leaving no room for alternative structures such as (8b).

(8)       One-terminal trees with a φ stem

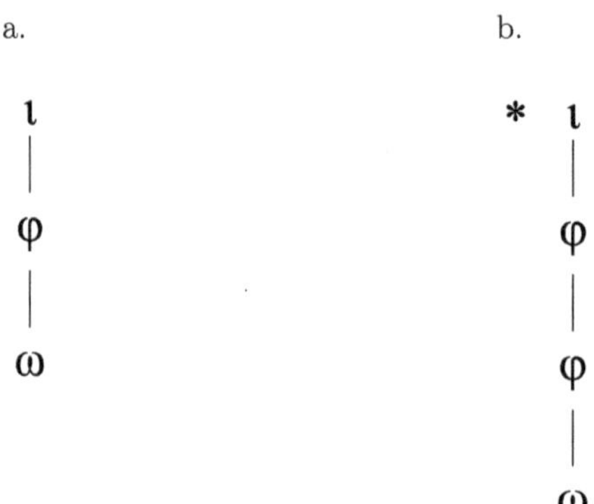

In the case of [+Branching] GEN, then the candidate set for $n=1$ is the empty set because the root φ cannot branch. (The empty set is not counted as a candidate, here and throughout the paper.) The cardinalities of these two constant or nearly constant GEN functions are shown in (9).

(9)       Cset cardinalities for GEN[+NonRec, +φ stem]

| | $n =$ 1 | 2 | 3 | 4 | 5 |
|---|---|---|---|---|---|
| \| GEN[+NonRec, +φ stem] \| | 1 | 1 | 1 | 1 | 1 |
| \| GEN[+NonRec, +φ stem, +Branching] \| | 0 | 1 | 1 | 1 | 1 |

### 2.2.1.2.  [+Headed] GEN functions: The effects of Headedness

Headedness is only active when violations of Exhaustivity are permitted. Even for GEN[−Exh], however, [Hd] has an extremely minor effect. Enforcing [+Hd] only removes a single tree from the corresponding [−Hd] candidate set. The [+Hd] parameter setting removes any tree where an intonational phrase does not contain a valid head, that is, any phonological phrase. Since intonational phrases cannot be recursive under the settings considered here,[1]

---

[1] As discussed above, this paper's scope is restricted to the core GEN function in SPOT, in which candidates may only contain recursive structures of a single prosodic category, namely

only a single unheaded tree is possible for any set of terminals. Unlike the other parameter settings, which have a multiplicative effect on the number of possible candidates, Headedness has only an additive effect. Therefore, Headedness will be ignored in the remainder of this chapter, and all GEN functions described from here on will be treated as [–Hd]. As indicated in (10), the reader can deduce the formula for the number of candidates given by any [–Exh, +Hd] version of GEN by subtracting 1 from the formula given for the [–Exh, –Hd] equivalent. For all [+Exh] GEN functions, GEN[+Hd] is the same as GEN[–Hd].

(10)    Effect of [+Hd] on cset cardinalities

| GEN[+Headedness] | Cardinality in relation to [–Hd] counterpart |
|---|---|
| \| GEN[+Exh, +Hd, $\alpha$Branching, $\beta$NonRec] \| | = \| GEN[+Exh, –Hd, $\alpha$Branching, $\beta$NonRec] \| (because [+Exh] $\rightarrow$ [+Hd]) |
| \| GEN[–Exh, +Hd, $\alpha$Branching, $\beta$NonRec] \| | = \| GEN[–Exh, –Hd, $\alpha$Branching, $\beta$NonRec] \| – 1 |

## 2.2.2 Preview of the GEN functions and cardinalities

The ten more complex GEN functions and the cardinality of their candidate sets remain to be described. For each of these GEN definitions, there is an approximately exponential[2] increase in cardinality for the candidate sets at each value of $n$, as can be seen in the table in (11). The numbers in the table reflect the observed size of the candidate sets produced by SPOT's GEN algorithm for those parameter settings. The remainder of this paper is devoted to proving that these numbers are indeed the values predicted by formulas that characterize the cardinality of the intended candidate sets. We first address the non-recursive GEN functions (the first four rows, grey background; §2.3), and then the remaining six recursive GEN functions (§2.4), which are arranged in the table in the order in which we discuss them, based on the complexity of the explanation. For each GEN function, (11) lists only the restrictions that are enforced (parameters with a positive value); parameters that are not explicitly listed in a GEN specification are

---

$\varphi.$

[2] The Fibonacci sequence, which we will see characterizes the rate of increase of some [+NonRec] GEN functions, is not, strictly speaking, exponential, but its rate of increase is similar to that of genuinely exponential functions. Thanks to Nazarré Merchant for this point.

restrictions that are not enforced (i.e., they have a negative value for that GEN).

(11)    GEN cardinality for $n$ from 1 to 6, where $n$ = the number of words

| GEN specification | $n = 1$ | $n = 2$ | $n = 3$ | $n = 4$ | $n = 5$ | $n = 6$ |
|---|---|---|---|---|---|---|
| $\begin{bmatrix} +\text{NonRec} \\ +\text{Branching} \\ +\text{Exhaustive} \end{bmatrix}$ | 0 | 1 | 1 | 2 | 3 | 5 |
| $\begin{bmatrix} +\text{NonRec} \\ +\text{Branching} \end{bmatrix}$ | 1 | 2 | 4 | 8 | 16 | 32 |
| $\begin{bmatrix} +\text{NonRec} \\ +\text{Exhaustive} \end{bmatrix}$ | 1 | 2 | 4 | 8 | 16 | 32 |
| $[+\text{NonRec}]$ | 2 | 5 | 13 | 34 | 89 | 233 |
| $\begin{bmatrix} +\varphi\ \text{root} \\ +\text{Branching} \end{bmatrix}$ | 0 | 1 | 3 | 11 | 45 | 197 |
| $[+\varphi\ \text{stem}]$ | 1 | 4 | 24 | 176 | 1,440 | 12,608 |
| $[+\text{Branching}]$ | 1 | 2 | 6 | 22 | 90 | 394 |
| $[\varnothing]$ | 2 | 8 | 48 | 352 | 2,880 | 25,216 |
| $\begin{bmatrix} +\text{Exhaustive} \\ +\text{Branching} \end{bmatrix}$ | 0 | 1 | 3 | 12 | 51 | 229 |
| $[+\text{Exhaustive}]$ | 1 | 5 | 33 | 253 | 2,121 | 18,853 |

## 2.3    Non-recursive GEN functions

The GEN[+NonRecursive] functions yield fewer candidates than those that allow recursive parses, because of their fixed depth. A non-recursive tree cannot have more layers than it has categories, whereas the depth of a recursive tree is restricted primarily by the number of terminals, rather than by the number of categories available. Due to the stronger restrictions on the structures created by GEN[+NonRec], the formulas describing the number of possible non-recursive trees are simpler than those describing the number of possible recursive trees. We begin, therefore, with the non-recursive GEN functions, proceeding from the most restrictive to the least.

### 2.3.1    *Branching Strict Layering GEN: GEN[+NonRec, +Exh, +Branching]*

The most restrictive and slowest-growing GEN function in SPOT is GEN[+NonRec, +Exh, +Branching]. The parameter setting [+NonRec] prohibits phonological phrases from dominating another phonological phrase, while [+Exh] prohibits the root intonational phrase from being the immediate parent of a word. The trees produced by this GEN, therefore, all satisfy the principles of Strict Layering (Selkirk 1984). In addition, the setting [+Branching] for this GEN means that every phonological phrase has at least two children; all trees produced by this GEN satisfy MINIMALBINARITY (12). An analyst seeking to create an OT system to account for the phrasing patterns in a language where all $\varphi$s are minimally binary, and working from the assumption of Strict Layering, might use this GEN in order to study the subset of a typology where BINMIN is undominated.

(12)     MINIMALBINARITY($\varphi$) = BINMIN($\varphi$): Assign a violation for every $\varphi$ that has less than two children.

The growth in the cardinality of GEN[+NonRec, +Exh, +Branching] is shown in (13), for trees with $n$ terminal nodes (that is, $n$ words in the prosodic tree, corresponding to $n$ $X^0$ terminals in the syntactic tree). There are zero non-recursive, exhaustive parses of a single word into a branching $\varphi$; there is one exhaustive, non-recursive parse of two words into branching $\varphi$s; one such parse of three words; two such parses of four words; and so on. The reader may recognize this as the Fibonacci sequence, which can be described with the formula in (14).

(13)     | GEN[+NonRec, +Exh, +Branching]($n$ from 1 to 8) | = 0, 1, 1, 2, 3, 5, 8, 13

(14)     / GEN[+NonRec, +Exh, +Branching] at $n$ terminals | = $a(n)$
         = $a(n-1) + a(n-2)$, for $n \geq 2$, with $a(1) = 0$ and $a(2) = 1$.
         (https://oeis.org/A000045, with 1-indexing rather than the 0-indexing of the Online Encyclopedia of Integer Sequences (OEIS): i.e., $F(0)$ on OEIS = $a(1)$ here.)

Why does the number of minimally binary, strictly layered trees with three prosodic categories grow according to the Fibonacci sequence? To answer this question, let us consider the ways in which an $n$th terminal may be added to a tree that starts out with $n-1$ terminals, taking GEN(5) as an example. For a sequence of five terminals, GEN[+Exh, +NonRec, +Branching] yields the three trees in (15). So $a(5) = 3$.

(15)      Gen[+Exh, +NonRec, +Branching](5)

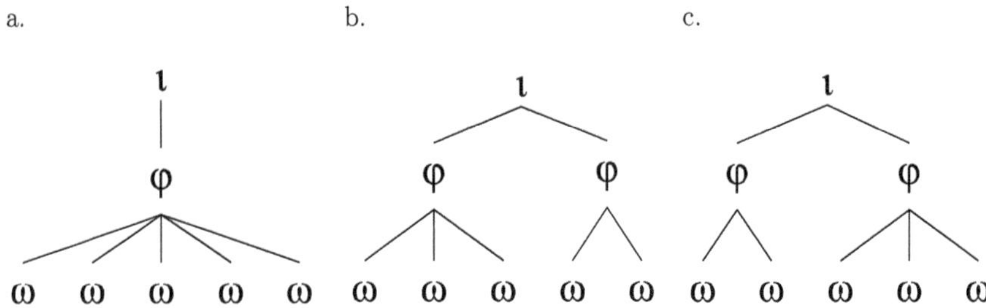

There are two strategies for adding a sixth terminal (terminal $n$) to the right
edge of the trees in (15) to produce trees that belong to the candidate set of
Gen[+NonRec, +Exh, +Branching] for six terminals. The first strategy is to
parse the sixth word into the rightmost phonological phrase. We will call the
function that does this IncludeInPhrase (16). IncludeInPhrase is the first of
several tree-expansion operations that will be defined in this chapter; they
are listed together in a table in the Appendix. While their definitions will
be phrased in terms of operations on a single tree, we will also apply these
functions to sets of trees, with the intended meaning being that the function
applies to each of the trees in the input set, yielding a set of output trees.

(16)      IncludeInPhrase($t$), where the input $t$ is a tree with $n - 1$ terminals
          = $t'$, a tree with $n$ terminals, where terminal $n$ is parsed into the
          rightmost phonological phrase

Applying IncludeInPhrase to the trees in Gen(5) yields the three trees depicted in (17). Newly added ω are identified by boxes. IncludeInPhrase can
apply to every tree from Gen($n - 1$), and therefore produces $a(n - 1)$ trees
with $n$ terminals. This is the source of the term $a(n - 1)$ in the recurrence
relation in (14). In these trees, the rightmost φ has a minimum of three
daughters, and a maximum of $n$ daughters, because IncludeInPhrase adds a
word to the rightmost φ which initially had at least two daughters, due to
the [+Branching] requirement of this Gen.

(17)    Incorporating a sixth terminal: IncludeInPhrase(Gᴇɴ[+Exh, +NonRec, +Branching](5))

a.                                b.                                c.

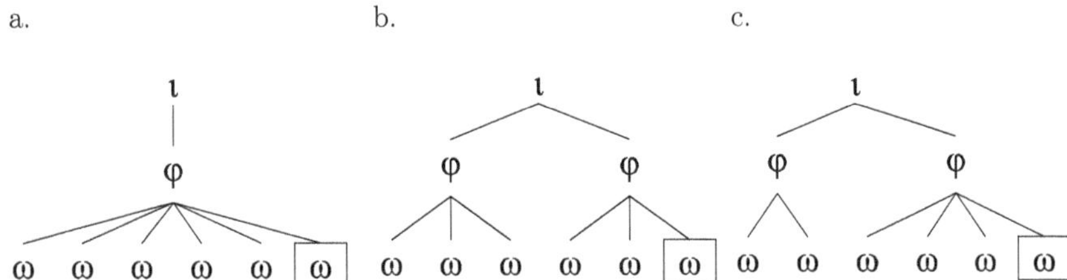

The second method of parsing an $n$th word into a tree is to remove the rightmost child from the rightmost phonological phrase, and phrase it with the appended word under a new phonological phrase. We call this operation Recouple (18).

(18)    Recouple($t$),
        where input $t$ is a tree with $n - 1$ terminals, in which the rightmost φ has > 2 daughters
        = $t'$, a tree with $n$ terminals, in which the rightmost φ has two daughters, terminals $n - 1$ and $n$.

The rightmost phonological phrase in $t$ must have at least three daughters for Recouple($t$) to apply, otherwise the penultimate phonological phrase in $t'$ would be unary, disqualifying it as a candidate for Gᴇɴ[+NonRec, +Exh, +Branching]. The new trees created by applying Recouple to the set of trees with five terminals are depicted in (19) (new structure created by the tree-building operation is shown with a grey background, and a grey dashed line connecting two nodes indicates a connection that existed in the input to the latest tree-building operation, but has been broken in the output of the tree-building function). Although there are three input trees in Gᴇɴ[+Exh, +NonRec, +Branching](5), as seen in (15), one of them, (15), has only two words in its rightmost φ, and is not a valid input to Recouple. For this reason, Recouple(Gᴇɴ[+Exh, +NonRec, +Branching](5)) creates only two output trees. Note that every tree created by Recouple has exactly two daughters in its rightmost φ.

(19)    Recouple(GEN[+Exh, +NonRec, +Branching](5))

a.                                                    b.

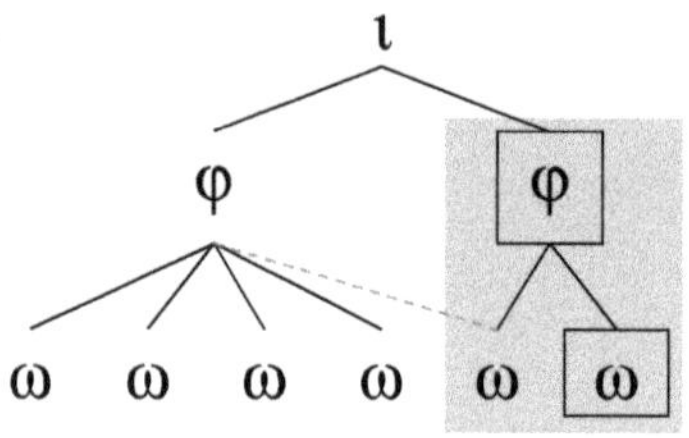

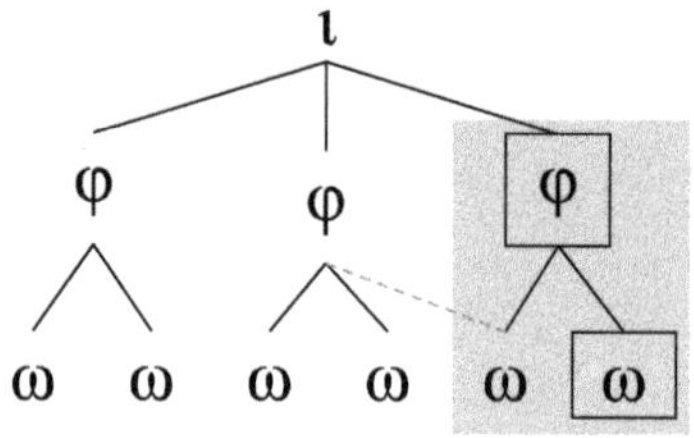

How many trees of [+NonRec, +Exh, +Branching] GEN$(n-1)$ have a right-most $\varphi$ with at least three daughters, and can undergo Recoupling? All candidates produced by IncludeInPhrase satisfy this criterion, and no candidates produced by Recouple do. Therefore, Recouple can apply to all the trees in GEN$(n-1)$ that were created by IncludeInPhrase. This is $a((n-1)-1) = a(n-2)$, the second term in the recurrence relation in (14). The current candidate set, $a(n)$, is the number of trees having undergone IncludeInPhrase, $a(n-1)$, plus the number of trees having undergone Recoupling, $a(n-2)$. Therefore, $a(n) = a(n-1) + a(n-2)$.

### 2.3.2 *Non-recursive branching GEN*

The next two GEN functions (GEN[+NonRec, +Branching], GEN[+NonRec, +Exh]) come as a pair, because both functions yield the same number of candidates. We discuss GEN[+NonRec, +Branching] first. The number of candidates generated by this GEN for $n$ terminals is given by the function in (20), called $b(n)$ throughout this section.

(20)    | GEN[+NonRec, +Branching]$(n$ words$)$ | $= b(n) = 2^{n-1} = 2b(n-1)$,
        for $n > 1$, where $n(1) = 1$

These two formulas are functionally equivalent because the cardinality at $n$ is always double the cardinality at $n-1$. We can understand why the number of candidates doubles with the addition of an $n$th terminal with an example. We begin with the candidates of GEN[+NonRec, +Branching] at $n = 3$, depicted in (21).

(21)    Gᴇɴ[+NonRec, +Branching](3 words)

a.                          b.                          c.                          d.

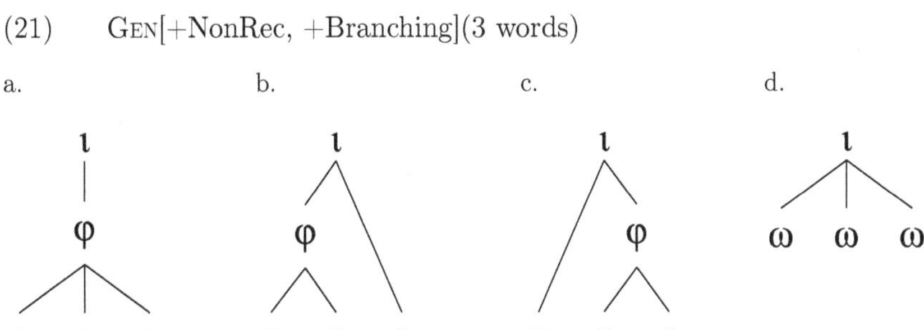

In these trees, [+NonRec] limits the number of intermediate phrase layers to one, and [+Branching] keeps the intermediate layers from being unary. Words that are not parsed into a φ are directly dominated by ι. Two more construction strategies are necessary to handle the possibility of "free" words at the right edge of the tree. The first is to parse the $n$th word being added to a tree directly into the intonation phrase as a free word, an operation termed AssociateToRoot (22).

(22)    AssociateToRoot($t$), where $t$ is a tree with $n - 1$ terminals
        $= t'$, a tree with $n$ terminals, in which the $n$th terminal is parsed
        directly into the intonational phrase

AssociateToRoot can apply to any tree in Gᴇɴ[+NonRec, +Branching] $(n - 1)$ to create a valid member of Gᴇɴ[+NonRec, +Branching]$(n)$, meaning that AssociateToRoot creates $b(n - 1)$ trees with $n$ terminals, as shown in (23).

(23)    AssociateToRoot(Gᴇɴ[+NonRec, +Branching](3 words))

a.                          b.                          c.                          d.

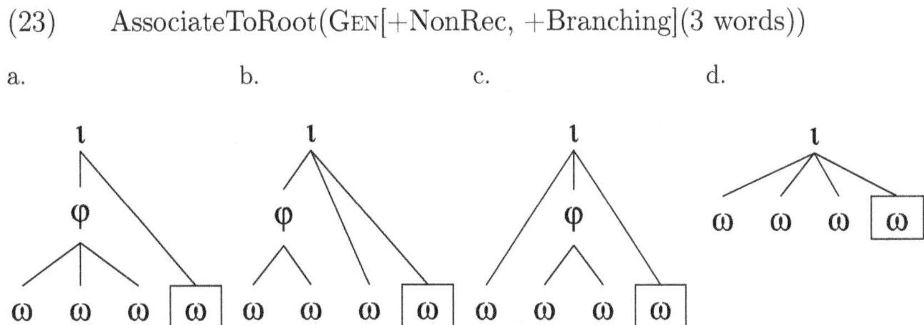

The second new construction strategy is Pair, defined in (24). If a tree has a free word on its right edge, an $n$th word can be incorporated by parsing it into a new binary φ whose daughters are terminals $n - 1$ and $n$.

(24)      Pair($t$),

        where $t$ is a tree with $n-1$ terminals, such that terminal $n-1$ (the penultimate terminal) is not contained in any $\varphi$

        $= t'$, a tree with $n$ terminals, whose rightmost child is a $\varphi$ with two daughters, terminals $n-1$ and $n$

Like Recouple from the previous subsection, Pair creates trees with a binary rightmost $\varphi$. These two parsing strategies can create identical trees. For example, either Recoupling $\{(\omega\ \omega\ \omega)\}$ (21) and Pairing $\{(\omega\ \omega)\ \omega\}$ (21) both create the candidate $\{(\omega\ \omega)(\omega\ \omega)\}$. Fortunately, we can ignore Recoupling as a parsing strategy for GEN[+NonRec, +Branching], because for every tree with a $\varphi$ containing three words on the right edge, there is a minimally different tree in GEN[+NonRec, +Branching] whose rightmost $\varphi$ contains two words, and has a free word as its righthand sister, to which Pairing can apply to create the same structure that Recoupling of the ternary $\varphi$ would have produced. (Another way to frame this is that Recoupling can be decomposed into two operations: releasing a word, and then Pairing. Since the result of releasing a word already exists in the set of trees as those with free words on the right edge, we only need to consider the Pairing step of Recoupling.) Thus, for GEN[+NonRec, +Branching]($n$), we will consider the results of IncludeInPhrase, Pair, and AssociateToRoot.

Both IncludeInPhrase and Pair parse the new word into a $\varphi$. If the rightmost word in the tree with $n-1$ terminals is parsed into a $\varphi$, then IncludeInPhrase can apply. If the rightmost word in the tree with $n-1$ terminals is free, then the two free words (terminals $n-1$ and $n$) can form a new $\varphi$ through Pair. All trees can undergo either IncludeInPhrase or Pair, but not both. Thus, IncludeInPhrase and Pair together create $b(n-1)$ trees (25). In the case of the three-word trees depicted in (21), IncludeInPhrase applies to (21a, c) to produce the four-word trees in (26a, b), while Pair applies to (21b, d) to yield (26c, d). As above, grey backgrounds indicate newly created structure, and a dashed grey line between two nodes indicates a connection that was broken by the structure-building operation.

(25)      $|$ IncludeInPhrase(GEN[+NonRec, +Branching]($n-1$ words))

        $+$ Pair(GEN[+NonRec, +Branching]($n-1$ words)) $| = b(n-1)$ (see (20))

(26)    IncludeInPhrase(GEN[+NonRec, +Branch](3)) ∪
        Pair(GEN[+NonRec, +Branch](3))

Outputs of IncludeInPhrase                    Outputs of Pair

a.                    b.                    c.                    d.

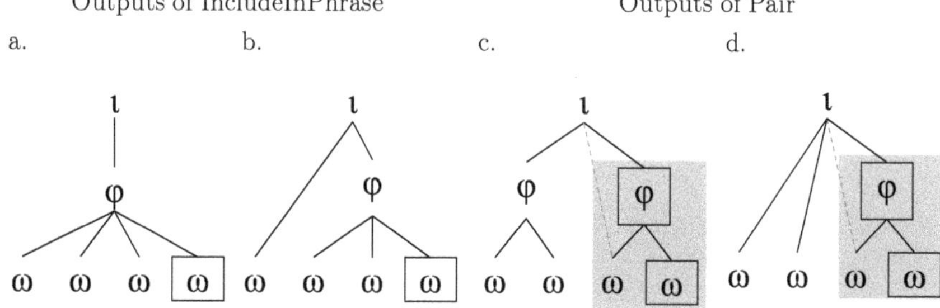

Combining the $b(n-1)$ trees created by AssociateToRoot and the $b(n-1)$ trees created by IncludeInPhrase and Pairing, we derive the formula for $b(n)$ that we began with in (20): $b(n) = b(n-1) + b(n-1) = 2 * b(n-1)$.

### 2.3.3   Strict Layering GEN (Non-recursive, exhaustively phrased)

The number of candidates generated by canonical Strict Layering GEN[+NonRec, +Exh] can be captured with the same formula as GEN[+NonRec, +Branching].

(27)    | GEN[+NonRec, +Exh]($n$ words) | $= b(n) = 2^{n-1} = 2 * b(n-1)$,
        for $n > 1$, where $n(1) = 1$

This equivalence in the size of the candidate sets owes to the tradeoff between enforcing Exhaustivity and enforcing Branchingness. For each tree $t$ in GEN[+NonRec, +Branching] that violates Exhaustivity, there is a single equivalent tree $t'$ in GEN[+NonRec, +Exh] that conforms to Exhaustivity by wrapping each free word of $t$ in a unary φ, with all branching φs remaining identical in the transformation from $t$ to $t'$. Compare the candidates of GEN[+NonRec, +Exh](3) in (28) to those of GEN[+NonRec, +Branching] (3) in 0. Conversely, for each tree $u$ in GEN[+NonRec, +Exh] that includes a unary φ, there is a single equivalent tree $u'$ in GEN[+NonRec, +Branching] that conforms to minimal binarity (i.e., [+Branching]) while violating Exhaustivity, by converting every unary φ in $u$ to a free word parsed directly into the ι in $u'$. All other trees are common to both GEN[+NonRec, +Branching] and GEN[+NonRec, +Exh], thus explaining the equivalence in the sizes of their candidate sets.

(28)    Gen[+NonRec, +Exh](3 words) — compare to 0

a.                b.                c.                d.

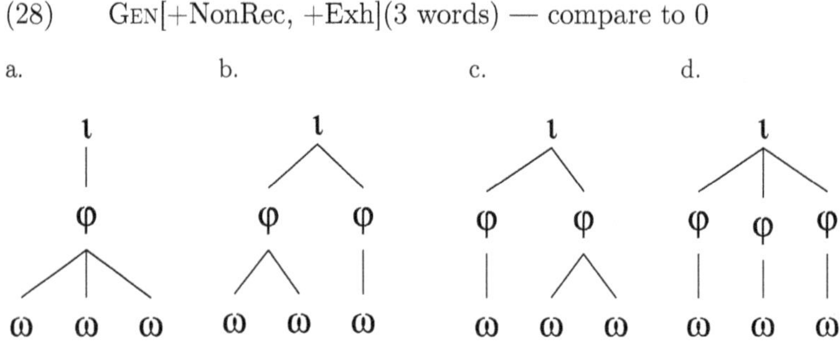

(29)    Gen[+NonRec, +Branching](3 words). Repeated from (21)

a.                b.                c.                d.

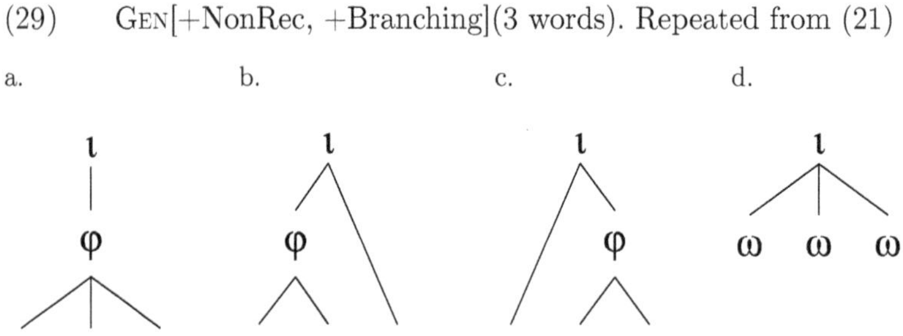

We can re-prove the validity of the formula for $b(n)$ for Gen[+NonRec, +Exh] as well. Let $E$ be the candidate set of Gen[+NonRec, +Exh] for $n-1$ words. There are two ways to add an $n$th word to each of the $b(n-1)$ trees in $E$: IncludeInPhrase (16), and ExhaustivelyAssociate (30). With Exhaustively Associate, rather than being parsed directly into the ι, terminal $n$ is parsed into a new unary φ. Each parsing strategy produces $b(n-1)$ new trees, with the result that $b(n) = b(n-1) + b(n-1) = 2b(n-1)$, as originally claimed in (27).

(30)    ExhaustivelyAssociate($t$), where $t$ is a tree of $n-1$ terminals
        $= t'$, a tree with $n$ terminals, such that the first $n-1$ terminals
        have the same constituent structure as in $t$, while the $n$th terminal
        is parsed into a unary φ immediately dominated by the root ι

### 2.3.4    Non-recursive Gen

The fourth non-recursive Gen enforces Non-Recursivity, but not Exhaustivity or Branchingness: Gen[+NonRec, −Br, −Exh]. Its cardinality grows as in (31), in a pattern described by the formula in (32).

(31)      | GEN[+NonRec] ($n$ from 1 to 6)| = 2, 5, 13, 34, 89, 233

(32)      | GEN[+NonRec]($n$ words) | = $c(n) = 3 * c(n-1) - c(n-2)$, where
          $c(1) = 2$ and $c(2) = 5$
          (A001519 in OEIS, with OEIS's $a(n)$ equal to our $c(n-1)$ )

This is a bisection of the Fibonacci sequence. That is, this sequence consists of every other Fibonacci number. One bisection (B1) progresses [1, 3, 8, 21, 55, ...] while the bisection under question (B2) progresses [2, 5, 13, 34, 89, 233, ...]. To understand why this formula applies, let us consider all the ways to build GEN($n$) from the $c(n-1)$ trees created by GEN($n-1$), with the trees of GEN(2 words) in (33) as a visual aid.

(33)      GEN[+NonRec](2 words)

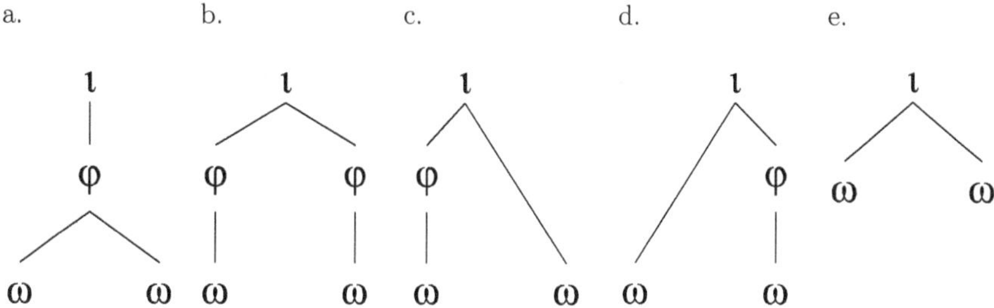



There are three ways to incorporate a third terminal into these trees: AssociateToRoot (22), ExhaustivelyAssociate (30), and IncludeInPhrase (16). AssociateToRoot and ExhaustivelyAssociate can apply to all $c(n-1)$ trees in GEN($n-1$), to create $2c(n-1)$ trees. The transformation IncludeInPhrase cannot apply to all $c(n-1)$ trees, however, only to trees in which the right-most word is parsed into a $\varphi$. The number of trees in GEN($n-1$) that IncludeInPhrase can apply to—call this $d(n-1)$—is the total number of trees, $c(n-1)$, *minus* those that IncludeInPhrase cannot apply to, $x$.

(34)      $c(n)$ = AssociateToRoot(GEN($n-1$)) +
          ExhaustivelyAssociate(GEN($n-1$)) + IncludeInPhrase(GEN($n-1$))
   a.     | AssociateToRoot(GEN($n-1$)) | = $c(n-1)$
   b.     | ExhaustivelyAssociate(GEN($n-1$)) | = $c(n-1)$
   c.     | IncludeInPhrase(GEN($n-1$)) | = $d(n-1) = c(n-1) - x$, where $x$
          = the number of trees in GEN($n-1$) that IncludeInPhrase cannot
          apply to.
   d.     $c(n) = c(n-1) + c(n-1) + d(n-1) = 2\,c(n-1) + d(n-1)$

The trees IncludeInPhrase cannot apply to are those that have free words at their right edge. These trees are the subset of the trees in $\textsc{Gen}(n-1)$ that were created by AssociateToRoot($\textsc{Gen}(n-2)$). As noted above, AssociateToRoot can apply to any tree in $\textsc{Gen}$, meaning that there are $c(n-2)$ trees in AssociateToRoot($\textsc{Gen}(n-2)$), and therefore $x$ in (34) is $c(n-2)$. Substituting $c(n-2)$ for $x$ yields (35a). The value of $c(n)$ is $2 * c(n-1) + d(n-1)$. Replacing $d(n-1)$ in (34d) with $c(n-1) - c(n-2)$ from (35a) yields (32), the recursive formula given in OEIS.

(35)      Deriving $c(n)$

     a.    $d(n-1) = c(n-1) - c(n-2)$

     b.    $c(n) = 2 * c(n-1) + d(n-1)$

             $= 2 * c(n-1) + (c(n-1) - c(n-2))$

             $= 3 * c(n-1) - c(n-2)$

             $= (32)$

We can also understand why this is a bisection of the Fibonacci sequence (which describes the cardinality of $\textsc{Gen}[+\text{NonRec}, +\text{Exh}, +\text{Branching}]$), by approaching $d(n)$ from another angle. The number of trees to which IncludeInPhrase can apply is the number of trees that previously underwent either ExhaustivelyAssociate ($= c(n-1)$), or IncludeInPhrase ($= d(n-1)$), because these are the two tree-building operations that create trees with φs at their right edges. This gives us the formula in (36).

(36)      $d(n) = c(n-1) + d(n-1)$

The formulas for $d(n)$ in (36) and $c(n)$ in (34) are interdependent. As shown in 0, the series can be developed by passing values back and forth, starting with the candidates of $\textsc{Gen}[+\text{NonRec}]$ at $n = 1$ in (37), and at $n = 2$ in (33).

(37)      $\textsc{Gen}[+\text{NonRec}]$(1 word)

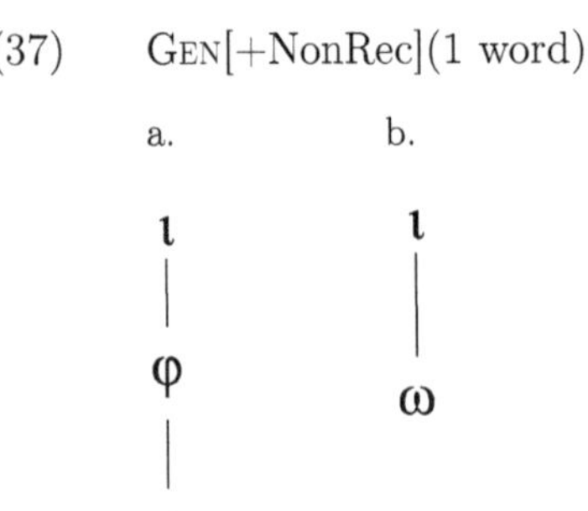

(38)      Growth of $c(n)$ and $d(n)$

|  | $n=1$ | $n=2$ | $n=3$ | $n=4$ | $n=5$ | $n=6$ | $n=7$ |
|---|---|---|---|---|---|---|---|
| $d(n) = c(n-1) + d(n-1)$ | 1 | 3 | 8 | 21 | 55 | 144 | 377 |
| $c(n) = 2 * c(n-1) + d(n-1)$ | 2 | 5 | 13 | 34 | 89 | 233 | 610 |

Reading (38) from top down, left to right, the Fibonacci sequence appears. The $d(n)$ formula shows the alternative bisection of the Fibonacci sequence, B1. Knowing this, a succinct way to write the formula for the cardinality of GEN[+NonRec] formula is:

(39)      $c(n) = a(2n + 2)$, where $a(n)$ is the $n$th term of the Fibonacci sequence F(n), where F(1...8) = 0, 1, 1, 2, 3, 5, 8, 13, as in (13) and (14)

This is not an interdependence like the one between $c(n)$ and $d(n)$, as $c(n)$ relies on $a(n)$ but $a(n)$ does not rely on $c(n)$.

## 2.4   GEN with prosodic recursion

The remaining six GEN functions allow prosodic recursion. We first discuss GEN[+φ stem, +Branching] and GEN[+φ stem]. These two set the foundation for understanding the final four parameter combinations.

### 2.4.1   GEN[+φ stem, +Branching]

GEN[+φ stem, +Branching] produces sets of trees with a φ stem, in which all non-terminal nodes are branching. The cardinality of these sets grows as shown below in (40). Apart from the value for $n = 1$, this well-studied sequence is known as the little Schröder numbers, or the super-Catalan numbers; its formula (41) is given by OEIS (https://oeis.org/A001003).[3]

(40)      Cardinality of GEN[+φ stem, +Branching]

|  | $n=$ | 1 | 2 | 3 | 4 | 5 | 6 |
|---|---|---|---|---|---|---|---|
| \| GEN[+φ stem, +Branching]$(n)$\| |  | 0 | 1 | 3 | 11 | 45 | 197 |

---

[3] The first little Schröder number is 1, not 0. The authors gratefully acknowledge that the discovery of the connection between GEN[+φ stem, +Branching] and the little Schröder numbers is due to Nick Kalivoda, who is also the original source for the mathematical reasoning in the following subsections on GEN[+φ stem] (§4.2) and GEN[−φ stem, −Branching] (§4.3).

(41)    $S(n) = ((6n - 9) * S(n - 1) - (n - 3) * S(n - 2))/n$

This formula, derived by combinatorics much more involved than the kind used for the first four formulas, produces the little Schröder numbers. According to Qi and Guo (2017):

> the little Schröder numbers form an integer sequence that can be used to count the number of plane trees with a given set of leaves, the number of ways of inserting parentheses into a sequence, and the number of ways of dissecting a convex polygon into smaller polygons by inserting diagonals.

Although the third description of the little Schröder numbers is unrelated to the kinds of representations involved in linguistics, the first two are commonplace representations of hierarchical linguistic structures. The key description is of "plane trees," which map perfectly onto our prosodic trees. When the tree is rooted in $\varphi$ and all intermediate nodes are branching, we get "the number of plane trees with a given set of leaves" assuming that these plane trees have no unary-branching nodes. All possible hierarchical groupings of leaves are accounted for. This paper will not go into the mathematics of deriving $S(n)$, but using the $S(n)$ formula we can discuss the remaining parameter combinations.

### 2.4.2   GEN[+φ stem]

GEN[+φ stem] maintains the requirement that trees have a $\varphi$ stem, but removes the requirement that all $\varphi$s be branching. The number of trees that GEN[+φ stem] produces is shown in (42), and this sequence can be described with the formula in (43).

(42)    | GEN[+φ stem](1 to 6 words) | = 1, 4, 24, 176, 1440, 12608

(43)    | GEN[+φ stem]$(n)$ | $= Z(n) = S(n) * 2^n$,
        where $S(n)$ is the $n$th little Schröder number, defined in (41)

Removing the [+Branching] requirement increases the number of possible minimal $\varphi$s, but does not alter the possible non-minimal $\varphi$s. Non-minimal $\varphi$s (those containing another $\varphi$) cannot be unary, because a $\varphi$ cannot have a single $\varphi$ as its sole daughter, due to the general prohibition of vacuous recursion in SPOT. Non-branching $\varphi$s are restricted to dominating a singular prosodic word.

For every terminal node in a [+Branching] tree, a [−Branching] tree may or may not have an additional minimal, unary $\varphi$ containing that terminal node. For example, consider the single tree produced by Gen[+φ stem, +Branching] at $n = 2$ (44). Gen[+φ stem, –Branching] admits this tree, as well as three additional trees created through admitting structures with unary φs (44). That is, Gen[+φ stem, –Branching] admits $2^2$ trees for two terminals, compared to a single tree admitted by Gen[+φ stem, +Branching].

(44)     Gen[+φ stem](2)

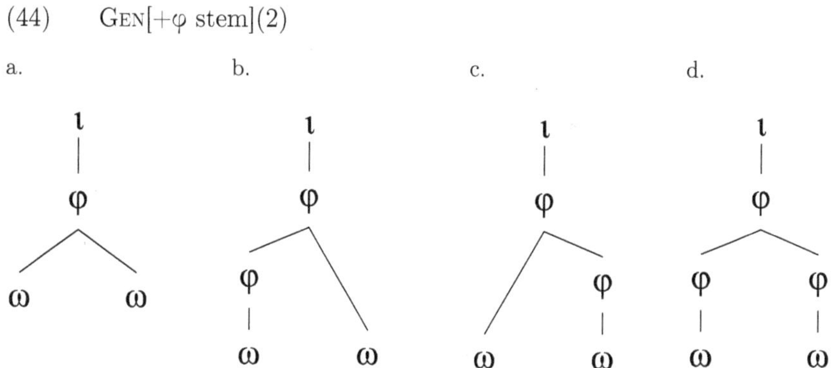


In Gen[–Branching] there are two choices for how to treat each terminal node in trees produced by Gen[+Branching], because each terminal node may or may not have an extra unary-branching φ parent in [–Branching] trees. This doubles the number of trees for every terminal node in the tree, hence the multiplication of $S(n)$ by $2^n$ in the formula shown in (43).

### 2.4.3   Gen[–φ stem, ±Branching]

We turn now to the Gen functions that do not require prosodic trees to be rooted in φ, but still allow recursion, beginning with Gen[+Branching] and the entirely unrestricted Gen[–Branching], or Gen[∅] in the overview table (7). The relationships among these functions and the cardinalities of their candidate sets are shown in the table in (45). Removing the [+φ stem] requirement doubles the cardinality of the candidate set, because every output $p$ in Gen[+φ stem] yields two valid outputs in Gen[–φ stem]: $p$ itself, unchanged, and Relink($p$). Relink, defined in (46), converts a φ-stemmed tree to its non-φ-stemmed counterpart. When Relink applies, the children of a maximal φ become children of the root intonational phrase, creating a tree that has no φ-stem, as in (47). This change of category causes previously non-maximal φs in $p$ to become maximal in $q$. Word daughters of the maximal φ in $p$ are parsed directly into the ι in $q$, creating violations of Exhaustivity. Gen[±Branching] allows such violations, however, so every $p$ in Gen[+Branching, +φ stem] can be converted into a valid $q$ belonging to

GEN[+Branching] by Relinking, and likewise for GEN[−Branching, +φ stem] with GEN[−Branching]. The original φ-stemmed outputs of Gen[+φ stem], schematized in (47b), are equally valid for GEN[−φ stem].

(45)    Converting from GEN[+φ stem] to GEN[−φ stem]

|                | [+φ stem]                                          | [−φ stem]                                    |
| -------------- | -------------------------------------------------- | -------------------------------------------- |
| [+Branching]   | \| GEN[+φ stem, +Branching] \|  $= S(n)$           | \| GEN[−φ stem, +Branching] \|  $= S(n) * 2 = e(n)$ |
| [−Branching]   | \| GEN[+φ stem, −Branching] \|ˊ  $= S(n) * 2^n = Z(n)$ | \| GEN[−φ stem, −Branching] \|  $= Z(n) * 2 = f(n)$ |

(46)    Relink($p$): Delink all the children of the φ-stem in $p$ and reattach
        them to the root ι to create $q$, a tree that does not have a φ-stem.

Combining the φ-stemless candidates produced by Relink and the φ-stemmed candidates GEN[+φ stem], we can see that the number of trees in GEN[−φ stem, αBranching] will be twice the number of trees in GEN[+φ stem, αBranching], as indicated in (45). The [+Branching] parameter does not apply to ιs, so this doubling of the candidate set from GEN[+φ stem] to GEN[−φ stem] occurs for both [+Branching] and [−Branching] GEN functions.

(47)    GEN[−φ stem]

        a.                          b.

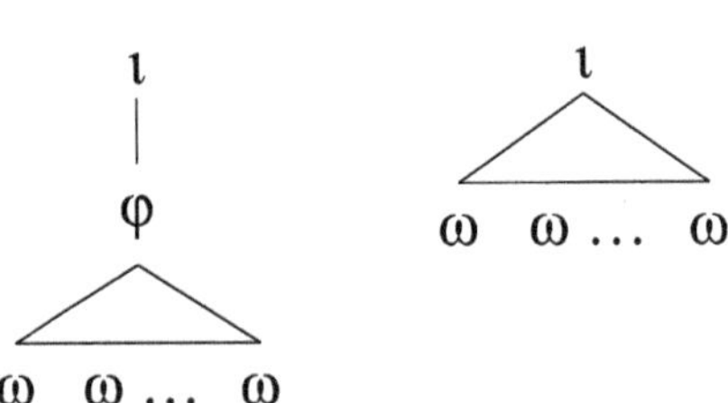

### 2.4.4  GEN[+Exh, ±Branching]

The remaining two GEN functions create trees that are rooted in an intonational phrase, but enforce Exhaustivity, requiring every word to be parsed into at least one phonological phrase. There are two such GEN functions, because one also enforces [+Branching], while the other does not.

(48)      Growth in cardinality of GEN[+Exhaustivity]

| $n =$ | 1 | 2 | 3 | 4 | 5 | 6 | 7 | 8 |
|---|---|---|---|---|---|---|---|---|
| GEN[+Exh, +Branching] | 0 | 1 | 3 | 12 | 51 | 229 | 1,068 | 5,125 |
| GEN[+Exh] | 1 | 5 | 33 | 253 | 2,121 | 18,853 | 174,609 | 1,667,021 |

The first of these sequences, for GEN[+Exhaustivity, +Branching], does not appear in OEIS, but the second, for GEN[+Exhaustivity, −Branching], does. Deriving the number of Exhaustivity-satisfying trees rooted in $\iota$ from the number of $\varphi$-rooted trees (which vacuously satisfy Exhaustivity) is much more complex than deriving the number of $\iota$-rooted trees without the Exhaustivity requirement, which was a simple matter of multiplying by two. With the requirement of Exhaustivity, every $\varphi$-rooted tree can still become a valid $\iota$-rooted tree through Iota-wrapping, but not every $\varphi$-rooted tree can do so through Relinking. Relinking a $\varphi$-stemmed tree in which the maximal $\varphi$ directly dominates one or more prosodic words will produce Exhaustivity violations when Relink makes those words the immediate children of the root $\iota$. The number of trees that do satisfy Exhaustivity is twice the number of $\varphi$-rooted trees, less $e(n)$, the number of Exhaustivity-violators.

(49)      $\mid \mathrm{GEN}[+\mathrm{Exh}, \alpha\mathrm{Branching}] \mid = 2^* \mid \mathrm{GEN}[+\varphi \text{ stem}, \alpha\mathrm{Branching}] \mid - e(n)$,
where $e(n)$ is the number of Exhaustivity-violating structures created by Recategorization

Unfortunately, calculating $e(n)$ is non-trivial. Although we currently do not have a full proof that these numbers are correct, we offer some partial explanations below in the form of summations that characterize the cardinalities of these two GEN functions.

### 2.4.4.1   GEN[+Exh, +Branching]

GEN[+Exh, +Branching] allows all trees in which all intermediate nodes are branching and every word is parsed into a phonological phrase. These trees are similar to those created by GEN[+$\varphi$ stem, +Branching], in that both GEN functions require all phonological words to be parsed into $\varphi$s. They differ in that GEN[+Exh, −$\varphi$ stem, +Branching] does not require the tree to contain a phonological phrase that dominates all terminals. The cardinality of GEN[+$\varphi$ stem, +Branching] is described by the Schröder–Hipparchus series, or little Schröder numbers (see §2.4.1), but no sequence in OEIS matches the cardinality of GEN[+Exhaustivity, +Branching]. However, if we consider the procedure for creating the trees of this GEN (50), we can derive a recursive equation for its cardinality (51).

(50)      Procedure for calculating GEN[+Exh, +Branching]
   a.     Choose a parenthesization of the $n$ terminals (i.e., one of the non-
          recursive tree structures that would be created by GEN[+NonRec,
          +Exh, +Branching]). This parenthesization determines the maximal
          φs.
   b.     Run each of the subsets of terminals created by the parenthesization
          in the previous step through GEN[+φ stem, +Branching].
   c.     Cross the sets of subtrees from each of the parenthesizations in
          Step (b) to get full trees for that parenthesization. That is, for each
          possible subtree in the first maximal φ, build a candidate with each
          possible subtree from the second maximal φ, and so on.
   d.     Repeat for each of the other parenthesizations from Step (a), and
          sum all the products, to get the whole candidate set.

This procedure can be translated into an equation for the cardinality of
GEN[+Exh, +Branching] (51).

(51)      | GEN[+Exh, +Branching]($n$ words) |
          $= g(n) = S(n) + \sum_{k=2}^{n-2} S(k) * g(n - k)$

The first possible parenthesization of the terminals puts all $n$ of them in
a single φ, the sole daughter of the ι root. The number of possible subtrees rooted in this $n$-terminal φ is $S(n)$, the cardinality of GEN[+φ stem,
+Branching]($n$ terminals). This is the first term in the equation above. The
remaining parenthesizations divide the $n$ terminals between two or more
maximal φs. The summation accounts for these trees, with $k$ standing for
the number of terminals in the leftmost φ. The smallest admissible φ in this
GEN must contain at least two terminals, so the minimum value of $k$ in this
expression is two. The maximum value of $k$ is $n - 2$ for the same reason,
since the righthand side of the tree will have $n - k$ terminals, and so $n - k$
must be at least two, and $k$ can be no more than $n - 2$, in order to fulfill
the requirement that all φ nodes be branching. Thus, if $n < 4$, $g(n) = S(n)$,
because the summation will not be evaluated, since there is no number $k$
such that $2 \leq k \leq n - 2$.

   The $k$ terminals in the leftmost maximal φ can be structured into $S(k)$
trees rooted in a maximal φ, in which each node is minimally binary-branching. As for the remaining $n - k$ terminals, they may be grouped into a single
maximal φ, or multiple maximal φs. For example, for $n = 6$ and $k = 2$, it
is possible to group the last four terminals into a single four-terminal φ, or
two binary-branching φs, while satisfying the requirements of GEN[+Exh,
+Branching]. $S(n - k)$ would account for all the structures in which the last

$n - k$ terminals are grouped into a single maximal φ, but will not count any structures where they are split up into two φs (or potentially more than two φs, if $n > 7$).

(52)     Two maximal φ structures for $n = 6$, $k = 2$
    a.    (a b)(c d e f)     *Last four terminals are contained in a single φ*
    b.    (a b)(c d)(e f)     *Last four terminals are not contained in a single φ*

Rather than counting all the branching substructures rooted in a φ, we need to count all the branching substructures in which every word is parsed into at least one φ—that is, structures that satisfy Branchingness and Exhaustivity. Hence the recursive factor in the summation expression, $g(n - k)$.

Any of the $S(k)$ substructures for the first $k$ terminals can be combined with any of the $g(n - k)$ substructures for the last $n - k$ terminals for a unique and valid [+Exh, +Branching] parse of all $n$ terminals, and so the total number of parses for any given values of $n$ and $k$ is the product of $S(k)$ and $g(n - k)$.

Let us consider the 229 trees of GEN[+Exh, +Branching](6 terminals) as an example. Setting $n = 6$, we derive the formula on the first line of (53), which can be simplified as shown on the following lines to arrive at the correct value, 229.

(53)     $g(6) = S(6) + \sum_{k=2}^{6-2} S(k) * g(6 - k)$

| | |
|---|---|
| $= S(6) + (S(2) * g(4) + S(3) * g(3) + S(4) * g(2))$ | *Expanding the summation* |
| $= S(6) + S(2) * (S(4) + S(2) * g(2)) + S(3) * g(3) + S(4) * g(2)$ | *Expanding $g(4)$* |
| $= S(6) + S(2) * (S(4) + S(2) * S(2)) + S(3) * S(3) + S(4) * S(2)$ | *$g(n)$ where $n < 4 = S(n)$* |
| $= 197 + 1 * (11 + 1 * 1) + (3 * 3) + (11 * 1)$ | *Substituting for $S$* |
| $= 197 + 12 + 9 + 11$ | |
| $= 229$ | |

We have verified that this formula correctly derives the first seven terms of the sequence $g(n)$. Given its use of $S(n)$, we believe it has some connection to other sequences derived from the Schröder triangle, and therefore likely has an interpretation in the domain of lattice paths as well, but we leave further simplification or extension of this formula for future research.

*2.4.4.2   GEN[+Exhaustivity]*

The final variation on GEN is GEN[+Exh], which enforces Exhaustivity and no other additional parameters. GEN[+Exh] is similar to GEN[+Exh, +Branching], but allows non-branching $\varphi$s. We can straightforwardly adjust the formula for GEN[+Exh, +Branching] (54) to remove the restriction on Branchingness (55). Removing the requirement of Branchingness involves two changes. First, $h(n)$ in (55) uses $Z(n)$, the number of $\varphi$-stemmed trees, where $g(n)$ in (54) uses $S(n)$, the number of branching $\varphi$-stemmed trees. (See §2.4.2 for an explanation of why $Z(n) = 2^n S(n)$.) Second, where [+Branching] $g(n)$ begins the summation at $k = 2$ and ends it at $k = n - 2$, so as to always keep at least two words in the maximal $\varphi$, [–Branching] $h(n)$ begins at $k = 1$ and includes $k = n - 1$. Both of these changes are shown in (a) in (55). The next line, (b) in (55), shows a further simplification. Since the summation does not need to skip $k = n - 1$, it can continue all the way up to $k = n$, unlike in $g(n)$ where the $\varphi$-stemmed phrasings must be calculated in separate terms (the first term in (54)). At $k = n$, $h(n - k) = h(0) = 1$, such that this $n$th term of the sequence evaluates to $Z(n)$, which no longer needs to be a separate term outside of the summation.

(54)      | GEN[+Exh, +Branching]($n$ words) |

$$= g(n) = S(n) + \sum_{k=2}^{n-2} S(k) * g(n - k) \qquad \text{Repeated from (51)}$$

(55)      | GEN[+Exh]($n$ words) | $= h(n) =$

a.      $= Z(n) + \sum_{k=1}^{n-1} Z(k)h(n - k)$

b.      $= \sum_{k=1}^{n} Z(k)h(n - k)$

The sequence produced by GEN[+Exh] matches A330802 in OEIS, for which OEIS gives the formula in (56).

(56)      $g(n) = \dfrac{(24 - 12n)g(n - 3) + (32n - 10)g(n - 2) + (9n - 9)g(n - 1)}{n + 1}$

where $g(1)=1$, $g(2)=5$, $g(3) = 33$  https://oeis.org/A330802

The OEIS entry, authored by Peter Luschny, also provides a note indicating that this sequence represents evaluation of the Big Schröder polynomials at ½ and normalized with $2^n$. The Big Schröder polynomials are given by the formula in (57). According to Wikipedia, the hypergeometric function is defined as a power series, shown in (58a), which reduces to the polynomial in (58b) if $a$ or $b$ is a non-positive integer. This holds in (54), where $a = k - n$, which is guaranteed to be a non-positive integer since $k \leq n$. As shown in (59), setting $x$ to ½ and multiplying by $2^n$ yields the observed sequence.

(57)   Big Schröder polynomials

   a.   *Adapted from Mathematica notation provided by Peter Luschny (p.c.)*

$P(n, x) = \text{Sum}[\text{ Binomial}(n, k)\ \text{Hypergeometric2F1}[k - n, n + 1, k + 2, -1]\ x^k, \{k, 0, n\}]$

   b.   *Substituting in the binomial coefficients and changing notation*

$$P(n, x) = \sum_{k=0}^{n} \frac{n!}{k!(n-k)!} \times {}_2F_1(k - n, n + 1, k + 2, -1) \times x^k$$

   c.   *P(n, x) evaluated with n from 0 to 8 (Peter Luschny, p.c.):*

     i.   $h(0, x) = 1$

     ii.   $h(1, x) = 2 + x$

     iii.   $h(2, x) = 6 + 4\,x + x^2$

     iv.   $h(3, x) = 22 + 16\,x + 6\,x^2 + x^3$

     v.   $h(4, x) = 90 + 68\,x + 30\,x^2 + 8\,x^3 + x^4$

     vi.   $h(5, x) = 394 + 304\,x + 146\,x^2 + 48\,x^3 + 10\,x^4 + x^5$

     vii.   $h(6, x) = 1806 + 1412\,x + 714\,x^2 + 264\,x^3 + 70\,x^4 + 12\,x^5 + x^6$

     viii.   $h(7, x) = 8558 + 6752\,x + 3534\,x^2 + 1408\,x^3 + 430\,x^4 + 96\,x^5 + 14\,x^6 + x^7$

     ix.   $h(8, x) = 41586 + 33028\,x + 17718\,x^2 + 7432\,x^3 + 2490\,x^4 + 652\,x^5 + 126\,x^6 + 16\,x^7 + x^8$

(58)   Hypergeometric   function   (https://en.wikipedia.org/wiki/Hypergeometric_function)

   a.   As a power series, for $|z| < 1$:

$$_2F_1(a, b; c; z) = \sum_{n=0}^{\infty} \frac{(a)_n (b)_n}{(c)_n} \frac{z^n}{n!} = 1 + \frac{ab}{c} \frac{z}{1!} + \frac{a(a + 1)b(b + 1)}{c(c + 1)} \frac{z^2}{2!} + \dots$$

   b.   Reduced to a polynomial if $a$ or $b$ in the power series in (53a) is a non-positive integer

$$_2F_1(-m, b; c; z) = \sum_{n=0}^{m} (-1)^n \binom{m}{n} \frac{(b)_n}{(c)_n} z^n$$

(59)      Evaluating at ½ and normalizing by $2^n$

    a.      Evaluating at x = ½

$$P(n, \tfrac{1}{2}) = \sum_{k=0}^{n} \frac{n!}{k!(n-k)!} \frac{z^n}{n!}\, {}_2F_1(k-n,\, n+1,\, k+2,\, -1)\, (\tfrac{1}{2})^k$$

    b.      Normalizing by $2^n$

$$h(n) = \sum_{k=0}^{n} \frac{n!}{k!(n-k)!} \frac{z^n}{n!}\, {}_2F_1(k-n,\, n+1,\, k+2,\, -1)\, (\tfrac{1}{2})^k\, 2^n$$

$$2^n \sum_{k=0}^{n} \frac{n!}{k!(n-k)!} \frac{z^n}{n!}\, {}_2F_1(k-n,\, n+1,\, k+2,\, -1)\, (\tfrac{1}{2})^k$$

We leave for future work the task of explaining the connection between the summation in (55) that we adapted from (51), and the formulations in (55–57) given in OEIS by Peter Luschny, which will most likely reveal a connection between (51) and the Big Schröder polynomials as well.


## 2.5      Conclusion

When phonological structure is assumed to conform to Strict Layering, the number of possible prosodies for a given string of phonological words is very limited. Non-recursivity and Exhaustivity are inviolable, and so is Headedness. It is relatively simple to calculate the number of possible parses, and to check that the generated candidate set is correct and complete for up to six terminals (32 possible parses). If this assumption of Strict Layering is abandoned, however, such that Non-recursivity and Exhaustivity become violable constraints, the number of possible parses explodes. Removing Exhaustivity as a requirement results in 233 possible parses of six terminals (or 232 if Headedness is still enforced); removing Non-Recursivity as a requirement but retaining Exhaustivity results in close to nineteen thousand possible parses of six terminals; and removing both restrictions means over 25,000 parses are possible. Since all of these numbers are so large, it is not feasible to verify that the generated candidate sets are complete by checking them against a manually generated list. Requiring all φs to be minimally binary, however, dramatically slows the growth rate, as shown by the contrast between the magnitudes of the candidate sets at six terminals, with and without the [+Branching] requirement, in the final and penultimate columns of (60). Applying the [+Branching] restriction on GEN makes it possible to generate candidate sets for much longer sentences without running up against computational limits, and is useful for examining subsets of the typology in which a constraint on minimal binarity is undominated.

(60)    GEN functions without branching as a parameter

| | | $n=1$ | $n=2$ | $n=3$ | $n=4$ | $n=5$ | $n=6$ | GEN[+Branching], $n=6$ |
|---|---|---|---|---|---|---|---|---|
| Strictest Layering | [+NonRec, +Exh] | 1 | 2 | 4 | 8 | 16 | 32 | 5 |
| | [+NonRec] | 2 | 5 | 13 | 34 | 89 | 233 | 32 |
| | [+$\varphi$ stem] | 1 | 4 | 24 | 176 | 1440 | 12608 | 197 |
| | [+Exh] | 1 | 5 | 33 | 253 | 2121 | 18853 | 229 |
| Weakest Layering | [∅] | 2 | 8 | 48 | 352 | 2880 | 25216 | 394 |

When using SPOT, the analyst is reasonably likely to notice if an ill-formed structure that should have been excluded from GEN was included in the candidate set by mistake. It is much harder to detect an omitted candidate, however. Therefore, in this paper, we have provided evidence that SPOT's generated candidate sets are indeed complete through a different means: by reasoning through the number of ways to build structures of $n$ terminals from those of $n-1$ terminals and thereby deriving a recurrence relation between the cardinality of the candidate set for smaller values of $n$, and larger values.

We found that the cardinalities of the candidate sets produced by all GEN functions investigated here represent mathematically sensible sequences, as shown in (61). The non-recursive versions of GEN grow in ways that are connected to the Fibonacci sequence (rows a, f in (61)), or to the exponential function $2^{n-1}$ (rows b, c). Recursive versions, on the other hand, grow as a function of the little Schröder numbers or super-Catalan numbers. Previous work had already established that the little Schröder numbers represent the number of trees with $n$ terminals, in which every non-terminal node has two or more children (mentioned in, e.g., Guo and Qi 2017, Stanley 1999); this is exactly GEN[+$\varphi$ stem, +Branching] (d). Three other recursive GEN sequences can be derived simply from this one (g, h, j). In structures produced by these three GEN functions, the category labels of the nodes are irrelevant, because a node's category can be inferred from its position in the tree. When the root node is a $\varphi$ (d, h), all non-terminals are also $\varphi$s, and so the distinction between $\varphi/\omega$ amounts to a distinction between non-terminals and terminals. When the root node is an ɩ, we have a three-way distinction between root $\sim$ ɩ, intermediate levels $\sim$ $\varphi$, and terminals $\sim$ $\omega$. When Exhaustivity is enforced, the category labels become relevant, although they can still be read off the tree directly. Exhaustivity can be interpreted as a requirement that a non-root, non-terminal node intervene on any path from a terminal to the root; or in other words, as a requirement that the tree be at least three levels deep at every point.

(61)      Formulas for the cardinality of GEN functions, in order of how fast they grow

| | Parameter Combination | Function | Related to |
|---|---|---|---|
| a. | [+NonRec, +Exh, +Branching] | Fibonacci sequence: $a(n) = a(n-1) + a(n-2)$ | Fibonacci sequence |
| b. | [+NonRec, +Branching] | $2^{(n-1)}$ | Exponential |
| c. | [+NonRec, +Exh] | $2^{(n-1)}$ | Exponential |
| d. | [+φ stem, +Branching] | Little Schröder numbers: $S(n) = ((6n-9){*}S(n-1) - (n-3){*}S(n-2))/n$ | Little Schröder numbers |
| e. | [+Exh, +Branching] | $S(n) + \Sigma(\text{for } k \text{ from 2 to } (n-2))[S(k) * g(n-k)]$ | Little Schröder numbers |
| f. | [+NonRec] | Bisection of the Fibonacci sequence: $c(n) = 3 * c(n-1) - c(n-2)$ | Fibonacci sequence |
| g. | [+Branching] | Twice the little Schröder numbers: $2{*}S(n)$ | Little Schröder numbers |
| h. | [+φ stem] | Little Schröder numbers multiplied by $2^n$: $Z(n) = 2^n * S(n)$ | Little Schröder numbers |
| i. | [+Exh] | Big Schröder polynomials evaluated at ½ and normalized by $2^n$: $h(n) = ((24{-}12{*}n) * h(n-3) + (32 * n - 10) * h(n-2) + (9 * n - 9) * h(n-1))/(n+1)$ or: $h(k) = \Sigma(\text{for } k \text{ from 1 to } n)[Z(k) * h(n-k)]$ | Little Schröder numbers, Big Schröder numbers |
| j. | [∅] | Twice the number of φ-rooted candidates: $2\,Z(n)$, or $2^{n+1} S(n)$ | Little Schröder numbers |

All of these functions describe the actual number of trees produced by SPOT's GEN functions for the given parameter settings, as well as the number of trees that they *should* produce, if the candidate sets are complete. This validates the logic in SPOT's code and is evidence that SPOT's candidate sets are complete.

While this chapter was able to discover a formula for every GEN under consideration, no attempt was made to simplify the formulas for GEN[+Exh, +Branching], or to show why the two formulas for GEN[+Exh] are equivalent. This is left for future research. Furthermore, SPOT also has other GEN settings not considered here, such as versions of GEN that allow reordering of the terminals, or movement of a single terminal, as well as other variations that arise with the cancelation of the starting assumption here that all terminals are prosodic words (i.e., when clitics that are parsed as syllables are included in the syntactic input). Future work could provide a more complete description of these other candidate sets and their rates of growth. Finally, a recently added feature of SPOT is a version of the GEN algorithm that creates trees in which two prosodic categories are allowed to be recursive—i.e., recursive words and recursive phonological phrases in the same structure, as occurs in the prosodic structure of long compound words (see Ito and Mester 2021). Such candidate sets grow even more rapidly than the ones considered here, making it even more essential to discover a function describing the expected number of candidates, to aid in development and validation of the code that actually generates the tree structures. This, too, is a project for future investigation.

## References


Bellik, Jennifer, Bellik, Ozan, and Kalivoda, Nick (2015–2021). Syntax-Prosody in Optimality Theory (SPOT). Javascript application. http:// spot.sites.ucsc.edu. Codebase at https://github.com/syntax-prosody-ot.

Bennett, Ryan, Elfner, Emily, and McCloskey, James (2016). Lightest to the right: An apparently anomalous displacement in Irish. *Linguistic Inquiry* 47: 169–234.

Elfner, Emily (2012). *Syntax-Prosody Interactions in Irish.* PhD dissertation, University of Massachusetts Amherst.

Ito, Junko and Mester, Armin (1992/2003). Weak layering and word binarity. In Takeru Honma, Masao Okazaki, Toshiyuki Tabata and Shin-ichi Tanaka (eds.) *A New Century of Phonology and Phonological Theory: A Festschrift for Professor Shosuke Haraguchi on the Occasion of His Sixtieth Birthday* 26–65. Tokyo: Kaitakusha.

Ito, Junko and Mester, Armin (2013). Prosodic subcategories in Japanese. *Lingua* 124: 20–40

Ito, Junko and Mester, Armin (2021). Recursive prosody and the prosodic form of compounds. *Languages* 6: 65.

Jun, Sun-Ah (1998). The accentual phrase in the Korean prosodic hierarchy. *Phonology* 15: 189–226.

Kalivoda, Nick (2018). *Syntax-Prosody Mismatches in Optimality Theory.* PhD dissertation, University of California, Santa Cruz.

Ladd, D. Robert (1986). Intonational phrasing: the case for recursive prosodic structure. *Phonology Yearbook* 3: 311–340.

Ladd, D. Robert (1988). Declination "reset" and the hierarchical organization of utterances. *Journal of the Acoustical Society of America* 84: 530–544.

Nespor, Marina and Vogel, Irene (1983). Prosodic structure above the word. In Anne Cutler and D. Robert Ladd (eds.) *Prosody: Models and Measurements* 123–140. Berlin, Heidelberg, New York, Tokyo: Springer.

Nespor, Marina and Vogel, Irene (1986). *Prosodic Phonology.* Dordrecht: Foris.

OEIS Foundation Inc (2020). The On-Line Encyclopedia of Integer Sequences. http://OEIS.org.

Pierrehumbert, Janet and Beckman, Mary (1988). *Japanese Tone Structure.* Cambridge, MA: MIT Press.

Prince, Alan (2017). OT Checklist. ROA 1306, Rutgers Optimality Archive, http://roa.rutgers.edu.

Prince, Alan (2018). Counting parses. In Ryan Bennett, Andrew Angeles, Adrian Brasoveanu, Dhyana Buckley, Nick Kalivoda, Shigeto Kawahara, Grant McGuire and Jaye Padgett (eds.) *Hana-bana (花々): A Festschrift for Junko Ito and Armin Mester.* Santa Cruz: Linguistics Research Center.

Prince, Alan and Smolensky, Paul (1993/2004). *Optimality Theory: Constraint Interaction in Generative Grammar.* Malden, MA: Blackwell Publishing.

Qi, Feng and Guo, Bai-Ni (2017). Explicit and recursive formulas, integral representations, and properties of the Large Schröder numbers. *Kragujevac Journal of Mathematics* 41: 121–141.

Selkirk, Elisabeth (1984). *Phonology and Syntax: the Relation between Sound and Structure.* Cambridge, MA: MIT Press.

Selkirk, Elisabeth (2011). The syntax–phonology interface. In John A. Goldsmith, Jason Riggle, and Alan C. L. Yu (eds.) *The Handbook of Phonological Theory* 435–484. Blackwell Publishing.

Stanley, Richard P. (1999). Exercises on Catalan and Related Numbers, (39b). In Richard P. Stanley, *Enumerative Combinatorics, vol. 2* 221–247. Cambridge University Press 1999. Available at http://www-math.mit.edu/~rstan/ec/catalan.pdf.

## About the authors

*Edward Shingler*

Undergraduate research assistant and programmer for the SPOT project, Linguistics BA 2021, University of California, Santa Cruz. Research interests: syntax–prosody interface, psycholinguistics and attention.

*Jennifer Bellik*

Postdoctoral researcher and lecturer, Department of Linguistics, UC Santa Cruz. Research interests: syntax-prosody interface, Optimality Theory,

Articulatory Phonology, and Turkish phonology. Recent publications: "An acoustic study of vowel intrusion in Turkish onset clusters", *Laboratory Phonology* 2018; "Automated tableau generation with SPOT" with N.Kalivoda, *Linguistics Vanguard* 2019; and "The effect of speech style and deaccentuation on vowel intrusion in Turkish complex onsets", *Proceedings of ICPhS* 2019.

## Appendix: Tree operations

The following table lists all the tree-modifying operations named throughout
the chapter.

| | | |
|---|---|---|
| Add a $\omega$ terminal | IncludeInPhrase (16) | Add new terminal (word) into rightmost $\varphi$ |
| | Recouple (18) | Remove a single word from rightmost $\varphi$ (rightmost $\varphi$'s $\omega$-count $> 2$) to form a new $\varphi$ with new $\omega$ (new rightmost $\varphi$'s $\omega$-count $= 2$) |
| | AssociateToRoot (22) | Add $\omega$ immediately below the root $\iota$ on the right |
| | Pair (24) | Take rightmost $\omega$ and create new $\varphi$ with new word (new $\varphi$'s $\omega$-count $= 2$) |
| | ExhaustivelyAssociate (30) | Add a unary $\varphi$ immediately below the root $\iota$ on the right, with a new $\omega$ as its sole child (new $\varphi$'s $\omega$-count $= 1$) |
| Convert $\varphi$-stem tree to a non-$\varphi$-stemmed tree | Relink($p$) 0 | Detach all the children of the maximal $\varphi$ in $p$ (a [+$\varphi$ stem] tree), and reattach them to the root $\iota$ to create $q$ (a [−$\varphi$ stem] tree). |

# Chapter 3

# Branching sensitivity, prosodic recursion, and mapping constraints

Max Tarlov[*]

## 3.1 Introduction

Phrasal phenomena in phonology are often sensitive to syntactic structure, requiring that phrasal phonology have an interface with syntax (Bennett and Elfner 2019, Elordieta 2008). In the research which investigates this interface within the framework of Optimality Theory (OT, Prince and Smolensky 1993/2004), there are two main approaches: Alignment Theory, which posits that there is correspondence between the *edges* of syntactic and prosodic structures, and Match Theory, which posits a correspondence between the *constituents* of syntactic and prosodic structure. (For Alignment, see Chen 1987, Selkirk 1986, and Truckenbrodt 1995; for the idea of matching, see Liberman and Prince 1977, and for Match Theory, see Selkirk 2011.) In both frameworks, the posited mapping constraints interface with constraints on prosodic well-formedness, such as binarity constraints that impose requirements on the size of prosodic constituents.

In pursuit of a better understanding of the implications of this fundamental difference between Match and Alignment Theories, this chapter compares the typological predictions of two constraint sets, each consisting of syntax–prosody mapping constraints and two markedness constraints. Since

[*] This chapter would never have been started, much less completed, if not for the inspiration and guidance of the editors, especially Jennifer Bellik and Nick Kalivoda. I am also grateful to the researchers associated with the SPOT project at UCSC and two anonymous reviewers, as well as the organizers and participants of the SOTA II conference—especially Alan Prince.

Alignment was conceived of with the Strict Layer Hypothesis (Selkirk 1984) in mind and Match with the growing acceptance of analyses using prosodic recursivity, I combine the two constraint sets with two distinct GEN functions, resulting in four total *systems* (1). (In this chapter, "system" refers to a fully defined CON set, GEN function, and the resulting factorial typologies.) In two of the systems (Match.Rec and Align.Rec), GEN allows recursion, where one system uses MATCH and the other uses ALIGN constraints. In the other two systems (Match.NR and Align.NR), GEN does not allow recursion. Once again, one system uses MATCH and the other uses ALIGN. The table in (1) shows the intersection of these parameters and the naming system used in this chapter to refer to each combination.

(1)　　　　Systems analyzed in this chapter

|  | MATCH constraints | ALIGN constraints |
| --- | --- | --- |
| Recursive GEN | Match.Rec | Align.Rec |
| Non-recursive GEN | Match.NR | Align.NR |

I anchor discussion of these systems with a simple type of real-world phenomenon I refer to as subject-branchingness sensitivity. Subject-branchingness sensitivity is cross-linguistically common and appears in various forms throughout this volume (e.g., Bellik and Van Handel, Chapter 10). The four typologies examined in this chapter each contain at least one language which emulates this behavior, but, as we will see, only to varying degrees. Since subject-branchingness sensitivity (henceforth SBS) is well-attested across languages, it provides a useful test case for whether a given system predicts an empirically sufficient typology.

SBS is exemplified by Kinyambo, a Bantu language documented by Bickmore (1989, 1990) and analyzed in OT by Bellik and Kalivoda (2016). In Kinyambo, a subject and its accompanying verb are mapped into the same phonological phrase when the subject consists of only one word (i.e., the subject is non-branching) and phrases apart from the verb when the subject consists of two words (i.e., the subject is branching), as seen in (2) and (3). The high tone is marked with an acute accent when present, and underlined where absent. Parentheses ( ) show the phonological phrase boundaries proposed by Bickmore (1989, 1990), who first described and analyzed this behavior in the language.

(2)　　　　(abak͟ozi bákajúna)
　　　　　　workers they-helped
　　　　　　'The workers helped'

(3)      (*abak<u>o</u>zi bakúru*) (*bákajúna*)
         workers mature they-helped
         'The mature workers helped'

The phrasing shown above is Bickmore's explanation for why *abakozi* is pronounced without the lexical high tone which can be observed in its citation form in (4), whereas *bakúru* and *bákajúna* retain their high tones above in (2) and (3).

(4)      Kinyambo words in isolation
     a. *abakózi*     'workers'
     b. *bákajúna*    'they helped'
     c. *bakúru*      'mature'

Bickmore's conclusion is that High Tone Deletion operates on all prosodic words that are non-final within a phonological phrase, so because *bakúru* appears with its lexical high tones intact in (3), it must not be final within the phrase, and *abakozi* and *bakúru* must form a phonological phrase separate from *bákajúna*. This pattern exemplifies subject-branchingness sensitivity: the syntactic branchingness of the subject determines its phonological phrasing. SBS is also observed in Xitsonga (Lee and Selkirk 2022) and Connemara Irish (Elfner 2012, 2015). Similar sensitivity to other kinds of syntactic structure is also common. Sensitivity to the branchingness of a prepositional phrase can be seen in Spanish (Prieto 2006) and Italian (Ghini 1993, Van Handel 2021). Sensitivity to object branchingness can be seen in Catalan (Prieto 2005).

The remainder of this section develops a formal definition of SBS. The definition of SBS should account for whether a phonological structure is caused by the branchingness of the subject. For example, if Kinyambo phrased all two-word sentences as the structure in (2) and all three-word sentences as the structure in (3), we would describe Kinyambo as sensitive to the length of the sentence, not the branchingness of the subject.

This chapter uses two definitions of SBS, presented in (5). Square brackets [ ] represent XP boundaries, here and throughout the chapter. The less stringent definition (5a) abandons the notion of causality described above and looks only for surface-level similarities to other SBS languages. The more stringent definition in (5b) attempts to set a measurable standard for causality by employing the notion of a STRONG MISMATCH. A strong mismatch occurs 'where descending syntactic structure maps onto ascending (and thereby contradictory) prosodic structure" (Kalivoda 2018, p. 52). In other words, a strong mismatch is the phrasing together in the prosody of two or more words that do not form a syntactic constituent and, in fact, belong to separate syntactic constituents, contradicting the overarching shape of the syntactic tree. By comparison, a WEAK MISMATCH occurs where a syntactic constituent is simply not present in the prosodic structure, and any prosodic structure which is not represented in the syntactic exponent is non-branching (a single word cannot belong to a separate constituent from itself).

(5)      Subject-branchingness sensitivity (SBS)

    a.   *Less stringent definition:* A language L displays SBS iff

       i.    In L, there is no $\varphi$ boundary between the subject and verb when the subject is non-branching.

       ii.   In L, there *is* a $\varphi$ boundary between the subject and verb when the subject is branching.

          I.e., [[N] [V]] $\rightarrow$ (N V)

          but [[[N] [A]] [V]] $\rightarrow$ ...N A) V... or ...N A) (V...

    b.   *More stringent definition:* A language L displays SBS iff

       i.    L conforms to (a)

       ii.   Let $x$ be L's prosodic parse of the branching-subject sentence [[[N][A]] [V]]. $x$ does not occur as a strong mismatch anywhere in L.

          E.g., [[[N][A]] [V]] $\rightarrow$ (N A)(V) and [V [[N] [N]]] $\rightarrow$ (V N) (N)

In (5b), the notion of a strong mismatch is used as a benchmark for SBS because strong mismatches indicate that something other than syntactic structure is primarily motivating a prosodic structure. If a particular phonological structure surfaces even when it contradicts the overarching shape of its syntactic input, we cannot confidently say that a syntactic structure like subject branchingness is causing that phrasing in that grammar when it happens to surface for non-mismatching input/output pairs as well.

This chapter employs subject-branchingness sensitivity as a window into the concrete typological consequences of Alignment and Match theories, as well as their assumed GEN functions. Treating both the mapping constraint regime and the GEN function as variable parameters sheds light on the complex relationship between GEN and CON—a relationship which has not, to my knowledge, been systematically studied in the domain of syntax–prosody mapping. I find that a definition of GEN which allows prosodic recursion yields better emulation of subject-branchingness sensitivity, and a simpler property analysis of the resulting typology (Alber and Prince 2021) when paired with Match Theory than when paired with Alignment Theory. Conversely, a definition of GEN which does not allow prosodic recursion, when paired with Alignment Theory, yields better emulation of subject-branchingness sensitivity, and a simpler property analysis than it does when it is paired with Match Theory. These differences between MATCH and ALIGN are even greater in the non-recursive systems than in the recursive systems.

The remainder of the chapter is organized as follows. Section 3.2 formally defines the systems whose typologies I analyze. Sections 3.3 and 3.4 discuss the typologies of the recursive systems (Match.Rec and Align.Rec, respectively), and §§3.5 and 3.6, the typologies of the non-recursive systems (Match.NR and Align.NR). For each of the four systems, I provide an overview of the factorial typology, a detailed description of the languages in each typology, a property analysis (see Albert and Prince 2021, Alber and Prince 2017, and Alber et al. 2016) and a discussion of subject-branchingness sensitivity in that system. Section 3.7 discusses and concludes.

## 3.2   Formal definitions of systems

A rigorous investigation of the typologies of an OT system requires thorough definitions of the component parts: GEN, CON and EVAL (see Prince 2017). This section defines the GEN and CON functions used in the systems in this chapter. I use the definition of EVAL originally proposed by Prince and Smolensky (1993/2004).

### 3.2.1   GEN

A complete definition of GEN defines both the set of possible outputs and the set of possible inputs, as dictated in Prince (2017). This section first defines the set of possible inputs and discusses why these particular inputs were chosen (2.1.1), then defines the output sets (2.1.2).

### 3.2.1.1   Inputs

The inputs to GEN for the four systems defined here are generated from the phrase structure grammar in (6).

(6)      Phrase structure grammar for syntactic inputs:
    a.   $XP \rightarrow X^0\ XP$
    b.   $XP \rightarrow XP\ X^0$
    c.   $XP \rightarrow XP\ XP$
    d.   $XP \rightarrow X^0$

This phrase structure grammar is the result of the list of principles in (7);[1] (8) lists the substructures that the principles in (7) were designed to prohibit.

(7)      Input syntax requirements:
    a.    Every word is a terminal $X^0$.
    b.    Every terminal $X^0$ is a word.
    c.    Every non-terminal is an XP.
    d.    Every XP is either binary-branching or unary-branching.
    e.    Every binary-branching XP immediately dominates at most one terminal. (No XP introduces more than one head.)
    f.    Every unary-branching XP immediately dominates a terminal.
    g.    Every tree is rooted in an XP.
    h.    Inputs are maximally four words long.

(8)      Excluded syntactic structures (Square brackets represent XP boundaries)
    a.    Recursion that does not add new syntactic terminals: [XP]
    b.    Adjacent heads: $[X^0\ X^0]$
    c.    Ternary branching: $[XP\ X^0\ XP]$

The substructure in (8a) is excluded by the principle in (7f) because (8a) is an example of vacuous recursion. While this may be syntactically well-formed, the two nodes dominate the same string of terminals and are both XPs, so any mapping constraint should only map one of them and ignore the other (see Elfner 2012 for discussion). Since the invisibility of one of the nodes in structure (8a) to the mapping constraints makes (8a) equivalent to $[_{XP}\ X^0]$, a structure that is generated by the system anyway, we can simply prohibit the vacuous recursion structure. The structures characterized by (8b) are excluded by (7e) because they are syntactically ill-formed; no XP can have more than one head. The structure in (8c) is excluded by (7d) to keep the typologies of this system small. Finally, (7h) limits inputs to four words since longer sentences would generate larger typologies which would be impractical to fully explore in this chapter alone. The limited size of the input set is further discussed in §3.7.

The principles in (7) and the phrase structure rules in (6) generate 72 licit syntactic structures, three of which are particularly important for this

---

[1] These principles were first proposed to me by Nick Kalivoda and further refined with the help of Jennifer Bellik.

chapter. These three structures, enumerated in (9), are the same inputs used above to identify SBS in Kinyambo, and serve as the prototypical structures which distinguish SBS languages. While category labels are given in the trees below to clarify their connection to the Kinyambo examples in (2) and (3), the prosodic mapping process ignores these categories.

(9)      Prototypical structures for distinguishing SBS

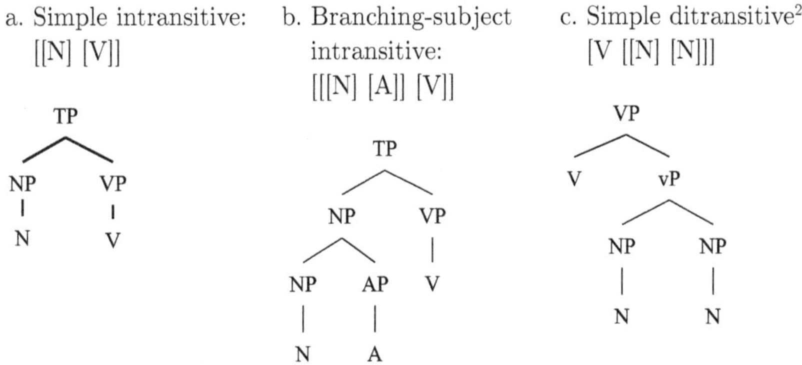

The principles for the syntactic inputs laid out above do not allow for X′ constituents, only XP constituents and X⁰s. This chapter assumes that X′ constituents are treated as if they were XP constituents by syntax–prosody mapping constraints (as proposed by Ito and Mester 2018). Thus, [XP X′] would be treated as [XP XP], the same as an adjunction structure. This view of syntactic visibility allows the simple and constrained set of phrase structure rules in (7) to plausibly generate all possible syntactic structures.[3] Another viable view of syntactic visibility which is not used in this chapter is that the X′ is invisible to syntax–prosody mapping constraints. This view would predict ternary structures such as [XP X⁰ XP]—a head with a complement and a specifier. Since this chapter relies on the maximal simplicity

---

[2] I identify the structure [X⁰ [[X⁰] [X⁰]]] as that of a simple V-N-N ditransitive, assuming a Larsonian VP-shell structure (Larson 1988) in which the trace or lower copy of V is invisible at the syntax-prosody interface. However, even if ditransitives are assumed to have a different structure, [X⁰ [[X⁰] [X⁰]]] is an input admitted by GEN, and hence forms a part of the four OT systems explored in this chapter.

[3] These phrase structure rules do generate both head-complement and complement-head structures; Kinyambo, our test case, only makes use of the head-complement order, but other languages use complement-head structures or a mix of both orders. Since the systems discussed here are intended to be general, I choose to allow them to generate the complement-head structure despite it being illicit in Kinyambo.

of its systems to compare their fundamental properties, I will not use this
alternative assumption.

### 3.2.1.2  Outputs

Candidates were generated and evaluated using SPOT (Bellik et al. 2015–
2021). For all four systems discussed here, only exhaustive parses were
generated (i.e., all prosodic words are children of phonological phrases, not
intonational phrases). While it would have been possible to examine systems
where Exhaustivity is not enforced, it is more straightforward to, for the
most part, follow the assumptions made by Bickmore (1989, 1982) for our
prime example of SBS, Kinyambo.

While §§3.3 and 3.4 detail systems that allow recursivity at the level of
the phonological phrase, the GEN function used in §§3.5 and 3.6 enforces
Non-Recursivity for its outputs. These latter systems most closely resemble the Kinyambo analyses in Bellik and Kalivoda (2016), which, following
Bickmore (1989, 1990), assume that phrasing is non-recursive.

Following the formal definition of the inputs laid out in 2.1.1, I formally
define the outputs generated by SPOT in (10) and (11). (10) defines the
outputs for the first two systems, which do allow recursion, and (11) defines
the outputs for the last two systems, which do not.

(10)     Recursive GEN outputs: All prosodic trees where...
   a.    Every prosodic word ω is a terminal.
   b.    Every terminal is an ω.
   c.    Every ω is the daughter of a phonological phrase φ.
   d.    Every tree is rooted in an intonational phrase ι (not shown).

(11)     Non-recursive GEN outputs: All prosodic trees where...
   a.    The requirements in (10) are met and
   b.    Every φ is the daughter of an ι.

### 3.2.2  CON

Two different constraint sets are used in this chapter, the MATCH CON and
the ALIGN CON. These two constraint sets have been pared down significantly
compared to the larger constraint sets used by other analyses such as Bellik
and Kalivoda (2016). As discussed further in §3.2.2.1 and §3.2.2.2, the more
common constraints which have been removed from the systems are either
MATCH-specific, ALIGN-specific, or specific to recursive definitions of GEN.
These constraints would have confounded the differences between the four
typologies. Other constraints which have been removed, such as EQUALSISTERS

(Myrberg 2013), would have inflated the typologies and further obscured the basic behaviors of MATCH and ALIGN.

### 3.2.2.1   MATCH *constraint set*

The MATCH constraint set uses only three constraints, defined in (12). These definitions are adapted from the definitions found on the SPOT interface (Bellik et al. 2015–2021). I use the convention of the 'sp." prefix to denote a syntax to prosody mapping constraint and the 'm." prefix to denote a markedness constraint, at the suggestion of Alan Prince (p.c.).

(12)    MATCH constraint set
  a.   **sp.MATCH**: Assign one violation for every XP such that there is no $\varphi$ that dominates all and only the same terminal nodes as it (Selkirk 2011, Elfner 2012).
  b.   **m.BINMIN**: Assign one violation for every $\varphi$ with only one immediate child.
  c.   **m.BINMAX**: Assign one violation for every $\varphi$ with more than two immediate children.

First note that sp.MATCH could alternatively be defined in terms of correspondence, where a $\varphi$ corresponds to some XP if and only if the $\varphi$ and XP dominate the same terminal nodes. As this is not common practice in the literature, I have not used correspondence in the definition above. Note also that the binarity constraints in (12) and throughout the chapter are defined as branch-counting binarity constraints, as opposed to leaf-counting binarity constraints. That is, they count the number of immediate descendants of any category in a $\varphi$, rather than counting the number of $\omega$s in the $\varphi$ (Bellik and Van Handel, Chapter 10). As established in Chapter 10, branch-counting binarity yields size-driven structure building, of which SBS is an example, whereas leaf-counting binarity does not. Furthermore, the larger typologies that arise from the use of leaf-counting binarity constraints would serve only to obscure the differences between Alignment, MATCH, recursivity and Strict Layering (see §3.2.1; Bellik and Kalivoda 2016; and Bellik and Van Handel, Chapter 10).[4]

The most notable omission from this constraint set is a prosody-to-syntax version of MATCH, for instance, ps.MATCH (Selkirk 2011). This was left out because ALIGN systems do not have a comparable prosody-to-syntax

---

[4] I use the categorical versions of binarity in this chapter, and not the gradient definitions, as the categorical definitions are standard in the literature.

mapping constraint standardly used in the literature.[5] Furthermore, to include prosody-to-syntax Alignment constraints in the ALIGN systems would have increased the size of these typologies and complicated their analysis.

The asymmetry introduced by including a prosody-to-syntax mapping constraint in the MATCH systems but not the ALIGN systems would have obscured the main differences between the MATCH and ALIGN approaches. The constraint set in (12) also lacks a non-recursivity constraint. NONRECURSIVITY would have been inactive in the non-recursive system, introducing another asymmetry between typologies, so it was left out as well.

### 3.2.2.2  *ALIGN constraint set*

The ALIGN constraint set replaces the single mapping constraint in the MATCH systems with the two Alignment constraints, but keeps the minimal and maximal binarity constraints for a total of four constraints, enumerated in (13).

(13)     ALIGN constraint set
- a.   **sp.ALIGNL**: Assign one violation for every word which falls on the *left* edge of an XP but not the *left* edge of a φ (Selkirk 1986, Chen 1987).
- b.   **sp.ALIGNR**: Assign one violation for every word which falls on the *right* edge of an XP but not the *right* edge of a φ (Selkirk 1986, Chen 1987).
- c.   **m.BINMIN**: Assign one violation for every φ with only one immediate daughter (Elfner 2012).
- d.   **m.BINMAX**: Assign one violation for every φ with more than two immediate daughters (Elfner 2012).

The omission of note for the ALIGN constraint set is sp.WRAP (Truckenbrodt 1995, 1999). sp.WRAP does not seem to be entirely necessary for many syntax-prosody analyses in the Alignment framework (see, for example, Downing and Mtenje 2011), so it was left out so as to not unnecessarily complicate the typologies. However, it is worth considering in future work.

---

[5] While allowed by McCarthy and Prince's (1993) schema for Generalized Alignment, the syntax–prosody mapping literature makes little use of this option. Cheng and Downing (2016) and Bellik et al. (2022) are examples of the few works which do make use of prosody-to-syntax Alignment constraints.

## 3.3   Recursive Match system (Match.Rec)

This section and the following one examine the recursive Match system (Match.Rec) and the recursive Align system (Align.Rec), respectively. These systems are presented before the non-recursive systems due to their simpler typologies. Because Match.Rec and Align.Rec both use the Gen from (10) which allows recursive phonological phrases, the candidate sets for these two systems are larger than those of the non-recursive systems in §§3.5 and 3.6. The formal definition of the outputs of this Gen function is reproduced from (10) as (14), and (15) provides a list of all of the allowed parses for a two-word sentence as a summary. The constraint set for Match.Rec, the system discussed first, is repeated in (16).

(14)    Recursive Gen outputs:
    a.    Every $\omega$ is a terminal.
    b.    Every terminal is an $\omega$.
    c.    Every $\omega$ is the daughter of a $\varphi$.
    d.    Every tree is rooted in an $\iota$ (not shown).

(15)    All candidates for two-word inputs in recursive systems:
    a.    (a) (b)
    b.    (a (b))
    c.    ((a) b)
    d.    ((a) (b))
    e.    (a b)

(16)    Match constraint set (full definitions in (12)): sp.Match, m.BinMin, m.BinMax

The typology for Match.Rec (17) contains only two languages: L.1 contains fully isomorphic parses and L.2 contains minimally different parses which are strictly binary-branching. Isomorphic prosodic parses are shown with white backgrounds, while grey backgrounds indicate non-isomorphic parses. A universal support[6] for this typology can be formed with a single input, as there are only two languages in the typology and each input is parsed differently by each language. Inputs beyond those necessary for a universal support are given here to illustrate the broader behavior of each language. All of

_______________

[6] Here, 'universal support" refers to a set of inputs which completely differentiate the languages in the typology for this system which is limited to four-word inputs.

the factorial typologies in this chapter were calculated using OTWorkplace (Prince et al. 2007–2020). The property analyses presented in this chapter were also created with the aid of OTWorkplace.

(17)    Typology of Match.Rec

|       | [[a] [b]] | [a [b [c]]] | [[a [b]] c] | [a [b [c [d]]]] |
|-------|-----------|-------------|-------------|-----------------|
| L.1   | ((a) (b)) | (a (b (c))) | ((a (b)) c) | (a (b (c (d)))) |
| L.2   | (a b)     | (a (b c))   | ((a b) c)   | (a (b (c d)))   |

### 3.3.1  Languages of Match.Rec

All of the prosodic parses in L.1 are isomorphic with the syntactic structure, so for every XP in the syntax, there is a φ which contains all and only the same terminal nodes, and for every φ, there is an XP dominating all and only these same nodes. The first language of Match.Rec might be described as maximally faithful, as none of the optima violate the mapping constraint sp.MATCH.

(18)    ERC showing the only ranking in L.1: sp.MATCH ≫ m.BinMin

| Input     | Winner    | Loser | sp.MATCH | m.BinMin | m.BinMax |
|-----------|-----------|-------|----------|----------|----------|
| [[a][b]]  | ((a)(b))  | (a b) | W        | L        |          |

As shown in the above elementary ranking condition (ERC, Prince 2002a,b et seq.), sp.MATCH is the highest ranked constraint of this language, and for each input, there is a recursive output which fully satisfies sp.MATCH. Since isomorphic parses never violate sp.MATCH, other parses are filtered out, with the exception of the parse ((a)(b)) which has an 'inserted' φ, as shown in (19). This behavior will not be seen in the non-recursive systems, since isomorphic parses are always recursive, due to the recursive nature of the syntactic inputs.

(19)    Non-isomorphic candidates are filtered out by sp.MATCH

| [a [b]]    | sp.MATCH | m.BinMin | m.BinMax |
|------------|----------|----------|----------|
| (a) (b)    | 1        | 2        | 0        |
| (a (b))    | 0        | 1        | 0        |
| ((a) b)    | 1        | 1        | 0        |
| ((a) (b))  | 0        | 2        | 0        |
| (a b)      | 1        | 0        | 0        |

L.2 chooses minimally different parses for each input when compared to the parses chosen by L.1: only branching XPs are mapped to φs. For example, [[a][[b][c]]] is mapped to (a (b c)). As a result, unary φs are are banned from sentences longer than one ω.[7] This is because m.BinMin is the highest ranked constraint in the language and candidates which contain unary φs are filtered out (20). Since the [X⁰ X⁰] substructure is excluded from the systems analyzed here, as explained in 2.1.1, every syntactic tree contains at least one unary XP. As a result, all multi-word optima in L.2 are non-isomorphic.

(20)     ERC showing the ranking of m.BinMin ≫ sp.Match in L.2 of Match. Rec

| Input | Winner | Loser | sp.Match | m.BinMin | m.BinMax |
|---|---|---|---|---|---|
| [[a][b]] | (a b) | ((a)(b)) | L | W | |

### 3.3.2  Property analysis of Match.Rec

An examination of the optima in (17) reveals that none of the possible optima in this system violate m.BinMax, which therefore cannot be crucially ranked against either of the other two constraints. Additionally, every candidate in this system to which m.BinMax does assign a violation would be harmonically bounded as a result of violations of sp.Match, so m.BinMax can be ignored entirely.[8] Since m.BinMax is not ranked in the system, there are only two constraints at play: sp.Match and m.BinMin. This leaves us with a simple property analysis consisting of only one property, p.MapUnary, defined in (21). The values for the single property in this system can be seen in (22).

(21)     **p.MapUnary**: sp.Match <> m.BinMin
   a.   unary.allowed: Every XP constituent, including unary XPs, is faithfully mapped to a φ.
   b.   unary.banned: Unary XPs are not mapped (except in the case of a one-word input). Only binary-branching XPs are mapped to a φ.

---

[7] The one-word input [X⁰] necessarily maps to a unary φ as a result of the Exhaustivity condition on Gen. All children of ιs must be φs, and all children of φs must be ωs, so when only one syntactic terminal is present in the input, the sole prosodic terminal must be phrased as a unary φ.

[8] In section 4, I show that m.BinMax is similarly unrankable in Align.Rec, but that it cannot be completely ignored; its omission from the system would yield a slightly different typology since some candidates are harmonically bounded as a result of a m.BinMax violation.

(22)     PA table for Match.Rec

|       | **p.MapUnary** |
|-------|----------------|
| L.1   | unary.allowed  |
| L.2   | unary.banned   |

### 3.3.3  *Subject-branchingness sensitivity in Match.Rec*

In this system, L.2 exhibits SBS at both levels of stringency, demonstrating that MATCH can model SBS even in a very simple system with only two active constraints. Both languages' optima for the prototypical SBS inputs in (9) are shown in (23).

(23)     SBS effects in Match.Rec typology

|       | Simple Intransitive | Branching-subject Intransitive | Simple Ditransitive |
|-------|---------------------|--------------------------------|---------------------|
|       | [[N] [V]]           | [[[N] [A]] [V]]                | [V [[N] [N]]]       |
| L.1   | ((N) (V))           | (((N) (A)) (V))                | (V ((N) (N)))       |
| L.2   | (N V)               | ((N A) V)                      | (V (N N))           |

L.2 (grey background) meets the less stringent requirements enumerated in (5a) by phrasing the subject and verb together for the simple intransitive but phrasing the subject and its adjoining adjective together in the branching-subject intransitive. In order to meet the more stringent definition of SBS laid out in (5b), L.2 must also not allow the structure ((X X) X) to surface for any inputs where this structure would be a strong mismatch. This structure does not surface as a strong mismatch anywhere in the language and, in fact, strong mismatches are impossible in this language: since all phonological phrases which surface in L.2 have a syntactic counterpart, there are no strong mismatches anywhere in the language.

## 3.4    Recursive ALIGN system (Align.Rec)

Like Match.Rec, the system Align.Rec includes recursive φs in its candidate set. Its constraint set is shown in (24); see (13) for definitions.

(24)     ALIGN constraint set: sp.ALIGNL, sp.ALIGNR, m.BINMIN, m.BINMAX

For the recursive ALIGN system, the resulting typology is five languages, three more than Match.Rec. This typology is summarized in (25), where the first three inputs constitute a universal support. The final four-word input is included to show the kinds of optima that arise in the longer inputs. A white background indicates that the isomorphic parse is a possible optimum. Light grey indicates a parse that is isomorphic apart from not mapping unary or suprabinary XPs. Dark grey indicates a strong mismatch.

(25)   Summary of Align.Rec typology

|       | [[a] b]   | [a [b]]   | [a [[b] c]]  | [[[a] b] [c [d]]]   |
|-------|-----------|-----------|--------------|--------------------|
| L.1   | ((a) b)   | (a (b))   | (a ((b) c))  | ((a) b) (c (d))    |
|       |           |           | ((a (b)) c)  | (((a) b) (c (d)))  |
| L.2   | (a b)     | (a (b))   | (a (b c))    | (a b) (c (d))      |
|       |           |           |              | ((a b) (c (d)))    |
| L.3   | ((a) b)   | (a b)     | ((a b) c)    | ((a) b) (c d)      |
|       |           |           |              | (((a) b) (c d))    |
| L.4   | (a b)     | (a b)     | (a (b c))    | (a b) (c d)        |
|       |           |           |              | ((a b) (c d))      |
| L.5   | (a b)     | (a b)     | ((a b) c)    | (a b) (c d)        |
|       |           |           |              | ((a b) (c d))      |

### 3.4.1   Languages of Align.Rec

In L.1 of Align.Rec (26), both Alignment constraints outrank m.BINMIN.

(26)   Hasse diagram for L.1 in Align.Rec

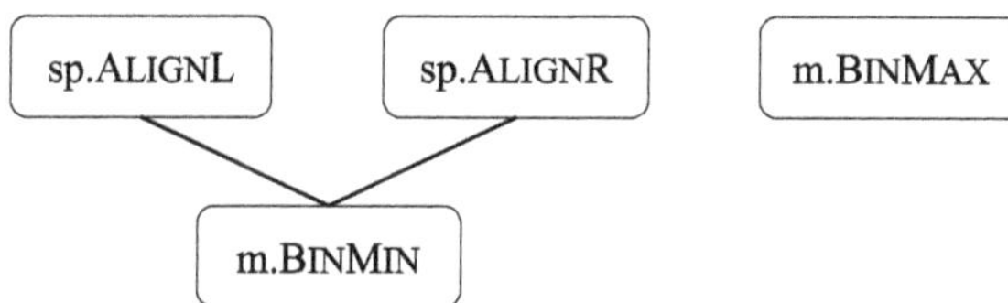


As in Match.Rec, the first language in the Align.Rec typology might be described as being maximally faithful, but maximally faithful candidates in an ALIGN system look different from maximally faithful candidates in Match.Rec. Specifically, there are more candidates that obey all sp.ALIGN constraints than candidates that obey sp.MATCH. This is because two or more coinciding edges are seen by the Alignment constraints to be the same edge, whereas for the sp.MATCH constraints, these edges belong to different syntactic or prosodic units which must be separately mapped. This proliferation of optima for L.1 is quite pervasive, occurring in all but the uniformly left-branching and uniformly right-branching inputs (cf. the "Ambivalence Problem" discussed by Bellik et al. 2022). For an input like the one pictured

in (27), almost every prosodic parse such that each word belongs to a unary
φ is an optimum of L.1. Only the parse in (29) is not a possible optimum in
L.1, as it is harmonically bounded by the candidates in (28) due to a violation of m.BinMax.[9]

(27)    L.1 of Align.Rec allows five distinct parses for this single syntactic
        structure

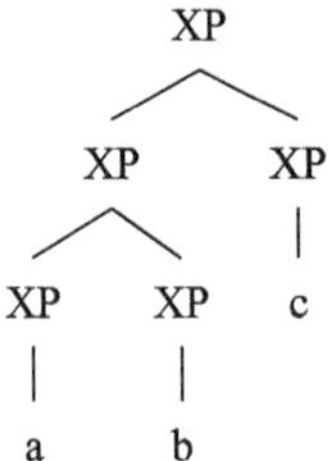

(28)    Allowed parses for structure in (27) in Align.Rec's L.1

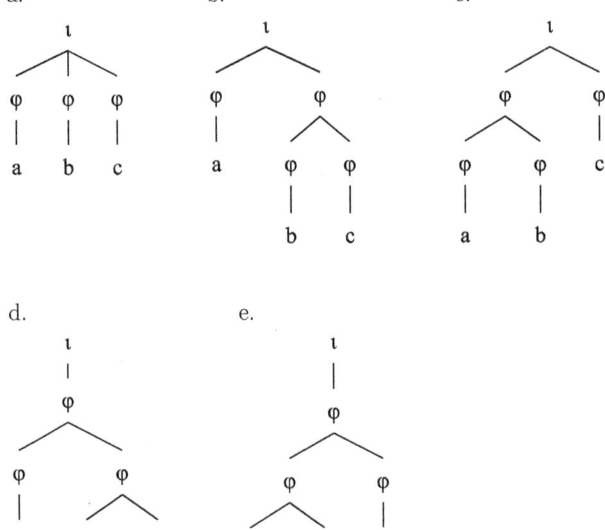

---

[9] Note that the ternary branching ɩ in (28a) is not harmonically bounded like the ternary
branching φ in (29), since m.BinMax is parameterized to the φ; see (12c) and (13d).

(29)     Harmonically bounded parse of (27)

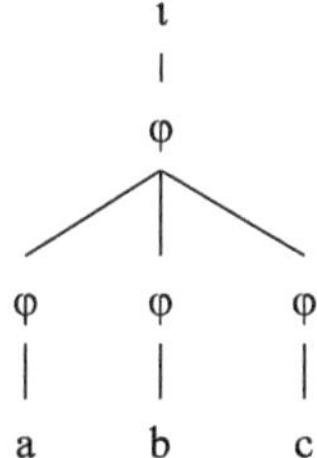

The optima in L1 could be constructed by the following process: find all left edges and all right edges of the syntactic structure and create the prosodic parse with the minimum amount of structure which maps each of these to prosodic left edges and right edges respectively. Once this is done, any additional structure may be added to the list of optima for a given input as long as that additional structure does not create more marked structures (unary- or ternary-branching $\varphi$s) than those which are present in the minimally mapped parse.

The next language, L.2, prioritizes sp.AlignL over all other constraints (30), so all left edges must be mapped from syntax to prosody. Next, L.2 prioritizes binary-branching parses, and maps right edges only in service of these other two priorities, as m.BinMin outranks sp.AlignR. In this way, left-branching [[[[a] [b]] [c]] [d]] can be mapped to right-branching (a (b (c (d)))) (31), where five right edges are not faithfully mapped, but all left edges are, and the resulting parse contains only a single unary $\varphi$. Unary $\varphi$s in L.2 only appear on the right edge of the sentence, because the left edge of a unary XP must be always mapped, but the right edge can generally be left unmapped in order to create parses with fewer violations of m.BinMin. The only exception is that, at the right edge of the sentence, a $\varphi$ boundary must be placed anyway.

(30)     Hasse diagram for L.2 in Align.Rec

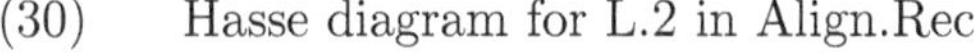
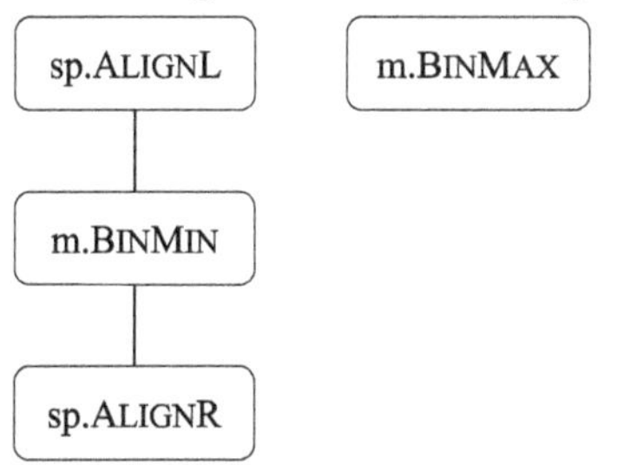

(31)    sp.ALIGNL and m.BINMIN crucially ranked over sp.ALIGNR in L.2 of
        Align.Rec

| Input | Winner | Loser | sp. ALIGNL | m. BINMIN | sp. ALIGNR | m. BINMAX |
|---|---|---|---|---|---|---|
| [[[[a] [b]] [c]] [d]] | (a (b (c (d)))) | (a) (b) (c) (d) | | W | L | |
| [[[[a] [b]] [c]] [d]] | (a (b (c (d)))) | (a) (b) (c) (d) | W | L | | |

L.3 follows a mirrored version of the principles of L.2: all right edges are
faithfully mapped, unary φs are only allowed at the left edge, and left edges
are ignored except when they allow for binary-branching φs. The ranking
that produces this pattern is depicted in (32).

(32)    Hasse diagram for L.3 of Align.Rec

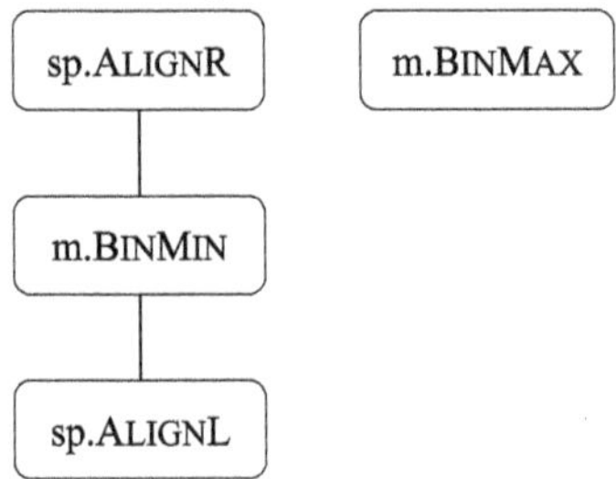



L.4 only allows binary-branching structure, but like L.2, prioritizes mapping left edges and only ever maps right edges in service of markedness
constraints (33a). This results in some very interesting mismatches, such as
the mapping of [[[a] [b]] c] to (a (b c)). While this mapping does not preserve the constituent structure, it does faithfully map all of the left edges
without creating unary structure. If the process for L.2 is to map all left
edges and then find the maximally binary parse that satisfies the left-edge
mapping condition, the process for L.4 is to map all of the left edges, and
then delete left edges that create unary φs. Finally, L.5 mirrors L.4, just as
L.3 mirrors L.2 (33).

(33)    Hasse diagrams for L.4 (left) and L.5 (right) in Align.Rec

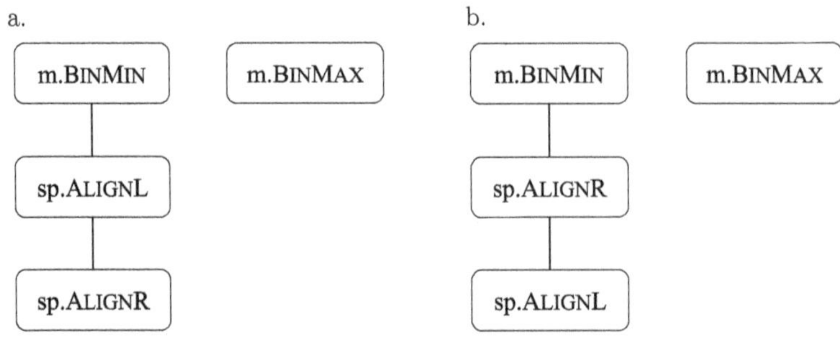

### 3.4.2  *Property analysis of Align.Rec*

All of the languages in Align.Rec except for L.1 can be categorized as either left-favoring or right-favoring; all else being equal, L.2 and L.4 will choose a candidate which maps more left edges at the expense of mapping right edges, while L.3 and L.5 will choose a candidate which maps more right edges at the expense of mapping left edges. To formalize this typological dichotomy, I define the property p.LR (left/right), which is simply the opposition of sp.AlignL and sp.AlignR. This definition can be seen in (34). This property is also useful in defining the other two properties for this typology.

(34)   **p.LR**: sp.AlignL $<>$ sp.AlignR
    a.   L: Prioritize mapping left edges over mapping right edges.
    b.   R: Prioritize mapping right edges over mapping left edges.

Since L.1 is exceptional with respect to the dichotomy characterized by p.LR above in that it always maps all left edges and all right edges, directional indifference should also be a property which distinguishes L.1 from the other four languages of the typology. I formalize this property as p.AlignAll in (35).

(35)   **p.AlignAll**: LR.sub $<>$ m.BinMin
    a.   align.all: Every XP edge is mapped to the edge of a $\varphi$
    b.   align.some: Not every XP edge is mapped to the edge of a $\varphi$

In the case of L.1, where sp.AlignL and sp.AlignR are the two highest ranked constraints, all non-maximally faithful candidates are filtered out, regardless of which of the two mapping constraints a given candidate violates. In (36), we can see that whether the sub-optimal candidate is filtered out by sp.AlignL or sp.AlignR is determined by the input, not the relative ranking of these two constraints.

(36)   sp.AlignL and sp.AlignR outrank m.BinMin in L.1 of Align.Rec

| Input | Winner | Loser | sp.AlignL | sp.AlignR | m.BinMax | m.BinMin |
|---|---|---|---|---|---|---|
| [a [b]] | (a (b)) | (a b) | W | | | L |
| [[a] b] | ((a) b) | (a b) | | W | | L |

For this reason, the relative ranking of the two Align constraints does not matter, and L.1 does not have a value for the property p.LR. This is consistent with the exceptionality of L.1 with respect to p.LR.

One final property is needed to differentiate L.2 and L.3 from L.4 and L.5. The former two languages differ from the latter two in their treatment of unary XPs, as seen in tableaux (37)–(40). Given the right input, a candidate containing a unary φ will emerge in L.2 and L.3, whereas L.4 and L.5 never allow a candidate with a unary φ to surface.

(37)    sp.ALIGNL ≫ m.BINMIN and m.BINMIN ≫ sp.ALIGNR in L.2 of Align.Rec

| Input | Winner | Loser | sp.ALIGNL | m.BINMAX | m.BINMIN | sp.ALIGNR |
|---|---|---|---|---|---|---|
| [a [b]] | (a (b)) | (a b) | W | | L | |
| [[a] b] | (a b) | ((a) b) | | | W | L |

(38)    sp.ALIGNR ≫ m.BINMIN and m.BINMIN ≫ sp.ALIGNL in L.3 of Align.Rec

| Input | Winner | Loser | sp.ALIGNR | m.BINMAX | m.BINMIN | sp.ALIGNL |
|---|---|---|---|---|---|---|
| [[a] b] | ((a) b) | (a b) | W | | L | |
| [a [b]] | (a b) | (a (b)) | | | W | L |

(39)    m.BINMIN ≫ sp.ALIGNL in L.4 of Align.Rec

| Input | Winner | Loser | m.BINMIN | m.BINMAX | sp.ALIGNL | sp.ALIGNR |
|---|---|---|---|---|---|---|
| [a [b]] | (a b) | (a (b)) | W | | L | |

(40)    m.BINMIN ≫ sp.ALIGNR in L.5 of Align.Rec

| Input | Winner | Loser | m.BINMIN | m.BINMAX | sp.ALIGNR | sp.ALIGNL |
|---|---|---|---|---|---|---|
| [[a] b] | (a b) | ((a) b) | W | | L | |

Since the two languages in Match.Rec differ in the same way that L.2 and L.3 differ from L.4 and L.5, I posit the same property here, p.MapUnary, with some minor contextual modifications. First, since the definition in (21) makes reference to sp.MATCH, a constraint which does not exist in the ALIGN systems, Alignment constraints must be substituted in. This can be done with whichever ALIGN constraint is higher ranked in a given language as in (41), using the constraint class defined by p.LR to refer to both ALIGN constraints together.

(41)   **p.MapUnary**: LR.dom $<>$ m.BɪɴMɪɴ
   a.   unary.allowed: The left and right edges of a single unary XP may be mapped, resulting in a unary φ.
   b.   unary.banned: The left and right edges of a single unary XP may not *both* be mapped, resulting in a prohibition of unary φs.

The second change to the definition of p.MapUnary for the Align.Rec system is in the descriptions of the property's two values in (41a) and (41b). While the description of p.MapUnary in (41a) states that languages with the *unary.allowed* value for this property in Align.Rec *may* map unary XPs to unary φs, it does not stipulate that all unary XPs will necessarily be mapped. By contrast, the description of p.MapUnary in (21a) states that languages with the '*unary.allowed*' value for this property will always map all unary XPs isomorphically in Match.Rec. The descriptions of the '*unary. banned*' values for p.MapUnary in (21b) and (41b) are equivalent; they both describe languages where unary φs are prohibited.

Notice that the formalization of p.MapUnary in (41) is very similar to the formalization of p.AlignAll in (35) above, as both properties oppose the Alignment constraints with m.BɪɴMɪɴ. The difference between these two properties is that p.AlignAll picks out the subordinate Alignment constraint while p.MapUnary picks out the dominant Alignment constraint. This also makes clear that any language in the system which aligns all edges also maps all unary XPs; if a language ranks the subordinate member of p.LR above m.BɪɴMɪɴ—meaning it has the 'align.all' value of the property p.AlignAll— then the dominant member of p.LR must also outrank m.BɪɴMɪɴ, entailing the 'unary.allowed' value of p.MapUnary.

The three properties detailed above fully characterize the grammars in the recursive Aʟɪɢɴ typology. The property analysis is summarized in (42), where angle brackets $<\ >$ denote that the property value is entailed by the definition of another property, in this case p.AlignAll. This relationship can also be seen in the treeoid provided in (43).

(42)   Property analysis for Align.Rec

|       | **p.AlignAll** | **p.MapUnary**         | **p.LR** |
|-------|----------------|------------------------|----------|
| L.1   | align.all      | $<$unary.allowed$>$    | *moot*   |
| L.2   | align.some     | unary.allowed          | L        |
| L.3   | align.some     | unary.allowed          | R        |
| L.4   | align.some     | unary.banned           | L        |
| L.5   | align.some     | unary.banned           | R        |

(43)      Treeoid for Align.Rec

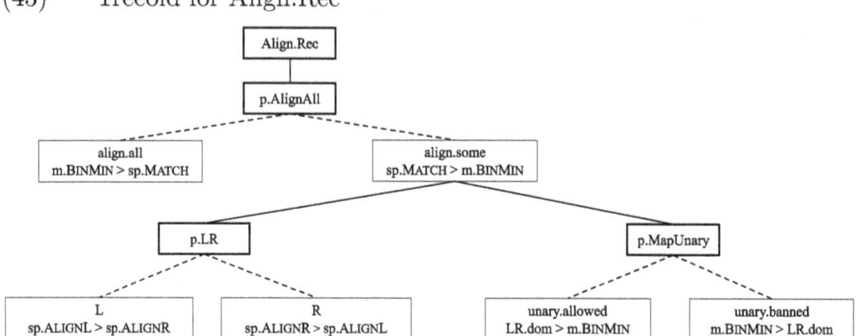

As in Match.Rec, m.BINMAX does not assign any violations to any of the possible optima for the system and therefore is not crucially ranked against any of the other three constraints. For further discussion, see §3.7.2.

### 3.4.3  Subject-branchingness sensitivity in Align.Rec

L.5 meets the less strict definition of SBS used in this chapter, but it fails the more stringent test of (5b). As shown in the typology provided in (44), L.5 does exhibit the basic pattern of SBS: the subject and verb are phrased together for the simple intransitive and apart for the branching-subject intransitive (grey cells). However, the same phonological structure surfaces for both the branching-subject intransitive and the simple ditransitive, the latter of which is a strong mismatch.

(44)      Typology of known Kinyambo mappings in Align.Rec

|  | Simple Intransitive | Branching-subject Intransitive | Simple Ditransitive |
|---|---|---|---|
|  | [[N] [V]] | [[[N] [A]] [V]] | [V [[N] [N]]] |
| L.1 | (N) (V) <br> ((N) (V)) | (N) (A) (V) <br> (N) ((A) (V)) <br> ((N) (A)) (V) <br> ((N) ((A) (V))) <br> (((N) (A)) (V)) | (V (N)) (N) <br> (V ((N) ((N))) <br> ((V (N)) (N)) |
| L.2 | (N (V)) | (N (A (V))) | (V (N (N))) |
| L.3 | ((N) V) | (((N) A) V) | ((V N) N) |
| L.4 | (N V) | (N (A V)) | (V (N N)) |
| L.5 | (N V) | ((N A) V) | ((V N) N) |

Because the ((a b) c) structure surfaces even when it contradicts the shape of its syntactic input (a strong mismatch), we cannot conclude that it is the branchingness of the subject which causes that same structure to arise in the case of the branching-subject intransitive. L.5 thus fails the more stringent definition of SBS given in (5b).

Conflict between the two ALIGN constraints is what prevents any language in Align.Rec from conforming to the more stringent definition of SBS. The comparative tableau (45) exemplifies this: sp.ALIGNL prefers (a (b c)) for both inputs and sp.ALIGNR prefers ((a b) c) for both inputs. Since there is no other constraint in Align.Rec which prefers or disprefers either structure, there is no ranking such that both structures emerge in the same language.

(45)    ALIGN constraints in Align.Rec cannot drive SBS

| Input | Winner | Loser | sp.ALIGNL | sp.ALIGNR | m.BINMIN | m.BINMAX |
|---|---|---|---|---|---|---|
| [V [[N] [N]]] | (V (N N)) | ((V N) N) | W | L | | |
| [[[N] [A]] [V]] | ((N A) V) | (N (A V)) | L | W | | |

Because sp.ALIGNL and sp.ALIGNR both prefer the same respective candidates in (45) regardless of the input, they cannot effectively motivate branchingness effects. While additional constraints could be added to the system to force it to model the more stringent definition of SBS used for this chapter, the ALIGN constraints remain themselves useless for this language feature in this system.

## 3.5   Non-recursive Match system (Match.NR)

This section presents Match.NR, and the following section presents Align.NR. Both systems use a definition of GEN which does not allow prosodic recursion. This results in much smaller candidate sets, but not smaller typologies. A formal definition of these outputs is provided in (46) (repeated from (11) above), and (47) provides a list of all of the allowed parses of a two-word sentence as a summary.

(46)    Non-recursive GEN outputs:
  a.   Every ω is a terminal.
  b.   Every terminal is an ω.
  c.   Every ω is the daughter of a φ.
  d.   Every tree is rooted in an ι (not shown).
  e.   Every φ is the daughter of an ι.

(47)     All candidates for two-word inputs in non-recursive systems
  a.    (a) (b)
  b.    (a b)

I start with Match.NR since it has fewer constraints, which results in a smaller typology. But as we will see, Match.NR is the most complicated and least intuitive system presented in this chapter. As an example of the counterintuitiveness of the Match.NR system, consider that, later on in this section (54), I need to enumerate seven steps in order to describe the mapping behavior of a single language (L.2). No other system in this chapter requires this. Furthermore, the other languages of Match.NR did not receive this treatment not because they are simpler to explain but because they are just as complex and such discussion would simply distract from the main point of this chapter.

Match.NR uses the MATCH constraint set in (48) (see (12) for full definitions). The Match.NR typology consists of five languages, which are summarized in (49). A white background indicates a parse that is the same as L.1's parse. Grey indicates a flat parse, which is a weak mismatch; dark grey indicates a strong mismatch (possibly co-optimal).

(48)     Match.NR constraints: sp.MATCH, m.BINMIN, m.BINMAX

(49)     Typology for Match.NR

|  | [[a] [b]] | [a [b]] | [a [b [c]]] | [[[a] b] c] | [[a [[b] c]] d] |
|---|---|---|---|---|---|
| L.1 | (a) (b) | (a b) | (a) (b c)<br>(a b) (c) | (a) (b c)<br>(a b) (c) | (a) (b) (c d)<br>(a) (b c) (d) |
| L.2 | (a) (b) | (a b) | (a b c) | (a b c) | (a b c d) |
| L.3 | (a b) | (a b) | (a) (b c)<br>(a b) (c) | (a) (b c)<br>(a b) (c) | (a b) (c d) |
| L.4 | (a b) | (a b) | (a b c) | (a b c) | (a b) (c d) |
| L.5 | (a b) | (a b) | (a b c) | (a b c) | (a b c d) |

Of the two-word inputs, only [[a] [b]] has more than one possible optimum across the five languages; the other two inputs, [a [b]] and [[a] b], always surface as (a b) under any ranking. Pairs of mirror-image inputs such as <[a[b]], [[a]b]> and <[a [b [c]]], [[[a] b] c]> prosduce exactly identical outputs within each of the five languages. In ALIGN systems, a flat parse (a b) of the input [a [b]] incurs a violation of sp.ALIGNL but not sp.ALIGNR, and vice versa for the mirror input [[a] b], but in MATCH systems, (a b) incurs a single violation of sp.MATCH, no matter which of the two inputs it is mapped from. This is because sp.MATCH looks only at the constituency, whereas the ALIGN constraints asymmetrically look at edges. Furthermore, the markedness constraints used here, m.BINMIN and m.BINMAX, are insensitive to left/right distinctions, so Match.NR makes no distinctions between left-branching and right-branching inputs. Only three inputs—[[a] [b]], [a [b [c]]] and [[a [[b] c]] d], for example—are needed to differentiate the five languages, forming a small universal support. To show more of the possibilities for mappings in the Match.NR typology, (50) provides a selection of the mappings for four-word inputs.

(50)      Summary of four-word inputs for Match.NR

|  | [a [[[b] [c]] d]] | [[[[a] b] c] d] | [[[[a] b] c] [d]] | [[a] [[[b] c] d]] |
|---|---|---|---|---|
| L.1 | (a) (b) (c) (d) | (a b) (c d) | (a) (b c) (d) <br> (a b) (c) (d) | (a) (b) (c d) <br> (a) (b c) (d) |
| L.2 | (a) (b) (c) (d) | (a b) (c d) | (a b c) (d) | (a) (b c d) |
| L.3 | (a b) (c d) | (a b) (c d) | (a b) (c d) | (a b) (c d) |
| L.4 | (a b) (c d) | (a b) (c d) | (a b) (c d) | (a b) (c d) |
| L.5 | (a b c d) | (a b) (c d) | (a b) (c d) | (a b c d) |

### 3.5.1   *Languages of Match.NR*

In order to describe the complex patterns of the Match.NR typology, I introduce three specialized terms for syntactic substructures which are discussed in this paragraph and illustrated in (51). The first term is TWIG, which is simply a unary XP (51a). The intuition here is that a unary XP is between a small branch ending in a single leaf. The second term is ADJUNCTION SUBSTRUCTURE (51b). While adjunction exists at many levels in syntax, adjunction substructure here refers specifically to a *minimal* adjunction substructure, that is, an XP that dominates exactly two twigs, $[[X^0] [X^0]]$. The final term is HEAD/COMPLEMENT SUBSTRUCTURE (51c, d), which similarly refers to the minimal structure of an XP which dominates exactly one twig and exactly one bare leaf, meaning an $X^0$ which is not the daughter of a unary XP. The term HEAD/COMPLEMENT SUBSTRUCTURE is particularly useful because it ignores the direction in which the structure branches. As we saw with the Match.Rec system, MATCH constraints exhibit symmetry, so being able to refer to both the $[X^0 [X^0]]$ substructure and the $[[X^0] X^0]$ substructure is useful in describing the behavior of this MATCH system. In referring to minimal substructures precisely in this section, we see that trends exhibited by a language in the treatment of smaller structures reveal behaviors in the larger structures as well.

(51)      Minimal substructures

a. Twig                                b. Adjunction substructure

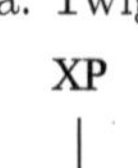

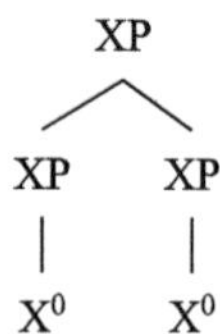

c. Head/Complement                    d. Head/Complement
   substructure                          substructure
   (left-headed)                         (right-headed)

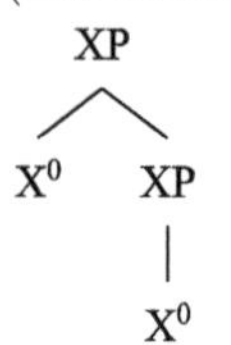

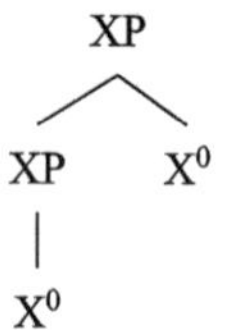

Hasse diagrams of the grammars of Match.NR are shown in (52).

(52)      Grammars of Match.NR

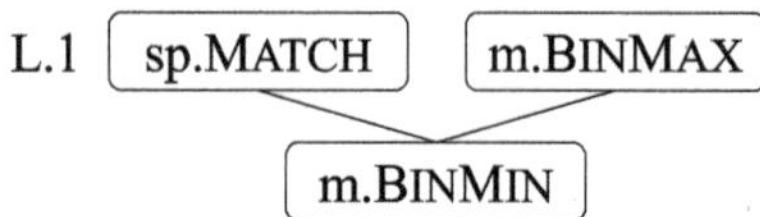

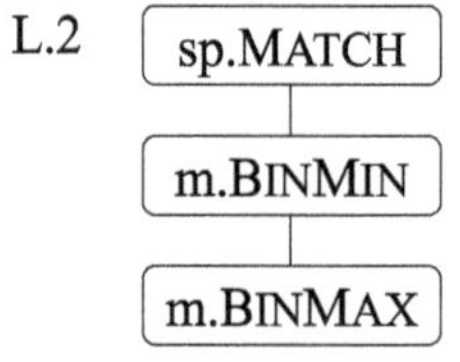

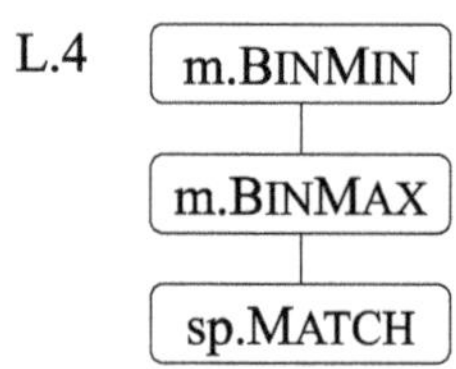

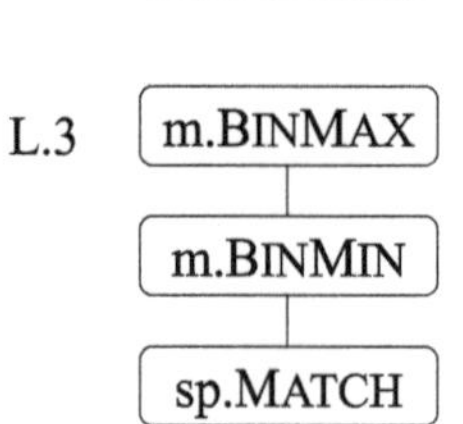

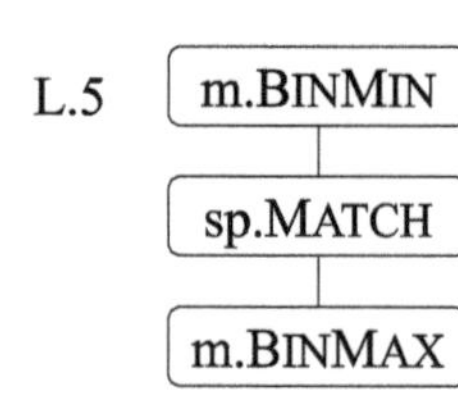

### 3.5.1.1  Languages 1 and 2 of Match.NR

In L.1 and L.2, sp.MATCH outranks m.BinMin, with the result that adjunction substructures like [[a][b]] always map to (a) (b), and head/complement substructures, such as [a [b]] or [[a] b], map to (a b). However, inputs with head/complement structures sometimes have two co-optima, in which case one optimum maps the head/complement structure to (ω ω) and the other optimum maps the two words of the head/complement substructure into different φs. All of the inputs which map to multiple co-optima in L.1 and L.2 contain a head/complement substructure, though not all inputs with head/complement substructures map to multiple optima. This can be seen in (53), where the syntactic head/complement substructure is bolded and underlined.

(53)     Co-optimal mappings in L.1 and L.2 of Match.NR

| Syntactic structure | L.1 mappings | L.2 mappings |
| --- | --- | --- |
| [[**a** **b**] c] | (a) (b c) | (a b c) |
| [a [**b** **c**]] | (a b) (c) | |
| [[[**a** **b**] c] [d]] | | (a b c) (d) |
| [[a [**b** **c**]] [d]] | | |
| [[a [**b** **c**]] d] | (a) (b c) (d) | (a b c d) |
| [a [[**b** **c**] d]] | (a b) (c) (d) | |
| [a [[**b** [**c**]] [d]]] | | (a) (b c) (d) <br> (a b) (c) (d) |
| [[[a] [[**b**] **c**]] d] | | (a) (b) (c d) <br> (a) (b c) (d) |
| [[a [[**b**] **c**]] d] | (a) (b) (c d) | (a b c d) |
| [a [[[**b**] **c**] d]] | (a) (b c) (d) | |
| [[a] [[[**b**] **c**] d]] | | (a) (b c d) |
| [[a] [b [**c** [**d**]]]] | | |

As we can see in (53), all inputs which map to multiple optima in L.2 map also to multiple optima in L.1, though, again, not vice versa. (There are only two inputs which map to multiple optima in L.2: [[[a] [[b] c]] d] and its mirror image [a [[b [c]] [d]]], depicted in (54a.i, ii).) To illustrate the logic of these two languages, (54) provides a procedure for finding the optimal parse in L.2.

(54)     Mapping procedure for L.2 in Match.NR

   a.    If the syntactic input is either [[[a] [[b] c]] d] (depicted in i.) or its mirror image [a [[b [c]] [d]]] (depicted in ii.), it will have two co-optima. The first optimum maps each twig to a unary φ (dashed boxes in i. and ii.) and wraps the remaining two terminals in a binary φ (dotted boxes in i. and ii.), resulting in (a) (b) (c d) for the first input and (a b) (c) (d) for the second. The other optimum is the same for both inputs: (a) (b c) (d).

i.    [[[a] [[b] c]] d] → (a) (b) (c d) ~ (a) (b c) (d)

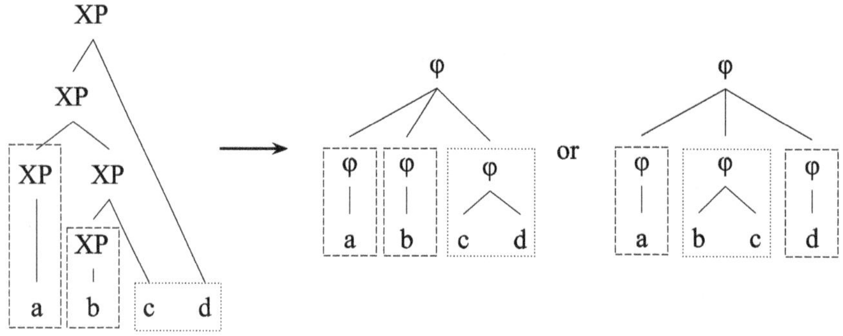

ii.    [a [[b [c]] [d]]] →(a b) (c) (d) ~ (a) (b c) (d)

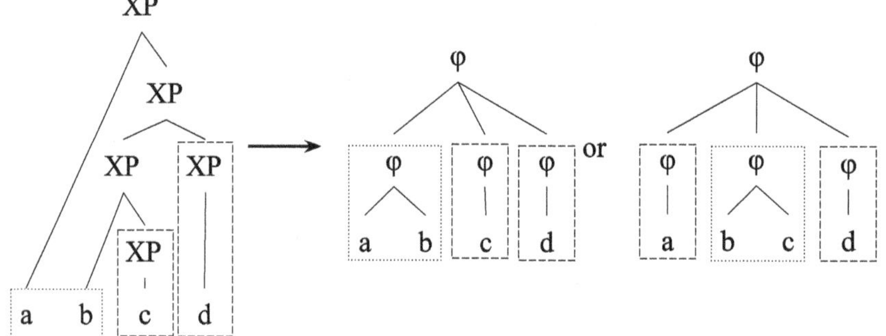

b.    Otherwise, start by mapping all of the adjunction structures to (ω) (ω).

c.    Next, map all of the head/complement substructures to (ω ω).

d.    If the sister of a head/complement structure is a bare leaf $X^0$, expand the φ mapped from the head/complement structure in Step c. to a ternary-branching φ which contains that leaf.

e.    If a substructure which is mapped to a ternary φ in Step d. is a sister to another bare leaf and that bare leaf is linearly adjacent to the head/complement substructure, again expand the ternary-branching φ to a quaternary φ (this excludes the uniformly right-branching syntax [a [b [c [d]]]] and its all-left branching mirror image).

f.    If there are any pairs of linearly-adjacent bare leaves which have not yet been parsed, parse them into binary φs.

g.    Map any remaining unparsed terminals to unary φs.

L.1 can be described with a similar procedure, which I will not enumerate, except that L.1 prohibits ternary- and quaternary-branching φs, so where a suprabinary φ appears in L.2, L.1 instead maps to binary-branching and unary φs. As L.2 is an Optimality-Theoretic grammar, the procedure in (54) reflects the constraint rankings of this grammar. Here I connect steps in the above procedure with the constraint rankings that give rise to these behaviors, and I then explain how the other four languages of this typology differ from L.2 both in behavior and in constraint ranking. In the following subsection, I formalize these constraint rankings and associated behaviors in a property analysis.

The first distinctive characteristic of L.2 is its mapping of adjunction substructures to (ω) (ω), as opposed to (ω ω). This behavior (54b) arises because sp.Match is ranked above m.BinMin: while the binary parse (ω ω) causes fewer violations of m.BinMin than (ω) (ω), it only matches the highest of the three XPs in the adjunction structure, whereas (ω) (ω) matches two of the three XPs, incurring fewer violations of sp.Match, which is higher ranked.

(55)    Crucial ranking sp.Match ≫ m.BinMin for L.2 of Match.NR

| Input | Winner | Loser | sp.Match | m.BinMin | m.BinMax |
|---|---|---|---|---|---|
| [[a] [b]] | (a) (b) | (a b) | W | L | |

In contrast, head/complement substructures are mapped to (ω ω) in L.2, as described in (54c), because both the binary parse (ω ω) and the unary parse (ω) (ω) incur the same number of violations of sp.Match.

(56)    sp.Match fails to distinguish between (a) (b) and (a b) for [a [b]]

| [a [b]] | sp.Match | m.BinMin | m.BinMax |
|---|---|---|---|
| (a) (b) | 1 | 2 | 0 |
| (a b) | 1 | 0 | 0 |

Head/complement substructures contain only two XPs; (ω) (ω) matches the lower of these two XPs while (ω ω) matches the higher XP. Each of these parses matches only one of the two XPs in the head/complement substructure and each incurs one violation of sp.Match. Since sp.Match fails to distinguish between these two parses, the unary parse is filtered out by the lower-ranked constraint m.BinMin. The difference between head/complement substructures and adjunction substructures in L.2 is shown in (57).

(57)     Differing treatment of head/complement vs. adjunction substructures

| Input | Winner | Loser | sp.Match | m.BinMin | m.BinMax |
|---|---|---|---|---|---|
| Adjunction: [[X⁰] [X⁰]] | (ω) (ω) | (ω ω) | W | L | |
| Head/complement: [X⁰ [X⁰]] | (ω ω) | (ω) (ω) | | W | |

Step (54d) reflects the ranking of m.BinMin over m.BinMax in L.2 of Match. NR. Given a string of three terminals, all non-recursive exhaustive parses result in marked structure: if two of the words are parsed into a binary-branching φ, the third must be parsed into a unary φ. Alternatively, all three words can be parsed into separate unary φs or into a single ternary-branching φ. Because m.BinMin is ranked above m.BinMax, (ω ω ω) is preferred over the other two alternatives as long as all three options equally satisfy the highest ranked constraint, sp.Match, as in (58). If there is more than one twig in the XP which the ternary φ matches, then sp.Match will no longer favor the flat parse over a candidate containing a unary φ, as in (59) and (60). Thus ternary-branching optima only arise in L.2 if a bare leaf is the sister to a head/complement substructure.

(58)     Ternary φ in L.2 of Match.NR when only one twig is present

| Input | Winner | Loser | sp.Match | m.BinMin | m.BinMax |
|---|---|---|---|---|---|
| [X⁰ [X⁰ [X⁰]]] | (ω ω ω) | (ω) (ω ω) | | W | L |
| [X⁰ [X⁰ [X⁰]]] | (ω ω ω) | (ω) (ω) (ω) | | W | L |

(59)     sp.Match prefers a unary φ when multiple twigs are present (L.2 of Match.NR)

| Input | Winner | Loser | sp.Match | m.BinMin | m.BinMax |
|---|---|---|---|---|---|
| [[X⁰] [X⁰ [X⁰]]] | (ω) (ω ω) | (ω ω ω) | W | L | W |
| [[X⁰] [X⁰ [X⁰]]] | (ω) (ω ω) | (ω) (ω) (ω) | | W | |

(60)     sp.Match prefer unary φs when multiple twigs are present (L.2 of Match.NR)

| Input | Winner | Loser | sp.Match | m.BinMin | m.BinMax |
|---|---|---|---|---|---|
| [X⁰ [[X⁰] [X⁰]]] | (ω) (ω) (ω) | (ω ω ω) | W | L | W |
| [X⁰] [[X⁰ [X⁰]]] | (ω) (ω) (ω) | (ω) (ω ω) | W | L | |

In (54e), we can see that the criteria for expanding a ternary-branching φ to a quaternary-branching φ are stricter than the criteria for expanding a binary-branching φ to a ternary-branching φ. This is because a string of four terminals *can* be mapped to an unmarked prosodic structure in a non-recursive, exhaustive system with the balanced binary parse (ω ω) (ω ω). Since the balanced binary parse is favored by m.BINMAX and both parses equally satisfy m.BINMIN, the quaternary-$\varphi$ parse only emerges when it is favored by sp.MATCH and sp.MATCH is higher ranked than m.BINMAX, as shown in (61).

In (61a), the quaternary parse only matches one XP, the root, but the balanced binary parse matches no XPs, so sp.MATCH favors the quaternary-branching $\varphi$ parse. In contrast, the two parses in (61b) both match a single XP: the quaternary-branching $\varphi$ matches the root of the syntactic tree and the second $\varphi$ of the balanced binary parse matches the head/complement substructure. Since neither sp.MATCH nor m.BINMIN distinguishes between the two candidates, m.BINMAX filters out the quaternary parse.

(61)    Selecting the balanced parse in L.2 of Match.NR

| Input | Winner | Loser | sp.MATCH | m.BINMIN | m.BINMAX |
|---|---|---|---|---|---|
| a. [a [[[b] c] d]] | (a b c d) | (a b) (c d) | W | | L |
| b. [a [b [c [d]]]] | (a b) (c d) | (a b c d) | | | W |

In addition to competing with the unmarked balanced binary parse, the quaternary-branching $\varphi$ candidate must also contend with parses which contain unary $\varphi$s. The quaternary-branching $\varphi$ only emerges when m.BINMIN is ranked higher than m.BINMAX, just as ternary-branching $\varphi$s only emerge under the same ranking condition, shown in (62).

(62)    Quartenary $\varphi$ in L.2 of Match.NR

| Input | Winner | Loser | sp.MATCH | m.BINMIN | m.BINMAX |
|---|---|---|---|---|---|
| [a [[[b] c] d]] | (a b c d) | (a) (b c d) | | W | L |

### 3.5.1.2  Language 3 of Match.NR

As depicted above in (52), Languages 1 and 2 both share the ranking of sp.MATCH above m.BINMIN; Languages 3, 4, and 5 all share the opposite ranking, m.BINMIN above sp.MATCH. As a result, L.3 maps both adjunction substructures and head/complement structures to (ω ω) for two- and three-word inputs, except where the sister of the head/complement structure is a bare leaf and there is an edge-aligned twig. In this case, both (a) (b c) and (a b) (c) are co-optima, since both match only one XP and incur only one violation of m.BINMIN. Just as is the case with the co-optima in L.1 and L.2, one of the optima does map the head/complement substructure, but the other does not. Unlike L.1 and L.2, m.BINMIN is ranked higher than sp.MATCH in L.3, so even though mapping the adjunction substructure to (ω ω) incurs more violations of sp.MATCH than mapping the same structure to (ω) (ω), the unary parse (ω) (ω) is filtered out by m.BINMIN before it is evaluated by sp.MATCH. All four-word inputs in L.3 map to (a b) (c d). This is because ternary and quaternary φs are not allowed in L.3 (as we saw in the description if L.2, ternary- and quaternary-branching φs only arise when sp.MATCH outranks m.BINMAX) so even in cases where the balanced parse does not map any XP, suprabinary parses which would better satisfy sp.MATCH are filtered out by m.BINMIN.

### 3.5.1.3   *Languages 4 and 5 of Match.NR*

L.4 and L.5 both allow ternary φs, as unary φs are completely prohibited. This is because m.BINMIN is the highest ranked constraint in both languages. As such, all two-word inputs are mapped to (a b) and all three-word inputs are mapped to (a b c).

L.5 allows quaternary φs in addition to ternary φs, as both m.BINMIN and sp.MATCH are ranked above m.BINMAX, but quaternary φs are only chosen in cases where there is no edge-aligned head/complement substructure. When there is a head/complement substructure, both the balanced parse (a b) (c d) and the quaternary parse (a b c d) match only one XP, so they incur the same number of violations of sp.MATCH. However, the balanced parse incurs one fewer violation of m.BINMAX, so it is preferred over the quaternary parse. On the other hand, when no head/complement or adjunction substructure is edge-aligned, (a b) (c d) does not map any XPs and is filtered out by sp.MATCH as the quaternary parse has fewer violations.

### 3.5.2   *Property analysis of Match.NR*

The first property for this system is p.HAM.a/b (High-Adjunction Mapping allowed/banned) which specifically characterizes the behavior described in (54b) above. As explained above, the higher XP of an adjunction substructure is mapped only when m.BINMIN outranks sp.MATCH, so p.HAM.a/b can be formulated as the opposition of these two constraints (63).

(63)      **p.HAM.a/b**: m.BINMIN <> sp.MATCH
       a.     HAM.a: Given an adjunction substructure, a language may map the highest XP to a binary φ rather than the two lower XPs to unary φs.
       b.     HAM.b: Given an adjunction substructure, a language may map the two lower XPs to unary φs rather than the higher XP to a binary φ.

The opposition of m.BINMIN and sp.MATCH is also the definition of p.MapUnary in Match.Rec, as defined in (21), but the description of the property is distinct. In Match.Rec, unary φs only ever emerge because they are mapped from a unary XP in the syntactic structure, so the property p.MapUnary can be broadly defined as the property of mapping twigs. In contrast, unary φs often emerge in Match.NR as a result of the Non-recursivity and Exhaustivity conditions of the Gen function. Because unary φs cannot be unambiguously connected to syntactic structures in Match.NR as in in Match.Rec, the property that is equivalent to p.MapAll in this system must be more narrowly defined. So while p.MapUnary and p.HAM.a/b both oppose m.BinMin and sp.Match and describe a grammar's permissiveness of unary φs, they must be defined as distinct properties.

The second and third properties of Match.NR relate to (54d) and (54e), which outline the criteria for the creation of ternary and quaternary φs, respectively. As described above, ternary φs only arise when m.BinMin outranks m.BinMax, so the property p.3φ.a/b (Ternary φ allowed/banned) can be formalized as (64).

(64)    **p.3φ.a/b**: m.BinMin $<>$ m.BinMax
    a.   3φ.a: Ternary-branching φs are allowed in the outputs.
    b.   3φ.b: Ternary-branching φs are banned from the outputs.

Ternary φs are a kind of marked structure that was not present in the recursive systems of the previous section, and consequently, there was no ranking for m.BinMax in Match.Rec or Align.Rec. However, as described above, no ranking of constraints in the non-recursive systems can avoid marked structure for the three-word inputs; there is no non-recursive, exhaustive parse of three words in which every φ is binary-branching. Given this fact, ternary-branching φs becomes viable optima for the system, and the ranking of m.BinMax determines whether these ternary-branching φs emerge for a given language.

Quaternary φs, as we saw above, also emerge in this typology, though under a more strict set of circumstances. For quaternary-branching φs to emerge at all for a given language, both sp.Match and m.BinMin must be ranked above m.BinMax. This is formalized as the property p.4φ.a/b (Quaternary φ allowed/banned) in (65).

(65)    **p.4φ.a/b**: {sp.Match, m.BinMin}.sub $<>$ m.BinMax
    a.   4φ.a: Quaternary-branching φs are allowed in the outputs.
    b.   4φ.b: Quaternary-branching φs are banned from the outputs.

These three properties fully characterize the typology of Match.NR. A summary table for this property analysis is provided in (66), and a treeoid illustrating the entailment relationships between p.3φ.a/b and p.4φ.a/b is provided in (67).

(66)     Property analysis for Match.NR

|      | p.HAM.a/b | p.3φ.a/b | p.4φ.a/b |
|------|-----------|----------|----------|
| L.1  | b         | b        | <b>  |
| L.2  | b         | a        | a        |
| L.3  | a         | b        | <b>  |
| L.4  | a         | a        | b        |
| L.5  | a         | a        | a        |

If quaternary φs are allowed by a language, this property analysis correctly entails that ternary φs are allowed as well, since 4φ.a requires that m.BɪɴMɪɴ dominate m.BɪɴMᴀx. Conversely, the prohibition of ternary φs entails the prohibition of quaternary φs. These entailments do not run both ways, though: allowing ternary φs does not entail the allowance of quaternary φs, and the prohibition of quaternary φs does not entail the prohibition of ternary φs. L.4 shows that this is the case, since it allows ternary φs in the three-word input but prohibits quaternary φs. In (66) and (67), I have chosen to represent how 3φ.b entails 4φ.b by displaying p.4φ.a/b as moot for Languages 1 and 3.

(67)     Treeoid for the Match.NR property analysis

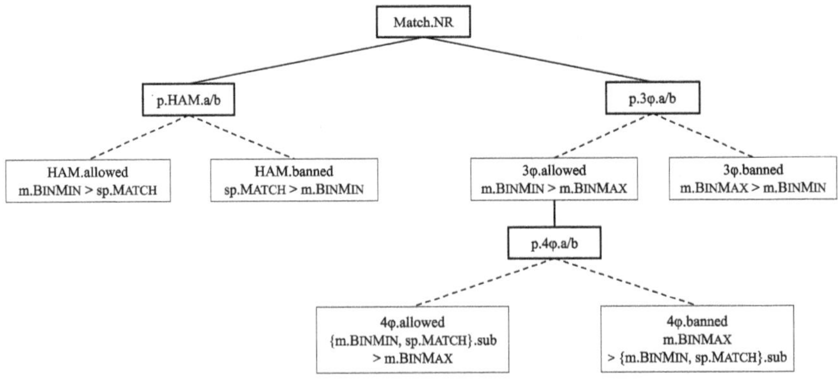


### 3.5.3   Subject-branchingness sensitivity in Match.NR

In Match.NR, only L.3 exhibits sensitivity to the branchingness of the subject: it phrases the subject and the verb together for the simple intransitive and the subject and adjective together for the branching-subject intransitive. This language only meets the less stringent definition of SBS in (5a), however, since a strong mismatch candidate appears as a co-optimum for the simple ditransitive.

(68)     Typology for known Kinyambo phrasings in Match.NR

|        | *Simple Intransitive*<br>**[[N] [V]]** | *Branching-subject Intransitive*<br>**[[[N] [A]] [V]]** | *Simple Ditransitive*<br>**[V [[N] [N]]]** |
|--------|--------------------|-------------------------------|----------------------|
| L.1    | (N) (V)            | (N) (A) (V)                   | (V) (N) (N)          |
| L.2    | (N) (V)            | (N) (A) (V)                   | (V) (N) (N)          |
| L.3    | (N V)              | (N A) (V)                     | (V) (N N)<br>(V N) (N) |
| L.4    | (N V)              | (N A V)                       | (V N N)              |
| L.5    | (N V)              | (N A V)                       | (V N N)              |

The parse (V N) (N) for the simple ditransitive is a strong mismatch from the simple ditransitive's syntax because the verb and the direct object do not form a constituent on their own in the syntactic exponent [V [[N][N]]]. Since the phonological structure ($\omega$ $\omega$) ($\omega$) surfaces in L.3 even as a strong mismatch, we cannot confidently state that it is the branchingness of the subject which causes its surfacing for the branching-subject intransitive.


## 3.6   Non-recursive Align system (Align.NR)

The final system of this chapter is Align.NR. Its constraint set appears in (69); see (13) for full constraint definitions.

(69)     ALIGN constraint set: sp.ALIGNL, sp.ALIGNR, m.BINMIN, m.BINMAX

The non-recursive ALIGN typology is nearly double the size of the Match.NR typology, at eight languages. A universal support for this typology is provided in (70), where a white background indicates a weak mismatch; dark grey indicates a completely flat parse; and light grey indicates a strong mismatch (possibly co-optimal). A support for this system is larger than the support for the MATCH typology, but does not require the four-word inputs. The increased size is to be expected since the ALIGN constraint set has four constraints as opposed to the MATCH constraint set, which has three. This means that, for the ALIGN constraint set, there are 24 linear orders of the constraints, whereas there are only six linear orders of the MATCH constraints. Additionally, Alignment constraints treat mirror-image inputs such as [a [b [c]]] and [[[a] b] c] differently, as opposed to MATCH constraints which treat them equivalently.

(70)      Typology for Align.NR

|        | [a [b [c]]]          | [[[a] b] c]          | [a [[b] [c]]]        | [[[a] [b]] c]        |
|--------|---------------------|---------------------|---------------------|---------------------|
| L.1    | (a) (b) (c)         | (a) (b) (c)         | (a) (b) (c)         | (a) (b c)           |
| L.2    | (a) (b) (c)         | (a) (b c)<br>(a b) (c) | (a) (b) (c)      | (a) (b) (c)         |
| L.3    | (a) (b) (c)         | (a b c)             | (a) (b) (c)         | (a) (b c)           |
| L.4    | (a) (b c)<br>(a b) (c) | (a) (b) (c)      | (a b) (c)           | (a) (b) (c)         |
| L.5    | (a b c)             | (a) (b) (c)         | (a b) (c)           | (a) (b) (c)         |
| L.6    | (a) (b c)<br>(a b) (c) | (a) (b c)<br>(a b) (c) | (a) (b c)     | (a) (b c)           |
| L.7    | (a) (b c)<br>(a b) (c) | (a) (b c)<br>(a b) (c) | (a b) (c)     | (a b) (c)           |
| L.8    | (a b c)             | (a b c)             | (a b c)             | (a b c)             |

As alluded to above, sp.ALIGNL and sp.ALIGNR prefer different optima between members of the mirror-image inputs. If we examine these mirror-image syntactic parses, we see that languages similarly mirror in their optima. For example, L.3 maps the uniformly right-branching three-word input [a [b [c]]] to (a b c) and the uniformly left-branching three-word input [[[a] b] c] to (a) (b) (c). L.5 conversely maps the uniformly right-branching input to (a) (b) (c) and the uniformly left-branching input to (a b c). A similar symmetry can be seen between L.2 and L.4.

Languages 6 and 7 often have mirror-image outputs (a) (b c) and (a b) (c), but they do not exhibit symmetry along the axis of the inputs, rather when Languages 6 and 7 have different outputs, L.6 always chooses (a) (b c) and L.7 always chooses (a b) (c) due to a different ranking of sp.ALIGNL and sp.ALIGNR.

Four-word inputs are not needed to define a support for this system, partly because quaternary-branching φs are not allowed in the typology at all. L.8, which chooses the (a b) parse for all of the two-word inputs and the (a b c) parse for all of the three-word inputs, chooses (a b) (c d) for all of the four-word inputs, as opposed to a quaternary φ. L.6 and L.7 also only output two binary phrases for each four-word input. L.1 continues to output only unary φs. These behaviors can be seen in (71), where a similar color-coding to (70) applies.

(71)    Summary of four-word Typology for Align.NR

|        | [[a [[b] c]] [d]] | [[[[a] b] c] [d]] | [[a] [b [c [d]]]] |
|--------|-------------------|-------------------|-------------------|
| L.1 | (a) (b) (c) (d) | (a) (b) (c) (d) | (a) (b) (c) (d) |
| L.2 | (a) (b c) (d) | (a) (b c) (d) <br> (a b) (c) (d) | (a) (b) (c) (d) |
| L.3 | (a) (b c) (d) | (a b c) (d) | (a) (b) (c) (d) |
| L.4 | (a b) (c) (d) | (a) (b) (c) (d) | (a) (b) (c d) <br> (a) (b c) (d) |
| L.5 | (a b) (c) (d) | (a) (b) (c) (d) | (a) (b c d) |
| L.6 | (a b) (c d) | (a b) (c d) | (a b) (c d) |
| L.7 | (a b) (c d) | (a b) (c d) | (a b) (c d) |
| L.8 | (a b) (c d) | (a b) (c d) | (a b) (c d) |

### 3.6.1  Languages of Align.NR

The grammars of the eight languages of Align.NR are depicted as Hasse diagrams in (72).

(72)    Grammars of Align.NR

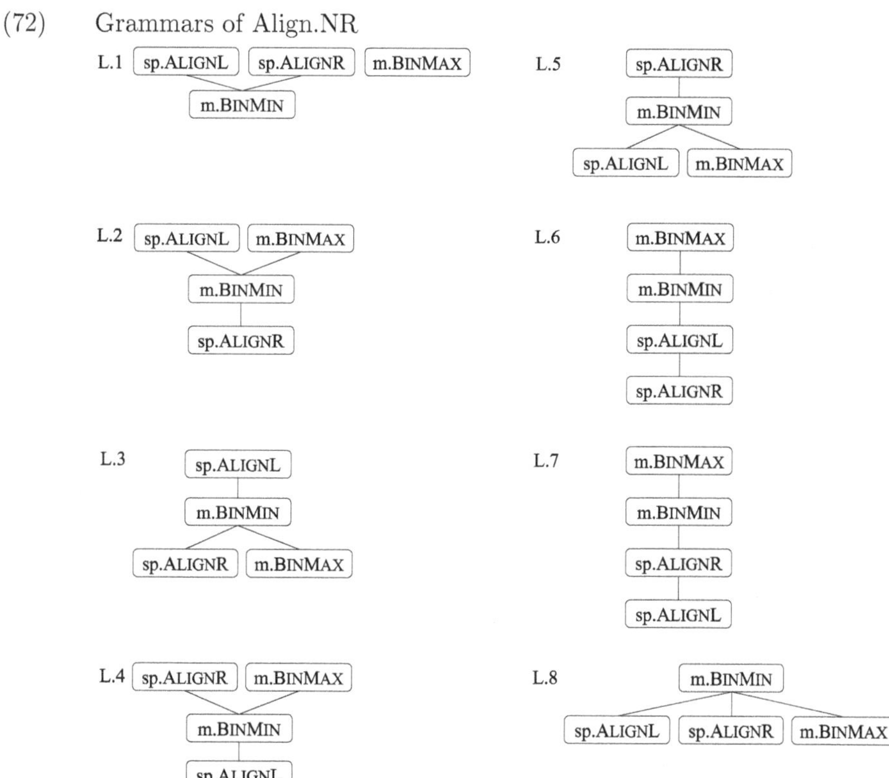

L.1 of Align.NR only has a single parse for each length of sentence: each word is parsed into a single unary $\varphi$. This is because both mapping constraints are ranked above m.BinMin. Since the substructure $[X^0\ X^0]$ is omitted from these systems, there is no case where a terminal is not separated from another terminal by some syntactic edge, so a maximally faithful parse also contains a prosodic edge between each terminal. Prosodic recursion is not permitted by Gen in this system, so the only way for each terminal to be separated from other terminals by a prosodic edge is by mapping each terminal to a unary $\varphi$.

L.3 is slightly more sophisticated, but not by much. Each left edge is mapped faithfully to the left edge of a single $\varphi$, then right edges are simply placed before each non-initial left edge and at the end of the sentence, regardless of where right edges fall in the syntactic structure. One caveat is added to this process: quaternary $\varphi$s are not allowed in this language, so in the case that the above generalization results in a parse containing a quaternary $\varphi$, the quaternary $\varphi$ is broken up into two binary-branching $\varphi$s. In this system, only one input demands this caveat: [[[[a] b] c] d]. If the caveat were not added, all the left edges would be faithfully mapped to the left edge of a single $\varphi$ at the left edge of the whole sentence and the right edge would only be placed at the end of the sentence, resulting in a quaternary $\varphi$: (a b c d). Instead, the resulting parse is (a b) (c d), as the omission of prosody-to-syntax constraints from Con means that the addition of structure does not incur any violations if it does not create marked structure, and is preferred when it helps to avoid marked structure, as shown in (73).

(73)　　　L.3's mappings for the purely right- and left-branching four-word inputs in Align.NR

| Input | Winner | Loser | sp.AlignL | m.BinMin | m.BinMax | sp.AlignR |
|---|---|---|---|---|---|---|
| [[[[a] b] c] d] | (a b) (c d) | (a b c d) | | | W | W |
| [a [b [c [d]]]] | (a) (b) (c) (d) | (a b) (c d) | W | L | | |

L.5 mirrors this behavior: every right syntactic edge is faithfully mapped, then left edges are placed at the beginning of the sentence and after each non-final right edge.

L.2 uses the same principles as L.3, but with another caveat: ternary $\varphi$s are not allowed, so where L.3 would parse three words into a ternary $\varphi$, L.2 must parse them into a unary $\varphi$ and a binary $\varphi$. The split between these unary and binary $\varphi$s means placing a left edge of a $\varphi$ where no XP left edge exists in the syntax, as L.3 and L.2 both faithfully map all left edges before this step. Since the addition of structure is not penalized by any faithfulness constraint, the placement of the boundary between the unary $\varphi$ and the binary $\varphi$ is determined by the location of the greatest number of right XP edges. For example, the structure [[[[a] [b]] c] d] is mapped to (a) (b c d) by L.3, but since L.2 prohibits ternary $\varphi$s, the ternary $\varphi$ must be broken up. By splitting between $c$ and $d$, one right edge is mapped which would not be matched otherwise. However, if the split is made between $b$ and $c$, two right edges are mapped. For this reason, (a) (b) (c d) harmonically bounds (a) (b c) (d) for this input. In the case that the number of right edges is the same for both splits, free variation arises.

(74)    Support for L.2 in Align.NR

| Input | Winner | Loser | sp.AʟɪɢɴL | m.BɪɴMᴀx | m.BɪɴMɪɴ | sp.AʟɪɢɴR |
|---|---|---|---|---|---|---|
| [a [b]] | (a) (b) | (a b) | W | | L | |
| [[[a] b] c] | (a) (b c) (a b) (c) | (a b c) | | W | L | W |
| [[a] b] | (a b) | (a) (b) | | | W | L |

L.4 follows the same principles as L.2 except that priority is given to left edges instead of right edges.

Languages 6 and 7 highly disfavor unary $\varphi$s, so both allow maximally one unary $\varphi$ for each parse. These unary $\varphi$s only arise in the three-word case, where, without the possibility of recursion, the output must contain either a unary or a ternary $\varphi$. Neither language allows ternary $\varphi$s, so a unary $\varphi$ is necessary. All two-word inputs are parsed as (a b), and all four-word cases are parsed as (a b) (c d). For L.6, the placement of the unary $\varphi$ is determined by which split results in more faithful mappings of left edges (75). L.7 determines the placement of the unary $\varphi$ by which split faithfully maps more right edges. L.8 maps two-word and four-word cases the same as L.6 and L.7, but maps all three-word cases to a single ternary $\varphi$ (76).

(75)    Support for L.6 in Align.NR

| Input | Winner | Loser | m.BɪɴMᴀx | m.BɪɴMɪɴ | sp.AʟɪɢɴL | sp.AʟɪɢɴR |
|---|---|---|---|---|---|---|
| [a [b [c]]] | (a) (b c) (a b) (c) | (a b c) | W | L | W | |
| [a [b]] | (a b) | (a) (b) | | W | L | |
| [a [[b] c]] | (a) (b c) | (a b) (c) | | | W | L |

(76)    Support for L.8 in Align.NR

| Input | Winner | Loser | m.BINMIN | sp.ALIGNL | sp.ALIGNR | m.BINMAX |
|---|---|---|---|---|---|---|
| [[a] b] | (a b) | (a) (b) | W | | L | |
| [a [b [c]]] | (a b c) | (a) (b) (c) | W | L | | L |

(77)    Mirror-image language pairs of Align.NR

| Left edges prioritized | Right edges prioritized |
|---|---|
| L.2 | L.4 |
| L.3 | L.5 |
| L.6 | L.7 |

### 3.6.2  Property analysis of Align.NR

The property analysis for Align.NR can be constructed using properties
from the preceding analyses. The first property is p.AlignAll, first defined
in (35) and reproduced below as (78). The property p.AlignAll specifically
distinguishes L.1 from the other languages in the same way that it does in
Align.Rec.

(78)    **p.AlignAll**: {sp.ALIGNL, sp.ALIGNR}.sub <> m.BINMIN
   a.    align.all: Every XP edge is mapped to the edge of a φ.
   b.    align.some: Not every XP edge is mapped to the edge of a φ.

The second property which can be recycled from Align.Rec is p.LR, which
distinguishes between left-preference and right-preference languages, first
defined in (34) and reproduced as (79) below.

(79)    **p.LR**: sp.ALIGNL <> sp.ALIGNR
   a.    L: Mapping of left edges is preferred over the mapping of right
         edges.
   b.    R: Mapping of right edges is preferred over the mapping of left
         edges.

The p.MapUnary property can also be recycled from the two recursive
systems. While p.MapUnary is defined both for Match.Rec in (21) and for
Align.Rec in (41), the definition needed in this case is the latter, which is
reproduced below as (80).

(80)    **p.MapUnary**: LR.dom $<>$ m.BinMin
   a.   unary.allowed: The left and right edges of a single unary XP may
       be mapped, resulting in a unary φ.
   b.   unary.banned: The left and right edges of a single unary XP may
       not *both* be mapped, resulting in a prohibition of unary φs.

Finally, p.3φ.a/b can be reused from Match.NR. Since p.3φ.a/b is defined
only with markedness constraints, which are consistent across systems in
this chapter, the original definition as it appears in (64) can be used. The
definition for p.3φ.a/b is reproduced below as (81).

(81)    **p.3φ.a/b**: m.BɪɴMɪɴ $<>$ m.BɪɴMᴀx
   a.   3φ.a: ternary-branching φs are allowed in the outputs.
   b.   3φ.b: ternary-branching φs are banned from the outputs.

These four properties constitute a complete characterization of the Align.NR
typology. A summary of the property analysis is provided in (82) and a
treeoid showing the entailment relationships is provided in (83), where the
dotted line indicates a disjunction, where the value of p.LR is non-moot
only where ternary φs are banned (p.3φ.b) or unary XPs are mapped. L.8
does not map unary XPs and does allow ternary φs, so the value of p.LR is
moot for that language. The values of all three of these properties are moot
for L.1, as all three properties scope under the negative value of p.AlignAll.

(82)    Property analysis for Align.NR

|       | **p.alignAll** | **p.LR** | **p.MapUnary** | **p.3φ.a/b** |
|-------|----------------|----------|----------------|--------------|
| L.1   | align.all      | *moot*   | <unary.allowed> | *moot*      |
| L.2   | align.some     | R        | unary.allowed  | b            |
| L.3   | align.some     | R        | unary.allowed  | a            |
| L.4   | align.some     | L        | unary.allowed  | b            |
| L.5   | align.some     | L        | unary.allowed  | a            |
| L.6   | align.some     | L        | unary.banned   | b            |
| L.7   | align.some     | R        | unary.banned   | b            |
| L.8   | align.some     | *moot*   | unary.banned   | a            |

(83)     Treeoid for Align.NR

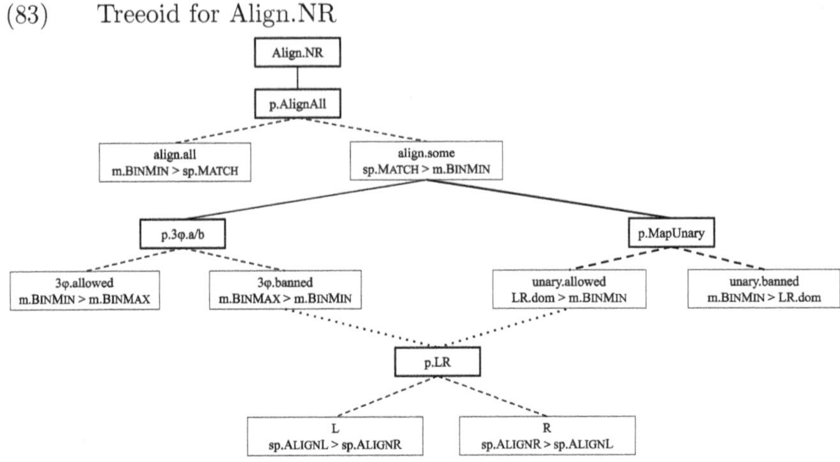

It is interesting to consider Languages 1 and 8 side by side. L.8 is characterized by m.BɪɴMɪɴ dominating all other constraints. This results in a
grammar that completely bans unary φs in multi-word inputs. L.1 is nearly
the opposite of L.8; m.BɪɴMɪɴ is outranked by both mapping constraints,
resulting in a language where every XP boundary is mapped to a φ boundary. The only thing that is not opposite about the grammars is that the
ranking of m.BɪɴMᴀx is moot, as represented by the mootness of p.HAM.a/b
and p.3φ.a/b.

### 3.6.3   Subject-branchingness sensitivity in Align.NR

L.6 and L.7 both exhibit SBS, but both only by the less stringent definition
given in (5a). While the former appears to meet the more stringent
requirements of (5b) in the table in (84), it falls short elsewhere in the
language, as I will illustrate further on in this section.

(84)     SBS in Align.NR

|  | Simple Intransitive | Branching-subject Intransitive | Simple Ditransitive |
|---|---|---|---|
|  | [[N] [V]] | [[[N] [A]] [V]] | [V [[N] [N]]] |
| L.1 | (N) (V) | (N) (A) (V) | (V) (N) (N) |
| L.2 | (N) (V) | (N) (A) (V) | (V N) (N) |
| L.3 | (N) (V) | (N) (A) (V) | (V N) (N) |
| L.4 | (N) (V) | (N) (A) (V) | (V) (N) (N) |
| L.5 | (N) (V) | (N) (A) (V) | (V) (N) (N) |
| L.6 | (N V) | (N A) (V) | (V) (N N) |
| L.7 | (N V) | (N A) (V) | (V N) (N) |
| L.8 | (N V) | (N A V) | (V N N) |

L.7 meets the less stringent definition of SBS from (5a) by phrasing the subject and verb together when the subject is non-branching, as in the simple intransitive, but separately when the subject branches, as in the branching-subject intransitive. This basic pattern has been seen in all three previous systems: Match.Rec, Align.Rec and Match.NR. L.7 fails to meet the more stringent definition of SBS from (5b) because the phonological structure we see in the branching-subject intransitive also surfaces for the simple ditransitive, where it is a strong mismatch. We have seen this same pattern in Align.Rec and Match.NR.

L.6 meets the less stringent definition of SBS from (5a) as L.7 does, but a strong mismatch candidate does not surface for the simple ditransitive. A strong mismatch candidate does surface on a purely right-branching syntax, shown in (85), which compares L.3 of Match.NR and L.6 and L.7 of Align. NR. All three languages phrase the subject and the adjective together for the branching-subject intransitive. The three languages all differ, though, for their parses of the simple ditransitive. Align.NR L.6 phrases the objects together, Align.NR L.7 phrases the verb and direct object together, forming a strong mismatch, and Match.NR L.3 has both of these phrasings as co-optima. Most interestingly, all three languages have the same co-optima for the purely right-branching input (N) (N N), which does not form a strong mismatch with the input, and (N N) (N), which does (the first and second terminals do not form a constituent in the syntactic input). Recall that §3.5.3 argued that L.3 of Match.NR failed to meet the more stringent definition of SBS from (4b) because a strong mismatch candidate surfaced as one of the optima for the simple ditransitive. By this same logic, L.6 from Align.NR must also fail the stringent definition of SBS for its mismatching phrasing of the purely right-branching syntax.

That both L.6 and L.7 of Align.NR meet the less stringent definition of SBS from (5a) but fall short of the more stringent definition of SBS from (5b) is unsurprising given that L.6 is the left-handed version of L.7 (see §3.6.1).

(85)     Comparison of Match.NR L.3 and Align.NR L.6, L.7

|  | Branching-subject Intransitive | Simple Ditransitive | Pure Right-branching |
|---|---|---|---|
|  | [[[N] [A]] [V]] | [V [[N] [N]]] | [N [N [N]]] |
| Match.NR L.3 | (N A) (V) | (V) (N N) (V N) (N) | (N) (N N) (N N) (N) |
| Align.NR L.6 | (N A) (V) | (V) (N N) | (N) (N N) (N N) (N) |
| Align.NR L.7 | (N A) (V) | (V N) (N) | (N) (N N) (N N) (N) |

## 3.7   Discussion

Aside from exploring subject-branchingness sensitivity, two major goals of
this chapter are to understand the differences in typological predictions of
Match and Alignment Theories, and to understand the differences between
the typological predictions of recursive and non-recursive GEN functions.
Section 7.1 summarizes the principal findings about subject-branchingness
sensitivity in the four systems explored in the chapter. Section 3.7.1 compares
other typological differences between the recursive and non-recursive systems,
and §3.7.3 similarly compares the MATCH and ALIGN systems. Finally, §3.7.4
summarizes and concludes with some directions for further research.

### 3.7.1   Subject-branchingness sensitivity

The table in (86) summarizes the adherence of languages in the four systems
to the two definitions of SBS in (5).

(86)     SBS in each of the four systems

|  | Less stringent SBS | More stringent SBS |
|---|---|---|
| Match.Rec | ✓ (L.2) | ✓ (L.2) |
| Align.Rec | ✓ (L.5) |  |
| Match.NR | ✓ (L.3) |  |
| Align.NR | ✓ (L.6, L.7) |  |

While all four systems produce at least one language which meets the less
stringent definition of SBS, only the Match.Rec typology contains a language which meets the more stringent definition. Note that L.2 of Match.Rec
overgeneralizes somewhat in meeting the more stringent definition of SBS:
no strong mismatches appear anywhere in L.2 or, indeed, anywhere in the

entire typology of Match.Rec. While the Align.NR typology also contains a language which prohibits strong mismatches (L.1), it fails to show SBS since it also prohibits binary φs, which are a necessary structure for SBS.

(87)    Languages prohibiting strong mismatches

|  | Simple Intransitive | Branching-subject Intransitive | Simple Ditransitive |
|---|---|---|---|
|  | [[N] [V]] | [[[N] [A]] [V]] | [V [[N] [N]]] |
| Match.Rec L.1 | ((N) (V)) | (((N) (A)) (V)) | (V ((N) (N))) |
| Match.Rec L.2 | (N V) | (N A) (V) | (V) (N N) |
| Align.NR L.1 | (N) (V) | (N) (A) (V) | (V) (N) (N) |

### 3.7.2  Recursive and non-recursive GEN

Perhaps the most surprising result of this chapter is that, while a non-recursive GEN produces a smaller candidate set, recursive GEN produces smaller and simpler typologies for both the Match systems and the Alignment systems. This can be partially attributed to the relative inactivity of m.BINMAX in both Align.Rec and Match.Rec. By this I mean that, while m.BINMAX does eliminate some candidates through harmonic bounding in Align.Rec, its ranking does not matter in either recursive system because none of the possible optima violates it. In Match.Rec, the relative inactivity of m.BINMAX means that, instead of three constraints producing six linear orders, ranking only matters for two constraints, with two linear orders of those two constraints, producing a two-language typology. In Align.Rec, four constraints produce 24 linear orders, but ranking only matters for three of these constraints, of which there are only six linear orders. The number of languages in the Align.Rec typology is further reduced since the relative ranking of sp.ALIGNL and sp.ALIGNR does not matter when they both dominate m.BINMIN.

A simple reason for the relative inactivity of m.BINMAX in the recursive systems is the lack of ternary-branching nodes in the input set. Ternary-branching inputs are not considered in the systems presented in this chapter (see §3.2.1.1), but if ternary-branching inputs were considered, the ranking of m.BINMAX would almost certainly matter in recursive systems, and the recursive systems would produce larger typologies.

While the lack of ternary-branching inputs helps explain why m.BINMAX is relatively inactive in the recursive systems, it does not explain why the ranking of m.BinMax *does* matter in the non-recursive systems. To understand why m.BinMax is more active in the non-recursive systems, let us consider the example of [a [b [c]]] in both Match.NR and Align.NR. The violation tableaux for this input in these two systems are provided in (88) and (89), respectively.

(88)     Violation Tableau for right-branching input in Match.NR

|   | [a [b [c]]] | sp.Match | m.BinMin | m.BinMax |
|---|---|---|---|---|
| a. | (a b) (c) | 2 | 1 | |
| b. | (a) (b c) | 2 | 1 | |
| c. | (a b c) | 2 | | 1 |

(89)     Violation Tableau for right-branching input in Align.NR

|   | [a [b [c]]] | sp.AlignL | sp.AlignR | m.BinMin | m.BinMax |
|---|---|---|---|---|---|
| a. | (a) (b) (c) | | | 3 | |
| b. | (a b) (c) | 1 | | 1 | |
| c. | (a) (b c) | 1 | | 1 | |
| d. | (a b c) | 2 | | | 1 |

We can see from (88) and (89) that non-recursive prosodic parses of three-word inputs must have either a unary $\varphi$ or a ternary $\varphi$; there is no non-recursive and exhaustive parse of a three-word input such that all $\varphi$s are binary-branching. (While (88) and (89) only show non-harmonically bounded candidates, the above generalization holds for the harmonically bounded candidates as well.) Because Gen in the NR systems does not allow recursive parses, the ternary-branching candidates are not harmonically bounded by binary-branching candidates such as (a (b c)) as they are in Match.Rec and Align.Rec.

The inactivity of m.BinMax in the recursive systems is reflected in its absence in the property analyses of those two systems. In the property analyses of the two non-recursive systems, m.BinMax opposes m.BinMin in the properties p.3$\varphi$.a/b and p.4$\varphi$.a/b, the latter only being used in Match.NR. Because the syntactic structure never directly motivates suprabinary prosodic structure, as discussed above, mapping constraints alone do not oppose m.BinMax. By contrast, m.BinMin opposes sp.Match by itself in both Match systems (p.MapUnary in Match.Rec, p.HAM.a/b in Match.NR) and both Align constraints in the two Alignment systems (p.MapUnary and p.AlignAll in both systems). This is because the syntactic structure *does* directly motivate unary prosodic structure in the four systems defined here.

The interaction between the non-recursive definition of GEN and m.BINMAX is interesting in that research in OT usually focuses on the interaction of constraints, not on properties of GEN. In the comparison of recursive and non-recursive systems, we can see that the candidate set determines not only which optima are available to the system and which candidates become harmonically bounded, but also which constraints are active and how constraints interact.

This interaction does not stray too far from established research tendencies, however, if one recalls that a system with a non-recursive GEN function is a subsystem of one in which NONRECURSIVITY is a constraint in CON rather than a condition in GEN. In languages where NONRECURSIVITY is the highest ranked constraint, candidates that would not be produced by the non-recursive GEN are filtered out before they need to be evaluated by any other constraint and only candidates that *would* be produced by the non-recursive GEN remain. The interaction of m.BINMAX with the non-recursive definition of GEN in Match.NR and Align.NR is then equivalent to the interaction of m.BINMAX and a higher-ranked NONRECURSIVITY constraint.

### 3.7.3   ALIGN and MATCH constraint sets

The most obvious difference between the MATCH systems and the ALIGN systems is that MATCH systems produce smaller typologies. Match.NR produced a five-language typology, while Align.NR produced an eight-language typology. Furthermore, Match.Rec produced the smallest typology with only two languages, while Align.Rec produced a five-language typology. A main factor in this difference in typology size is the size of the constraint sets—the MATCH systems have one fewer constraint than the ALIGN systems because the MATCH systems use a single mapping constraint, sp.MATCH, in place of the two mapping constraints required for the ALIGN systems, sp.ALIGNL and sp.ALIGNR. With fewer constraints, the MATCH systems have fewer linear orders of those constraints.

In addition to having fewer constraints, the MATCH typologies are smaller because sp.MATCH is satisfied by fewer candidates than the Alignment constraints. For example, tableaux (88) and (89) above show that, although no non-recursive candidate satisfies sp.MATCH, the mapping [a [b [c]]] → (a) (b) (c) satisfies sp.ALIGNL, and all candidates satisfy sp.ALIGNR. Furthermore, several candidates may be 'maximally faithful" for certain inputs in Align.Rec, whereas only a single candidate is maximally faithful for each input in Match.Rec, as discussed in §3.6. The relative permissiveness of the Alignment constraints helps account for their larger typologies since the

Alignment constraints generally filter out or harmonically bound fewer candidates than sp.MATCH.

Another difference between Match and Alignment Theories can be seen in the comparison of the two non-recursive systems. While the behavior of the Alignment constraints in Align.NR is fairly straightforward and familiar to those who have read classic Alignment analyses such as Truckenbrodt's (1999) analyses of Tohono O'odham and Chicheŵa, Match.NR is significantly less intuitive (though see Cao and Bibbs, Chapter 9, for an alternative viewpoint). Most clearly, this is demonstrated by the necessity to enumerate seven steps to describe the mapping process of a single language in Match.NR in (54), whereas the mapping processes for the languages of all of the other systems could be explained in-line.

As a further example, I return to (88), where we see that the mapping of [a [b [c]]] to (a) (b c) receives the same number of violations of sp.MATCH as the mapping to (a b) (c), even though the latter is a strong mismatch, a seemingly much more grievous rebracketing. While the first parse, (a) (b c), fails to map the XP constituent [c], the second parse, (a b) (c), fails to map the larger and more distinctive constituent [b [c]]. Since no markedness constraint in the system prefers one over the other, Match.NR predicts that, if one of these two parses surfaces for this input, it will be in free variation with the other. Furthermore, this is not simply a result of the omission of sp.MATCH's complementary constraint ps.MATCH, since ps.MATCH assigns only one violation to each of these candidates. Rather, it is a consequence of restricting the candidate set to non-recursive parses only.

While Alignment Theory, which was developed while prosodic structure was generally assumed to be non-recursive, makes sense in both recursive and non-recursive systems, Match Theory is only coherent when the prosodic structures considered are allowed to be recursive. This follows from Selkirk's (2011) original formulation of Match Theory as a reflection of the recursive nature of syntactic structures. This leads to the broader generalization that, within OT, a constraint set can only be fully understood in the context of a well-defined GEN function. This follows Bane and Riggle (2012), who illustrate the importance of considering all of the candidates produced by GEN, especially when studying the typological predictions of a system. The strange interaction between sp.MATCH and GEN in Match.NR, along with the interaction between m.BINMAX and GEN discussed in the previous subsection, further illustrate that, in addition to considering all of the candidates produced by a particular definition of GEN, an analyst must consider what candidates GEN does not produce, and whether the definition of GEN should be adjusted to include these candidates.

One final line of comparison between the MATCH and ALIGN systems can be made in their respective property analyses. The property analysis of Align.Rec is a subset of the property analysis for Align.NR, differing only in that Align.NR requires the property p.3φ.a/b with the emergence of ternary-branching φs in the non-recursive systems. In contrast, Match.Rec and Match.NR do not share any properties. While they both contain a property which is defined by the opposition m.BINMIN <> sp.MATCH, the descriptions of these properties must differ: in Match.Rec, this property is called p.MapUnary; in Match.NR, it is called p.HAM.a/b. This difference further points to the strange nature of Match.NR when compared to the other three systems presented in this chapter.

### 3.7.4   *Conclusion and directions for further research*

This chapter presented four OT typologies which illustrate the complex relationship between the definition of GEN (whether it allows recursivity or not) and the type of mapping constraints used (Alignment Theory and Match Theory). With the example of subject-branchingness sensitivity, a cross-linguistically common type of behavior exemplified by High Tone Deletion in Kinyambo, I hope to have shown the reader how to rigorously investigate basic assumptions about prosodic grammar such as these. Using property analysis, I have also explored the relationship between constraint sets and GEN. In comparing the four systems, I find that, while a definition of GEN which allows recursion generates far more candidates than a non-recursive GEN, recursive typologies are smaller. Additionally, I find that Match Theory is significantly less interpretable when paired with a non-recursive GEN function. In contrast, when Match Theory is paired with a recursive GEN, it not only becomes more interpretable, but yields the only system which meets the more stringent definition of subject-branchingness sensitivity.

In future research, the recursive systems might be expanded to include NONRECURSIVITY as a constraint. NONRECURSIVITY would certainly increase the size of the smaller typologies of the recursive systems, potentially providing greater insight into the behavior of MATCH and ALIGN. While NONRECURSIVITY as a constraint was not considered in this chapter, the property analyses presented here would provide a good starting point, as a definition of GEN which does not allow recursion is functionally equivalent to a system where a non-recursivity constraint is the highest ranked constraint. The constraint sets of all of the systems might also be expanded to include prosody-to-syntax constraints, sp.WRAP, or any of the other constraints proposed in the literature.

Another topic left for further research concerns expanded versions of the systems presented in which the length of the inputs is not limited to four words. This chapter may not establish universal support for such expanded systems. While the basic pattern of SBS would not appear in longer sentences, a universal support might refine the property analyses and shed further light on the behaviors of the SBS languages identified in this chapter.

## References

Alber, Birgit, Delbusso, Natalie, and Prince, Alan (2016). From intensional properties to universal support. *Language* 92: e88–e116.

Alber, Birgit and Prince, Alan (2017). *The Book of nGX*. ROA 1312, Rutgers Optimality Archive, http://roa.rutgers.edu.

Alber, Birgit and Prince, Alan (2021). *The Structure of OT Typologies.* Chapter 1: Introduction to Property Theory. Unpublished manuscript. ROA 1381, Rutgers Optimality Archive, http://roa.rutgers.edu.

Bane, Max and Riggle, Jason (2012). Consequences of candidate omission. *Linguistic Inquiry* 43: 695–706.

Bellik, Jennifer and Kalivoda, Nick (2016). Adjunction and branchingness effects in syntax-prosody mapping. In Gunnar Ólafur Hansson, Ashley Farris-Trimble, Kevin McMullin, and Douglas Pulleyblank (eds.) *Supplemental Proceedings of the 2015 Annual Meeting on Phonology,* Linguistic Society of America. http://doi.org/10.3765/amp.v3i0.3690

Bellik, Jennifer, Bellik, Ozan, and Kalivoda, Nick (2015–2021). Syntax-Prosody in Optimality Theory (SPOT). Javascript application. http:// spot.sites.ucsc.edu. Codebase at https://github.com/syntax-prosody-ot.

Bellik, Jennifer, Ito, Junko, Kalivoda, Nick and Mester, Armin (2022). Matching and alignment. In Haruo Kubozono, Junko Ito, and Armin Mester (eds.) *Prosody and Prosodic Interfaces.* Oxford University Press. 457–481.

Bennett, Ryan and Elfner, Emily (2019). The syntax-prosody interface. *Annual Review of Linguistics* 5: 151–171.

Bickmore, Lee (1989). *Kinyambo Prosody.* PhD dissertation, University of California, Los Angeles.

Bickmore, Lee (1990). Branching nodes and prosodic categories: evidence from Kinyambo. In Sharon Inkelas and Draga Zec (eds.) *The Phonology-Syntax Connection* 1–18. Chicago: University of Chicago Press.

Chen, Matthew (1987). The syntax of Xiamen tone sandhi. *Phonology Yearbook* 4: 109–149.

Cheng, Lisa Lai-Shen and Downing, Laura J. (2016). Phasal syntax = cyclic phonology? *Syntax* 19: 156–191.

Downing, Laura J. and Mtenje, Al (2011). Un-Wrap-ing prosodic phrasing in Chichewa. *Lingua* 121: 1965–1986

Elfner, Emily (2012). *Syntax-Prosody Interactions in Irish.* PhD dissertation, University of Massachusetts Amherst.

Elfner, Emily (2015). Recursion in prosodic phrasing: evidence from
Connemara Irish. *Natural Language and Linguistic Theory* 33: 1169–1208.

Elordieta, Gorka (2008). An overview of theories of the syntax-phonology
interface. *International Journal of Basque Linguistics and Philology* 42:
209–286.

Ghini, Mirco (1993). Φ-formation in Italian: a new proposal. In Carrie Dyck
(ed.) *Toronto Working Papers in Linguistics* 12: 41–78.

Ito, Junko and Mester, Armin (2018). Matching light elements. In Jason
Merchant, Line Mikkelsen, Deniz Rudin, and Kelsey Sasaki (eds.) *A
Reasonable Way to Proceed: Essays in Honor of Jim McCloskey* 169–
191. Santa Cruz: Linguistics Research Center. Retrieved from https://
escholarship.org/uc/item/7z29n70x

Kalivoda, Nick (2018). *Syntax-Prosody Mismatches in Optimality Theory.*
PhD dissertation, University of California, Santa Cruz.

Kalivoda, Nick, and Bellik, Jennifer (2018). Prosodic recursion and pseudo-
cyclicity in Danish compound stød. In Ryan Bennett, Andrew Angeles,
Adrian Brasoveanu, Dhyana Buckley, Nick Kalivoda, Shigeto Kawahara,
Grant McGuire and Jaye Padgett (eds.) *Hana-bana (花々): A Festschrift
for Junko Ito and Armin Mester.* Santa Cruz: Linguistics Research Center.

Larson, Richard K. (1988). On the double object construction. *Linguistic
Inquiry* 19: 335–391.

Lee, Seunghun and Selkirk, Elisabeth (2022). Xitsonga tone: The syntax-
phonology interface. In Haruo Kubozono, Junko Ito, and Armin Mester
(eds.) *Prosody and Prosodic Interfaces.* Oxford University Press. 337–374.

Liberman, Mark and Prince, Alan (1977). On stress and linguistic rhythm.
*Linguistic Inquiry* 8: 249–336.

McCarthy, John J. and Prince, Alan (1993). Generalized alignment. In
Geert Booij and Jaap van Marle (eds.) *Yearbook of Morphology* 79–153.
Dordrecht: Kluwer.

Myrberg, Sara (2013). Sisterhood in prosodic branching. *Phonology* 30:
73–124.

Prieto, Pilar (2005). Syntactic and eurhythmic constraints on phrasing
decisions in Catalan. *Studia Linguistica* 59: 194–222.

Prieto, Pilar (2006). Phonological phrasing in Spanish. In Fernando Martínez-
Gil and Sonia Colina (eds.) *Optimality-Theoretic Studies in Spanish
Phonology* 39–61. Amsterdam: John Benjamins.

Prince, Alan (2017). OT Checklist. ROA 1306, Rutgers Optimality Archive,
http://roa.rutgers.edu.

Prince, Alan (2002a). Arguing optimality. In Angela Carpenter, Andries
Coetzee, and Paul de Lacy (eds.) *Papers in Optimality Theory II*
(University of Massachusetts Occasional Papers in Linguistics 26) 269–304.
Amherst, MA: GLSA.

Prince, Alan (2002b). Entailed ranking arguments. Unpublished manuscript.
ROA 500, Rutgers Optimality Archive, http://roa.rutgers.edu.

Prince, Alan, Merchant, Nazarré, and Tesar, Bruce (2007–2020).
OTWorkplace. http://sites.google.com/site/otworkplace

Prince, Alan and Smolensky, Paul (1993/2004). *Optimality Theory: Constraint Interaction in Generative Grammar*. Malden, MA: Blackwell Publishing.

Selkirk, Elisabeth (1984). *Phonology and Syntax: the Relation between Sound and Structure*. Cambridge, MA: MIT Press.

Selkirk, Elisabeth (1986). On derived domains in sentence phonology. *Phonology Yearbook* 3: 371–405.

Selkirk, Elisabeth (2011). The syntax–phonology interface. In John A. Goldsmith, Jason Riggle, and Alan C. L. Yu (eds.) *The Handbook of Phonological Theory* 435–484. Blackwell Publishing.

Truckenbrodt, Hubert (1995). *Phonological Phrases: Their Relation to Syntax, Focus, and Prominence*. PhD dissertation, Massachusetts Institute of Technology.

Truckenbrodt, Hubert (1999). On the relation between syntactic phrases and phonological phrases. *Linguistic Inquiry* 30: 219–255.

Van Handel, Nicholas (2021). Matching overtly headed syntactic phrases in Italian. *Phonology* 38: 317–356.

## About the author

*Max Tarlov*

Undergraduate research assistant and programmer for the SPOT project, Linguistics BA 2020, University of California, Santa Cruz. Research interests: phonology, the syntax–prosody interface, Optimality Theory and computational linguistics.

# Part II

# Match Theory

# Chapter 4

# Overtly headed XPs and ι-initial STRONGSTART in Irish syntax–prosody mapping

Nick Kalivoda[*]

## 4.1 Introduction

Elfner (2012, 2015) develops a theory of phonological phrasing in Conamara Irish (henceforth Irish) within Match Theory (Selkirk 2011). On this theory, Irish phonological phrases ($\varphi$s) are recursive, and deviate from perfect syntax–prosody matching only insofar as is necessary to satisfy certain prosodic markedness constraints, primarily m.STRONGSTART, m.BINMIN($\varphi$,branches), and m.BINMAX($\varphi$,branches).[1]

Elfner's analysis goes a long way toward deriving the prosodic structures needed to account for various boundary tones in Irish, but within OT it runs into a ranking paradox, leading Elfner to recast the analysis within Harmonic Grammar (Legendre et al. 1990).

This chapter presents a reanalysis of the Irish facts in classic Optimality Theory with strict domination (Prince and Smolensky 1993/2004), resolving the ranking paradox between sp.MATCH(XP,$\varphi$) and m.STRONGSTART.

---

[*] This chapter builds upon work with Jennifer Bellik (Kalivoda and Bellik 2021), and I am grateful to Jennifer for her input and assistance throughout the project. Thanks are also due to Junko Ito, Armin Mester, Nicholas Van Handel, and the audience of AMP 2020 at UC Santa Cruz. All errors are my own.

[1] Constraints in this chapter are prefixed with either 'sp.' for 'syntax–prosody' or 'm.' for 'markedness'.

The analysis accounts for the phrasing of monoclausal transitive and intransitive sentences with subjects and objects of varying length (with one minor exception). While the analysis owes much to Elfner's, it involves two significantly different theoretical proposals: (i) that there are MATCH constraints which refer specifically to overtly headed constituents, and (ii) that m.STRONGSTART, or at least a version of it, applies only ι-initially. Singling out overtly headed constituents for matching has been argued to be necessary for Italian by Van Handel (2021). Our particular version of m.STRONGSTART restricted to ι-initial position is a novel proposal of this chapter (and of Kalivoda and Bellik 2021, an earlier version of this work).

## 4.2    Background on Irish

### *4.2.1   Tone patterns*

Elfner's (2012, 2015) theory of phonological phrasing in Irish is meant to account for the distribution of two phrasal tone contours: LH and HL. The first word of a declarative utterance generally bears an LH, and the last word an HL, suggesting that LH marks the left edge of some prosodic constituent, and that HL marks the right edge of one. For example, the three-word intransitive sentence in (1), which we call V-SS,[2] has an LH on the sentence-initial verb and an HL on the sentence-final adjective.

(1)     V-SS (Elfner 2012, p. 62)

| | | |
|---|---|---|
| ᴸᴴimeoidh | múinteoirí ᴴᴸ | banúla ᴴᴸ |
| leave.FUT | teachers | ladylike |
| 'Ladylike teachers will leave.' | | |

In addition to the sentence-initial LH and sentence-final HL, (1) contains an HL on the sentence-medial noun. This demonstrates that LH and HL contours are not simply paired, as would be expected if they marked the left and right edges, respectively, of non-overlapping constituents, as in $(_\alpha$ LH ... HL). Instead, they must either mark edges of nested constituents, as in $(_\alpha (_\alpha$ LH ... HL) ... HL), or be deployed differently in constituents of different categories, as in $(_\alpha$ LH ... HL$)(_\beta$ HL), where $\alpha \neq \beta$.

---

[2] Throughout the chapter, we refer to sentences with names of the form V-S(S)(S)-(O)(O)(O). 'V' is the verb; 'S' is any word contained in a subject; and 'O' is any word contained in an object. Within an argument, the first 'S' or 'O' is a noun, while every following 'S' or 'O' is an adjective.

That the distribution of LH and HL is at least indirectly sensitive to syntactic structure is shown by the fact that sentences of the same length but different structure can differ in tone placement. For example, while a three-word VSO sentence can optionally have the same LH-HL-HL pattern as (1), as in (2b), it can also differ, as in (2a).

(2)    V-S-O (Elfner 2012, pp. 170–171)
   a.    Option 1

   $^{LH}$cheannaigh      múinteoirí      málaí$^{HL}$
   bought           teachers        bags
   'Teachers bought bags.'

   b.    Option 2

   $^{LH}$cheannaigh      múinteoirí$^{HL}$   málaí$^{HL}$
   bought           teachers        bags
   'Teachers bought bags.'

From this distinction between V-SS and V-S-O, one can conclude that either syntax directly determines the distribution of tones, or does so indirectly via its relation to the prosodic hierarchy.

Four-word sentences also display different tonal patterns depending on syntactic structure. In a sentence with a verb, a two-word subject, and a one-word object, V-SS-O, each of the first two words hosts a rise, and each of the last two words a fall, as in (3). A sentence of the form V-S-OO, by contrast, has a rise on the verb, a fall on the subject, and a fall on the second word of the object, with no tones docked to the first word of the object, as shown in (4).

(3)    V-SS-O (Elfner 2012, p. 62)
   $^{LH}$díofaidh      $^{LH}$rúnaí      dathúil$^{HL}$      blathanna$^{HL}$
   sell.FUT        secretary     handsome        flowers
   'A handsome secretary will sell flowers.'

(4)    V-S-OO (Elfner 2015, p. 1198)
   $^{LH}$cheannaigh      múinteoirí$^{HL}$      málaí      bána$^{HL}$
   bought           teachers          bags      white
   'Teachers bought white bags.'

Since (2)–(4) all consist of a verb, a subject, and an object, but have different tonal patterns, the syntactic structure of the clause cannot be the only factor in determing tone placement. In addition, the number of words in each constituent plays a role.

When the subject and object each contain two words, as in (5), the verb has its usual rise; the first word of the subject has a rise; the second words of the subject and object have a fall; and the first word of the object is not specified for tone.

(5)      V-SS-OO (Elfner 2015, p. 1174)
   [LH]díofaidh    [LH]leabharlannaí    dathúil[HL]    blathanna    áille[HL]
   sell.FUT        librarian            handsome       flowers      beautiful
   'A handsome librarian will sell beautiful flowers.'

Incrementing the length of either argument by one word results in yet another pattern. Example (6) shows that when the subject contains three words and the object contains two, the pattern is LH-LH-Ø-HL-Ø-HL. When the lengths of the arguments are reversed, as in (7), the pattern is instead LH-LH-HL-LH-Ø-HL.

(6)      V-SSS-OO (Elfner 2015, p. 1195)
   [LH]cheannaigh  [LH]múinteoirí banúla    dathúla[HL]  blathanna áille[HL]
   bought          teachers       ladylike  handsome bags          white
   'Handsome ladylike teachers bought white bags.'

(7)      V-SS-OOO (Elfner 2015, p. 1195)
   [LH]díofaidh    [LH]rúnaí    dathúil[HL]    [LH]blathanna bána    áille[HL]
   sell.FUT        secretary    handsome       flowers       white   beautiful
   'A handsome secretary will sell beautiful white flowers.'

Elfner (2012, 2015) presents data for many other sentence-types, including ditransitives and sentences with embedded clauses. These too display sequences of words bearing LH, HL, and no tones at all, with the same curious property of not always having an equal number of rises and falls, also on display in (1)–(7). In this chapter, we provide a reanalysis of the data in (1)–(7), and leave consideration of additional data for future work. Doing so allows us to investigate three factors in isolation: intransitivity versus transitivity, subject length, and object length.

Elfner (2012, 2015) analyzes these patterns within Prosodic Hierarchy Theory (PHT; Selkirk 1986, Nespor and Vogel 1986), according to which the influence of syntax on phonology is mediated by a sentence's prosodic structure. While PHT originally posited a wide array of prosodic categories, without the possibility of recursion, Elfner (2012, 2015) follows Ito and Mester (2007, 2009a, 2009b, 2012, 2013) in restricting the inventory of prosodic categories at or above the word level to the intonational phrase ι, the phonological phrase φ, and the prosodic word ω. Taking of the notion of prosodic recursion from Ladd (1986) and Gussenhoven (1991, 2005), Ito and Mester (2007, 2009a, 2009b, 2012, 2013) argue that phonological phenomena previously associated with distinct levels of the prosodic hierarchy are in fact associated only with ι, φ, and ω, but at various levels of embedding. Specifically, a prosodic constituent π bears two features determined by its hierarchical relation to other constituents of the same category: [±minimal] and [±maximal]. If π dominates another node of category π, it is [−minimal], and if it does not, it is [+minimal]. Similarly, if π is dominated by another node of category π, it is [−maximal], and if not, it is [+maximal]. These features freely combine, as shown for φ in the tree in (8), where all four combinations are present.

(8)      Minimality and maximality features of phonological phrases

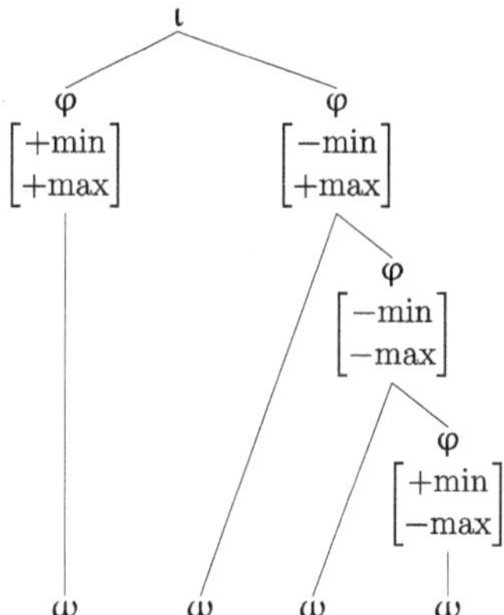

Elfner (2012, 2015) takes up the insight from Ito and Mester (2007, 2009a, 2009b, 2012, 2013) that a phonological process may occur in a configuration determined by a prosodic category π with a particular value or combination of values for [±minimal] and/or [±maximal]. For Irish, Elfner proposes that while HL associates to the rightmost ω of any φ, LH associates to the leftmost ω in a non-minimal φ, but not a minimal φ.

(9)      Prosodically Conditioned Tones in Irish (Elfner 2012, 2015)

  a.    LH    leftmost ω of non-minimal φ

  b.    HL    rightmost ω of φ

Given the patterns of (1)–(7), the theory of tone distribution in (9) indicates that these sentences have the prosodic structures in (10).

(10)     Irish phrasings proposed by Elfner (2012)

  a.    V-SS        →    ((V S) S)

  b.    V-S-O       →    (V (S O)) or ((V S) O)

  c.    V-SS-O      →    (V ((S S) O))

  d.    V-S-OO      →    ((V S) (O O))

  e.    V-SS-OO     →    (V ((S S) (O O)))

  f.    V-SSS-OO    →    (V ((S (S S)) (O O)))

  g.    V-SS-OOO    →    (V ((S S) (O (O O))))

For the most part, these phonological phrasings relate to the syntactic structures of (1)–(7) very straightforwardly, though there are some syntax–prosody mismatches, as shown in the discussion of Irish syntax in the following subsection.

### 4.2.2    Irish syntax

Elfner (2012, 2015) adopts the syntactic analysis of Irish clause structure developed by Chung and McCloskey (1987) and McCloskey (1991, 1996, 2001, 2011), which we also assume here. In an Irish finite main clause, the verb undergoes successive head movement through $v$ and T to a polarity head $\Sigma$. The subject moves to Spec,TP, and if there is an object, it remains *in situ*. This is shown in (11).[3]

---

[3] The plus sign indicates head-adjunction. $V+v+T+\Sigma$ is an abbreviation for a complex head $[_\Sigma [_T [_v V\ v]\ T]\ \Sigma]$, and N+F abbreviates $[_F N\ F]$.

(11)    Irish clause structure

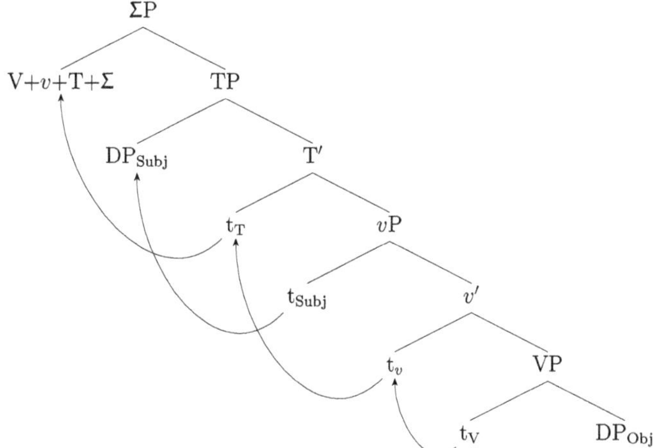

Within the DP, we follow Elfner (2012, 2015) and McCloskey (personal communication) in positing a functional head F between D and N, to which N obligatorily moves. If all Irish XPs are left-headed and APs are left-adjoined to NP, then N-to-F movement correctly derives noun–adjective word order.[4] Thus, a DP containing a noun and a single adjective has the structure in (12), and one containing a noun and two adjectives has the structure in (13).

(12)    Irish DP with one adjective

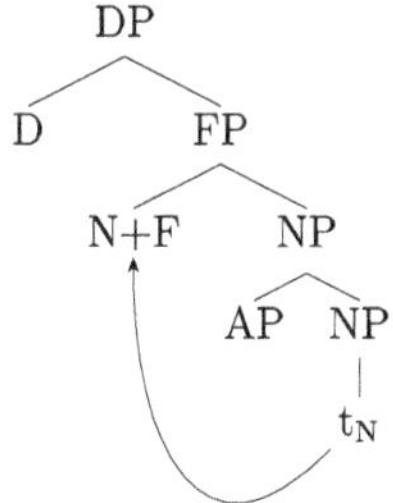

---

[4] As will become apparent in §4.3.1.1, it does not matter for our purposes whether APs are adjoined to N or are specifiers of dedicated functional projections above NP, as on a cartographic approach (Cinque 2010). What matters is that N raises past them to the higher head F.

(13)    Irish DP with two adjectives

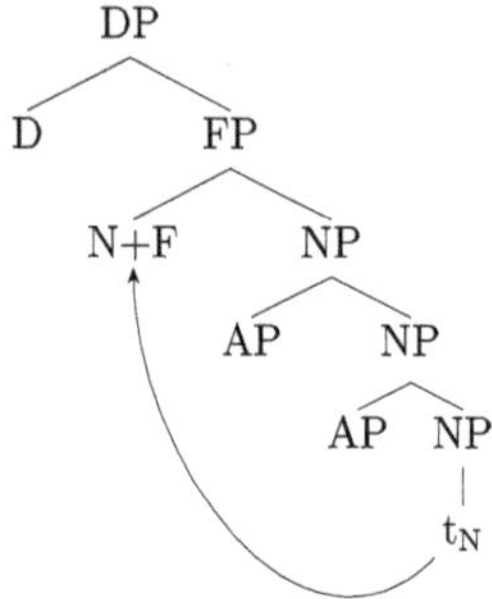

In the next section, we define an OT system which takes certain combinations of the trees in in (11)–(13) as inputs.

## 4.3    An OT system with modified MATCH and STRONGSTART

Elfner (2012, 2015) analyzes the phonological phrasing of Irish in terms of Match Theory (Selkirk 2011), an Optimality-Theoretic approach to the syntax–prosody interface which posits two types of constraints: mapping constraints of the MATCH family, and prosodic markedness constraints. A constraint MATCH($\alpha$,$\beta$)—prefixed with either 'sp.' for syntax-to-prosody or 'ps.' for prosody-to-syntax—is violated once for every input (or output) constituent $\alpha$ that lacks a matching output (or input) constituent $\beta$. Two constituents $\alpha$ and $\beta$ are *matching* if and only if they exhaustively dominate the same terminal string.[5]

Elfner (2012, 2015) employs the two basic phrase-level MATCH constraints from Selkirk (2011): sp.MATCH(XP,$\varphi$) and ps.MATCH($\varphi$,XP). These interact with markedness constraints favoring binary-branching $\varphi$s, and a constraint m.STRONGSTART which penalizes prosodic constituents beginning with a weak element. The markedness constraints compel certain deviations from the perfect syntax–prosody isomorphism demanded by sp.MATCH(XP,$\varphi$) and ps.MATCH($\varphi$,XP).

However, as will be shown in §4.4, these constraints do not entirely derive the patterns from §4.2 in classic OT with strict domination. In particular, there is no strict ranking that will select both the mismatched parse ((V S) (O O)) in (10d) while also selecting the matching parse (V ((SS) O)) in

---

[5] The notion of terminal string identity must in fact be spelled out in terms of a correspondence relation between terminal nodes. See (22) below for a more precise definition.

(10c) or matching parses with a three-word subject or object. This problem prompts Elfner to switch to Harmonic Grammar (Legendre et al. 1990), a theory related to OT in which constraints are weighted rather than strictly ranked. In this section, we define an OT system in the sense of Alber et al. (2016) and Alber and Prince (2021), eschewing constraint weighting and capitalizing instead on the distinction between overtly and covertly headed XPs proposed by Van Handel (2021). We also address an issue with the precise formulation of m.STRONGSTART, presenting a new version of this constraint with certain salutary effects for Irish phrasing and, *ex hyp.*, for the typology of phonological phrasing more generally.

An OT system $S$ is a pair $\langle S.\text{GEN}, S.\text{CON} \rangle$. $S.\text{GEN}$ specifies the candidate sets (csets) of $S$, while $S.\text{CON}$ is the system's constraint set. The factorial typology of $S$ is fully determined by the definition of $S.\text{GEN}$ and $S.\text{CON}$. We define a system VSO.Oh in §4.3. Candidates in the csets of VSO.Oh.GEN are triplets $\langle in, out, corr \rangle$, where *in* is a syntactic input tree, *out* is a prosodic output tree, and *corr* is an input–output correspondence relation. The inputs of VSO.Oh are defined in §4.3.1.1, while the outputs and correspondence relation are given in §4.3.1.2. The constraints of VSO.Oh.CON are defined in §4.3.1.3. The factorial typology of VSO.Oh is presented in §4.3.2, and its structure is elucidated in terms of Property Theory in §4.3.3 (Alber et al. 2016; Alber and Prince 2021). One language in the typology resembles Irish in all but one detail, and this language is discussed in §4.3.4. Remaining challenges for the system VSO.Oh are discussed in §4.3.5.

### 4.3.1   GEN

### 4.3.1.1   Inputs

Elfner (2012, 2015) and Bennett et al. (2016) analyze the prosody of many different syntactic constructions in Irish. In the OT system VSO.Oh, we restrict our attention to a small and well-defined subset of these input structures, namely those trees which meet the specifications in (14).

(14)    Inputs in VSO.Oh (syntactically detailed version)
       A tree is an input in VSO.Oh if it has the form
       $[_{\Sigma P}\ \text{V}+v+\text{T}+\Sigma\ [_{TP}\ \text{DP}_i\ [_{T'}\ \text{t}_T\ [_{vP}\ \text{t}_i\ [_{v'}\ \text{t}_v\ [_{VP}\ \text{t}_V\ (\text{DP}_j)]]]]]]$,
       where each DP is of the form (a), (b), or (c):
   a.   $[_{DP}\ \text{D}\ [_{FP}\ \text{N}+\text{F}\ [_{NP}\ \text{t}_N]]]]$
   b.   $[_{DP}\ \text{D}\ [_{FP}\ \text{N}+\text{F}\ [_{NP}\ [_{AP}\ \text{A}]\ [_{NP}\ \text{t}_N]]]]]$
   c.   $[_{DP}\ \text{D}\ [_{FP}\ \text{N}+\text{F}\ [_{NP}\ [_{AP}\ \text{A}]\ [_{NP}\ [_{AP}\ \text{A}]\ [_{NP}\ \text{t}_N]]]]]]$
       and terminal nodes D, t, are silent, and every other maximal $\text{X}^0$ is pronounced.

That is, an input is a transitive or intransitive Irish clause where each argument contains either one, two, or three words. The specifications in (14) are met by the following twelve trees ("V" is an abbreviation for 'V+$v$+T+$\Sigma$" and "N" is an abbreviation for 'N+F"; overt words are emphasized).

(15)    Inputs of VSO.Oh enumerated (syntactically detailed version)

    a.    V-S (no example)

$[_{\Sigma P}\ \mathbf{\underline{V}}\ [_{TP}\ [_{DPi}\ D\ [_{FP}\ \mathbf{\underline{N}}\ [_{NP}\ t_N]]]\ [_{T'}\ t_T\ [_{vP}\ t_i\ [_{v'}\ t_v\ [_{VP}\ t_V]]]]]]$

    b.    V-SS (cf. (1))

$[_{\Sigma P}\ \mathbf{\underline{V}}\ [_{TP}\ [_{DPi}\ D\ [_{FP}\ \mathbf{\underline{N}}\ [_{NP}\ [_{AP}\ \mathbf{\underline{A}}]\ [_{NP}\ t_N]]]]\ [_{T'}\ t_T\ [_{vP}\ t_i\ [_{v'}\ t_v\ [_{VP}\ t_V]]]]]]$

    c.    V-S-O (cf. (2))

$[_{\Sigma P}\ \mathbf{\underline{V}}\ [_{TP}\ [_{DPi}\ D\ [_{FP}\ \mathbf{\underline{N}}\ [_{NP}\ t_N]]]\ [_{T'}\ t_T\ [_{vP}\ t_i\ [_{v'}\ t_v\ [_{VP}\ t_V\ [_{DPj}\ D\ [_{FP}\ \mathbf{\underline{N}}\ [_{NP}\ t_N]]]]]]]]$

    d.    V-SSS (no example)

$[_{\Sigma P}\ \mathbf{\underline{V}}\ [_{TP}\ [_{DPi}\ D\ [_{FP}\ \mathbf{\underline{N}}\ [_{NP}\ [_{AP}\ \mathbf{\underline{A}}]\ [_{NP}\ [_{AP}\ \mathbf{\underline{A}}]\ [_{NP}\ t_N]]]]]\ [_{T'}\ t_T\ [_{vP}\ t_i\ [_{v'}\ t_v\ [_{VP}\ t_V]]]]]]$

    e.    V-SS-O (cf. (3))

$[_{\Sigma P}\ \mathbf{\underline{V}}\ [_{TP}\ [_{DPi}\ D\ [_{FP}\ \mathbf{\underline{N}}\ [_{NP}\ [_{AP}\ \mathbf{\underline{A}}]\ [_{NP}\ t_N]]]]\ [_{T'}\ t_T\ [_{vP}\ t_i\ [_{v'}\ t_v\ [_{VP}\ t_V\ [_{DPj}\ D\ [_{FP}\ \mathbf{\underline{N}}\ [_{NP}\ t_N]]]]]]]]$

    f.    V-S-OO (cf. (4))

$[_{\Sigma P}\ \mathbf{\underline{V}}\ [_{TP}\ [_{DPi}\ D\ [_{FP}\ \mathbf{\underline{N}}\ [_{NP}\ t_N]]]\ [_{T'}\ t_T\ [_{vP}\ t_i\ [_{v'}\ t_v\ [_{VP}\ t_V\ [_{DPj}\ D\ [_{FP}\ \mathbf{\underline{N}}\ [_{NP}\ [_{AP}\ \mathbf{\underline{A}}]\ [_{NP}\ t_N]]]]]]]]]$

    g.    V-SSS-O (no example)

$[_{\Sigma P}\ \mathbf{\underline{V}}\ [_{TP}\ [_{DPi}\ D\ [_{FP}\ \mathbf{\underline{N}}\ [_{NP}\ [_{AP}\ \mathbf{\underline{A}}]\ [_{NP}\ [_{AP}\ \mathbf{\underline{A}}]\ [_{NP}\ t_N]]]]]\ [_{T'}\ t_T\ [_{vP}\ t_i\ [_{v'}\ t_v\ [_{VP}\ t_V\ [_{DPj}\ D\ [_{FP}\ \mathbf{\underline{N}}\ [_{NP}\ t_N]]]]]]]]$

    h.    V-SS-OO (cf. (5))

$[_{\Sigma P}\ \mathbf{\underline{V}}\ [_{TP}\ [_{DPi}\ D\ [_{FP}\ \mathbf{\underline{N}}\ [_{NP}\ [_{AP}\ \mathbf{\underline{A}}]\ [_{NP}\ t_N]]]]\ [_{T'}\ t_T\ [_{vP}\ t_i\ [_{v'}\ t_v\ [_{VP}\ t_V\ [_{DPj}\ D\ [_{FP}\ \mathbf{\underline{N}}\ [_{NP}\ [_{AP}\ \mathbf{\underline{A}}]\ [_{NP}\ t_N]]]]]]]]]$

    i.    V-S-OOO (no example)

$[_{\Sigma P}\ \mathbf{\underline{V}}\ [_{TP}\ [_{DPi}\ D\ [_{FP}\ \mathbf{\underline{N}}\ [_{NP}\ t_N]]]\ [_{T'}\ t_T\ [_{vP}\ t_i\ [_{VP}\ t_V\ [_{DPi}\ D\ [_{FP}\ \mathbf{\underline{N}}\ [_{NP}\ [_{AP}\ \mathbf{\underline{A}}]\ [_{NP}\ [_{AP}\ \mathbf{\underline{A}}]\ [_{NP}\ t_N]]]]]]]]]$

    j.    V-SSS-OO (cf. (6))

$[_{\Sigma P}\ \mathbf{\underline{V}}\ [_{TP}\ [_{DPi}\ D\ [_{FP}\ \mathbf{\underline{N}}\ [_{NP}\ [_{AP}\ \mathbf{\underline{A}}]\ [_{NP}\ [_{AP}\ \mathbf{\underline{A}}]\ [_{NP}\ t_N]]]]]\ [_{T'}\ t_T\ [_{vP}\ t_i\ [_{v'}\ t_v\ [_{VP}\ t_V\ [_{DPj}\ D\ [_{FP}\ \mathbf{\underline{N}}\ [_{NP}\ [_{AP}\ \mathbf{\underline{A}}]\ [_{NP}\ t_N]]]]]]]]]$

    k.    V-SS-OOO (cf. (7))

$[_{\Sigma P}\ \mathbf{\underline{V}}\ [_{TP}\ [_{DPi}\ D\ [_{FP}\ \mathbf{\underline{N}}\ [_{NP}\ [_{AP}\ \mathbf{\underline{A}}]\ [_{NP}\ t_N]]]]\ [_{T'}\ t_T\ [_{vP}\ t_i\ [_{v'}\ t_v\ [_{VP}\ t_V\ [_{DPj}\ D\ [_{FP}\ \mathbf{\underline{N}}\ [_{NP}\ [_{AP}\ \mathbf{\underline{A}}]\ [_{NP}\ [_{AP}\ \mathbf{\underline{A}}]\ [_{NP}\ t_N]]]]]]]]]$

    l.    V-SSS-OOO (no example)

$[_{\Sigma P}\ \mathbf{\underline{V}}\ [_{TP}\ [_{DPi}\ D\ [_{FP}\ \mathbf{\underline{N}}\ [_{NP}\ [_{AP}\ \mathbf{\underline{A}}]\ [_{NP}\ [_{AP}\ \mathbf{\underline{A}}]\ [_{NP}\ t_N]]]]]\ [_{T'}\ t_T\ [_{vP}\ t_i\ [_{v'}\ t_v\ [_{VP}\ t_V\ [_{DPj}\ D\ [_{FP}\ \mathbf{\underline{N}}\ [_{NP}\ [_{AP}\ \mathbf{\underline{A}}]\ [_{NP}\ [_{AP}\ \mathbf{\underline{A}}]\ [_{NP}\ t_N]]]]]]]]]$

Given the definition of GEN and the constraint sets used in this chapter (both for VSO.Oh and the systems in §4.4), only certain nodes in these syntactic input trees are relevant to the syntax–prosody mapping. We follow Elfner (2012, 2015) and Bennett et al. (2016) in simplifying the system by building m.BINMIN($\varphi$) into GEN (see §4.3.1.2 below), such that no candidate includes a $\varphi$ that dominates only one $\omega$. Thus, no unary-branching XP is matched in any candidate, meaning that every candidate incurs an equal number of sp.MATCH violations for unary XPs (for all constraints in the sp.MATCH family used in this chapter). No other constraints in the chapter refer to unary XPs, so these XPs can be safely omitted from input representations for the sake of simplicity.

A further simplification of input representations is obtained when we consider which branching XPs are conflated in Elfner's (2012, 2015) version of Match Theory, which we adopt. On Elfner's theory, if two XPs have the same overt terminal string, they are counted as a single XP by the MATCH constraints, and if an XP does not dominate any overt terminals, the MATCH constraints ignore it completely. Thus, in an intransitive clause, the TP is conflated with the subject DP, since they have the same overt terminal string, and the $v$P and VP are ignored, since they contain no overt material. In a transitive clause, the $v$P, VP, and object DP are conflated, since all three have the same overt terminal string. Within the DP, the DP and FP are conflated; since D is silent, they have the same overt terminal string. If we take the trees in (15) and prune away unary XPs, conflate co-terminous XPs, and delete XPs that lack overt terminals, we arrive at the following simplified representations:

(16)    Input trees, simplified by pruning, conflation, and deletion

    a.  V-S (no example)

        $[_{\Sigma P}$ V N]

    b.  V-SS (cf. (1))

        $[_{\Sigma P}$ V $[_{TP/DP/FP}$ N A]]

    c.  V-S-O (cf. (2))

        $[_{\Sigma P}$ V $[_{TP}$ N N]]

    d.  V-SSS (no example)

        $[_{\Sigma P}$ V $[_{TP/DP/FP}$ N $[_{NP}$ A A]]]

    e.  V-SS-O (cf. (3))

        $[_{\Sigma P}$ V $[_{TP}$ $[_{DP/FP/vP/VP}$ N A] N]]

    f.  V-S-OO (cf. (4))

        $[_{\Sigma P}$ V $[_{TP}$ N $[_{DP/FP/vP/VP}$ N A]]]

    g.  V-SSS-O (no example)

        $[_{\Sigma P}$ V $[_{TP}$ $[_{DP/FP}$ N $[_{NP}$ A A]] N]

h. V-SS-OO (cf. (5))

$[_{\Sigma P}\ V\ [_{TP}\ [_{DP/FP}\ N\ A]\ [_{DP/FP/vP/VP}\ N\ A]]]$

i. V-S-OOO (no example)

$[_{\Sigma P}\ V\ [_{TP}\ N\ [_{DP/FP/vP/VP}\ N\ [_{NP}\ A\ A]]]]$

j. V-SSS-OO (cf. (6))

$[_{\Sigma P}\ V\ [_{TP}\ [_{DP/FP}\ N\ [_{NP}\ A\ A]]\ [_{DP/FP/vP/VP}\ N\ A]]]$

k. V-SS-OOO (cf. (7))

$[_{\Sigma P}\ V\ [_{TP}\ [_{DP/FP}\ N\ A]\ [_{DP/FP/vP/VP}\ N\ [_{NP}\ A\ A]]]]$

l. V-SSS-OOO (no example)

$[_{\Sigma P}\ V\ [_{TP}\ [_{DP/FP}\ N\ [_{NP}\ A\ A]]\ [_{DP/FP/vP/VP}\ N\ [_{NP}\ A\ A]]]]$

Given VSO.Oh.Con (defined in §4.3.2), the XPs' category labels in (16) play no role; what matters is whether a constituent is an XP, not what category it has (a common assumption of Prosodic Hierarchy Theory; see Nespor and Vogel 1986). However, one constraint in VSO.Oh.Con will distinguish between overtly headed and covertly headed XPs. Of the branching XPs in the input trees admitted by VSO.Oh.Gen, every ΣP and FP is overtly headed, and all other branching XPs (TPs, DPs, NPs, $v$Ps, and VPs) are covertly headed. ΣP is headed by the moved verb, and FP is headed by the moved noun. All other XPs either have inherently silent heads, or heads that have moved. In a final round of representational simplification, we settle on the trees in (17) to be used as the inputs in the rest of the discussion of VSO.Oh. "OhP" stands for "overtly headed XP", and "ShP" stands for "silently headed XP".

(17) Fully simplified input trees in VSO.Oh.Gen

a. V-S (no example)

$[_{OhP}\ V\ N]$

b. V-SS (cf. (1))

$[_{OhP}\ V\ [_{OhP}\ N\ A]]$

c. V-S-O (cf. (2))

$[_{OhP}\ V\ [_{ShP}\ N\ N]]$

d. V-SSS (no example)

$[_{OhP}\ V\ [_{OhP}\ N\ [_{ShP}\ A\ A]]]$

e. V-SS-O (cf. (3))

$[_{OhP}\ V\ [_{ShP}\ [_{OhP}\ N\ A]\ N]]$

f. V-S-OO (cf. (4))

$[_{OhP}\ V\ [_{ShP}\ N\ [_{OhP}\ N\ A]]]$

g. V-SSS-O (no example)

$[_{OhP}\ V\ [_{ShP}\ [_{OhP}\ N\ [_{ShP}\ A\ A]]\ N]]$

h. V-SS-OO (cf. 5)

$[_{OhP}\ V\ [_{ShP}\ [_{OhP}\ N\ A]\ [_{OhP}\ N\ A]]]$

   i.   V-S-OOO (no example)
$[_{OhP}$ V $[_{ShP}$ N $[_{OhP}$ N $[_{ShP}$ A A]]]]

   j.   V-SSS-OO (cf. (6))
$[_{OhP}$ V $[_{ShP}$ $[_{OhP}$ N $[_{ShP}$ A A]] $[_{OhP}$ N A]]]

   k.   V-SS-OOO (cf. (7))
$[_{OhP}$ V $[_{ShP}$ $[_{OhP}$ N A] $[_{OhP}$ N $[_{ShP}$ A A]]]]

   l.   V-SSS-OOO (no example)
$[_{OhP}$ V $[_{ShP}$ $[_{OhP}$ N $[_{ShP}$ A A]] $[_{OhP}$ N $[_{ShP}$ A A]]]]

The distinction between OhPs and ShPs is reminescent of part of Truckenbrodt's (1995, 1999) Lexical Category Condition:

(18)     Lexical Category Condition (Truckenbrodt 1999, p. 226)
Constraints relating syntactic and prosodic categories apply to lexical syntactic elements and their projections, but not to functional elements and their projections, or to empty syntactic elements *and their projections.*

The part of the LCC referring to 'empty syntactic elements *and their projections*' identifies what we have called ShPs as invisible to the syntax–prosody mapping constraints. However, we do not adopt the LCC, since our definition of XP-visibility differs in two crucial ways. First, we follow Elfner (2012, 2015) in treating functional XPs like TP as visible for mapping. Second, ShPs are not invisible to all of the constraints in VSO.Oh.Con (§4.2.3), but are ignored by only one particular mapping constraint.

Note also that we treat every segment of an adjunction structure as an XP that is visible to the syntax–prosody mapping constraints, as argued to be necessary by Bellik and Kalivoda (2016), *pace* Truckenbrodt (1995, 1999) and Selkirk (2011, fn. 38). That is, in a structure $[_{NP}$ AP NP], both segments of NP are visible for mapping, which is why two-adjective sequences in (17) are treated as XPs (specifically ShPs) rather than as non-XPs.

### 4.3.1.2 Outputs

Having specified which syntactic trees can be *in* in a candidate ⟨*in, out, corr*⟩, we now specify which trees can be *out*, and how these are related to *in* by *corr*. Output prosodic trees in VSO.Oh.Gen obey two inviolable conditions—Exhaustivity and Branchingness—but allow recursive phonological phrases ($_\varphi$ ...φ...). The Exhaustivity condition bans output representations in which a prosodic word ω is immediately dominated by the intonational phrase ι, and the Branchingness condition rules out unary φs. These and several other conditions are spelled out in (19).

(19)     Outputs and correspondence relation of VSO.Oh.Gen

 For an input tree *sTree*, an output *pTree* is a prosodic tree such that:

  a. Every maximal, overt syntactic word $X^0$ in *sTree* stands in a correspondence relation *corr* with an ω in *pTree*.

  b. Every ω in *pTree* stands in a correspondence relation *corr* with a maximal, overt syntactic word $X^0$ in *sTree*.

  c. The linear order of maximal, overt $X^0$s in *sTree* is preserved among their output correspondents in *pTree*.

  d. The root node of *pTree* is of category ι.

  e. All non-terminal non-root nodes in *pTree* are of category φ.

  f. Every node of category φ immediately dominates at least two other nodes.

  g. Every node of category ω in *pTree* is dominated by a node of category φ.

  h. Every terminal node in *pTree* is of category ω.

In our notation, parentheses indicate φ-edges: $(_\varphi \ ...)$. Since every tree is rooted in ι and every other non-terminal is a φ, we routinely omit outer ι brackets $\{_\iota \ ...\}$. We use single capital letters "V", "N", and "A" both for syntactic words $X^0$ and for prosodic words ω, since the category of these nodes is clear from context. Since linear order is preserved between correspondent terminal nodes, we do not include correspondence indices.

With the Gen specifications in (19), we get the following numbers of trees on *n* words (see Shingler and Bellik, this volume, Ch. 2 for proof).

(20)     Numbers of candidates

| n | Output Trees |
|---|---:|
| 2 | 1 |
| 3 | 3 |
| 4 | 12 |
| 5 | 51 |
| 6 | 229 |
| 7 | 1068 |

Since VSO.Oh.Gen admits 1 input with 2 words, 2 inputs with 3 words, 3 inputs with 4 words, 3 inputs with 5 words, 2 inputs with 6 words, and 1 input with 7 words, the system contains 1722 candidates across 12 candidate sets. All 1722 candidates were generated using SPOT (Bellik et al. 2015–2021).

*4.3.1.3   Con*

The constraint set of VSO.Oh includes two constraints familiar from Elfner (2012, 2015): sp.Match(XP,$\varphi$) and m.BinMax($\varphi$,branches). The other two constraints are not used by Elfner, though they are inspired by her work. All four are presented in (21).

(21)    VSO.Oh.Con

  a.    sp.Match(XP,$\varphi$)                                        (sp.Match-XP)
        Violated by an input XP that does not have a matching $\varphi$ in the output.

  b.    sp.Match(XP$_{\text{OvertlyHeaded}}$,$\varphi$)                      (sp.Match-OhP)
        Violated by an input OhP (overtly headed XP) that does not have a matching $\varphi$ in the output.

  c.    m.BinMax($\varphi$,branches)                                  (m.BinMax)
        Violated by a $\varphi$ that immediately dominates more than two nodes.

  d.    m.StrongStart$_{\text{Initial}}$                          (m.StrongStart$_{\text{Init}}$)
        Violated by an $\iota$-initial $\omega$ that is sister to a $\varphi$.

The definitions of the two sp.Match constraints include the term "matching", which is defined in (22).

(22)    Definition of Matching (cf. Elfner 2012)
        A node $\alpha$ and a node $\beta$ are *matching* iff there is a correspondence bijection between the overt nodes in their terminal strings. When $\alpha$=XP and $\beta$=$\varphi$, these nodes are matching if $\alpha$ has the form $[_{\text{XP}}\ X^0_1\ X^0_2...X^0_n]$ and $\beta$ has the form $(_\varphi\ \omega_1\ \omega_2...\omega_n)$.

sp.Match(XP$_{\text{OvertlyHeaded}}$,$\varphi$), or sp.Match-OhP for short, differs from plain sp.Match(XP,$\varphi$) in only seeing overtly headed XPs. That is, it counts the number of OhPs that are not matched by output $\varphi$s, but ignores unmatched ShPs. This constraint originates in Van Handel (2021).

The constraint m.StrongStart$_{\text{Initial}}$ is based on the standard m.StrongStart (Selkirk 2011, Elfner 2012), which penalizes each prosodic constituent whose leftmost daughter is lower on the prosodic hierarchy than its second-to-leftmost daughter. But m.StrongStart$_{\text{Initial}}$ differs from classic m.StrongStart in several important ways. The most obvious difference is that it looks for weak starts only at the beginning of an intonational phrase ɩ, rather than everywhere throughout the tree. A sequence ωφ violates the constraint if it is ɩ-initial, but not elsewhere.[6]

A less obvious difference between m.STRONGSTART$_{\text{Initial}}$ and m.STRONGSTART is that it penalizes any ɩ-initial configuration ω...φ in which ω and φ are sisters, including ɩ-initial sequences of sisters like ωωφ in which the initial two sisters are of the same category. This is to prevent the constraint from being satisfied by "doubly weak starts", an unfortunate unintended consequence of classic m.STRONGSTART (a fact previously observed in passing by Kalivoda 2018 and discussed at length by Bellik Ch. 11, this volume and by Chen 2021). Due to this property, m.STRONGSTART$_{\text{Initial}}$ is a version of Chen's (2021) m.STRONGSTRONGSTART.

### 4.3.2    Factorial typology of VSO.Oh

The system VSO.Oh has a factorial typology consisting of three languages, shown in (23). This was calculated using OTWorkplace (Prince et al. 2007–2021) with the violation tableau generated using SPOT (Belilk et al. 2015–2021). For reasons of space, "OhP" is suppressed in the input, and "ShP" is replaced with "s"; that is, [...] stands for [$_{\text{OhP}}$ ...] and [$_s$ ...] stands for [$_{\text{ShP}}$ ...]. The word "match" in an output cell indicates that the output prosodic tree is isomorphic to the input syntactic tree, with every input XP (whether OhP or ShP) matched to a φ.

(23)      Factorial typology of VSO.Oh

| | Input | L.1 | L.2 | L.3 |
|---|---|---|---|---|
| a. | *V-S*<br>[V N] | match | | |
| b. | *V-SS*<br>[V [N A]] | ((V N) A) | match | |
| c. | *V-S-O*<br>[V [$_s$ N N]] | ((V N) N) | | match |
| d. | *V-SSS*<br>[V [N [$_s$ A A]]] | ((V N) (A A)) | match | |

---

[6] The definition of m.STRONGSTART$_{\text{Initial}}$ is unique to this chapter and its predecessor (Kalivoda and Bellik 2021). However, Harizanov (2014) defines a similar version of STRONGSTART which penalizes ɩ-initial clitics, i.e., ɩ-initial sub-ω prosodic constituents that are not contained within an ω. m.STRONGSTART$_{\text{Initial}}$ as defined here differs from Harizanov's definition in also penalizing an ɩ-initial ω when it is followed by a sister of a higher prosodic category. Thanks to Junko Ito for bringing Harizanov's constraint to my attention.

| | Input | L.1 | L.2 | L.3 |
|---|---|---|---|---|
| e. | *V-SS-O* <br> [V [$_s$ [N A] N]] | (((V N) A) N) <br> ((V N) (A N)) | match | |
| f. | *V-S-OO* <br> [V [$_s$ N [N A]]] | ((V N) (N A)) | | match |
| g. | *V-SSS-O* <br> [V [$_s$ [N [$_s$ A A]] N] | (((V N) (A A)) N) | match | |
| h. | *V-SS-OO* <br> [V [$_s$ [N A] [N A]]] | (((V N) A) (N A)) <br> ((V N) (A (N A))) | match | |
| i. | *V-S-OOO* <br> [V [$_s$ N [N [$_s$ A A]]]] | ((V N) (N (A A))) | | match |
| j. | *V-SSS-OO* <br> [V [$_s$ [N [$_s$ A A]] [N A]]] | (((V N) (A A)) (N A)) <br> ((V N) ((A A) (N A))) | match | |
| k. | *V-SS-OOO* <br> [V [$_s$ [N A] [N [$_s$ A A]]]] | (((V N) A) (N (A A))) <br> ((V N) (A (N (A A)))) | match | |
| l. | *V-SSS-OOO* <br> [V [$_s$ [N [$_s$ A A]] [N [$_s$ A A]]]] | (((V N) (A A)) (N (A A))) <br> ((V N) ((A A) (N (A A)))) | match | |

Of these three languages, L.2 is the closest to Elfner's proposals for Irish (see (10) above). In rows (c), (e), (f), (h), (j), and (k), L.2 displays the correct mappings for V-S-O, V-SS-O, V-S-OO, V-SS-OO, V-SSS-OO, and V-SS-OOO, respectively. Since we have no data for V-S, V-SSS, V-SSS-O, V-S-OOO, and V-SSS-OOO, the L.2 mappings in rows (d), (g), (i), and (l) are testable predictions, and are discussed further in §4.3.4. L.2 is only incorrect for Irish on row (b), i.e., for V-SS. While L.1 has the correct Irish mapping in row (b), it differs from Irish on almost every other row.

While each of L.2 and L.3 has a uniquely determined output for every input in (23), L.1 contains five cases of co-optimality, where two candidates with equivalent violation profiles survive filtration. Such cases arise due to the simplicity of VSO.Oh.Con. An expanded OT system, based on VSO.Oh.Con, but with additional constraints such as ps.Match($\varphi$,XP), might cut down on co-optima, but we aim here to provide a firm understanding of VSO.Oh as a first step. The typology of VSO.Oh has a simple structure in terms of Property Theory (Alber et al. 2016; Alber and Prince 2021), elucidated in the next subsection. We emphatically do not propose that a full theory of syntax–prosody mapping should include only the constraints in VSO.Oh.Con. We restrict our attention to the constraints in (21) in order to understand this simple system, which can serve as a basis for understanding more complex systems in the future.

*4.3.3   Grammars and property analysis*

The three languages of VSO.Oh shown in (23) have the grammars in (24).

(24)     Grammars of VSO.Oh
    a.    Grammar of L.1

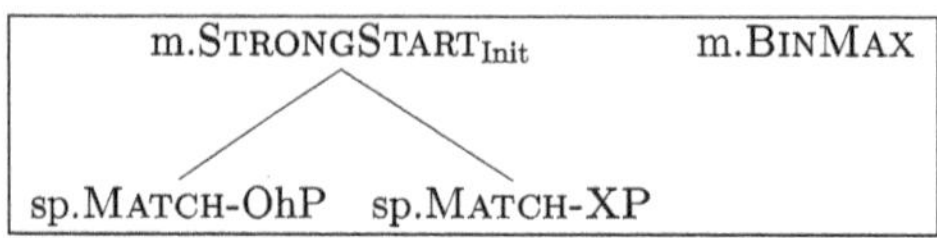

    b.    Grammar of L.2

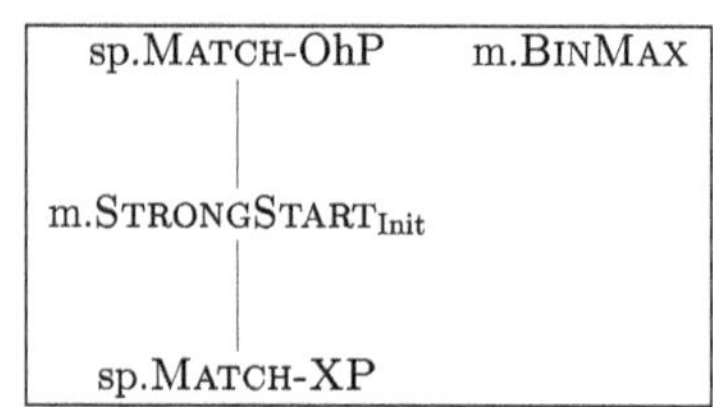

    c.    Grammar of L.3

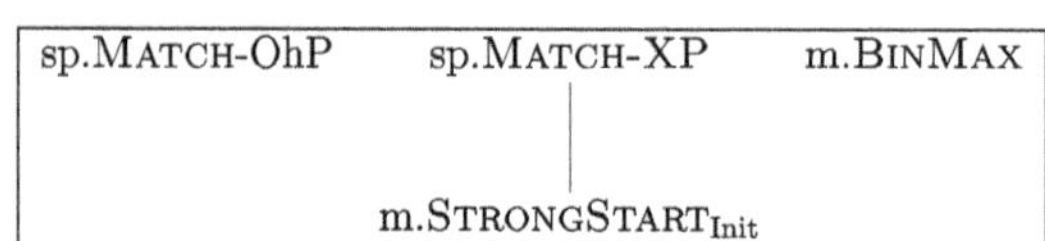

A property analysis (PA) of an OT system $S$ is a set of antagonisms X $<>$ Y, where X and Y are constraints or constraint classes, and each grammar in the typology is fully determined by selecting which antagonist dominates the other in each property (Alber et al. 2016; Alber and Prince 2021; Del-Busso 2018). The grammars in (24) are identified by their values for the two properties in (25). A property 'p.PROPERTY.a/b' has prefix 'p.' and values 'a' and 'b'; the '.a/b' will occasionally be omitted in the property name.

(25)     Properties of VSO.Oh

| Property | a | b | Scope |
|---|---|---|---|
| p.VS.mis/iso | m.STRONGSTART$_{\text{Init}}$ | sp.MATCH-XP | wide |
| p.VS+.mis/iso | m.STRONGSTART$_{\text{Init}}$ | c.MATCH.dom | wide |

*Constraint class:* c.MATCH $=$ {sp.MATCH-XP, sp.MATCH-OhP}

The first property in (25), p.VS, pits two individual constraint against each other. If a grammar includes the ranking m.STRONGSTART$_{\text{Init}}$ $\gg$ sp.MATCH-XP, then it has the value p.VS.mis. If it includes the reverse ranking, sp.Match-XP $\gg$ m.StrongStart$_{\text{Init}}$, then it has the value p.VS.iso. The name of the property alludes to the syntactic configuration $[_{\text{OhP}}$ V $[_{\text{ShP}}$ N]...], in which a verb precedes a one-word subject, and the values "mis" and "iso" stand for "mismatch" and "isomorphism", respectively. How this property and its values determine extensional traits in the languages of VSO.Oh is discussed below.

The second property, p.VS+, is so named because it determines a language's extensional mappings when the verb is followed by a multi-word subject. As with p.VS, the values "mis" and "iso" for p.VS+ stand for "mismatch" and "isomorphism," respectively. The "a" side of p.VS+ is again the single constraint m.StrongStart$_{\text{Init}}$, but the "b" side is a constraint class defined using the ".dom" operator (Alber and Prince 2021). For a constraint class Y and a grammar G, Y.dom(G) returns the constraint in Y that is highest ranked in G. In this case, the class c.Match is the set of both sp.Match constraints: {sp.Match-XP, sp.Match-OhP}. This means that c.Match.dom(G) is the highest ranked sp.Match constraint in a grammar G. The grammar of L.1 has the value p.VS.mis because m.StrongStart$_{\text{Init}}$ dominates both sp.Match constraints, while L.2 and L.3 have the value p.VS.iso, because in each, one of the sp.Match constraints dominates m.StrongStart$_{\text{Init}}$.

The fourth column in (25) gives the typological scope of each property. In this case, both properties are wide scope, meaning that every grammar in the typology has either an a-value or b-value for both of them. There is in fact a narrow-scope version of p.VS+.mis/iso in which c.Match.dom is replaced by the single constraint sp.Match-Oh, but while this property would have a simpler structure, p.VS+.mis/iso as currently stated relates more simply to the extensional traits of the languages of VSO.Oh discussed below.

The property values of the three languages in the typology of VSO.Oh are presented in the following property analysis table.

(26)    Property analysis table for VSO.Oh

|     | p.VS | p.VS+ |
| --- | --- | --- |
| L.1 | mis | mis |
| L.2 | mis | iso |
| L.3 | iso | iso |

L.1 is maximally mismatching, with the value "mis" for both p.VS and p.VS+. At the other extreme is L.3, which has the value "iso" for both properties. L.2, which we have identified with Irish, falls in between; while it is p.VS.mis, it is also p.VS+.iso.

Each property value of a grammar determines an extensional trait of that grammar's corresponding language. The traits associated with each value are given in (27).

(27)   Property values and extensional traits of VSO.Oh

| **p.VS.mis** | **p.VS.iso** |
|---|---|
| The verb phrases with a following one-word subject: $[_{\text{OhP}}\ \text{V}\ [_{\text{ShP}}\ \text{N}]...] \rightarrow (_\varphi\ (_\varphi\ \text{V N})\ ...)$ | All syntactic inputs undergo perfect matching. |
| **p.VS+.mis** | **p.VS+.iso** |
| The verb phrases with the first word of a following multi-word subject; every output contains $(_\varphi\ (_\varphi\ \text{V N})\ ...)$. | If the subject contains multiple words, then the syntactic input undergoes perfect matching. |

There are two entailment relations of note in (26) and (27). The first is that the value p.VS+.mis entails the value p.VS.mis, which concretely means that any language in which the verb phrases with the first word of a multi-word subject, leaving the subject unmatched, will also phrase the verb with a one-word subject. The second is that p.VS.iso entails p.VS+.iso. Extensionally, this means that if the verb does not phrase with a one-word subject, disrupting a following ShP, it will not phrase with part of a multi-word subject, which would mean disrupting a following OhP.

### 4.3.4   The grammar of Irish (p.VS.mis, p.VS+.iso) in VSO.Oh

We now take a closer look at language L.2 (p.VS.mis, p.VS+.iso), which accords with nearly all of Elfner's proposed structures for Irish in (10), and makes predictions for the phrasing of the sentences in (15)–(17) for which data is lacking. As shown in (24), the grammar of this language is sp.MATCH(OhP,$\varphi$) $\gg$ m.STRONGSTART$_{\text{Init}}$ $\gg$ sp.MATCH(XP,$\varphi$), with m.BINMAX($\varphi$,branches) not crucially ranked.

As shown in (23), every language in the typology of VSO.Oh contains the mapping $[_{\text{OhP}}\ \text{V N}] \rightarrow (\text{V N})$. This is guaranteed by the fact that this is the only candidate admitted by VSO.Oh.GEN for this cset. There is therefore no need to show a tableau for this mapping.

L.2's mapping in (23) differs from the reported phrasing in (10), mapping $[_{\text{OhP}}\ \text{V}\ [_{\text{OhP}}\ \text{N A}]]$ to non-Irish (V (N A)) instead of Irish ((V N) A). We return to this issue below, but first consider mappings on which L.2 does accord with Irish (10), and mappings in (23) that make predictions for Irish phrasing.

L.2's mapping of a V-S-O sentence in (23) is $[_{\text{OhP}}$ V $[_{\text{ShP}}$ N N]] $\rightarrow$ ((V N) N). This constitutes a strong syntax–prosody mismatch (in the sense of Kalivoda 2018), since the input ShP (the TP of (15c)) is not matched, and the two-word $\varphi$ in the output does not match an input constituent. The violation tableau (VT) in (28) contains all three candidates admitted by VSO.Oh.GEN for this cset. The first two are possible optima in the system, while (28c) is harmonically bounded. Here and in all subsequent violation tableaux, harmonic bounds are preceded by 'HB'; the L.2 winner is marked as optimal using an arrow; and non-L.2 optima are left unmarked. For space reasons, the tableaux use extreme constraint abbreviations: sp.OhP for sp.MATCH-OhP, m.SS$_\text{I}$ for m.STRONGSTART$_{\text{Init}}$, sp.XP for sp.MATCH-XP, and m.BM for m.BINMAX($\varphi$,branches).

(28)    VT for V-S-O (2/2 optima, 1/1 HBs)

| $[_{\text{OhP}}$ V $[_{\text{ShP}}$ N N]] | sp.OhP | m.SS$_\text{I}$ | sp.XP | m.BM |
|---|---|---|---|---|
| a. $\rightarrow$ ((V N) N) | 0 | 0 | 1 | 0 |
| b. (V (N N)) | 0 | 1 | 0 | 0 |
| c. HB (V N N) | 0 | 0 | 1 | 1 |

The L.2 winner (28a) does not violate sp.MATCH-OhP, because the input's sole OhP (the $\Sigma$P) is matched; it does not violate m.STRONGSTART$_{\text{Init}}$, because its first $\omega$ has no sister of category $\varphi$; and it does not violate m.BINMAX($\varphi$,branches), because each $\varphi$ in the output is binary-branching. The harmonically bounded candidate (28c) ties with (28a) on all but m.BINMAX($\varphi$,branches), where it performs worse, since the output is a ternary-branching $\varphi$. The competition therefore comes down to (28a) versus (28b). The latter ties with (28a) on sp.MATCH-OhP and m.BINMAX($\varphi$,branches), performs worse on m.STRONGSTART$_{\text{Init}}$, and performs better on sp.MATCH-XP. By matching the input ShP, (28b) incurs a violation of m.STRONGSTART$_{\text{Init}}$, since the first $\omega$ has a sister $\varphi$.

Converting the VT in (28) to a comparative tableau (CT; Prince 2002) yields the following result.

(29)    CT for Irish V-S-O

| Input | Winner | Loser | sp.OhP | m.SS$_\text{I}$ | sp.XP | m.BM |
|---|---|---|---|---|---|---|
| $[_{\text{OhP}}$ V $[_{\text{ShP}}$ N N]] | ((V N) N) | (V (N N)) | | W | L | |
| $[_{\text{OhP}}$ V $[_{\text{ShP}}$ N N]] | ((V N) N) | (V N N) | | | | W |

The first line shows that m.$\textsc{StrongStart}_{\text{Init}}$ must dominate plain sp.$\textsc{Match}$-XP in this language; the second merely shows that (28c) is harmonically bounded by (28a).

Next, we consider a V-SS-O sentence, which in L.2 exhibits perfect matching $[_{\text{OhP}}$ V $[_{\text{ShP}}$ $[_{\text{OhP}}$ N A] N]] $\rightarrow$ (V ((N A) N)). This accounts for the tonal pattern $^{\text{LH}}$V $^{\text{LH}}$N N$^{\text{HL}}$ A$^{\text{HL}}$, given Elfner's tone assignment algorithm in (9). V is the leftmost word of a non-minimal $\varphi$, so it receives LH. Although the subject N is at the left edge of a minimal $\varphi$ (N A), it is also at the left edge of a non-minimal $\varphi$ ((N A) N), so it too receives LH. The adjective and object noun are both $\varphi$-final, so they receive HL.

The tableau in (30) contains the L.2 mapping (30a), as well as the eleven other candidates admitted by VSO.Oh.$\textsc{Gen}$. Of the non-Irish candidates, only (30b–c) are possible optima; (30d–l) are harmonically bounded.

(30)       VT for V-SS-O (3/3 optima; 9/9 HBs)

| $[_{\text{OhP}}$ V $[_{\text{ShP}}$ $[_{\text{OhP}}$ N A] N]] | | sp.OhP | m.SS$_{\text{I}}$ | sp.XP | m.BM |
|---|---|---|---|---|---|
| a. $\rightarrow$ | (V ((N A) N)) | 0 | 1 | 0 | 0 |
| b. | (((V N) A) N) | 1 | 0 | 2 | 0 |
| c. | ((V N) (A N)) | 1 | 0 | 2 | 0 |
| d. HB | (V N A N) | 1 | 0 | 2 | 1 |
| e. HB | ((V N A) N) | 1 | 0 | 2 | 1 |
| f. HB | ((V (N A)) N) | 0 | 1 | 1 | 0 |
| g. HB | ((V N) A N) | 1 | 0 | 2 | 1 |
| h. HB | (V N (A N)) | 1 | 1 | 2 | 1 |
| i. HB | (V (N A N)) | 1 | 1 | 1 | 1 |
| j. HB | (V (N (A N))) | 1 | 1 | 1 | 0 |
| k. HB | (V (N A) N) | 0 | 1 | 1 | 1 |
| l. HB | (V N) (A N) | 2 | 0 | 3 | 0 |

The Irish candidate (30a) undergoes perfect matching, and thus satisfies sp.$\textsc{Match}$-OhP and sp.$\textsc{Match}$-XP. Its prosodic output, like its input syntax, is perfectly binary-branching, so it also satisfies m.$\textsc{BinMax}$($\varphi$,branches). But since (30a) matches the ShP to a $\varphi$, it contains the m.$\textsc{StrongStart}_{\text{Init}}$-violating configuration ($_\varphi$ V $\varphi$). The non-Irish viable candidates (30b–c) satisfy m.$\textsc{StrongStart}_{\text{Init}}$, but at the cost of violating both sp.$\textsc{Match}$ constraints, failing to match both the ShP and the subject OhP. Like (30a), (30b–c) fully satisfy m.$\textsc{BinMax}$($\varphi$,branches). Converting (30) to a CT in which (30a) is asserted to be optimal, we obtain the following result (with harmonic bounds excluded):

(31)     CT for Irish V-SS-O

| Input | Winner | Loser | sp.OhP | m.SS$_1$ | sp.XP | m.BM |
|---|---|---|---|---|---|---|
| [$_{OhP}$ V [$_{ShP}$ [$_{OhP}$ N A] N]] | (V ((N A) N)) | (((V N) A) N) <br> ((V N) (A N)) | W | L | W | |

The elementary ranking condition (ERC; Prince 2002) in (31) shows that in L.2, either sp.MATCH-OhP or sp.MATCH-XP dominates m.STRONGSTART$_{Init}$. The contentful ERC from (29) states that m.STRONGSTART$_{Init}$ dominates sp.MATCH-XP. Combining these, we arrive at the full grammar of Irish, sp.MATCH-OhP $\gg$ m.STRONGSTART$_{Init}$ $\gg$ sp.MATCH-XP.

Although the ERCs from (29) and (31) provide the entire grammar of L.2, it is instructive to consider why this grammar produces mismatches in other cases as well—in fact, whenever the subject is just a single word— and why this does not occur when the subject contains multiple words. We explain this in some detail since it is problematic given Elfner's constraint set, and provides the motivation for sp.MATCH-OhP in our system. Recall from (4), repeated here as (32), that the verb in a V-S-OO sentence has the usual rise, but that the second and fourth words bear a fall, while the third word has no tones at all.

(32)     V-S-OO (Elfner 2015, p. 1198)

| $^{LH}$cheannaigh | múinteoirí$^{HL}$ | málaí | bána$^{HL}$ |
|---|---|---|---|
| bought | teachers | bags | white |

'Teachers bought white bags.'

According to Elfner's assumptions about tone assignment in (9), the tone-less word *málaí* 'bags' is not at the left edge of a non-minimal φ, and it is not at the right edge of any φ. That is, it is either medial within its minimal φ, or initial within a minimal φ that is not itself the leftmost daughter of a non-minimal φ. The second and fourth words, *múinteoirí* 'teachers' and *bána* 'white' must of course be φ-final. Thus, the tones in (32) are accounted for by the phrasing ((V N) (N A)), where the verb and subject (a syntactic non-constituent) form the first minimal φ, and the object forms the second.

The VT in (33) shows the Irish/L.2 mapping in (33a) alongside the L.3 winner (33b) and all ten of the other candidates admitted by VSO.Oh.GEN, (33c–l), which are harmonically bounded.

(33)   VT for V-S-OO (2/2 optima, 10/10 HBs)

| $[_{\text{OhP}}$ V $[_{\text{ShP}}$ N $[_{\text{OhP}}$ N A]]] | | | sp.OhP | m.SS$_{\text{I}}$ | sp.XP | m.BM |
|---|---|---|---|---|---|---|
| a. | $\rightarrow$ | ((V N) (N A)) | 0 | 0 | 1 | 0 |
| b. | | (V (N (N A))) | 0 | 1 | 0 | 0 |
| c. | HB | (V N N A) | 1 | 0 | 2 | 1 |
| d. | HB | ((V N N) A) | 1 | 0 | 2 | 1 |
| e. | HB | (((V N) N) A) | 1 | 0 | 2 | 0 |
| f. | HB | ((V (N N)) A) | 1 | 1 | 2 | 0 |
| g. | HB | ((V N) N A) | 1 | 0 | 2 | 1 |
| h. | HB | (V N (N A)) | 0 | 1 | 1 | 1 |
| i. | HB | (V (N N A)) | 1 | 1 | 1 | 1 |
| j. | HB | (V ((N N) A)) . | 1 | 1 | 1 | 0 |
| k. | HB | (V (N N) A) | 1 | 1 | 2 | 1 |
| l. | HB | (V N) (N A) | 1 | 0 | 2 | 0 |

The L.2 mapping, (33a), violates sp.MATCH-XP once, since it fails to match the ShP containing the subject and object. However, it does not violate sp.MATCH-OhP, since the OhP containing all four words and the OhP containing the object are both matched. The perfectly matching (33b) does not violate an sp.MATCH constraint, either, but unlike rebracketed (33a) it violates m.STRONGSTART$_{\text{Init}}$ due to the ι-initial configuration ($_{\varphi}$ V $\varphi$). The situation with V-S-OO is therefore the same as that with V-S-O; for rebracketing to beat matching, m.STRONGSTART$_{\text{Init}}$ must dominate sp.MATCH-XP, and these outcomes tie on sp.MATCH-OhP. This is shown in the CT in (34).

(34)   CT for Irish V-S-OO

| Input | Winner | Loser | sp.OhP | m.SS$_{\text{I}}$ | sp.XP | m.BM |
|---|---|---|---|---|---|---|
| $[_{\text{OhP}}$ V $[_{\text{ShP}}$ N $[_{\text{OhP}}$ N A]]] | ((V N) (N A)) | (V (N (N A)) | | W | L | |

The ERC here is exactly that provided by the first line of (29). The commonality is due to the fact that whenever the verb phrases with a one-word subject to avoid a violation of m.STRONGSTART$_{\text{Init}}$, it leaves the ShP containing everything but the verb unmatched, but does not prevent any OhPs from being matched.

The L.2 ranking sp.MATCH-OhP $\gg$ m.STRONGSTART$_{\text{Init}}$ forces the isomorphic V-SS-O mapping $[_{\text{OhP}}$ V $[_{\text{ShP}} [_{\text{OhP}}$ N A] N]] $\rightarrow$ (V ((N A) N)) in (30)–(31), and matching also occurs when a word is added to the object, as in V-SS-OO below. In fact, since L.2 is p.VS+.iso, every input with a branching subject undergoes perfect matching. Another instance of this is shown in (35).

(35)    VT for Irish V-SS-OO (3/3 optima, 0/48 HBs)

| $[_{OhP}$ V $[_{ShP}$ $[_{OhP}$ N A] $[_{OhP}$ N A]]] | sp.OhP | m.SS$_I$ | sp.XP | m.BM |
|---|---|---|---|---|
| a.   →   (V ((N A) (N A))) | 0 | 1 | 0 | 0 |
| b.      (((V N) A) (N A)) | 1 | 0 | 2 | 0 |
| c.      ((V N) (A (N A))) | 1 | 0 | 2 | 0 |

While the isomorphic L.2 mapping (35a) violates m.STRONGSTART$_{Init}$, it satifies sp.MATCH-OhP. In the non-matching L.1 co-optima (35b–c), rebracketing leads to satisfaction of m.STRONGSTART$_{Init}$, but leaves the subject OhP unmatched. The ERC obtained from (35) is the same as that from (30)–(31), as shown in the CT in (36).

(36)    CT for Irish V-SS-OO

| Input | Winner | Loser | sp.OhP | m.SS$_I$ | sp.XP | m.BM |
|---|---|---|---|---|---|---|
| $[_{OhP}$ V $[_{ShP}$<br>$[_{OhP}$ N A]<br>$[_{OhP}$ N A]]] | *match*<br>= (35) | (((V N) A) (N A))<br>((V N) (A (N A))) | W | L | W | |

Again, whenever the subject contains multiple words, it is an OhP which sp.MATCH-OhP protects from being broken up by phrasing the verb with the first word of the subject. Since sp.MATCH-OhP outranks m.STRONGSTART$_{Init}$, the ι-initial weak start ($_φ$ V φ) is tolerated in these cases.

Exactly the same reasoning applies to the matching V-SSS-OO and V-SS-OOO mappings, correctly deriving their tonal patterns by (9). Since in each case the subject is a branching OhP, it must be matched. However, the introduction of three-word arguments raises an important point about the constraint m.STRONGSTART$_{Init}$. Elfner's general m.STRONGSTART is violated twice in the matching parses for V-SSS-OO and V-SS-OOO, since these contain not only an ι-initial sequence ωφ, but also medial cases of φ-initial ωφ in phrases of the form (N (A A)). These medial cases do not violate m.STRONGSTART$_{Init}$. This point is discussed in detail in §4.4.2 below.

The p.VS.mis, p.VS+.iso pattern of L.2 continues for the rest of the csets in VSO.Oh. When the subject contains only one word, it phrases with the verb. When the subject contains more than one word, everything is matched. This makes predictions for the pronunciation of Irish V-SSS, V-SSS-O, V-S-OOO, and V-SSS-OOO, for which we have no data. In L.2, these map to the outputs shown in (37). While VSO.Oh.GEN itself says nothing about tones, the prosodic trees in (37) are annotated with the tones derived by (9) in order to show the exact predictions for pronunciation. Since every output admitted by VSO.Oh.GEN is rooted in ι, the ι is not shown.

(37)     Predictions of VSO.Oh for Irish phrasings and tones
    a.    V-SSS

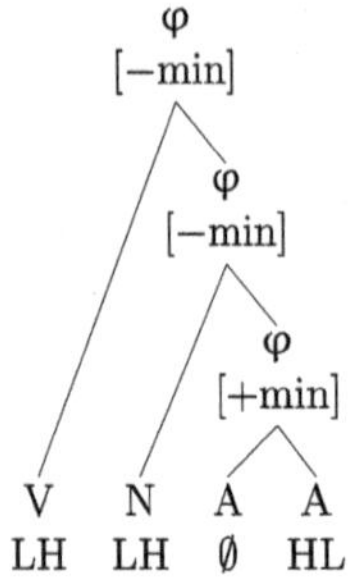


    b.    V-SSS-O

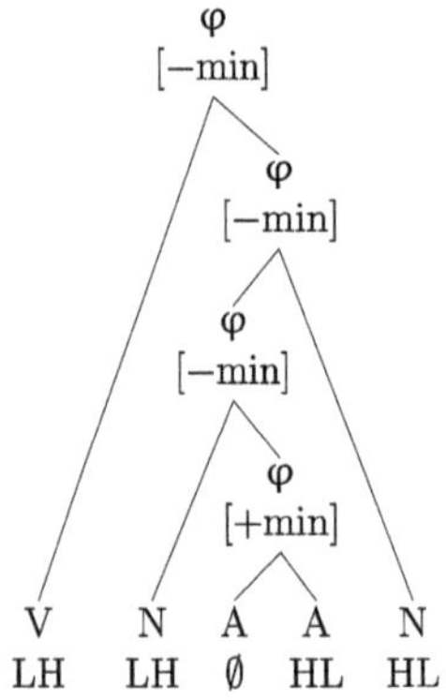


    c.    V-S-OOO

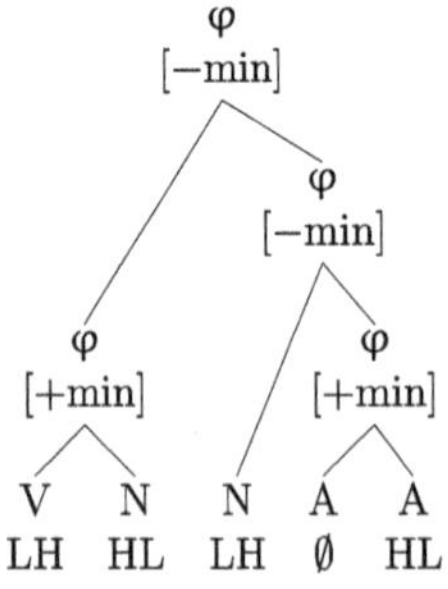

d.   V-SSS-OOO

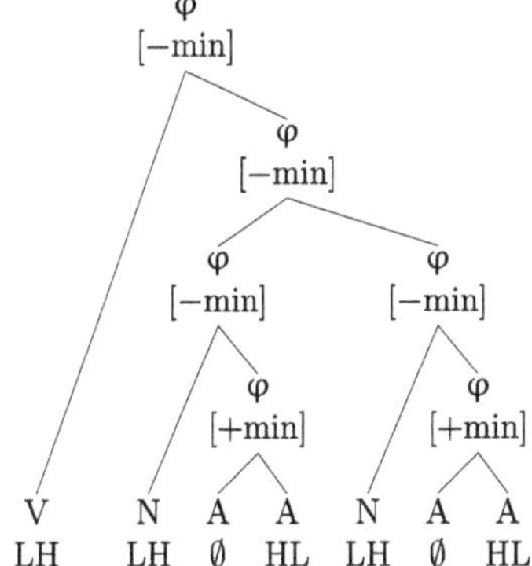

If these predictions are correct, this would be striking confirmation of the
analysis of Irish in terms of the system VSO.Oh.

### 4.3.5   Remaining challenges for VSO.Oh

Before we conclude this discussion of Irish and its relation to the p.VS.mis,
p.VS+.iso language L.2 of VSO.Oh, we must address L.2's main incorrect
prediction, namely the phrasing of V-SS. Elfner reports that each word
of the subject hosts a fall, as in (1), indicating the phrasing ((V N) A).
This phrasing fails to match the subject OhP, and therefore runs afoul of
sp.Match-OhP. This is a puzzle that finds no solution in VSO.Oh. Given
the reported variability in phrasings of the three-word sentence V-S-O, we
might wonder whether there is also variability in the phrasing of V-SS.
Alternatively, a full analysis of Irish phrasing may require an additional
constraint not included in VSO.Oh. We leave this issue for future research.

A second outstanding issue for the relationship between L.2 and Irish is
the fact that certain Irish sentences have variable phrasing. Elfner proposes
to account for these via co-optimality in Harmonic Grammar. Since each
mapping of L.2 in VSO.Oh has a uniquely determined output (unlike L.1,
which does include co-optima), this option is not available here. And we
cannot say that Irish involves a variable ranking of any of the constraints in
this system, since both L.1 and L.3 contain multiple mappings that are not
attested in Irish. However, this does not mean that classic OT is in principle unable to capture the attested variation. The system we have presented
contains only four constraints, among many others that we consider to plausibly belong to the wider constraint set of a descriptively adequate theory.
It is entirely possible that the factorial typology of a system like VSO.Oh,
but with an expanded constraint set, contains additional languages which

include variant phrasings attested in Irish, without including unattested variants. We leave this possibility open for future research.


## 4.4   Problems for classic Match Theory

### 4.4.1   Match Theory without the OhP/ShP distinction

We now compare VSO.Oh with another system based on Elfner's (2012, 2015) work, VSO.C (where the 'C' stands for 'classic'). We keep GEN constant, as defined in (19), which seems to accord with Elfner's practice in enumerating candidates. That is, VSO.C.GEN = VSO.Oh.GEN. But since Elfner does not distinguish between OhPs and ShPs, we need not label input brackets in VSO.C, and we instead use square brackets to stand for the boundaries of all XPs, both OhPs and ShPs. The only difference between VSO.Oh and VSO.C is CON; VSO.C.CON includes only Elfner's sp.MATCH(XP,$\varphi$), m.BINMAX($\varphi$,branches), and the original version of m.STRONGSTART. Elfner also posits ps.MATCH($\varphi$,XP), but does not include it in many tableaux. We exclude it here for simplicity. VSO.C.CON is defined in (38).


(38)    VSO.C.CON
  a.    sp.MATCH(XP,$\varphi$)                                      (sp.MATCH-XP)
        Violated by an input XP that does not have a matching $\varphi$ in the
        output.
  b.    m.BINMAX($\varphi$,branches)                                   (m.BINMAX)
        Violated by a $\varphi$ that immediately dominates more than two nodes.
  c.    m.STRONGSTART
        Violated by every node $\omega$ that is leftmost within its immediately
        containing $\varphi$ and whose right-adjacent sister is of category $\varphi$, i.e.,
        *($_\varphi$ $\omega$ $\varphi$.

The definition of matching relevant for (38) is that given in (22).

   The factorial typology of VSO.C, shown in (39), contains only two languages. In L.1, m.STRONGSTART dominates sp.MATCH(XP,$\varphi$), and in L.2, the reverse holds. Irish-compatible phrasings in (39) are prefixed with '✓', and Irish-incompatible phrasings are prefixed with '✗'. Cells for which we have no Irish data contain neither symbol.

(39)      Factorial typology of VSO.C

|     |                        | L.1 | L.2 |
|-----|------------------------|-----|-----|
| a.  | [V N]                  | match | |
| b.  | [V [N A]]              | ✓ ((V N) A) | ✗ match |
| c.  | [V [N N]]              | ✓ ((V N) N) | ✗ match |
| d.  | [V [N [A A]]]          | ((V N) (A A)) | match |
| e.  | [V [[N A] N]]          | ✗ (((V N) A) N)<br>✗ ((V N) (A N)) | ✓ match |
| f.  | [V [N [N A]]]          | ✓ ((V N) (N A)) | ✗ match |
| g.  | [V [[N [A A]] N]       | (((V N) (A A)) N)<br>((V N) ((A A) N)) | match |
| h.  | [V [[N A] [N A]]]      | ✗ (((V N) A) (N A)) | ✓ match |
| i.  | [V [N [N [A A]]]]      | (((V N) N) (A A))<br>((V N) ((N A) A)) | match |
| j.  | [V [[N [A A]] [N A]]]  | ✗ (((V N) (A A)) (N A))<br>✗ ((V N) ((A A) (N A))) | ✓ match |
| k.  | [V [[N A] [N [A A]]]]  | ✗ ((((V N) A) N) (A A))<br>✗ (((V N) (A N)) (A A))<br>✗ (((V N) A) ((N A) A))<br>✗ ((V N) ((A N) (A A))) | ✓ match |
| l.  | [V [[N [A A]] [N [A A]]]] | (((((V N) (A A)) N) (A A))<br>((((V N) ((A A) N)) (A A))<br>(((V N) (A A)) ((N A) A))<br>((V N) (((A A) N) (A A)))<br>((V N) ((A A) ((N A) A))) | match |

Neither L.1 nor L.2 is fully compatible with Irish. L.1 is compatible with
Irish on (39b,c,f), but not on (39e,h,j,k). The reverse holds for L.2. The
problem with L.1 is that it indiscriminately phrases the verb with the first
word of the subject, regardless of subject length, satisfying m.STRONGSTART
at the expense of sp.MATCH. In L.2, there is perfect matching, which is incorrect when the subject consists of a single word.

The problem is illustrated by a comparative tableau with two contradictory ERCs, the first showing what it takes for V-SS-O to be matched, and
the second what it takes for V-S-OO to be mismatched.

(40)      Contradictory ERCs for Irish in VSO.C

| Input | Winner | Loser | m.SS | sp.XP | m.BM |
|-------|--------|-------|------|-------|------|
| [V [[N A] N]] | (V ((N A) N)) | (((V N) A) N) ((V N) (A N)) | L | W | |
| [V [N [N A]]] | ((V N) (N A)) | (V (N (N A))) | W | L | |

For the matching V-SS-O candidate to win, sp.MATCH-XP must dominate m.STRONGSTART, but for the mismatching V-S-OO candidate to win,
m.STRONGSTART must dominate sp.MATCH-XP. This is the problem that
VSO.Oh solves by distinguishing between overtly and silently headed XPs,
treating the former as more important for matching than the latter, since
VSO.Oh.CON contains sp.MATCH-OhP alongside sp.MATCH-XP. Without this
distinction, VSO.C yields all-or-nothing behavior; either the TP containing
every word but the verb is matched (L.2), or it never is (L.1).

### 4.4.2  Match Theory without m.StrongStart$_{Initial}$

The preceding subsection showed that sp.MATCH(OhP,$\varphi$) is needed alongside
plain sp.MATCH(XP,$\varphi$), but the necessicity of m.STRONGSTART$_{Initial}$ remains
to be demonstrated. Its importance is made apparent by the phrasing of
three-word arguments, as in V-SSS-OO, repeated in (41), and V-SS-OOO,
repeated in (42).

(41)      V-SSS-OO (Elfner 2015, p. 1195)
          $^{LH}$cheannaigh $^{LH}$múinteoirí banúla    dathúla$^{HL}$ blathanna áille$^{HL}$
          bought        teachers      ladylike  handsome bags       white
          'Handsome ladylike teachers bought white bags.'

(42)      V-SS-OOO (Elfner 2015, p. 1195)
          $^{LH}$díofaidh $^{LH}$rúnaí    dathúil$^{HL}$    $^{LH}$blathanna bána    áille$^{HL}$
          sell.FUT      secretary handsome    flowers       white    beautiful
          'A handsome secretary will sell beautiful white flowers.'

By (9), we know that the phrasing of the three-word subject in (41) and
the three-word object in (42) is ($^{LH}$N (A A$^{HL}$)). The $\varphi$ containing all three
words is non-minimal, so its first word, N, receives LH. The second adjective
is $\varphi$-final, so it receives HL. Crucially, the first adjective is not in a position
that receives tone, being neither initial in a non-minimal $\varphi$ nor final in a $\varphi$.
    The phrase ($^{LH}$N (A A$^{HL}$)) violates classic m.STRONGSTART, since it contains
a $\varphi$-initial $\omega$ whose sister immediately to its right is a $\varphi$. A syntax–prosody

mismatch in which the noun phrased with the first adjective would satisfy m.STRONGSTART, but this cannot be correct for Irish, since on this parse, each adjective would be $\varphi$-final and therefore bear HL: *(($^{LH}$N A$^{HL}$) A$^{HL}$). Thus, m.STRONGSTART's ability to override syntax–prosody matching, on display in phrasings like ((VS)(OO)), cannot extend to these cases.

While we have explained the inability of m.STRONGSTART to disrupt multi-word subjects as an effect of sp.MATCH-OhP, this constraint is silent on the ungrammaticality of *(($^{LH}$N A$^{HL}$) A$^{HL}$). The syntactic input structure of a three-word argument is [$_{OhP}$ N [$_{ShP}$ A A]], where ShP is silent because N has raised out of it (as shown in (13)), so sp.MATCH-OhP does not object to phrasing the two adjectives apart, even though they form a syntactic constituent.

There must therefore be another explanation for perfectly matched subjects and objects. The system VSO.Oh accounts for this because instead of m.STRONGSTART, it employs m.STRONGSTART$_{Init}$, which is not violated by constituents ($_\varphi$ $\omega\varphi$...) unless they are $\iota$-initial. A system with classic m.STRONGSTART and without m.STRONGSTART$_{Init}$ fails to produce a language compatible with Irish. We demonstrate this formally by defining a third and final system, VSO.Oh.StStC, where 'StStC" stands for 'm.STRONGSTART – classic". This system differs from VSO.Oh only in replacing m.STRONGSTART$_{Init}$ with m.STRONGSTART, as shown by the definitions in (43) and (44).

(43)   VSO.Oh.StStC.GEN = VSO.Oh.GEN

(44)   VSO.Oh.StStC.CON
    a.   sp.MATCH(XP,$\varphi$)                                      (sp.MATCH-XP)
       Violated by an input XP that does not have a matching $\varphi$ in the output.
    b.   sp.MATCH(XP$_{OvertlyHeaded}$,$\varphi$)                          (sp.MATCH-OhP)
       Violated by an input OhP (overtly headed XP) that does not have a matching $\varphi$ in the output.
    c.   m.BINMAX($\varphi$,branches)                                  (m.BINMAX)
       Violated by a $\varphi$ that immediately dominates more than two nodes.
    d.   m.STRONGSTART
       Violated by every node $\omega$ that is leftmost within its immediately containing $\varphi$ and whose right-adjacent sister is of category $\varphi$, i.e., *($_\varphi$ $\omega$ $\varphi$.

The factorial typology of VSO.Oh.StStC contains three languages, with the same grammars as VSO.Oh, swapping m.STRONGSTART$_{Init}$ for m.STRONGSTART in each grammar. However, it differs from VSO.Oh in its concrete mappings. Unlike in VSO.Oh, there is no language in VSO.Oh.StStC with the phrasing ((VS)(OO)) that also perfectly matches three-word subjects and objects. This is demonstrated by the comparative tableau in (45).

(45)      Contradictory ERCs for Irish in VSO.Oh.StStC

| Input | Winner | Loser | sp. OhP | m. SS | sp. XP | m. BM |
|---|---|---|---|---|---|---|
| V-S-OO = (17f) | ((V N) (N A)) | (V (N (N A)) | | W | L | |
| V-SSS-OO = (17j) | (V ((N (A A)) (N A))) | (V (((N A) A) (N A))) | | L | W | |

There is something intolerable about the $\varphi$-initial sequence $\omega\varphi$ in the V-S-OO case, but not in the V-SSS-OO case, but in the system VSO.Oh.StStC, with classic m.STRONGSTART, there is no way to distinguish these. VSO.Oh, the system proposed in this chapter to account for Irish phrasing, avoids the problem by localizing m.STRONGSTART to the beginning of the $\iota$, with the constraint m.STRONGSTART$_{\text{Init}}$.

## 4.5   Conclusion

In conclusion, we have shown that classical OT is capable of resolving the ranking paradox of m.STRONGSTART and sp.MATCH(XP,$\varphi$) for Irish. The key to the solution lies in distinguishing the mapping of overtly headed XPs from silently headed XPs. This proposal, first made by Van Handel (2021), hearkens back to previous observations that motivated the Lexical Category Condition (Truckenbrodt 1995, 1999), while still recognizing Elfner's discovery that functional projections are visible to MATCH constraints and are sometimes mapped to $\varphi$s in Irish. By combining the specialized sp.MATCH(OhP,$\varphi$) and more general sp.MATCH(XP,$\varphi$), antagonizing both with m.STRONGSTART$_{\text{Initial}}$, the system VSO.Oh is able to capture a range of faithfulness in mapping: perfectly matching all XPs (L.3); matching overtly headed XPs but rebracketing when the subject contains only one word (L.2); and always rebracketing to avoid violating m.STRONGSTART$_{\text{Initial}}$ (L.1).

We have also shown how Property Theory (Alber and Prince 2021) sheds light on the structure of VSO.Oh. Two properties, p.VS.mis/iso and p.VS+.mis/iso, characterize the three grammars of the typology, and each value determines an extensional pattern found in the concrete mappings of VSO.

Oh's languages. Irish, with the value combination p.VS.mis and p.VS+.iso, lies between the extremes of universal mismatching and universal matching.

Finally, the mappings in L.2 of VSO.Oh make novel predictions for Irish which remain to be tested. No matter how long the subject and object are, Irish is predicted to phrase the verb with a one-word subject and to otherwise have perfect XP-to-φ matching. Combined with Elfner's tone assignment algorithm in (9), the trees from L.2 of VSO.Oh make testable predictions for the pronunciation of Irish sentences, which we hope will stimulate future work.

# References


Alber, Birgit and Prince, Alan (2021). *The Structure of OT Typologies.* Chapter 1: Introduction to Property Theory. Unpublished manuscript. ROA 1381, Rutgers Optimality Archive, http://roa.rutgers.edu.

Alber, Birgit, Delbusso, Natalie, and Prince, Alan (2016). From intensional properties to universal support. *Language* 92: e88–e116.

Bellik, Jennifer, Bellik, Ozan, and Kalivoda, Nick (2015–2021). Syntax-Prosody in Optimality Theory (SPOT). Javascript application. http:// spot.sites.ucsc.edu. Codebase at https://github.com/syntax-prosody-ot.

Bellik, Jennifer and Kalivoda, Nick (2016). Adjunction and branchingness effects in syntax-prosody mapping. In Gunnar Ólafur Hansson, Ashley Farris-Trimble, Kevin McMullin, and Douglas Pulleyblank (eds.) *Supplemental Proceedings of the 2015 Annual Meeting on Phonology*, Linguistic Society of America. http://doi.org/10.3765/amp.v3i0.3690

Bennett, Ryan, Elfner, Emily, and McCloskey, James (2016). Lightest to the right: An apparently anomalous displacement in Irish. *Linguistic Inquiry* 47: 169–234.

Chen, Fulang (2021). On the left-/right-branching asymmetry in Mandarin tone 3 sandhi. In Ryan Bennett, Richard Bibbs, Mykel L. Brinkerhoff, Max J. Kaplan, Stephanie Rich, Amanda Rysling, Nicholas Van Handel, and Maya Wax Cavallero (eds.) *Proceedings of the 2020 Annual Meeting on Phonology*, Washington, DC: Linguistic Society of America. https:// doi.org/10.3765/amp.v9i0.4881

Chung, Sandra and McCloskey, James (1987). Government, barriers and small clauses in Modern Irish. *Linguistic Inquiry* 18: 173–237.

Cinque, Guglielmo (2010). *The Syntax of Adjectives: A Comparative Study.* Cambridge, MA: MIT Press.

DelBusso, Natalie R. (2018). *Typological Structure and Properties of Property Theory.* PhD dissertation, Rutgers University.

Elfner, Emily (2012). *Syntax-Prosody Interactions in Irish.* PhD dissertation, University of Massachusetts Amherst.

Elfner, Emily (2015). Recursion in prosodic phrasing: evidence from Connemara Irish. *Natural Language and Linguistic Theory* 33: 1169–1208.

Gussenhoven, Carlos (1991). The English rhythm rule as an accent deletion rule. *Phonology* 8: 1–35.

Gussenhoven, Carlos (2005). Procliticized phonological phrases in English: Evidence from rhythm. *Studia Linguistica* 59(2): 174–193.

Harizanov, Boris (2014). The role of prosody in the linearization of clitics: evidence from Bulgarian and Macedonian. In Cassandra Chapman, Olena Kit, and Ivona Kučerová (eds.) *Formal Approaches to Slavic Linguistics 22: The McMaster Meeting 2013* 109–130. Ann Arbor, MI: Michigan Slavic Publications.

Ishihara, Shinichiro (2014). Match theory and the recursivity problem. In Shigeto Kawahara and Mika Igarashi (eds.) *MIT Working Papers in Linguistics 73: Proceedings of Formal Approaches to Japanese linguistics 7* 69–88. Cambridge, MA.

Ito, Junko and Mester, Armin (2007). Prosodic adjunction in Japanese compounds. In Yoichi Miyamoto and Masao Ochi (eds.) *MIT Working Papers in Linguistics 55: Proceedings of Formal Approaches to Japanese Linguistics 4* 97–111. Cambridge, MA.

Ito, Junko and Mester, Armin (2009a). The extended prosodic word. In Janet Grijzenhout and Barış Kabak (eds.), *Phonological Domains: Universals and Deviations* 135–194. Berlin: Mouton de Gruyter.

Ito, Junko and Mester, Armin (2009b). The onset of the prosodic word. In Steve Parker (ed.), *Phonological Argumentation: Essays on Evidence and Motivation* 227–260. London: Equinox.

Ito, Junko and Mester, Armin (2012). Recursive prosodic phrasing in Japanese. In Toni Borowsky, Shigeto Kawahara, Takahito Shinya, and Mariko Sugahara (eds.) *Prosody Matters: Essays in Honor of Elisabeth Selkirk* 280–303. London: Equinox Publishing.

Ito, Junko and Mester, Armin (2013). Prosodic subcategories in Japanese. *Lingua* 124: 20–40.

Kalivoda, Nick (2018). *Syntax-Prosody Mismatches in Optimality Theory.* PhD dissertation, University of California, Santa Cruz.

Kalivoda, Nick and Bellik, Jennifer (2021). Overtly headed XPs and Irish syntax–prosody mapping. In Ryan Bennett, Richard Bibbs, Mykel L. Brinkerhoff, Max J. Kaplan, Stephanie Rich, Amanda Rysling, Nicholas Van Handel, and Maya Wax Cavallero (eds.) *Proceedings of the 2020 Annual Meeting on Phonology*, Washington, DC: Linguistic Society of America. https://doi.org/10.3765/amp.v9i0.4906

Ladd, D. Robert (1986). Intonational phrasing: the case for recursive prosodic structure. *Phonology Yearbook* 3: 311–340.

Legendre, Geraldine, Miyata, Yoshiro, and Smolensky, Paul (1990). Can connectionism contribute to syntax? Harmonic grammar, with an application. In Michael Ziolkowski, Manuela Noske, and Karen Deaton (eds.) *Proceedings of the 26th Regional Meeting of the Chicago Linguistic Society* 237–252. Chicago: Chicago Linguistic Society.

McCloskey, James (1991). Clause structure, ellipsis and proper government in Irish. *Lingua* 85: 259–302.

McCloskey, James (1996). Subjects and subject positions in Irish. In Robert
    Borsley and Ian Roberts (eds.) *The Syntax of the Celtic Languages: A
    Comparative Perspective* 241–283. Cambridge: Cambridge University
    Press.
McCloskey, James (2001). On the distribution of subject properties in Irish.
    In William D. Davies and Stanley Dubinsky (eds.) *Objects and Other
    Subjects* 157–192. Dordrecht: Kluwer.
McCloskey, James (2011). The shape of Irish clauses. In Andrew Carnie (ed.)
    *Formal Approaches to Celtic Linguistics* 143–178. Cambridge: Cambridge
    Scholars Publishing.
Nespor, Marina and Vogel, Irene (1986). *Prosodic Phonology.* Dordrecht: Foris.
Prince, Alan (2002). Arguing optimality. In Angela Carpenter, Andries
    Coetzee, and Paul de Lacy (eds.) *Papers in Optimality Theory II*
    (University of Massachusetts Occasional Papers in Linguistics 26) 269–304.
    Amherst, MA: GLSA.
Prince, Alan, Merchant, Nazarré, and Tesar, Bruce (2007–2021).
    OTWorkplace. http://sites.google.com/site/otworkplace
Prince, Alan and Smolensky, Paul (1993/2004). *Optimality Theory: Constraint
    Interaction in Generative Grammar.* Malden, MA: Blackwell Publishing.
Selkirk, Elisabeth (1986). On derived domains in sentence phonology.
    *Phonology Yearbook* 3: 371–405.
Selkirk, Elisabeth (2011). The syntax–phonology interface. In John A.
    Goldsmith, Jason Riggle, and Alan C. L. Yu (eds.) *The Handbook of
    Phonological Theory* 435–484. Blackwell Publishing.
Truckenbrodt, Hubert (1995). *Phonological Phrases: Their Relation to Syntax,
    Focus, and Prominence.* PhD dissertation, Massachusetts Institute of
    Technology.
Truckenbrodt, Hubert (1999). On the relation between syntactic phrases and
    phonological phrases. *Linguistic Inquiry* 30: 219–255.
Van Handel, Nicholas (2021). Matching overtly headed syntactic phrases in
    Italian. *Phonology* 38: 317–356.


## About the author

*Nick Kalivoda*

Postdoctoral researcher, Centre for Languages and Literature, Lund University. Research interests: syntax–prosody interface, syntax, phonology, and Optimality Theory. Recent publications: "Automated tableau generation using SPOT (Syntax Prosody in Optimality Theory)", with J. Bellik, *Linguistics Vanguard* 2019, "XP- and X⁰-movement in the Latin verb: Evidence from mirroring and anti-mirroring" with E. Zyman, *Glossa* 2020, and "Match Theory: An overview", with S. Ishihara, *Language and Linguistics Compass* 2022.

# Chapter 5

# Constraining subcategory-sensitive MATCH constraints

Nicholas Van Handel, Dan Brodkin, and Ben Eischens[*]

## 5.1   Introduction

Recent work at the syntax-prosody interface has argued that prosodic structure is built from a restricted inventory of recursive categories (Ito and Mester 2007, 2009, 2012, 2013; Selkirk 2011, inter alia). In the Prosodic Adjunction Theory of Ito and Mester (2007), for instance, recursive prosodic constituents are taken to be organized into subcategories based on their position in the prosodic tree, as shown in (1). For instance, $\varphi$ are maximal when they are not dominated by any other $\varphi$ and non-maximal when they are dominated by another $\varphi$. Similarly, $\varphi$ are non-minimal when they dominate another $\varphi$ and minimal when they do not. These subcategories can serve as the domains for different phonological processes, allowing for the identification of distinct prosodic domains without expanding the inventory of categories above the level of the foot beyond the phonological word ($\omega$), phonological phrase ($\varphi$), and intonational phrase ($\iota$) (Ito and Mester 2012, 2013; Elfner 2015; Elordieta 2015).

---

[*] We thank Jenny Bellik and Junko Ito for helpful comments and suggestions on an earlier version of this chapter, and Eric Baković, Ryan Bennett, Richard Bibbs, Nick Kalivoda, Armin Mester, and Amanda Rysling for useful discussion of this work.

(1)     Recursive φs are organized into prosodic subcategories (from Ito and
        Mester 2013, (5))

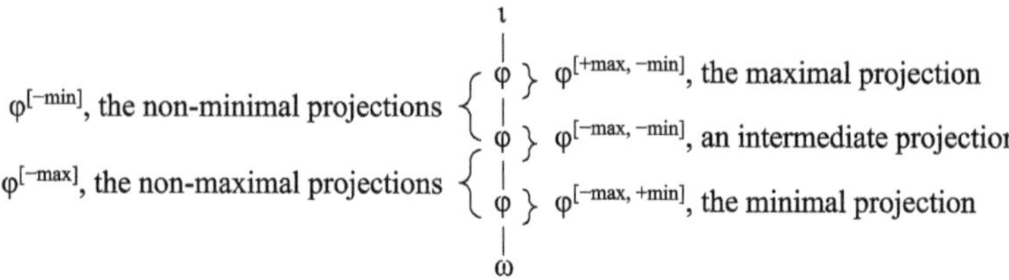

This understanding of prosodic structure forms the theoretical basis for
the simplification of the process which relates syntactic structure to prosodic form in Selkirk's (2009, 2011) Match Theory. This theory holds that
the mapping between syntactic and prosodic constituents is mediated by a
set of Optimality-Theoretic constraints which enforce isomorphism between
syntactic structures, organized into heads ($X^0$), phrases (XP), and clauses
(CP), and prosodic structures, organized into ωs, φs, and ιs. This framework
employs two types of these constraints. The first type governs the mapping
from syntax to prosody and ensures that $X^0$s, XPs, and CPs are mapped
to ωs, φs, and ιs. The second type governs the correspondence of prosody-
to-syntax and ensures that ωs, φs, and ιs correspond to $X^0$s, XPs, and CPs,
respectively. We provide examples of Match constraints at the phrasal level,
along with their informal definitions, in (2).

(2)     Match constraints at the phrasal level
    a.  sp.Match(XP, φ)                                      (syntax-to-prosody)
        'Ensure that each XP in the syntax corresponds to a φ in the
        prosody."
    b.  ps.Match(φ, XP)                                      (prosody-to-syntax)
        'Ensure that each φ in the prosody corresponds to an XP in the
        syntax."

Recent work has extended prosodic subcategories to the mapping constraints
themselves, resulting in Match constraints that target specific subcategories (Ishihara 2014; Ito and Mester 2013, 2020; Kalivoda 2018). In his analysis of Japanese, for instance, Ishihara (2014) introduced the constraint
sp.Match($XP^{[+max]}$, $φ^{[+max]}$), which is defined in (3) below.

(3)     sp.Match($XP^{[+max]}$, $φ^{[+max]}$): Assign one violation for each [+max] XP
        in the syntactic input that does not have a matching [+max] φ in
        the prosodic output.

This constraint differs from sp.MATCH(XP, $\varphi$) in two ways. Like all MATCH constraints, it contains a first argument (XP)[1] which delimits the set of constituents that need to be matched. In this case, the argument $\text{XP}^{[+\text{max}]}$ targets the set of maximal XPs (i.e., those XPs that are not dominated by another XP) rather than all XPs. The constraint also contains a second argument which expresses a requirement which holds over the correspondent. This second argument, $\varphi^{[+\text{max}]}$, also makes reference to subcategories: the correspondent must be a maximal $\varphi$. In short, this constraint targets only a subset of the XPs targeted by general sp.MATCH(XP, $\varphi$) and places an additional requirement on the corresponding $\varphi$s.

Ishihara introduced sp.MATCH($\text{XP}^{[+\text{max}]}$, $\varphi^{[+\text{max}]}$) in order to derive the mapping from the left-branching input in (4) to the balanced structure in (4a). The perfectly matched candidate, (4c), is ruled out by BINMAX($\varphi$, $\omega$), which requires $\varphi$ to contain at most two words. However, BINMAX($\varphi$, $\omega$) favors the flat candidate (4b) over the desired winner (4a), in which the $\varphi$ corresponding to ZP contains four $\omega$s. Ishihara concludes that matching ZP, which is maximal, is more important than respecting binarity. Ranking sp.MATCH($\text{XP}^{[+\text{max}]}$, $\varphi^{[+\text{max}]}$) above BINMAX($\varphi$, $\omega$) ensures that the $\varphi$ corresponding to ZP is preserved, while still allowing the ranking of BINMAX($\varphi$, $\omega$) over sp.MATCH(XP, $\varphi$) to rule out the perfectly isomorphic candidate.

(4)      The constraint sp.MATCH($\text{XP}^{[+\text{max}]}$, $\varphi^{[+\text{max}]}$) prioritizes matching ZP

| $[_{\text{ZP}}\ [_{\text{YP}}\ [_{\text{WP}}\ [_{\text{UP}}\ \text{u}]\ \text{w}]\ \text{y}]\ \text{z}]$ | sp.MATCH($\text{XP}^{[+\text{max}]}$, $\varphi^{[+\text{max}]}$) | BINMAX($\varphi$, $\omega$) | sp.MATCH(XP, $\varphi$) |
|---|---|---|---|
| a.   $(_1\ (_2\ \text{u w})\ (_3\ \text{y z}))$ | 0 | 1<br>$\varphi_1$ | 2<br>YP, UP |
| b.   $(_1\ \text{u w})\ (_2\ \text{y z})$ | $\text{W}_1$<br>ZP | $\text{L}_0$ | $\text{W}_3$<br>ZP, YP, UP |
| c.   $(_1\ (_2\ (_3\ (_4\ \text{u})\ \text{w})\ \text{y})\ \text{z})$ | $\text{e}_0$ | $\text{W}_2$<br>$\varphi_1$, $\varphi_2$ | $\text{L}_0$ |

This example demonstrates a key feature of subcategory-sensitive MATCH constraints: they target only a subset of XPs, which is useful when a prosodic markedness constraint prevents perfect matching. Other analyses have adopted Ishihara's constraint (Kalivoda 2018; Ito and Mester 2020; Bellik

---

[1] In the prosody-to-syntax constraint ps.MATCH($\varphi$, XP), the first argument is $\varphi$ instead of XP, but it has the same role of identifying those constituents that need a correspondent. Similarly, the second argument in this constraint is XP instead of $\varphi$, but it has the same role of stating what the correspondent needs to be.

et al. 2022),[2] and Ito and Mester (2013) have proposed sp.MATCH(XP$^{[-min]}$, $\varphi$), which requires all non-minimal XPs to have a $\varphi$ correspondent. In the same vein, subcategory-sensitive ALIGN constraints have also been proposed (Selkirk and Elordieta 2010, Martínez-Paricio and Kager 2015). These analyses show that there is interest in the literature in augmenting CON with subcategory-sensitive constraints. However, opening the door to subcategory sensitivity allows for the possibility of constraints that favor theoretically implausible mappings, such as matching non-maximal XPs to maximal $\varphi$s. The aim of this chapter is to systematically investigate the consequences of including such constraints in CON.

In §5.2, we show that subcategory sensitivity leads to a proliferation of MATCH constraints, some of which cause deviations from the syntax (*Anti-Match* effects) rather than enforcing syntax-prosody isomorphism. To determine which feature specifications cause Anti-Match effects, we systematically investigated the behavior of subcategory-sensitive constraints (SSCs) using the Syntax-Prosody in Optimality Theory (SPOT) application, which automatically generates and assigns violations to candidates (Bellik et al. 2015–2021). The methods and results of this investigation are described in §§5.3 and 5.4. In §5.5, we propose a ban on feature specifications that cause Anti-Match effects, arguing that this follows from MATCH constraints being part of the theory of Faithfulness. Section 5.6 outlines various approaches to extending the proposal that Anti-Match constraints do not belong in the theory, highlighting their advantages and disadvantages. Section 5.7 concludes.

## 5.2    The problem: Unintended consequences of subcategory-sensitive MATCH

While subcategory-sensitive MATCH constraints can be useful, this augmentation of CON raises theoretical issues that have so far gone unaddressed. The first issue involves a proliferation of MATCH constraints. Consider the constraint sp.MATCH(XP, $\varphi$). Once subcategory sensitivity is allowed, both arguments, XP and $\varphi$, can be specified for [min] and [max] status. For each feature, there are three possible values: [+, −, unspecified]. Four features (two for each argument) with three possible values each leads to $3^4$, or 81, possible syntax-to-prosody MATCH constraints. This number doubles to 162 once prosody-to-syntax constraints are included. Though

---

[2] Bellik et al. (2022) build the requirement that all maximal XPs are matched into GEN, but this is equivalent to having sp.MATCH(XP$^{[+max]}$, $\varphi^{[+max]}$) undominated in CON.

these constraints are logically possible, a theory that admits this many MATCH constraints introduces redundancy, and only a small fraction of these constraints have been motivated in the literature.

This proliferation of MATCH constraints is not merely an issue of parsimony. Many of the logically possible constraints predicted by this theory favor implausible mappings that directly enforce non-isomorphism between syntactic and prosodic structures, e.g., sp.MATCH($XP^{[-min]}$, $\varphi^{[+min]}$). We call constraints of this type *Anti-Match* because they favor at least one non-isomorphic candidate to the perfectly matching one. The inclusion of Anti-Match constraints in the theory would undermine the claim that MATCH constraints enforce syntax-prosody correspondence, while mismatches are the consequence of high-ranking prosodic markedness constraints (e.g., BINARITY, STRONGSTART) overriding MATCH constraints. Anti-Match constraints are also problematic from the perspective that MATCH constraints belong to the theory of Faithfulness. We return to these objections in detail in §5.5.

Anti-Match constraints come in two types. *Flattening* constraints favor ignoring at least one XP in the syntax, resulting in a prosodic output with fewer levels of embedding than the syntactic input. For instance, the constraint sp.MATCH($XP^{[-min]}$, $\varphi^{[+min]}$), defined in (5), attempts to map non-minimal XPs to minimal $\varphi$s. For the right-branching input in (6), this constraint favors a non-isomorphic mapping. The SSC assigns a violation to the isomorphic candidate (6a): though non-minimal WP is matched, its correspondent $\varphi_1$ is not minimal, and the constraint is violated. Moreover, the SSC is satisfied by the flattened candidate (6b): failure to match the minimal YP ensures that the non-minimal WP corresponds to a minimal $\varphi$. Thus, if sp.MATCH($XP^{[-min]}$, $\varphi^{[+min]}$) were ranked above general sp.MATCH(XP, $\varphi$), a non-isomorphic candidate would win. This is a clear Anti-Match effect.

(5)    sp.MATCH($XP^{[-min]}$, $\varphi^{[+min]}$): Assign one violation for each [−min] XP in the syntactic input that does not have a matching [+min] $\varphi$ in the prosodic output.

(6)    The constraint sp.MATCH($XP^{[-min]}$, $\varphi^{[+min]}$) favors flattening over isomorphism.

| $[_{WP}$ w $[_{YP}$ y z] ] | sp.MATCH(XP, $\varphi$) | ps.MATCH ($\varphi$, XP) | sp.MATCH ($XP^{[-min]}$, $\varphi^{[+min]}$) |
|---|---|---|---|
| → a. $(_1$ w $(_2$ y z) ) <br> Isomorphic | 0 | 0 | 1 <br> WP |
| b. $(_1$ w y z) <br> Flattened | $W_1$ <br> YP | $e_0$ | $L_0$ |

*Expanding* constraints work in the opposite direction: they favor building additional $\varphi$s that are unmotivated by the syntax, thereby creating outputs with *more* levels of embedding than the syntactic input. Consider the constraint sp.MATCH(XP$^{[+min]}$, $\varphi^{[-min]}$), defined in (7). As shown in (8), this SSC favors mapping the same right-branching input to outputs like (8b) and (8c) in which either $y$ or $z$ is parsed into a $\varphi$, even though neither $y$ nor $z$ constitutes an XP. Building this unmotivated $\varphi$ structure ensures that the $\varphi$ corresponding to YP is non-minimal, satisfying the SSC. In contrast, the isomorphic candidate is penalized because the minimal YP is matched to a minimal $\varphi$. This is another Anti-Match effect: (8b) and (8c) would win if sp.MATCH(XP$^{[+min]}$, $\varphi^{[-min]}$) were ranked above ps.MATCH($\varphi$, XP).

(7)      sp.MATCH(XP$^{[+min]}$, $\varphi^{[-min]}$): Assign one violation for each [+min] XP in the syntactic input that does not have a matching [−min] $\varphi$ in the prosodic output.

(8)      The constraint sp.MATCH(XP$^{[+min]}$, $\varphi^{[-min]}$) favors expanding over isomorphism.

| $[_{WP}$ w $[_{YP}$ y z] ] | sp.MATCH(XP, $\varphi$) | ps.MATCH($\varphi$, XP) | sp.MATCH(XP$^{[+min]}$, $\varphi^{[-min]}$) |
|---|---|---|---|
| → a. $(_1$ w $(_2$ y z$)$ ) <br> Isomorphic | 0 | 0 | 1 <br> YP |
| b. $(_1$ w $(_2$ $(_3$y$)$ z$)$ ) <br> Expanded | e$_0$ | W$_1$ <br> $\varphi_3$ | L$_0$ |
| c. $(_1$ w $(_2$ y $(_3$z$)$ ) ) <br> Expanded | e$_0$ | W$_1$ <br> $\varphi_3$ | L$_0$ |

Though Flattening and Expanding constraints are clearly antithetical to the idea that MATCH constraints enforce isomorphism, it is less clear whether Anti-Match behavior is widespread, and determining the extent of the problem is non-trivial given that there exist many possible SSCs. For this reason, we carried out an investigation in SPOT aimed at uncovering when Anti-Match effects arise.


## 5.3    SPOT investigation

The Syntax-Prosody in Optimality Theory application is ideal for systematically studying SSCs because it allows for automatic generation and evaluation of candidates (Bellik et al. 2015–2021), which can then be used in OTWorkplace to calculate factorial typologies (Prince, Merchant, and

Tesar 2007–2020). As discussed in §5.2, there are at least 81 logically possible syntax-to-prosody MATCH constraints. Given that each SSC must be tested across various syntactic inputs with a large set of possible prosodic outputs, investigating these constraints by hand would not have been feasible.

The goal of the investigation was to uncover which SSCs favor non-isomorphic candidates (*Anti-Match* constraints) and which ones favor the perfectly matched candidate (*Lawful Match* constraints). For each SSC under investigation, we developed an OT system. We kept GEN (i.e., the syntactic inputs and prosodic outputs) constant across all systems, while CON always contained sp.MATCH(XP, φ), ps.MATCH(φ, XP), and one SSC. For each system, we calculated a factorial typology.

If the factorial typology contained a single language, then the SSC was a Lawful Match constraint. This is because Lawful Match constraints never favor a non-isomorphic parse over the perfectly matched one. When CON contains sp.MATCH(XP,φ), ps.MATCH(φ, XP), and a Lawful Match SSC, the isomorphic candidate will emerge as the winner under any constraint ranking, resulting in one language.

If the factorial typology contained two languages, then the SSC was an Anti-Match constraint. To be Anti-Match, there must exist at least one syntactic input for which the constraint favors a non-isomorphic candidate over the isomorphic one. The constraint will therefore conflict with either sp.MATCH(XP, φ), if it prefers a flattened parse, or with ps.MATCH(φ, XP), if it prefers an expanded one. When CON contains sp.MATCH(XP,φ), ps.MATCH(φ, XP), and an Anti-Match constraint, different candidates will win depending on the ranking, resulting in a factorial typology with two languages.

In the results, we report whether each SSC was Lawful Match or Anti-Match, and if each Anti-Match constraint was a Flattening constraint or an Expanding constraint. With the logic of the study in place, we now define GEN and CON.

## 5.3.1   GEN

### 5.3.1.1   *Inputs*

Syntactic inputs were generated using SPOT's automatic tree generator. The set of input trees consisted of all logically possible recursive nestings of 2–5 word strings with the properties in (9), such that all possible [max] and [min] specifications for XPs were included in the inputs. The complete list of all 24 inputs is provided in the Appendix.

(9)      Inputs: all syntactic trees with the following properties:
   a.    The root node is a CP.
   b.    All intermediate nodes are XPs.
   c.    All terminal nodes are $X^0$s.
   d.    There are between 2–5 terminal nodes.
   e.    All XP nodes are binary-branching.
   f.    Heads can be anywhere.
   g.    Mirror-image trees are excluded (e.g., the input {a [b c]} is included, but {[a b] c} is not, because these are mirror images).[3]

Trees were rooted in CP in order to include inputs like (10a), in which the maximal syntactic phrases, UP and YP, do not include the entire string of terminals.[4] This allows for the possibility of mapping a maximal XP to a non-maximal φ by building an even larger φ, as in (10b).

(10)     a.                           b.

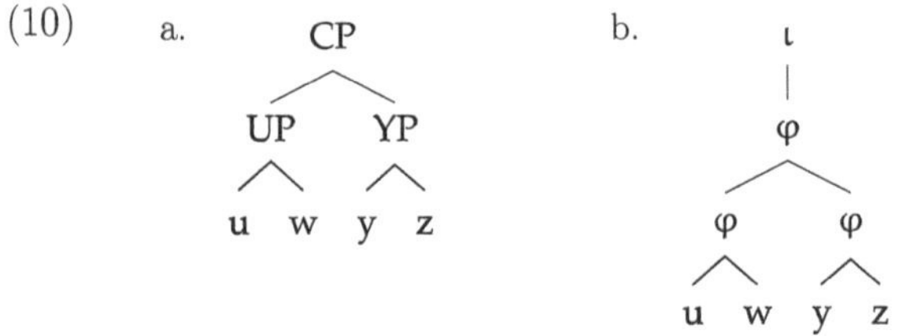

For a similar reason, XP nodes are required to be binary-branching so that all minimal XPs include more than one terminal node, as in (11a).[5] This allows for the possibility of mapping a minimal XP to a non-minimal φ by building an additional internal φ, as in (11b). If the minimal XP instead consisted of a single terminal node, it would be impossible to map the minimal XP to a non-minimal φ, because a single terminal node is already the

---

[3] Mirror image inputs are excluded because MATCH constraints are symmetrical, privileging neither the left nor right edge, and will assign the same number of violations to mirror image candidates. Omitting mirror images reduces the number of inputs without affecting the conclusions of the analysis.

[4] Following the distinction drawn between CP and other XPs in Match Theory, we assume that a maximal syntactic phrase is an XP (not CP) that is not dominated by any other XP. See also Ishihara (2014), who defines sp.MATCH(XP[+max], φ[+max]) to see the maximal *lexical* phrase.

[5] In trees and tableaux, CP and ɩ are shown only when CP is binary-branching, as in (10). CP and ɩ are otherwise omitted, as in (11), to reduce visual clutter, but are assumed to be present in all structures.

smallest possible grouping. Without these inputs, we would miss potential Anti-Match effects due to an insufficiently rich GEN, threatening the validity of our conclusions about which constraints cause Anti-Match effects.

(11)    a.   YP              b.   φ

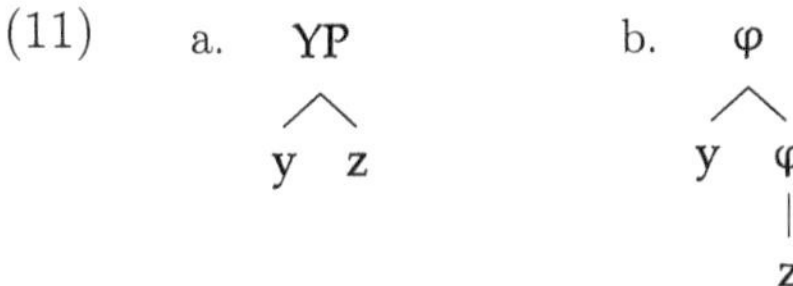

5.3.1.2  *Outputs*

For each syntactic input, prosodic output candidates were generated with the properties in (12).

(12)    Outputs: all prosodic trees with the following properties:
   a.   The root node is ι.
   b.   The intermediate nodes are φs.
   c.   The terminal nodes are ωs.
   d.   Every $X^0$ terminal node in the syntactic input is mapped to an ω terminal node in the prosodic output.
   e.   ι can immediately dominate ω (i.e., non-exhaustive parsing is allowed).
   f.   φ can dominate other φs (i.e., φ-recursion is allowed).
   g.   No φ dominates a φ with the same terminal nodes (i.e., vacuous recursion is prohibited).
   h.   The linear order of terminal nodes in the prosodic output is identical to the order in the syntactic input (i.e., movement is prohibited).

These settings allow for prosodic recursion and non-exhaustive parsing, resulting in a large number of candidates. This corresponds to the completely unrestricted core GEN in SPOT; see Shingler and Bellik (this volume, Ch. 2) for an explanation of the mathematics behind the number of candidates for an input with $n$ terminal nodes, summarized in (13) for $n=2$ through $n=5$. Once 5-word inputs are considered, there are 2880 possible outputs given these GEN settings, underscoring the need for automation of candidate generation and constraint evaluation.

(13)     Number of candidates for a tree with $n$ terminal nodes.

| Number of terminal nodes | Number of candidates |
| --- | --- |
| 2 | 8 |
| 3 | 48 |
| 4 | 352 |
| 5 | 2880 |

### 5.3.2  CON

Each system's CON contained three constraints: sp.MATCH(XP, $\varphi$), ps.MATCH($\varphi$, XP), and one of the SSCs. Given the large number of SSCs, we restricted ourselves to constraints that included either [max] or [min] specifications, but not both. That is, constraints like sp.Match(XP$^{[+\text{max}, -\text{min}]}$, $\varphi$) and sp.Match(XP$^{[+\text{max}]}$, $\varphi^{[+\text{min}]}$), which involve both [min] and [max] features, were not considered.

In the presentation of the results, we divide the constraints into four groups based on their feature specifications: (i) *Conflicting*: constraints in which the first and second arguments have opposite feature values, e.g., sp.MATCH(XP$^{[+\text{max}]}$, $\varphi^{[-\text{max}]}$), (ii) *Second Argument Only*: constraints with feature specifications only on their second argument, e.g., sp.MATCH(XP, $\varphi^{[-\text{max}]}$), (iii) *First Argument Only*: constraints with specifications only on their first argument, e.g., sp.MATCH(XP$^{[+\text{max}]}$, $\varphi$), and (iv) *Identical*: constraints in which the two arguments have the same feature values, e.g., sp.MATCH(XP$^{[+\text{max}]}$, $\varphi^{[+\text{max}]}$). Each of these categories had four possible combinations of features, resulting in 4*4 = 16 syntax-to-prosody constraints.

## 5.4     Classifying subcategory-sensitive MATCH constraints

In this section, we present the results of the SPOT investigation for the 16 syntax-to-prosody constraints, classifying each constraint as Anti-Match or Lawful Match. We make additional distinctions within each class. As discussed above, there are two types of Anti-Match constraints: Flattening and Expanding. There are also three types of Lawful Match constraints. The *Specialized* constraints only care about matching a subset of XPs and are in a special-general relationship with sp.MATCH(XP, $\varphi$) because they always assign a subset of the violations assigned by the general constraint sp.MATCH(XP, $\varphi$). The *superset* constraints are also in a special-general relationship with sp.MATCH(XP, $\varphi$), but assign a *superset* of the violations assigned by sp.MATCH(XP, $\varphi$); that is, the SSC is the general constraint. The *Dominance-Preserving* constraints are usually not in a special-general relationship with sp.MATCH(XP, $\varphi$) because they also prioritize the preservation of dominance relations by requiring XPs and $\varphi$s to be in the same relative position in the tree.

We find that Anti-Match effects arise in two configurations: Conflicting and Second Argument Only specifications. In contrast, Lawful Match effects arise with Identical and First Argument Only specifications. We show that these patterns are related to the different roles of each argument: the first delimits the set of XPs that needs to be matched, and the second places requirements on the corresponding $\varphi$. After reviewing the generalizations from the SPOT investigation, we motivate principled limits on the use of SSCs in §5.5.

### 5.4.1 Conflicting specifications

We first consider those constraints for which the first and second arguments have conflicting feature specifications. We have already seen two of these constraints in §5.2: sp.MATCH(XP$^{[-min]}$, $\varphi^{[+min]}$), a Flattening constraint, and sp.MATCH(XP$^{[+min]}$, $\varphi^{[-min]}$), an Expanding constraint. Our investigation found that the other two syntax-to-prosody constraints with conflicting feature specifications are also Anti-Match: sp.MATCH(XP$^{[+max]}$, $\varphi^{[-max]}$) is an Expanding constraint, while sp.MATCH(XP$^{[-max]}$, $\varphi^{[+max]}$) is a Flattening constraint. The findings for this group are summarized in (14).

(14)     Constraints with conflicting specifications cause Anti-Match effects.

| Constraint Name | Effect |
| --- | --- |
| sp.MATCH(XP$^{[+max]}$, $\varphi^{[-max]}$) | Anti-Match: Expanding |
| sp.MATCH(XP$^{[-max]}$, $\varphi^{[+max]}$) | Anti-Match: Flattening |
| sp.MATCH(XP$^{[+min]}$, $\varphi^{[-min]}$) | Anti-Match: Expanding |
| sp.MATCH(XP$^{[-min]}$, $\varphi^{[+min]}$) | Anti-Match: Flattening |

Conflicting feature specifications are an explicit call for a change in dominance relations, such that an XP's relative position in the syntactic input differs from the relative position of the correspondent $\varphi$ in the prosodic output. It is therefore unsurprising that these constraints cause Anti-Match effects. However, the Anti-Match problem is not limited to SSCs with opposite feature values: in the next section we show that Anti-Match effects arise even when feature specifications are limited to the second argument of the MATCH constraint.

### 5.4.2    *Specifications on the Second Argument Only*

The Anti-Match problem generalizes to constraints that only have feature specifications on the second argument. Consider how the constraint sp.Match(XP, $\varphi^{[-max]}$) treats potential prosodic parses of the right-branching input in (15). The first argument of the constraint lacks any feature specification and therefore picks out all XPs: maximal WP and non-maximal YP. The second argument states that a violation is incurred for each one of these XPs that fails to map to a non-maximal $\varphi$. Because the maximal WP is included in the set of all XPs, this constraint still calls for a change in dominance relations; this call is simply implicit, hidden by the lack of any features on the constraint's first argument.

(15)

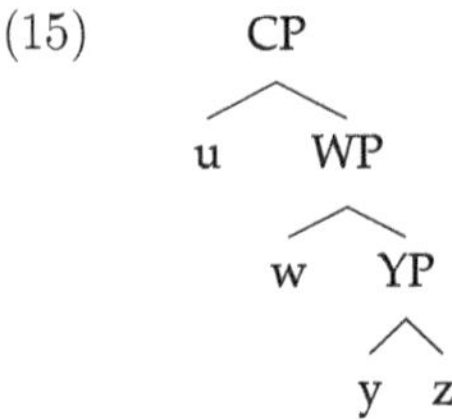

The tableau in (16) shows that this is an Expanding constraint, as expected given the implicit call for a change in dominance relations. The isomorphic candidate (16a) violates sp.Match(XP, $\varphi^{[-max]}$) once because WP is not matched to a non-maximal $\varphi$. In contrast, the expanded candidate (16b) avoids this violation by building an additional $\varphi$ above the one corresponding to WP, at the cost of incurring a violation of ps.Match($\varphi$, XP). As with other Expanding constraints, sp.Match(XP, $\varphi^{[-max]}$) will choose the non-isomorphic candidate (16b) when ranked above ps.Match($\varphi$, XP).

(16)     sp.Match(XP, $\varphi^{[-max]}$) favors the expanded candidate.

| $\{_{\text{CP}}$ u $[_{\text{WP}}$ w $[_{\text{YP}}$ y z]]$\}$ | sp.Match(XP, $\varphi$) | ps.Match($\varphi$, XP) | sp.Match(XP, $\varphi^{[-max]}$) |
|---|---|---|---|
| $\rightarrow$   a.   $\{$u $(_1$ w $(_2$ y z)$)\}$ <br> Isomorphic | 0 | 0 | 1 <br> WP |
| b.   $\{_{\iota}$ $(_1$ u $(_2$ w $(_3$ y z)$)))\}$ <br> Expanded | e$_0$ | W$_1$ <br> $\varphi_1$ | L$_0$ |

The constraint sp.Match(XP, $\varphi^{[-min]}$) is an Expanding constraint for a similar reason: the first argument, XP, picks out all XPs in the syntactic tree, and this set will always include at least one minimal XP. This SSC will favor expanded candidates in which the minimal XP is mapped to a non-minimal $\varphi$ by building an additional $\varphi$ below the one corresponding to the minimal XP.

Specifications on the second argument can also cause Flattening. For the input in (17), the SSC sp.MATCH(XP, $\varphi^{[+max]}$) once again has an implicit call for a change in dominance relations: the set of XPs delimited by the first argument includes non-maximal UP and non-maximal YP, which the constraint favors mapping to maximal $\varphi$.

(17)

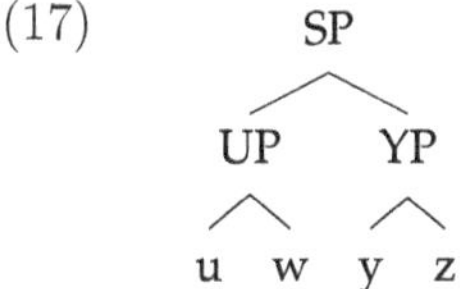

Again, the pressure to change the [max] feature in the prosody leads to Anti-Match effects: the isomorphic candidate (18a) violates the SSC twice because it maps neither UP nor YP to maximal $\varphi$, while the non-isomorphic candidate (18b) only violates the SSC once by ignoring the top layer SP. When the SSC is ranked above sp.MATCH(XP, $\varphi$), the flattened candidate will win.

(18)     sp.MATCH(XP, $\varphi^{[+max]}$) favors the flattened candidate.

| $[_{SP} [_{UP}$ u w$] [_{YP}$ y z$]]$ | sp.MATCH(XP, $\varphi$) | ps.MATCH($\varphi$, XP) | sp.MATCH(XP, $\varphi^{[+max]}$) |
|---|---|---|---|
| $\rightarrow$  a.  $(_1 (_2$ u w$) (_3$ y z$))$<br>Isomorphic | 0 | 0 | 2<br>UP, YP |
| b.  $(_1$ u w$) (_2$ y z$)$<br>Flattened | $W_1$<br>SP | $e_0$ | $L_1$<br>SP |

Finally, sp.MATCH(XP, $\varphi^{[+min]}$) never causes Anti-Match effects, unlike the other constraints in this category. However, this constraint also has an implicit call for a change in dominance relations: whenever the input contains non-minimal XPs, sp.MATCH(XP, $\varphi^{[+min]}$) introduces a pressure to map these non-minimal XPs to minimal $\varphi$s. The lack of Anti-Match effects is therefore an unexpected result.

The reason sp.MATCH(XP, $\varphi^{[+min]}$) does not cause Anti-Match effects lies in tree geometry. First, consider how sp.MATCH(XP, $\varphi^{[+min]}$) assigns violations. An isomorphic parse will map all and only the non-minimal XPs in the input to non-minimal $\varphi$, thereby incurring a violation for each non-minimal XP. A flattened candidate will try to perform better by matching non-minimal XPs to minimal $\varphi$s. However, non-minimal XPs always contain one or more XPs by definition. Any benefit from matching a non-minimal XP to a minimal $\varphi$ will be offset by the failure to match the one or more XPs that it dominates, so flattening can never improve on the isomorphic parse.

To see how this works concretely, the tableau in (19) shows how sp.MATCH(XP, $\varphi^{[+min]}$) prefers to parse the structure from (17). The isomorphic parse (19a) incurs a single violation of the SSC for failing to map non-minimal SP to a minimal $\varphi$. The flattened (19b) successfully maps SP to a minimal $\varphi$, but ends up performing worse because it fails to match both UP and YP. Thus, the isomorphic candidate wins despite the constraint's implicit call for a change in dominance relations.

(19)    sp.MATCH(XP, $\varphi^{[+min]}$) does not favor the flattened parse, even when the input contains non-minimal XPs whose feature value could be reversed.

| $[_{SP} [_{UP} \text{ u w}] [_{YP} \text{ y z}]]$ | sp.MATCH(XP, $\varphi$) | ps.MATCH($\varphi$, XP) | sp.MATCH(XP, $\varphi^{[+min]}$) |
|---|---|---|---|
| →    a.   $(_1 (_2 \text{ u w}) (_3 \text{ y z}))$ <br> Isomorphic | 0 | 0 | 1 <br> SP |
| HB   b.   $(_1 \text{ u w y z})$ <br> Flattened | $W_2$ <br> UP, YP | $e_0$ | $W_2$ <br> UP, YP |

Before moving on, we point out that sp.MATCH(XP, $\varphi^{[+min]}$) is also in a special-general relationship with sp.MATCH(XP, $\varphi$). This stringency relationship arises when the violations assigned by the special constraint are a subset of those assigned by the general one. In this case, sp.MATCH(XP, $\varphi$) is the special constraint, because its violations are a subset of those assigned by the SSC. In both constraints, the first argument dictates that all XPs need to be mapped to some $\varphi$; thus, whenever an XP is not matched in the output, both constraints are violated. However, the constraints differ in how they assign violations when XPs *are* matched in the output. The constraint sp.MATCH(XP, $\varphi$) is satisfied as long as there is some $\varphi$, regardless of its position in the tree, while the second argument of the SSC requires that the matching $\varphi$ be minimal. XPs mapped to non-minimal $\varphi$ will satisfy sp.MATCH(XP, $\varphi$) but not the SSC, explaining why the latter's violations are a superset of those assigned by sp.MATCH(XP, $\varphi$).[6]

---

[6] In fact, the three other Second Argument Only constraints investigated in this section also assign a superset of the violations assigned by sp.MATCH(XP, $\varphi$), for similar reasons. As

Intuitively, it may seem strange that sp.MATCH(XP, $\varphi$) is the special constraint: we have informally referred to sp.MATCH(XP, $\varphi$) as a general constraint, and sp.MATCH(XP, $\varphi^{[+\text{min}]}$) may seem "special" since its second argument bears an additional feature specification. Nevertheless, the terminology reflects the formal definition based on the violations assigned by each constraint. We call sp.MATCH(XP, $\varphi^{[+\text{min}]}$) a *superset* constraint, to differentiate it from the SSCs in §5.4.3, which assign a subset of the violations assigned by sp.MATCH(XP, $\varphi$).

Zooming out, we find that Anti-Match effects still arise when only the second argument of a SSC has feature specifications, with one exception due to tree geometry; these findings are summarized in the table in (20). We showed that Anti-Match effects arise despite the absence of an explicit feature conflict between the two arguments in the constraint definitions, because the set of all XPs may still contain an XP with a feature value opposite of the one specified on the second argument. These findings suggest that Anti-Match effects are not always immediately apparent from a constraint definition. They also suggest that SSCs that have feature specifications on the second argument that are not also present on the first argument should be avoided; we take this up in more detail in §5.5.

(20)   Constraints with Second Argument Only specifications often, but not always, cause Anti-Match effects.

| Constraint Name | Behavior |
|---|---|
| sp.MATCH(XP, $\varphi^{[-\text{max}]}$) | Anti-Match: Expanding |
| sp.MATCH(XP, $\varphi^{[+\text{max}]}$) | Anti-Match: Flattening |
| sp.MATCH(XP, $\varphi^{[-\text{min}]}$) | Anti-Match: Expanding |
| sp.MATCH(XP, $\varphi^{[+\text{min}]}$) | Lawful Match: Superset |

*5.4.3   Specifications on the First Argument Only*

In contrast to the previous group of constraints, no Anti-Match effects are found when the feature specification is only on the first argument. Instead, these SSCs assign a subset of the violations assigned by sp.MATCH(XP, $\varphi$), with which they are in a special-general relationship. This is because the first argument of a SSC like sp.MATCH($\text{XP}^{[+\text{min}]}$, $\varphi$) picks out a subset of XPs to match, while the general sp.MATCH(XP, $\varphi$) cares about matching all XPs.

---

described earlier, they differ from sp.MATCH(XP, $\varphi^{[+\text{min}]}$) in that they also cause Anti-Match effects. We reserve the term *Superset* for sp.MATCH(XP, $\varphi^{[+\text{min}]}$) in order to distinguish it from these Anti-Match constraints.

We therefore call SSCs with First Argument Only specifications *Specialized* constraints.

The tableau in (21) illustrates the special-general relationship between sp.MATCH(XP, $\varphi$) and sp.MATCH(XP$^{[+min]}$, $\varphi$) with a right-branching input. The isomorphic (21a) satisfies both constraints by matching everything. The partially flattened (21b), which fails to match YP, incurs one violation of both sp.MATCH(XP, $\varphi$) and the SSC. The completely flattened (21c) incurs two violations of sp.MATCH(XP, $\varphi$) by failing to match WP and YP but only one violation of the SSC. Across all three candidates, we see that sp.MATCH(XP$^{[+min]}$, $\varphi$) assigns only a subset of the violations assigned by sp.MATCH(XP, $\varphi$), as expected.

(21)    sp.MATCH(XP$^{[-min]}$, $\varphi$) and sp.MATCH(XP, $\varphi$) are in a special-general relationship.

| [$_{UP}$ u [$_{WP}$ w [$_{YP}$ y z]]] | sp.M(XP, $\varphi$) | ps.M($\varphi$, XP) | sp.M(XP$^{[+min]}$, $\varphi$) |
|---|---|---|---|
| → a. ($_1$ u ($_2$ w ($_3$ y z))) <br> Isomorphic | 0 | 0 | 0 |
| HB b. ($_1$ u ($_2$ w y z)) <br> Partially flattened | W$_1$ <br> YP | e$_0$ | W$_1$ <br> YP |
| HB c. ($_1$ u w y z) <br> Completely flattened | W$_2$ <br> WP, YP | e$_0$ | W$_1$ <br> YP |

Although we only demonstrate the special-general relationship for sp.MATCH(XP$^{[+min]}$, $\varphi$), we found that the same relationship holds between sp.MATCH(XP, $\varphi$) and the other three SSCs with specifications on the first argument, as summarized in (22). The lack of Anti-Match effects due to the special-general relationship suggests that constraints with specifications only on the first argument may not be a problematic addition to the inventory of Match constraints.

(22)    Constraints with First Argument Only specifications are Specialized.

| Constraint Name | Behavior |
|---|---|
| sp.MATCH(XP$^{[+max]}$, $\varphi$) | Lawful Match: Specialized |
| sp.MATCH(XP$^{[-max]}$, $\varphi$) | Lawful Match: Specialized |
| sp.MATCH(XP$^{[+min]}$, $\varphi$) | Lawful Match: Specialized |
| sp.MATCH(XP$^{[-min]}$, $\varphi$) | Lawful Match: Specialized |

### 5.4.4   Identical specifications

SSCs in which the arguments have identical feature specifications are also Lawful Match constraints, but the majority of them are not in a special-general relationship with sp.MATCH(XP, $\varphi$). Consider the constraint sp.MATCH(XP$^{[+min]}$, $\varphi^{[+min]}$). Like the SSCs in §5.4.3, this SSC only attempts to match a subset of those XPs targeted by sp.MATCH(XP, $\varphi$) due to the [+min] feature on the first argument. However, this SSC sometimes assigns more violations than sp.MATCH(XP, $\varphi$) because it also requires the XP and $\varphi$ to share certain features, whereas sp.MATCH(XP, $\varphi$) is satisfied as long as some matching $\varphi$ exists. We call this type of constraint Dominance-Preserving, because requiring XP and $\varphi$ to have identical feature specifications ensures that their relative position is the same in both syntax and prosody.

This dominance preservation is shown in (23) for a four-word right-branching syntactic input. The fully flattened (23b) incurs violations of both sp.MATCH(XP, $\varphi$) and the SSC by failing to match certain XPs. The expanded constraint (23c) satisfies sp.MATCH(XP, $\varphi$), because all XPs are matched to some $\varphi$. However, it violates the SSC: although YP is matched, its corresponding $\varphi$ is minimal, so its relative position in the tree structure has changed.

(23)    sp.MATCH(XP$^{[+min]}$, $\varphi^{[+min]}$) and sp.MATCH(XP, $\varphi$) are not in a special-general relationship.

| $[_{UP}$ u $[_{WP}$ w $[_{YP}$ y z$]\,]\,]$ | sp.M(XP, $\varphi$) | ps.M($\varphi$, XP) | sp.M(XP$^{[+min]}$, $\varphi^{[+min]}$) |
|---|---|---|---|
| $\rightarrow$    a.   $(_1$ u $(_2$ w $(_3$ y z$)))$ <br> Isomorphic | 0 | 0 | 0 |
| HB   b.   $(_1$ u w y z$)$ <br> Flattened | W$_2$ <br> WP, YP | e$_0$ | W$_1$ <br> YP |
| HB   c.   $(_1$ u $(_2$ w $(_3$ y $(_4$ z$))))$ <br> Expanded | e$_0$ | W$_1$ <br> $\varphi_4$ | W$_1$ <br> YP |

Thus, Dominance-Preserving constraints sometimes assign more violations than sp.MATCH(XP, $\varphi$) because they place additional requirements on matching $\varphi$s. In addition to sp.MATCH(XP$^{[+min]}$, $\varphi^{[+min]}$), we found that sp.MATCH(XP$^{[+max]}$, $\varphi^{[+max]}$), sp.MATCH(XP$^{[-max]}$, $\varphi^{[-max]}$), and sp.MATCH(XP$^{[-min]}$, $\varphi^{[-min]}$) were also Dominance-Preserving constraints.

Interestingly, sp.MATCH(XP$^{[-min]}$, $\varphi^{[-min]}$) turned out to be in a special-general relationship with sp.MATCH(XP, $\varphi$), unlike the other Dominance-Preserving constraints. That is, the number of violations assigned by sp.MATCH(XP$^{[-min]}$, $\varphi^{[-min]}$) is always a subset of those assigned by sp.MATCH(XP, $\varphi$). In order to understand why, consider the two ways to violate sp.MATCH($XP^{[-min]}$, $\varphi^{[-min]}$). First, a non-minimal XP could fail to be mapped to *any* $\varphi$; this will violate both the SSC and general sp.MATCH(XP, $\varphi$), so does not affect the special-general relation. Alternatively, a non-minimal XP could be mapped to a minimal $\varphi$; this minimal $\varphi$ would violate the SSC but would satisfy sp.MATCH(XP, $\varphi$). However, this mapping will be accompanied by one or more violations of sp.MATCH(XP, $\varphi$), because it requires ignoring all XPs inside the non-minimal XP, which contains at least one XP by definition. Thus, the total violations assigned by sp.MATCH(XP, $\varphi$) will always be greater than or equal to those assigned by the SSC, resulting in the special-general relationship.

This type of mapping is illustrated in (24): the non-minimal SP in (24a) is mapped to a minimal $\varphi$ in (24b) by ignoring UP and YP. This leads to one violation of sp.MATCH($XP^{[-min]}$, $\varphi^{[-min]}$) due to SP and two violations of sp.MATCH(XP, $\varphi$) due to UP and YP. This demonstrates how a violation of sp.MATCH($XP^{[-min]}$, $\varphi^{[-min]}$) caused by mapping a non-minimal XP to a minimal $\varphi$ will always co-occur with one or more violations of sp.MATCH(XP, $\varphi$). It should also be noted that sp.MATCH($XP^{[-min]}$, $\varphi^{[-min]}$) is still a Dominance-Preserving constraint: it is only satisfied when non-minimal SP is mapped to a non-minimal $\varphi$. In contrast, the Specialized constraint sp.MATCH($XP^{[-min]}$, $\varphi$) would be satisfied by the Flattened (24b) because it does not care whether SP retains its non-minimal status as long as it is matched.

(24)    sp.MATCH($XP^{[-min]}$, $\varphi^{[-min]}$) is both Dominance-Preserving and in a special-general relationship with sp.MATCH(XP, $\varphi$)

| $[_{SP}\ [_{UP}\ \text{u w}\ ]\ [_{YP}\ \text{y z}]\ ]$ | sp.M(XP, $\varphi$) | ps.M($\varphi$, XP) | sp.M($XP^{[-min]}$, $\varphi^{[-min]}$) |
|---|---|---|---|
| →   a.   $(_1\ (_2\ \text{u w})\ (_3\ \text{y z})))$ <br> Isomorphic | 0 | 0 | 0 |
| HB   b.   $(_1\ \text{u w y z})$ <br> Flattened | $W_2$ <br> UP, YP | $e_0$ | $W_1$ <br> SP |

As summarized in (25), identical feature specifications lead to a second type of Lawful Match, the Dominance-Preserving constraints, which aim not only to match constituents but to preserve the relative position of nodes in the tree. Unlike Specialized constraints, Dominance-Preserving constraints are not necessarily in a special-general relationship with sp.MATCH(XP, $\varphi$). As with Specialized constraints, the absence of Anti-Match effects suggests that Dominance-Preserving constraints can be permitted in the theory without causing issues, and we briefly consider how Specialized and Dominance-Preserving constraints might be teased apart in §5.6.1.

(25)    Constraints with Identical specifications are Dominance-Preserving.

| Constraint Name | Behavior |
| --- | --- |
| sp.MATCH(XP$^{[+max]}$, $\varphi^{[+max]}$) | Lawful Match: Dominance-Preserving |
| sp.MATCH(XP$^{[-max]}$, $\varphi^{[-max]}$) | Lawful Match: Dominance-Preserving |
| sp.MATCH(XP$^{[+min]}$, $\varphi^{[+min]}$) | Lawful Match: Dominance-Preserving |
| sp.MATCH(XP$^{[-min]}$, $\varphi^{[-min]}$) | Lawful Match: Dominance-Preserving |

### 5.4.5   Interim summary

The SPOT investigation showed that Anti-Match effects are fairly
widespread: we found multiple Flattening and Expanding constraints among
the 16 SSCs investigated here. The summary in (26) shows the number
of Anti-Match and Lawful Match constraints for each configuration; as a
reminder, four constraints were tested in each configuration. This summary
shows that Anti-Match effects are limited to two configurations: Conflicting
and Second Argument Only feature specifications. In the following section,
we argue that these configurations should be excluded from the theory in
order to avoid Anti-Match effects.

(26)    Number of Anti-Match and Lawful Match SSCs for each
        configuration.

| Feature Specifications | Anti-Match | Lawful Match |
| --- | --- | --- |
| Conflicting | 4 | 0 |
| Second Argument Only | 3 | 1 |
| First Argument Only | 0 | 4 |
| Identical | 0 | 4 |

## 5.5   Constraining subcategory-sensitive constraints

The results of this investigation lead to an architectural conclusion about the
licit shapes of MATCH constraints in the grammar. In the preceding sections,
we have seen that the allowance for unconstrained feature specifications
yields a drastic increase in the generative capacity of the system, resulting
in MATCH constraints that militate against syntax-prosody isomorphism.
This observation suggests that the theory must be constrained in some way
to rule out the presence of Anti-Match constraints.

   To achieve this goal, we propose that Conflicting and Second Argument Only specifications are prohibited. These configurations cause the

problematic Anti-Match effects because they require, either explicitly or implicitly, for XPs and their $\varphi$ correspondents to have conflicting feature values. We refer to this proposal as the *Ban on Anti-Match Constraints*, stated in (27). As a consequence of this ban, MATCH constraints can only place a specification on their second argument if the same specification is also present on the first argument.[7]

(27)     The Ban on Anti-Match Constraints: MATCH constraints must not...
    a.    place conflicting subcategory specifications on their first and second arguments.

(Conflicting)

    b.    place a feature specification on their second argument without a parallel specification on the first argument.

(Second Argument Only)

This proposal addresses the problem of overgeneration identified in §§5.3 and 5.4 and flows from the logic of the theory of syntax–prosody mapping which has emerged from work in Prosodic Adjunction Theory (Ito and Mester 2007, 2009) and Match Theory (Selkirk 2011; Ishihara 2014; Elfner 2012, 2015; Elordieta 2015). In §5.6, we will discuss several ways in which this proposal might be extended. Before taking up this task, we lay out two arguments, both within the theoretical framework which we adopt, which we take to motivate its necessity.

### 5.5.1    *The nature of the syntax–prosody mapping*

The principal consideration which militates against the Anti-Match constraints above is an observation about the nature of divergence between syntactic and prosodic structure. Since the earliest period of work at this interface, it has been recognized that prosodic organization mirrors the syntax which underlies it in a close but imperfect manner (Chomsky and Halle 1968, Clements 1978, Chen 1987, Selkirk 1986). In light of this fact,

---

[7] Note that the Ban on Anti-Match Constraints also prohibits constraints like sp.MATCH(XP$^{[+min]}$, $\varphi^{[-max]}$) and sp.MATCH(XP$^{[+min]}$, $\varphi^{[-max, +min]}$). While these constraints have specifications on both arguments, the feature [−max] is specified only for the second argument, and we predict that such constraints will give rise to Anti-Match effects. In contrast, sp.MATCH(XP$^{[-max, +min]}$, $\varphi^{[-max]}$) would be allowed, because the [−max] specification on the second argument is also present on the first; we predict that such constraints will belong to the family of Lawful Match constraints. Since we have not yet tested constraints with both [max] and [min] specifications, we set these cases aside and continue to focus only on those constraints that have either a [max] or a [min] specification, but not both.

it has become a theoretical priority to understand the nature of such divergences between syntactic and prosodic form. The leading strand of thought in this literature, which assumes the existence of a distinct level of prosodic representation, has historically approached this type of discrepancy in one of two ways.

The earliest approach to this puzzle proposed to connect such syntax-prosody mismatches to properties of the mapping itself. The pioneering investigations of the interface in the 1980s, for instance, typically assumed a view of prosodic structure, now referred to as the Strict Layer Hypothesis (Nespor and Vogel 1986, Selkirk 1986), which held that prosodic organization differed from syntactic structure in fundamental respects (lacking, for instance, the capacity for recursion). As a natural consequence of this assumption, the literature of this era generally did not envision the existence of a system of mapping which produced prosodic structures with the same organization as the syntax which underlies them. Rather, these works often assumed a system of translation which rearranged syntactic structures into geometries that complied with constraints on prosodic organization. The end-based theory of Selkirk (1986), for instance, is one model of this type.

These approaches contrast with an alternative which assumes that mismatches between the syntax and prosody do not arise from constraints on mapping itself, but rather from independent pressures which govern prosodic form. This alternative, which maintains the central intuition of Match Theory, differs from its predecessors in several respects. First, it recognizes the observation—one which has now been defended at every level of the prosodic hierarchy above the foot[8]—that prosodic structure permits recursion (Ladd 1986; Booij 1996; Peperkamp 1997; Vigário 1999, 2003; Ito and Mester 2007, 2009, 2013; Wagner 2005; Elfner 2012, 2015; Bennett 2018) and other deviations from the structural ideal once assumed by proponents of Strict Layering. Second, it adopts the theoretical stance that prosodic structure above the foot is organized into a restricted set of recursive categories: the prosodic word, phonological phrase, and intonational phrase (Ito and Mester 2007, 2009; Elfner 2015; Elordieta 2015; Bennett 2018).

These two advances reflect the central theoretical insights of the papers which laid out the theory of prosodic structure known as Prosodic Adjunction Theory (Ito and Mester 2007, 2009). Their adoption, in turn, paves the way for a drastic simplification of the process which maps syntactic structure into prosodic form, as developed in Match Theory (Selkirk 2011).

---

[8] Prosodic recursion has also been argued for at the level of the foot (Bennett 2012, Martínez-Paricio and Kager 2015, Kager and Martínez-Paricio 2018, i.a.).

Should prosodic structure support recursion and be organized into categories with direct analogues in the syntax, it becomes possible to understand the process of mapping as one which prefers a one-to-one translation of the constituent structure of a syntactic input into an analogous prosodic output. This is a view on which the mapping itself does not impose deviations between the syntactic input and the prosodic output, and syntax-prosody mismatches are instead linked to independent prosodic well-formedness constraints.[9]

Proponents of Match Theory have formalized the workings of this mapping in several different ways (Selkirk 2009, 2011; Elfner 2015; Ito and Mester 2019; Lee and Selkirk 2022). What is important at present, however, is that the intuition above reflects a central tenet of the theory. In our view, there are good reasons for this to be so: the notion that the mapping constraints do not drive mismatches fits well with the observation that prosodic structure can be organized much like syntax and yields genuine theoretical simplification in terms of the mapping between the two.

In light of this stance, we arrive at a theoretical consideration which suggests the need to rule out Anti-Match constraints. This is the observation that Anti-Match constraints explicitly drive mismatches between the syntax and the prosody via Flattening and Expanding, contra the claim that such deviations are the responsibility of prosodic markedness constraints.

### 5.5.2   Match and the theory of Faithfulness

The arguments above lead us to the view that Anti-Match constraints run against the spirit of Match Theory. As such, we submit that they have no place in the theory at all. Simple as this conclusion may seem, it yields immediate benefits. First, it excludes the constraints which the SPOT investigation identified as motivating mismatches for non-phonological reasons in §5.4. Second, it leads to a substantial reduction in the number of

---

[9] The one exception is that certain XPs, like functional phrases (FuncP), may be invisible to mapping constraints (Nespor and Vogel 1986, Selkirk 1986, Truckenbrodt 1999, Lee and Selkirk 2022, Van Handel this volume, Ch. 6, i.a.). While sp.Match(LexP, $\varphi$) introduces a pressure to match lexical XPs (LexP), it does not drive mismatches because it does not penalize $\varphi$s that correspond to FuncP's. Like Specialized SSCs, it only introduces the pressure to match a subset of XPs. However, ps.Match($\varphi$, LexP) can drive mismatches, because it militates against all $\varphi$s that lack a LexP correspondent, including $\varphi$s that correspond to FuncP's. This is similar to Flattening SSCs: ps.Match($\varphi$, LexP) prefers a structure with fewer levels of embedding than if all XPs were matched. We view this as a principled exception, different from Anti-Match SSCs, because (i) lexical-only Match constraints still prefer perfect matching of LexP's, and (ii) there is ample evidence that a Lex/Func distinction (or a similar restriction) is needed.

MATCH constraints in the theory and delivers a more constrained typology of predicted languages. Third and finally, it allows MATCH constraints to be integrated into the theory of Faithfulness.

This final point, though theory-internal in nature, provides another motivation for the exclusion of Anti-Match constraints from the theory. In essence, it turns on the formal implementation of Match Theory in Optimality Theory. Within this framework, the constraints which enforce isomorphism between syntax and prosody are typically taken to fall under the umbrella of *Faithfulness*: that is, they enforce a type of cross-modular correspondence between syntactic and prosodic constituents. In the formulation of these constraints, for instance, Selkirk (2009:17) writes,

> The first type—call them S-P faithfulness constraints—require that syntactic constituency be faithfully reflected in prosodic constituency, and the second—call them P-S faithfulness constraints—require that prosodic constituency be a faithful reflection of syntactic constituency.

The formalization of MATCH constraints as a part of the theory of Faithfulness leads to two implications about the properties of these constraints. The first is that the theory must allow these constraints to treat certain elements of syntactic and prosodic structure as "correspondent" in some way. At the lowest level, MATCH constraints treat the pairings of $X^0$:ω, XP:φ, and CP:ι to reflect fundamentally faithful mappings. In this sense, these constraints are held to enforce correspondence between categorial labels. At a higher level, it follows from a theory which assumes the possibility for exact mapping that these constraints may force the preservation of dominance relations as well: under ideal circumstances, they may require that the phrases which are undominated in the syntax ("syntactically maximal") be similarly undominated in the prosody ("prosodically maximal") and that the phrases dominated in the syntax ("syntactically non-maximal") be similarly dominated in the prosody ("prosodically non-maximal"). In this respect, we might assume that MATCH constraints bear responsibility for the correspondence of subcategory labels as well.

A second concern follows from the inclusion of MATCH constraints in the theory of Faithfulness. This lies in the types of requirements which can licitly be imposed on outputs by constraints of this type. In Optimality Theory, faithfulness constraints serve as the formal machinery which ensures minimal difference between input and output. As their role is to preserve properties of the input, it is a definitional property of such constraints that they cannot force outputs to differ from inputs in any way. This observation leads to a clear conclusion about the shapes of MATCH constraints: if they are understood as faithfulness constraints in any meaningful sense, they should be unable to force differences between XPs and their $\varphi$ correspondents.

With this conclusion in hand, we arrive at a second strike against the Anti-Match constraints above: they do not behave like faithfulness constraints, because they can require XPs and $\varphi$s that are in a correspondence relationship to have conflicting subcategory feature specifications. As such, they cannot be included in the theory of Faithfulness with the Lawful Match constraints.

We take this observation to provide theoretical motivation for the elimination of the Anti-Match constraints above. The general profile of the mapping from syntax to prosody is one where prosodic structure appears faithful to syntactic constituency, and as such, the constraints which govern this mapping should be conceptualized as part of the theory of Faithfulness. However, the admission of Anti-Match constraints would render it impossible to categorically associate MATCH constraints with Faithfulness in this way. To allow them in at this cost would appear to be a mistake. As such, we suggest, they must be ruled out from the theory.

These two arguments lead us to the Ban on Anti-Match Constraints, stated earlier in (27), which prohibits Conflicting and Second Argument Only specifications. This proposal ensures that MATCH constraints do not impose subcategory specifications on their second argument that are not also present on their first argument. As a result, the sole MATCH constraints allowed in CON are those which bear the shapes in (28).[10, 11]

(28)     Permissible constraint shapes under the Ban on Anti-Match Constraints

     a.     Licit SP constraints:

         i.     sp.MATCH($X^0$, $\omega$), sp.MATCH(XP, $\varphi$), sp.MATCH(CP, $\iota$)

         ii.     sp.MATCH($XP^{[+max]}$, $\varphi$), sp.MATCH($XP^{[+min]}$, $\varphi$), ...

         iii.     sp.MATCH($XP^{[+max]}$, $\varphi^{[+max]}$), sp.MATCH($XP^{[+min]}$, $\varphi^{[+min]}$), ...

     b.     Licit PS constraints:

         i.     ps.MATCH($\omega$, $X^0$), ps.MATCH($\varphi$, XP), ps.MATCH($\iota$, CP)

---

[10] Though not discussed here for reasons of space, we found that prosody-to-syntax SSCs show similar behavior to the syntax-to-prosody SSCs: only Conflicting and Second Argument Only specifications cause Anti-Match effects. Again, this is because specifications on the second argument that are not also present on the first require correspondents to have different feature values. The Ban on Anti-Match constraints is therefore general, applying to both syntax-to-prosody and prosody-to-syntax constraints.

[11] We only show subcategory-sensitive constraints at the $\varphi$ level in the list of permissible MATCH constraints because these were the focus of our investigation. However, Ishihara (2014) suggests that there could also be specific MATCH constraints for $\iota$ and $\omega$, and we leave this possibility open.

 ii.  ps.Match($\varphi^{[+\text{max}]}$, XP), ps.Match($\varphi^{[+\text{min}]}$, XP), ...

 iii.  ps.Match($\varphi^{[+\text{max}]}$, XP$^{[+\text{max}]}$), ps.Match($\varphi^{[+\text{min}]}$, XP$^{[+\text{min}]}$), ...

## 5.6 Extending the proposal

The discussion above has led us to the proposal that, on the grounds of general considerations on the nature of Faithfulness and Match Theory, the subcategory-sensitive Match constraints which lead to Anti-Match effects should be excluded from Con. As shown in the SPOT investigation, these constraints are those in which the second argument has a feature specification that is not also present on the first, e.g., sp.Match(XP$^{[+\text{max}]}$, $\varphi^{[-\text{max}]}$) and sp.Match(XP, $\varphi^{[+\text{max}]}$). Eliminating these constraints narrows down the number of logically possible Match constraints, simplifying Con and the resulting typology. More importantly, it prevents Anti-Match effects, solving the main theoretical issue raised in this chapter.

However, one might extend the proposal outlined above in various ways, some of which are more restrictive than others. In this section, we outline possible extensions, as well as one alternative that lies outside the purview of this proposal but nonetheless merits discussion.

### 5.6.1 *Specialized vs. Dominance-Preserving constraints*

The prohibition on Anti-Match constraints in §5.5 still allows for two distinct types of Lawful Match constraints: Specialized constraints, which arise with First Argument Only specifications (e.g., sp.Match(XP$^{[+\text{max}]}$, $\varphi$), and Dominance-Preserving constraints, which arise with identical specifications (e.g., sp.Match(XP$^{[+\text{max}]}$, $\varphi^{[+\text{max}]}$). However, one might further constrain the inventory of subcategory-sensitive Match constraints by only allowing one type and not the other. For example, one might suppose that either Specialized or Dominance-Preserving constraints are necessary, but not both. This point is especially apparent when one considers that Specialized and Dominance-Preserving Match constraints often do the same work. For example, Kalivoda (2018) and Ito and Mester (2020) use the Specialized constraint sp.Match(XP$^{[+\text{max}]}$, $\varphi$) to account for the same phenomenon as the Dominance-Preserving constraint sp.Match(XP$^{[+\text{max}]}$, $\varphi^{[+\text{max}]}$) adopted in Ishihara (2014).

There are two possible forms of this approach. The first, which we refer to as the Specialized Hypothesis, limits the inventory of SSCs to Specialized constraints. On such an approach, only the constraints with the shape in (29) would be allowed.

(29)		The Specialized Hypothesis
	a.	Licit SP constraints:
		i.	sp.MATCH($X^0$, ω), sp.MATCH(XP, φ), sp.MATCH(CP, ι)
		ii.	sp.MATCH($XP^{[+max]}$, φ), sp.MATCH($XP^{[+min]}$, φ), ...
	b.	Licit PS constraints:
		i.	ps.MATCH(ω, $X^0$), ps.MATCH(φ, XP), ps.MATCH(ι, CP)
		ii.	ps.MATCH($φ^{[+max]}$, XP), ps.MATCH($φ^{[+min]}$, XP), ...

An alternative is the Dominance-Preserving Hypothesis, which states that Dominance-Preserving constraints are the only permissible subcategory-sensitive MATCH constraints. Under this view, constraints of the shape in (30) would be allowed, and the Specialized constraints in (29) would be prohibited.

(30)		The Dominance-Preserving Hypothesis
	a.	Licit SP constraints:
		i.	sp.MATCH($X^0$, ω), sp.MATCH(XP, φ), sp.MATCH(CP, ι)
		ii.	sp.MATCH($XP^{[+max]}$, $φ^{[+max]}$), sp.MATCH($XP^{[+min]}$, $φ^{[+min]}$), ...
	b.	Licit PS constraints:
		i.	ps.MATCH(ω, $X^0$), ps.MATCH(φ, XP), ps.MATCH(ι, CP)
		ii.	ps.MATCH($φ^{[+max]}$, $XP^{[+max]}$), ps.MATCH($φ^{[+min]}$, $XP^{[+min]}$), ...

Though we do not take a position on these two approaches here, it is important to point out that whether the theory should include only Specialized or only Dominance-Preserving constraints is ultimately an empirical question, since each type of constraint favors slightly different prosodic structures for certain inputs. For example, imagine a hypothetical language in which the input structure in (31) is prosodified as shown.

(31)		$[_{WP}$ w $[_{YP}$ y z]] → (w y z)

This mapping could be modeled by ranking NONRECURSIVITY over sp.MATCH(XP, φ), motivating flattening, as shown in (32).

(32)		NONREC favors the flattened candidate.

| $[_{WP}$ w $[_{YP}$ y z]] | NONREC | sp.MATCH(XP, φ) |
|---|---|---|
| → a. $(_1$ w y z)<br>Flattened | 0 | 1<br>YP |
| b. $(_1$ w $(_2$ y z))<br>Isomorphic | $W_1$ | $L_0$ |

However, imagine that in this same language, a syntactic input like the one in (33) is prosodified faithfully, with partial flattening. As shown in (34), this would not be predicted by the ranking of NONRECURSIVITY over sp.MATCH(XP,$\varphi$), since NONRECURSIVITY would prefer the completely flattened candidate (34b).

(33)     $[_{UP}$ u $[_{WP}$ w $[_{YP}$ y z]]] $\rightarrow$ (u (w y z))

(34)     NONREC $\gg$ sp.MATCH(XP,$\varphi$) favors the completely flattened candidate.

| $[_{UP}$ u $[_{WP}$ w $[_{YP}$ y z]]] | NONREC | sp.MATCH(XP, $\varphi$) |
|---|---|---|
| ☹ a.  $(_1$ u $(_2$ w y z)) <br> Partially flattened | 1 | 1 <br> YP |
| 💣* b.  $(_1$ u w y z) <br> Completely flattened | $L_0$ | $W_2$ <br> WP, YP |
| c.  $(_1$ u $(_2$ w $(_3$ y z))) <br> Isomorphic | $W_2$ | $L_0$ |

In this case, a subcategory-sensitive MATCH constraint could be introduced to select the correct winner. In (35), ranking sp.MATCH(XP$^{[-min]}$, $\varphi$) over NONRECURSIVITY would ensure that candidate (35a) wins. This is because both non-minimal XPs are matched in candidate (35a), while only one is in candidate (35b).

(35)     sp.MATCH(XP$^{[-min]}$, $\varphi$) $\gg$ NONREC favors the partially flattened candidate.

| $[_{UP}$ u $[_{WP}$ w $[_{YP}$ y z]]] | sp.MATCH(XP$^{[-min]}$, $\varphi$) | NONREC | sp.MATCH(XP, $\varphi$) |
|---|---|---|---|
| → a.  $(_1$ u $(_2$ w y z)) <br> Partially flattened | 0 | 1 | 1 <br> YP |
| b.  $(_1$ u w y z) <br> Completely flattened | $W_1$ <br> WP | $L_0$ | $W_2$ <br> WP, YP |
| c.  $(_1$ u $(_2$ w $(_3$ y z))) <br> Isomorphic | $e_0$ | $W_2$ | $L_0$ |

In this case, the Specialized constraint would predict the correct output. However, the analogous Dominance-Preserving constraint sp.MATCH(XP$^{[-min]}$, $\varphi^{[-min]}$) instead favors the isomorphic candidate (36c), because it is the only one that both matches the non-minimal XPs and preserves their relative position in the tree, as shown in (36).

(36)      sp.Match($XP^{[-min]}$, $\varphi^{[-min]}$) $\gg$ NonRec does not favor partial flattening.

| $[_{UP}$ u $[_{WP}$ w $[_{YP}$ y z]]] | sp.Match($XP^{[-min]}$, $\varphi^{[-min]}$) | NonRec | sp.Match(XP, $\varphi$) |
|---|---|---|---|
| ☹ a. $(_1$ u $(_2$ w y z)) <br> Partially flattened | 1 <br> WP | 1 | 1 <br> YP |
| b. $(_1$ u w y z) <br> Completely flattened | $W_2$ <br> UP, WP | $L_0$ | $W_2$ <br> WP, YP |
| 💣* c. $(_1$ u $(_2$ w $(_3$ y z))) <br> Isomorphic | $L_0$ | $W_2$ | $L_0$ |

Since the Specialized and Dominance-Preserving Match constraints some-times prefer different output candidates, there will be times where only one constraint can select the right output. In the hypothetical example, the Specialized constraint was needed because it was only necessary for the non-minimal XP to be matched; it did not matter whether its relative position in the tree was preserved. There may also be cases where a Dominance-Preserving constraint is needed instead. This example shows the type of evidence one might bring to bear on the question of whether both types of constraint are needed in Con.

Future work should also investigate the different typological predictions of these constraints by comparing the factorial typologies of systems that contain sp.Match(XP, $\varphi$), a prosodic markedness constraint, and either a Specialized or a Dominance-Preserving constraint, and seeing which pro-sodic outputs are unique to each typology. These predictions should then be paired with further empirical investigation.

### 5.6.2    Eliminate subcategories altogether

Another extension of the Ban on Anti-Match Constraints would be to ban subcategory-sensitive Match constraints altogether, and not only those that produce Anti-Match effects. We refer to this hypothesis as the No Subcategory-Sensitive Match Hypothesis. This would mean that only the constraints in (37) are present in Con.

(37)      The No Subcategory-Sensitive Match Hypothesis
     a.    Licit SP constraints: sp.Match($X^0$, $\omega$), sp.Match(XP, $\varphi$), sp.Match(CP, $\iota$).
     b.    Licit PS constraints: ps.Match($\omega$, $X^0$), ps.Match($\varphi$, XP), ps.Match($\iota$, CP).

Such an approach might be preferred by some on grounds of parsimony, since a simple ban on subcategory-sensitive MATCH constraints provides an architecturally simpler means to deal with the Anti-Match problem, while vastly simplifying the repertoire of MATCH constraints and the resulting typology.

This hypothesis receives both potential support and tentative pushback from a survey of existing analyses using subcategory-sensitive MATCH constraints. The support comes from the fact that very few analyses have used SSCs: only sp.MATCH(XP$^{[+\text{max}]}$, $\varphi^{[+\text{max}]}$), sp.MATCH(XP$^{[+\text{max}]}$, $\varphi$), and sp.MATCH(XP$^{[-\text{min}]}$, $\varphi$) have been proposed, all in analyses of prosodic phrasing in Japanese (Ishihara 2014; Kalivoda 2018; Ito and Mester 2020; Bellik et al. 2022). Moreover, SSCs can sometimes be replaced by other more general constraints: for example, Ito and Mester's (2013) sp.MATCH(XP$^{[-\text{min}]}$, $\varphi$) was replaced in Ito and Mester (2020) with ps.MATCH($\varphi$, XP). We have also encountered anecdotal evidence that SSCs may sometimes be replaced. For example, an earlier version of Kalivoda and Bellik's (2021) analysis of Irish made use of sp.MATCH(XP$^{[-\text{min}]}$, $\varphi$), but this was later replaced by sp.MATCH(XP$_{\text{OvertlyHeaded}}$, $\varphi$) (Kalivoda and Bellik, p.c.). Additionally, Van Handel's (2021) analysis of Italian at one point included sp.MATCH(XP$_{\text{OH}}^{[+\text{max}]}$, $\varphi^{[+\text{max}]}$) but later replaced it with ps.MATCH($\varphi$, XP$_{\text{OH}}$).

However, the MATCH constraints sensitive to maximal XPs appear crucial in the analyses of Japanese (Ishihara 2014; Kalivoda 2018; Ito and Mester 2020; Bellik et al. 2022), which might suggest that we cannot entirely do away with SSCs. At the same time, Ishihara (2014) points out that sp.MATCH(XP$^{[+\text{max}]}$, $\varphi^{[+\text{max}]}$) is conceptually similar to and performs many of the same functions as WRAP(XP), which requires each XP to be contained in a $\varphi$ (Truckenbrodt 1999). A proponent of the No Subcategory-Sensitive Match Hypothesis could try to limit the set of mapping constraints to sp.MATCH(XP, $\varphi$), ps.MATCH($\varphi$, XP), and WRAP(XP). If some version of WRAP(XP) could replace sp.MATCH(XP$^{[+\text{max}]}$, $\varphi^{[+\text{max}]}$) in the analyses of Japanese, then the empirical motivation for the inclusion of subcategory-sensitive MATCH constraints would disappear, since no other analyses have needed them.

Still, it is certainly plausible that subcategory-sensitive MATCH constraints could prove useful in analyses of other languages, and additional empirical support may be found once more languages have been thoroughly analyzed within Match Theory. Indeed, evidence from a larger sample of languages shows that reference to prosodic subcategories is necessary for markedness constraints, as will be seen in the following section. It would therefore be premature to conclude that all subcategory-sensitive MATCH constraints should be eliminated from the theory based on the small sample. That is, even though SSCs may be replaced in some cases by more general constraints, and even though the only currently adopted constraints of this type could possibly be replaced by WRAP(XP), there is simply not enough typological coverage to confidently state that subcategory-sensitive MATCH constraints can always be replaced by other constraints. However, this possibility leads us to tentatively recommend that researchers consider alternative analyses before settling on SSCs, given the potential issues they introduce.

### 5.6.3 *Binary vs. privative features*

One final approach to the issue of SSCs deserves mention here, though it is not necessarily an extension of the Ban on Anti-Match Constraints. Specifically, one might propose that subcategory-sensitive MATCH constraints do exist in CON, but that they may only be defined in terms of privative features, not binary features. This approach would somewhat ameliorate the proliferation of MATCH constraints, since the features [max] and [min] would have two possible values (specified or unspecified), as opposed to the three possible values for binary features $(+, -,$ unspecified). Since there are four features (two for each argument), this means that there would be $2^4 = 16$ possible syntax-to-prosody constraints, instead of the $3^4 = 81$ constraints allowed with binary features. This number would be even smaller if specifications were limited to Specialized or Dominance-Preserving constraints.

This approach would eliminate the Anti-Match effects caused by conflicting feature values in constraints like sp.MATCH($XP^{[+max]}, \varphi^{[-max]}$), since privative features do not allow for conflicting values—features are either specified or unspecified. However, Anti-Match effects could still arise with privative features, because this system would still allow for constraints in which there is a feature specification on the second argument that is not also present on the first, e.g., sp.MATCH($XP^{[max]}, \varphi^{[min]}$), as in (38). If the constraint sp.MATCH($XP^{[max]}, \varphi^{[min]}$) were ranked over both sp.MATCH($XP, \varphi$) and ps.MATCH($\varphi, XP$), the flattened candidate (38b) would win: ignoring ZP allows the maximal YP to be mapped to a minimal $\varphi$. This means that we would still need the Ban on Anti-Match Constraints to prohibit specifications on the second argument that are not present on the first.

(38)    Privative features can still cause Anti-Match effects

| $[_{YP}\ y\ [_{ZP}\ z]]$ | sp.MATCH(XP, $\varphi$) | ps.MATCH($\varphi$, XP) | sp.MATCH(XP$^{[max]}$, $\varphi^{[min]}$) |
|---|---|---|---|
| $\rightarrow$ a. $(_1\ y\ (_2\ z))$ <br> Isomorphic | 0 | 0 | 1 <br> YP |
| b. $(_1\ y\ z)$ <br> Flattened | W$_1$ <br> ZP | e$_0$ | L$_0$ |

Independent difficulties arise with privative features. The primary issue is that there are numerous analyses that depend on the expressive power of binary features. For example, Elfner (2015) argues that LH accents in Connemara Irish appear at the left edge of non-minimal $\varphi$s, and Elordieta (2015) shows that the domain of pitch reset in Lekeitio Basque is also the non-minimal $\varphi$. In order to explain why these processes apply within the non-minimal $\varphi$, it is likely that the constraints involved in these cases would need to make reference to $\varphi^{[-min]}$, which is something that a privative feature system for prosodic subcategories would be unable to express. Additionally, Martínez-Paricio and Kager's (2015) account of ternary rhythm using recursive feet includes ALIGN constraints that reference non-minimal feet, which would likewise not be possible in a privative feature system. Finally, the survey of previous analyses in the table in (39) shows additional markedness constraints that crucially reference [–min] or [–max] features. Though constraints (39e-k) might be definable in terms of privative features, binary features are independently needed for at least some prosodic markedness constraints.

(39)      Survey of previous analyses using subcategory-sensitive markedness
          constraints

| Constraints | Language | Subcategory |
|---|---|---|
| a.  WordMaxAccent | Japanese (Ito and Mester 2021) | $\omega^{[+max, -min]}$ |
| b.  BinMaxHead($\omega^{[+max, -min]}$) | Japanese (Ito and Mester 2021) | $\omega^{[+max, -min]}$ |
| c.  EqualSisters2 | Japanese (Ito and Mester 2020) | Any category, [±min, ±max] |
| d.  Subcategory-sensitive StrongStart | Italian (Van Handel 2021) | Any category, [±min] |
| e.  BinMax($\varphi^{[+min]}$) | Japanese (Ito and Mester 2021) | $\varphi^{[+min]}$ |
| f.  NonFinality($\omega^{[+max]}$) | Chukchansi Yokuts (Guekguezian 2017) | $\omega^{[+max]}$ |
| g.  Onset-word-max | Non-rhotic varieties of English (Ito and Mester 2009) | $\omega^{[+max]}$ |
| h.  CrispEdge[+ATR, $\varphi^{[+max]}$] | Akan (Kügler 2015) | $\varphi^{[+max]}$ |
| i.  If-accented-then-head-of-$\varphi^{[+min]}$ | Tokyo Japanese, Northern Bizkaian Basque (Selkirk and Elordieta 2010) | $\varphi^{[+min]}$ |
| j.  IP-Initial-$\varphi$-Binarity | Northern Bizkaian Basque (Selkirk and Elordieta 2010) | $\varphi^{[+min]}$ |
| k.  AccentAsHead | Japanese (Ito and Mester 2013) | $\varphi^{[+min]}$ |

To uphold the privative feature hypothesis, one would have to posit that
Match constraints may only reference privative features, while markedness constraints may reference binary features, resulting in an unprincipled
distinction between classes of constraints in Con. This does not seem well
motivated, so we do not pursue this approach.

## 5.7   Conclusion

Over the past 15 years, research on recursive prosodic structure has delivered an impressive range of empirical results. As the status of recursive prosodic subcategories has come to the fore, however, a range of theoretical questions have arisen over their interaction with the broader architecture of Match Theory. In cases where general MATCH constraints do not straightforwardly yield correct results, researchers have proposed subcategory-sensitive constraints like sp.MATCH($XP^{[+max]}$, $\varphi^{[+max]}$) (Ishihara 2014) which make reference to these subcategories. While constraints of this type may ultimately play a role in the theory, their introduction raises a number of questions about the licit shapes of MATCH constraints. Left unchecked, the possibility for unconstrained subcategory specification leads to a proliferation of logically possible MATCH constraints, including MATCH constraints that motivate non-isomorphism between syntax and prosody. In this chapter, we have argued that the existence of such Anti-Match constraints is theoretically undesirable for two reasons: first, they undermine the impulse to simplify the mapping between syntax and prosody which has driven much of the work in Match Theory; and second, they complicate the task of integrating MATCH constraints into the theory of Faithfulness. As such, we propose that they must be ruled out by the Ban on Anti-Match Constraints. Whether the extensions discussed in §5.6 are also needed remains an empirical matter to be investigated in future work.

Before drawing this chapter to a close, we would like to highlight four points which have come up in the course of this investigation. The first of these points concerns the status of prosodic subcategories in the theory of prosodic structure at large. With much recent work, we take the notions of prosodic recursion and reference to prosodic subcategories to reflect theoretically legitimate and empirically productive extensions of the classical Prosodic Hierarchy Theory (Ito and Mester 2009, 2013; Elfner 2015; Bennett 2018; i.a.). We would therefore like to emphasize that this chapter is not meant as an argument against the use of prosodic subcategories in work on the syntax-prosody interface. Rather, we call for caution in extending the use of subcategories to MATCH constraints.

The second point involves the status of subcategory-sensitive MATCH constraints in the literature. Although these constraints have not been invoked with great frequency, the most compelling evidence for their existence involves the matching of maximal constituents (Ishihara 2014, Kalivoda 2018, Ito and Mester 2020). This may suggest that maximal XPs have a special status in the mapping from syntax to prosody, and this pattern deserves further investigation. At the same time, we have pointed out that it is sometimes possible to replace SSCs with more general constraints. In light of this fact and the issues of constraint proliferation and Anti-Match effects highlighted in this chapter, we tentatively advise researchers to pursue alternatives to SSCs when possible. Of course, further research may show that SSCs are a necessary component of the theory, but this is not clear at present.

The third point concerns the generality of the problem that we have addressed in this work. While we have focused on the effects of subcategory specifications on MATCH constraints, these issues are not restricted to Match Theory: subcategory-sensitive ALIGN constraints have also been proposed (Selkirk and Elordieta 2010, Martínez-Paricio and Kager 2015, Bennett et al. 2018). While a fuller discussion is outside the scope of this chapter, we note that the use of these constraints could potentially introduce some of the same issues with the SSCs discussed here. Subcategory-sensitive ALIGN constraints present the same problem of constraint proliferation, since each constraint contains two arguments, each of which may be specified for a subcategory, as well as the directionality of alignment. Additionally, they may give rise to undesirable predictions similar to Anti-Match effects. Given that the focus of this chapter is on the use of subcategories in MATCH constraints, we leave it to future research to determine whether any pathological predictions are made by the allowance of subcategory specification at the $\varphi$ level for ALIGN constraints.

The fourth and final point concerns the value of SPOT as a tool for carrying out the types of investigation which inform the theory in this way. To determine the particular feature specifications that do and do not give rise to Anti-Match effects, we considered 16 different OT systems, each with thousands of candidates. Such work would not have been feasible by hand, but is made possible by the automatic generation of candidates in SPOT. We expect SPOT to continue to be a useful resource, both for further investigation into SSCs—such as the different predictions made by Specialized versus Dominance-Preserving constraints—and, more broadly, for comparing different approaches to the syntax-prosody interface.

## References

Bellik, Jennifer, Bellik, Ozan, and Kalivoda, Nick (2015–2021). Syntax-Prosody in Optimality Theory (SPOT). Javascript application. http:// spot.sites.ucsc.edu. Codebase at https://github.com/syntax-prosody-ot.
Bellik, Jennifer, Ito, Junko, Kalivoda, Nick and Mester, Armin (2022). Matching and alignment. In Haruo Kubozono, Junko Ito, and Armin

Mester (eds.) *Prosody and Prosodic Interfaces* 457–481. Oxford University Press.

Bennett, Ryan (2012). Foot-conditioned Phonotactics and Prosodic Constituency. PhD dissertation, University of California, Santa Cruz.

Bennett, Ryan (2018). Recursive prosodic words in Kaqchikel (Mayan). *Glossa: A Journal of General Linguistics* 3: 67.

Bennett, Ryan, Harizanov, Boris, and Henderson, Robert (2018). Prosodic smothering in Macedonian and Kaqchikel. *Linguistic Inquiry* 49: 195–246.

Booij, Geert (1996). Cliticization as prosodic integration: the case of Dutch. *The Linguistic Review* 13: 219–242.

Chen, Matthew (1987). The syntax of Xiamen tone sandhi. *Phonology Yearbook* 4: 109–149.

Chomsky, Noam and Halle, Morris (1968). *The Sound Pattern of English.* New York: Harper & Row.

Clements, George N. (1978). Tone and syntax in Ewe. In Donna Jo Napoli (ed.) *Elements of Tone, Stress, and Intonation* 21–99. Washington, DC: Georgetown University Press.

Elfner, Emily (2012). *Syntax-Prosody Interactions in Irish.* PhD dissertation, University of Massachusetts Amherst.

Elfner, Emily (2015). Recursion in prosodic phrasing: evidence from Connemara Irish. *Natural Language and Linguistic Theory* 33: 1169–1208.

Elordieta, Gorka (2015). Recursive phonological phrasing in Basque. *Phonology* 32: 49–78.

Guekguezian, Peter Ara (2017). Templates as the interaction of recursive word structure and prosodic well-formedness. *Phonology* 34: 81–120.

Ishihara, Shinichiro (2014). Match theory and the recursivity problem. In Shigeto Kawahara and Mika Igarashi (eds.) *MIT Working Papers in Linguistics 73: Proceedings of Formal Approaches to Japanese linguistics 7* 69–88. Cambridge, MA.

Ito, Junko and Mester, Armin (2007). Prosodic adjunction in Japanese compounds. In Yoichi Miyamoto and Masao Ochi (eds.) *MIT Working Papers in Linguistics 55: Proceedings of Formal Approaches to Japanese Linguistics 4* 97–111. Cambridge, MA.

Ito, Junko and Mester, Armin (2009). The extended prosodic word. In Janet Grijzenhout and Barış Kabak (eds.) *Phonological Domains: Universals and Deviations* 135–194. Berlin: Mouton de Gruyter.

Ito, Junko and Mester, Armin (2012). Recursive prosodic phrasing in Japanese. In Toni Borowsky, Shigeto Kawahara, Takahito Shinya, and Mariko Sugahara (eds.) *Prosody Matters: Essays in Honor of Elisabeth Selkirk* 280–303. London: Equinox Publishing.

Ito, Junko and Mester, Armin (2013). Prosodic subcategories in Japanese. *Lingua* 124: 20–40

Ito, Junko and Mester, Armin (2019). Match as syntax-prosody Max/Dep: prosodic enclisis in English. *English Linguistics* 36: 1–28.

Ito, Junko, and Mester, Armin (2020). Match theory and prosodic wellformedness constraints. In Hongming Zhang and Youyong Qian (eds.)

*Prosodic Studies. Challenges and Prospects* 252–274. London and New York: Routledge.

Ito, Junko and Mester, Armin (2021). Recursive prosody and the prosodic form of compounds. *Languages* 6: 65.

Kager, René and Martínez-Paricio, Violeta (2018). The internally layered foot in Dutch. *Linguistics* 56: 69–114.

Kalivoda, Nick (2018). *Syntax-Prosody Mismatches in Optimality Theory.* PhD dissertation, University of California, Santa Cruz.

Kügler, Frank (2015). Phonological phrasing and ATR vowel harmony in Akan. *Phonology* 32: 177–204.

Ladd, D. Robert (1986). Intonational phrasing: the case for recursive prosodic structure. *Phonology Yearbook* 3: 311–340.

Lee, Seunghun and Selkirk, Elisabeth (2022). Xitsonga tone: The syntax-phonology interface. In Haruo Kubozono, Junko Ito, and Armin Mester (eds.) *Prosody and Prosodic Interfaces* 337-374. Oxford University Press.

Martínez-Paricio, Violeta and Kager, René (2015). The binary-to-ternary rhythmic continuum in stress typology: layered feet and non-intervention constraints. *Phonology* 32: 459–504.

Nespor, Marina and Vogel, Irene (1986). *Prosodic Phonology.* Dordrecht: Foris.

Peperkamp, Sharon (1997). *Prosodic Words.* The Hague: Holland Academic Graphics.

Prince, Alan, Merchant, Nazarré, and Tesar, Bruce (2007–2020). OTWorkplace. http://sites.google.com/site/otworkplace

Selkirk, Elisabeth (1986). On derived domains in sentence phonology. *Phonology Yearbook* 3: 371–405.

Selkirk, Elisabeth (2009). On clause and intonational phrase in Japanese: the syntactic grounding of prosodic constituent structure. *Gengo Kenkyu* 136: 35–73.

Selkirk, Elisabeth (2011). The syntax–phonology interface. In John A. Goldsmith, Jason Riggle, and Alan C. L. Yu (eds.) *The Handbook of Phonological Theory* 435–484. Blackwell Publishing.

Selkirk, Elisabeth and Elordieta, Gorka (2010). The role for prosodic markedness constraints in phonological phrase formation in two pitch accent languages. Presentation at Tone and Intonation in Europe 4, Stockholm University.

Truckenbrodt, Hubert (1999). On the relation between syntactic phrases and phonological phrases. *Linguistic Inquiry* 30: 219–255.

Van Handel, Nicholas (2021). Matching overtly headed syntactic phrases in Italian. *Phonology* 8: 317–356.

Vigário, Marina (1999). On the prosodic status of stressless function words in European Portuguese. In T. Alan Hall and Urula Kleinhenz (eds.) *Studies on the Phonological Word* 255–294. Amsterdam: John Benjamins.

Vigário, Marina (2003). *The Prosodic Word in European Portuguese.* Berlin: Mouton de Gruyter.

Wagner, Michael (2005). *Prosody and Recursion.* PhD dissertation, Massachusetts Institute of Technology.

## About the authors

*Nicholas Van Handel*

Graduate research assistant for the SPOT project, Ph.D. student, Department of Linguistics, UC  Santa Cruz. Research interests: Psycholinguistics and phonology, with a focus on implicit prosody, sentence processing, and the syntax-prosody interface. Recent publications: 'Matching overtly headed syntactic phrases in Italian" 2021, *Phonology.*

*Dan Brodkin*

Graduate research assistant for the SPOT project, Ph.D. student, Department of Linguistics, UC Santa Cruz. Research interests: Syntax, Ergativity, Prosodic Structure, and Phonological Displacement, with an empirical focus on Mandar (Austronesian, ISO: mdr). Recent publications: 'Perception Verb Complements in Mandar" 2022, *Syntax and Semantics at Santa Cruz V*; 'Ergative Anaphors and High Absolutive Syntax" 2022, *Proceedings of WCCFL 39*; 'Second Position and Prosodic Recursion" 2021, *Supplementary Proceedings of AMP 2020.*

*Ben Eischens*

Graduate research assistant for the SPOT project, Ph.D. student, Department of Linguistics, UC Santa Cruz. Research interests: Phonology and phonetics, with a focus on tone and laryngealization in San Martín Peras Mixtec (Otomanguean, ISO: jmx). Recent publications: 'Polar question formation in San Martín Peras Mixtec" 2021, *Proceedings of WSCLA 25*; 'Negative features in San Martín Peras Mixtec" 2020, *Proceedings of NELS 50*; 'Decomposing negative indefinites in San Martín Peras Mixtec" 2020, *Proceedings of WSCLA* 24.

## Appendix: Syntactic inputs for all systems

| # of terminal nodes | Syntactic inputs | |
|---|---|---|
| 2-word inputs (2 total) | {y z} | {[y z]} |
| 3-word inputs (2 total) | {w [y z]} | {[w [y z]]} |
| 4-word inputs (6 total) | {u [w [y z]]} | {u [[w y] z]} |
| | {[u w] [y z]} | {[u [w [y z]]]} |
| | {[u [[w y] z]]} | {[[u w] [y z]]} |
| 5-word inputs (14 total) | {s [u [w [y z]]]} | {s [u [[w y] z]]} |
| | {s [[u w] [y z]]} | {s [[u [w y]] z]} |
| | {s [[[u w] y] z]} | {[s u] [w [y z]]} |
| | {[s u] [[w y] z]} | {[s [u [w [y z]]]]} |
| | {[s [u [[w y] z]]]} | {[s [[u w] [y z]]]} |
| | {[s [[u [w y]] z]]} | {[s [[[u w] y] z]]} |
| | {[[s u] [w [y z]]]} | {[[s u] [[w y] z]]} |

# Chapter 6

# Visibility settings for Match Theory

Nicholas Van Handel[*]

## 6.1    Introduction

Match Theory (Selkirk 2011) calls for a close correspondence between syntactic and prosodic constituents: syntactic words ($X^0$) map onto prosodic words ($\omega$), syntactic phrases (XP) map onto phonological phrases ($\varphi$), and syntactic clauses map onto intonational phrases ($\iota$). The simplicity of the proposal hides the more complicated question of which syntactic constituents are "visible" to MATCH constraints. The answer to this question is essential in order to understand the predictions of Match Theory, yet there is debate at each level ($X^0$, XP, and clause). At the word level, Elfner (2012) assumes that only lexical words are visible to MATCH($X^0$, $\omega$), while Tyler (2019) argues that MATCH($X^0$, $\omega$) does not distinguish lexical and functional heads. At the clausal level, Selkirk (2011) discusses the possibility of two MATCH(Clause, $\iota$) constraints: a general constraint that attempts to match all clauses, and a more specific constraint that only matches clauses with illocutionary force. Several formulations have also been proposed at the phrasal level, and these proposals are the focus of this chapter.

In the original formulation of Match Theory, Selkirk (2011) suggests that MATCH(XP, $\varphi$) may distinguish lexical and functional projections, such that only lexical projections are visible to MATCH constraints, following much previous work (Selkirk and Shen 1990, Truckenbrodt 1999, i.a.). Selkirk and Lee

[*] I would like to thank Jenny Bellik, Dan Brodkin, Junko Ito, and Armin Mester for helpful feedback on previous versions of this chapter, as well as Ryan Bennett, Nick Kalivoda, and Amanda Rysling for discussion of the issues covered in this chapter.

(2017; Lee and Selkirk 2022) formalize this as $\text{MATCH}(\text{XP}_{\text{Lexical}}, \varphi)$, defined in (1).[1] $\text{MATCH}(\text{LexP}, \varphi)$ only requires XPs whose head is a word containing a lexical category root (N, V, or A) to be matched to $\varphi$s. Under this view, empty-headed phrases like VP are not visible to $\text{MATCH}(\text{LexP}, \varphi)$ once the verb has raised to a higher projection because their head no longer contains V (Elordieta and Selkirk 2022). This definition is similar to Truckenbrodt's (1999) Lexical Category Condition (LCC), which claims that the syntax–prosody mapping ignores both functional and empty-headed projections.

(1)      $\text{MATCH}(\text{XP}_{\text{Lexical}}, \varphi) = \text{MATCH}(\text{LexP}, \varphi)$: Assign one violation for each XP in the syntactic representation that is headed by a word containing a lexical category root (N, V, A) and that is not matched by a corresponding $\varphi$ in the phonological representation.

There is also a prosody-to-syntax constraint, $\text{MATCH}(\varphi, \text{XP}_{\text{Lexical}})$, which requires all $\varphi$ to be matched by a lexical projection. This constraint is defined in (2).

(2)      $\text{MATCH}(\varphi, \text{XP}_{\text{Lexical}}) = \text{MATCH}(\varphi, \text{LexP})$: Assign one violation for each $\varphi$ in the phonological representation that is not matched by a corresponding XP in the syntactic representation that is headed by a word containing a lexical category root (N, V, A).

In this chapter, I assume Elfner's (2012, 2015) definition of matching, which states that an XP and a $\varphi$ 'match' if the $\varphi$ dominates all and only the phonological exponents of the terminal nodes dominated by XP. An example of a prosodic output that satisfies both $\text{MATCH}(\text{LexP}, \varphi)$ and $\text{MATCH}(\varphi, \text{LexP})$ is provided in (3). (3a) shows a hypothetical syntax tree with functional and lexical projections; boxes surround the lexical projections. $\text{MATCH}(\text{LexP}, \varphi)$ will be satisfied by the structure in (3b), because the two lexical projections, WP and YP, are both matched in the prosody; failure to match WP and YP would have violated this constraint. The structure also satisfies $\text{MATCH}(\varphi, \text{LexP})$ because both $\varphi$ correspond to lexical XPs; building additional $\varphi$s corresponding to the functional projections, XP and ZP, would have violated this constraint.

---

[1] This definition deviates from Lee and Selkirk's in assuming that MATCH constraints regulate correspondence between a syntactic input and a prosodic output. In their system, MATCHPHRASELEX first maps the morphosyntax to a prosodic input, and the constraints $\text{MAX}(\varphi)$ and $\text{DEP}(\varphi)$ regulate the relationship between $\varphi$s in the phonological input and output. This is discussed in more detail in §4.1.1.

(3)      a.

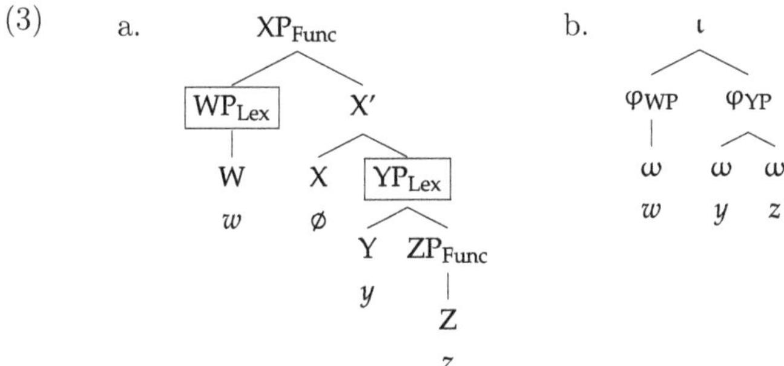

On the other end of the continuum, Elfner (2012, 2015) proposes that every syntactic XP that dominates a unique set of terminal nodes is visible to MATCH(XP, $\varphi$); I call this proposal "general matching" since it does not discriminate between different classes of XPs. The syntax-to-prosody and prosody-to-syntax constraints consistent with this proposal are defined in (4) and (5), respectively.

(4)      MATCH($\text{XP}_{\text{General}}$, $\varphi$) = MATCH(XP, $\varphi$): Assign one violation for each XP in the syntactic representation that is not matched by a corresponding $\varphi$ in the phonological representation.

(5)      MATCH($\varphi$, $\text{XP}_{\text{General}}$) = MATCH($\varphi$, XP): Assign one violation for each $\varphi$ in the phonological representation that is not matched by a corresponding XP in the syntactic representation

By eschewing the traditional distinction between functional and lexical projections, the general MATCH constraints demand an even tighter correspondence between syntax and prosody. The mapping that satisfies both MATCH(XP, $\varphi$) and MATCH($\varphi$, XP) is shown in (6): both lexical (WP, YP) and functional (XP, ZP) projections are matched to $\varphi$, and all $\varphi$ have an XP correspondent.

(6)    a.                                              b.

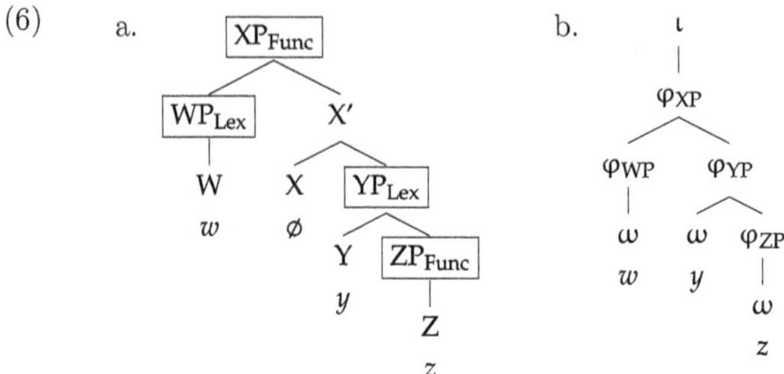

More recently, an alternative formulation has been proposed, according to
which only those XPs with overt heads are visible to MATCH constraints
(Kalivoda and Bellik 2021; Kalivoda, Chapter 4; Van Handel 2021). The cor-
responding constraints, MATCH(XP$_{\text{OvertlyHeaded}}$, $\varphi$) and MATCH($\varphi$, XP$_{\text{OvertlyHeaded}}$),
are defined in (7) and (8), respectively.

(7)    MATCH(XP$_{\text{OvertlyHeaded}}$, $\varphi$) = MATCH(OhP, $\varphi$): Assign one violation for
       each XP in the syntactic representation that has a phonologically
       overt head and that is not matched by a corresponding $\varphi$ in the
       phonological representation.

(8)    MATCH($\varphi$, XP$_{\text{OvertlyHeaded}}$) = MATCH($\varphi$, OhP): Assign one violation
       for each $\varphi$ in the phonological representation that is not matched
       by a corresponding XP in the syntactic representation that has a
       phonologically overt head.

MATCH(OhP, $\varphi$) stakes out an intermediate position: like MATCH(LexP, $\varphi$), it
does not require all XPs to be matched, but like MATCH(XP, $\varphi$), it does not
distinguish between functional and lexical projections. Put differently, this
version of MATCH recognizes that Truckenbrodt's (1999) LCC addresses two
related but separable issues: visibility of functional projections and visibility
of projections with silent heads. The mapping that satisfies both constraints
is shown in (9): MATCH(OhP, $\varphi$) is satisfied because all three overtly headed
phrases, WP, YP, and ZP, are matched to $\varphi$s, while MATCH($\varphi$, OhP) is satisfied because all $\varphi$s have overtly headed XP correspondents in the syntax.

(9)     a.

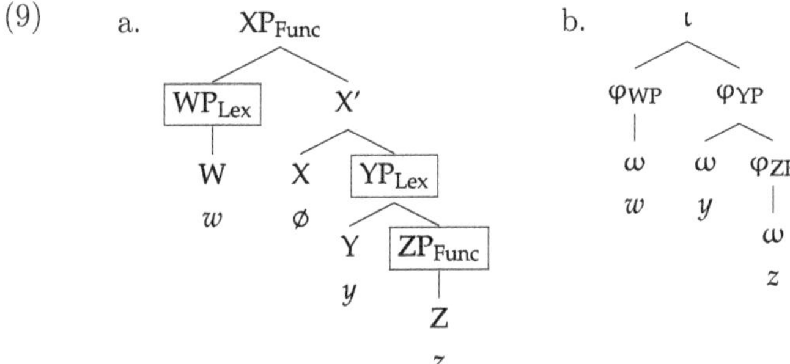

Establishing which syntactic constituents are visible to MATCH constraints is necessary in order to determine the full range of prosodic structures that Match Theory predicts to be possible cross-linguistically. This task requires comparing the predictions of each formulation both within and across languages. In this chapter, I provide such a comparison, focusing on data from Italian, Irish, and Xitsonga. I argue that MATCH(OhP, $\varphi$) usually can and sometimes must be used instead of MATCH(LexP, $\varphi$), raising the question of whether a lexical/functional distinction is needed.

The chapter is organized as follows. Section 6.2 reviews recent analyses of Italian and Irish that have employed MATCH(OhP, $\varphi$), and §6.3 presents a survey of visibility settings in various Match Theoretic analyses, showing that MATCH(OhP, $\varphi$) and MATCH(LexP, $\varphi$) are often interchangeable. Section 6.4 provides a reanalysis of Xitsonga, for which it has been claimed that MATCH(LexP, $\varphi$) is needed over MATCH(OhP, $\varphi$) (Lee and Selkirk 2022). This reanalysis shows that either visibility setting is compatible with the Xitsonga data, and so the data are not a decisive case against MATCH(OhP, $\varphi$). Section 6.5 considers potential objections to abandoning the lexical/functional distinction, and §6.6 concludes.

## 6.2    Matching overtly headed XPs

As described in the introduction, recent work has proposed a new type of MATCH constraint that attempts to match all overtly headed XPs but ignores any XPs with silent heads (Kalivoda and Bellik 2021, Kalivoda, Chapter 4, Van Handel 2021). In this section, I briefly review these analyses of Italian and Irish to show the empirical motivation behind this visibility setting.

### 6.2.1   Overtly headed XPs in Italian

Van Handel (2021) argues that MATCH(OhP, φ) is needed in Italian to avoid matching silently headed phrases (FP, VP) while ensuring that overtly headed functional phrases like quantifier phrases (QP) get matched. This section reviews two pieces of evidence showing that neither MATCH(LexP, φ) nor MATCH(XP, φ) is sufficient. The phrasings reported here are motivated by final lengthening and non-application of stress retraction (Nespor and Vogel 1986, Ghini 1993), which Van Handel argues are diagnostic of the right edge of maximal φ (a φ that is not dominated by any other φ).

In addition to MATCH(OhP, φ) and MATCH(φ, OhP), the analysis employs several markedness constraints. BINMIN(φ, ω) and BINMAX(φ, ω), defined in (10) and (11), penalize φs that contain less or more than two ω, respectively (Ghini 1993, Zec and Inkelas 1990, Bellik and Van Handel, Chapter 10). STRONGSTART, defined in (12), penalizes prosodic constituents whose leftmost daughter is lower on the prosodic hierarchy than the sister to its immediate right; this militates against structures like $(\omega_1 \ (\omega_2 \ \omega_3))$ in which $\omega_1$ is φ-initial and has a φ sister (Selkirk 2011, Elfner 2012, Bellik, Chapter 11).

(10)    LEAF-COUNTING MINIMAL BINARITY(φ, ω) = BINMIN(φ, ω): Assign one violation for each φ that does not contain at least two ω.

(11)    LEAF-COUNTING MAXIMAL BINARITY(φ, ω) = BINMAX(φ, ω): Assign one violation for each φ that contains more than two ω.

(12)    STRONGSTART: Assign a violation for every prosodic constituent whose leftmost daughter is lower on the prosodic hierarchy than the sister to its immediate right.

First, Van Handel argues that QP, which is overtly headed and functional, must be matched. In (13), a verb followed by a quantifier taking a DP complement will be parsed into its own maximal φ: lengthening of the verb *vaccinerò* indicates that the verb is phrased separately from the following QP (Ghini 1993). The syntax is given in (13a), the prosody is given in (13b), and an abstracted mapping in which each ω is replaced by its category label, i.e., V, Q, and N, is given in (13c). In all examples, the category labels are appended with "-f" for functional phrases and with "-s" for silently headed phrases, and parentheses indicate φ boundaries.

(13)

   a.   $[_{TP}$ vaccinerò $[_{QP\text{-}f}$ tutte $[_{DP}$ le scimmie $]]]$
       'I will vaccinate all the monkeys'

   b.   (vaccineròo) (tutte (le-sciimmie))

   c.   Abstracted mapping: $[_{TP}$ V $[_{QP\text{-}f}$ Q $[_{DP}$ N $]]] \rightarrow$ (V) (Q (N))

In (13), the head of TP is both overt and lexical, because the verb *vaccin-erò* has raised to T. DP is overtly headed because of the determiner *le*; Van Handel assumes that the determiner has procliticized onto the noun *scimmie*, forming a recursive ω, such that matching DP places *le-scimmie* in a φ.[2] Crucially, QP is overtly headed and functional because it is headed by the quantifier *tutte*. QP is therefore visible to MATCH(OhP, φ) and MATCH(φ, OhP) but not to the lexical-only MATCH constraints.

Based on the mapping in (13), Van Handel argues that QP must be visible to MATCH constraints to rule out a parse in which V and Q phrase together to the exclusion of N, i.e., (V Q) (N). The tableau in (14) shows that this parse, candidate (14b), performs better than or as well as the winning candidate (14a) on every constraint except MATCH(OhP, φ). MATCH(OhP, φ) favors candidate (14a) over (14b) because the former incurs only one violation for failing to match TP, while the latter fails to match both TP and QP. In contrast, MATCH(LexP, φ) cannot distinguish the two candidates because it does not care whether QP is matched. Thus, it is necessary for functional QP to be visible to MATCH(OhP, φ) in order to eliminate (14b). Additionally, the isomorphic candidate (14c) is ruled out by BINMAX(φ, ω), because the φ corresponding to TP contains three ωs. For reasons of space, category labels are omitted in all tableaux except where functional and/or silent status are indicated.

(14)    MATCH(OhP, φ), but not MATCH(LexP, φ), favors the desired winner

| $[V\ [_{QP\text{-}f}\ Q\ [N]]]$ | BMAX | M(OhP,φ) | SS | BMIN | M(φ,OhP) | M(LexP,φ) | M(φ,LexP) |
|---|---|---|---|---|---|---|---|
| →a.  (V) (Q (N)) | 0 | 1 | 1 | 2 | 1 | 1 | 2 |
| b.  (V Q) (N) | $e_0$ | $W_2$ | $L_0$ | $L_1$ | $e_1$ | $e_1$ | $L_1$ |
| c.  (V (Q (N))) | $W_1$ | $L_0$ | $W_2$ | $L_1$ | $L_0$ | $L_0$ | $L_1$ |

---

[2] Alternatively, an account using MATCH(LexP, φ) could assert that *le-scimmie* is parsed into a φ because the determiner has procliticized into the φ corresponding to NP. This is orthogonal to the main point of this example, which is that the overtly headed functional QP is matched.

While (14) shows that overtly headed functional phrases like QP need to be matched, subject-verb sequences provide evidence that silently headed XPs are not matched. In (15), both the subject and the verb undergo lengthening and stress retraction does not occur despite a potential clash (Ghini 1993), which indicates that they are in separate maximal $\varphi$s. In the syntax, the subject has raised to the specifier of a functional projection FP located above TP (Cardinaletti 2004, Frascarelli 2007, Dehé and Samek-Lodovici 2009). This FP has a silent functional head, while DP and TP are overtly headed.

(15)

    a.    $[_{\text{FP-f-s}}\ [_{\text{DP}}\ \text{la verità}]\ [_{\text{TP}}\ \text{vince}]]$
          'The truth wins'

    b.    (la-verit<u>àa</u>) (v<u>ii</u>nce)

    c.    Abstracted mapping: $[_{\text{FP-f-s}}\ [_{\text{DP}}\ \text{N}]\ [_{\text{TP}}\ \text{V}]] \rightarrow$ (N) (V)

As shown in (16), this phrasing requires the silently headed FP to be invisible to MATCH constraints. The desired winner (16a) only performs better than candidate (16b) on the prosody-to-syntax constraint MATCH($\varphi$, OhP), which penalizes (16b) for phrasing N and V together in a $\varphi$ that lacks an overtly headed XP correspondent. The general MATCH($\varphi$, XP) does not penalize (16b), because from its point of view this $\varphi$ is motivated by FP. Moreover, the syntax-to-prosody constraint MATCH(XP, $\varphi$) favors the losing candidate (16b) because it matches the silently headed FP. Van Handel concludes that both syntax-to-prosody and prosody-to-syntax MATCH constraints must only see overtly headed XPs in Italian: functional phrases like QP must be matched, while silently headed phrases like FP must not be.

(16)      MATCH($\varphi$, OhP), but not MATCH($\varphi$, XP), favors the desired winner

| $[_{\text{FP-f-s}}$ [N] [V]] | M(OhP,$\varphi$) | SS | BMIN | M($\varphi$,OhP) | M(XP,$\varphi$) | M($\varphi$,XP) |
|---|---|---|---|---|---|---|
| →a.   (N) (V) | 0 | 0 | 2 | 0 | 1 | 0 |
| b.   ((N) (V)) | $e_0$ | $e_0$ | $e_2$ | $W_1$ | $L_0$ | $e_0$ |

### 6.2.2   Overtly headed XPs in Irish

Kalivoda and Bellik (2021; Kalivoda, Chapter 4), henceforth K&B, also use MATCH(OhP, $\varphi$) in their analysis of Irish phrasing (Elfner 2012, 2015). The phrasings discussed in this section are diagnosed by the presence of LH phrase accents at the left edge of non-minimal $\varphi$ and HL phrase accents at the right edge of $\varphi$, as described in Elfner (2012, 2015).

K&B's primary concern is addressing a ranking paradox first noticed by Elfner (2012). In Irish, a four-word sentence with a branching subject and non-branching object (BrS), as in (17), is perfectly matched. The two arguments are phrased together to the exclusion of the verb, indicating that the silently headed TP is matched. However, a four-word sentence with a non-branching subject and a branching object (BrO), as in (18), has a mismatched prosody. The subject phrases with the verb rather than the object, so TP is not matched.

(17)    Branching subject, non-branching object (BrS):
   a.   $[_{\Sigma P}$ díofaidh $[_{\text{TP-f-s}}$ $[_{\text{FP}}$ rúnaí      dathúil]      blathanna]]
            sell.FUT             secretary handsome      flowers
         'A handsome secretary will sell flowers'
   b.   (díofaidh$^{\text{LH}}$ ((rúnaí$^{\text{LH}}$ dathúil$^{\text{HL}}$) blathanna$^{\text{HL}}$))
   c.   Abstracted mapping: $[_{\Sigma P}$ V $[_{\text{TP-f-s}}$ $[_{\text{FP}}$ S S] O]] → (V ((S S) O))

(18)    Non-branching subject, branching object (BrO):
   a.   $[_{\Sigma P}$ cheannaigh $[_{\text{TP-f-s}}$ múinteoirí $[_{\text{FP}}$ málaí bána ] ] ]
            bought               teachers        bags white
         'Teachers bought white bags'
   b.   ((cheannaigh$^{\text{LH}}$ múinteoirí$^{\text{HL}}$) (málaí bána$^{\text{HL}}$))
   c.   Abstracted mapping: $[_{\Sigma P}$ V $[_{\text{TP-f-s}}$ S $[_{\text{FP}}$ O O]]] → ((V S) (O O))

The paradox arises because these two mappings require opposite rankings of MATCH(XP, φ) and STRONGSTART. The elementary ranking conditions (ERCs) in (19) show that the matching parse for BrS requires MATCH(XP, φ) to be ranked over STRONGSTART: the winner matches TP and the subject FP, but violates STRONGSTART because V is φ-initial and sister to a φ.

However, the mismatched parse for BrO requires the opposite ranking: the winner satisfies STRONGSTART but fails to match TP. K&B conceptualize the problem as follows: BrS shows that matching FP is more important than satisfying STRONGSTART, while BrO shows that satisfying STRONGSTART takes priority over matching TP. They conclude that a constraint that prioritizes matching FP is needed. MATCH(OhP, φ), which ignores silently headed TP but sees overtly headed FP, is such a constraint.

(19)    Ranking paradox in Irish

| Input | | Winner | Loser | SS | M(XP,$\varphi$) |
|---|---|---|---|---|---|
| BrS | [V [$_{\text{TP-s}}$ [S S] O]] | (V ((S S) O)) | (((V S) S) O) ((V S) (S O)) | L | W |
| BrO | [V [$_{\text{TP-s}}$ S [O O]]] | ((V S) (O O)) | (V (S (O O))) | W | L |

K&B resolve the paradox by introducing MATCH(OhP, $\varphi$) into CON. The ERCs in (20) show that MATCH(OhP, $\varphi$) will favor the correct winner for BrS when ranked over STRONGSTART, because the winner matches the subject FP. Unlike MATCH(XP, $\varphi$), MATCH(OhP, $\varphi$) ignores TP and does not penalize the desired winner for BrO. This allows MATCH(OhP, $\varphi$) to be ranked over STRONGSTART for BrS without affecting the phrasing of BrO. Then, STRONGSTART can be ranked above MATCH(XP, $\varphi$) as needed to derive the phrasing of BrO.

(20)    Adding MATCH(OhP, $\varphi$) solves the ranking paradox

| Input | | Winner | Loser | M(OhP,$\varphi$) | SS | M(XP,$\varphi$) |
|---|---|---|---|---|---|---|
| BrS | [V [$_{\text{TP-s}}$ [S S] O]] | (V ((S S) O)) | (((V S) S) O) ((V S) (S O)) | W | L | W |
| BrO | [V [$_{\text{TP-s}}$ S [O O]]] | ((V S) (O O)) | (V (S (O O))) | e | W | L |

The idea that CON could contain multiple MATCH constraints with different visibility settings in a single language is novel, and the analysis shows yet another use for MATCH(OhP, $\varphi$): prioritizing a subset of XPs when a markedness constraint ranked over MATCH(XP, $\varphi$) prevents perfect matching. However, it should be noted that this use is not specific to MATCH(OhP, $\varphi$): MATCH(LexP, $\varphi$) also targets a subset of XPs and could achieve a similar effect. In fact, MATCH(LexP, $\varphi$) would be compatible with K&B's analysis. The FP targeted by MATCH(OhP, $\varphi$) is overtly headed because N has adjoined to its head, but the raising of N to F also makes FP lexical under Lee and Selkirk's (to appear) definition of lexical matching, which I employ throughout this chapter. Under this view, the analysis does not provide evidence to decide between MATCH(OhP, $\varphi$) and MATCH(LexP, $\varphi$), although it does establish that both MATCH(XP, $\varphi$) and a second MATCH constraint are needed.[3]

---

[3] Nick Kalivoda (p.c.) suspects that additional data from the phrasing of overtly headed functional phrases (e.g., PP, CP, QP) may provide support for MATCH(OhP, $\varphi$), but this is

*6.2.3   Interim summary*

The Italian and Irish analyses demonstrate the different uses of Match(OhP, φ): ignoring silently headed XPs without ruling out all functional phrases, and targeting a subset of XPs with specialized Match constraints. Moreover, both Kalivoda and Bellik (2021) and Van Handel (2021) point out that Truckenbrodt's (1999) Lexical Category Condition combines two distinctions, the lexical/functional (Lex/Func) and the silently/overtly headed (SH/OH) distinction. They ask whether both distinctions are needed, or if Match(OhP, φ) could also be used in analyses employing Match(LexP, φ). To address this question, the next section surveys the use of visibility settings in previous Match Theoretic analyses.


## 6.3   Cross-linguistic survey

To determine whether previous analyses employing Match(LexP, φ) are also compatible with Match(OhP, φ), a survey of previous work was conducted. Since the focus of this chapter is on different definitions of Match constraints, the survey was limited to papers that adopted Match Theory, provided an OT analysis, and made a specific claim about visibility settings for Match. The findings of this survey are summarized in (21). This table indicates the visibility settings employed in each paper, the desired effect of the visibility settings (e.g., matching or ignoring certain XPs), and whether each of the three different visibility settings would be compatible with the desired effect, indicated with a checkmark.

Throughout the discussion, I use Match(XP), Match(OhP), and Match(LexP) as blanket terms for the three visibility settings rather than referring to specific constraints, because some analyses do not employ both syntax-to-prosody and prosody-to-syntax constraints. Additionally, Ito and Mester (2019) use the constraints Max(φ) and Dep(φ) instead of Match(XP, φ) and Match(φ, XP), though these constraints still regulate the correspondence between XPs in the input and φs in the output. Similarly, Elordieta and Selkirk (2022) and Lee and Selkirk (2022) adopt a version of Match Theory in which the morphosyntax is mapped to a prosodic input, and the constraints Max(φ) and Dep(φ) enforce correspondence between φs in the input and output. These differences do not affect the conclusions about visibility settings.

---

an area for future work.

(21)     Survey of visibility settings in previous Match Theoretic analyses

| Language | Source Visibility Settings | Desired effect | M(XP) | M(OhP) | M(LexP) |
|---|---|---|---|---|---|
| a. Akan (Kügler 2015) | Match(LexP) | Ignore: $vP_{SH,Func}$ $TP_{SH,Func}$ | - | ✓ | ✓ |
| b. Basque (Elordieta and Selkirk, to appear) | Match(LexP) | Ignore: $PredP_{SH,Func}$ $vP_{SH,Func}$ $VP_{SH,Func}$ [4] $FinP_{SH,Func}$ | - | ✓ | ✓ |
| c. English (Ito and Mester 2019) | Match(XP) | Match: $TP_{OH,Func}$ $DP_{OH,Func}$ $PP_{OH,Func}$ | ✓ | ✓ | - |
| d. Irish (Elfner 2012, 2015) | Match(XP) | Match: $CP_{OH,Func}$ $TP_{SH,Func}$ $VP_{SH,Func}$ | ✓ | - | - |
| e. Irish (Kalivoda and Bellik 2021; Kalivoda, Chapter 4) | Match(XP) Match(OhP) | Prioritize matching: $FP_{OH,Lex}$ over: $TP_{SH,Func}$ | ✓ with M(OhP) or M(LexP) | ✓ with M(XP) | ✓ with M(XP) |
| f. Italian (Van Handel 2021) | Match(OhP) | Match: $QP_{OH,Func}$ Ignore: $VP_{SH,Func}$ $FP_{SH,Func}$ | - | ✓ | - |
| g. Japanese, Chicheŵa (Ishihara 2014) | Match(LexP) | Ignore: $TP_{SH,Func}$ | - | ✓ | ✓ |

---

[4] VP is labeled as functional in this table when its head is occupied by a trace; as described earlier, VP would not be visible under Lee and Selkirk's definition of Match(LexP, $\varphi$) because its head no longer contains V.

| Language | Source Visibility Settings | Desired effect | M(XP) | M(OhP) | M(LexP) |
|---|---|---|---|---|---|
| h. Kinyambo (Bellik and Kalivoda 2016) | Match(XP) | Match: $TP_{SH,Func}$ $vP_{SH,Func}$ | ✓ | - | - |
| i. Norwegian (Brinkerhoff and Tengesdal 2021) | Match(LexP) | Ignore: $DP_{OH,Func}$ $vP_{SH,Func}$ | - | - | ✓ |
| j. Various (Kalivoda 2018) | Match(LexP) | Ignore: $VP_{SH,Func}$ $TP_{SH,Func}$ | - | ✓ | ✓ |
| k. Xitsonga (Selkirk and Lee 2017; Lee and Selkirk, to appear) | Match(LexP) | Ignore: $applP_{SH,Func}$ $clP_{OH,Func}$ | - | - | ✓ |

Before discussing the findings of the survey, some caveats are necessary. The checkmark in each column only indicates that the corresponding visibility settings would be capable of achieving the desired effect of rendering the listed XPs (in)visible. However, the absence of a checkmark does *not* indicate that an analysis using alternative visibility settings would be impossible. Though it may be true that certain XPs need to be matched or ignored, it could be that markedness constraints, not visibility settings, are responsible for this effect.

As an example, Ishihara (2014) and Kügler (2015) use lexical-only Match constraints to ensure that an empty-headed TP is not matched to φ, such that a subject NP and a VP phrase separately. However, this can also be achieved with the general visibility settings if Match(XP, φ) is ranked below a constraint like BinMin(ι), defined in (22), which penalizes ι that only dominate a single constituent. This is shown in (23): BinMin(ι) rules out the candidate in which TP is matched.

(22)    Branch-counting Minimal Binarity(ι) = BinMin(ι): Assign one
        violation for each ι with less than two branches (immediate children,
        of any category).

(23)    BɪɴMɪɴ($\iota$) can prevent TP from being matched

| [$_{\text{TP-f-s}}$ [$_{\text{NP}}$ N] [$_{\text{VP}}$ V [$_{\text{NP}}$ N ]]] | BɪɴMɪɴ($\iota$) | Mᴀᴛᴄʜ(XP, $\varphi$) |
|---|---|---|
| →     a.     (N) (V (N)) | 0 | 1 |
|     b.     ((N) (V (N))) | W$_1$ | L$_0$ |

My intention with the preceding example is not to suggest that the analyses using Mᴀᴛᴄʜ(LexP, $\varphi$) are incorrect—indeed, BɪɴMɪɴ($\iota$) by itself would be insufficient to account for the full range of structures considered in these analyses. Rather, I point out that augmenting Cᴏɴ with additional markedness constraints is always an available strategy to prevent certain XPs from being matched, which is why alternative analyses using those visibility settings that lack a checkmark in (21) may still be possible.

Another concern is that some analyses might not have considered all possible candidates, which could affect the validity of their conclusions (Karttunen 2006; Bane and Riggle 2012; Kalivoda 2018; Bellik et al. 2022); as discussed in Bellik et al. (Chapter 1), this risk is prevalent in Match Theoretic analyses, where typical assumptions about Gᴇɴ quickly lead to hundreds and thousands of candidates for a single input. The results of this survey should be interpreted with caution, but it is still useful to see why different visibility settings have been proposed in the literature.

Of the eleven analyses surveyed, three use Mᴀᴛᴄʜ(XP), six use Mᴀᴛᴄʜ(LexP), one uses Mᴀᴛᴄʜ(OhP), and one uses both Mᴀᴛᴄʜ(XP) and Mᴀᴛᴄʜ(OhP). The two analyses employing Mᴀᴛᴄʜ(OhP) were already reviewed in §6.2. Van Handel's (2021) account requires Mᴀᴛᴄʜ(OhP) because only silently headed phrases fail to map to $\varphi$ in Italian. Kalivoda and Bellik's (2021) analysis of Irish employs both Mᴀᴛᴄʜ(XP, $\varphi$) and Mᴀᴛᴄʜ(OhP, $\varphi$); the latter is needed to prioritize matching the overtly headed FP. As already noted, N has raised to the head of FP in their analysis; FP is therefore lexical, so either Mᴀᴛᴄʜ(OhP, $\varphi$) or Mᴀᴛᴄʜ(LexP, $\varphi$) could account for the data.

Of the three analyses employing Mᴀᴛᴄʜ(XP), Elfner's (2012, 2015) analysis of Irish requires the general visibility setting because silently headed TP and VP must be matched; however, as described above, Kalivoda and Bellik (2021) argue that both Mᴀᴛᴄʜ(XP, $\varphi$) and Mᴀᴛᴄʜ(OhP, $\varphi$) are needed in this language to solve a ranking paradox. Ito and Mester's (2019) analysis of English would be compatible with Mᴀᴛᴄʜ(OhP, $\varphi$) instead of Mᴀᴛᴄʜ(XP, $\varphi$), because all of the functional phrases that need to be matched also have overt heads. The remaining analysis, Bellik and Kalivoda's (2016) investigation of Kinyambo phrasing, requires Mᴀᴛᴄʜ(XP) in order to render silently headed TP and $v$P visible to Mᴀᴛᴄʜ. However, it is unclear whether this is necessary to capture Kinyambo phrasing: their use of MATCH(XP) was a simplifying assumption based on Elfner (2012) that allowed them to hold visibility settings constant while varying other parameters of CON.

Of the six analyses employing MATCH(LexP), four were also compatible with MATCH(OhP), because they only needed to render silently headed XPs invisible. The other two analyses, Brinkerhoff and Tengesdal's (2021) analysis of Norwegian and Lee and Selkirk's (2022) analysis of Xitsonga, appear to need MATCH(LexP) because both silently and overtly headed functional phrases lack φ correspondents. However, both analyses have potential alternative analyses: failure to match an XP is not necessarily due to visibility settings. I briefly discuss Norwegian here and provide a more detailed discussion of Xitsonga in §6.4.

In Brinkerhoff and Tengesdal's (2021) analysis of Norwegian, MATCH(LexP) renders overtly headed functional DPs (pronouns) and silently headed $v$P invisible to the MATCH constraints. However, their account assumes a highly ranked HEADEDNESS constraint, which requires each φ to dominate an ω. This constraint penalizes candidates in which the pronominal DPs are matched, because the pronouns are not full prosodic words. Because highly ranked HEADEDNESS already prevents pronominal DPs from being mapped to φs, it is not necessary to make these DPs invisible to the MATCH constraints. In contrast, it appears crucial that MATCH ignores silently headed $v$P in their analysis. Thus, this is a case where either MATCH(LexP) or MATCH(OhP) could account for the data, because a markedness constraint could be responsible for the failure to match overtly headed functional phrases.[5]

Though the sample size of the survey is small, some languages require MATCH(XP), while others require more restrictive visibility settings. It appears that MATCH(LexP) is the most frequently used visibility setting, and it is most often used to render empty-headed phrases invisible. This suggests that MATCH(OhP) may be able to supplant the Lex/Func distinction, since it also ignores these phrases. However, Lee and Selkirk (2022) claim that the classifier phrase, an overtly headed functional phrase, must be invisible in Xitsonga, and explicitly argue against MATCH(OhP) based on this data point. In §6.4, I test the validity of this argument by building three systems

---

[5] Brinkerhoff and Tengesdal (2021) also assume that phrasal MATCH constraints ignore CP, because CP should instead correspond to ι. However, the verb has raised to C in the structures they consider, and we might expect CP to be visible to all versions of MATCH(XP, φ) because it has a phonologically overt lexical head. Under this alternative view, a markedness constraint such as BINMIN(ι) would be needed to prevent CP from being mapped to a φ. Whether CPs are visible to MATCH(XP, φ) when their head is occupied by a lexical verb is an open question for future work.

in SPOT, testing whether each visibility setting can capture the phrasing data in Xitsonga.

## 6.4    Case study: Xitsonga

In their analysis of Xitsonga, Lee and Selkirk (2022), henceforth L&S, explicitly argue against MATCH(OhP) based on phrasing data showing that the classifier phrase (clP) is not mapped to a φ. This is a potential test case for differentiating MATCH(LexP) and MATCH(OhP): being both functional and overtly headed, clP will be invisible to the former but not the latter. However, L&S do not provide a tableau showing that the wrong output would be chosen if the classifier were visible to MATCH constraints. Moreover, as discussed in the previous section, markedness constraints can prevent an XP from having a corresponding φ in the output, even if that XP is visible to MATCH constraints, so the absence of a φ corresponding to clP does not necessarily mean that clP is invisible.

Three OT systems were created to determine whether each of the three visibility settings, MATCH(OhP), MATCH(LexP), and MATCH(XP), could capture the data in Xitsonga. The GEN, CON, and factorial typologies of each system are presented in the following sections. For each system, candidates were generated and violations were assigned in SPOT (Bellik et al. 2015–2021), and the factorial typology was calculated in OTWorkplace (Prince et al. 2007–2020).

To preview the findings, both MATCH(OhP) and MATCH(LexP) are shown to be compatible with Xitsonga, while MATCH(XP) is not. The findings about MATCH(LexP) and MATCH(XP) validate L&S's analysis, although the finding about MATCH(OhP) challenges one of their conclusions and shows that these data do not distinguish between these two visibility settings. Though the main points of their analysis are confirmed, the MATCH(LexP) system also reveals that the constraint ranking required for Xitsonga is slightly different from the ranking in their paper, underlining the importance of considering all candidates.

### 6.4.1    GEN

#### 6.4.1.1    Inputs

The input syntactic structures were the four structures used by L&S to motivate the ranking of MATCH and prosodic markedness constraints in Xitsonga. These structures are provided in (24–27); the full syntax is in the (a) examples, an abstracted syntax in which words are replaced by category labels is in the (b) examples, and the phrasing posited by L&S is in the (c) examples. They diagnose φ structure on the basis of High Tone Spread: H tone spreads rightward to the penultimate syllable of a φ and is blocked at left φ edges. Since the focus of this chapter is determining which definition(s) of MATCH can derive the correct phrasings, I adopt L&S's input and output structures wholesale. The reader is referred to their paper for details of the syntactic analysis and their account of the distribution of High Tone Spread.

The first two structures in (24) and (25) involve a verb followed by an NP object containing one and two words, respectively. As shown in the contrast between (24c) and (25c), the verb phrases with a following noun when the NP consists of a single word, but the NP is contained in its own φ when it consists of two words.

(24)    Verb + unary object
  a.    Full syntax: $[_{VP} [_V$ ni $[_V$ lava]] $[_{NP} [_N$ nguluve]]]
                    1sg-want-FV        pig
                    'I want a pig'
  b.    Abstracted syntax: $[_{VP}$ V $[_{NP}$ N]]
  c.    Phrasing: (V N)

(25)    Verb + binary object
  a.    Full syntax: $[_{VP} [_V$ hi $[_V$ lava]] $[_{NP} [_N$ hlambeto] $[_{AP} [_A$ yi ntsongo]]]]
                    1pl-want-FV      cooking.pot      cl9-small
                    'We want a small cooking pot'
  b.    Abstracted syntax: $[_{VP}$ V $[_{NP}$ N $[_{AP}$ A]]]
  c.    Phrasing: (V (N A))

The next structure is the double object construction in (26). As described by L&S, the verb in (26) undergoes head movement from VP to applP and through a series of functional heads (indicated by the ellipsis) before ending up at the head of the extended verbal projection, leaving the two NP objects behind in a functional, empty-headed applP.[6]

---

[6] In the prosodic input for the double object construction, L&S show that the classifier *ti* and the noun stem *nguvu* are placed in an ω and a φ together, e.g., $(_\varphi [_\omega$ *tinguvu*]), which implies that the classifier is inside N2 and NP2 with the noun stem. Additionally, their abstract syntactic structure only shows a NP for the second object. However, this seems at odds with their analysis that noun classifiers are introduced in a class marker phrase (clP) outside of NP, as in (27); in their analysis, the position of the classifier outside of NP is necessary to explain why the classifier encliticizes to the verb in (27). If the classifier is actually outside of NP2 in (26), then it is not clear why we do not also find encliticization of the classifier to the preceding N1 in the double object construction. Right-edge alignment might provide an answer: perhaps the classifier cannot encliticize into (V N1) because the right φ boundary is aligned with the right edge of NP. The alternative parse with encliticization, (V N1+Cl),

(26)     Double object construction
   a.    Full syntax:
         $[_{VP}$ $[_V$ va xavela] ... $[_{applP}$ $[_{NP}$ $[_N$ munhu ]] $[t_{i,j}$ $[_{VP}$ $t_i$ $[_{NP}$ $[_N$ ti nguvu ]]]]]]
         3pl-buy-appl                        someone                          cl10-cloth
         'They are buying clothes for someone'
   b.    Abstracted syntax: $[_{VP}$ V $[_{applP\text{-}f\text{-}s}$ $[_{NP1}$ N1] $[_{NP2}$ N2]]]
   c.    Phrasing: ((V N1) N2)

The double object construction is of particular interest for the question
of visibility settings, because the applP dominating the two NPs does not
correspond to a φ in (26c). L&S argue that MATCH(LexP, φ) is necessary to
derive this phrasing because MATCH(LexP, φ), unlike MATCH(XP, φ), ignores
functional phrases like applP. Another possibility is that applP is invisible
to MATCH(OhP, φ) because it has a silent head.

The final structure in (27) shows that a noun class marker phrases separately from a following NP containing a noun and a modifier. L&S analyze
the noun classifier as the head of a functional class marker phrase, clP, but
remain agnostic about the internal structure of the modifier phrase following
the noun, although they assume that it maps to a φ in the prosodic input.
For clarity, I use the labels 'ModP and 'Mod" for the phrase and word, respectively. Finally, the classifier is labeled "Cl-clitic" to indicate that it will
map to a syllable rather than an ω, unlike the other input words.

(27)     Noun class marker + multi-word NP
   a.    Full syntax: $[_{VP}$ $[_V$ ni languta] $[_{clP}$ mu $[_{NP}$ $[_N$ lungu] $[_{ModP}$ lo-nkulu]]]]
         1sg-look.at        cl1         European   cl1 big
         'I look at a big European'
   b.    Abstracted syntax: $[_{VP}$ V $[_{clP\text{-}f}$ Cl-clitic $[_{NP}$ N $[_{ModP}$ Mod ]]]]
   c.    Phrasing: (V+Cl (N Mod))

The structure in (27) is also relevant for the question of visibility settings: clP
is functional but has an overt head, so it should be visible to MATCH(OhP),
but not to MATCH(LexP). As (27c) shows, clP is not matched; instead, the
class marker encliticizes onto the preceding verb (indicated with the "+"

----

would prevent alignment and perform worse on ALIGNR(XP, φ). Pursuing such an analysis is
outside the scope of this chapter. Since the aim here is to determine which visibility settings
are compatible with L&S's analysis, and the crucial point of this example is that the applP
containing both objects is not matched, I set aside the potential issue with the classifier and
adopt their syntactic structure, [V [[N1] [N2]]].

sign). L&S contend that the absence of a φ corresponding to clP is evidence for Match(LexP) over Match(OhP).

It should be mentioned that L&S employ a modular version of Match Theory in which MatchPhrase is a spell-out constraint that first maps the morphosyntax onto a prosodic structure that acts as the input to phonology. The inputs to phonology are therefore prosodic trees that are isomorphic to the syntactic trees, with the exception that any XPs invisible to the version of MatchPhrase being used are not mapped to φ in the input. For instance, MatchPhraseLex ignores functional XPs, so only φs corresponding to LexPs are present in the input to phonology. Faithfulness constraints Max(φ) and Dep(φ) replace Match(XP, φ) and Match(φ, XP), respectively, and regulate the relationship between the phonological input and output. For ease of exposition, I continue to use the more traditional theory in which Match constraints directly regulate the relationship between the syntactic input and the prosodic output; this is not a statement on the relative merit of the two architectures.[7]

### 6.4.1.2 Outputs

Specifying Gen also requires defining the output prosodic trees. To ensure comparability with L&S's analysis, the prosodic tree outputs had the same properties as the candidates in their tableaux, as outlined in (28).

(28)    Outputs: all prosodic trees with the following properties:
    a.    The root node is ι.
    b.    The intermediate nodes are φ.
    c.    The terminal nodes are ω or σ.
    d.    All children of ι are φ.
    e.    All children of φ are either ω or σ.
    f.    φ can dominate other φ, i.e., φ-recursion is permitted.
    g.    No φ dominates a φ with the same terminal nodes, i.e., vacuous recursion is prohibited.
    h.    The linear order of terminal nodes in the output is identical to the order in the input, i.e., movement is prohibited.
    i.    The terminal nodes in the output are identical to the terminal nodes in the input, i.e., the prosodic trees involve all parses of the string

---

[7] The architecture does not affect the outcome of the results, and the presentation here can be translated into L&S's terms in the following way: (i) input syntactic trees are replaced by prosodic trees, and XPs only have a φ correspondent in these inputs if they are visible to whichever version of Match is being used, (ii) Match(XP, φ) is replaced by Max(φ), and (iii) Match(φ, XP) is replaced by Dep(φ).

of terminals in the syntactic input, with one exception, described below.

There is one exception to the properties in (28). For the structure in (27) involving class markers, L&S consider candidates in which the classifier remains a stray clitic as well as candidates in which it encliticizes into the preceding word.[8] For this reason, the output trees for the input in (27) deviate from property (28i) by including all prosodic parses of the input string, i.e., <V Cl-clitic N Mod>, as well as all parses of the string in which the classifier forms an ω with V, i.e., <V+Cl N Mod>; these prosodic parses still conform to the properties in (28a-h).

### 6.4.2. Con

The Con of each system was based on the four constraints used by L&S. First, there were two mapping constraints, Match(XP, φ) and Match(φ, XP), which correspond to L&S's Max(φ) and Dep(φ). A different version of the Match constraints was used for each system, and there was one system for each visibility setting: System.OvertHeads (S.OvertHeads), System. Lexical (S.Lexical), and System.General (S.General). There were also two prosodic markedness constraints. Binarity(φ) requires φ to immediately dominate two constituents, and StrongStart penalizes φ whose leftmost daughter is lower on the prosodic hierarchy than the sister to its immediate right. The Con for S.OvertHeads, S.Lexical, and S.General are provided in (29), (30), and (31).

(29)    Con for S.OvertHeads:
   a.    Match(OhP, φ)
   b.    Match(φ, OhP)
   c.    Branch-counting Binarity(φ) = BinBr(φ): Assign a violation for every node of category φ with more than two branches (immediate children, of any category).
   d.    StrongStart: Assign a violation for every node of category φ whose leftmost daughter is lower on the prosodic hierarchy than the sister to its immediate right.

---

[8] L&S do not consider candidates in which the clitic procliticizes onto the following noun, i.e., [ω [ω Cl] [ω N]]. Systems in which procliticization candidates are included show the same pattern of results (i.e., the Match(OhP) and Match(LexP) systems generate Xitsonga, but the Match(XP) system does not), provided that StrongStart is also defined to penalize weak starts within ω. Only the systems without procliticization candidates are reported here, for reasons of space and comparability with L&S's analysis.

(30)    CON for S.Lexical:
   a.    MATCH(LexP, φ)
   b.    MATCH(φ, LexP)
   c.    BINBR(φ)
   d.    STRONGSTART

(31)    CON for S.General:
   a.    MATCH(XP, φ)
   b.    MATCH(φ, XP)
   c.    BINBR(φ)
   d.    STRONGSTART

### *6.4.3   S.OvertHeads*

#### *6.4.3.1   Factorial typology*

We first examine S.OvertHeads, whose factorial typology is presented in
(32). Though all syntactic trees were rooted in CP, and all prosodic trees
in ι, I omit curly braces from the representations because ι structure is not
relevant. The classifier 'Cl' has a subscript 'σ' whenever it stands alone
by itself (as opposed to encliticizing into the preceding V). The factorial
typology contains 11 languages, one of which (L.7) is compatible with
Xitsonga. Phrasings compatible with Xitsonga have a white background[9],
incompatible phrasings that have a φ corresponding to applP or clP have
a dark grey background, and all other incompatible phrasings have a light
grey background.

---

[9] For the input with the class marker, Lee and Selkirk note that there is no phonological
evidence to determine whether the class marker is stray or an enclitic, but the candidate with
an enclitic wins in their analysis because it satisfies BINBR(φ). The candidate with an enclitic
is also the optimum in the Xitsonga-compatible languages in S.OvertHeads and S.Lexical.
However, a white background is also used for the candidate with a stray classifier that is
compatible with the data, i.e., (V Cl$_\sigma$ (N Mod)).

(32)      Factorial typology of S.OvertHeads

| | [V [N]] | [V [N [A]]] | [V [$_{\text{applP-f-s}}$ [N1] [N2]]] | [V [$_{\text{clP-f}}$ Cl-clitic [N [Mod]] |
|---|---|---|---|---|
| L.1 | (V N) | (V N A) | (V N1 N2) | (V Cl$_\sigma$ (N Mod)) |
| L.2 | (V N) | ((V N) A) | ((V N1) N2) | ((V Cl$_\sigma$)(N Mod)) |
| L.3 | (V N) | (V N (A)) | (V N1 (N2)) | (V Cl$_\sigma$ (N Mod)) |
| L.4 | (V N) | (V (N A)) | (V N1 N2) | (V (Cl$_\sigma$ (N Mod)) |
| L.5 | (V N) | (V (N A)) | ((V N1) N2) | (V (Cl$_\sigma$ (N Mod)) |
| L.6 | (V N) | (V (N A)) | (V N1 N2) | (V+Cl (N Mod)) |
| L.7 | (V N) | (V (N A)) | ((V N1) N2) | (V+Cl (N Mod)) |
| L.8 | ((V)(N)) | ((V)((N)(A))) | (((V)(N1))(N2))<br>((V)((N1)(N2))) | ((V)((Cl$_\sigma$)((N)(Mod)))) |
| L.9 | ((V)(N)) | ((V)((N)(A))) | ((V)(N1)(N2)) | ((V)((Cl$_\sigma$)((N)(Mod)))) |
| L.10 | (V (N)) | (V (N (A))) | ((V(N1))(N2))<br>(V((N1)(N2))) | (V (Cl$_\sigma$ (N (Mod)))) |
| L.11 | (V (N)) | (V (N (A))) | (V(N1)(N2)) | (V (Cl$_\sigma$ (N (Mod)))) |

The typology of S.OvertHeads includes Xitsonga, contra L&S's claim that the lack of a φ corresponding to clP is evidence in favor of Match(LexP) over Match(OhP). In fact, five of the eleven languages (L.1, L.2, L.3, L.6, and L.7) fail to match clP even though there is an explicit pressure from Match(OhP) to do so. This highlights an important point: just because an XP lacks a φ in the prosodic output does not mean that it is invisible to Match constraints, since markedness constraints can also drive absence of a φ.

If we consider the phrasings of the double object construction (3$^{\text{rd}}$ column in (32)), we see that the silently headed applP has a corresponding φ in only two languages, L.8 and L.10. This applP has a φ correspondent even though Match(OhP, φ) does not introduce a pressure to match applP and Match(φ, OhP) militates *against* this φ. This raises another important point: making an XP invisible to Match constraints does not necessarily prevent the creation of a φ dominating the same terminal nodes as said XP. Moreover, the existence of a φ that corresponds to an XP in the input does not entail that this XP is visible to Match constraints. Together, the possible optima for these two inputs show that caution is needed when drawing conclusions about the (in)visibility of a group of XPs based on whether an XP has a φ correspondent in the output.

### 6.4.3.2  Ranking

The constraint ranking for L.7, the language corresponding to Xitsonga, is in (33).

(33)    Constraint ranking for L.7 in S.OvertHeads

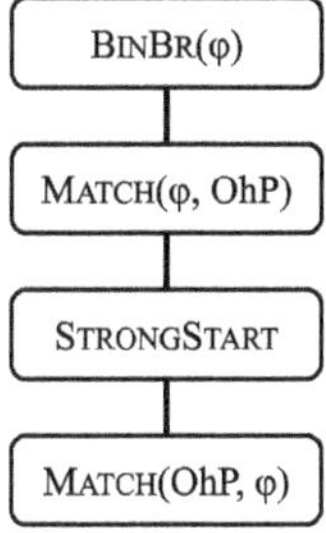


To understand this ranking, first consider the tableau in (34), which shows why the class marker encliticizes onto the preceding verb. Candidate (34b) performs better than the winner on MATCH(OhP, $\varphi$) by matching clP to a $\varphi$, but performs worse on STRONGSTART because this $\varphi$ begins with a syllable that is sister to a $\varphi$. Thus, STRONGSTART must be ranked above MATCH(OhP, $\varphi$), and failure to match clP does not require the invisibility of functional phrases. Candidate (34c) shows that MATCH($\varphi$, OhP) must be ranked above STRONGSTART to avoid placing the verb and the class marker into a $\varphi$.

(34)    Tableau showing encliticization of the class marker in L.7 of S.OvertHeads

| [V [$_{\text{clP-f}}$ Cl-clitic [N [Mod]] | BINBR($\varphi$) | M($\varphi$, OhP) | STRONGSTART | M(OhP, $\varphi$) |
|---|---|---|---|---|
| → a.  (V+Cl (N Mod)) | 0 | 0 | 1 | 2 |
| b.  (V (Cl$_\sigma$ (N Mod)) | e$_0$ | e | W$_2$ | L$_1$ |
| c.  ((V Cl$_\sigma$) (N Mod)) | e$_0$ | W$_1$ | L$_0$ | e$_2$ |

The tableau in (35) shows why the verb and the first noun are phrased together in the double object construction. Candidate (35c), in which VP and the second NP are matched, performs better than the desired winner candidate (35a) on MATCH($\varphi$, OhP) because it does not build any $\varphi$ that are unmotivated by the syntax. Candidate (35c) also performs better than (35a) on MATCH(OhP, $\varphi$) because it only incurs a single violation. However, (35c) performs worse on BINBR($\varphi$), incurring two violations because it has both a ternary and a unary $\varphi$; this means that BINBR($\varphi$) must be ranked above MATCH($\varphi$, OhP) and MATCH(OhP, $\varphi$). Candidate (35b) is harmonically bounded by the winner because it incurs the same number of MATCH($\varphi$, OhP) and MATCH(OhP, $\varphi$) violations while also incurring a violation of STRONGSTART.

(35)    Tableau showing phrasing of the double object construction in L.7
        of S.OvertHeads

| [V [$_{applP\text{-}f\text{-}s}$ [N1] [N2]]] | BINBR($\varphi$) | M($\varphi$, OhP) | STRONGSTART | M(OhP, $\varphi$) |
|---|---|---|---|---|
| →   a.   ((V N1) N2) | 0 | 1 | 0 | 2 |
| HB  b.   (V (N1 N2)) | e$_0$ | e$_1$ | W$_1$ | e$_2$ |
|     c.   (V N1 (N2)) | W$_2$ | L$_0$ | e$_0$ | L$_1$ |

Though the previous two examples have provided all the information needed to motivate the constraint ranking, it is worth considering the verb followed by the branching NP in (36) to see why its phrasing is different from that of the double object construction in (35). The winner (36a) phrases the noun and the adjective together at the expense of violating STRONGSTART, but satisfies MATCH($\varphi$, OhP) because both $\varphi$s are motivated by the syntax. Candidate (36b) avoids the STRONGSTART violation by phrasing the verb and noun together, but this causes it to be eliminated by higher ranking MATCH($\varphi$, OhP). This differs from what we saw in (35), where the STRONGSTART-compliant candidate won because MATCH($\varphi$, OhP) could not distinguish (35a) and (35b) due to the invisibility of applP.

(36)    Tableau showing phrasing of the verb and binary object in L.7 of
        S.OvertHeads

| [V [N [A]]] | BINBR($\varphi$) | M($\varphi$, OhP) | STRONGSTART | M(OhP, $\varphi$) |
|---|---|---|---|---|
| →   a.   (V (N A)) | 0 | 0 | 1 | 1 |
|     b.   ((V N) A) | e$_0$ | W$_1$ | L$_0$ | W$_2$ |
|     c.   (V (N (A))) | W$_1$ | e$_0$ | W$_2$ | L$_0$ |

Thus, we have seen that a system in which overtly headed XPs are visible to MATCH constraints can capture Xitsonga. Contra L&S's argument, the lack of a $\varphi$ corresponding to clP can still be accounted for with this definition of MATCH, although the explanation is different: here, a STRONGSTART violation prevents clP from being matched, rather than the invisibility of functional phrases.

### 6.4.4   S.Lexical

#### 6.4.4.1   Factorial typology

Having seen that S.OvertHeads can generate Xitsonga, we now turn to the factorial typology of S.Lexical in (37). One of the 12 languages, L.6, corresponds to Xitsonga. This confirms that the phrasing of Xitsonga can be derived using MATCH(LexP), validating one of L&S's main claims.

Unlike the typology for S.OvertHeads, none of the languages in S.Lexical's typology has an output in which clP is matched. It is clear that MATCH(LexP) introduces a much greater pressure to avoid mapping clP to a $\varphi$. However, given that both systems contained languages with these optima, this only shows that MATCH(LexP) is sufficient, but not necessary, to derive phrasings in which clP is not matched.

(37)   Factorial typology of S.Lexical

| | [V [N]] | [V [N [A]]] | [V [$_{applP\text{-}f\text{-}s}$ [N1] [N2]]] | [V [$_{clP\text{-}f}$ Cl-clitic [N [Mod]] |
|---|---|---|---|---|
| L.1 | (V N) | (V N A) | (V N1 N2) | (V Cl$_\sigma$ (N Mod)) |
| L.2 | (V N) | ((V N) A) | ((V N1) N2) | ((V Cl$_\sigma$)(N Mod)) |
| L.3 | (V N) | (V N (A)) | (V N1 (N2)) | (V Cl$_\sigma$ (N Mod)) |
| L.4 | (V N) | (V (N A)) | ((V N1) N2) | ((V Cl$_\sigma$)(N Mod)) |
| L.5 | (V N) | (V (N A)) | (V N1 N2) | (V+Cl (N Mod)) |
| L.6 | (V N) | (V (N A)) | ((V N1) N2) | (V+Cl (N Mod)) |
| L.7 | ((V)(N)) | ((V)((N) (A))) | (((V)(N1))(N2)) ((V)((N1)(N2))) | ((V Cl$_\sigma$)((N) (Mod))) |
| L.8 | ((V)(N)) | ((V)((N) (A))) | ((V)(N1)(N2)) | (V Cl$_\sigma$ ((N) (Mod))) |
| L.9 | (V (N)) | (V (N (A))) | ((V(N1))(N2)) (V((N1)(N2))) | ((V Cl$_\sigma$)(N (Mod))) |
| L.10 | (V (N)) | (V (N (A))) | (V (N1)(N2)) | (V Cl$_\sigma$ (N (Mod))) |
| L.11 | (V (N)) | (V (N (A))) | ((V(N1))(N2)) (V((N1)(N2))) | (V+Cl (N (Mod))) |
| L.12 | (V (N)) | (V (N (A))) | (V (N1)(N2)) | (V+Cl (N (Mod))) |

#### 6.4.4.2   Ranking

The constraint ranking for L.6, the language corresponding to Xitsonga, is in (38). This ranking is slightly different from L.7 in S.OvertHeads: whereas STRONGSTART dominated MATCH(OhP, $\varphi$), here STRONGSTART and MATCH(LexP, $\varphi$) are not crucially ranked. This ranking also differs

from L&S's analysis: they assert that MATCH(LexP, φ) is ranked above
STRONGSTART, and do not comment on the relative ranking of MATCH(φ,
LexP) and STRONGSTART.[10]

(38)     Constraint ranking for L.6 in S.Lexical

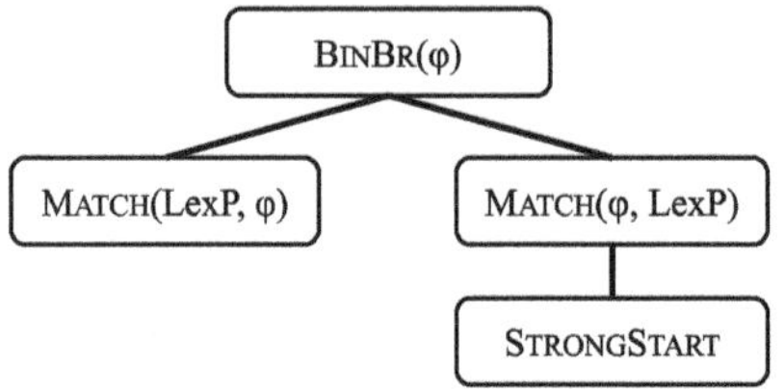


The tableau in (39) shows how the candidate with encliticization of the
class marker is chosen. As in L.7 of S.OvertHeads, MATCH(φ, LexP) must be
ranked above STRONGSTART in order to prevent the verb and the classifier
from forming a φ together, as in (39c). However, the different visibility settings cause candidate (39b), in which there is a φ corresponding to clP, to be
harmonically bounded by the winner, because candidate (39b) now incurs a
MATCH(φ, LexP) violation in addition to its extra violation of STRONGSTART.
This harmonic bounding also explains why the candidate did not emerge as
an optimum in any of the languages in the factorial typology in (38).

(39)     Tableau showing encliticization of the class marker in L.6 of
         S.Lexical

| [V [$_{\text{clP-f}}$ Cl-clitic [N [Mod]] | BINBR(φ) | M(φ, LexP) | STRONGSTART | M(LexP, φ) |
|---|---|---|---|---|
| →    a.   (V+Cl (N Mod)) | 0 | 0 | 1 | 1 |
| HB   b.   (V (Cl$_\sigma$ (N Mod)) | e$_0$ | W$_1$ | W$_2$ | e$_1$ |
| c.   ((V Cl$_\sigma$)(N Mod)) | e$_0$ | W$_1$ | L$_0$ | e$_1$ |

The tableau in (40) shows that the phrasing of the double object construction is derived in exactly the same way as in S.OvertHeads, since
both MATCH(LexP) and MATCH(OhP) ignore the empty-headed applP.
Again, we see that BINBR(φ) must be ranked above MATCH(φ, LexP) and

---

[10] As a reminder, I continue to refer to the traditional MATCH constraints for ease of exposition, but L&S's analysis actually employs MAX(φ) instead of MATCH(LexP, φ) and DEP(φ) instead of MATCH(φ, LexP). Translated into the terms of their analysis, their claim is that MAX(φ) is ranked over STRONGSTART.

Match(LexP, $\varphi$) to prevent a candidate that only matches the VP and the second NP from winning.

(40)   Tableau showing phrasing of the double object construction in L.6 of S.Lexical

| [V [$_{\text{applP-f-s}}$ [N1] [N2]]] | BinBr($\varphi$) | M($\varphi$, LexP) | StrongStart | M(LexP, $\varphi$) |
|---|---|---|---|---|
| $\rightarrow$   a.   ((V N1) N2) | 0 | 1 | 0 | 2 |
| HB   b.   (V (N1 N2)) | e$_0$ | e$_1$ | W$_1$ | e$_2$ |
| c.   (V N1 (N2)) | W$_2$ | L$_0$ | e$_0$ | L$_1$ |

The phrasing of the verb and binary object, shown in (41), is also derived in the same way as in S.OvertHeads. Still, it is worth pointing out that L&S assert that Match(LexP, $\varphi$) must be ranked over StrongStart to explain why the $\varphi$ corresponding to NP is retained, as in candidate (41a). However, the StrongStart-compliant parse, candidate (41b), performs worse than candidate (41a) on both Match($\varphi$, LexP) and Match(LexP, $\varphi$). Moreover, the ranking of Match($\varphi$, LexP) over StrongStart is independently motivated by the phrasing of the class marker in (39). Thus, Match($\varphi$, LexP) will already choose candidate (41a) over (41b), so the relative ranking of Match(LexP, $\varphi$) and StrongStart does not actually matter. This explains the discrepancy between L&S's analysis and the ranking in (38). Additionally, candidate (39c) showing the need for Match($\varphi$, LexP) to be ranked over StrongStart was not considered by L&S, highlighting once more the importance of generating all possible candidates in SPOT.

(41)   Tableau showing phrasing of the verb and binary object in L.6 of S.Lexical

| [V [N [A]]] | BinBr($\varphi$) | M($\varphi$, LexP) | StrongStart | M(LexP, $\varphi$) |
|---|---|---|---|---|
| $\rightarrow$   a.   (V (N A)) | 0 | 0 | 1 | 1 |
| b.   ((V N) A) | e$_0$ | W$_1$ | L$_0$ | W$_2$ |
| c.   (V (N (A))) | W$_1$ | e$_0$ | W$_2$ | L$_0$ |

### 6.4.5   *General.System*

#### 6.4.5.1   *Factorial typology*

Both S.OvertHeads and S.Lexical have been shown to generate a language compatible with Xitsonga, though the details of the analyses vary slightly. Here, we verify that S.General is incapable of generating Xitsonga, as argued by L&S.

The factorial typology of S.General is presented in (42). With only seven languages, this typology is slightly smaller than the others, likely because general matching allows fewer opportunities for deviations from the syntax by requiring a greater number of XPs to be in correspondence relations with φs. Of the seven languages, none fully captures the phrasing of Xitsonga, although L.5 has the right phrasing for three out of four inputs. Additionally, there are three languages in which applP fails to map to a φ, and four languages in which clP fails to map to a φ, even though both are visible to Match(XP, φ).

(42)     Factorial typology for S.General

|  | [V [N]] | [V [N [A]]] | [V [$_{\text{applP-f-s}}$ [N1] [N2]]] | [V [$_{\text{clP-f}}$ Cl-clitic [N [Mod]] |
|---|---|---|---|---|
| L.1 | (V N) | (V N A) | (V N1 N2) | (V Cl$_\sigma$ (N Mod)) |
| L.2 | (V N) | ((V N) A) | ((V N1) N2) | ((V Cl$_\sigma$)(N Mod)) |
| L.3 | (V N) | (V N (A)) | (V N1 (N2)) | (V Cl$_\sigma$ (N Mod)) |
| L.4 | (V N) | (V (N A)) | (V (N1 N2)) | (V (Cl$_\sigma$ (N Mod))) |
| L.5 | (V N) | (V (N A)) | (V (N1 N2)) | (V+Cl (N Mod)) |
| L.6 | ((V)(N)) | ((V)((N)(A))) | ((V)((N1)(N2))) | ((V)((Cl$_\sigma$)((N)(Mod)))) |
| L.7 | (V (N)) | (V (N (A))) | (V ((N1)(N2))) | (V (Cl$_\sigma$ (N (Mod)))) |

### 6.4.5.2  Ranking

To understand why L.5 fails to fully capture Xitsonga, consider the contradictory ERCs in (43). For input (a), L.5 selects the right-branching (V (NA)). This candidate requires ranking either Match(φ, XP) or Match(XP, φ) over StrongStart. However, this prevents L.5 from selecting the left-branching candidate for input (b): as the ERC shows, the left-branching candidate requires the contradictory ranking of StrongStart over both Match constraints. The issue is that Match(XP, φ) and Match(φ, XP) have no way of distinguishing NP from applP, and any ranking that causes NP in input (a) to be matched will also cause applP in input (b) to be matched. S.OvertHeads and S.Lexical avoid this problem by making applP invisible to Match, allowing the Match constraints to treat NP and applP differently.

(43)     Contradictory ERCs in S.General

| Input | Winner | Loser | BinBr(φ) | M(φ,XP) | SS | M(XP,φ) |
|---|---|---|---|---|---|---|
| a.  [V [N [A]]] | (V (N A)) | ((V N) A) | e | W | L | W |
| b.  [V [$_{\text{applP-f-s}}$ [N1] [N2]]] | ((V N1) N2) | (V (N A)) | e | L | W | L |

### 6.4.6   Xitsonga summary

The results from this study show that the Xitsonga data do not provide a decisive case for choosing between MATCH(LexP) and MATCH(OhP), at least for the structures considered here. It remains possible, as originally suggested by Kalivoda and Bellik (2021) and Van Handel (2021), that MATCH(OhP) could replace MATCH(LexP). Though the results reviewed are promising, firm conclusions will require further testing of these two visibility settings on additional data within and across languages.

A recurring theme of this study has been that the lack of a $\varphi$ correspondent does not necessarily mean that an XP is invisible to MATCH constraints. Arguments about visibility settings therefore require systematic testing of alternative constraint definitions, as made possible in SPOT. In addition, the results from Xitsonga suggest two ways to guide future work on visibility settings.

First, the failure for S.General to generate a Xitsonga-compatible language showed that applP must be invisible to MATCHXP. In §6.4.5.2, it was suggested that applP needed to be invisible so that the Match constraints could differentiate $[_{\text{applP-f-s}}$ [N1] [N2]] from $[_{\text{NP}}$ N [A]]: since the underlying syntax is nearly identical, the only way to make sure that the phrasing of applP and NP differ is to have the MATCH constraints treat them differently.

This speaks to a larger point about visibility settings: the strongest way to argue that a particular visibility setting is needed is to find two (near-) identical syntactic structures that differ solely in the Lex/Func or SH/OH status of a single XP. For instance, the structures in (44) are identical except for BP, which is functional in (44a) but lexical in (44b). If both lexical and functional XPs are visible to MATCH(XP) in this hypothetical language, then the MATCH constraints will treat the inputs identically, and they will be phrased in the same way. If instead MATCH(LexP) ignores functional phrases, then MATCH will treat the two inputs differently, because BP will be ignored in (44a) but not (44b); here, the phrasings will likely be different.[11] Thus, showing that there is a different phrasing for two syntactic structures that differ only in the functional or silently headed status of a single XP is the clearest way to argue for restrictive visibility settings.

---

[11] The phrasing is not guaranteed to be different, because markedness constraints ranked over MATCH can cause two different syntactic structures to be mapped to the same prosodic output. For instance, BINMIN($\varphi$) $\gg$ MATCH(XP, $\varphi$) will favor the same parse (a b) for the distinct inputs [a [b]] and [[a] b].

(44)

   a.   [$_{AP}$ a [$_{BP-f}$ b [$_{CP}$ c]]]
   b.   [$_{AP}$ a [$_{BP}$ b [$_{CP}$ c]]]

Second, the phrasing of clP showed that an XP can fail to be matched without requiring a particular visibility setting. In this case, it was important that the clP had a clitic at its left edge, such that matching clP violated STRONGSTART; this allowed for an alternative markedness-based account of clP's lack of a $\varphi$ correspondent. More generally, this suggests that functional phrases that begin with a clitic might not be the most informative test case for distinguishing MATCH(LexP) and MATCH(OhP). Since clitics are prosodically weak, phrases headed by clitics may be more likely to induce violations of STRONGSTART and other markedness constraints such as HEADEDNESS, which requires all $\varphi$s to dominate an $\omega$ and would penalize $\varphi$s that only dominate a clitic, and EXHAUSTIVITY, which requires all $\sigma$s to be parsed into feet and all feet to be parsed into $\omega$s and would penalize structures in which clitics attach directly to $\varphi$ (Selkirk 1996, Ito and Mester 2009). Deviations from perfect matching may be licensed in order to avoid structures that violate these markedness constraints, such that it may be more difficult to determine whether failure to match functional phrases headed by a clitic is driven by markedness constraints or by visibility settings.

Instead, functional phrases headed by a prosodic word rather than a clitic may be more useful for establishing whether MATCH constraints in a given language see overtly headed functional XPs. Of course, finding the right function words to test could be difficult; as will be discussed in §6.5.1, function words have idiosyncratic prosodic behavior and are typically (but not always) prosodically weak. Again, the main point is that some inputs are more informative about visibility settings than others, and the analyst should evaluate markedness-based explanations before ascribing the absence of a $\varphi$ to visibility settings.

## 6.5    Potential objections to abandoning the Lex/Func distinction

We have seen that MATCH(LexP) and MATCH(OhP) are often interchangeable, and in some languages, like Italian, MATCH(OhP) is needed. Moreover, at least one language in which MATCH(LexP) appeared to be necessary, Xitsonga, was amenable to reanalysis. This is promising for the idea that the SH/OH distinction could replace the Lex/Func distinction, but the evidence needed to decide between the two is admittedly sparse, and it remains possible that both MATCH(LexP) and MATCH(OhP) are needed for full empirical coverage.

This is a question for future work. With this in mind, I turn my attention to potential objections to abandoning the Lex/Func distinction. I argue that other phenomena typically ascribed to the Lex/Func distinction, such as word-level prosody, do not necessarily require this distinction.

### 6.5.1   Word-level prosody

One might object that MATCH(LexP) should not be replaced by MATCH(OhP) because the Lex/Func distinction is independently needed to capture other empirical phenomena. Perhaps the biggest motivation for a Lex/Func distinction comes from word-level prosody. It is well known that lexical and functional words tend to have different prosodic behavior: lexical words map to ω by default, while function words are usually prosodically weak and tend not to map to ω (Nespor and Vogel 1986; Selkirk 1986, 1996, 2011; Ito and Mester 2009; Peperkamp 1997; i.a.). This asymmetry has been explained by stipulating that function words are invisible to syntax–prosody mapping constraints (Selkirk 1986, 1996; Truckenbrodt 1999), an assumption adopted by much work in Match Theory (Selkirk 2011; Elfner 2012; Ito and Mester 2019; Guekguezian 2017; Lee and Selkirk, to appear).

First, it should be emphasized that it is possible to abandon the Lex/Func distinction at the phrasal level while retaining it at the word level; this option is pursued by Elfner (2012) and Ito and Mester (2019). Moreover, Ito and Mester (2019) show that having distinct visibility settings for phrases and words allows for an insightful treatment of why English function words do not reduce in phrase-final position.

In their account, MATCH($Lex^0$) ignores function words and militates against parsing them into ωs. However, the same function word can be promoted to an ω when it sits alone in a functional phrase, as with the preposition *at* in (45). Here, MATCH(XP, φ) favors matching PP and HEADEDNESS requires all φ to contain at least one ω. In order to satisfy both constraints, *at* is promoted to an ω even though this violates the prosody-to-syntax constraint MATCH(ω, $Lex^0$). Crucially, this explanation requires PP to be visible and $P^0$ to be invisible to the mapping constraints. Thus, enforcing the Lex/Func distinction at the word level but not at the phrasal level is not only theoretically possible but in fact necessary for their account to work. This casts doubt on the claim that word-level prosody motivates retention of the Lex/Func distinction at the phrasal level.

(45)    HEADEDNESS causes phrase-final *at* to be promoted to an $\omega$

| $[_{\text{VP}}$ look $[_{\text{PP}}$ at _ $]]$ | HEADEDNESS | MATCH(XP, $\varphi$) | MATCH($\omega$, Lex$^0$) |
|---|---|---|---|
| →    a.    (lóok$_\omega$ (æ̀t$_\omega$)) | 0 | 0 | 1 |
|    b.    (lóok$_\omega$ (ət$_\sigma$)) | W$_1$ | e$_0$ | L$_0$ |
| HB    c.    (lóok$_\omega$ æ̀t$_\omega$) | e$_0$ | W$_1$ | e$_1$ |
|    d.    (lóok$_\omega$ ət$_\sigma$) | e$_0$ | W$_1$ | L$_0$ |

Another option is to also abandon the Lex/Func distinction at the word level. Tyler (2019) shows that a version of MATCH($X^0$) that attempts to map all heads to $\omega$, regardless of functional status, is capable of accounting for the Lex/Func asymmetry without encoding it in mapping constraints. Tyler points out that MATCH(Lex$^0$) does not explain why function words do not behave as a uniform class: depending on the item and the syntactic context, they can be proclitics or enclitics attaching at the level of $\omega$, $\varphi$, or $\iota$, and can sometimes map to full $\omega$s (Selkirk 1996, Zec and Inkelas 1991, Zec 2005, Ito and Mester 2009).

Instead, Tyler proposes that MATCH($X^0$) attempts to map all $X^0$s onto $\omega$ by default, regardless of functional status. The lexical entries of certain morphemes are associated with a prosodic subcategorization frame that requires them to procliticize or encliticize onto an adjacent $\omega$ (Inkelas 1990, Zec and Inkelas 1991, Zec 2005, Bennett et al. 2018). Adherence to the subcategorization frame is enforced by the constraint SUBCAT; when ranked above MATCH($X^0$), SUBCAT will force a functional item to cliticize onto a neighboring $\omega$ instead of being mapped to its own $\omega$.

To explain how functional items acquire subcategorization frames, Tyler appeals to a usage-based account: function words tend to be more frequent and predictable, both of which are associated with phonetic reduction (Zipf 1929, Lieberman 1963, Bybee 2000, 2006, Aylett and Turk 2004, i.a.). This reduction is eventually phonologized in the form of prosodic subcategorization frames. Not all function words will acquire a prosodic subcategorization frame, because not all function words are reduced. Tyler shows how this system accounts for the behavior of various English function words. By eschewing a blunt Lex/Func distinction, the account readily predicts the idiosyncratic behavior of function words, because we no longer expect all function words to behave as a class. This account is arguably more explanatory than MATCH(Lex$^0$): function words typically develop reduced forms because they tend to be frequent and predictable, but their reduction is not caused by their functional status *per se*.[12]

Thus, Tyler's analysis shows that the word-level Lex/Func asymmetry can be derived without lexical-only mapping constraints. This analysis fits well with the suggestion of replacing MATCH(LexP, φ) with MATCH(OhP, φ): together, these approaches can account for much of the data used to motivate encoding the Lex/Func distinction in the phonological grammar, suggesting that abandoning this distinction is not as drastic a move as one might have expected.

### 6.5.2   The prosody of pronouns

A related concern involves pronouns. Like other function words, pronouns tend to be prosodically weak; in the following examples from Truckenbrodt (2007), the lexical subject *mayor* in (46) receives phrasal stress (indicated by underlining), but the pronominal subject *he* in (47) does not. In Truckenbrodt's account, functional XPs are invisible to the constraint STRESS-XP, which requires each XP to contain a beat of stress on the φ level. In (47), STRESS-XP ignores the functional subject DP, so the pronoun is unstressed.

(46)    [$_{DP}$ the [$_{NP}$ mayor]] won their support

(47)    [$_{DP}$ he] won their support

If we did away with the Lex/Func distinction, then DP would be visible to STRESS-XP, and we could risk not being able to account for the lack of stress on the pronoun in (47). However, the behavior of pronouns is not knockdown evidence in favor of the Lex/Func distinction. As Truckenbrodt points out, pronouns are also contextually given, and given elements are typically deaccented (Ladd 1980, 1983; Selkirk 1995; Féry and Samek-Lodovici 2006; i.a.). An alternative analysis presents itself: constraints governing the relationship between givenness and stress/accents are responsible for the reduction of

---

[12] A potential objection to this account is that prosodic subcategorization frames are themselves stipulative because they specify not only which words will reduce but also how they are parsed into the overall prosodic structure (i.e., as enclitics or proclitics). It is possible to imagine a similar approach in which propensity to reduce is a property of each lexical item, but the way the reduced word is integrated into the prosodic structure is determined by the interaction of independent constraints rather than being stated in a subcategorization frame. Determining the best way to analyze word-level prosody is beyond the scope of this chapter; the main point is that there are alternatives to encoding a Lex/Func distinction in the mapping constraints.

pronouns, rather than the Lex/Func distinction. This would explain the lack of accent on the subject in (47) without needing to stipulate the invisibility of functional projections to mapping constraints. Truckenbrodt ultimately concludes that both the lexical/functional distinction and an appeal to givenness are needed, though his reasoning for retaining the former is based on the invisibility of functional words and phrases to mapping constraints, which I have already argued may not be necessary.

The behavior of pronouns is therefore not grounds for retaining the Lex/Func distinction, as long as the role of givenness is recognized. Providing an account of givenness effects is outside the scope of this chapter (see Selkirk 1995, Schwarzschild 1999, Féry and Samek-Lodovici 2006, Kratzer and Selkirk 2020, i.a.). The important point is that an alternative account is available for yet another phenomenon previously attributed to the Lex/Func distinction. Again, the Lex/Func distinction is a useful heuristic because it often correlates with other properties driving phonological patterning, but it is not strictly necessary to derive those patterns.

### 6.5.3 *Encliticization out of FuncP*

Selkirk (2011) argues that a Lex/Func distinction could explain why functional heads often encliticize to preceding words outside of the phrase that they head. Selkirk cites various languages in which this occurs: determiners encliticize onto a preceding verb in Chamicuro (Parker 1999) and Kwakwala (Boas 1947, Anderson 1984), prepositions encliticize onto a preceding verb in Shanghai Chinese (Selkirk and Shen 1990), and English has various contractions in which function words encliticize onto a preceding lexical word (e.g., *wanna* < *want to*, *kinda* < *kind of*).

As Selkirk points out, these instances of encliticization would be predicted if FuncP were invisible to MATCH(LexP). If a syntactic input like (48) preferentially mapped to a prosodic output like (49), then there would be no φ boundary intervening between V and Func to prevent encliticization, and prosodic markedness constraints could force Func into an ω with V.

(48)      [$_{\text{VP}}$ V [$_{\text{FuncP}}$ Func [$_{\text{NP}}$ N]]]

(49)      (V Func (N))

In fact, this was one of the arguments that Lee and Selkirk (2022) used to motivate MATCH(LexP) in Xitsonga, in which the class marker encliticizes onto the preceding verb, as discussed in §6.4. However, we have already seen that the invisibility of functional phrases is not the only way to account for this type of pattern: encliticization in Xitsonga can be derived in a system that replaces Match(LexP) with Match(OhP), provided that a higher-ranking markedness constraint overrides the pressure to match FuncP. In the re-analysis of Xitsonga, this constraint was StrongStart, which disfavored the candidate that matched FuncP because its corresponding $\varphi$ began with a $\sigma$.

As shown in (50), a similar analysis could potentially apply to the other languages cited by Selkirk (2011) with structures like (48). This tableau shows that a candidate matching FuncP will lose under any definition of Match as long as StrongStart is ranked higher.[13] This suggests that these encliticization structures may not be informative about visibility settings, unless it can independently be shown that StrongStart (and any other markedness constraint that would penalize the $\varphi$ corresponding to FuncP) must be ranked below Match(XP, $\varphi$) in the language in question. Only by ruling out alternative accounts that invoke markedness constraints could we state with confidence that Match(LexP) is responsible for the lack of a $\varphi$ corresponding to FuncP.[14] Since encliticization can arise even with Match(XP, $\varphi$) and Match(OhP, $\varphi$), I conclude that this cross-linguistic pattern does not constitute decisive evidence in favor of a Lex/Func distinction, although it is certainly possible that the Lex/Func distinction is (partially) responsible for encliticization out of FuncP in at least some languages.

(50)    StrongStart can prevent FuncP from having a $\varphi$ correspondent under any definition of Match

| $[_{VP}$ V $[_{FuncP}$ Func $[_{NP}$ N$]]]$ | StrongStart | M(XP, $\varphi$) | M(OhP, $\varphi$) | M(LexP, $\varphi$) |
|---|---|---|---|---|
| a.    $(V_\omega$ Func$_\sigma$ $(N_\omega))$ | 0 | 1 | 1 | 0 |
| b.    $(V{+}Func_\omega$ $(N_\omega))$ | 1 | 1 | 1 | 0 |
| c.    $(V_\omega$ $(Func_\sigma$ $(N_\omega)))$ | 2 | 0 | 0 | 0 |

---

[13] StrongStart and the Match constraints are insufficient to choose candidate (50b), in which Func is an enclitic, over candidate (50a), in which Func attaches to $\varphi$. Encliticization is presumably driven by additional markedness constraints; in both Lee and Selkirk's (2022) analysis of Xitsonga and my reanalysis, this was due to BinBr($\varphi$).

[14] The tableau in (50) shows that Match(LexP, $\varphi$) does not rule out candidate (50c), but Match($\varphi$, LexP) *would* rule out (50c) because it would consider the $\varphi$ corresponding to FuncP to be unmotivated by the syntax.

## 6.6    Conclusion

At least three different visibility settings for Match constraints have been
proposed in the literature. The most general formulation, Match(XP), calls
for all XPs that dominate a unique terminal string to have a matching φ,
without discriminating between lexical and functional projections (Elfner
2012, 2015). The strictest formulation, Match(LexP), requires any XP headed
by a word containing a lexical category root (N, V, A) to have a matching φ
(Selkirk and Lee 2017; Lee and Selkirk 2022). Finally, Match(OhP), requires
any XP with a phonologically overt head to have a matching φ, but does
not distinguish lexical and functional projections (Kalivoda and Bellik 2021,
Kalivoda, Chapter 4, Van Handel 2021).

This chapter has addressed the question of whether all three visibility settings are needed. Match(OhP) is needed in Italian (Van Handel 2021), and
Irish requires Match(XP) and either Match(OhP) or Match(LexP) (Kalivoda and Bellik 2021, Kalivoda, Chapter 4). However, Match(OhP) and
Match(LexP) are often interchangeable. Crucially, it was argued that Xitsonga can be analyzed with either Match(OhP) or Match(LexP), contra Lee
and Selkirk's claim that Match(LexP) is needed instead of Match(OhP).

These findings raise the possibility that Match(OhP) could provide an
alternative and potentially more explanatory account of data previously covered by the Lex/Func distinction. It is well known that the syntax–prosody
mapping appears to treat lexical and functional material differently, which
has led to theories in which only lexical material is visible to the mapping
(Nespor and Vogel 1986; Truckenbrodt 1999; Lee and Selkirk 2022). However, recent work suggests that this Lex/Func distinction is too broad and
that there are clear exceptions where functional projections are mapped to
φ (Elfner 2012, 2015; Ito and Mester 2019; Van Handel 2021) and function
words are mapped to ω (Tyler 2019). Match(OhP) continues this trend of
pushing back on the coarse Lex/Func distinction while potentially providing
an explanation for those cases in which lexical and functional projections do
in fact appear to behave differently. Functional projections may simply be
more likely to have silent heads and to be ignored by Match(OhP). Similarly, functional phrases often introduce prosodically weak material that violates markedness constraints like StrongStart, Headedness, and Exhaustivity; when highly ranked, these markedness constraints can prevent perfect
matching. The correlation between functional status and having a silent
head or introducing prosodically weak material may then give rise to an apparent Lex/Func distinction when failure to match all XPs is actually driven
by markedness constraints and the invisibility of silently headed phrases.

While this suggestion is purely speculative, it has intuitive appeal. On the one hand, it is unclear why MATCH constraints should care whether an XP's head is from a lexical or a functional category, given that the phonology does not make distinctions between phrases of different categories within these classes, such as NP versus VP. On the other hand, it is well-established that the syntax–prosody mapping ignores silent elements (Nespor and Vogel 1986, Truckenbrodt 1999), and it makes sense that the phonology, as the system that governs the sound patterns of language, would be perfectly content to ignore (phrases projected by) elements that are unpronounced. This parallels Tyler's (2019) explanation of why function words get reduced: the phonology itself does not care about functional status. Rather, being functional correlates with frequency and predictability, which leads to reduction and has consequences for phonology.

The force of these potential explanations depends on the findings of the survey being representative of cross-linguistic trends. However, the survey is a small sample, and future work should continue to test the different formulations of MATCH on data from additional languages before drawing any firm conclusions. Consideration of languages analyzed in frameworks other than Match Theory are a potentially rich source of relevant data, though caution is needed in interpreting their results. Such analyses were not included in the survey, because work in other frameworks, particularly those predating Match Theory, often make different assumptions about the shape of possible prosodic structures or posit syntactic structures that do not conform to contemporary syntactic theory. Reanalyzing these data in Match Theory to test whether their claims about visibility settings hold for MATCH constraints is therefore non-trivial. Moreover, Bellik and Kalivoda's (2016) study of Kinyambo, which compared systems with MATCH versus ALIGN/WRAP, suggests that visibility settings may interact with mapping constraints in unexpected ways. They made all XPs visible to mapping constraints and found that systems involving MATCH were able to (mostly) capture the phrasing of Kinyambo, while ALIGN/WRAP systems were unsuccessful. This shows that claims about visibility settings in one theory may not hold true in another, so care is needed when drawing conclusions based on work in other frameworks. Even if it turns out that MATCH(LexP) is a necessary component of CON once more languages are considered, it is still worthwhile to reexamine long-held assumptions, and comparing different versions of MATCH will help us understand which syntax-prosody mismatches arise because certain phrases are invisible to MATCH constraints and which are driven by prosodic markedness constraints.

Beyond theory, the present study makes an important methodological point: precise constraint definitions and rigorous testing of the consequences of alternative formulations is necessary in syntax-prosody work. The results from the Xitsonga investigation also demonstrate that constraint comparison is not merely a theoretical exercise but rather has important analytical consequences: minor differences in MATCH constraints affect the size and contents of the predicted typology. Future work should continue to look for evidence that could distinguish MATCH(OhP) and MATCH(LexP) in other languages. At present, few studies have conducted an extensive comparison of the consequences of each formulation, likely due in part to the difficulty of generating and evaluating all possible candidates. This theory comparison is made possible in SPOT (Bellik et al. 2015–2021), and the present study provides a template for similar work in other languages. These comparisons should be pursued in order to refine Match Theory and gain a better understanding of cross-linguistic variation in the syntax–prosody mapping.

## References

Anderson, Stephen R. (1984). Kwakwala syntax and the Government-Binding theory. In Eung-Do Cook and Donna B. Gerdts (eds.) *The Syntax of Native American Languages* 21–75. New York: Academic Press.

Aylett, Matthew and Turk, Alice (2004). The smooth signal redundancy hypothesis: A functional explanation for relationships between redundancy, prosodic prominence, and duration in spontaneous speech. *Language and Speech* 47: 31–56.

Bane, Max and Riggle, Jason (2012). Consequences of candidate omission. *Linguistic Inquiry* 43: 695–706.

Bellik, Jennifer, Bellik, Ozan, and Kalivoda, Nick (2015–2021). Syntax-Prosody in Optimality Theory (SPOT). Javascript application. http:// spot.sites.ucsc.edu. Codebase at https://github.com/syntax-prosody-ot.

Bellik, Jennifer, Ito, Junko, Kalivoda, Nick and Mester, Armin (to appear). Matching and alignment. In Haruo Kubozono, Junko Ito, and Armin Mester (eds.) *Prosody and Prosodic Interfaces*. Oxford University Press.

Bellik, Jennifer and Kalivoda, Nick (2016). Adjunction and branchingness effects in syntax- prosody mapping. In Gunnar Ólafur Hansson, Ashley Farris-Trimble, Kevin McMullin, and Douglas Pulleyblank (eds.) *Supplemental Proceedings of the 2015 Annual Meeting on Phonology*, Linguistic Society of America. http://doi.org/10.3765/amp.v3i0.3690

Bennett, Ryan, Harizanov, Boris, and Henderson, Robert (2018). Prosodic smothering in Macedonian and Kaqchikel. *Linguistic Inquiry* 49: 195–246.

Boas, Franz (1947). Kwakiutl grammar with a glossary of the suffixes. *Transactions of the American Philosophical Society* 37: 203–377.

Brinkerhoff, Mykel L. and Tengesdal, Eirik (2021). MATCHING phrases in Norwegian object shift. In Ryan Bennett, Richard Bibbs, Mykel L. Brinkerhoff, Max J. Kaplan, Stephanie Rich, Amanda Rysling, Nicholas Van Handel, and Maya Wax Cavallaro (eds.) *Supplemental Proceedings of the 2020 Annual Meeting on Phonology.* Washington, DC: Linguistic Society of America.

Bybee, Joan (2000). The phonology of the lexicon: evidence from lexical diffusion. In Michael Barlow and Suzanne Kemmer (eds.) *Usage-Based Models of Language* 65–85. Stanford: CSLI.

Bybee, Joan (2006). From usage to grammar: the mind's response to repetition. *Language* 82: 711–733.

Cardinaletti, Anna (2004). Towards a cartography of subject positions. In Luigi Rizzi (ed.) *The Structure of CP and IP* 115–165. New York: Oxford University Press.

Dehé, Nicole and Samek-Lodovici, Vieri (2009). On the prosody and syntax of DPs: evidence from Italian noun-adjective sequences. *Natural Language and Linguistic Theory* 27: 45–75.

Elfner, Emily (2012). *Syntax-Prosody Interactions in Irish.* PhD dissertation, University of Massachusetts Amherst.

Elfner, Emily (2015). Recursion in prosodic phrasing: evidence from Connemara Irish. *Natural Language and Linguistic Theory* 33: 1169–1208.

Elordieta, Gorka and Selkirk, Elisabeth (2022). Unaccentedness and the formation of prosodic structure in Leikeitio Basque. In Haruo Kubozono, Junko Ito, and Armin Mester (eds.) *Prosody and Prosodic Interfaces* 374–420. Oxford University Press.

Féry, Caroline and Samek-Lodovici, Vieri (2006). Focus projection and prosodic prominence in nested foci. *Language* 82: 131–150.

Frascarelli, Mara (2007). Subjects, topics and the interpretation of referential pro: an interface approach to the linking of (null) pronouns. *Natural Language and Linguistic Theory* 25: 691–734.

Ghini, Mirco (1993). Φ-formation in Italian: a new proposal. In Carrie Dyck (ed.) *Toronto Working Papers in Linguistics* 12: 41–78.

Guekguezian, Peter Ara (2017). Templates as the interaction of recursive word structure and prosodic well-formedness. *Phonology* 34: 81–120.

Inkelas, Sharon (1990). *Prosodic Constituency in the Lexicon.* New York: Garland.

Ishihara, Shinichiro (2014). Match theory and the recursivity problem. In Shigeto Kawahara and Mika Igarashi (eds.) *MIT Working Papers in Linguistics 73: Proceedings of Formal Approaches to Japanese linguistics 7* 69–88. Cambridge, MA.

Ito, Junko and Mester, Armin (2009). The extended prosodic word. In Janet Grijzenhout and Barış Kabak (eds.) *Phonological Domains: Universals and Deviations* 135–194. Berlin: Mouton de Gruyter.

Ito, Junko and Mester, Armin (2013). Prosodic subcategories in Japanese. *Lingua* 124: 20–40

Ito, Junko and Mester, Armin (2019). Match as syntax-prosody Max/Dep: prosodic enclisis in English. *English Linguistics* 36: 1–28.

Kalivoda, Nick (2018). *Syntax-Prosody Mismatches in Optimality Theory.* PhD dissertation, University of California, Santa Cruz.

Kalivoda, Nick and Bellik, Jennifer (2021). Overtly headed XPs and Irish syntax–prosody mapping. In Ryan Bennett, Richard Bibbs, Mykel L. Brinkerhoff, Max J. Kaplan, Stephanie Rich, Amanda Rysling, Nicholas Van Handel, and Maya Wax Cavallero (eds.) *Proceedings of the 2020 Annual Meeting on Phonology*, Washington, DC: Linguistic Society of America. https://doi.org/10.3765/amp.v9i0.4906

Karttunen, Lauri (2006). The insufficiency of paper-and-pencil linguistics: the case of Finnish prosody. In Miriam Butt, Mary Dalrymple, and Tracy Holloway King (eds.) *Intelligent Linguistic Architectures: Variations on Themes by Ronald M. Kaplan* 287–300. Stanford: CSLI.

Kratzer, Angelika and Selkirk, Elisabeth (2020). Deconstructing information structure. *Glossa: A Journal of General Linguistics* 5: 113.

Kügler, Frank (2015). Phonological phrasing and ATR vowel harmony in Akan. *Phonology* 32: 177–204.

Ladd, D. Robert (1980). *The Structure of Intonational Meaning: Evidence from English*. Bloomington, IN: Indiana University Press.

Ladd, D. Robert (1983). Even, focus, and normal stress. *Journal of Semantics* 2: 157–170.

Lee, Seunghun and Selkirk, Elisabeth (2022). Xitsonga tone: The syntax-phonology interface. In Haruo Kubozono, Junko Ito, and Armin Mester (eds.) *Prosody and Prosodic Interfaces* 337–374. Oxford University Press.

Lieberman, Philip (1963). Some effects of semantic and grammatical context on the production and perception of speech. *Language and Speech* 6: 172–187.

Nespor, Marina and Vogel, Irene (1986). *Prosodic Phonology*. Dordrecht: Foris.

Parker, Stephen (1999). On the behavior of definite articles in Chamicuro. *Language* 75: 552–562.

Peperkamp, Sharon (1997). *Prosodic Words*. The Hague: Holland Academic Graphics.

Prince, Alan, Merchant, Nazarré, and Tesar, Bruce (2007–2020). OTWorkplace. http://sites.google.com/site/otworkplace

Schwarzchild, Roger (1999). Givenness, AvoidF and other constraints on the placement of accent. *Natural Language Semantics* 7: 141–177.

Selkirk, Elisabeth (1986). On derived domains in sentence phonology. *Phonology Yearbook* 3: 371–405.

Selkirk, Elisabeth (1995). Sentence prosody: intonation, stress, and phrasing. In John A. Goldsmith (ed.) *The Handbook of Phonological Theory* 550–569. London: Blackwell.

Selkirk, Elisabeth (1996). The prosodic structure of function words. In James L. Morgan and Katherine Demuth (eds.) *Signal to Syntax: Bootstrapping from Speech to Grammar in Early Acquisition* 187–213. Mahwah, NJ: Erlbaum.

Selkirk, Elisabeth (2011). The syntax–phonology interface. In John A. Goldsmith, Jason Riggle, and Alan C. L. Yu (eds.) *The Handbook of Phonological Theory* 435–484. Blackwell Publishing.

Selkirk, Elisabeth and Lee, Seunghun (2017). Syntactic constituency spell-out through Match constraints. Presentation at SPOT1 Workshop, University of California, Santa Cruz. Available at https://thi.ucsc.edu/wp-content/uploads/2017/10/Selkirk_SPOT_11_18_2017.pdf

Selkirk, Elisabeth and Shen, Tong (1990). Prosodic domains in Shanghai Chinese. In Sharon Inkelas and Draga Zec (eds.) *The Phonology-Syntax Connection* 313–337. Chicago: University of Chicago Press.

Truckenbrodt, Hubert (1999). On the relation between syntactic phrases and phonological phrases. *Linguistic Inquiry* 30: 219–255.

Truckenbrodt, Hubert (2007). The syntax-phonology interface. In Paul de Lacy (ed.) *The Cambridge Handbook of Phonology* 435–456. Cambridge: Cambridge University Press.

Tyler, Matthew (2019). Simplifying Match Word: evidence from English functional categories. *Glossa: A Journal of General Linguistics* 4: 15.

Van Handel, Nicholas (2021). Matching overtly headed syntactic phrases in Italian. *Phonology* 38: 317–356.

Zec, Draga and Inkelas, Sharon (1990). Prosodically constrained syntax. In Sharon Inkelas and Draga Zec (eds.) *The Phonology-Syntax Connection* 365–378. Chicago: University of Chicago Press.

Zec, Draga and Inkelas, Sharon (1991). The place of clitics in the prosodic hierarchy. In Dawn Bates (ed.) *Proceedings of the 10th West Coast Conference on Formal Linguistics* 505–519. Stanford: CSLI.

Zec, Draga (2005). Prosodic differences among function words. *Phonology* 22: 77–112.

Zipf, George K. (1929). Relative frequency as a determinant of phonetic change. *Harvard Studies in Classical Philology* 40: 1–95.

## About the author

*Nicholas Van Handel*

Graduate research assistant for the SPOT project, Ph.D. student, Department of Linguistics, UC Santa Cruz. Research interests: Psycholinguistics and phonology, with a focus on implicit prosody, sentence processing, and the syntax-prosody interface. Recent publications: 'Matching overtly headed syntactic phrases in Italian" 2021, *Phonology*.

# Part III

# Align Theory

# Chapter 7

# Interactions of matching, alignment, and binarity in Japanese and beyond

Nick Kalivoda[*]

## 7.1    Introduction

Match Theory holds that although sp.MATCH and ps.MATCH constraints promote syntax-prosody isomorphism, they may be outranked by markedness constraints which compel mismatches (Selkirk 2011). MATCH constraints have the same effects as faithfulness constraints, so this amounts to the usual situation in Optimality Theory (OT; Prince and Smolensky 1993/2004): a ranking MARKEDNESS ≫ FAITHFULNESS results in an unfaithful input–output mapping.

Kubozono (1989) discovered a syntax–prosody mismatch in Japanese which, in isolation, finds a ready explanation within Match Theory. A four-word left-branching syntactic structure maps to a prosodic tree with balanced branching, as in (1).

[*] I am grateful to Alan Prince, Jennifer Bellik, Junko Ito, and Armin Mester for comments and suggestions. All errors are my own.

(1)    Japanese mismatch from four-word left-branching input (Kubozono 1989)[1]

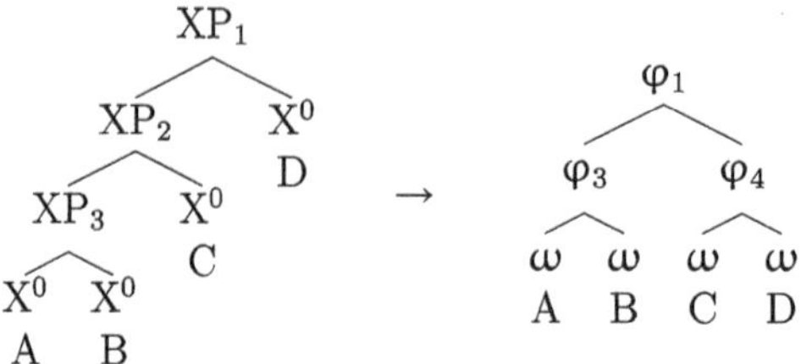

The mapping in (1) violates the MATCH constraints sp.MATCH(XP,$\varphi$) and ps.MATCH($\varphi$,XP). The input constituent $XP_2$ has no matching $\varphi$ in the output—i.e., no ($_\varphi$ A B C)—and the output constituent $\varphi_4$ has no matching XP in the input—i.e., no [$_{XP}$ C D].

The mismatch in (1) has been analyzed as resulting from a markedness constraint m.BINMAX($\varphi$,$\omega$) dominating the basic MATCH constraints (Selkirk 2011, Ishihara 2014, Kalivoda 2018). This constraint penalizes every $\varphi$ that dominates more than two words, at any level of depth. If the input in (1) underwent perfect matching, its output would contain a phonological phrase dominating three words: ($_\varphi$ A B C). The conflict between the actual Japanese mapping in (1), and the ungrammatical faithful mapping, is shown in the following comparative tableau (CT; Prince 2002a,b et seq.). Here and elsewhere, XP boundaries are represented by square brackets, and $\varphi$ boundaries by parentheses.

(2)    Comparative tableau for Japanese mismatch

| Input | Winner | Loser | m.BINMAX ($\varphi$,$\omega$) | sp.MATCH (XP,$\varphi$) | ps.MATCH ($\varphi$,XP) |
|---|---|---|---|---|---|
| [[[A B] C] D] | ((A B) (C D)) | (((A B) C) D) | W | L | L |

While the losing matching candidate violates m.BINMAX($\varphi$,$\omega$) twice with its three-word ($_\varphi$ A B C) and four-word ($_\varphi$ A B C D), the winner violates it only once, with ($_\varphi$ A B C D). Thus in this comparison, m.BINMAX($\varphi$,$\omega$) assigns a "W", meaning that it prefers the winner over the loser. Taken with the fact

---

[1] Kubozono proposed representations involving Major and Minor phrases, rather than recursive $\varphi$s. The prosodic tree in (1) is derived from Kubozono's by replacing Major and Minor phrase labels with '$\varphi$', as proposed by Ito and Mester (2013).

that the MATCH constraints assign 'L", meaning that they prefer the matching loser, this gives us an elementary ranking condition (ERC) stating that m.BINMAX($\varphi$,$\omega$) dominates the basic MATCH constraints in Japanese.

While this analysis nicely accounts for the mismatch in (1), Bellik et al. (2022; henceforth BIKM) point out that it misses a fundamental left/right asymmetry in Japanese. The constraints in (2) wrongly predict that the right-branching mirror image of the input should also map to balanced-branching ($_\varphi$ ($_\varphi$ A B) ($_\varphi$ C D)), resulting in neutralization. Instead, a four-word right-branching tree is perfectly matched in the prosody, as shown in (3).

(3)      Japanese match from four-word right-branching input

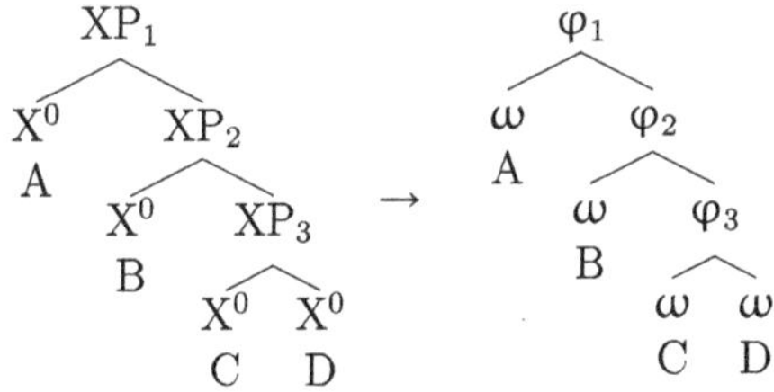


Here the MATCH constraints prefer the actual Japanese mapping, while m.BINMAX($\varphi$,$\omega$) prefers the balanced-branching output. When an ERC expressing this is added to the comparative tableau in (2), the result is the ranking paradox in (4).

(4)      Ranking paradox for Japanese: contradictory ERCs

| Input | Winner | Loser | m.BINMAX ($\varphi$,$\omega$) | sp.MATCH (XP,$\varphi$) | ps.MATCH ($\varphi$,XP) |
|---|---|---|---|---|---|
| *Left-branching* [[[A B] C] D] | *Balanced* ((A B) (C D)) | *Matched* (((A B) C) D) | W | L | L |
| *Right-branching* [A [B [C D]]] | *Matched* (A (B (C D))) | *Balanced* ((A B) (C D)) | L | W | W |

No ranking of the constraints in (4) gives the correct result in both cases. If m.BINMAX($\varphi$,$\omega$) outranks the MATCH constraints, then both inputs neutralize to ($_\varphi$ ($_\varphi$ A B) ($_\varphi$ C D)). If either of the MATCH constraints outranks m.BINMAX($\varphi$,$\omega$), then both inputs undergo perfect matching. An additional constraint is therefore needed.

According to Match Theory, the only constraints are MATCH constraints and markedness constraints. The definition of MATCH (discussed in §7.2) entails that no MATCH constraint can solve the paradox in (4). And no commonly used markedness constraint like STRONGSTART (Selkirk 2011, Elfner 2012) or EQUALSISTERS (Myrberg 2013) makes the necessary distinctions, either.[2] From this, BIKM conclude that syntax–prosody and/or prosody–syntax alignment constraints should be rehabilitated (McCarthy and Prince 1993; Truckenbrodt 1995, 1999), and show that the paradox in (4) is resolved by the introduction of sp.ALIGN(XP,L,$\varphi$,L), which demands that the left edge of every XP align with the left edge of some $\varphi$, or ps.ALIGN($\varphi$,R,XP,R), which demands that the right edge of every $\varphi$ align with the right edge of some XP. The former is shown in (5).

(5)        Japanese ranking paradox resolved with Alignment

| Input | Winner | Loser | sp.ALIGN (XP,L,$\varphi$,L) | m.BIN MAX ($\varphi$,$\omega$) | sp.MATCH (XP,$\varphi$) | ps.MATCH ($\varphi$,XP) |
|---|---|---|---|---|---|---|
| *Left-branching* [[[AB]C]D] | *Balanced* ((AB)(CD)) | *Matched* (((AB)C)D) | e | W | L | L |
| *Right-branching* [A[B[CD]]] | *Matched* (A(B(CD))) | *Balanced* ((AB)(CD)) | W | L | W | W |

To the alignment constraint sp.ALIGN(XP,L,$\varphi$,L), it does not matter whether the left-branching input maps to a balanced or matched output, hence the 'e' in the comparative tableau. This is because the left edge of every XP in this input is initial, so the constraint is satisfied by both the winner and loser, each of which begins with the left edge of a $\varphi$. However, for the right-branching input, sp.ALIGN(XP,L,$\varphi$,L) prefers matching over balancing. While the matched candidate satisfies alignment perfectly, the balanced loser fails to align the left edge of the phrase [$_{\mathrm{XP}}$ B C D]. The combination of ERCs in (5) yields the successful ranking sp.ALIGN(XP,L,$\varphi$,L) $\gg$ m.BINMAX($\varphi$,$\omega$) $\gg$ sp.MATCH(XP,$\varphi$), ps.MATCH($\varphi$,XP). This solution is in line with previous research proposing that Japanese aligns the left edges of XPs (cf. Selkirk and Tateishi 1991), and avoids positing an *ad hoc* markedness constraint.

Pursuing an analysis of Japanese in terms of asymmetric alignment, the question arises whether MATCH constraints are called for at all. Pure Match Theory and pure Align/Wrap theory are surely conceptually more

---

[2] BIKM also show that a constraint STRONGEND does not resolve the paradox.

parsimonious than their union, so MATCH constraints must make a significant contribution to earn their keep. BIKM show that two more mappings of four-word XPs in Japanese cannot be explained without either a syntax–prosody constraint sp.MATCH(XP,φ) or a prosody–syntax constraint ps.MATCH(φ,XP). Specifically, the two "mixed-branching" inputs in (6) both undergo perfect matching.

(6)      Matching of Four-Word Mixed-Branching Inputs in Japanese
   a.    Matching of Four-Word Left-over-Right Branching Syntax

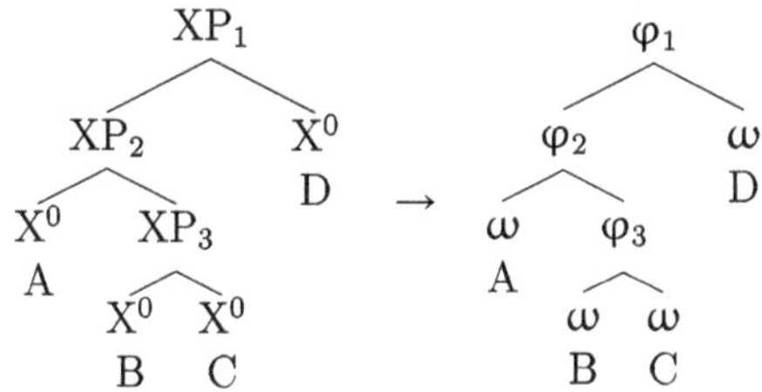

   b.    Matching of Four-Word Right-over-Left Branching Syntax

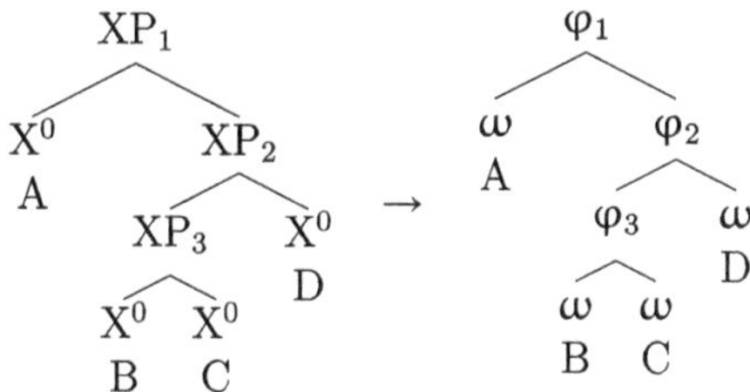

The pattern in (6) constitutes what BIKM dub the Ambivalence Problem. No syntax–prosody or prosody–syntax alignment constraint disfavors mapping the input in (6a) to the output in (6b), or the input in (6b) to the output in (6a). The markedness constraint m.BINMAX(φ,ω) does not decide in favor of matching either. Thus, without MATCH constraints, matching and mismatching tie for these structures. This is shown in the comparative tableau in (7) for the input in (6a).[3]

---

[3] For space reasons, the constraint names in (7) are abbreviated. sp.AL-L = sp.ALIGN(XP,L,φ,L); sp.AL-R = sp.ALIGN(XP,R,φ,R); ps.AL-L = ps.ALIGN(φ,L,XP,L); ps.AL-R = ps.ALIGN(φ,R,XP,R); m.BINMAX = m.BINMAX(φ,ω).

(7)       Ambivalence Problem (Bellik et al. 2022)

| Input | Winner | Loser | sp. Al-L | sp. Al-R | ps. Al-L | ps. Al-R | m. BinMax |
|---|---|---|---|---|---|---|---|
| *L-over-R-Branching* [[A [B C]] D] | *Matching* ((A (B C)) D) | *R-over-L Branching* (A ((B C) D)) | e | e | e | e | e |

In (7), no constraint prefers matching the input in (6a) over mapping it to the mismatched output from (6b). In both the winning and losing mappings, every XP edge aligns with an appropriate φ edge, and vice versa. The binarity constraint is violated once by each candidate, since each output contains two suprabinary φs. Thus, just like pure Match Theory, pure Alignment Theory does not account for Japanese phrasing either.[4]

Adding one of the Match constraints from (2)–(5) solves the Ambivalence Problem of (7). Both sp.Match(XP,φ) and ps.Match(φ,XP) favor matching rather than mismatching, providing the "W" necessary to ensure that some constraint favors the winner over the loser. This is demonstrated with sp.Match(XP,φ) in (8).[5]

(8)       Match solves the Ambivalence Problem (Bellik et al. 2022)

| Input | Winner | Loser | sp. Match | sp. Al-L | sp. Al-R | ps. Al-L | ps. Al-R | m. BinMax |
|---|---|---|---|---|---|---|---|---|
| *L-over-R-Branching* [[A[BC]]D] | *Matching* ((A(BC))D) | *R-over-L Branching* (A((BC)D)) | W | e | e | e | e | e |

Thus, BIKM show that alignment is needed for the Japanese edge asymmetry, and Match is needed to account for matching in certain recursive structures. This leads to a hybrid theory involving two types of mapping constraints: both Match constraints and the Align constraints they were intended to replace (Selkirk 2011).

This hybrid theory proposed by BIKM has yet to be studied on its own terms. While BIKM show that combining Match, Align, and Binarity

---

[4] Syntax–prosody alignment constraints often work in concert with a constraint sp.Wrap(XP), which demands that every XP be contained within a φ (Truckenbrodt 1995, 1999). This constraint would not help in (7). Since every input XP is contained within the maximal φ in both the winning and losing candidates, sp.Wrap(XP) would also assign 'e', favoring neither the winner nor the loser.

[5] In (8), sp.Match stands for sp.Match(XP,φ).

constraints addresses an issue in the phonology of Japanese, the theory itself cries out for elucidation in terms of the analytic method (Prince 2007). Once its premises are fully defined within the context of an OT system, a rich array of theoretical facts await discovery. For a system $S_{M/A}$ in the hybrid MATCH/ALIGN theory, immediate questions include: (i) What are the languages in the factorial typology of $S_{M/A}$? (ii) What are the grammars of those languages? (iii) How do intensional properties of those grammars relate to extensional traits of mappings? and (iv) What is the structure of $S_{M/A}$'s typology?

The present chapter seeks to answer these questions for a MATCH/ALIGN system called SB. (The name alludes to the "Strict Binarity" requirement on SB.GEN, introduced below.) Although SB involves only four constraints—a syntax–prosody MATCH constraint, two syntax–prosody ALIGN constraints, and a BINARITY constraint—its typology reveals numerous subtle constraint interactions that require careful study. The typology of SB, and the relation between grammars and phrasing patterns, are studied below in terms of Property Theory (Alber and Prince 2021). The constraint interactions that make up the grammars of the languages of SB are shown both to impose a structure on the typology itself, and to elucidate the syntax–prosody mappings in the individual languages.

## 7.2   Definition of SB and its subsystems

An OT system S is a pair ⟨S.GEN, S.CON⟩ (Alber et al. 2016). S.GEN gives the candidate sets (csets) in S, which are generally sets of triples ⟨*in*,*out*,*corr*⟩, where *in* is an input, *out* is an output, and *corr* is a correspondence relation between *in* and *out*. In syntax–prosody mapping, a candidate's input is a syntactic tree, and its output is a prosodic tree. SB.GEN and its subsets $SB_n$.GEN are defined in §7.2.1.

S.CON is the constraint set of S. A constraint in S.CON is a function which assigns a non-negative integer to each candidate admitted by S.GEN. The constraint set SB.CON is defined in §7.2.2. Both SB.GEN and SB.CON are computationally implemented using the SPOT application  (Bellik, Bellik, and Kalivoda 2015–2021). The violation tableaux for SB generated by SPOT were then imported into OTWorkplace (Prince, Merchant, and Tesar 2007–2021), in which the factorial typologies, grammars, and property analyses were calculated.

### 7.2.1   G*EN*

SB.G*EN*, which generates the candidate sets to be considered in this chapter, is defined in (9).

(9)    SB.G*EN*
    a.   Inputs in SB

An input is any syntactic tree with $m$ terminal nodes, $2 \leq m$, in which:
      i.   Every non-terminal node is of category XP.
      ii.   Every terminal node is of category $X^0$.
      iii.   Every non-terminal node has exactly two children.

    b.   Outputs in SB

For an input $S$ with $m$ terminal nodes, an output $P$ is a prosodic tree with $m$ terminal nodes in which:
      i.   Every non-terminal node is of category φ.
      ii.   Every terminal node is of category ω.
      iii.   Every non-terminal node has exactly two children.

    c.   C*ORR* in SB

For an input tree $S$ and an output tree $P$, a correspondence relation holds such that the $n^{\text{th}}$ terminal node of $S$ corresponds to the $n^{\text{th}}$ terminal node of $P$. Notationally, we highlight this correspondence by using capital letters A, B, C, ... to represent terminal nodes of both $S$ and $P$, though in $S$ these have category $X^0$ and in $P$ they have category ω. Because A, B, C, ... in $S$ correspond to A, B, C, ... in $P$, we omit correspondence indices.

A subsystem SB$_n$ is defined as in (10).

(10)    SB$_n$.G*EN*
    a.   An input is a syntactic tree with $m$ terminal nodes, $2 \leq m \leq n$, which obeys the conditions in (9a).
    b.   For each input, an output tree is a prosodic tree that obeys the conditions in (9b).
    c.   For an input tree $S$ and an output tree $P$, a correspondence relation holds such that the $n^{\text{th}}$ terminal node of $S$ corresponds to the $n^{\text{th}}$ terminal node of $P$.

The verbose conditions on input and output trees in (9)–(10) can be restated using phrase structure rules as in (11).

(11)    Phrase structure rules for trees in SB.Gen

    a.   For inputs:    XP     →     $\{$XP, X$^0\}$ $\{$XP, X$^0\}$

    b.   For outputs:  $\varphi$     →     $\{\varphi, \omega\}$ $\{\varphi, \omega\}$

In other words, both the input and output trees are perfectly binary-branching. This condition makes SB.Gen stricter than Gen as defined by BIKM and makes the mappings easier to analyze. Of course, neither (11a) nor (11b) is totally realistic for natural languages; future work will need to take into account the fact that $[_{\text{XP}}$ X$^0$ X$^0]$ is not generally considered a valid syntactic structure, and that phonological phrases often have more than two branches, e.g. ($_\varphi$ $\omega$ $\omega$ $\omega$).

That being said, these simplifications are not so wide of the mark. Various researchers have treated one-word XPs as phonologically inert (Tokizaki 2006, Bennett, Elfner, and McCloskey 2016), and the imperative for strict binary branching, though frequently rejected in Prosodic Hierarchy Theory, is a recurring theme in work from metrical phonology (see, e.g., Liberman and Prince 1977, a.m.o.).[6] Furthermore, although not generally considered part of Gen, the violable markedness constraints m.BinMin($\varphi$,branches) and m.BinMax($\varphi$,branches) are often placed in Con (Selkirk 2011, Elfner 2012, Ito and Mester 2013). We could easily define a new system in which such constraints are not part of Gen, but part of Con instead. Although we follow Merchant and Prince (to appear) in defining a system that "stands on its own and is not to be understood as a fragment of something else", it is nevertheless reasonable to assume that learning about the system SB with its extreme simplifications could facilitate understanding a more complicated system derived from it in the future.

### 7.2.2   Con

The constraint set SB.Con is given in (12). Although every constraint in SB.Con is taken from previous literature, we provide our own unambiguous definitions, and prefix the constraint names to show what kind of constraints they are: 'sp" for syntax→prosody mapping (faithfulness), and 'm" for markedness.[7]

---

[6] Though prosodic structure could turn out to be strictly binary branching, this would involve positing large amounts of hitherto undetected structure in apparent cases of flat, super-binary constituents.

[7] We use the terms 'mapping", 'syntax→prosody", and 'faithfulness" interchangeably, even though there is an important sense in which such constraints differ from usual faithfulness constraints. While faithfulness constraints demand input-output identity for items of the same

(12)     SB.Con

   a.    sp.MATCH(XP,φ)                                                   (sp.M)
         Violated by every XP in $S$ for which there is no matching φ in $P$.

   b.    sp.ALIGN(XP,L,φ,L)                                               (sp.AL)
         Violated by every XP in $S$ that does not share a left edge with some
         φ in $P$.

   c.    sp.ALIGN(XP,R,φ,R)                                               (sp.AR)
         Violated by every XP in $S$ that does not share a right edge with
         some φ in $P$.

   d.    m.BINMAX(φ,ω)                                                    (m.BW)
         Violated by every φ in $P$ that dominates more than two ωs.[8]

In the discussion that follows, we frequently abbreviate the constraints
of SB.CON. Henceforth, sp.MATCH(XP,φ) can be abbreviated as sp.M or
sp.MATCH; sp.ALIGN(XP,L,φ,L) as sp.AL or sp.ALIGN-L; sp.ALIGN(XP,R,φ,R)
as sp.AR or sp.ALIGN-R; and m.BINMAX(φ,ω) as m.BW or m.BIN-ω.

   The mapping constraint definitions in (13) contain two terms, 'matching"
and 'sharing a left/right edge," which require definition.


(13)     Definitions of mapping relations

   a.    Matching (cf. Elfner 2012)
         A node XP and a node φ are *matching* iff there is a correspondence
         bijection between the nodes in the terminal strings of XP and φ,
         i.e., $[_{XP} X^0_1 X^0_2 ... X^0_n]$ and $(_φ \omega_1 \omega_2 ... \omega_n)$.

   b.    Edge-Sharing (cf. McCarthy and Prince 1993)
         A node XP and a node φ share a left/right edge iff the leftmost/
         rightmost terminal node in XP corresponds to the leftmost/right-
         most terminal node in φ.

-----

type (e.g. input segments and output segments), mapping constraints compare items of different types (e.g. XP and φ). However, if we ignore the type distinction and equate CP with
ι, XP with φ, and $X^0$ with ω, then mapping constraints are simply ordinary faithfulness constraints from Correspondence Theory (McCarthy and Prince 1995).

[8] m.BINMAX(φ,ω) in this system is categorical, not gradient; it assigns one violation for every
φ dominating more than two words, so $(_φ \omega\omega\omega)$, $(_φ \omega\omega\omega\omega)$, $(_φ \omega\omega\omega\omega\omega)$, etc. all induce exactly
one violation. Replacing categorical m.BW with gradient m.B̂W results in a different typology,
the study of which we leave to future research. m.BINMAX(φ,ω) also differs from another
commonly invoked binarity constraint, m.BINMAX(φ,branches), which assigns a violation for
every φ that immediately dominates more than two nodes. This constraint is satisfied by every
candidate admitted by SB.GEN, since all trees in SB are perfectly binary branching. See Bellik
and Kalivoda (2016), Kalivoda and Bellik (2018), and Bellik and Van Handel (Chapter 10)
for discussion of this important distinction among binarity constraints.

In trees throughout this chapter, we sometimes place arbitrary indices on XPs and $\varphi$s. When an XP and a $\varphi$ have the same index, they are matching (and therefore share both left and right edges). When an XP and a $\varphi$ bear different indices, they are not matching, but this does not preclude the possibility that they share exactly one edge.

The alignment constraints sp.ALIGN(XP,L,$\varphi$,L) and sp.ALIGN(XP,R,$\varphi$,R) are exactly those of Truckenbrodt (1995, 1999). While they take the form dictated by the theory of Generalized Alignment (McCarthy and Prince 1993), they differ from many of the most commonly encountered alignment constraints, such as ALL-FEET-LEFT and ALL-FEET-RIGHT, in two important ways. First, they are mapping constraints—i.e., essentially a type of faithfulness constraint—not markedness constraints. To avoid confusion with markedness constraints like ALL-FEET-LEFT, we assiduously include the type prefix 'sp" on all occasions. Second, sp.ALIGN(XP,L,$\varphi$,L) and sp.ALIGN(XP,R,$\varphi$,R) are not distance-sensitive; for each XP in an input, an sp.ALIGN constraint assigns either 0 violations or 1 violation. An XP edge does not incur more violations the further it is from the closest $\varphi$ edge of the same type; i.e., AB]CD $\rightarrow$ ABC)D is not better than AB]CD $\rightarrow$ ABCD) on sp.ALIGN-R.

Although SB.CON contains the syntax$\rightarrow$prosody mapping constraint sp.MATCH(XP,$\varphi$), it does not contain its prosody$\rightarrow$syntax counterpart ps.MATCH($\varphi$,XP), which is also a key component of Match Theory (Selkirk 2011). However, it turns out that with the strict binarity restrictions of SB.GEN, the two MATCH constraints are equivalent. For every candidate $k$ admitted  by SB.GEN, sp.M($k$) = ps.M($k$). So substituting ps.M for sp.M in SB, or including both constraints, has no effect on the typology. In every grammar and property analysis discussed below for SB, or for one of its subsystems SB$_n$, ps.MATCH can take the place of sp.MATCH. If both are included, then {sp.MATCH, ps.MATCH}.dom takes the place of sp.MATCH. This is an artifact of the extreme restrictions placed on SB.GEN. In a system without strict binary branching built into GEN, sp.MATCH and ps.MATCH do not generally assign the same number of violations, or partition the csets equivalently.

Having spelled out SB.GEN and SB.CON, we now turn to the analysis of the simplest subsystems of SB, namely SB$_2$ and SB$_3$.


## 7.3   Subsystems SB$_2$ and SB$_3$

The typologies of SB$_2$ and SB$_3$ both contain exactly one language, in which every input maps to an isomorphic output. The mappings of the language in SB$_3$ are shown in (14). (We henceforth omit the XP and $\varphi$ labels in bracketed string notation, since the label of a constituent in square brackets is always XP, and the label of a constituent in parentheses is always $\varphi$.)

(14)     The one language of $SB_3$
    a.   [A B]      $\rightarrow$   (A B)
    b.   [[A B] C] $\rightarrow$   ((A B) C)
    c.   [A [B C]] $\rightarrow$   (A (B C))

The mapping in (14a) from [AB] to (AB) follows trivially, since the cset for [AB] contains only one candidate. There is only one strictly binary-branching tree on two terminals, so $SB_2$ has only one input and one output. For completeness, a trivial tableau is shown in (15).

(15)     VT for two-word input (full candidate set)

| $XP_1$<br>A  B | sp.M | sp.AL | sp.AR | m.BW |
|---|---|---|---|---|
| $\varphi_1$<br>A  B | 0 | 0 | 0 | 0 |

The single candidate in (15) does not violate any of the constraints. $XP_1$ and $\varphi_1$ are matching, and they therefore share both their left and right edges. m.Bin-$\omega$ (m.BW in the tableau) is satisfied since $\varphi_1$ contains exactly two $\omega$s. However, the candidate's perfection is a moot point, since it has no competitors anyway.

The isomorphic mappings in (14b–c) are guaranteed by the equivalent markedness profiles of left-branching ((A B) C) and right-branching (A (B C)), these being the only two outputs in each three-word cset. The lone markedness constraint in SB, the binarity constraint m.Bin-$\omega$, assigns one violation to each, since each contains only one suprabinary $\varphi$: the maximal $\varphi$ containing A, B, and C. Thus, mapping either three-word input to a non-isomorphic output does not improve on markedness. Furthermore, mismatching by definition worsens a candidate's fate on the three syntax$\rightarrow$prosody (faithfulness) constraints. Since a three-word mismatch is unfaithful but does not improve on markedness, it is harmonically bounded, leaving the unique matching candidate in each cset victorious. This is shown in the following tableau for the left-branching input.

(16)   VT for three-word L-branching input (1/1 optima, 1/1 HBs)

| 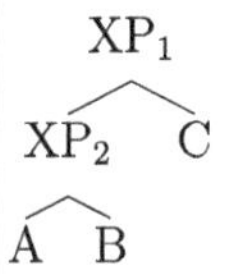 $XP_1$ [ $XP_2$ C / A B ] | sp.M | sp.AL | sp.AR | m.BW |
|---|---|---|---|---|
| a. 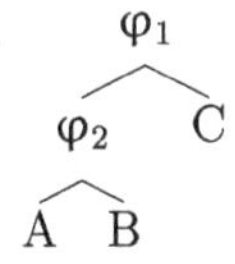   $\varphi_1$ [ $\varphi_2$ C / A B ] | | | | 1 $(\varphi_1)$ |
| b. 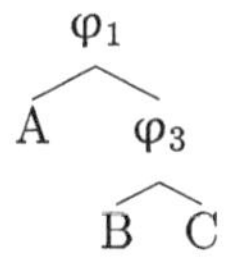   $\varphi_1$ [ A   $\varphi_3$ / B C ] | 1 $(XP_2)$ | | 1 $(XP_2)$ | 1 $(\varphi_1)$ |

Both candidates (16a) and (16b) violate m.Bin-$\omega$ once, since $\varphi_1$ dominates three $\omega$s. But while (16a) satisfies all three mapping constraints, (16b) violates sp.MATCH once for failing to match $XP_2 = [AB]$, and sp.Align-R once since $XP_2$ does not share a right edge with any $\varphi$.

An analogous tableau with the input [A[BC]] would show that [A[BC]] → (A(BC)) harmonically bounds [A[BC]] → ((AB)C), outperforming it on sp.MATCH and sp.Align-L, and tying with it on sp.Align-R and m.Bin-$\omega$.

In the larger systems discussed below, the mappings in (14) are present in every language, regardless of ranking. They are therefore omitted from tables showing factorial typologies. Since  the typologies of $SB_2$ and $SB_3$ contain only one language, there is no need to undertake a property analysis of them, so we now move on to $SB_4$, where things get more interesting.


## 7.4   Subsystem $SB_4$

As per (9) in §7.2.1, $SB_4$ includes the three csets of $SB_3$, plus csets for all strictly binary-branching input trees containing four words, of which there are five:

(17)      The five four-word input trees of SB$_4$

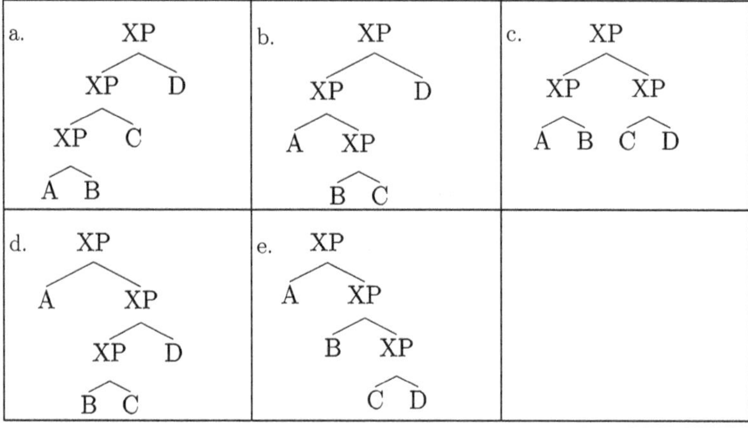

These five trees are also the five possible output trees for a four-word input, when "XP" is replaced with "φ." (We do not visually represent the additional difference in terminal node category between input and output trees.)

(18)      The five four-word prosodic trees admitted by SB$_4$.GEN

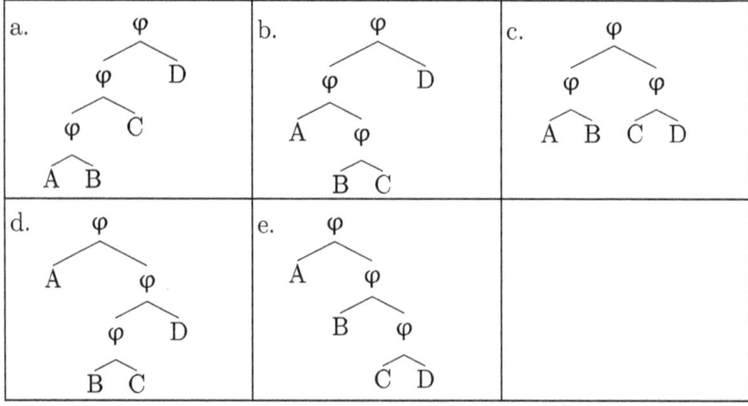

As in every subsystem of SB, the constraints of SB$_4$ are sp.MATCH(XP,φ), sp.ALIGN(XP,L,φ,L), sp.ALIGN(XP,R,φ,R), and m.BINMAX(φ,ω).

### 7.4.1    Typology of SB$_4$

The factorial typology of SB$_4$ consists of four languages, shown in (19). To improve readability, the word "match" is used to indicate that the winning output in a cell is the unique prosodic tree isomorphic to that column's input. The input–output mappings from $SB_3$ are not included in the table, since they are constant across languages.

(19)     Factorial typology of $SB_4$

|          | [A[B[CD]] | [[A[BC]]D] | [[AB][CD]] | [A[[BC]D]] | [[[AB]C]D] |
|----------|-----------|------------|------------|------------|------------|
| Iso      | match     | match      | match =    | match      | match      |
| EP.L     | match     | match      | ((AB)(CD)) | match      | ((AB)(CD)) |
| EP.R     | ((AB)(CD))| match      | ((AB)(CD)) | match      | match      |
| Bal      | ((AB)(CD))| ((AB)(CD)) | ((AB)(CD)) | ((AB)(CD)) | ((AB)(CD)) |

Foreshadowing the property analysis of $SB_4$, the languages in (19) are named in ways that allude to their grammars and traits. Representing the two extremes of faithfulness and non-markedness are the first language, Iso (named for 'isomorphism"), which maps every input to a perfectly matching output, and the fourth language, Bal (named for 'balancing"), in which every input is neutralized to the 'balanced" prosodic parse ((AB)(CD)). The second and third languages, EP.L and EP.R (named for 'edge-preserving left/right"), map some inputs to isomorphic outputs, and others to ((AB)(CD)). Which inputs the EP languages map faithfully depends on the placement of left and/or right edges.

The grammars of the languages in (19) are given in (20) as disjunctive sets of Hasse diagrams. The grammar of Iso is not a partial order, and therefore cannot be represented as a single Hasse diagram (see Prince 2017 on both the limitations and the excesses of Hasse diagrams, and other popular devices, in representing OT grammars). Filtering candidates according to either of the two disjunctive partial orders yields the mappings of Iso. The order of languages in (20) is changed relative to the order in (19) to facilitate comparison of the twin grammars of EP.L and EP.R.

(20)     Grammars of the languages of SB$_4$

a. Iso                                                          b. Bal

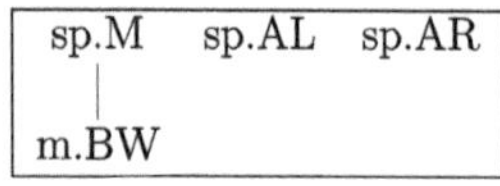

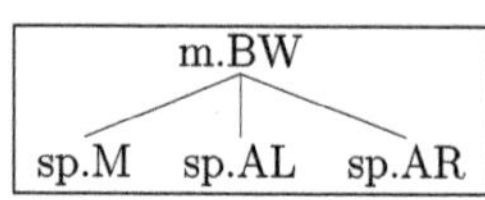

c. EP.L                                                        d. EP.R

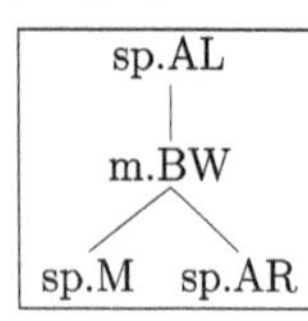

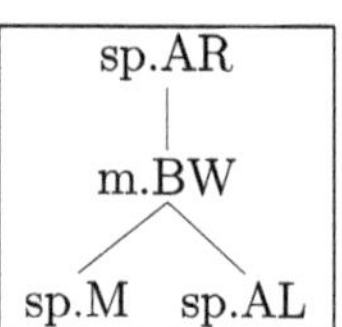

We will justify these grammars below by examining the rankings responsible
for the various mappings in (19). We examine the structure of the typology
itself in §7.4.2.

In SB$_4$, every mismatch involves mapping a tree to ((AB)(CD)), and no
language maps [[AB][CD]] to a mismatching output. This follows from the
way the markedness constraint m.Bɪɴ-ω partitions each cset: it considers
((AB)(CD)) the best output, and the four other trees tie in last place. In
the balanced tree in (21), only the root node offends m.Bɪɴ-ω by dominating more than two words.

(21)     Best 4ω tree on m.Bɪɴ-ω (1 violation)

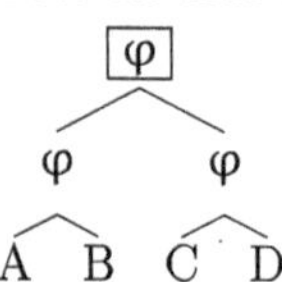

The trees in (22), by contrast, each contain two such nodes: the root node,
and the φ immediately dominated by the root node.

(22)      Worst 4ω trees on m.Bɪɴ-ω (2 violations each)

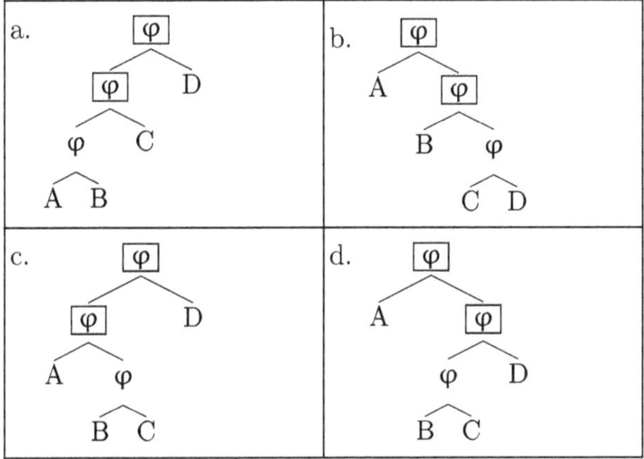

The five trees in (21)–(22) are the only four-word prosodic trees in SB, so the partition imposed by m.Bɪɴ-ω is bipartite: *balanced* $>_{\text{m.BW}}$ *unbalanced*.[9] It is significant that there is a unique tree preferred  by m.Bɪɴ-ω. If an input deviates from matching, then it must map to this uniquely least marked tree. This is guaranteed by OT's property of *Harmonic Ascent*, discovered by Moreton (2004), since syntax→prosody markedness constraints are faithfulness constraints,[10] and there is a perfectly faithful (isomorphic,  matching) candidate in every cest of SB. Harmonic Ascent is defined in (23).

(23)      Harmonic Ascent (Moreton 2004, Prince 2007)
          Suppose for y≠x, x → y is optimal for some hierarchy H, where
          x → x is also a candidate. Then for H|M, the subhierarchy of M
          [markedness –NK] constraints ranked as they are in H, it must be
          that  y≻x on H|M.

As Prince (2007) puts it, 'if things do not stay the same, they must get better (markedness-wise)." In SB, the markedness subhierarchy M contains exactly one constraint, m.Bɪɴ-ω, for every constraint hierarchy H. Thus, if a tree in SB does not stay the same, it must improve on m.Bɪɴ-ω. This explains the universality of the mapping [[AB][CD]] → ((AB)(CD)) in SB_4,

---

[9] An expression x $>_{\text{C}}$ y is to be read as 'x is more harmonic than y on constraint C" (Merchant and Prince to appear).

[10] See fn. 3 for a caveat which does not affect the line of reasoning pursued here.

as well as the fact that every mismatch in every language of $SB_4$ involves mapping a syntactic tree to $((AB)(CD))$.

In the remainder of this subsection, we consider the ranking conditions that determine whether non-balanced input trees undergo matching or balancing. The violation tableau in (24) shows the possible ways of mapping four-word left-branching $[[[AB]C]D]$ to a prosodic output. Candidate (24a) is perfectly matching, while mismatching (24b) is less marked on m.Bɪɴ-ω.

(24)    VT for four-word L-branching input (2/2 optima, 0/3 HBs)

| $\begin{matrix} & XP_1 & \\ XP_2 & & D \\ XP_3 & C & \\ A & B & \end{matrix}$ | sp.M | sp.AL | sp.AR | m.BW |
|---|---|---|---|---|
| a. $\begin{matrix} & \varphi_1 & \\ \varphi_2 & & D \\ \varphi_3 & C & \\ A & B & \end{matrix}$ | | | | $2\ (\varphi_1,\varphi_2)$ |
| b. $\begin{matrix} & \varphi_1 & \\ \varphi_3 & & \varphi_4 \\ A\ B & & C\ D \end{matrix}$ | $1\ (XP_2)$ | | $1\ (XP_2)$ | $1\ (\varphi_2)$ |

The matching candidate (24a) fully satisfies the faithfulness constraints sp.Mᴀᴛᴄʜ, sp.Aʟɪɢɴ-L, and sp.Aʟɪɢɴ-R, and incurs two violations of m.Bɪɴ-ω, as discussed above. Candidate (24b), while less marked on m.Bɪɴ-ω, violates sp.Mᴀᴛᴄʜ and sp.Aʟɪɢɴ-R. In (24b), the input constituent $XP_2 = [ABC]$ does not align to the right edge of any $\varphi$.[11] The following diagrams illustrate the (un)faithfulness of (24b) more vividly. Dashed arrows represent successful mappings, while solid arrows pointing to empty set symbols indicate faithfulness violations.

---

[11] In writing $XP_2 = [ABC]$, the expression to the right of the equals sign is the terminal string of $XP_2$, which in one sense *is* $XP_2$. Note that '=' here does not indicate strict identity in the hierarchical sense, since the expression '[ABC]' does not indicate that [AB] are themselves $XP_3$. We adopt this convention throughout the chapter.

(25)    (Un)faithfulness in candidate (24b)
   a.    sp.MATCH: 1 violation

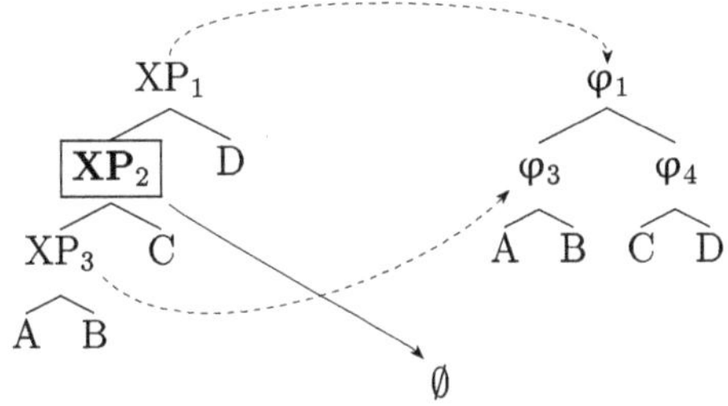

   b.    sp.ALIGN-L: 0 violations

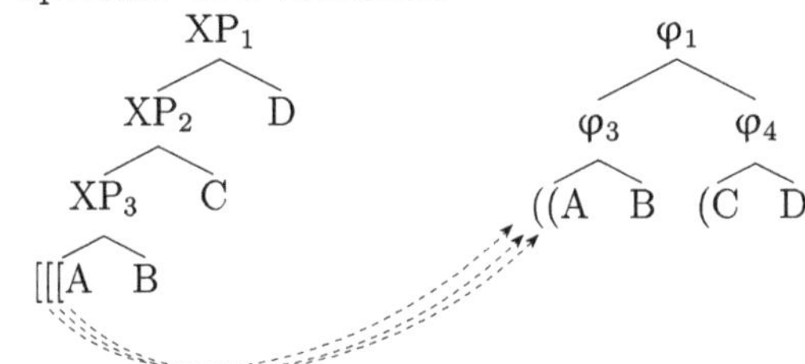

   c.    sp.ALIGN-R: 1 violation

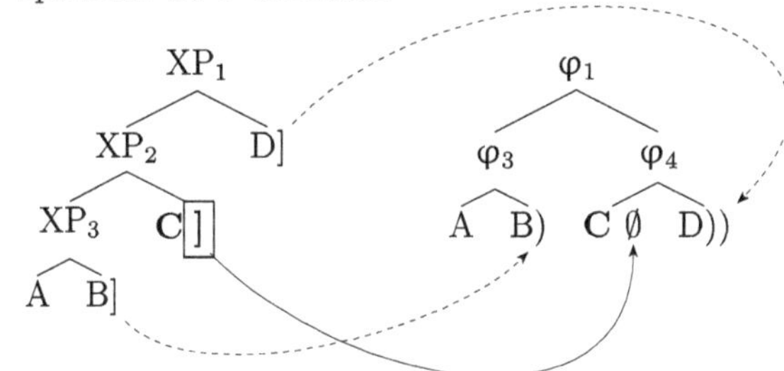

As (25b) shows, (24b) fully satisfies sp.ALIGN-L, a consequence of the left-branching structure of the input. The left edges of $XP_1$=[ABCD], $XP_2$=[ABC], and $XP_3$=[AB] are all initial in the terminal string, hence necessarily aligned to the left edge of the maximal $\varphi$ in each output. It does not matter to sp.ALIGN-L that word A is at the left edge of three XPs, but only at the left edge of two $\varphi$s; all sp.ALIGN-L asks is whether each left XP edge is aligned with *some* left $\varphi$-edge. Thus sp.ALIGN-L is silent on the choice between isomorphic (24a) and balanced (24b).

Deriving comparative tableau from (24) reveals the elementary ranking conditions associated with each possible mapping (ERCs; Prince 2002a,b et seq.). Empty cells have the 'e' value.

(26)     CTs for mappings from four-word L-branching input

     a.     Matching winner: (24a) > (24b)

| Input | Winner | Loser | sp.M | sp.AL | sp.AR | m.BW |
|---|---|---|---|---|---|---|
| 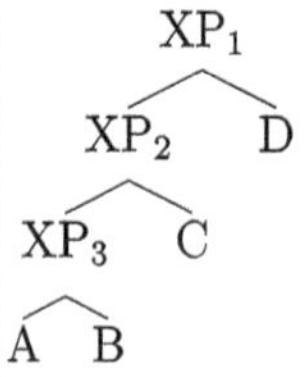 $XP_1$ [ $XP_2$, D ]; $XP_2$ [ $XP_3$, C ]; $XP_3$ [ A, B ] | 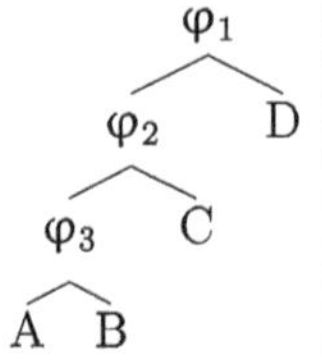 $\varphi_1$ [ $\varphi_2$, D ]; $\varphi_2$ [ $\varphi_3$, C ]; $\varphi_3$ [ A, B ] | 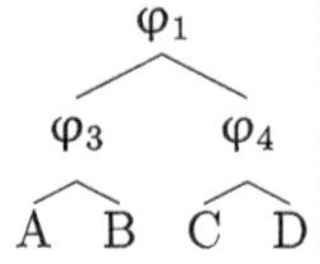 $\varphi_1$ [ $\varphi_3$, $\varphi_4$ ]; $\varphi_3$ [ A, B ]; $\varphi_4$ [ C, D ] | W |  | W | L |

     b.     Balanced winner: (24b) > (24a)

| Input | Winner | Loser | sp.M | sp.AL | sp.AR | m.BW |
|---|---|---|---|---|---|---|
| 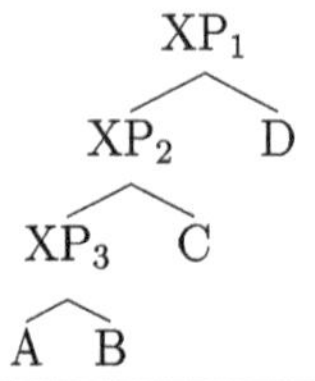 $XP_1$ [ $XP_2$, D ]; $XP_2$ [ $XP_3$, C ]; $XP_3$ [ A, B ] | 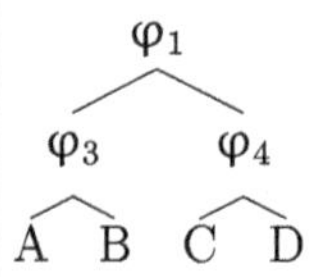 $\varphi_1$ [ $\varphi_3$, $\varphi_4$ ]; $\varphi_3$ [ A, B ]; $\varphi_4$ [ C, D ] | 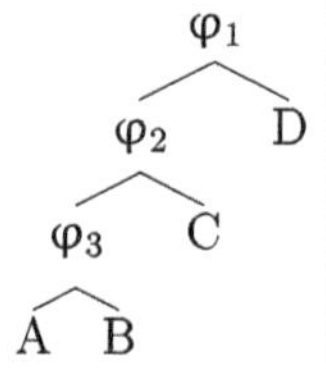 $\varphi_1$ [ $\varphi_2$, D ]; $\varphi_2$ [ $\varphi_3$, C ]; $\varphi_3$ [ A, B ] | L |  | L | W |

In comparative tableaux, the intended winner on a given row beats the intended loser if some constraint assessing "W" outranks every constraint assessing "L." Thus, the matching candidate (26a) wins if sp.MATCH or sp.ALIGN-R dominates m.BIN-ω (as in Iso and EP.R), and the balanced candidate (26b) wins if m.BIN-ω dominates both sp.MATCH and sp.ALIGN-R (as in EP.L and Bal).

Having dealt with the four-word left-branching input, we turn to its mirror image, the strictly right-branching four-word input. The VT containing its possible optimal mappings is given in (27).

(27)    VT for four-word R-branching input (2/2 optima, 0/3 HBs)

| XP$_1$ tree | sp.M | sp.AL | sp.AR | m.BW |
|---|---|---|---|---|
| a. matching tree ($\varphi_1$ / A $\varphi_2$ / B $\varphi_3$ / C D) | | | | 2 ($\varphi_1,\varphi_2$) |
| b. balanced tree ($\varphi_1$ / $\varphi_3$ $\varphi_4$ / A B C D) | 1 (XP$_2$) | 1 (XP$_2$) | | 1 ($\varphi_1$) |

VT (27) is exactly like VT (24), except the trees have mirror image shapes, and the mapping to the balanced tree (27b) violates sp.ALIGN-L instead of sp.ALIGN-R. As before, the matching candidate satisfies sp.MATCH while the balancing candidate violates it once. And of course, the matching (27a) violates m.BIN-ω twice, while balanced (27b) does so only once.

The faithful and unfaithful aspects of (27b) are illustrated in (28).

(28)    (Un)faithfulness in candidate (27b)
    a.    sp.MATCH: 1 violation

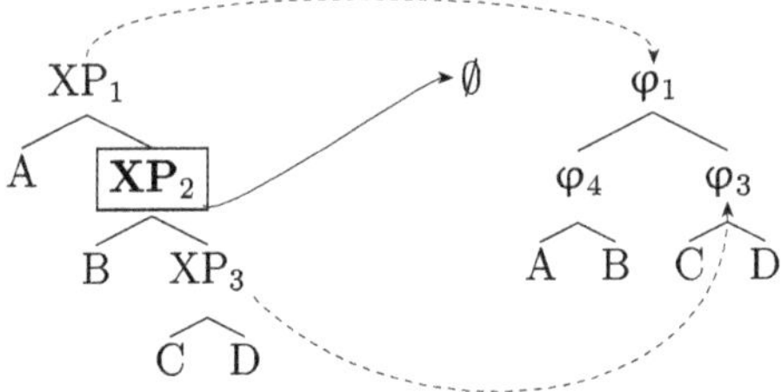

b.    sp.ALIGN-L: 1 violation

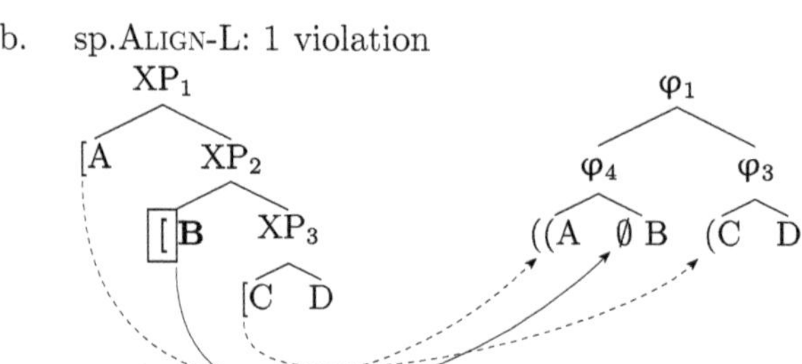

c.    sp.ALIGN-R: 0 violations

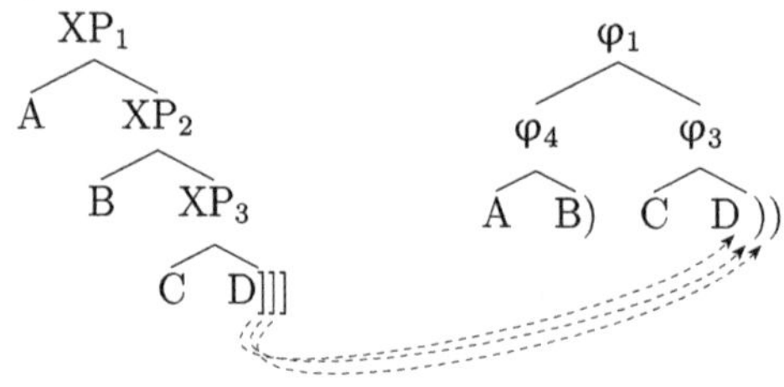

The comparative tableaux in (29) show the ERCs for the matching and balancing mappings from [A[B[CD]]].

(29)      CTs for mappings from four-word R-branching input

     a.     Matching winner: (27a) ≻ (27b)

| Input | Winner | Loser | sp.M | sp.AL | sp.AR | m.BW |
|---|---|---|---|---|---|---|
| $XP_1$ / A $XP_2$ / B $XP_3$ / C D | $\varphi_1$ / A $\varphi_2$ / B $\varphi_3$ / C D | $\varphi_1$ / $\varphi_3$ $\varphi_4$ / A B C D | W | W | | L |

     b.     Balanced winner: (27b) ≻ (27a)

| Input | Winner | Loser | sp.M | sp.AL | sp.AR | m.BW |
|---|---|---|---|---|---|---|
| $XP_1$ / A $XP_2$ / B $XP_3$ / C D | $\varphi_1$ / $\varphi_3$ $\varphi_4$ / A B C D | $\varphi_1$ / A $\varphi_2$ / B $\varphi_3$ / C D | L | L | | W |

The matching candidate [A[B[CD]]] → (A(B(CD))) beats the balancing candidate [A[B[CD]]] → ((AB)(CD)) when sp.MATCH or sp.ALIGN-L dominates m.BIN-ω ((29a)), as in Iso and EP.L. Balancing beats matching when m.BIN-ω dominates both sp.MATCH and sp.ALIGN-L ((29b)), as in EP.R and Bal.

Finally, we turn to one of the 'mixed-branching" inputs, [[A[BC]]D], which contains one left-branching phrase [$_{XP}$ XP D] and one right-branching phrase [$_{XP}$ A XP]. We call this the L-over-R-branching input. This input is matched in Iso, EP.L, and EP.R, and only undergoes rebracketing in Bal. The VT in (30) contains the two possible optima.

(30)    VT for four-word L-over-R-branching input (2/2 optima, 0/3 HBs)

| XP$_1$ tree | sp.M | sp.AL | sp.AR | m.BW |
|---|---|---|---|---|
| a. $\varphi_1$ tree | | | | 2 ($\varphi_1,\varphi_2$) |
| b. $\varphi_1$ tree | 2 (XP$_2$,XP$_3$) | 1 (XP$_3$) | 2 (XP$_2$,XP$_3$) | 1 ($\varphi_1$) |

Unlike in the uniformly branching cases, balancing (30b) violates both syntax→prosody alignment constraints, because both types of edges occur phrase-medially. This is illustrated in (31).

(31)     (Un)faithfulness in candidate (30b)

    a.    sp.MATCH: 2 violations

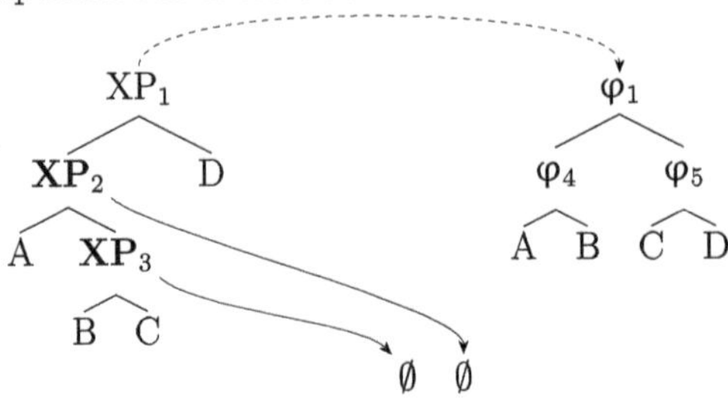

    b.    sp.ALIGN-L: 1 violation

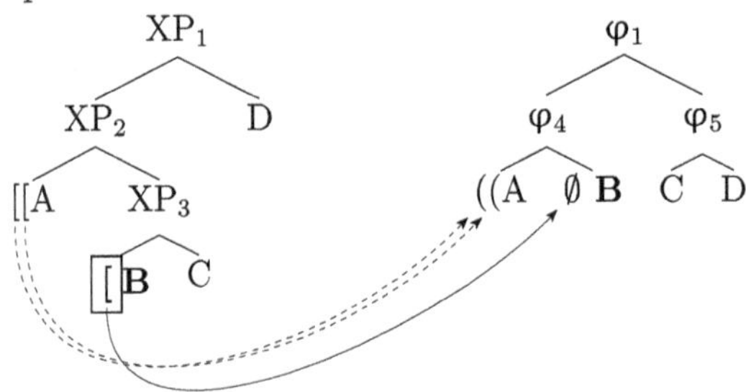

    c.    sp.ALIGN-R: 2 violations

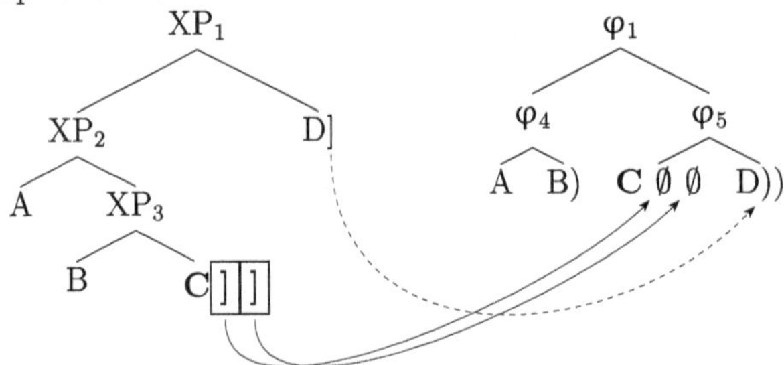

Here, every constraint prefers one optimum or the other. Every faithfulness constraint prefers matching (30a) over balancing (30b). As usual, m.BIN-ω has the opposite preference. This is shown in the following CTs derived from (30).

(32)    CTs for mappings from four-word L-over-R-branching input
  a.    Matching winner: (30a) ≻ (30b)

| Input | Winner | Loser | sp.M | sp.AL | sp.AR | m.BW |
|---|---|---|---|---|---|---|
| $[_{XP_1}\ [_{XP_2}\ A\ [_{XP_3}\ B\ C]]\ D]$ | $[_{\varphi_1}\ [_{\varphi_2}\ A\ [_{\varphi_3}\ B\ C]]\ D]$ | $[_{\varphi_1}\ [_{\varphi_4}\ A\ B]\ [_{\varphi_5}\ C\ D]]$ | W | W | W | L |

  b.    Balanced winner: (30b) ≻ (30a)

| Input | Winner | Loser | sp.M | sp.AL | sp.AR | m.BW |
|---|---|---|---|---|---|---|
| $[_{XP_1}\ [_{XP_2}\ A\ [_{XP_3}\ B\ C]]\ D]$ | $[_{\varphi_1}\ [_{\varphi_4}\ A\ B]\ [_{\varphi_5}\ C\ D]]$ | $[_{\varphi_1}\ [_{\varphi_2}\ A\ [_{\varphi_3}\ B\ C]]\ D]$ | L | L | L | W |

These CTs show that the L-over-R-branching input only undergoes a mismatch if m.Bin-ω dominates all other constraints, as in Bal. All it takes for it to undergo matching is for sp.Match, sp.Align-L, or sp.Align-R to dominate m.Bin-ω, as is the case in Iso, EP.L, and EP.R.

There is one four-word input that we have not yet examined, namely [A[[BC]D]], which we call R-over-L-branching due to right-branching [$_{XP}$ A XP] and left-branching [$_{XP}$ XP D]. As (19) shows, this input always shares the fate of L-over-R. The faithfulness constraints sp.Match, sp.Align-L, and sp.Align-R prefer [A[[BC]D]] → (A((BC)D)) over [A[[BC]D]] → ((AB)(CD)), and m.Bin-ω prefers the opposite. The ERCs are the same as those for [[A[BC]]D] in (32).

### 7.4.2   *Property analysis of SB$_4$*

In this subsection we present a property analysis (PA) of SB$_4$, the grammars of whose languages are repeated in (33) below.

(33)      Grammars of the languages of SB$_4$

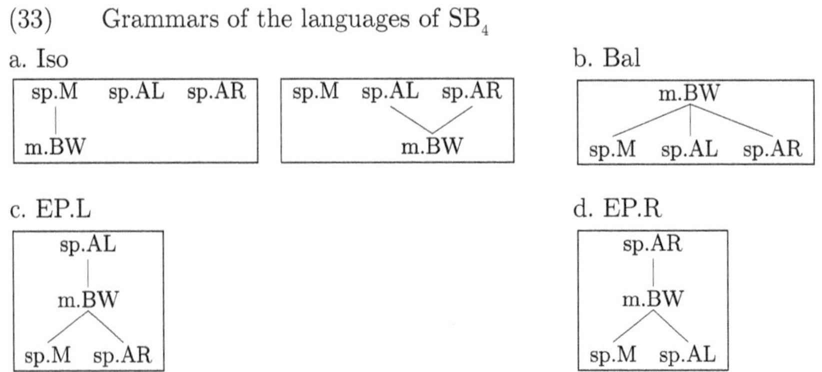

The languages are characterized by the following three properties.

(34)      Properties of SB$_4$

| Property | a | b | Scope |
|---|---|---|---|
| p.MATCH.iso/mis | {sp.M, c.ALIGN.sub}.dom | m.BW | wide |
| p.MAINEDGE.pres/del | c.ALIGN.dom | m.BW | under p.MATCH.mis |
| p.ALIGN.L/R | sp.AL | sp.AR | under p.MAINEDGE.pres |

The first property, p.MATCH.iso/mis, pits {sp.M, c.ALIGN.sub}.dom against
m.BIN-ω, and takes wide scope. The a-side, {sp.M, c.ALIGN.sub}.dom, refers to a public class, c.ALIGN = {sp.AL, sp.AR}.[12] The meaning of {sp.M,
c.ALIGN.sub}.dom is "the dominant constraint in the set containing sp.M and
the subordinate alignment constraint." The language Iso is p.MATCH.iso, and
the other three languages are p.MATCH.mis.

   p.MAINEDGE.pres/del scopes under p.MATCH.mis, meaning that it is moot
for Iso. In EP.L and  EP.R, the dominant syntax→prosody alignment constraint dominates m.BIN-ω, and in Bal, m.BIN-ω dominates both alignment
constraints.

   Finally, p.ALIGN.L/R scopes under p.MAINEDGE.pres, and serves only to
distinguish EP.L from EP.R. In EP.L, sp.ALIGN-L dominates sp.ALIGN-R,
and in EP.R, sp.ALIGN-R dominates sp.ALIGN-L.

   The property values for each language are shown in the PA table in (35).

---

[12] In Property Theory (Alber and Prince 2021:41), a *public class* is a constraint class whose
members are themselves antagonists of a property. In the case of p.MATCH.iso/mis, which can
be spelled out fully as {sp.M, {sp.AL, sp.AR}.sub}.dom, the two alignment constraints are
the antagonists of the property p.ALIGN.L/R = sp.AL <> sp.AR, so c.ALIGN is a public class.

(35)     Property analysis table for SB$_4$

|       | p.MATCH | p.MAINEDGE | p.ALIGN |
|-------|---------|------------|---------|
| Iso   | iso     | *moot*     | *moot*  |
| Bal   | mis     | del        | *moot*  |
| EP.L  | mis     | pres       | L       |
| EP.R  | mis     | pres       | R       |

As indicated in the "scope" column of (34) and the "moot" cells in (35), not all properties of SB$_4$ apply to all languages. p.MAINEDGE is applicable only to languages with mismatching, and p.ALIGN only to those which preserve their main edge. These relations are represented in the property *treeoid* in (36). As in Alber and Prince (2021), "the single lines terminate in properties of which values must be chosen and the double lines mark the inconsistent values of a single property, where one and only one is chosen." When a property in the treeoid is dominated by another property, it is within its scope.

(36)     Property Treeoid for SB$_4$

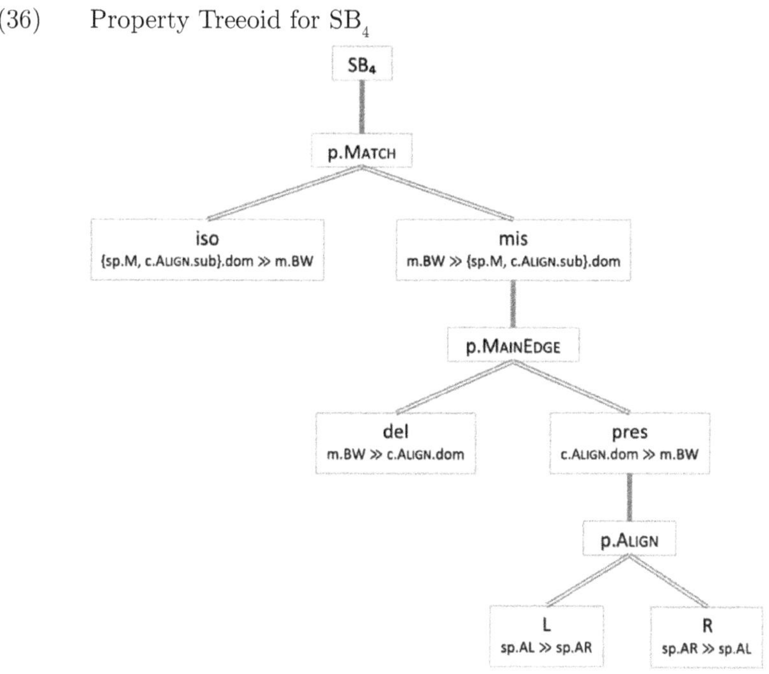


We will see below that property treeoids for larger subsystems of SB maintain most of the structure of (36), but with some widening of scope (in SB$_5$) and with a new property added (in SB$_7$). Property treeoids and Universal

Violation Tableaux for all systems discussed in the chapter are provided in an Appendix.

The property values from this analysis of $SB_4$ are paired as follows with extensional traits in the languages:

(37)      Property values and extensional traits for $SB_4$

| p.MATCH.iso | p.MATCH.mis |
|---|---|
| The input and output trees are isomorphic. | At least one input unfaithfully maps to $((AB)(CD))$. |
| p.MAINEDGE.pres | p.MAINEDGE.del |
| The main edge of every XP aligns with the main edge of some $\varphi$. (Whether the main edge is left or right is determined by p.ALIGN.L/R.) | Every 4-word input maps to $((AB)(CD))$. |
| p.ALIGN.L | p.ALIGN.R |
| An XP's left edge is its main edge. | An XP's right edge is its main edge. |

In other words, p.MATCH.iso/mis determines whether any unfaithfulness is permitted at all. If a language is not perfectly faithful (i.e., not Iso), then p.MAINEDGE.pres/del determines whether it faithfully aligns one edge of each XP (p.MAINEDGE.pres) or ignores XP edges (p.MAINEDGE.del). If the latter, then the language is maximally unfaithful (Bal), and as unmarked as possible, allowing only one faithful mapping: $[[AB][CD]] \rightarrow ((AB)(CD))$. The two p.MAINEDGE.pres languages are distinguished by which XP edge is the main edge: left or right.

The terminology regarding the property values p.ALIGN.L and p.ALIGN.R is of necessity somewhat counterintuitive. It is easy to remember that p.ALIGN.L is characterized by the ranking sp.ALIGN-L $\gg$ sp.ALIGN-R, and sp.ALIGN-R by the opposite—hence the names 'EP.L" and 'EP.R." But EP.L faithfully maps the strictly *right*-branching input $[A[B[CD]]]$ and rebrackets the strictly left-branching input $[[[AB]C]D]$. EP.R does the opposite; it is faithful to left-branching $[[[AB]C]D]$ but rebrackets right-branching $[A[B[CD]]]$. This is because there are candidates with R-branching input $[A[B[CD]]]$ that violate sp.ALIGN-L by failing to align the left edges before B and C, but no candidates that violate sp.ALIGN-R, since the three right edges after D are aligned to the right edge of the maximal $\varphi$ in every candidate. Similarly, $[[[AB]C]D]$ contains two violable right edges, one after B and one after C, but no violable left edges. Its three left edges are initial, and thus align to the left edge of the maximal $\varphi$ in every candidate.

Although it does not readily extend to larger subsystems of SB, there is in fact a more minimal possible property analysis of $SB_4$ than the one given in (34)–(36). This alternative consists of the two properties in (38), where "fth" stands for "faithfulness" and "unf" for "unfaithfulness."

(38)     Alternative properties of $SB_4$

| Property | a | b | Scope |
|---|---|---|---|
| p.4ωL.fth/unf | {sp.M, sp.AR}.dom | m.BW | wide |
| p.4ωR.fth/unf | {sp.M, sp.AL}.dom | m.BW | wide |

The first separates Iso and EP.R from Bal and EP.L; the second Iso and EP.L from Bal and EP.R:

(39)     Alternative property analysis table for $SB_4$

|  | p.4ωL | p.4ωR |
|---|---|---|
| Iso | fth | fth |
| Bal | unf | fth |
| EP.L | fth | unf |
| EP.R | unf | unf |

The traits associated with these alternative property values are the following:

(40)     Traits associated with alternative property values in $SB_4$

| p.4ωL.fth <br> [[[AB]C]D] → (((AB)C)D) | p.4ωL.unf <br> [[[AB]C]D] → ((AB)(CD)) |
|---|---|
| p.4ωR.fth <br> [A[B[CD]]] → (A(B(CD))) | p.4ωR.unf <br> [A[B[CD]]] → ((AB)(CD)) |

In $SB_4$, the mappings for the L-branching and R-branching input trees suffice to determine a language's mappings for all other inputs as well. The property values p.4ωL.fth and p.4ωR.fth both separately entail faithful mappings for [[A[BC]]D], [[AB][CD]], and [A[[BC]D]]. The conjunction of p.4ωL.unf and p.4ωR.unf entails that every 4-word input maps to ((AB)(CD)). Again, the use of "L" and "R" is somewhat counterintuitive here, since p.4ωL.fth is the value for EP.R, not EP.L, referring as it does  to faithfulness to the left-branching input.

Although the PA in (38)–(40) is pithier than the first PA from (34)–(37), only the latter extends nicely to the system $SB_5$, which is the topic of the next section.

## 7.5 Subsystem SB$_5$

Subsystem SB$_5$ contains five languages instead of four. The grammars from SB$_5$ and SB$_6$ are equivalent, so at an abstract level the typologies themselves are equivalent. Thus, everything said about intensional grammars in this section carries over to SB$_6$, although at the extensional level, the section deals only with the mappings of SB$_5$.

The subsystem SB$_5$ contains all the csets of SB$_4$, plus fourteen more for the inputs in (41).

(41)     Five-word input trees in SB$_5$

| | | | | | | |
|---|---|---|---|---|---|---|
| (XP A (XP B (XP C (XP D E)))) | (XP A (XP B (XP (XP C D) E))) | (XP A (XP (XP B C) (XP D E))) | (XP A (XP (XP B (XP C D)) E)) | (XP A (XP (XP (XP B C) D) E)) | (XP (XP A B) (XP C (XP D E))) | (XP (XP A B) (XP (XP C D) E)) |
| (XP (XP A (XP B C)) (XP D E)) | (XP (XP (XP A B) C) (XP D E)) | (XP (XP A (XP B (XP C D))) E) | (XP (XP A (XP (XP B C) D)) E) | (XP (XP (XP A B) (XP C D)) E) | (XP (XP (XP A (XP B C)) D) E) | (XP (XP (XP (XP A B) C) D) E) |

The cset for each five-word input consists of the fourteen prosodic trees isomorphic to the input trees in (41): $(_\varphi$ A $(_\varphi$ B $(_\varphi$ C $(_\varphi$ D E)))), $(_\varphi$ A $(_\varphi$ B $(_\varphi$ $(_\varphi$ C D) E))), etc.

### 7.5.1 Typology of SB$_5$

The factorial typology of SB$_5$ contains five languages instead of four. Iso, EP.L, and EP.R carry over directly from SB$_4$, but SB$_4$'s Bal splits into two new languages: Bal.L and Bal.R. For space reasons, (42) contains only a support for SB$_5$. It includes a combination of columns that suffice (in fact, more than suffice) to distinguish all five languages, but does not show the mapping for each of the 22 inputs.

(42)     Factorial typology for $SB_5$ (support)

|  | 'RR'<br>[A[B[CD]]] | 'RL'<br>[A[[BC]D]] | 'LR'<br>[[A[BC]]D] | 'LL'<br>[[[AB]C]D] | 'RLR'<br>[A[[B[CD]]E]] | 'LRL'<br>[[A[[BC]D]]E] |
|---|---|---|---|---|---|---|
| Iso | match | match | match | match | match | match |
| EP.L | match | match | match | ((AB)(CD)) | match | ((A(BC))(DE))<br>(A((BC)(DE))) |
| EP.R | ((AB)(CD)) | match | match | match | (((AB)(CD))E)<br>((AB)((CD)E)) | match |
| Bal.L | ((AB)(CD)) | ((AB)(CD)) | ((AB)(CD)) | ((AB)(CD)) | (A((BC)(DE))) | ((A(BC))(DE))<br>(A((BC)(DE))) |
| Bal.R | ((AB)(CD)) | ((AB)(CD)) | ((AB)(CD)) | ((AB)(CD)) | (((AB)(CD))E)<br>((AB)((CD)E)) | (((AB)(CD))E) |

Iso, EP.L, and EP.R have the same grammars in $SB_5$ as they do in $SB_4$. The grammars of Bal.L and Bal.R in $SB_5$ are refinements of the grammar of Bal in $SB_4$. In simple Bal, m.BIN-ω dominates all three mapping constraints, but there are no further requirements. Bal.L and Bal.R are the same, except that in the former sp.ALIGN-L dominates sp.ALIGN-R, and in the latter sp.ALIGN-R dominates sp.ALIGN-L. The grammars of $SB_5$ are given in (43).

(43)     Grammars of $SB_5$

a. Iso

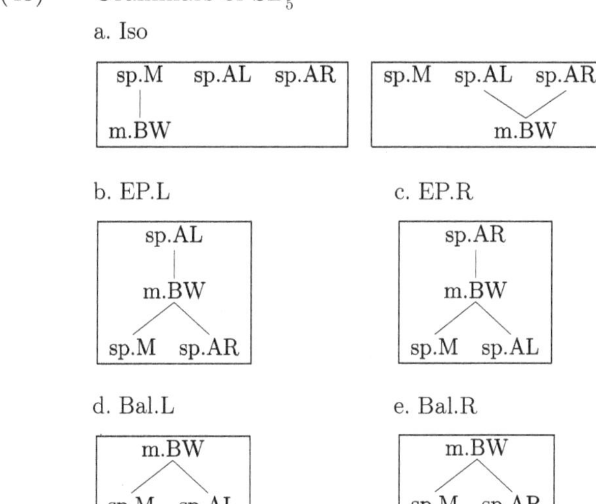

b. EP.L          c. EP.R

d. Bal.L         e. Bal.R

As in $SB_4$, the language Iso of $SB_5$ maps every input to a perfectly matching output. For the four-word inputs, EP.L and EP.R have the same mappings that they do in SB$_4$, and both Bal.L and Bal.R of SB$_5$ have the mappings of Bal from SB$_4$. The new information here comes from the last two columns of (42), which involve five-word trees.

Both of the five-word inputs in (42) are maximally "mixed" in branchingness. The first, [A[[B[CD]]E]], displays R-over-L-over-R (RLR) branching, and the second, [[A[[BC]D]]E], L-over-R-over-L (LRL) branching. RLR undergoes matching in Iso and EP.L, while LRL undergoes matching in Iso and EP.R.

RLR undergoes mismatching in EP.R, Bal.L, and Bal.R, but in different ways. In Bal.L, the mapping is [A[[B[CD]]E]] → (A((BC)(DE))). At the level of [$_{XP}$ A XP], this is faithful, but within the XP sister to A, the mixed-branching subtree [[B[CD]]E] balances to ((BC)(DE)), just as isomorphic [[A[BC]]D] does in isolation in this language. In EP.R and Bal.R (which, anticipating somewhat, are the p.ALIGN.R languages), there is co-optimality between two mappings: [A[[B[CD]]E]] → (((AB)(CD))E) and [A[[B[CD]]E]] → ((AB)((CD)E)). These mappings are unfaithful at the level of [$_{XP}$ A XP], but in each, every right XP edge is aligned to a right $\varphi$ edge; D]] → D) or D]] → D)). And of course, the edges after E are aligned to the right edge of the maximal $\varphi$ in every output allowed by SB.GEN.

The situation is the same for input LRL, *mutatis mutandis*. Here, it is EP.R that joins Iso in enforcing perfect matching, while EP.L, Bal.L, and Bal.R are unfaithful. Bal.R is faithful at the [$_{XP}$ XP E] level, but rebrackets internal to E's sister. The p.ALIGN.L languages EP.L and Bal.L are unfaithful at the [$_{XP}$ XP E] level, but in each of their co-optima, every left edge is properly aligned: [[B → (B or [[B → (B, and [[A → (A or [[A → ((A.

The factorial typology table in (42) shows six of the 22 inputs in SB$_5$. Of the remaining 16, nine undergo perfect matching in every language. These nine are the three inputs of SB$_3$, the balanced-branching input [[AB][CD]] of SB$_4$, and the six 5-word trees in (44).

(44)     Universally matched five-word inputs in SB$_5$

Like the balanced ((AB)(CD)) discussed above, the matching outputs for the trees in (44) are the best outputs in terms of m.Bin-ω within their csets. Each incurs two violations of m.Bin-ω, as shown in (45), where offending nodes are boxed.

(45)     The six best 5ω trees on m.Bin-ω (2 violations each)

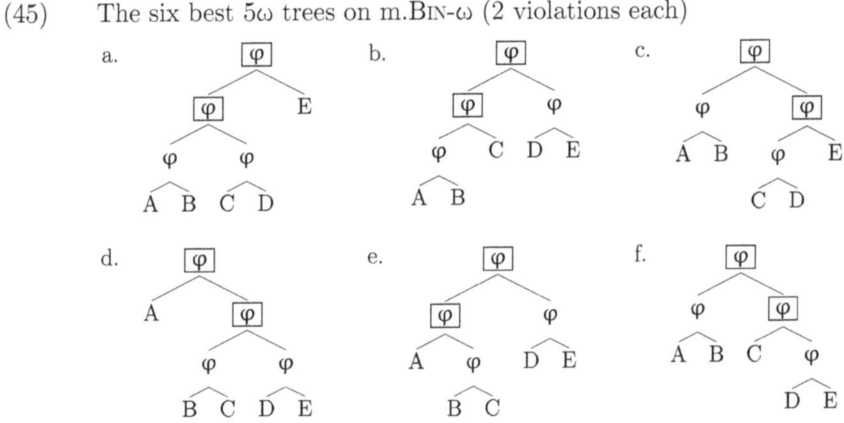

The six trees in (45) contrast with the other eight 5-word prosodic trees, each of which incurs three violations of m.Bin-ω rather than two. These eight trees are shown in (46), condensed into four diagrams by means of the triangle notation. When a φ dominates terminals P Q R via a triangle, this stands for either of two distinct subtrees: (P (Q R)) or ((P Q) R).

(46)     The worst 5ω trees on m.Bɪɴ-ω (3 violations each)

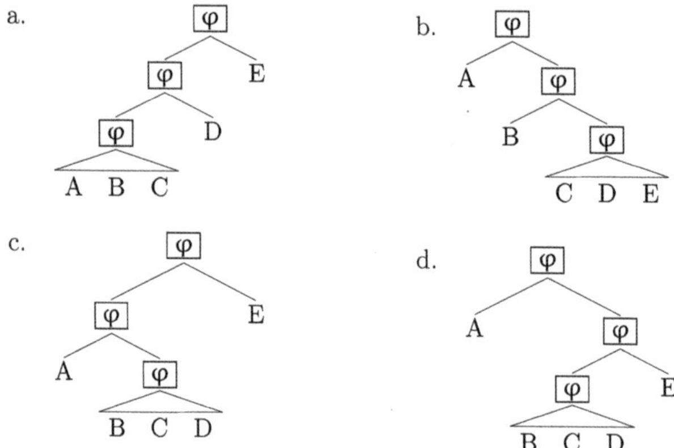

The trees in (45) and (46) exhaust the set of 5-word output trees admitted by SB.Gᴇɴ. As with the 4-word csets, m.Bɪɴ-ω partitions a 5-word cset into two blocks: *best* and *worst*. The best are those in (45), and the worst those in (46). Just as [[AB][CD]] maps to an isomorphic output in every language of SB, so do the inputs isomorphic to the trees in (44), i.e., exactly those in (45). Only inputs isomorphic to the m.BW-dispreferred trees in (46) map to mismatching outputs in some languages of SB₅. This is guaranteed by the principle of Harmonic Ascent in (23).

But there is also an important difference between m.Bɪɴ-ω's partitioning of the four- and five-word csets. There is only one best four-word output on m.Bɪɴ-ω—((AB)(CD))—while on five words, there are six trees that tie for best on m.Bɪɴ-ω: those in (45). This means that if m.Bɪɴ-ω compels an unfaithful mapping from one of the trees in (46), there are six options remaining, and the choice among them is left to the syntax→prosody mapping constraints. The behavior of the eight five-word inputs that sometimes undergo mismatches is shown in (47).

(47)     Mappings of mismatchable five-word trees

a.     Matched in Iso and EP.L

| | "RRR" [A[B[C[DE]]]] | "RRL" [A[B[[CD]E]]] | "LRR" [[A[B[CD]]]E] | "RLR" [A[[B[CD]]E]] |
|---|---|---|---|---|
| Iso | match | match | match | match |
| EP.L | match | match | match | match |
| EP.R | ((AB)(C(DE))) (A((BC)(DE))) | ((AB)((CD)E)) | (((AB)(CD))E) | (((AB)(CD))E) ((AB)((CD)E)) |
| Bal.L | ((AB)(C(DE))) (A((BC)(DE))) | ((AB)((CD)E)) | (((AB)(CD))E) | (A((BC)(DE))) |
| Bal.R | ((AB)(C(DE))) (A((BC)(DE))) | ((AB)((CD)E)) | (((AB)(CD))E) | (((AB)(CD))E) ((AB)((CD)E)) |

b.     Matched in Iso and EP.R

| | "LLL" [[[[AB]C]D]E] | "LLR" [[[A[BC]]D]E] | "RLL" [A[[[BC]D]E]] | "LRL" [[A[[BC]D]]E] |
|---|---|---|---|---|
| Iso | match | match | match | match |
| EP.L | (((AB)(CD))E) (((AB)C)(DE)) | ((A(BC))(DE)) | (A((BC)(DE))) | ((A(BC))(DE)) (A((BC)(DE))) |
| EP.R | match | match | match | match |
| Bal.L | (((AB)(CD))E) (((AB)C)(DE)) | ((A(BC))(DE)) | (A((BC)(DE))) | ((A(BC))(DE)) (A((BC)(DE))) |
| Bal.R | (((AB)(CD))E) (((AB)C)(DE)) | ((A(BC))(DE)) | (A((BC)(DE))) | (((AB)(CD))E) |

The two inputs in (47) of greatest interest are RLR and LRL, previously shown in (42), since these are the ones that distinguish Bal.L and Bal.R. Since each of RLR and LRL distinguishes the two Bal languages, we only examine the intricacies of one of them here, namely LRL, for which a VT is given in (48). As always, the VT contains all optima from the relevant cset.

(48)　　VT for input LRL (4/4 optima, 0/10 harmonic bounds)

| [tree: XP₁ → XP₂ E; XP₂ → A XP₃; XP₃ → XP₄ D; XP₄ → B C] | sp.M | sp.AL | sp.AR | m.BW |
|---|---|---|---|---|
| a. [tree: $\varphi_1$ → $\varphi_2$ E; $\varphi_2$ → A $\varphi_3$; $\varphi_3$ → $\varphi_4$ D; $\varphi_4$ → B C] | | | | 3 ($\varphi_1$, $\varphi_2$, $\varphi_3$) |
| b. [tree: $\varphi_1$ → $\varphi_2$ E; $\varphi_2$ → $\varphi_5$ $\varphi_6$; $\varphi_5$ → A B; $\varphi_6$ → C D] | 2 (XP$_3$, XP$_4$) | 2 (XP$_3$, XP$_4$) | 1 (XP$_4$) | 2 ($\varphi_1$, $\varphi_2$) |
| c. [tree: $\varphi_1$ → $\varphi_5$ $\varphi_6$; $\varphi_5$ → A $\varphi_4$; $\varphi_4$ → B C; $\varphi_6$ → D E] | 2 (XP$_2$, XP$_3$) | | 2 (XP$_2$, XP$_3$) | 2 ($\varphi_1$, $\varphi_5$) |
| d. [tree: $\varphi_1$ → A $\varphi_5$; $\varphi_5$ → $\varphi_4$ $\varphi_6$; $\varphi_4$ → B C; $\varphi_6$ → D E] | 2 (XP$_2$, XP$_3$) | | 2 (XP$_2$, XP$_3$) | 2 ($\varphi_1$, $\varphi_5$) |

The matching candidate (48a), which wins in Iso and EP.R, violates m.BIN-ω three times, once for each of $\varphi_1$=(ABCDE), $\varphi_2$=(ABCD), and $\varphi_3$=(BCD). Candidates (b-d) do better on m.BIN-ω, incurring two violations each.

While the m.Bɪɴ-ω violations of (48a-d) are easy to ascertain, closer inspection is needed to explain the faithfulness violations of the non-matching (48b-d). First consider the mapping in (48b), which violates sp.Mᴀᴛᴄʜ twice, sp.Aʟɪɢɴ-L twice, and sp.Aʟɪɢɴ-R once. The diagrams in (49) illustrate unfaithfulness with solid arrows, and faithful mappings with dashed arrows.

(49)    (Un)faithfulness in candidate (48b)
   a.    sp.MATCH: 2 violations

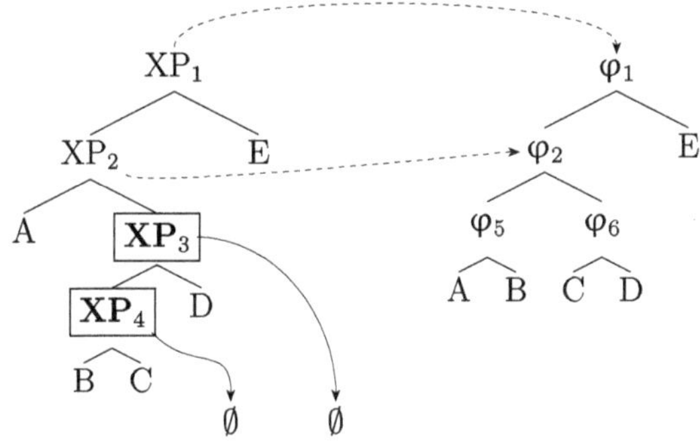

   b.    sp.Aʟɪɢɴ-L: 2 violations

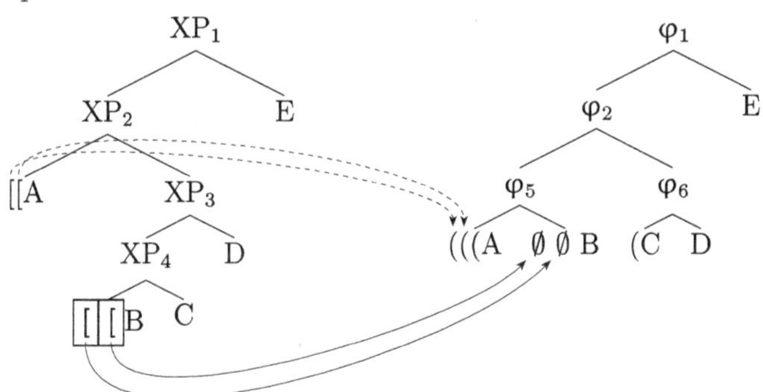

   c.    sp.Aʟɪɢɴ-R: 1 violation

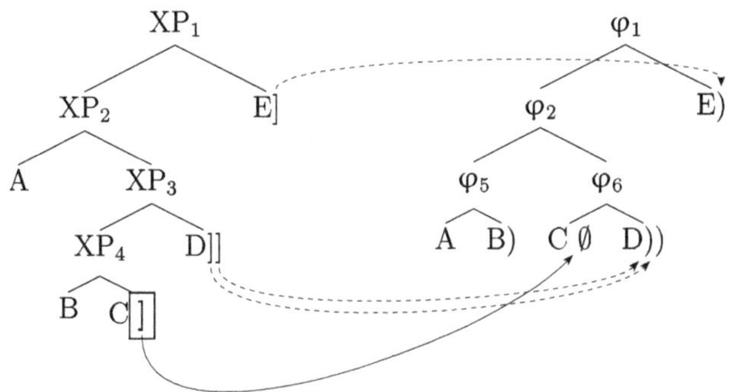

In (49a), $XP_1$=[ABCDE] maps to $\varphi_1$=(ABCDE), and $XP_2$=[ABCD] maps to $\varphi_2$=(ABCD). There is no $\varphi_3$=(BCD) to match $XP_3$, and no $\varphi_4$=(BC) to match $XP_4$.

In (49b), the left edges of $XP_1$ and $XP_2$, both before A, align with one of the left $\varphi$-edges before A in the output. But the left edges of $XP_3$ and $XP_4$, both before B, do not align with any left $\varphi$ edge in the output, because B is non-initial in $\varphi_5$=(AB).

In (49c), the right edge of $XP_1$ aligns with the right edge of $\varphi_1$, as guaranteed by SB.GEN. The right edges of $XP_2$ and $XP_3$, both after D, align with the right edge of $\varphi_2$ (and $\varphi_6$, though only one edge is needed for satisfaction). The unmatched edge is that of $XP_4$ after C, since C is initial in $\varphi_6$=(CD).

Candidates (48c) and (48d) tie on all constraints, but they violate and satisfy them in different ways. The diagrams in (47) show the fate of (48c).

(50)　　　(Un)faithfulness in candidate (48c)

　　a.　　sp.MATCH: 2 violations

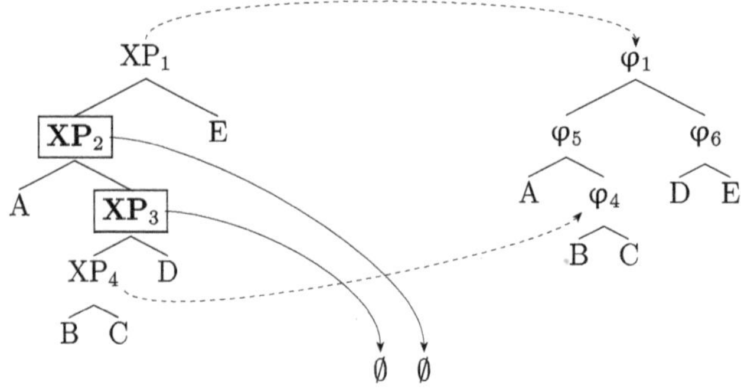

　　b.　　sp.ALIGN-L: 0 violations

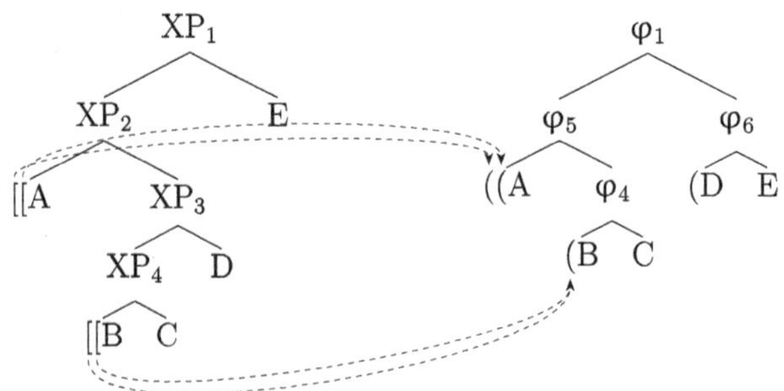

   c.   sp.ALIGN-R: 2 violations

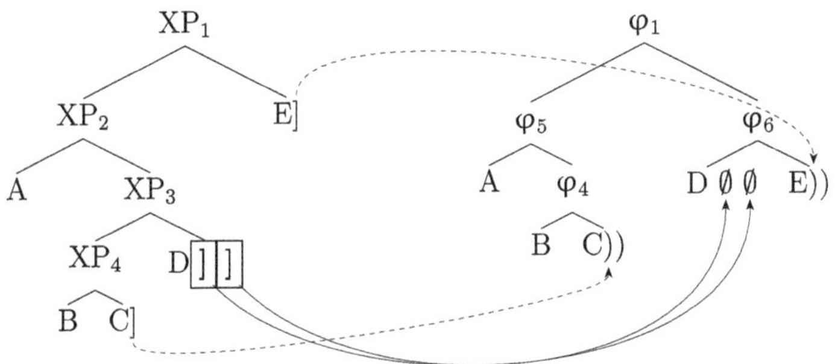

(50a) shows that $XP_1$=[ABCDE] and $XP_4$=[BC] map to $\varphi_1$=(ABCDE) and $\varphi_4$=(BC), respectively. $XP_2$=[ABCD] and $XP_3$=[BCD] are not matched.

In (50b), we see that the left edges of $XP_1$ and $XP_2$ before A align to the left edge of $\varphi_1$ (and $\varphi_5$), while the left edges of $XP_3$ and $XP_4$, both before B, map to the left edge of $\varphi_4$. Thus, candidate (48c) does not violate sp.ALIGN-L.

Finally, (50c) shows that while the right edges $XP_1$ and $XP_4$ are aligned to right $\varphi$ edges, those of $XP_2$ and $XP_3$ after D are not, since D is initial in $\varphi_6$=(DE).

The diagrams in (51) show the provenance of violation counts for candidate (48d), which are equal to those of (48c).

(51)    (Un)faithfulness in candidate (48d)

   a.   sp.MATCH: 2 violations

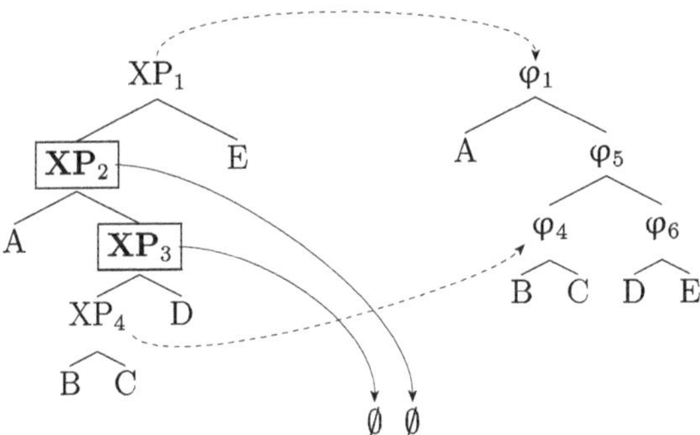

b.    sp.ALIGN-L: 0 violations

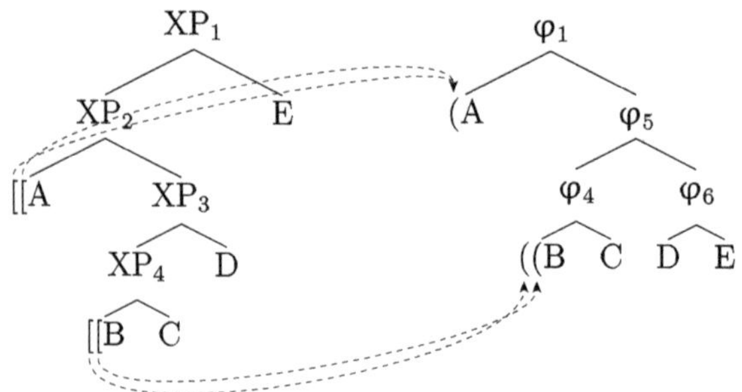

c.    sp.ALIGN-R: 2 violations

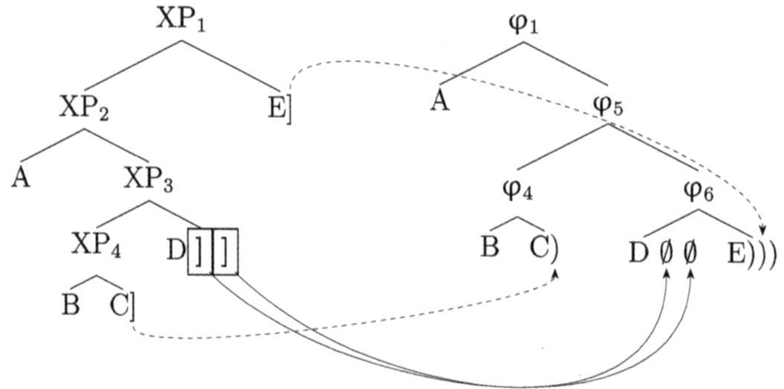

Here too, $XP_2$ and $XP_3$ are the only unmatched XPs. As in (50b), the left
XP edges in (51b) all align to left φ-edges, though here A is at the edge only
of $φ_1$, and B is at the left edges of $φ_5$ and $φ_4$. Likewise, (51c) shows the successful alignment of the right edges of $XP_1$ and $XP_4$, and the misalignment
of the right edges of $XP_2$ and $XP_3$.

The comparative tableau in (52) shows the ERCs that arise when the
matching candidate for LRL is asserted to be optimal.

(52)     CT for Matching winner: (48a) > (48b,c,d)

| Input | Winner | Loser | sp.M | sp.AL | sp.AR | m.BW |
|---|---|---|---|---|---|---|
| a.<br>$[_{XP_1}\ [_{XP_2}\ A\ [_{XP_3}\ [_{XP_4}\ B\ C]\ D]]\ E]$ | $[_{\varphi_1}\ [_{\varphi_2}\ A\ [_{\varphi_3}\ [_{\varphi_4}\ B\ C]\ D]]\ E]$ | $[_{\varphi_1}\ [_{\varphi_2}\ [_{\varphi_5}\ A\ B]\ [_{\varphi_6}\ C\ D]]\ E]$ | W | W | W | L |
| b.<br>$[_{XP_1}\ [_{XP_2}\ A\ [_{XP_3}\ [_{XP_4}\ B\ C]\ D]]\ E]$ | $[_{\varphi_1}\ [_{\varphi_2}\ A\ [_{\varphi_3}\ [_{\varphi_4}\ B\ C]\ D]]\ E]$ | $[_{\varphi_1}\ [_{\varphi_5}\ A\ [_{\varphi_4}\ B\ C]]\ [_{\varphi_6}\ D\ E]]$<br><br>$[_{\varphi_1}\ A\ [_{\varphi_5}\ [_{\varphi_4}\ B\ C]\ [_{\varphi_6}\ D\ E]]]$ | W |  | W | L |

The matching winner in (52a) beats the mismatched ($\varphi_2$ E) when any one of the faithfulness constraints dominates m.BW. For matching to win on row (52b), either sp.Match or sp.Align-R must dominate m.Bin-ω. The second ERC is more informative than (i.e., entails) the first; WeWL → WWWL by W-extension (Prince 2002b).

The CT in (53) gives the conditions under which the ($\varphi_2$ E) mismatch wins.

(53)    CT for φE-mismatching winner: (48b) ≻ (48a,c,d)

| Input | Winner | Loser | sp.M | sp.AL | sp.AR | m.BW |
|---|---|---|---|---|---|---|
| a. [XP₁ [XP₂ A [XP₃ [XP₄ B C] D]] E] | [φ₁ [φ₂ [φ₅ A B] [φ₆ C D]] E] | [φ₁ [φ₂ A [φ₃ [φ₄ B C] D]] E] | L | L | L | W |
| b. [XP₁ [XP₂ A [XP₃ [XP₄ B C] D]] E] | [φ₁ [φ₂ [φ₅ A B] [φ₆ C D]] E] | [φ₁ [φ₅ A [φ₄ B C]] [φ₆ D E]] ; [φ₁ A [φ₅ [φ₄ B C] [φ₆ D E]]] |  | L | W |  |

Row (53a), in which the matching candidate loses, is simply the negation of (52a): LLLW = ¬(WWWL). To mismatch with the $(\varphi_2\ \text{E})$ output, m.BIN-ω must dominate every faithfulness constraint; m.BIN-ω ≫ sp.M, sp.ALIGN-L, sp.ALIGN-R. And this time, the second row of the CT provides an ERC not entailed by or entailing the first. For $(\varphi_2\ \text{E})$ to beat the co-optima containing a subtree (A φ), sp.ALIGN-R must dominate sp.ALIGN-L.

Finally, (54) shows how the (A φ)–containing co-optima (48c) and (48d) beat LRL-matching (48a) and the alternatively mismatched (48b). Of course, the rows here are simply the negation of rows (52b) and (53b).

(54)    CT for Aφ-mismatching winners: (48c,d) ≻ (48a,b)

| Input | Winner | Loser | sp.M | sp.AL | sp.AR | m.BW |
|---|---|---|---|---|---|---|
| a. $XP_1$ [ $XP_2$ [ A, $XP_3$ [ $XP_4$ [ B C ], D ] ], E ] | $\varphi_1$ [ $\varphi_5$ [ A, $\varphi_4$ [ B C ] ], $\varphi_6$ [ D E ] ]; $\varphi_1$ [ A, $\varphi_5$ [ $\varphi_4$ [ B C ], $\varphi_6$ [ D E ] ] ] | $\varphi_1$ [ $\varphi_2$ [ A, $\varphi_3$ [ $\varphi_4$ [ B C ], D ] ], E ] | L | | L | W |
| b. $XP_1$ [ $XP_2$ [ A, $XP_3$ [ $XP_4$ [ B C ], D ] ], E ] | $\varphi_1$ [ $\varphi_5$ [ A, $\varphi_4$ [ B C ] ], $\varphi_6$ [ D E ] ]; $\varphi_1$ [ A, $\varphi_5$ [ $\varphi_4$ [ B C ], $\varphi_6$ [ D E ] ] ] | $\varphi_1$ [ $\varphi_2$ [ $\varphi_5$ [ A B ], $\varphi_6$ [ C D ] ], E ] | | W | L | |

For these optima to win, m.Bin-ω must dominate both sp.Match and
sp.Align-R, as shown in (54a), and sp.Align-L must dominate sp.Align-R,
as shown in (54b).

Although there are three options for how to prosodify the LRL input, they
do not mix freely with the languages from $SB_4$, which would triple that four-
language typology to a twelve-language one. Only the ERCs from the LRL-
match in (52) are compatible with Iso and EP.R, and only the ERCs for the
(A φ)–containing co-optima in (54) are compatible with EP.L. But while the
grammar of Bal from $SB_4$ demands one of the mismatching winners, it does
not decide between them, since it merely asserts that m.Bin-ω dominates the
highest ranking faithfulness constraint, and m.Bin-ω does not distinguish the
winner and loser in (54b). Only the alignment constraints make this distinction, so Bal from $SB_4$ splits into the two languages Bal.L and Bal.R in $SB_5$.
Supports for these new languages are provided in (55) and (56).

(55)    Support for Bal.L

| Input | Winner | Loser | m.BW | sp.M | sp.AL | sp.AR |
|---|---|---|---|---|---|---|
| a. 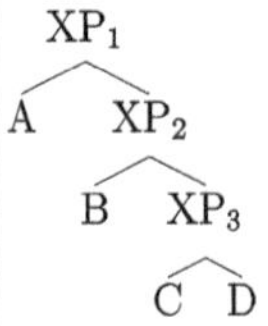<br><br>XP$_1$ [ A , XP$_2$ [ B , XP$_3$ [ C D ] ] ] | 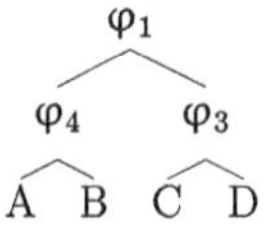 $\varphi_1$ [ $\varphi_4$ , $\varphi_3$ ] ; A B C D | 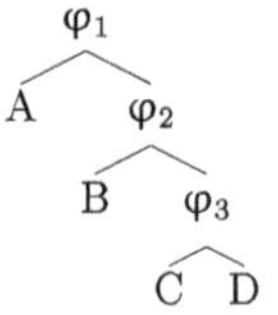 $\varphi_1$ [ A , $\varphi_2$ [ B , $\varphi_3$ [ C D ] ] ] | W | L | L | |
| b. 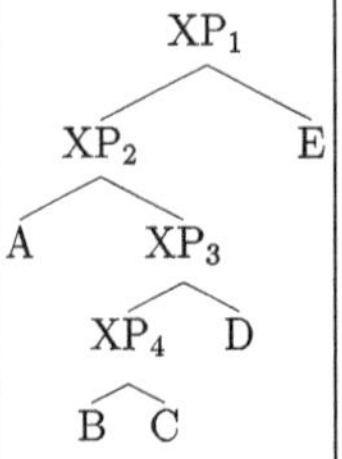<br><br>XP$_1$ [ XP$_2$ [ A , XP$_3$ [ XP$_4$ [ B C ] , D ] ] , E ] | 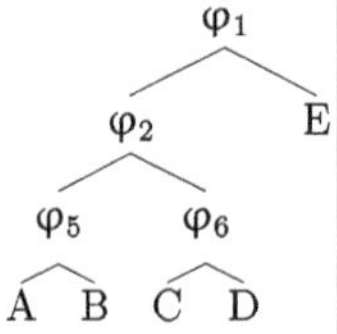 $\varphi_1$ [ $\varphi_2$ [ $\varphi_5$ , $\varphi_6$ ] , E ] ; A B C D | 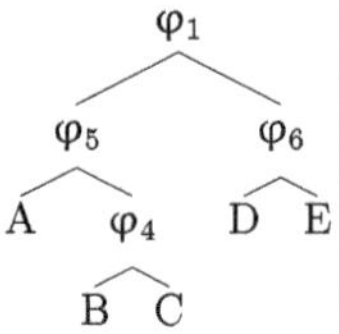 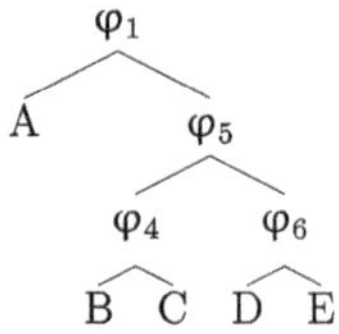 $\varphi_1$ [ $\varphi_5$ [ A , $\varphi_4$ [ B C ] ] , $\varphi_6$ [ D E ] ] ; $\varphi_1$ [ A , $\varphi_5$ [ $\varphi_4$ , $\varphi_6$ ] ] ; B C D E | | | W | L |

(56)    Support for Bal.R

| Input | Winner | Loser | m.BW | sp.M | sp.AR | sp.AL |
|---|---|---|---|---|---|---|
| a. 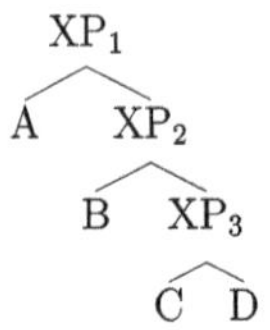<br><br>XP$_1$ [ A , XP$_2$ [ B , XP$_3$ [ C D ] ] ] | 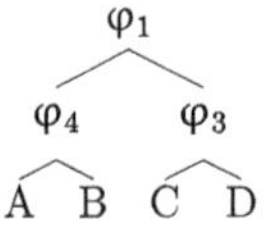 $\varphi_1$ [ $\varphi_4$ , $\varphi_3$ ] ; A B C D | 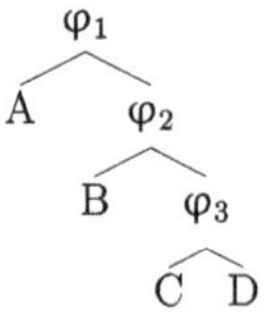 $\varphi_1$ [ A , $\varphi_2$ [ B , $\varphi_3$ [ C D ] ] ] | W | L | L | |
| b. 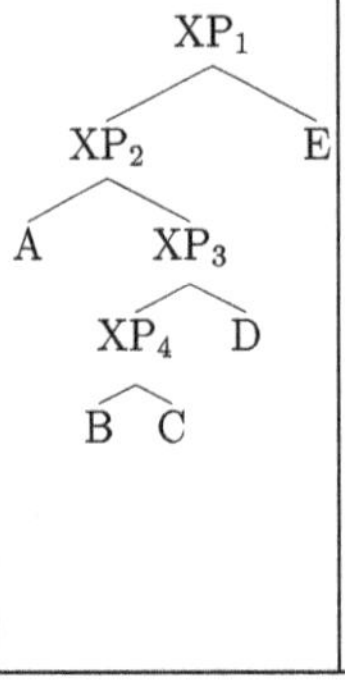<br><br>XP$_1$ [ XP$_2$ [ A , XP$_3$ [ XP$_4$ [ B C ] , D ] ] , E ] | 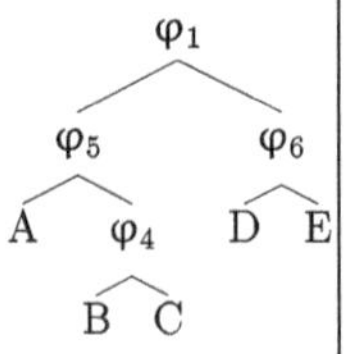 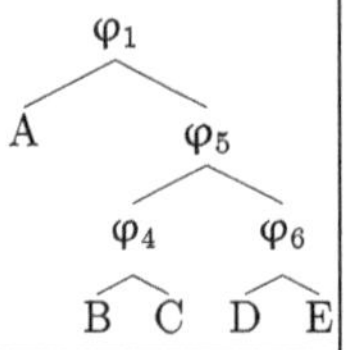 $\varphi_1$ [ $\varphi_5$ [ A , $\varphi_4$ [ B C ] ] , $\varphi_6$ [ D E ] ] ; $\varphi_1$ [ A , $\varphi_5$ [ $\varphi_4$ , $\varphi_6$ ] ] ; B C D E | 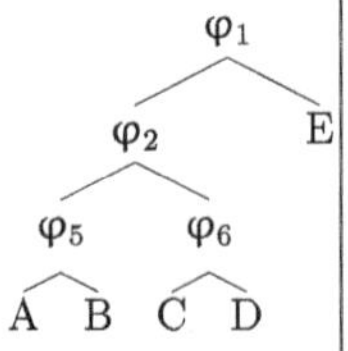 $\varphi_1$ [ $\varphi_2$ [ $\varphi_5$ , $\varphi_6$ ] , E ] ; A B C D | | | W | L |

The relative ranking of the alignment constraints in Bal.L and Bal.R, absent in Bal of $SB_4$, means that the scope of the p.ALIGN.L/R property from $SB_4$ extends in $SB_5$, as discussed in the next subsection.

### 7.5.2   Property analysis of $SB_5$

The property analysis of $SB_5$ employs exactly the same properties as that of $SB_4$, but with a wider scope for p.ALIGN.L/R. In $SB_4$, p.ALIGN.L/R scoped under p.MAINEDGE.pres, and in $SB_5$ it scopes under MATCH.mis.

(57)   Properties of $SB_5$

| Property | a | b | Scope |
|---|---|---|---|
| p.MATCH.iso/mis | {sp.M, c.ALIGN.sub}.dom | m.BW | wide |
| p.MAINEDGE.pres/del | c.ALIGN.dom | m.BW | under MATCH.mis |
| p.ALIGN.L/R | sp.AL | sp.AR | under MATCH.mis |

The properties in (57)  divide the languages of the typology as in (58).

(58)   Property analysis table for $SB_5$

|  | p.MATCH | p.MAINEDGE | p.ALIGN |
|---|---|---|---|
| Iso | iso | *moot* | *moot* |
| EP.L | mis | pres | L |
| EP.R | mis | pres | R |
| Bal.L | mis | del | L |
| Bal.R | mis | del | R |

The change in the scope of p.ALIGN between $SB_4$ and $SB_5$ is shown by the treeoid in (59).

(59)   Property Treeoid for $SB_5$

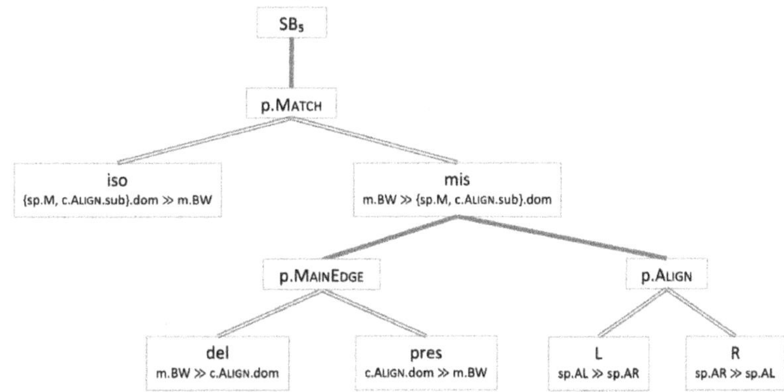

The property values in SB$_5$ correspond to traits similar to those from SB$_4$, laid out in (34). These traits are given in (60). The key difference is in the interpretation of MAINEDGE.del, which must be elaborated to cover the various prosodically "best" output options.

(60)     Property values and extensional traits for SB$_5$

| p.MATCH.iso<br>The input and output trees are<br>isomorphic. | p.MATCH.mis<br>Some inputs are mismatched. |
|---|---|
| p.MAINEDGE.pres<br>The main edge of every XP aligns with<br>the main edge of some φ. | p.MAINEDGE.del<br>Every 4ω input maps to ((AB)(CD)).<br>Every 5ω input maps to an output that<br>is violates m.BIN-ω exactly twice. |
| p.ALIGN.L<br>An XP's left edge is its main edge. | p.ALIGN.R<br>An XP's right edge is its main edge. |

As stated in (60), the traits do not fully account for the details of each mapping. In the following subsection, we elaborate on them to clarify these details.

### 7.5.3   Traits of SB$_5$ languages

In this subsection, we explain in depth the extensional traits of two languages of SB$_5$: the p.ALIGN.L languages EP.L and Bal.L. These languages' grammars are repeated in (61).

(61)     Grammars of p.ALIGN.L languages of SB$_5$

   a. Grammar of EP.L                          b. Grammar of Bal.L

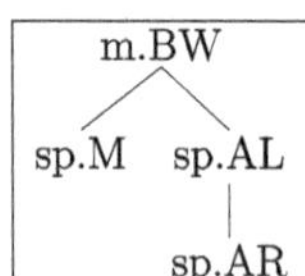



The extensional pattern of Iso needs no explanation, and the traits of EP.R and Bal.R are the same as those of their p.ALIGN.L counterparts, *mutatis mutandis*, so the traits of EP.L and Bal.L hold the key to understanding the extensional patterns of the entire typology.

   Several new terms will prove useful in the account to follow, specifically *treelet, odd word out*, and *even word out*, as defined in (62).

(62)    Terminology for analysis of traits in $SB_5$

    a.    Treelet: A treelet is a (sub)tree consisting of one non-terminal node and two terminals, i.e., $[_{XP} \ X^0 \ X^0]$ or $(_\varphi \ \omega \ \omega)$. The category labels XP, $\varphi$, $X^0$, and $\omega$ do not matter.

    b.    Odd Word Out (OWO): A terminal node $W_k$ in a terminal string $[W_1 \ W_2 \ldots W_k \ldots W_{n-1} \ W_n]$ is an odd word out (OWO) iff $k$ is odd and $W_k$ is not contained in a treelet.

    c.    Even Word Out (EWO): A terminal node $W_k$ in a terminal string $[W_1 \ W_2 \ldots W_k \ldots W_{n-1} \ W_n]$ is an even word out (EWO) iff $k$ is even and $W_k$ is not contained in a treelet.

In the five-word trees of $SB_5$, the outputs that perform best on m.BIN-$\omega$ contain two treelets and one OWO. These trees are repeated from (41) in (63), with the top nodes of treelets in boxes and OWOs labeled as such.

(63)    Best 5-word trees on m.BIN-$\omega$ (2 violations each)

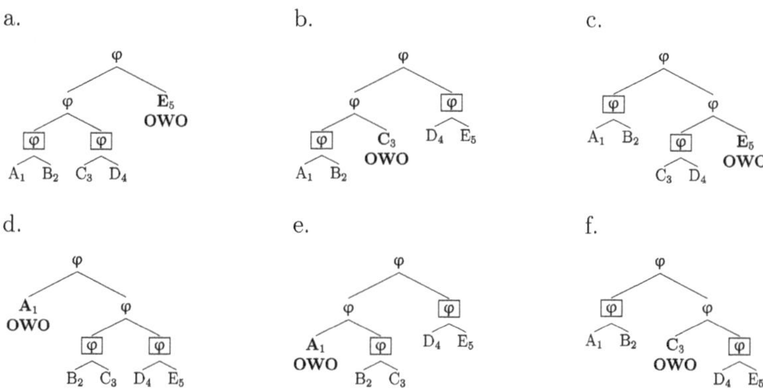

In (63a), there are two treelets: $(_\varphi \ A_1 \ B_2)$ and $(_\varphi \ C_3 \ D_4)$. The odd word out is $E_5$; it is the fifth word in the terminal string, and is not contained in a treelet. Words $A_1$ and $C_3$, while odd, are not OWOs, since they are in treelets. There are no even words out, since the two even words, $B_2$ and $D_4$, are both contained in treelets. Similar remarks apply to (63b–f).

    The *worst* five-word trees on m.BIN-$\omega$, which contain three suprabinary $\varphi$s each, differ   from those in (63) in that they contain one treelet, two OWOs, and one EWO, as shown in (64).

(64)      Worst 5-word trees on m.Bɪɴ-ω (3 violations each)

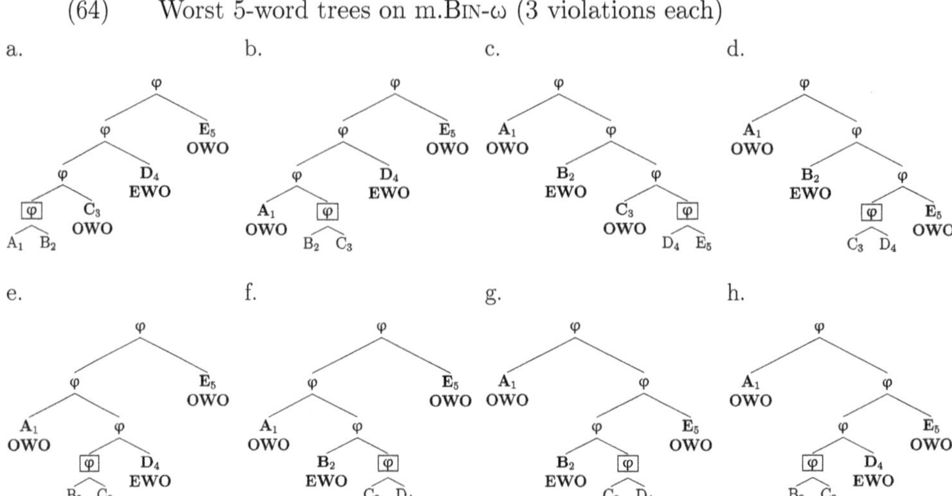

Thus, if a five-word input tree contains two OWOs, it either undergoes matching, or maps to an output tree with only one OWO. Equivalently, a five-word input tree containing an EWO is matched, or maps to a tree with no EWOs. A third equivalent formulation is: A five-word input tree containing one treelet matches or maps to an output containing two treelets.

Having defined treelets, odd words out, and even words out, we now examine the  extensional traits of EP.L and Bal.L.

### 7.5.3.1  Traits of EP.L in $SB_5$

In EP.L, the property value p.Mᴀᴛᴄʜ.mis means that some trees are mismatched. By Harmonic Ascent (23), mismatches only occur if they improve on markedness, and in SB the only markedness constraint is m.Bɪɴ-ω. So every mismatch involves maximizing the number of  treelets, and minimizing the number of OWOs and EWOs. This is accomplished by taking two adjacent words, one an OWO and the other an EWO, and placing them in a treelet together, as in (65).

(65)    Unfaithful mapping of RLL in EP.L

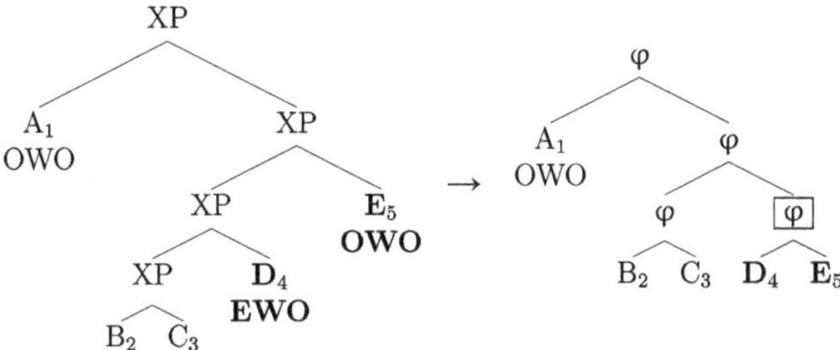

In the RLL input $[A_1 \ [[[B_2 \ C_3] \ D_4] \ E_5]]$ in (65), $D_4$ is an EWO and $E_5$ is an OWO. In the output tree, $D_4$ and $E_5$ form a treelet, and only $A_1$ is left as an OWO. $A_1$ is not adjacent to an EWO in the input, since $B_2$ is in a treelet with $C_3$, so it remains an OWO in the output.

The mismatch of RLL in (65) is in fact the same as the familiar mismatch of LL from $SB_4$: $[[[A_1 \ B_2] \ C_3] \ D_4] \to ((A_1 \ B_2)(C_3 \ D_4))$. In this mapping, $C_3$ is an OWO, $D_4$ is an EWO, and the  output contains a new treelet $(_\varphi \ C_3 \ D_4)$. But in $SB_5$, not every mismatch involves the subtrees $[[[X^0 \ X^0] \ X^0] \ X^0]$ and $((\omega \ \omega)(\omega \ \omega))$. In LLR, the EWO and OWO that join to form a new treelet are not both contained in a four-word XP.

(66)    Unfaithful mapping of LLR in EP.L

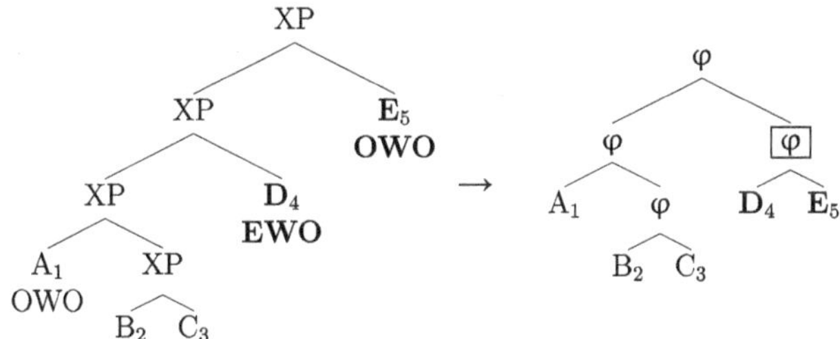

There are two more five-word mismatches in EP.L, but unlike those in (65)–(66), these involve co-optimality. These are shown in (67).

(67)    Unfaithful mappings to co-optima in EP.L

   a. Mapping from input LRL

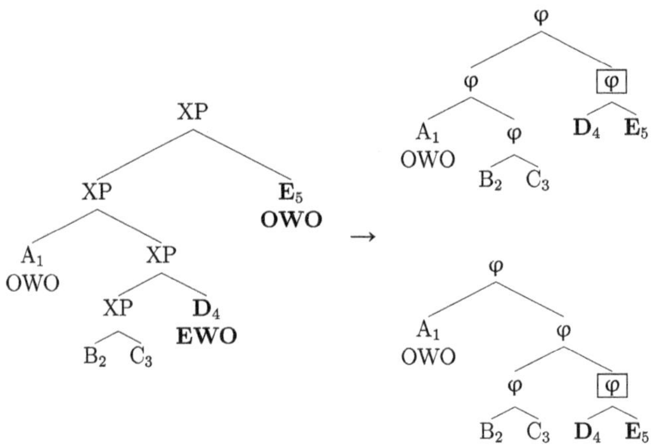

   b. Mapping from input RLR

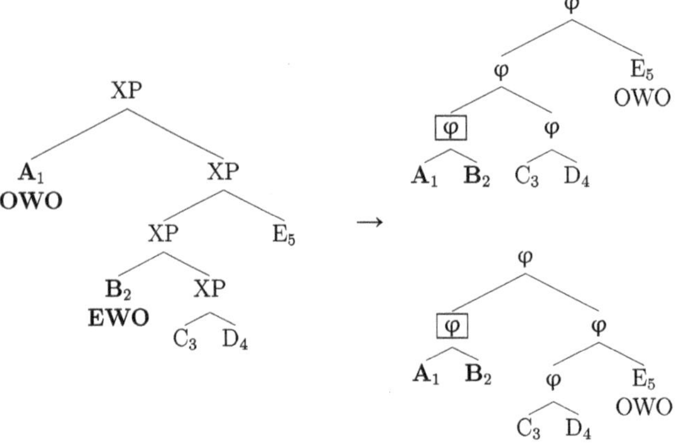

In (67a), $D_4$ and $E_5$ join to form a treelet in both outputs. Thus, both outputs contain the subtrees $A_1$, $(B_2\ C_3)$, and $(D_4\ E_5)$. Due to the SB.GEN requirement that trees be strictly binary-branching, there must either be a constituent $(A_1\ (B_2\ C_3))$ or a constituent $((B_2\ C_3)\ (D_4\ E_5))$. Neither possibility violates sp.ALIGN-L, and neither choice is better on m.BIN-ω, according to which a φ containing A, B, and C is just as bad as a φ containing B, C,

D, and E.[13] The question, then, is whether sp.MATCH or sp.ALIGN-R has a preference. Neither does. Creating the treelet $(D_4 E_5)$ makes it impossible to match the XP $[A_1 B_2 C_3 D_4]$, and equally impossible to match the XP $[B_2 C_3 D_4]$, so either output will violate sp.MATCH twice. The right edges of these two XPs are likewise unalignable. Since $D_4$ is at the end of both, and $D_4$ is non-final in an output treelet, it is impossible to align them. Thus, the two outputs in (67a) are co-optimal. The same can be said of the mappings in (67b), *mutatis mutandis*.

The drive to improve on m.BIN-ω is checked in EP.L by the ranking sp.ALIGN-L ≫ m.BIN-ω, i.e., by the property values p.MAINEDGE.pres and p.ALIGN.L. This means that in EP.L, an adjacent EWO and OWO cannot join to form a treelet if they are separated by the left edge of an XP. If two words Y and Z form a treelet $(_\varphi Y Z)$, and Z is at the left edge of an XP in the input, then that XP's left edge is not aligned to the left edge of a φ. This is impossible in EP.L, which properly aligns all left edges of XPs. This fact accounts for RRR, RRL, RLR, and LRR being matched in EP.L, as shown in (68).

(68)   Faithful mapping to m.BIN-ω-dispreferred trees in EP.L, respecting
       sp.ALIGN-L

   a.   RRR
        $[A_1 [B_2 [C_3 [D_4 E_5]]]] \rightarrow (A_1 (B_2 (C_3 (D_4 E_5))))$
        OWO EWO OWO

   b.   RRL
        $[A_1 [B_2 [[C_3 D_4] E_5]]] \rightarrow (A_1 (B_2 ((C_3 D_4) E_5)))$
        OWO EWO        OWO

   c.   RLR
        $[A_1 [[B_2 [C_3 D_4]] E_5]] \rightarrow (A_1 ((B_2 (C_3 D_4)) E_5))$
        OWO EWO        OWO

   d.   LRR
        $[[A_1 [B_2 [C_3 D_4]]] E_5] \rightarrow ((A_1 (B_2 (C_3 D_4))) E_5)$
        OWO EWO        OWO

In every tree in (68), the OWO $A_1$ is separated from the EWO $B_2$ by the left edge of an XP, so $A_1$ and $B_2$ cannot join to form a treelet in EP.L. In (68a), $C_3$ is the second OWO, and although it is adjacent to EWO $B_2$, they

---

[13] This is an instance in which the use of categorical rather than gradient m.BINMAX(φ,ω) is crucial. If the gradient version were used, then building a φ over $A_1$ and $(B_2 C_3)$ would be preferable to building one over $(B_2 C_3)$ and $(D_4 E_5)$, and the outputs in (67a) could no longer be co-optimal.

are separated by the left edge of an XP. In (68b–d), the second OWO is $E_5$, and since the preceding word $D_4$ is not an EWO (it is contained in a treelet), the two cannot form an output treelet.

### 7.5.3.2 Traits of Bal.L in $SB_5$

In Bal.L, the property value p.MAINEDGE.del guarantees that every five-word tree containing two OWOs maps to a tree containing exactly one OWO, even if this means that the left edge of an XP must be misaligned. An output with no OWOs at all would be even better, but this is impossible in forms with an odd number of words due to SB.GEN. The question, then, is which of the one-OWO trees each input maps to. The following table shows each unfaithful mapping from a five-word input.

(69)    Unfaithful five-word mappings in Bal.L (OWOs and EWOs emphasized)

| Input | | Output(s) | Input OWOs | Output OWO |
|---|---|---|---|---|
| a. RRR | [**A** [**B** [**C** [D E]]]] | ((A B) (**C** (D E))) <br> (**A** ((B C) (D E))) | A, C | A ∨ C |
| b. LLL | [[[[A B] **C**] **D**] **E**] | (((A B) (C D)) **E**) <br> (((A B) **C**)( D E)) | C, E | C ∨ E |
| c. LRL | [[**A** [[B C] **D**]] **E**] | ((**A** (B C)) (D E)) <br> (**A** ((B C) (D E))) | A, E | A |
| d. RLR | [**A** [[**B** [C D]] **E**]] | (**A** ((B C) (D E))) | | |
| e. LLR | [[[**A** [B C]] **D**] **E**] | ((**A** (B C)) (D E)) | | |
| f. RLL | [**A** [[[B C] **D**] **E**]] | (**A** ((B C) (D E))) | | |
| g. RRL | [**A** [**B** [[C D] **E**]]] | ((A B) ((C D) **E**)) | | E |
| h. LRR | [[**A** [**B** [C D]]] **E**] | (((A B) (C D)) **E**) | | |

In every mapping other than (69d), an output treelet is formed from an input OWO and an input EWO, and the treelet present in the input is preserved. In (69c) and (69e–f), the new treelet in the output is (D E), and the input treelet [C D] is mapped to the other output treelet. In (69g–h), it is A and B that join to form output (A B), and [C D] is faithfully mapped to (C D). In (69a–b), there is an input sequence OWO–EWO–OWO; forming a treelet from input OWO–EWO results in one co-optimum, while forming a treelet from input EWO–OWO results in another.

This leaves only the strange case of [**A** [[**B** [C D]] **E**]] in (69d), where input [C D] is broken up in the output. To its left is the EWO B, and to its right the OWO E, and in the output (B C) and (D E) are the two treelets. The question is why this is the outcome when input A and B  are an OWO and EWO which we might expect to form an output treelet. The answer is that breaking up [C D] to form (A ((B C) (D E))) is the best option in terms of sp.ALIGN-L, that sp.MATCH is neutral on the choice, and that sp.ALIGN-L dominates sp.ALIGN-R.

(70)    Unfaithfulness to treelet in (69d) (4/4 optima, 0/10 HBs)

|  | [**A** [[**B** [C D]] **E**]] | m.BW | sp.AL | sp.AR | sp.M |
|---|---|---|---|---|---|
| a. → | (**A** ((B C) (D E))) | 2 | 1 | 2 | 2 |
| b. | ((A B) ((C D) **E**)) | 2 | 2 | 0 | 2 |
| c. | (((A B) (C D)) **E**) | 2 | 2 | 0 | 2 |
| d. | (**A** ((**B** (C D)) **E**)) | 3 | 0 | 0 | 0 |

(71)    VT (70) converted to CT

| Input | Winner | Loser | m.BW | sp.AL | sp.AR | sp.M |
|---|---|---|---|---|---|---|
| [**A** [[**B** [C D]] **E**]] | (**A** ((B C) (D E))) | ((A B) ((C D) **E**)) <br> (((A B) (C D)) **E**) |  | W | L |  |
| [**A** [[**B** [C D]] **E**]] | (**A** ((B C) (D E))) | (**A** ((**B** (C D)) **E**)) | W | L | L | L |

In (70a), one left edge of XP is misaligned: that between B and C. When (A B) and (C D) are the output treelets, as in (70b-c), two left edges are misaligned: those separating input A and B.

### 7.5.3.3   Interim summary

In the preceding discussion, we have seen that the best trees on m.BIN-ω maximize treelets ($_\varphi$ ω ω), and minimize odd/even words out ($_\varphi$ ω φ), ($_\varphi$ φ ω). In p.MATCH.mis languages, input trees containing only one treelet [$_{XP}$ X⁰ X⁰] undergo adjustments (when allowed), which increase the number of treelets, and hence decrease the number of m.BIN-ω violations. Usually this involves taking an input OWO and input EWO and merging them into an output treelet, and in p.MAINEDGE.pres languages, this is always the case, since destroying an input treelet necessarily violates both sp.ALIGN-L and sp.ALIGN-R. In MAINEDGE.del languages, the situation is more complicated. The discussion around (70)–(71) above shows that input treelets can be destroyed in these  languages, but the conditions under which this occurs are difficult to characterize succinctly.

This notion of treelet maximization in p.MATCH.mis languages, though absent from our discussion of SB$_4$, can be retro-applied to make sense of the sole mismatch in that subsystem, which takes one-treelet inputs and maps them onto the two-treelet ($_\varphi$ ($_\varphi$ ωω)($_\varphi$ ωω)). The next section briefly discusses its applicability to the next subsystem, $SB_6$, which contains exactly the same grammars as $SB_5$.

## 7.6    Subsystem $SB_6$

Subsystem $SB_6$ contains all the csets of $SB_5$, plus csets for the 42 six-word inputs admitted by SB.GEN. As always, each of these syntactic trees is isomorphic to a prosodic tree that is a possible output in each cset for one of the inputs, so each cset contains 42 candidates.

Remarkably, like $SB_5$, $SB_6$ has five languages: Iso, EP.L, EP.R, Bal.L, and Bal.R. Their grammars are the same as in $SB_5$, so the property analysis of $SB_6$ is that of $SB_5$ as well. Extensionally, the p.MATCH.mis languages of $SB_6$ are like those of $SB_5$ in showing an increase in treelets from input to output (and therefore a decrease in OWOs/EWOs) in all cases of mismatching.

## 7.7    Subsystems $SB_7$ and $SB_8$

We have also used SPOT and OTWorkplace to calculate the typologies for $SB_7$ and $SB_8$, and have ascertained that each contains 7 languages (with grammars the same in each). $SB_7$ introduces 132 csets of seven-word trees, and $SB_8$ introduces 429 csets of eight-word trees. Thus, $SB_7$ contains 196 csets, and $SB_8$ contains 625.

Three grammars of $SB_7$ and $SB_8$ are those of Iso, EP.L, and EP.R from $SB_4$ and $SB_5$. The other four derive from the p.MAINEDGE.del languages of $SB_5$. Bal.L of $SB_5$ gives rise to M.Bal.L and A.Bal.L of $SB_7$/$SB_8$, and Bal.R gives rise to M.Bal.R and A.Bal.R. The grammars of these languages are given in (72).

(72)    Grammars of $SB_7$ and $SB_8$
        a. Iso

        b. EP.L                        c. EP.R

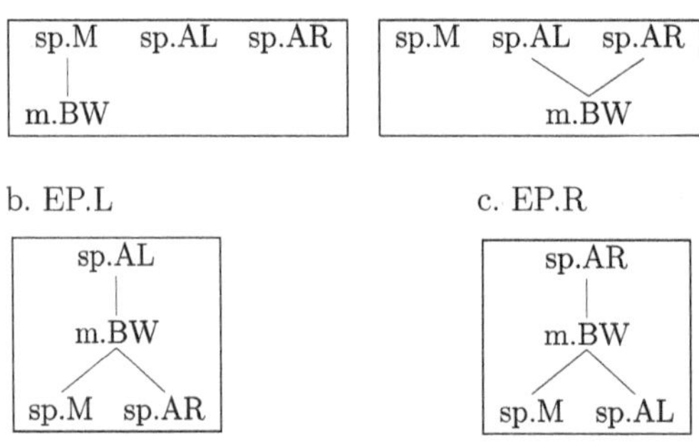

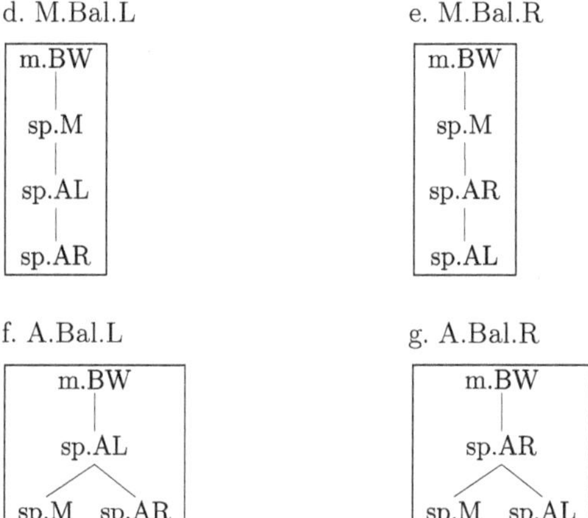

These grammars are subject to a property analysis with the three properties from SB$_5$, plus one more: p.MAP.M/A, which has antagonists sp.MATCH and c.ALIGN.dom. The conflict between sp.MATCH and the dominant alignment constraint (c.ALIGN.dom) is entirely new in SB$_7$; in smaller subsystems of SB, sp.MATCH and c.ALIGN.dom faced off only against m.BIN-ω, never against each other. At a pre-theoretical intuitive level, the sudden emergence of conflict between them is perhaps surprising, since MATCH constraints favor double-sided alignment. And yet, as we shall see below, the conflict has major consequences.

The properties are defined in (73) below.

(73)    Properties of grammars of SB$_7$ and SB$_8$

| Property | a | b | Scope |
|---|---|---|---|
| p.MATCH.iso/mis | {sp.M, c.ALIGN.sub}.dom | m.BW | wide |
| p.MAINEDGE/pres.del | c.ALIGN.dom | m.BW | under p.MATCH.mis |
| p.ALIGN.L/R | sp.AL | sp.AR | under p.MATCH.mis |
| p.MAP.M/A | sp.M | c.ALIGN.dom | under p.MAINEDGE.del |

MAP.M/A is only needed to make distinctions among the balancing languages (p.MAINEDGE.del). It is moot for Iso, since Iso contains linear extensions of the grammar (legs; Merchant and Prince, to appear) with sp.M highest ranked and c.ALIGN.dom highest ranked. Technically, EP.L and EP.R could be classified as p.MAP.A, but this specification is redundant, so we analyze p.MAP.M/A as scoping under p.MAINEDGE.del rather than under p.MATCH.mis; this is indicated by the use of <A> in angled brackets in the following PA table.

(74)     PA table for $SB_7$ and $SB_8$

|        | p.Match | p.MainEdge | p.Align | p.Map |
|--------|---------|------------|---------|-------|
| Iso    | iso     | *moot*     | *moot*  | *moot* |
| EP.L   | mis     | pres       | L       | <A> |
| EP.R   | mis     | pres       | R       | <A> |
| M.Bal.L | mis    | del        | L       | M     |
| M.Bal.R | mis    | del        | R       | M     |
| A.Bal.L | mis    | del        | L       | A     |
| A.Bal.R | mis    | del        | R       | A     |

The structure of the property analysis is further elucidated by the treeoid in (75).

(75)     Property treeoid for $SB_7$ and $SB_8$

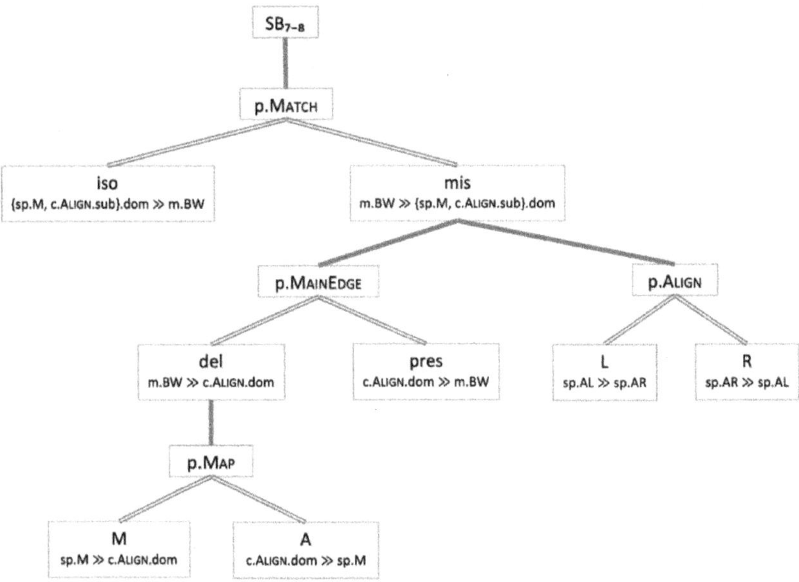


Examining all 625 mappings of $SB_8$ is beyond the scope of this chapter. However, it is worth considering how sp.M can suddenly come into conflict with the dominant alignment constraint, when this conflict did not arise in $SB_5$. The following table shows how each language treats two inputs: RLRRR and LRLLL.

(76)      RLRRR and LRLLL in $SB_7$ and $SB_8$

| | RLRRR<br>[**A** [[B [**C** [D [E F]]]] **G**]] | LRLLL<br>[[**A** [[[[B C] D] **E**] F]] **G**] |
|---|---|---|
| Iso | | match |
| EP.L | match | ((**A** ((B C) (D E))) (F G))<br>(**A** (((B C) (D E)) (F G))) |
| EP.R | (((A B) ((C D) (E F))) **G**)<br>((A B) (((C D) (E F)) **G**)) | match |
| M.Bal.L | | |
| M.Bal.R | | ((**A** ((B C) (D E))) (F G)) |
| A.Bal.L | (**A** (((B C) (D E)) (F G)))<br>(**A** ((B C) ((D E) (F G)))) | (**A** (((B C) (D E)) (F G))) |
| A.Bal.R | (((A B) ((C D) (E F))) **G**)<br>((A B) (((C D) (E F)) **G**)) | ((((A B) (C D)) (E F)) **G**)<br>(((A B) ((C D) (E F))) **G**) |

The RLRRR input has three OWOs: A, C, and G. In EP.R, M.Bal.L, M.Bal.R, and A.Bal.R, it maps to trees in which G is the sole OWO, while in A.Bal.L it maps to trees in which A is the sole OWO. This distinguishes M.Bal.L from A.Bal.L. Mapping RLRRR to trees where G is the OWO satisfies sp.MATCH in preference to sp.ALIGN-L, since this mapping preserves the XP [EF] as treelet (EF), but fails to align B with a left $\varphi$-edge in the output. The opposite choice, mapping RLRRR to trees where A is the OWO, improves performance on sp.ALIGN-L by putting B (which is at the left edge of two XPs in the input) at the left edge of a $\varphi$ in the output, at the expense of failing to match XP=[EF]. This exemplifies the conflict between sp.MATCH and sp.ALIGN-L that becomes possible when six terminals and five levels of embedding are allowed in the candidate set.

Similar logic applies to LRLLL, but for a conflict between sp.MATCH and sp.ALIGN-R. The LRLLL input also has three OWOs: A, E, and G. In EP.L, M.Bal.L, M.Bal.R, and A.Bal.L, it maps to trees in which A is the sole OWO. This preserves the treelet (B C), improving performance on sp.MATCH. In A.Bal.R, LRLLL maps to trees in which G is the OWO, improving performance on sp.ALIGN-R by putting F (which is at the right edge of two XPs in the input) at the right edge of a $\varphi$ in the output as well. Thus, M.Bal.R is distinguished from A.Bal.R.[14]

---

[14] The table in (76) does not demonstrate that M.Bal.L and M.Bal.R are distinct languages, but this can be ascertained through examination of Bal.L and Bal.R of $SB_5$.

## 7.8  The full system SB

We do not currently know how many languages are in the typology of SB, but in this section we narrow down the possibilities, and show that there are no fewer than 7, and no more than 11.

$SB_9$ is the first subsystem $SB_n$ whose typology we have not yet calculated. The number of trees on $n$ terminals admitted by SB.Gen is the $(n-1)^{st}$ Catalan number, $C_{n-1}$, when $n \geq 2$.[15] This means that $SB_9$ introduces 1430 more csets, each containing 1430 candidates, on top of the 625 csets of $SB_8$. The resulting 2055 csets, with 2,248,355 candidates, presents challenges for computation, since it exceeds the number of rows allowed in Microsoft Excel. Although there are ways of overcoming this challenge, we leave them for future work.

In $SB_{10}$, there are 4862 csets for ten-word trees, each containing 4862 candidates, making for a total of 6917 csets and 25,887,399 candidates in $SB_{10}$. The numbers of candidates, csets, and languages for subsystems $SB_2$ through $SB_{10}$ are given in (77).

(77)  Numerics of subsystems $SB_n$

| System | Csets | Candidates | Languages |
|---|---|---|---|
| $SB_2$ | 1 | 1 | 1 |
| $SB_3$ | 3 | 5 | |
| $SB_4$ | 8 | 30 | 4 |
| $SB_5$ | 22 | 226 | 5 |
| $SB_6$ | 64 | 1990 | |
| $SB_7$ | 196 | 19,414 | 7 |
| $SB_8$ | 625 | 203,455 | |
| $SB_9$ | 2055 | 2,248,355 | $7 \leq i \leq 11$ |
| $SB_{10}$ | 6917 | 25,887,399 | $7 \leq k \leq 11$ |

Although we have not calculated the typologies of $SB_9$ and $SB_{10}$, we list them in (77) as $i$ and $k$, and know that $7 \leq i \leq k \leq 11$. The total number of languages in the full system SB is $m$, and $7 \leq i \leq k \leq m \leq 11$. We refer to $m$ as |Typ.SB|, the cardinality of the typology of SB.

The proof that $7 \leq$ |Typ.SB| is by construction. It is given in (78).

---

[15] See Wikipedia, "Catalan Numbers" (https://en.wikipedia.org/wiki/Catalan_number), and sequence A000108 in *The On-Line Encyclopedia of Integer Sequences* (https://oeis.org/A000108).

(78)     $7 \leq |\text{Typ.SB}|$

     *Proof.* We have calculated the factorial typology of $\text{SB}_8$, and it contains 7 languages. SB makes all the distinctions made by $\text{SB}_8$, so SB contains at least 7 languages.

As a step on the way to proving that $|\text{Typ.SB}| \leq 11$, we observe that $|\text{Typ.SB}| \leq 24$.

(79)     $|\text{Typ.SB}| \leq 24$

     *Proof.* SB.Con contains 4 constraints, and $4! = 24$.

We can prove that $|\text{Typ.SB}| \leq 11$ by showing that certain languages of $\text{SB}_8$ are not subject to further refinement. Borrowing the term "refinement" from order theory we define it for OT typologies as in (80). Here, the letter $\lambda$ means "linear extension of a grammar" or "leg" (Alber et al. 2016; Merchant and Prince, to appear; Alber and Prince 2021).

(80)     Typological refinement

     A grammar $G = \{\lambda_1, \lambda_2, ..., \lambda_n\}$ in typology $T$ is *refined* in typology $T'$ iff there are two distinct grammars $H$, $I$ in $T'$ such that $H \subset G$ and $I \subset G$.

As an example, Bal in $\text{SB}_4$ is refined into Bal.L and Bal.R in $\text{SB}_5$, because three legs of Bal are legs of Bal.L, and the other three are legs of Bal.R; and Bal.L and Bal.R are further refined in $\text{SB}_7$.

(81)     Refinement of Bal from $\text{SB}_4$ through $\text{SB}_8$

| Linear Extension of Grammar (Leg) | | | | | | $\text{SB}_4$ | $\text{SB}_{5,6}$ | $\text{SB}_{7,8}$ |
|---|---|---|---|---|---|---|---|---|
| m.BW | $\gg$ | sp.M | $\gg$ | sp.AL | $\gg$ sp.AR | | | M.Bal.L |
| m.BW | $\gg$ | sp.AL | $\gg$ | sp.M | $\gg$ sp.AR | | Bal.L | A.Bal.L |
| m.BW | $\gg$ | sp.AL | $\gg$ | sp.AR | $\gg$ sp.M | Bal | | |
| m.BW | $\gg$ | sp.M | $\gg$ | sp.AR | $\gg$ sp.AL | | | M.Bal.R |
| m.BW | $\gg$ | sp.AR | $\gg$ | sp.M | $\gg$ sp.AL | | Bal.R | A.Bal.R |
| m.BW | $\gg$ | sp.AR | $\gg$ | sp.AL | $\gg$ sp.M | | | |

We now show that the grammar of Iso is not refined in the full system SB. Recall that Iso has the following grammar, here presented as a Skeletal Basis (Brasoveanu and Prince 2011), a comparative tableau which provides Iso's entire ERC grammar:

(82)      Grammar of Iso in $SB_4$, $SB_5$, $SB_6$, $SB_7$, $SB_8$ (Skeletal Basis)

| sp.M | sp.AL | sp.AR | m.BW |
|------|-------|-------|------|
| W    |       | W     | L    |
| W    | W     |       | L    |

The grammar of Iso is fully determined by the property value p.MATCH.iso, which means {sp.M, c.ALIGN.sub}.dom $\gg$ m.BW. The grammar has 14 legs, given in (83).

(83)      The 14 legs of Iso

    a.    sp.M $\gg$ sp.AL $\gg$ sp.AR $\gg$ m.BW

    b.    sp.M $\gg$ sp.AL $\gg$ m.BW $\gg$ sp.AR

    c.    sp.M $\gg$ sp.AR $\gg$ sp.AL $\gg$ m.BW

    d.    sp.M $\gg$ sp.AR $\gg$ m.BW $\gg$ sp.AL

    e.    sp.M $\gg$ m.BW $\gg$ sp.AL $\gg$ sp.AR

    f.    sp.M $\gg$ m.BW $\gg$ sp.AR $\gg$ sp.AL

    g.    sp.AL $\gg$ sp.M $\gg$ sp.AR $\gg$ m.BW

    h.    sp.AL $\gg$ sp.M $\gg$ m.BW $\gg$ sp.AR

    i.    sp.AL $\gg$ sp.AR $\gg$ sp.M $\gg$ m.BW

    j.    sp.AL $\gg$ sp.AR $\gg$ m.BW $\gg$ sp.M

    k.    sp.AR $\gg$ sp.M $\gg$ sp.AL $\gg$ m.BW

    l.    sp.AR $\gg$ sp.M $\gg$ m.BW $\gg$ sp.AL

    m.    sp.AR $\gg$ sp.AL $\gg$ sp.M $\gg$ m.BW

    n.    sp.AR $\gg$ sp.AL $\gg$ m.BW $\gg$ sp.M

The first thing to observe is that any leg in which sp.M dominates m.BW will map every input to a matching output. There are 12 such legs: every leg in (83) except for (83j) and (83n). Since each of these 12 determines an isomorphic mapping from every input, they never produce extensionally distinct results, and are therefore legs of the grammar of a single language in the full system SB (and in all of its subsystems).

To prove that Iso from $SB_8$ is not refined in SB, we must still demonstrate that (83j) and (83n) will never split off from Iso to yield a refinement. Although we have not yet undertaken a formal proof of this fact, it is evident that c.ALIGN.sub indeed functions as an enforcer of perfect isomorphism, just like sp.MATCH.

If Iso is not refined in SB, 14 of SB's 24 legs will always be part of a single grammar: the grammar of Iso. This leaves 10 legs about which we are less certain; these belong to 6 different grammars in $SB_8$ (the p.MATCH.mis grammars), but we cannot as of yet rule out further refinements in $SB_9$ and beyond. However, since each grammar must contain at least one leg, these 10 legs must belong to no more than 10 different grammars. If there ultimately turns out to be 10 p.MATCH.mis grammars, then there will be 11 languages in SB. Thus, SB contains at most 11 languages.

## 7.9   Some predictions for Japanese

EP.L of $SB_4$ through $SB_8$ contains the three- and four-word phrasings found in Japanese, at a certain level of abstraction (i.e., ignoring one-word constituents and effects of lexical accent; Kubozono 1989; Bellik et al. 2022). Abstractly identifying Japanese with EP.L in $SB_8$ provides 617 novel predictions for syntax–prosody mappings in Japanese. We do not know if these are borne  out, but we hope that they can direct future experimental work.

Here we provide just a few mappings from EP.L to give a taste of the sort of behavior predicted for Japanese. Every left edge of an XP is aligned in EP.L, so all strictly right-branching phrases are matched, e.g. [A [B [C [D E]]]] → (A (B (C (D E)))). But strictly left-branching structures undergo mismatching. The EP.L mappings for 5-word LLL through 9-word LLLLLLL are given  in (84).[16]

(84)     Mappings from strictly left-branching inputs in EP.L

| | Input | Output(s) |
|---|---|---|
| a. | 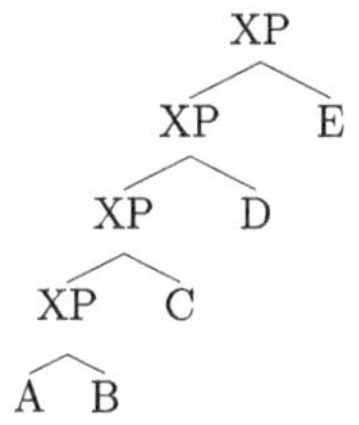 [[[[A B] C] D] E] (strictly left-branching XP tree) | 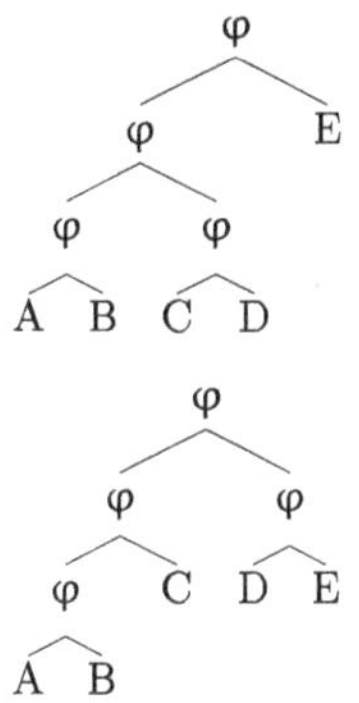 (φ ((φ (A B) (φ C D)) E)) and (φ ((φ (φ (A B)) C) (φ D E))) |

---

[16] Although we have not calculated the typology of $SB_9$, we have calculated a typology containing all of $SB_8$ plus the nine-word input [[[[[[[A B] C] D] E] F] G] H] I]. Whether or not EP.L is refined in $SB_9$, we know the mapping from [[[[[[[A B] C] D] E] F] G] H] I] that is determined by the grammar of EP.L from $SB_8$.

| | Input | Output(s) |
|---|---|---|
| b. | 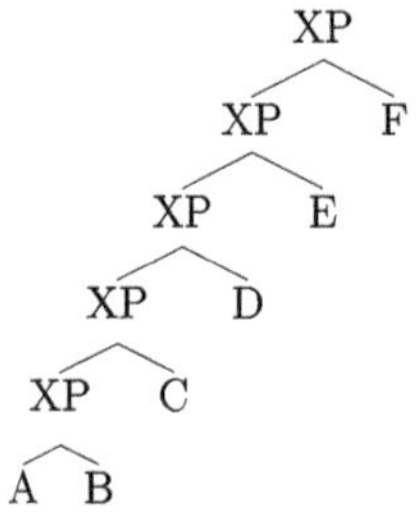 XP → XP F → XP E → XP D → XP C → A B | 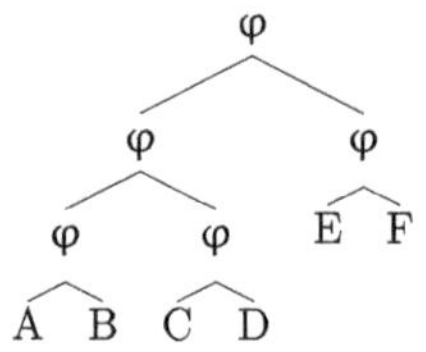 φ → [φ → [φ A B] [φ C D]] [φ E F] |
| c. | 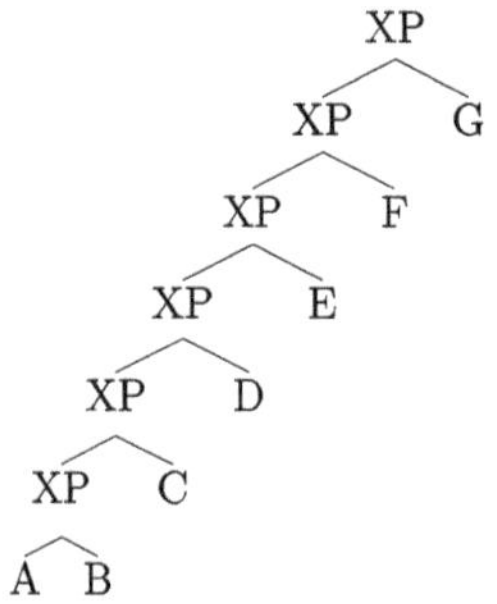 XP → XP G → XP F → XP E → XP D → XP C → A B | 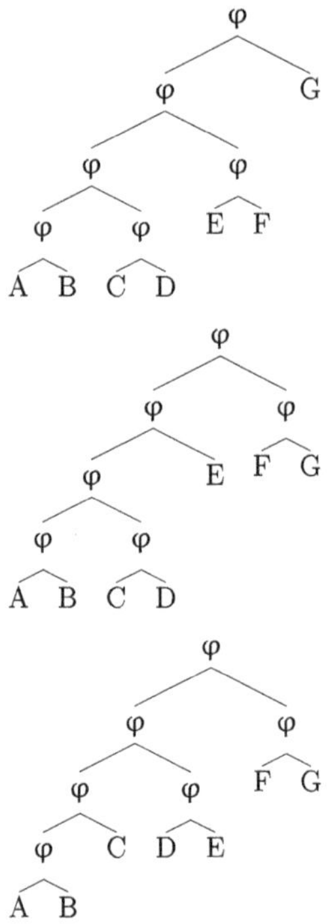 φ → [φ → [φ → [φ A B] [φ C D]] [φ E F]] G<br><br>φ → [φ → [φ → [φ A B] [φ C D]] E F G] [φ E F G]<br><br>φ → [φ → [φ → [φ A B] C D E] [φ F G]] |
| d. | 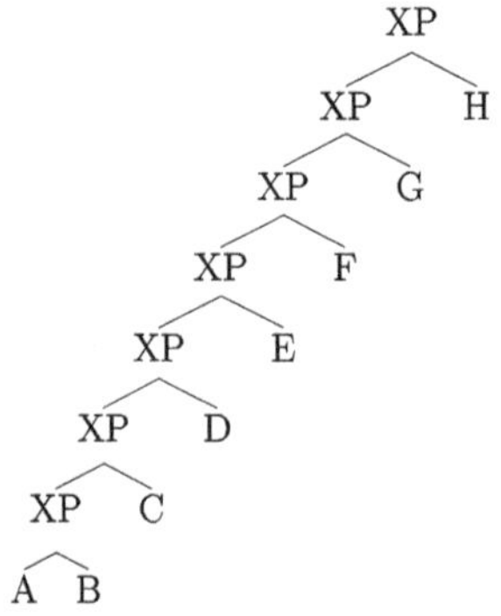 XP → XP H → XP G → XP F → XP E → XP D → XP C → A B | 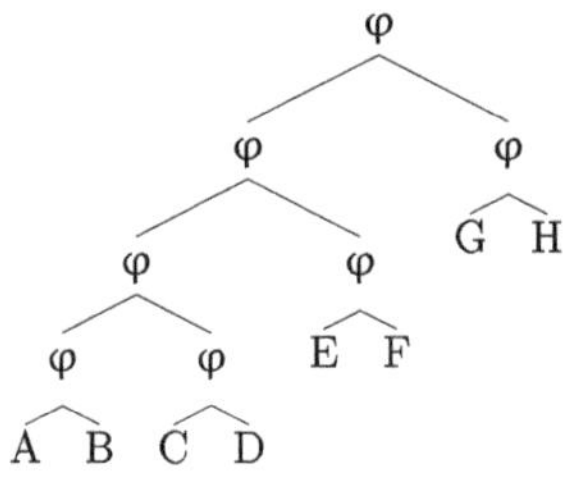 φ → [φ → [φ → [φ A B] [φ C D]] [φ E F]] [φ G H] |

| Input | Output(s) |
|---|---|
| e. 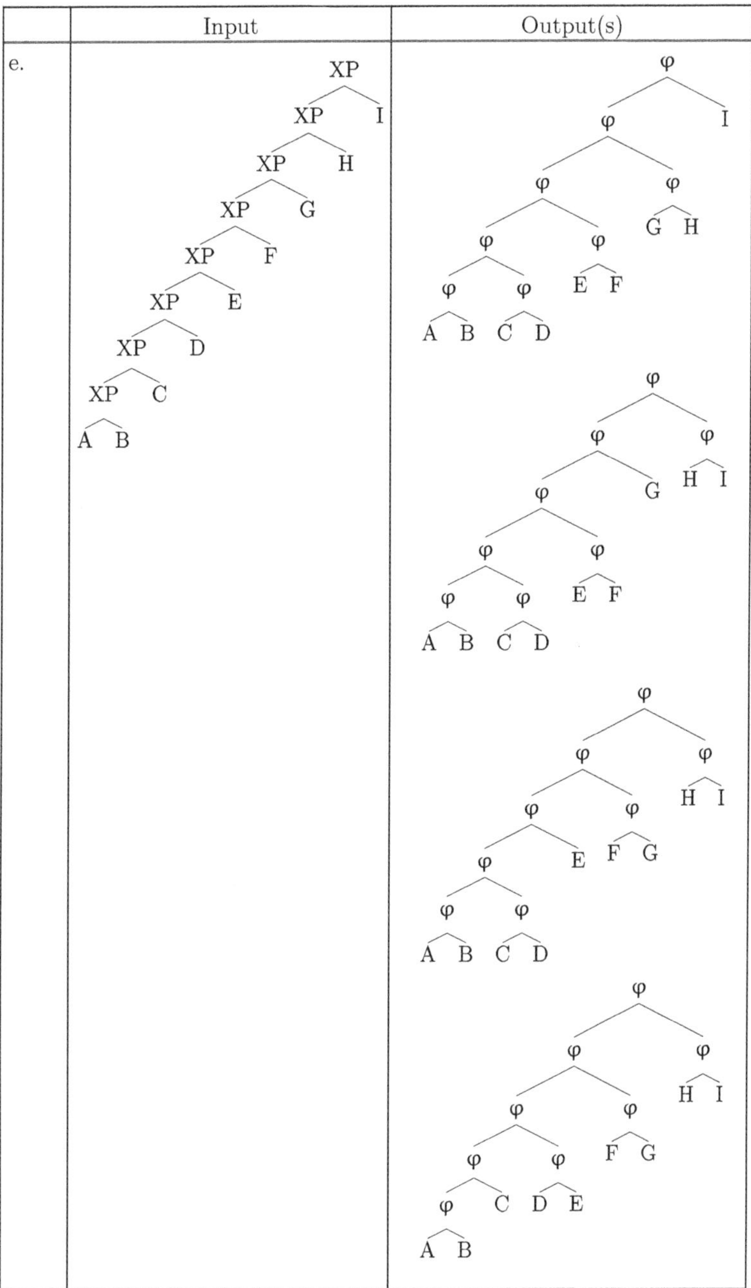 | |

In (84), an input treelet [A B] is always mapped faithfully to (A B). When the number of words is an even number $n$, there is a unique output containing $n/2$ treelets and no OWOs. When the number of words is an odd number

$m$, there are $(m-1)/2$ outputs, each containing $(m-1)/2$ treelets and one OWO. The OWO can be any odd-numbered word other than A, which is always in a treelet with B. For example, nine-word [[[[[[[A B] **C**] D] **E**] F] **G**] H] **I**] contains four OWOs, and it has four outputs: one in which the OWO is C, one in which it is E, one in which it is G, and one in which it is I. Non-treelet subtrees in all of the outputs are always left-branching, with one exception: the balanced-branching subtree $((\omega\omega)(\omega\omega))$. By "left-branching" here we mean that the non-treelet subtrees $(_\varphi\ \alpha\ \beta)$ other than $((\omega\omega)(\omega\omega))$ are such that that $\alpha$ dominates more leaves than $\beta$ does.

A striking prediction here is that phrases with an even number of words have a unique output, while phrases with an odd number of words are subject to variation in phrasing. The situation with OWOs is reminiscent of the phenomenon of unparsed syllables in the weakly dense languages of the footing system nGX (Alber et al. 2016). In weakly dense languages, even-parity words are exhaustively parsed into binary feet (i.e., treelets), while odd-parity words have one odd syllable out. But while the position of the OWO is often unsettled in SB, the position of the unparsed syllable is always uniquely determined in the weakly dense languages of nGX. When ALL-FEET-LEFT (AFL) dominates ALL-FEET-RIGHT (AFR), the unparsed syllable is at the right edge of the word, as in $[_\omega\ (_F\ \sigma\sigma)(_F\ \sigma\sigma)\sigma]$. When the ranking of AFL and AFR is reversed, the unparsed syllable appears at the left edge, as in $[_\omega\ \sigma(_F\ \sigma\sigma)(_F\ \sigma\sigma)]$. In SB, the only constraints that affect the positioning of the OWO are sp.MATCH, sp.ALIGN-L, and sp.ALIGN-R, but as we have seen, these are not always decisive on this point.

This leads us to a word of caution regarding the predictions made by SB for Japanese. As we have mentioned, SB is already at a high level of abstraction, setting aside many aspects of structure that are relevant in natural languages. One must also keep in mind that SB contains only a small handful of the constraints proposed by researchers working on syntax–prosody mapping. The addition of any other constraint is likely to have major consequences for the typology of the resulting system. Since we do not claim that the constraints of SB are the only constraints in CON for the human faculty for language, we cannot claim with confidence that the predictions of EP.L will be fully borne out in Japanese. In addition, the longer the input phrases become, the more we can expect performance factors like memory, attention, etc. to obscure the data obtained by experiment.

Having listed all of these caveats, we do consider it a virtue of SB that it makes definite predictions for Japanese. If these predictions are ultimately falsified, this will define the direction for future research, and will undoubtedly provide important clues regarding the full nature of the syntax–prosody interface. Pending such empirical discoveries, we hope to have contributed with this chapter toward the general understanding of the formal predictions that follow from an OT system involving some commonly invoked constraints of the MATCH, ALIGN, and BINARITY families.


## 7.10   Conclusion

This chapter has followed up on a finding from Bellik et al. (2022), the ramifications of which we did not explore there. In that work, we demonstrated that both MATCH and ALIGN constraints are needed to account for a phonological phrasing asymmetry in Japanese, in which left-branching XPs are mismatched and right-branching XPs are matched. Here, we have elucidated the ways in which MATCH and ALIGN constraints interact in an OT system called SB, using SPOT and OTWorkplace to achieve full clarity and explicitness.

Using Property Theory (Alber and Prince 2021), we have found that while sp.MATCH and sp.ALIGN-L and sp.ALIGN-R conflict indirectly due to ranking $vis$-$\grave{a}$-$vis$ m.BINMAX($\varphi,\omega$) in subsystems of SB in which inputs have fewer than seven words, they suddenly come into direct conflict in $SB_7$. Once $SB_7$ is reached, some mismatching languages are actually distinguished from each other by a property pitting sp.MATCH against the dominant sp.ALIGN constraint. This result comes as something of a surprise, and underscores the importance of checking the behavior of every candidate set admitted by GEN in a given system.

Every language in SB is either perfectly matching, or allows some mismatching in order to improve on the markedness constraint m.BINMAX($\varphi,\omega$). Among the mismatchers, there are those which require alignment to their main XP edge, and those that do not. The main edge is either the left edge, if sp.ALIGN-L dominate sp.ALIGN-R, or the right edge, if the reverse holds. Among the edge-disrespecting mismatchers, there is the further question of whether matching or alignment is more important. These properties uncovered for $SB_7$ and $SB_8$ are guaranteed to hold for the full system SB as well, but we do not yet know whether $SB_7$ constitutes a *universal support* for the full typology of SB. However, it is clear that $SB_7$ and $SB_8$'s seven languages will not refine to exceed eleven in the full typology.

Returning to the concrete linguistic motivation for this line of inquiry, we again note SB's predictions for phonological phrasing in Japanese. Like in the four-word left-branching case, we expect every purely left-branching XP in Japanese to undergo a process of binarization, making the tree flatter and maximizing the number of two-word phonological phrases. Whether these predictions are borne out, and whether any other languages of SB

can be identified with attested natural languages, will show whether the
MATCH+ALIGN hypothesis is worth pursuing further.


## References

Alber, Birgit, Delbusso, Natalie, and Prince, Alan (2016). From intensional
    properties to universal support. *Language* 92: e88–e116.
Alber, Birgit and Prince, Alan (2021). *The Structure of OT Typologies.*
    Chapter 1: Introduction to Property Theory. Unpublished manuscript.
    ROA 1381, Rutgers Optimality Archive, http://roa.rutgers.edu.
Bellik, Jennifer and Kalivoda, Nick (2016). Adjunction and branchingness
    effects in syntax-prosody mapping. In Gunnar Ólafur Hansson, Ashley
    Farris-Trimble, Kevin McMullin, and Douglas Pulleyblank (eds.)
    *Supplemental Proceedings of the 2015 Annual Meeting on Phonology,*
    Linguistic Society of America. http://doi.org/10.3765/amp.v3i0.3690
Bellik, Jennifer, Bellik, Ozan, and Kalivoda, Nick (2015–2021). Syntax-
    Prosody in Optimality Theory (SPOT). Javascript application. http://
    spot.sites.ucsc.edu. Codebase at https://github.com/syntax-prosody-ot.
Bellik, Jennifer, Ito, Junko, Kalivoda, Nick and Mester, Armin (2022).
    Matching and alignment. In Haruo Kubozono, Junko Ito, and Armin
    Mester (eds.) *Prosody and Prosodic Interfaces.* Oxford University Press.
Bennett, Ryan, Elfner, Emily, and McCloskey, James (2016). Lightest to the
    right: An apparently anomalous displacement in Irish. *Linguistic Inquiry*
    47: 169–234.
Brasoveanu, Adrian and Prince, Alan (2011). Ranking and necessity: the
    Fusional Reduction Algorithm. *Natural Language and Linguistic Theory*
    29: 3–70.
Chen, Matthew (1987). The syntax of Xiamen tone sandhi. *Phonology
    Yearbook* 4: 109–149.
DelBusso, Natalie R. (2018). *Typological Structure and Properties of Property
    Theory.* PhD dissertation, Rutgers University.
Elfner, Emily (2012). *Syntax-Prosody Interactions in Irish.* PhD dissertation,
    University of Massachusetts Amherst.
Ishihara, Shinichiro (2014). Match theory and the recursivity problem. In
    Shigeto Kawahara and Mika Igarashi (eds.) *MIT Working Papers in
    Linguistics 73: Proceedings of Formal Approaches to Japanese linguistics 7*
    69–88. Cambridge, MA.
Ishihara, Shinichiro (2015). Syntax–phonology interface. In Haruo Kubozono
    (ed.) *Handbook of Japanese Phonetics and Phonology* 569–618. Berlin:
    Mouton de Gruyter.
Ishihara, Shinichiro and Myrberg, Sara (2018). The asymmetry problem
    and Match Theory: an example from Stockholm Swedish. Presentation
    at the International Conference on Tone and Intonation, University of
    Gothenburg.

Ito, Junko and Mester, Armin (2013). Prosodic subcategories in Japanese.
    *Lingua* 124: 20–40.
Kalivoda, Nick (2018). *Syntax-Prosody Mismatches in Optimality Theory.*
    PhD dissertation, University of California, Santa Cruz.
Kalivoda, Nick, and Bellik, Jennifer (2018). Prosodic recursion and pseudo-
    cyclicity in Danish compound stød. In Ryan Bennett, Andrew Angeles,
    Adrian Brasoveanu, Dhyana Buckley, Nick Kalivoda, Shigeto Kawahara,
    Grant McGuire and Jaye Padgett (eds.) *Hana-bana (花々): A Festschrift
    for Junko Ito and Armin Mester.* Santa Cruz: Linguistics Research Center.
Kubozono, Haruo (1989). Syntactic and rhythmic effects on downstep in
    Japanese. *Phonology* 6: 39–67.
Liberman, Mark and Prince, Alan (1977). On stress and linguistic rhythm.
    *Linguistic Inquiry* 8: 249–336.
McCarthy, John J. and Prince, Alan (1993). Generalized alignment. In
    Geert Booij and Jaap van Marle (eds.) *Yearbook of Morphology* 79–153.
    Dordrecht: Kluwer.
McCarthy, John J. and Prince, Alan (1995). Faithfulness and reduplicative
    identity. In Jill Beckman, Laura Walsh Dickey, and Suzanne Urbanczyk
    (eds.) *Papers in Optimality Theory* (University of Massachusetts
    Occasional Papers in Linguistics 18) 249–384. Amherst, MA: GLSA.
Merchant, Nazarré and Prince, Alan (to appear). *The Mother of All Tableaux:
    Order, Equivalence, and Geometry in the Large-scale Structure of
    Optimality Theory.* Equinox Press.
Moreton, Elliott (2004). Non-computable functions in optimality theory. In
    John J. McCarthy (ed.) *Optimality Theory in Phonology: A Reader* 141–
    164. Wiley-Blackwell.
Myrberg, Sara (2013). Sisterhood in prosodic branching. *Phonology* 30:
    73–124.
Prince, Alan (2002a). Arguing optimality. In Angela Carpenter, Andries
    Coetzee, and Paul de Lacy (eds.) *Papers in Optimality Theory II*
    (University of Massachusetts Occasional Papers in Linguistics 26) 269–304.
    Amherst, MA: GLSA.
Prince, Alan (2002b). Entailed ranking arguments. Unpublished manuscript.
    ROA 500, Rutgers Optimality Archive, http://roa.rutgers.edu.
Prince, Alan (2007). The pursuit of theory. In Paul de Lacy (ed.) *The
    Cambridge Handbook of Phonology* 33–60. Cambridge: Cambridge
    University Press.
Prince, Alan (2017). Representing OT Grammars. ROA 1309, Rutgers
    Optimality Archive, http://roa.rutgers.edu.
Prince, Alan and Smolensky, Paul (1993/2004). *Optimality Theory: Constraint
    Interaction in Generative Grammar.* Malden, MA: Blackwell Publishing.
Prince, Alan, Merchant, Nazarré, and Tesar, Bruce (2007–2021).
    OTWorkplace. http://sites.google.com/site/otworkplace
Selkirk, Elisabeth (1986). On derived domains in sentence phonology.
    *Phonology Yearbook* 3: 371–405.

Selkirk, Elisabeth (2011). The syntax–phonology interface. In John A. Goldsmith, Jason Riggle, and Alan C. L. Yu (eds.) *The Handbook of Phonological Theory* 435–484. Blackwell Publishing.

Selkirk, Elisabeth O. and Tateishi, Koichi (1991). Syntax and downstep in Japanese. In Carol Georgopoulos and Roberta Ishihara (eds.) *Interdisciplinary Approaches to Language: Essays in Honor of S.-Y. Kuroda* 519–544. Dordrecht: Springer.

Tokizaki, Hisao (2006). Linearizing structure with silence: A Minimalist theory of syntax-phonology interface. Ph.D. thesis, University of Tsukuba.

Truckenbrodt, Hubert (1995). *Phonological Phrases: Their Relation to Syntax, Focus, and Prominence.* PhD dissertation, Massachusetts Institute of Technology.

Truckenbrodt, Hubert (1999). On the relation between syntactic phrases and phonological phrases. *Linguistic Inquiry* 30: 219–255.


## About the author

*Nick Kalivoda*

Postdoctoral researcher, Centre for Languages and Literature, Lund University. Research interests: syntax–prosody interface, syntax, phonology, and Optimality Theory. Recent publications: "Automated tableau generation using SPOT (Syntax Prosody in Optimality Theory)", with J. Bellik, *Linguistics Vanguard* 2019, 'XP- and X⁰-movement in the Latin verb: Evidence from mirroring and anti-mirroring" with E. Zyman, *Glossa* 2020, and "Match Theory: An overview", with S. Ishihara, *Language and Linguistics Compass* 2022.

**Appendix: Universal Violation Tableaux and Property Treeoids**

(85)   Universal Violation Tableau for $SB_4$

| $SB_4$ | sp.M | sp.AL | sp.AL | m.BW |
|---|---|---|---|---|
| Iso | 0 | 0 | 0 | 2 |
| EP.L | 1 | 0 | 1 | 1 |
| EP.R | 1 | 1 | 0 | 1 |
| Bal | 2 | 2 | 2 | 0 |

(86)   Property Treeoids for $SB_4$

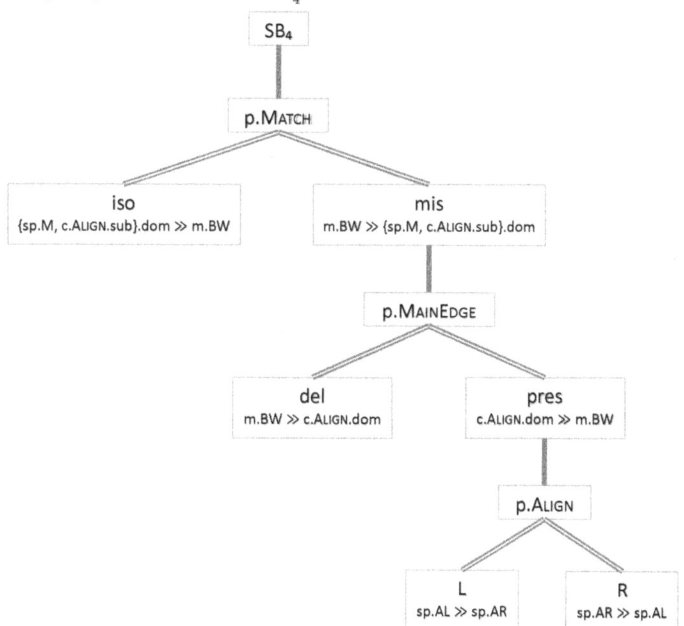


(87)   Universal Violation Tableau for $SB_{5-6}$

| $SB_{5-6}$ | sp.M | sp.AL | sp.AL | m.BW |
|---|---|---|---|---|
| Iso | 0 | 0 | 0 | 2 |
| EP.L | 1 | 0 | 1 | 1 |
| EP.R | 1 | 1 | 0 | 1 |
| Bal.L | 2 | 2 | 3 | 0 |
| Bal.R | 2 | 3 | 2 | 0 |

(88)      Property Treeoid for $SB_{5\text{–}6}$

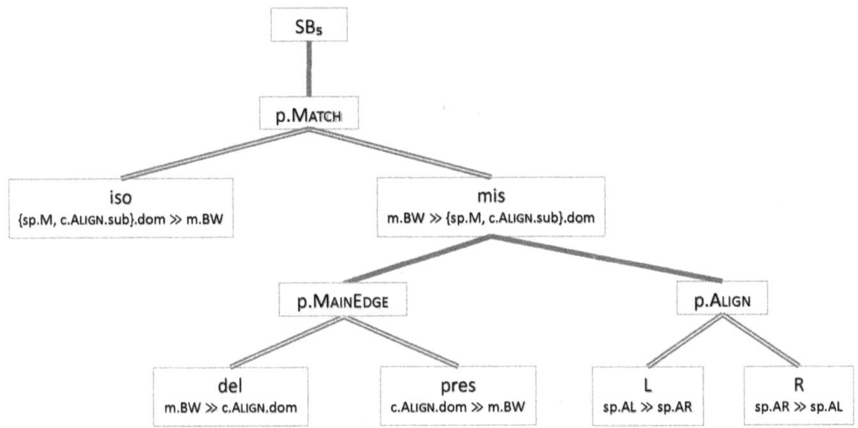


(89)      Universal Violation Tableau for $SB_{7\text{–}8}$

| $SB_{7\text{–}8}$ | sp.M | sp.AL | sp.AL | m.BW |
|---|---|---|---|---|
| Iso | 0 | 0 | 0 | 2 |
| EP.L | 1 | 0 | 1 | 1 |
| EP.R | 1 | 1 | 0 | 1 |
| M.Bal.L | 2 | 3 | 4 | 0 |
| M.Bal.R | 2 | 4 | 3 | 0 |
| A.Bal.L | 3 | 2 | 5 | 0 |
| A.Bal.R | 3 | 5 | 2 | 0 |

(90)      Property Treeoid for $SB_{7-8}$

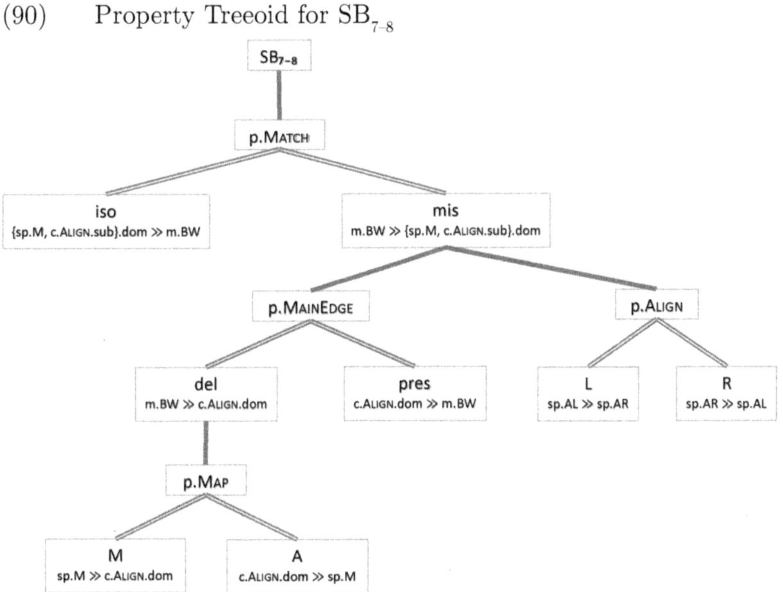

# Chapter 8

# Align-driven clitic movement in Chamorro

Richard Bibbs[*]

## 8.1 Introduction

Prosodically dependent material, in this case *clitics*, often has limited distributional patterns in languages. Where a clitic can appear is often subject to certain constraints, such as being unable to occur at the beginning of a sentence. Certain clitics are characterized as *second-position* (2P) clitics, a special type of clitic which typically occurs in the second string-linear position in a sentence. Previous work has demonstrated that purely syntactic movement may account for the position of 2P clitics in some languages (Anderson 1996, 2005). However, the position of some 2P clitics, and clitics generally, has been demonstrated to be the result of prosodic factors (Bennett et al., 2016. Chung 2003. Harizanov 2014, Schütze 1994). An early account of prosodically-driven clitic placement is Chung (2003), where the placement of weak pronouns in the language is motivated through the use of prosodic mapping and prosodic subcategorization. Another case of prosodically motivated weak pronoun placement is found in Irish. Bennett et al. (2016) provide an account of weak pronoun postposing, where the movement is driven primarily by the avoidance of proclitics through a high-ranking STRONGSTART constraint. While Irish does not have 2P clitics, it does demonstrate how the interaction of prosodic well-formedness constraints and

[*] I would like to thank Jenny Bellik, Dan Brodkin, Nick Kalivoda, and Nicholas Van Handel for helpful comments and suggestions on an earlier version of this chapter, and Ryan Bennett, Gorka Elordieta, Junko Ito, and Armin Mester for useful discussion of this work.

mapping constraints based in Match Theory can capture prosodic movement of clitics.

In this chapter, we will take another look at the placement of 2P weak pronoun clitics in Chamorro. While Chung (2003) demonstrates weak pronoun placement may be accounted for using prosodic subcategorization, this is not the only possible analysis. This chapter shows that movement of weak pronoun clitics in Chamorro can be motivated within Optimality Theory, through the interaction of prosodic well-formedness constraints and mapping constraints. This constraint-motivated prosodic movement has already been demonstrated in Bennett et al. (2016)'s account of Irish weak pronoun postposing, so extending it to another language case is a logical step forward. Notably Irish weak pronoun postposing was accounted for using the Match mapping constraint supposed under Match Theory (Selkirk 2011). The analysis uses Match, rather than Align-based mapping constraints (Bellik and Kalivoda 2016, Selkirk 1986; Truckenbrodt 1999), to remain consistent with prior work on the syntax–prosody mapping of Irish (Bennett et al. 2016, Elfner 2012). However, it is important to test whether prosodic movement can be motivated within both Match and Align Theory. Equally important is whether prosodic movement in different languages can be accounted for within the same theory. Chamorro serves as a convenient test case for addressing these questions, as it provides an empirically different case of prosodic movement than that of Irish. Irish weak pronoun movement is characterized by rightward postposing, whereas Chamorro weak pronouns appear to move leftward to 'second position."

The results of this analysis will demonstrate that in fact, prosodic movement of weak pronouns in Chamorro cannot be captured using Match constraints. Instead, syntax-prosody alignment constraints, and their interactions with prosodic well-formedness constraints, are required to motivate the leftward movement of weak pronoun clitics in Chamorro. This is because movement improves performance on the relatively flexible Alignment constraints, but is never favored by Match, which requires a stricter syntax-prosody correspondence. This result not only shows that weak pronoun placement in Chamorro can be accounted for without the use of subcategorization, but also that not all prosodic movement can be captured under Match Theory, at least using standardly assumed markedness constraints.

## 8.2    Data

Chamorro is an Austronesian language primarily spoken throughout the Mariana Islands, as well as in diasporic communities throughout the United States. The data throughout this chapter comes primarily from prior work on Chamorro, including various reference grammars on the language (Chung 2020, Topping and Dungca 1973). Chamorro is a head-initial language with the most common word order being VSO.

### 8.2.1   Weak pronoun distribution

Chamorro has a variety of pronoun types, including overt and null pronouns. Here we will focus entirely on the weak overt pronouns, provided in (1).

(1)      Overt pronouns in Chamorro

|              | Weak  | Independent |
|--------------|-------|-------------|
| 1 sg.        | yu'   | guahu       |
| 2 sg.        | hao   | hagu        |
| 3 sg. anim.  | gui'  | guiya       |
| 1 incl. pl.  | hit   | hita        |
| 1 excl. pl.  | häm   | hämi        |
| 2 pl.        | hämyu | hämyu       |
| 3 pl. anim.  | siha  | siha        |

I adopt the term *weak pronoun*, following Chung (2003), to refer to these pronominal elements throughout. Weak pronouns in Chamorro are most easily characterized as second-position clitics (2P clitics), a special type of clitic which typically occurs in the second string-linear position in a sentence. Weak pronouns are prosodically deficient enclitics, meaning they are unstressed and mostly monosyllables that must lean on material to their left (Chung 2003). Weak pronouns in Chamorro have a special distribution when compared to full DPs or independent pronouns in the language. Weak pronouns can surface where non-pronominal subjects and direct objects typically cannot (Chung 2003). For example, in (2), the weak pronoun *hao* can occur in "second position" immediately following *patgon-na* (2a), but the full DP *si Dolores* cannot (2b). Note the L in the glosses throughout this chapter marks the Chamorro linker; an in-depth overview of the linker can be found in Chung (2020).

(2) a.   Kao    patgon-ña    **hao**    ädyu    na    ma'estra?
       Q    child-AGR    you    that    L    teacher
       'Are you that teacher's child?'

   b.   *Kao    patgon-ña    si Dolores ädyu    na    ma'estra?
       Q    child-AGR    Dolores    that    L    teacher
       ('Is Dolores that teacher's child?')

Chung (2003) also states that the overt pronouns in Chamorro are in apparent complementary distribution: weak pronouns 'represent pronominal subjects and direct objects," whereas independent pronouns represent other pronominals such as obliques, conjoined pronominals, and objects of prepositions. This is demonstrated in (3), where the independent pronoun *hagu* serves as an oblique marked argument, but the weak pronoun *hao* cannot.

(3)     Ma'a'ñao      i      gä'-hu      ga'lagu   nu    hagu/***hao**.
        AGR.afraid   the    pet-AGR    dog        obl   you
        'My dog is afraid of you.'

However, this second-position characterization on its own is not entirely accurate for Chamorro weak pronouns, as the weak pronouns often fall outside of the canonical second position (i.e., after the first string-linear element). Whether or not the weak pronoun may violate the typical 2P clitic generalization is, on the surface, subject to various syntactic considerations.

The placement of weak pronouns depend on whether there is a head-complement structure, or an adjunction structure. With basic head-complement structures, the weak pronoun (bolded) obligatory follows the predicate head, as demonstrated in (4) and (5).

(4)     [$_{AP}$ Ma'a'nao    **yu'**    [cha'ka]]
            AGR.afraid   1.SG      rats
        'I am afraid of rats.'

(5)     [$_{VP}$ Malagu'    **gui'**    [nuebu   na      kareta]]
            AGR.want     she       new     L       car
        'She wants a new car.'

However, this restriction changes in adjunction structures; specifically, we see optionality in clitic placement, where one option is not the expected 'second position." This is where we find crucial differences from canonical 2P clitic behavior. As an example, we will use DP predicate structures, as the NPs of these predicates are often modified through adjunction. First, if the NP of a DP predicate is unmodified, the clitic must immediately follow the N head of the predicate, just as we've seen with the typical head-complement structures in (4) and (5). Second, this same distributional restriction also applies to when the NP predicate has a postnominal modifier as in (6), where the PP is an adjunct to NP.

(6) [$_{DP}$ [Famalao'an] **hit** [ginin todus i islas gi Pacifika]]
      women          we   from  all  the islands LOC  Pacific
      'We are women from all the islands of the Pacific.' (Chung 2003)

Third, if the NP has a *prenominal* modifier, the clitic may either follow the N
head of NP (7a), or follow the entire adjunct phrase modifying the NP (7b).
This behavior is notably distinct from that of head-complement structures
(4) and postnominal modifier structures (6).

(7) a.   [[$_{AP}$    Aguagat] [$_{NP}$   na    patgun]]        **gui'**
            naughty      L   child   he
         'He's a naughty child.'
    b.   [[$_{AP}$ Aguagat]      **gui'** [$_{NP}$ na    patgun]]
            naughty        he    L    child
         'He's a naughty child.'

This optionality is not exclusive to modified nominal predicates. Select adverbs which adjoin to the left of a VP in Chamorro also exhibit the optional
pattern of placement for the weak pronoun, as shown in (8). The pattern
in (8) shows a flexibility in the placement of weak pronouns for modified
structures where the head of the modified phrase is displaced from a leftmost
position. In (8a), the weak pronoun *gui'* is in third position immediately following the VP, *dinisfruta*. In (8b) the weak pronoun *hit* appears in second
position immediately following the adverb *duru*, the same adverb in (8a),
instead of appearing in second position immediately following the VP *man-
guput*. This optionality of placement is the principal distinction between
typical head-complement structures and adjunction structures in the deter-
mination of weak pronoun placement.

(8) a.   Duru  dinisfruta        **gui'**   as    Fulanu
         a.lot  AGR.PASS.criticize  he    by    So-and-so
         'So-and-so had said a lot of bad things about him.' (*Saipan Tribune
         8/31/99*, Chung 2003)
    b.   Duru  **hit**      man-guput
         a.lot  we      AGR-party
         'We partied a lot.' (*Saipan Tribune 5/13/99*, Chung 2003)

A summary of the distributional generalizations seen in (2) and (4)–(8) is
provided in (9). Note that the preverbal adverbial structure in (8) is functionally equivalent to that of the prenominal modifier, so only the prenominal modifier structure is provided in (9). This is not an exhaustive list of

possible structures in Chamorro, but will serve as a representative set of the relevant second and third positions to be accounted for by the analysis in §8.3.

(9)　　　Summary of weak pronoun positions

| Syntax | Structure | Weak pronoun position | Example |
|---|---|---|---|
| [[$_{VP}$ V [NP]] [$_{DP}$ clitic]] | Head-complement | second | (4), (5) |
| [[$_{DP}$ [NP] [DP]] [$_{DP}$ clitic]] | DP possessive | second | (2) |
| [[NP [AP] [NP]] [$_{DP}$ clitic]] | Prenominal AP modifier | second or third | (7a), (7b) |
| [[NP [NP] [PP]] [$_{DP}$ clitic]] | Postnominal PP modifier | second | (6) |

### 8.2.2　Modifiers and adjunct visibility

The structures involving modification (i.e., adjunction) require a bit more detailed discussion. Recall that there are two important generalizations about the placement of weak pronouns with modified nominal predicates: (a) if there is a prenominal modifier, the weak pronoun either immediately follows the modifier XP (second position) or immediately follows the N head of the modified NP (third position); (b) if there is a postnominal modifier, the weak pronoun can only immediately follow the N head of the modified NP (second position). The schematizations for these generalizations are repeated in (10) and (11).

(10)　　　Prenominal Modifier

           NP

       XP    NP

(11)　　　Postnominal Modifier

           NP

       NP    XP

These generalizations can be analyzed very cleanly if we assume that different levels of projections for modified XPs are visible in syntax–prosody mapping. Adjunction visibility to mapping constraints has been shown to act a bit differently than typical head-complement structures (Truckenbrodt 1995, 1999; Selkirk 2011; Bellik and Kalivoda 2016). Due to the segment theory of adjunction, researchers have found that different segments of an adjunction structure may be visible to mapping constraints: either the lowest segment, the highest segment, or all segments. Truckenbrodt and Selkirk suggest only the lowest segment of XP is visible to Match constraints. Bellik and Kalivoda find that certain visibility settings make unique predictions for both Align/Wrap Theory and Match Theory with respect to the prosodic phrasing of adjunction structures. Here I assert that during syntax–prosody mapping, the visibility of projections for modified XPs is either: both high and low projections are visible for mapping, or only the highest projection is visible for mapping. This differs from the suggestions of Truckenbrodt (1995, 1999) and Selkirk (2011), but seems to align with the possibility of varying projection visibility found in Bellik and Kalivoda (2016). Chung (2003) also assumes a choice to map to the highest or lowest φ is available.

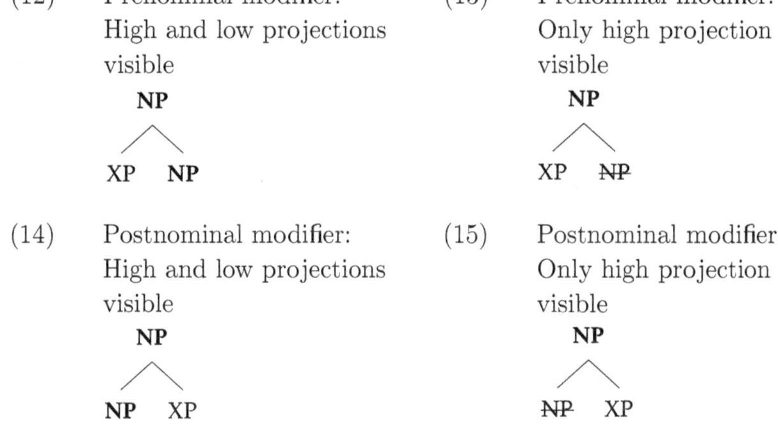

The structures in (12) and (14) that have high- and low-projection visibility result in every segment of the adjunct structure being visible to prosodic mapping. The structures in (13) and (15), where only the highest projection is visible, only allow the XP segment and the higher NP segment to be visible to prosodic mapping. The importance of these distinctions will be discussed further in §8.3 and §8.4.2.

## 8.3    System definitions

We define two separate OT systems for comparison: a Match system and an Align system. These systems will attempt to account for the same empirical facts overviewed in §8.2, but using different constraint sets. Both systems will share the same set of markedness constraints, but handle the syntax–prosody mapping constraints differently; the Match system will utilize MATCH, and the Align system will utilize ALIGN-R and ALIGN-L. Comparing these systems will reveal the viability of each theory (or lack thereof) in motivating the leftward prosodic movement of weak pronouns in Chamorro.

### 8.3.1    Defining GEN

#### 8.3.1.1 Inputs

Defining GEN for any OT system requires the careful specification of both the inputs and the outputs that will be considered within the analysis. Defining the inputs for this analysis requires the exhaustive consideration of all the relevant syntactic structures that may appear in Chamorro to ensure that we can both capture the empirical facts given weak pronoun placement in known Chamorro examples, and also determine what this analysis predicts for the placement of weak pronouns in previously unconsidered syntactic structures.

We consider a relatively small input set that consists predominately of two prosodic words alongside the weak pronoun. The inputs will be generated according to certain constraints on the syntax of Chamorro. In brief, inputs will be structures that consist of one- or two-word XPs + a weak pronoun. The direction of the head will not be constrained, and adjunction will be permitted.

An important note about the selected inputs, provided in (17), is that the weak pronoun, marked as "clitic", always appears as the rightmost element in the structure. This syntactic position for the weak pronoun is based on the assumption that specifiers of TPs (i.e., subjects) are rightward in Chamorro (Chung 1998, 2003). The only structures considered in this analysis are those with a weak pronoun subject;[1] this is also the most common syntactic role for weak pronouns in Chamorro (Chung 2003, 2020).

---

[1] If we assume weak pronouns in Chamorro also follow the typical absolutive pronoun distribution in other Austronesian languages, then both weak pronoun subjects and objects will have the same syntactic positioning. In this case, the analysis proposed here should account the same for either weak pronoun subjects or objects.

Another assumption regarding inputs is the 'flattening" of syntactic structure to prosodic structure (Elfner 2012). This takes place when multiple syntactic phrases dominate all and only the same unique phonologically overt terminal(s). An example of this is shown in (16). Because the DP and NP both dominate the same overt terminal *patgun*, the resulting prosodic structure will only result in a single phonological phrase dominating the terminal. In (16a) we see the syntactic structure for a DP containing *patgun*. The structure in (16b) is the pruned structure that has removed the DP level due to both the NP and the DP dominating all and only the same unique phonologically overt terminal (i.e., *patgun*). In (16c) we find the isomorphic prosodic parse of the structure in (16b). This 'flattening" is licensed both in MATCH (Bennett et al., 2016) and ALIGN mapping. Because of this, I have chosen to simplify the inputs to already represent this flattened structure, e.g. (16b), by removing syntactic XPs which redundantly dominate the same overt terminals as another syntactic XP.

(16) a.  Original syntax     b.  Flattened syntax     c.  Prosodic structure

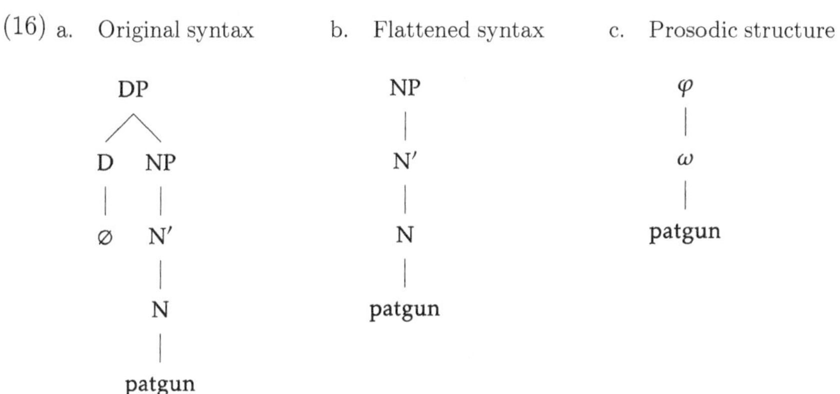

(17)    GEN Inputs

| | Inputs | Structure | Linear output |
|---|---|---|---|
| i. | [[a] [clitic]] | Predicate with no complement | a clitic (second position) |
| ii. | [[a [b]] [clitic]] | Predicate with single complement phrase or Nominal predicate with postnominal modifier (only high projection visible) | a clitic b (second position) |
| iii. | [[[a] [b]] [clitic]] | Nominal predicate with prenominal modifier (high and low projections visible) or Nominal predicate with postnominal modifier (high and low projections visible) | a clitic b (second position) |
| iv. | [[[a] b]] [clitic]] | Nominal predicate with prenominal modifier (only high projection visible) | a b clitic (third position) |

Each of the inputs in (17) serves as an important syntactic structure when considering the placement of weak pronouns in Chamorro. The input in (i), illustrating the structure of a predicate with no complement, can only correspond to an output where the clitic occurs in second position. The input in (ii) provides the syntax for a predicate with a single complement. This most closely represents verbal and adjectival predicate structures, but also represents the syntax for DP possessive structures, as in (2). The expected linear position of the clitic for the structure in (ii) is second position, immediately following the head of the predicate phrase. The structures in (i) and (ii) represent the most basic generalizations for weak pronoun placement.

The input in (ii) also corresponds to a postnominal modifier structure where only the highest projection is visible, (15), such that only the highest segment of NP is considered for mapping. The expected placement of the weak pronoun here is second position, immediately following the N head of the NP. The input in (iii) corresponds to both a postnominal and prenominal modifier structure where both the high and low projections are visible, (12) and (14). The expected placement for the weak pronoun for (iii) is again second position, this time following either the NP head if it is a postnominal structure, or following the XP modifier if it is a prenominal structure.

Finally, the input in (iv) corresponds to a prenominal modifier structure where only the highest projection is visible, (13). The expected linear position for the weak pronoun in this case is third position, immediately following the N head of the NP. By using differences in the visibility of projections, we're able to effectively illustrate why the weak pronoun is limited in its placement when there is difference in the direction of modification. This will become clear once we examine the systems and reveal how the improvement of prosodic well-formedness drives movement of the weak pronoun.

### 8.3.1.2  Outputs

I used the computational tool SPOT (Bellik et al., 2015–2021) to generate a candidate set consisting of all the licit prosodic parses for an input string of words, which is the terminal string of some well-formed syntactic tree. A licit prosodic parse in these two systems meets the requirements laid out in (18).

(18)   A prosodic tree P is an output of Gen(T) where T is an input syntactic tree, iff:
    a.   P is rooted in a node of category $\iota$ (intonational phrase).
    b.   Each non-terminal node of level $\alpha$ must contain a node of level $\alpha\text{--}1$ (Headedness).
    c.   Every terminal in T that is not a weak pronoun is mapped to a prosodic word.
    d.   Every weak pronoun in T is mapped to a syllable.
    e.   Every node in P that is neither a root nor a terminal is of category $\varphi$.

The prosodic hierarchy that is assumed here is essentially that of Selkirk (2011), Bellik and Kalivoda (2016), Bennett et al. (2016), and others. The prosodic categories included within the hierarchy are the intonational phrase ($\iota$), phonological phrase ($\varphi$), phonological (or prosodic) word ($\omega$), as well as lower-level prosodic categories such as the syllable and foot. The syllable and foot are included so that we may include prosodically dependent material (i.e., weak pronoun clitics). Additionally, we assume here that recursive structures are permitted (Bellik and Kalivoda 2016), allowing recursive $\varphi$ phrases.

An important point about the requirements in (18) is the inclusion of (18b). The restriction in (18b) is essentially a Headedness requirement, where each node must be 'headed" by a node of the next lowest prosodic category. For this analysis, this is important for ensuring that each phonological phrase is headed by a prosodic word. This also prevents a weak pronoun, which is just a foot or syllable, heading a phonological phrase. Weak pronouns, due to being prosodically dependent, cannot be the only terminal element within a phonological phrase, and the Headedness requirement in (18b) ensures this cannot occur.

The role of ordering of terminals must also be defined. Certain linear precedence relations must hold to allow the consideration of candidates that have moved the weak pronoun from its original syntactic position, to some new position in the prosodic output. The conditions on ordering of terminals are stated in (19).

(19)    *Linear precedence relation conditions*
   a.    Linear precedence relations between terminals that are not prosodically deficient (i.e., prosodic words) are preserved from input to output.
   b.    Linear precedence relations between prosodically weak material (i.e., weak pronouns) and other terminals are **not** preserved.

It is the condition in (19b) that admits clitic movement to the candidate set, allowing the consideration of candidates with the weak pronoun in positions other than its original syntactic position.

### 8.3.2   Con

In addition to GEN, which forms the inputs and outputs we consider, we must establish the sets of constraints used, i.e., CON. In this investigation we are primarily concerned with how constraint interactions motivate prosodic movement of the weak pronoun, without any reference to the weak pronoun itself. As we will see, this is primarily achieved through the interaction of syntax–prosody mapping constraints and constraints on prosodic well-formedness. However, this investigation will also demonstrate that not every prosodic mapping constraint is sufficient to motivate movement. The results will show that only mapping constraints which are alignment-based are able to motivate movement, whereas MATCH constraints are unable to drive movement of the weak pronoun.

We will be exploring two systems, MatchSystem and AlignSystem, that share the same GEN (inputs and outputs), as well as the same set of markedness constraints. The crucial difference will be in the mapping constraints, i.e., ALIGN or MATCH. The markedness constraints shared by both systems are typical constraints on prosodic well-formedness, as well as a constraint penalizing prosodic movement. In (20), I employ a binarity constraint on the minimum size of $\varphi$ phrases: all $\varphi$s must be minimally binary-branching (Elfner 2012).

(20)   $\textsc{BinMin}(\varphi)$
       Assign a violation for every node p of category $\varphi$ in the prosodic
       tree that has less than two children.

Binarity has been shown to be a driving force for prosodic movement in Irish
(Bennett et al., 2016), and will be important given the small constituent
sizes in the inputs. In addition to $\textsc{BinMin}$, we employ a constraint on the
equality of sisters in the prosodic tree, (21).

(21)   $\textsc{EqualSisters}$
       Assign one violation for every pair of adjacent sister nodes that are
       not of the same prosodic category.

$\textsc{EqualSisters}$ ensures that nodes within a prosodic tree are of the same
prosodic category (Myrberg 2013). This particular formulation of $\textsc{Equal-}$
$\textsc{Sisters}$ assigns violations based on adjacent pairs of nodes which differ in
prosodic category (Bellik and Kalivoda 2017). On the surface, it may not
be entirely obvious how $\textsc{EqualSisters}$ helps drive prosodic movement. However, we will see that moving the weak pronoun results in improved prosodic
well-formedness.

   Alongside these typical constraints is the also well-attested $\textsc{StrongStart}$,
provided in (22).

(22)   $\textsc{StrongStart}$
       Assign one violation for every node in the syntactic tree whose
       leftmost daughter is a syllable ($\sigma$), and is lower in the prosodic
       hierarchy than its sister constituent immediately to its right.

This particular formulation of $\textsc{StrongStart}$ penalizes syllables which appear as the leftmost daughter of a constituent if they have a sister constituent higher in the prosodic hierarchy to their immediate right (Elfner 2012,
Selkirk 2011). This version of $\textsc{StrongStart}$ will ensure that each prosodic
phrase has minimally a prosodic word at its left edge. This differs from some
versions of $\textsc{StrongStart}$ that would penalize any leftmost daughter that
was lower on the prosodic hierarchy than its sister constituent. This formalization of $\textsc{StrongStart}$ is functionally the same as the formulation used
in Bennett et al. (2016). This constraint will help to ensure that the weak
pronoun does not behave as a proclitic, also preventing the weak pronoun
from being sentence-initial.

   The last of the $\varphi$ constraints for both systems is provided in (23), and is a
mapping constraint that targets linear precedence relations.

(23)    NoShift
        Assign one violation if the terminals in the prosodic tree do not
        maintain the same precedence relations as those in the syntactic
        tree.

NoShift penalizes any change in the linear order of elements from the syntax to the prosody. This essentially penalizes prosodic movement, and is employed in this way following Bennett et al. (2016).

MatchSystem and AlignSystem share the set of constraints in (20)–(23), and differ purely in their mapping constraints. AlignSystem will have alignment mapping constraints as formulated in (24).

(24)    Align(XP, δ, φ, δ)
        Assign one violation for every node s of category XP such that there
        is no node p of category φ such that the δ edge of s corresponds to
        the δ edge of p, where δ is Left or Right.

The Align mapping constraint penalizes nodes which do not have a prosodic boundary that aligns with a syntactic boundary on a particular edge of the phrase, either left or right (Bellik and Kalivoda 2016, Selkirk 1986, Truckenbrodt 1999). Here we will consider both Align for the left edge of a phrase, Align(XP,L,φ,L), and the right edge of a phrase, Align(XP,R,φ,R).

The other mapping constraint we will consider, in a different system, is Match.

(25)    Match(XP,φ)
        Assign a violation for every node s of category XP in the syntactic
        tree for which there is no node p of category φ in the prosodic tree
        such that every terminal node dominated by s corresponds to a ter-
        minal node dominated by p, and vice versa.

The Match mapping constraint (Selkirk 2011, Elfner 2012), whose exact formulation is adopted from Bellik and Kalivoda (2016), differs from Align in that it cares more about isomorphism from the syntax to the prosody. This is because Match does not refer to a particular edge of a phrase, and instead requires that a phrase and its correspondent in the prosody share exactly the same terminal material (Bellik and Kalivoda 2016, Elfner 2012, Selkirk 2011).

(26)     Summary of systems: CON for AlignSystem and MatchSystem

| **AlignSystem** | **MatchSystem** |
| --- | --- |
| Align-L/R | Match |
| BinMin | BinMin |
| EqualSisters | EqualSisters |
| StrongStart | StrongStart |
| NoShift | NoShift |

A summary of the two systems is shown in (26). It is important to consider both the ALIGN and MATCH mapping constraints with respect to prosodic movement. The former has not yet been shown to motivate prosodic movement, and such a result would be novel. The latter has been shown to motivate rightward prosodic movement of clitic pronouns in Irish (Bennett et al., 2016). Finding a result in contrast to the Irish clitic pronoun behavior would also be novel, and would clearly differentiate Chamorro from Irish. We will in fact demonstrate both of these novel results; movement will be motivated through the interaction of ALIGN and markedness constraints, and MATCH will prove insufficient for the movement of weak pronouns in Chamorro, in contrast to Irish.

### 8.3.3   Computational tools

In this chapter I employ two computational tools for analysis and construction of inputs and outputs: OTWorkplace (Prince et al., 2007–2020) and SPOT (Bellik et al., 2015–2021). SPOT is a JavaScript application that has three primary functions for this analysis: first, it generates all of the possible syntactic inputs given constraints on syntactic structure (input generation); second, it generates all of the possible prosodic parses of a string of words, as well as all of the possible linear positions of a clitic in a string of words (candidate generation); and third, it automatically evaluates the violation counts of all candidates for various constraints (constraint evaluation).

The automation of the functions laid out above, especially those of input generations and candidate generation, are crucial for the systematic analysis of clitic positions given different syntactic structures. The manual generation and evaluation of candidates is extremely time-consuming if we consider all possible prosodic parses alongside all of the possible linear positions of a terminal element given a string of terminals. SPOT allows the generation of inputs and outputs for a syntax-prosody analysis, which can then be ported into the OT Workplace software for the analysis of typologies and constraint rankings.

## 8.4 Results

The analysis finds that MatchSystem fails to motivate any sort of prosodic movement, thereby proving insufficient. Instead, AlignSystem succeeds in motivating movement, with Align constraints interacting with markedness constraints to achieve the linear positions for weak pronoun clitics in Chamorro. Discussion of the Match system will happen alongside the Align system to show that the Match system is insufficient at motivating prosodic movement. Otherwise, the discussion will focus primarily on the Align system and the details of constraint interactions which allow prosodic movement and "second position" to be achieved.

AlignSystem provides a typology of 16 languages. By comparison, all candidates with movement are harmonically bounded in MatchSystem, so the Match typology will not be provided here. The full typology for the Align system is presented in Table 4, with color-coding indicating clitic position: lightest grey (off-white) is second position, medium grey is first-position, and the darkest grey is third position. Of the 16 languages, one matches the desired linear outputs (i.e., weak pronoun positions) as defined in (17), and that is Language 5. The prosodic outputs, and their respective inputs, for Language 5 are provided in (27).

(27)    16 language typology for AlignSystem

| | Solo Predicate | Head-complement / Right modifier (high visibility) | Left modifier (high visibility) | Left modifier (high/low visibility) / Right modifier (high/low visibility) |
|---|---|---|---|---|
| | [[a] [clitic]] | [[a [b]] [clitic]] | [[[[a] b]] [clitic]] | [[[a] [b]] [clitic]] |
| **L.01** | (a clitic) | ((a b) clitic) | ((a b) clitic) | ((a b) clitic) |
| **L.02** | (a clitic) | ((a) (b clitic)) <br> (a) (b clitic) | ((a b) clitic) | ((a) (b clitic)) <br> (a) (b clitic) |
| **L.03** | (a clitic) | (a (b clitic)) | ((a b) clitic) | (a (b clitic)) |
| **L.04** | (a clitic) | (a (b clitic)) | (clitic (a b)) | (a (b clitic)) |
| **L.05** | (a clitic) | ((a clitic) (b)) <br> (a clitic) (b) | ((a b) clitic) | ((a clitic) (b)) <br> (a clitic) (b) |
| **L.06** | (a clitic) | (clitic (a b)) | (clitic (a b)) | (clitic (a b)) |
| **L.07** | ((a) clitic) | ((a b) clitic) | (((a) (b)) clitic) <br> ((a) ((b) clitic)) <br> ((a) (b) clitic) <br> (a) ((b) clitic) | (((a) (b)) clitic) <br> ((a) ((b) clitic)) <br> ((a) (b) clitic) <br> (a) ((b) clitic) |
| **L.08** | ((a) clitic) | ((a b) clitic) | (((a) b) clitic) | (((a) b) clitic) |

|  | Solo Predicate | Head-complement / Right modifier (high visibility) | Left modifier (high visibility) | Left modifier (high/low visibility) / Right modifier (high/low visibility) |
|---|---|---|---|---|
|  | [[a] [clitic]] | [[a [b]] [clitic]] | [[[[a] b]] [clitic]] | [[[a] [b]] [clitic]] |
| **L.09** | ((a) clitic) | (((a) (b)) clitic)<br>((a) ((b) clitic))<br>((a) (b) clitic)<br>(a) ((b) clitic) | (((a) (b)) clitic)<br>((a) ((b) clitic))<br>((a) (b) clitic)<br>(a) ((b) clitic) | (((a) (b)) clitic)<br>((a) ((b) clitic))<br>((a) (b) clitic)<br>(a) ((b) clitic) |
| **L.10** | ((a) clitic) | ((a (b)) clitic)<br>(a ((b) clitic))<br>(a (b) clitic) | (((a) b) clitic) | (((a) (b)) clitic)<br>((a) ((b) clitic))<br>((a) (b) clitic)<br>(a) ((b) clitic) |
| **L.11** | ((a) clitic) | ((a clitic) (b))<br>(a clitic) (b) | (((a) (b)) clitic)<br>((a) ((b) clitic))<br>((a) (b) clitic)<br>(a) ((b) clitic) | (((a) (b)) clitic)<br>((a) ((b) clitic))<br>((a) (b) clitic)<br>(a) ((b) clitic) |
| **L.12** | ((a) clitic) | ((a clitic) (b))<br>(a clitic) (b) | (((a) b) clitic) | (((a) (b)) clitic)<br>((a) ((b) clitic))<br>((a) (b) clitic)<br>(a) ((b) clitic) |
| **L.13** | (clitic (a)) | ((a) (clitic (b)))<br>(a) (clitic (b))<br>((clitic (a)) (b))<br>(clitic ((a) (b)))<br>(clitic (a) (b))<br>(clitic (a)) (b) | ((a) (clitic b))<br>(a) (clitic b) | ((a) (clitic (b)))<br>(a) (clitic (b))<br>((clitic (a)) (b))<br>(clitic ((a) (b)))<br>(clitic (a) (b))<br>(clitic (a)) (b) |
| **L.14** | (clitic (a)) | ((a) (clitic (b)))<br>(a) (clitic (b))<br>((clitic (a)) (b))<br>(clitic ((a) (b)))<br>(clitic (a) (b))<br>(clitic (a)) (b) | (clitic (a b)) | ((a) (clitic (b)))<br>(a) (clitic (b))<br>((clitic (a)) (b))<br>(clitic ((a) (b)))<br>(clitic (a) (b))<br>(clitic (a)) (b) |
| **L.15** | (clitic (a)) | (a (clitic (b)))<br>(clitic (a (b))) | ((a) (clitic b))<br>(a) (clitic b) | ((a) (clitic (b)))<br>(a) (clitic (b))<br>((clitic (a)) (b))<br>(clitic ((a) (b)))<br>(clitic (a) (b))<br>(clitic (a)) (b) |
| **L.16** | (clitic (a)) | (a (clitic (b)))<br>(clitic (a (b))) | (clitic (a b)) | (a (clitic (b)))<br>(clitic (a (b))) |

Language 5, matching the desired linear outputs, is shown to be the language that best captures the Chamorro empirical pattern.

(28)　　　Inputs and corresponding prosodic outputs for Language 5

| Syntax | Prosody |
|---|---|
| [[a] [clitic]] | {(a clitic)} |
| [[a [b]] [clitic]] | {((a clitic) (b))} <br> {(a clitic) (b)} |
| [[[[a] b]] [clitic]] | {((a b) clitic)} |
| [[[a] [b]] [clitic]] | {((a clitic) (b))} <br> {(a clitic) (b)} |

While we consider a total of four inputs, capturing the descriptive generalizations defined in §8.2.1, only two inputs are necessary for providing support to this language's ranking arguments. This can be seen in the support in (29), where we see that all of the ranking arguments for this language can be proved with only the input involving a predicate with no complement ([[a] [clitic]], seen in rows 2 and 4), and the input that may be interpreted as a predicate and its complement, or a nominal predicate with a postnominal modifier with the highest projection visible ([[a [b]] [clitic]], seen in rows 1, 3, and 5).

(29)　　　Support in ERCs for L.5 of AlignSystem

| | Input | Winner | Loser | EqSis | SS | Al-L | BinMin | Al-R | NS |
|---|---|---|---|---|---|---|---|---|---|
| 1 | [[a [b]] [clitic]] | {((a clitic) (b))} <br> {(a clitic) (b)} | {(a (b clitic))} | W | | | L | W | L |
| 2 | [[a] [clitic]] | {(a clitic)} | {(clitic (a))} | | W | L | W | W | W |
| 3 | [[a [b]] [clitic]] | {((a clitic) (b))} <br> {(a clitic) (b)} | {((a b) clitic)} | | | W | L | | L |
| 4 | [[a] [clitic]] | {(a clitic)} | {((a) clitic)} | | | | W | L | |
| 5 | [[a [b]] [clitic]] | {((a clitic) (b))} <br> {(a clitic) (b)} | {((a) (b clitic))} <br> {(a) (b clitic)} | | | | | W | L |

These ranking arguments can be represented as a Hasse diagram (30).

(30)      Hasse diagram for L.5 of AlignSystem

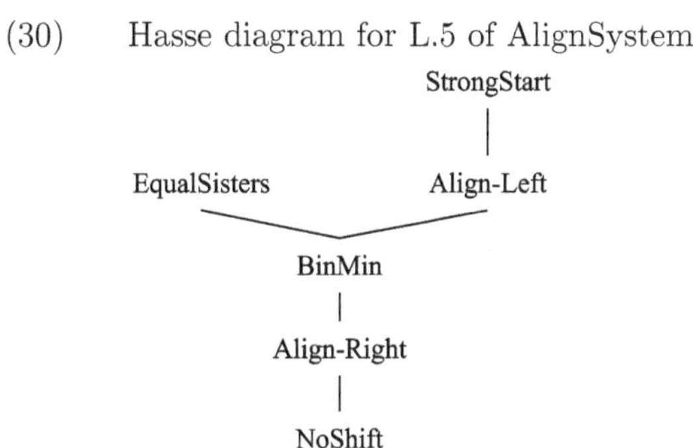


Each of these crucial ranking arguments contributes slightly different motivations towards movement and the ultimate prosodic structure we find for this Chamorro system. Here I will break down what each of these ranking arguments contribute, and how each of these are necessary for deriving the specific linear positions for weak pronouns in Chamorro.

Although all ranking arguments are essential, the ranking of ALIGN-R over NOSHIFT, shown in (31), is crucial to understanding why moving a weak pronoun actually benefits other prosodic structure. In (31) we can see that if the clitic is left in situ, as in candidate (b), the candidate incurs two ALIGN-R violations. This is due to the displacement of 'b" from the right edge of a φ-phrase boundary by the clitic, blocking the correct alignment of right boundaries between the syntax and prosody. However, if the clitic is moved to immediately follow 'a" as an enclitic, as in candidate (a), we see that the boundaries for 'b" are all correctly aligned, incurring no ALIGN-R violations for the winning candidate. Here we see that head-complement structures are informative for the work of ALIGN-R in motivating movement, as we improve the prosodic boundary alignment of the complement 'b" in exchange for moving the clitic to a neutral position in terms of alignment: immediately following the head 'a" which has no right boundary alignment requirements.

(31)    ALIGN-R dominates NOSHIFT; ERC 5

| (candidate) | EqSis | SS | ALIGN-L | BINMIN | **ALIGN-R** | NOSHIFT |
|---|---|---|---|---|---|---|
| a. | * |  | * | * |  | * |
| b. | * |  | * | * | **W | L |

Examining a tableau for MatchSystem in (32), we see that no ranking could possibly favor the candidate that has moved the clitic. Here we suppose a ranking of MATCH over BINMIN and NOSHIFT. We see that our desired candidate is favored over the alternative candidate that was also considered in (31). However, we also see that the desired candidate (a) is harmonically bounded by the superior candidate (c) which does not move the clitic, but has a different prosodic phrasing. This more optimal candidate incurs no violations of BINMIN or NOSHIFT, and has equal violations on MATCHXP to the desired candidate. Because of this, the desired candidate is unable to win unless we consider some markedness constraint directly tailored to prefer clitic movement—a prospect AlignSystem successfully avoids.

(32)     MatchSystem: harmonically bounded desired output

| | | EqSis | SS | MatchXP | BinMin | NoShift |
|---|---|---|---|---|---|---|
| ☹ a. | φ [ φ [ ω(a) clitic ] φ[ω(b)] ] | * | | ** | * | * |
| b. | φ [ φ[ω(a)] φ[ ω(b) clitic ] ] | * | | ***W | * | L |
| c. | φ [ φ[ω(a) ω(b)] clitic ] | * | | ** | L | L |

We have already seen in (31) that Align-R dominates NoShift in AlignSystem. Considering the other alignment constraint in AlignSystem, we observe
that Align-L dominates NoShift, but also BinMin. In (33), we can see that
if the clitic is left in situ as an enclitic sister to (a b), as in candidate (a), it
incurs two violations of Align-L. One of these violations is due to a lack of
left boundary for the clitic; this is shared between both candidates. However,
the inferior candidate (b) also incurs an additional Align-L violation in try-
ing to satisfy binarity while keeping the clitic in situ. If we move the clitic we
violate NoShift, but we can improve the alignment of prosodic boundaries

Syntax-Prosody in Optimality Theory

by giving 'b" its own φ. While this incurs a violation of BinMin, it more importantly improves Align-L. We see from this ranking condition that moving the clitic improves prosodic boundaries, which is ultimately prioritized over certain prosodic well-formedness, i.e., BinMin in AlignSystem.

(33)  Align-L dominates both BinMin and Noshift; ERC 3 in L.5 in AlignSystem

| | EqSis | SS | Align-L | BinMin | Align-R | NoShift |
|---|---|---|---|---|---|---|
| ☞ a. | * | | * | * | | * |
| b. | * | | **W | L | | L |
| c. | **W | | * | * | | L |

An expected ranking in any system motivating second position is found in the ranking of STRONGSTART over ALIGN-L. In (34), we can see that candidate (b) is ruled out due to the sentence-initial clitic that incurs a STRONGSTART violation, even though this would improve the alignment of leftward boundaries for the clitic. So even though the optimal candidate (a) is unable to maximize the left alignment of the prosodic boundaries for the clitic, it does correctly satisfy STRONGSTART. It should be noted that we also do not intend for the clitic to receive a totally matching prosodic structure, as it is prosodically dependent on other material and therefore cannot stand as the head of some $\varphi$ on its own. This is primarily what drives the weak pronoun to be some form of clitic.

(34)    STRONGSTART dominates ALIGN-L; ERC 2

| | TP (XP DP; a clitic) | EqSis | SS | ALIGN-L | BINMIN | ALIGN-R | NOSHIFT |
|---|---|---|---|---|---|---|---|
| ☞ a. | $\varphi$ ($\omega$ clitic; a) | * | | * | | * | |
| b. | $\varphi$ (clitic $\varphi$; $\omega$; a) | * | *W | L | *W | **W | *W |

The ranking argument provided in (35) provides the motivation for a ranking of BINMIN over ALIGN-R. Currently this ranking argument does not actually have any influence on the linear order of the clitic. However, this may change if longer inputs (e.g., three- to four-word inputs) are introduced. Another way that this ranking will play a significant role is if there is ever some way to distinguish the specific prosodic phrasing in Chamorro, which requires further phonetic investigation.

(35)     BINMIN dominates ALIGN-R; ERC 4

| | TP<br>XP   DP<br>\|    \|<br>a   clitic | EQSIS | SS | ALIGN-L | **BINMIN** | **ALIGN-R** | NOSHIFT |
|---|---|---|---|---|---|---|---|
| ☞ a. | φ<br>ω   clitic<br>\|<br>a | * | | * | | * | |
| b. | φ<br>φ   clitic<br>\|<br>ω<br>\|<br>a | * | | * | *W | L | |

Finally, the ranking seen in (36) is the motivation from ERC 1 in (29). If the clitic remains in situ in third position as in candidate (b), there are two EQUALSISTERS violations that are incurred, while binarity is also improved. However, moving the clitic to second position with a structure ((a clitic) (b)), as in candidate (a), EQUALSISTERS incurs one less violation, due to both 'a clitic" and 'b" having a φ. While this incurs a violation for BINMIN, the higher-ranked EQUALSISTERS ensures that a second-position clitic is better overall. This demonstrates that both alignment and prosodic well-formedness constraints are useful in determining the placement of weak pronouns.

(36)      EQUALSISTERS dominates BINMIN; ERC 1

| | 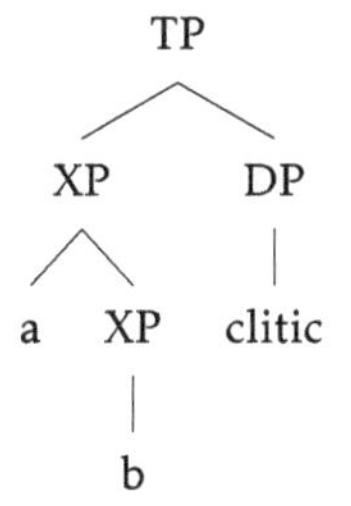 | EqSis | SS | Align-L | BinMin | Align-R | NoShift |
|---|---|---|---|---|---|---|---|
| ☞ a. | 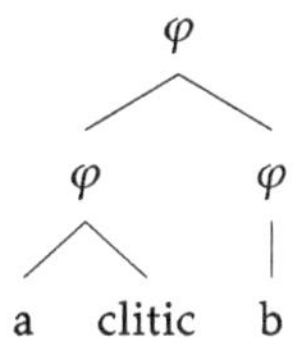 | * | | * | * | | * |
| b. | 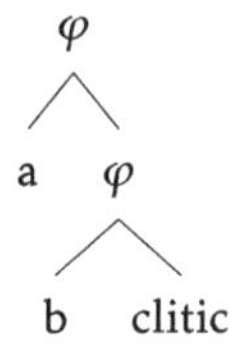 | **W | | * | L | **W | L |

The results from the investigation of MatchSystem and AlignSystem indicate that only ALIGN mapping constraints can be used to motivate movement of weak pronoun clitics in Chamorro. Match Theory requires more isomorphism between syntactic structure and prosodic structure. This often results in more strict violation assignment than ALIGN mapping constraints, as ALIGN mapping constraints only require a syntactic boundary to align with some prosodic boundary, rather than requiring the mapping of an entire syntactic constituent to a prosodic constituent. The strictness of MATCH does not allow movement of the weak pronoun improve prosodic boundaries, or somehow reduce MATCH violations. This results in a candidate which moves the weak pronoun incurring the same violations of MATCH as a candidate which leaves the weak pronoun in situ, while also incurring violations of NoShift and other prosodic well-formedness. As demonstrated by the tableaux in (32), the desired optima will be harmonically bounded, and this is exactly where MatchSystem fails. In contrast, ALIGN mapping constraints provide a flexibility for prosodic mapping, allowing the movement of a weak pronoun to actually benefit otherwise illicit syntax-to-prosody mappings.

Similar to the case of Irish weak pronoun postposing, prosodic markedness constraints also play a crucial role in weak pronoun placement in Chamorro. STRONGSTART restricts proclitic positions for the weak pronoun, ruling out any cases of sentence-initial weak pronouns or phrase-initial weak pronouns that may occur. While STRONGSTART does essential work in motivating postposing for Irish, weak pronoun movement in Chamorro is not motivated purely by markedness. This is primarily due to the final position of the weak pronoun in the syntax. In the Irish case, weak pronouns begin as objects that would normally be placed phrase-initially if left in situ. STRONGSTART restricts weak material at the left edge of a phrase, thereby motivating the postposing behavior. For Chamorro, weak pronouns originate in a rightward specifier of TP, making their initial syntactic position the rightmost element in a clause. This would typically be an ideal position for an enclitic, having no possibility of being the leftmost element in a phonological phrase. So while STRONGSTART does not necessarily motivate movement itself for Chamorro weak pronouns, it does play a significant role in determining the final landing site for the weak pronoun.

## 8.5  Alternative analyses

### 8.5.1  *Can the Match system be saved?*

Although MatchSystem has so far proved insufficient for accounting for the Chamorro facts, one might wonder if an alternative Match system could be proposed. Two possible alternatives come to mind that do not rely solely on MATCH and typical prosodic well-formedness. The first possibility is a Match system that employs a STRONGEND-type effect. A STRONGEND effect is a pressure exactly opposite to that of STRONGSTART, in that there is a pressure for strong material to end a prosodic constituent. One of the first conceptions of this style of effect in constraints is found as early as Selkirk (1996) with the formulation of edge alignment constraints. The prosody-to-prosody alignment constraint in (23) requires every phonological phrase to end in a full prosodic word (Ito and Mester 2019).

(37)    ALIGN-RIGHT-$\varphi$: ALIGN($\varphi$, R, $\omega$, R): Assign one violation for every $\varphi$ that does not have a $\omega$ at its right edge

On the surface, the presence of a STRONGEND effect seems like a plausible explanation for the Chamorro facts. Because there is leftward movement of the weak pronoun that always originates as the final terminal in a string, it seems reasonable to propose that a STRONGEND effect is causing the movement of the weak pronoun to allow for a strong element to occur finally. A similar sort of logic is discussed in Ito and Mester (2019), where it appears a STRONGEND effect is at play with the ungrammaticality of final enclisis in English.

However, there are several problems if we attempt to augment the Match system with the Align constraint in (37). I'll label the augmented system: MatchSystem.StrongEnd. This system has the same GEN as both MatchSystem and AlignSystem (refer to §8.3.1 for details). MatchSystem. StrongEnd's CON is the same as MatchSystem's Con, with the addition of ALIGN-RIGHT-φ (37). ALIGN-RIGHT-φ targets all φs, which correctly penalizes a weak pronoun at the right edge of the highest φ in the desired winner in (38), but equally prevents a weak pronoun from appearing at the right edge of an inner φ. This results in the same harmonic bounding situation as seen previously in the Match system (32), proving the augmented system to be insufficient.

(38)   Match system with harmonically bounded desired output

| | 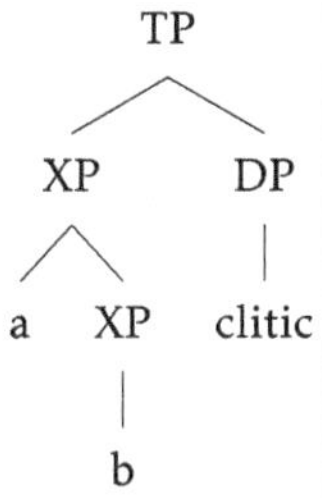 | EqSis | Align-Right-φ | MatchXP | BinMin | NoShift |
|---|---|---|---|---|---|---|
| ☞ a. | ((a clitic) (b)) | * | * | ** | * | * |
| b. | ((a b) clitic) | * | * | ** | L | L |

It is entirely possible to specify ALIGN-RIGHT-φ to only target maximal φ boundaries to avoid incorrectly penalizing weak pronouns at the edge of an internal φ. However, this reliance on maximal φs is not demonstrated by any other prosodic phenomena. We would prefer to see some independent evidence for maximal φs as a target for prosodic phenomena to further support this specification.

Even if we augment ALIGN-RIGHT-φ by specifying it to only target maximal φ, we've already seen evidence that Chamorro readily allows weak pronouns on the right edge of maximal φs. In (39), a repetition of (7a), the weak pronoun is the final terminal in the string, meaning it must necessarily occur finally in the φ.

(39)    [[$_{AP}$ Aguagat] [$_{NP}$ na      patgun]] **gui'**
        naughty      L       child    he
        'He's a naughty child.'

To allow for weak pronouns to appear word-finally, the Match system would
again need to be augmented to account the optionality of third position.
This is another complication for the Match system, that is already conveni-
ently accounted for in the Align system through the use of the variation in
projection visibility. Finally, Ito and Mester (2019) show that this account
of a STRONGEND type effect is merely a descriptive observation for English,
and the account provided in their analysis does not require any explicit reference to the edge of prosodic constituents. We see that STRONGEND is not
as parsimonious, empirically accurate, or externally supported as the Align
analysis already proposed.

A second possible alternative for revising the Match system is simply
pairing it with the already existing subcategorization account from Chung
(2003). This account would be empirically accurate, in that it properly
places the weak pronoun immediately following the leftmost φ phrase.
However, the empirical accuracy of this account comes at the expense of
stipulating the placement of the weak pronoun. This restatement of the
descriptive pattern does not explain why second position is derived. This is
the property that separates the Align account proposed in this chapter from
the previous accounts of Chamorro weak pronoun placement, and it is this
property that creates testable predictions which seek to explain how weak
pronoun placement comes about. While there are potential revisions to a
Match system for those that are loyal to Match Theory, the Align account
achieves the same empirical accuracy with the benefit of explaining the
phenomena at hand.

### 8.5.2    *Projection visibility*

A crucial insight this analysis provides for the syntax-prosody interface
is the requirements for projection visibility. Selkirk (2011), following
Truckenbrodt (1999), suggests that only the lowest segment of XP in an
adjunction structure should be visible to Match constraints. However, Bellik
and Kalivoda (2016) demonstrate that the highest projection must be visible
for the correct mappings for adjunction structures in Kinyambo. These
requirements change depending on whether Match constraints or Align
constraints are used. The present analysis of Chamorro has demonstrated
that having two visibility settings active, highest only and highest+lowest,
allows the correct weak pronoun placements to be obtained. The projection

visibilities take the form of different syntactic inputs, as can be seen in (17). Interestingly, the crucial visibility setting for Chamorro really turns out to be the highest-only visibility. The maximally isomorphic parses of pre- and post-modifier structures differ only under the high-only visibility setting. This is demonstrated by (12)–(15), reproduced in (40)–(43).

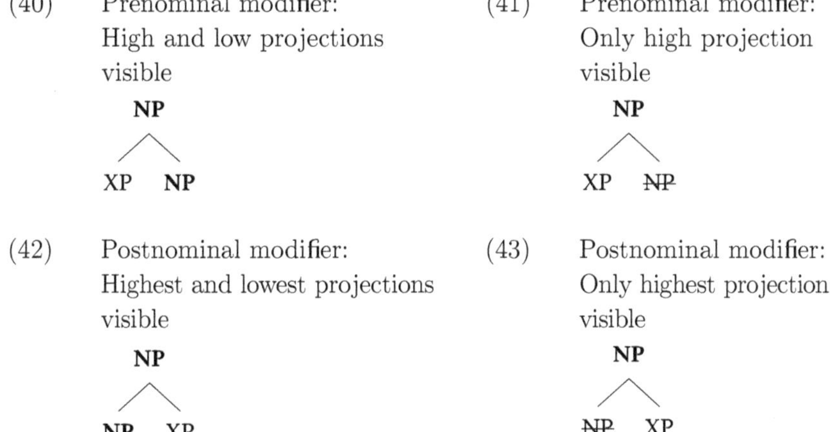

(40)   Prenominal modifier:
       High and low projections
       visible

(41)   Prenominal modifier:
       Only high projection
       visible

(42)   Postnominal modifier:
       Highest and lowest projections
       visible

(43)   Postnominal modifier:
       Only highest projection
       visible

The structures with only the high projection visible differentiate the pre- versus postnominal modifiers in terms of how the prosodic boundaries should be mapped. When only the highest projection is visible, the input to phonology for prenominal modifiers is [[a] b], and for postnominal modifiers is [a [b]]. But when both projections are visible, as in (40) and (42), both structures will share the same mappings, namely: [[a] [b]]. Crucially, if we consider having only the lowest projection visible, as in (44) and (45), we also obtain the same mapping between the two different modifier structures, namely: [a] [b]. Considering the three available options for projection visibility, we see that the highest projection is needed to properly differentiate the two different modifier structures. The other visibility option, which cause the structure to be treated the same, is also necessary for Chamorro to obtain the second linear position for the weak pronoun for each structure. However, choosing either the highest+lowest, or just the lowest, ends up being functionally the same, as these projections treat the structures as the same with regard to mapping.

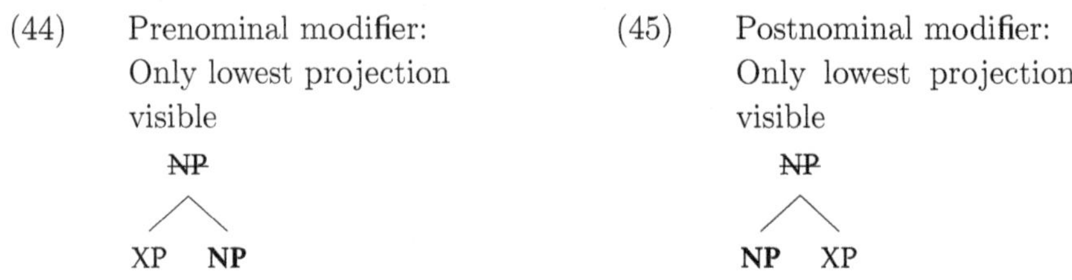

(44)    Prenominal modifier:          (45)    Postnominal modifier:
        Only lowest projection                Only lowest projection
        visible                               visible

To summarize this discussion, we find that Chamorro weak pronoun placement provides another case demonstrating that the highest projection must be visible to mapping, a finding previously demonstrated by Bellik and Kalivoda (2016) for Kinyambo. Chamorro also presents a unique case where optionality of projection visibility is required, as first suggested by Chung (2003).

### 8.5.3 *Constraint ranking reanalysis of optionality*

If one is committed to only having a single projection visibility setting available in a language, we may also entertain the proposal that optionality is captured through variable constraint ranking. Capturing the optionality of second vs. third position is possible with constraint reranking if we assume that the projection visibility is high+low, as shown in (25) and (27). The necessary constraint reranking that would need to occur is having ALIGN-R dominate ALIGN-L, rather than the ranking of ALIGN-L over ALIGN-R that we demonstrated in AlignSystem. If we examine the two languages in (46), taken from the languages in the typology in (46), we can see that with the same assumed projection visibility in the third column, we achieve second position in L.05 and third position in L.11.

(46)    Languages demonstrating constraint reranking for optionality

|        | [[a] [clitic]]   | [[a [b]] [clitic]] | [[[a] [b]] [clitic]]  |
|--------|------------------|--------------------|-----------------------|
| L.05   | (a clitic)       | ((a clitic) (b))   | ((a clitic) (b))      |
| L.11   | ((a) clitic))    | ((a clitic) (b))   | (((a) (b)) clitic))   |

These two different languages constitute a difference in constraint rankings, which is one way to achieve optionality in an OT system. The crucial ranking difference is between the two alignment constraints. In (47) we have the ranking seen previously of ALIGN-L dominating ALIGN-R, and in (48) we see ALIGN-R instead dominating ALIGN-L.

(47)    L.05 Hasse

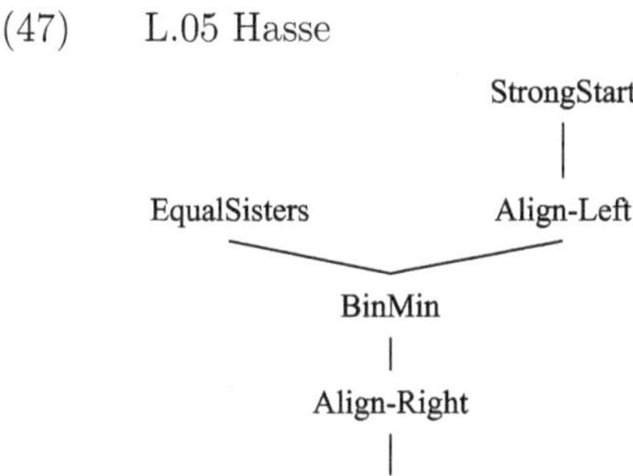

(48)    L.11 Hasse

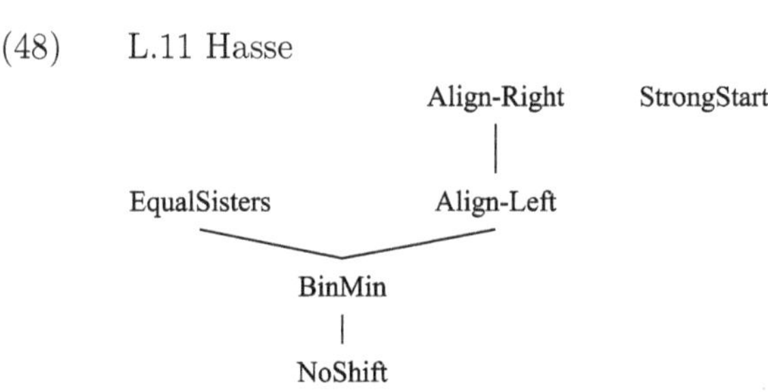

With this difference in constraint ranking, it is reasonable to propose that
the optionality in weak pronoun position can also be accounted for by assuming a single projection visibility, high+low, and also assuming that certain structures are marked to receive a different constraint ranking. Both
of these accounts of optionality require some specification of certain structures receiving either a different projection visibility or constraint ranking,
so theoretically they have similar stipulatory requirements. One benefit to
the projection visibility account is that it is already supported by the previous work of Chung (2003), and aligns well with the findings of Bellik and
Kalivoda (2016) that the highest level of projection visibility is required for
certain languages.

### 8.5.4   Three-word inputs

As this analysis only considered 1–2 word + clitic inputs, there might be
uncertainty as to whether this account succeeds when we have longer strings
of terminals. In a similar vein to infixation, we want to ensure that the weak
pronoun lands in the correct medial position, even when given alternate
medial positions. This is not tested very well when only one medial position
exists, such as in two-word inputs, especially when the other options may
be considered illicit. We can easily test whether the correct placement of a

weak pronoun is still achieved when there are three words, rather than two or one. An example of a three-word sentence with a second-position weak pronoun is provided in (49), repeated from (5).

(49)  Malagu'        **gui'**     nuebu    na       kareta
      AGR.want       she       new      L        car
      'She wants a new car.'

To test three-word inputs, a new system will be defined, named AlignSystem.3Word. This system's GEN is identical to that of AlignSystem, just with the addition of a three-word (+ clitic) input. The CON for the system is also identical to AlignSystem. If we use an input with three words + a weak pronoun clitic, we can see whether or not the analysis from AlignSystem correctly places the weak pronoun. In (49) the weak pronoun obligatorily occurs in second linear position, following the verbal predicate head. If we consider an input such as [[a [[b] [c]]] [clitic]], we can evaluate the outputs just as we did for the one- and two-word inputs. The results show that the constraint ranking for L.5 in AlignSystem still correctly places the weak pronoun in second position in this new system. The tableau in (50) reveals that Candidate a, where the clitic occurs in second linear position, performs best not only on markedness constraints like EqualSisters, but also on Align-Right. We see the same crucial motivations for one- and two-word inputs demonstrated by a three-word input, and the empirical point is captured correctly.

(50)

|  | [[a [[b] [c]]] [clitic]] | EqS | SS | Al-L | BinMin | Al-R | NS |
|---|---|---|---|---|---|---|---|
| ☞ a. | ((a clitic) ((b) (c))) | * |  | * | ** |  | * |
| b. | ((a ((b) (c))) clitic) | **W |  | * | ** |  | L |
| c. | {(a ((b clitic) (c)))} | **W |  | * | *L | *W | * |
| d. | {((a) ((b clitic) (c)))} | * |  | * | ** | *W | * |

The support for AlignSystem, provided in (29), is also a support for AlignSystem.3Word. This indicates that the positioning of weak pronouns can be easily determined from the most minimal of inputs, i.e., just one- and two-word inputs, in terms of number of terminals in a string

## 8.6   Directions for future research

### 8.6.1   Relative clauses

To ensure a careful investigation into whether movement was possible in either system considered, and in particular where the motivation for movement was stemming from, this analysis was constrained solely to one-to two-word inputs that represented a few key structures. The Align system was shown to account for the placement of weak pronouns in basic sentence structures in Chamorro, specifically head-complement and adjunction structures. However, there are other notable structures in Chamorro that affect the placement of weak pronouns. One notable construction that has not yet been discussed in this chapter are sentences involving relative clause (RC) modifiers, as in (51). Adjunction structures with RC modifiers behave similarly to other adjunction structures in that if the RC modifier follows the host, the weak pronoun must immediately follow the host, and if the RC modifier precedes the host, the weak pronoun may optionally follow the RC or the head of the host. The crucial point for RC structures, which may also be true for modifier XPs generally, is that weak pronouns never enter the RC modifier phrase. No matter the length of the RC, the weak pronoun never breaches the clause. Instead, the weak pronoun is placed immediately following the entire RC (if it is a prenominal modifier).

(51)   Mas     ya-hu                   **hao**    na      taotao
       most    WH[OBJ].like-AGR        you       L       person
       'You're the person I like most.'

This is an important data point as it shows that 'second position" is really not just second linear position, and instead is constrained by boundaries of entire phrases. However, accounting for the placement of the weak pronoun with a prenominal RC modifier is not entirely straightforward. The Align system as it is currently composed, with only the constraints given in §8.2.2, is insufficient. With only those constraints, the weak pronoun is incorrectly able to breach the RC, ending up in a position too far to the left. In accounting for this issue, one might suspect that prioritizing the boundary and terminal mappings of RCs would be sufficient for preventing the weak pronoun from entering. This prioritization of clause level boundaries over typical XP boundaries is more easily handled by Match constraints, as these require isomorphism and reference directly the terminal content of each phrase. Preventing the weak pronoun from breaching a relative clause is the next step for the Align account to show that the empirical facts can be handled completely outside of Match Theory.

### 8.6.2    Weak pronoun objects

Weak pronouns originating in direct object position were not considered in this analysis. Weak pronouns in Chamorro occur either as subjects or direct objects, the latter being evidenced in (52).

(52)    Ha    bisisita      **hit**       i      Ninu  Jesus  gi     gima'-ta
        AGR   visit.PROG    us.INCL   the    child  Jesus  LOC    house-AGR

        gi    durant-in    i      Krismas
        LOC   during-L     the    Christmas

        'The infant Jesus visits us at our homes during Christmas.' (Chung 2003)

Such cases were excluded merely to reduce the complexity of the overall system to get a better picture of what was motivating movement in basic cases. However, sentences with the weak pronoun in object position are very important, as we want to be sure leftward movement to "second position" is still preferred over other options. Weak pronouns in object position in Chamorro have the same "second-position" behavior as subject weak pronouns, but in fact they may not differ in their syntactic behavior. A reviewer points out that typically in Austronesian voice systems, the class of absolutive pronouns, which encompasses both direct object and subject pronouns (Chung 2003), end up in the same syntactic position.[2] For Chamorro, this position would be the typical subject position in a rightward specifier of TP. If we assume that weak pronouns end up in the same syntactic position, then their behavior in terms of the prosodic movement to second position will also be the same. Chung (2003) treats Chamorro weak pronouns as being absolutive pronouns, so strictly those pronouns which may serve as direct objects, or subjects of certain intransitives. Future work on the inner workings of the Chamorro pronouns may reveal a difference in weak pronoun objects versus subjects, but here I will adopt the assumption that the behavior of subject and object weak pronouns is parallel in the syntax, leading to parallel behavior for the Align account of prosodic movement.

### 8.6.3    Predictions about the movement of other clitics

As weak pronouns in Chamorro are not the only prosodically deficient material in the language, we must ask whether other clitic material is

---

[2] Thanks to Dan Brodkin for this point.

predicted to move in this account. The short answer would be yes, but only if the clitic material meets the same prosodic and structural criterion as weak pronouns. Weak pronouns, like most pronouns, are typically assumed to be determiner heads of a DP phrase (Chung 1998, 2003), but crucially have no complement sharing the DP. This means there is no immediate local dependency that must be satisfied in the syntax. Furthermore, weak pronouns are prosodically weak, and are not able to head their own phonological phrase, as we assume only prosodic words may head phonological phrases (Ito and Mester 1992/2003). Chamorro, unlike Irish (Bennett et al., 2016), has no option for strengthening the weak pronoun prosodically, and therefore it always seeks material to lean on prosodically. Because of these restrictions, weak pronouns are unique and are good candidates for being displaced prosodically. This predicts that any other weak prosodic material that shares the same restrictions as weak pronouns will move. However, there may be no instances of prosodically weak heads that function this way in Chamorro. The most likely candidate would be a prepositional head, which is often prosodically weak, that is able to stand alone (i.e., without a complement). To this author's knowledge, there are no prepositions that subcategorize for a null argument in Chamorro. All known non-pronominal prosodically deficient heads co-occur with a complement or other material within a phrase, and end up leaning on this material to satisfy prosodic dependence. Much of this reasoning for explaining the lack of movement from other clitics is shared in Bennett et al. (2016) for Irish.

We may ask then, what about material that is not prosodically deficient, but stands on its own? The simple answer is that material that is not prosodically deficient is predicted not to move simply because said material is able to head its own phonological phrase, and movement will actually disrupt prosodic well-formedness rather than improve it. An interesting question also arises when we consider languages that have multiple clitics moving to second position, such as the behavior of certain clitics in Mandar, an Austronesian language of West Sulawesi (Dan Brodkin, p.c.). In this case we find that aspectual, adverbial, and absolutive (nominal) clitics all seem to be able to move to second position. If we assume that aspectual and adverbial clitics might not stand alone in their own syntactic phrase (a potentially naive assumption), then it raises the question of why these clitics would move. Here, and also if a similar clitic is found in Chamorro, we may need to stipulate that only certain clitics could move. For now this question will be left to future work.

## 8.7 Conclusion

Similar to the prosodic account of weak pronoun postposing in Irish, Chamorro weak pronoun placement can be accounted for through interactions of syntax-to-prosody mapping, and prosodic well-formedness. The situation in Chamorro crucially differs from that of Irish in the clitic's origin in the syntax, the direction of movement, and also what is able to account for movement. A system based within Match Theory, MatchSystem, is shown to be insufficient for Chamorro weak pronoun placement. The successful system is one that makes use of syntax-prosody Align-based mapping constraints, driving movement through the improvement of prosodic boundary mapping elsewhere within a clause. While this analysis is not contrary to the initial proposal in Chung (2003) for prosodic subcategorization, it is an effective alternative that is consistent with the current theory of syntax-prosody. Some necessary assumptions still remain from Chung (2003), specifically the ideas of multiple projections being visible to mapping. However, this analysis does test those assumptions within an OT framework, and demonstrates that the use of both the highest and highest+lowest visibility settings is required for Chamorro. Much future work is required to test further empirical points in weak pronoun placement for Chamorro, but this analysis proves more than sufficient for capturing prosodic movement in basic cases and providing a renewed case study demonstrating the differences between Match- and Align-based theories of syntax–prosody mapping.

## References

Anderson, Stephen R. (1996). How to put your clitics in their place, or why the best account of second-position phenomena may be something like the optimal one. *The Linguistic Review* 13: 165–191.

Anderson, Stephen R. (2005). *Aspects of the Theory of Clitics.* Oxford: Oxford University Press.

Bellik, Jennifer, Bellik, Ozan, and Kalivoda, Nick (2015–2021). Syntax-Prosody in Optimality Theory (SPOT). Javascript application. http://spot.sites.ucsc.edu. Codebase at https://github.com/syntax-prosody-ot.

Bellik, Jennifer and Kalivoda, Nick (2016). Adjunction and branchingness effects in syntax-prosody mapping. In Gunnar Ólafur Hansson, Ashley Farris-Trimble, Kevin McMullin, and Douglas Pulleyblank (eds.) *Supplemental Proceedings of the 2015 Annual Meeting on Phonology,* Linguistic Society of America. http://doi.org/10.3765/amp.v3i0.3690

Bellik, Jennifer and Kalivoda, Nick (2017). Syntax prosody in OT. Presentation at SPOT1 Workshop, University of California, Santa Cruz. Available at https://thi.ucsc.edu/wp-content/uploads/2017/10/BellikKalivoda_SPOT_11_18_2017.pdf

Bennett, Ryan, Elfner, Emily, and McCloskey, James (2016). Lightest to the right: An apparently anomalous displacement in Irish. *Linguistic Inquiry* 47: 169–234.

Chung, Sandra (1998). *The Design of Agreement: Evidence from Chamorro.* Chicago: University of Chicago Press.

Chung, Sandra (2003). The syntax and prosody of weak pronouns in Chamorro. *Linguistic Inquiry* 34: 547–599.

Chung, Sandra (2020). *Chamorro Grammar.* eScholarship Repository: University of California. Available at https://escholarship.org/uc/item/2sx7w4h5

Elfner, Emily (2012). *Syntax-Prosody Interactions in Irish.* PhD dissertation, University of Massachusetts Amherst.

Harizanov, Boris (2014). The role of prosody in the linearization of clitics: evidence from Bulgarian and Macedonian. In Cassandra Chapman, Olena Kit, and Ivona Kučerová (eds.) *Formal Approaches to Slavic Linguistics 22: The McMaster Meeting 2013* 109–130. Ann Arbor, MI: Michigan Slavic Publications.

Ito, Junko and Mester, Armin (1992/2003). Weak layering and word binarity. In Takeru Honma, Masao Okazaki, Toshiyuki Tabata and Shin-ichi Tanaka (eds.) *A New Century of Phonology and Phonological Theory: A Festschrift for Professor Shosuke Haraguchi on the Occasion of His Sixtieth Birthday* 26–65. Tokyo: Kaitakusha.

Ito, Junko and Mester, Armin (2019). Match as syntax-prosody Max/Dep: prosodic enclisis in English. *English Linguistics* 36: 1–28.

Myrberg, Sara (2013). Sisterhood in prosodic branching. *Phonology* 30: 73–124.

Prince, Alan, Merchant, Nazarré, and Tesar, Bruce (2007–2020). OTWorkplace. http://sites.google.com/site/otworkplace

Schütze, Carson (1994). Serbo-Croatian second position clitic placement and the phonology-syntax interface. In Andrew Carnie, Heidi Harley, and Tony Bures (eds.) *MIT Working Papers in Linguistics* 21: 373–473.

Selkirk, Elisabeth (1986). On derived domains in sentence phonology. *Phonology Yearbook* 3: 371–405.

Selkirk, Elisabeth (1996). The prosodic structure of function words. In James L. Morgan and Katherine Demuth (eds.) *Signal to Syntax: Bootstrapping from Speech to Grammar in Early Acquisition* 187–213. Mahwah, NJ: Erlbaum.

Selkirk, Elisabeth (2011). The syntax–phonology interface. In John A. Goldsmith, Jason Riggle, and Alan C. L. Yu (eds.) *The Handbook of Phonological Theory* 435–484. Blackwell Publishing.

Topping, Donald M. and Dungca, Bernardita C. (1973). *Chamorro Reference Grammar.* Honolulu: University of Hawaii Press.

Truckenbrodt, Hubert (1995). *Phonological Phrases: Their Relation to Syntax, Focus, and Prominence.* PhD dissertation, Massachusetts Institute of Technology.

Truckenbrodt, Hubert (1999). On the relation between syntactic phrases and phonological phrases. *Linguistic Inquiry* 30: 219–255.

## About the author

*Richard Bibbs*

Graduate research assistant for the SPOT project, Ph.D. student, Department of Linguistics, UC Santa Cruz. Research interests: phonetics, phonology, perception, and (sentence) processing, focusing on the behavior of laryngeals, especially in Chamorro (Austronesian, ISO: cha). Recent presentations: 'Perceptual factors license vocalic contrasts in Chamorro", *Annual Meeting on Phonology (AMP)*, Stony Brook, New York, October 2019.

# Chapter 9

# Revisiting tone sandhi domains in Xiamen Chinese: MATCH vs. ALIGN with Strict Layering


Yaqing Cao, Richard Bibbs, and Jennifer Bellik[*]


## 9.1 Introduction

Current approaches to the syntax-prosody interface in the framework of Optimality Theory (Prince and Smolensky 1993/2003) have proposed a number of constraints on the mapping between syntactic structures and prosodic structures. Among these, there are two major approaches, Match Theory and Align/Wrap Theory. MATCH constraints require isomorphism between prosodic words ($\omega$) and $X^0$s; phonological phrases ($\varphi$) and syntactic XPs; and intonational phrases ($\iota$) and syntactic clauses (Selkirk 2011, Elfner 2012). ALIGN constraints, on the other hand, merely require the alignment of the edges of syntactic constituents ($X^0$s, XPs, CPs, etc.) and the edges of prosodic constituents ($\omega$s, $\varphi$s, $\iota$s, etc.), based on Selkirk's 1986 pre-OT theory (see also: Chen 1987). WRAP (Truckenbrodt 1995, 1999) is an even looser requirement that forces XPs to be encapsulated in $\varphi$s. Both Match Theory and Align/Wrap Theory also incorporate prosodic well-formedness constraints like BINARITY, EQUALSISTERS (Myrberg 2013), STRONGSTART, etc., that drive mismatches between syntactic and prosodic structure. MATCH and ALIGN/


[*] Our thanks to Emily Elfner, Armin Mester and Ben Eischens for their constructive comments. Special thanks to Nick Kalivoda for his thorough reviews of multiple drafts of this paper and for extensive discussions of the syntactic representations here. Thanks also to Junko Ito and participants in her Fall 2020 seminar on the syntax-prosody interface, for helpful feedback on earlier versions of this work.

WRAP are the syntax-prosody interface's version of input–output faithfulness constraints like MAX-IO, DEP-IO, and IDENT-IO, in that they require prosodic structures to stay as faithful as possible to the input syntactic structure. Prosodic well-formedness constraints resemble the markedness constraints that make up the requirements of phonology proper.

The original definition of MATCH constraints (Selkirk 2011) defined them in terms of alignment to both right and left edges. Subsequent work, however, has embraced correspondence-oriented definitions of MATCH (Elfner 2012, 2015), which demand a greater degree of isomorphism when possible reordering of terminals is taken into account. Conceptually, Match Theory is based on the idea that, by default (if mapping constraints are undominated), prosodic structure will be just as recursive as syntactic structure. That is, all mismatches are generally understood, in Match Theory, to be a consequence of prosodic well-formedness constraints. In Align Theory, on the other hand, the mapping constraints are less stringent, and can be perfectly satisfied without achieving isomorphism between syntax and prosody. For example, ALIGN-LEFT(XP) and ALIGN-RIGHT(XP) are both fully satisfied by the mapping in (1), since every left XP boundary in the input lines up with a left φ boundary in the output, and likewise for the right XP boundaries. MATCH(XP), on the other hand, is not satisfied by this non-recursive mapping, because there is no φ that contains the same terminal string as the VP in the input. In (1) and throughout, square brackets [ ] indicate syntactic phrase boundaries, parentheses ( ) indicate φ boundaries, and curly braces { } indicate ι boundaries.

(1)        $[_{TP}\ [_{DP}\ \text{subj}][_{VP}\ \text{verb}\ [_{DP}\ \text{obj}]]] \rightarrow \{_{\iota}\ (_{\varphi}\ \text{subj})(_{\varphi}\ \text{verb})(_{\varphi}\ \text{obj})\ \}$
           *Satisfies ALIGN, violates MATCH*

ALIGN constraints, then, can be perfectly satisfied by prosodic structures that conform to Strict Layering. The Strict Layer Hypothesis (Selkirk 1984) says that the parent of a prosodic node of level $k$ is always of level $k + 1$, and the child of a prosodic node of level $k$ is always of level $k - 1$. This prohibits recursive structure (level-doubling) in prosody, as well as non-exhaustive parsing (level-skipping).

Unlike ALIGN constraints, MATCH constraints cannot be satisfied by a non-recursive prosodic parse of a recursive syntactic input. As a consequence, when the candidate set is limited to non-recursive, strictly layered structures, or when a constraint on NONRECURSIVITY is undominated, MATCH will always be violated at least once, and can select some surprising candidates. For example, in the non-recursive MATCH system (Match.NR) in Tarlov (Chapter 3), MATCH(XP, φ) is equally satisfied by mapping *[a [b [c]]]* to *{(a)(b c)}*, *{(a b)(c)}*, or *{(a b c)}*, since each of those outputs matches a single XP to a φ. The first of these mappings, *[a [b [c]]]* → *{(a)(b c)}*, intuitively appears to be the best "match," since it contains a prosodic constituent corresponding to every syntactic constituent, albeit not a prosodic constituent of the category demanded by Match Theory. The $X^0$ *a* is mapped to a φ (a higher category than MATCH($X^0$, ω) demands—category promotion); the XP *[b c]* is mapped to a φ *(b c)* (the correct category), the XP *[c]* has a corresponding ω *c* (a lower category than MATCH(XP, φ) demands—category demotion); and the maximal XP is mapped to an intonational phrase (category promotion). The intuition that *{(a)(b c)}* is a superior prosody for *[a [b [c]]]* compared to rebracketed *{(a b)(c)}* or flattened *{(a b c)}* is not reflected in the formalization of MATCH(XP, φ), however, which is only satisfied by mappings of the correct category, and therefore does not care about the cross-category mappings. Tarlov goes on to suggest that applying MATCH to strictly non-recursive candidate sets is best avoided, since the results contradict the intended purpose of MATCH constraints, which is to prefer prosodies that better reflect the syntactic input structures.

This chapter further explores the interaction of MATCH constraints with strictly layered candidate sets, and compares this interaction to the behavior of ALIGN and WRAP constraints in the same context. Using Xiamen Chinese tone sandhi domains as a case study, it demonstrates the ability of MATCH constraints to select superficially mismatching optima, even without the intervention of prosodic well-formedness constraints.

In addition to investigating the mismatching effect of combining MATCH with non-recursive candidate sets, this chapter also investigates mismatches driven by subcategory-specific MATCH constraints. When recursion is present in prosodic structure, it is often useful to refer to prosodic subcategories—minimal, non-minimal, maximal, or non-maximal instances of a given prosodic category (Ito and Mester 1992, 2007, 2009a, 2009b, 2013). Match Theory's embrace of prosodic recursion has given rise to subcategory-specific constraints, such as MATCHMAX (Ishihara 2014), which requires matching of the highest (maximal) XP segment, but ignores mismatches of lower (non-maximal) XP segments. This finer distinction empowers subcategory-specific MATCH constraints with more flexible empirical and conceptual coverage. In principle, this subcategorization can be extended to Align Theory as well. Subcategory-specific mapping constraints as employed in the literature are intended to function as specialized versions of general MATCH—requiring isomorphism for some subset of the syntactic nodes. However, the theory of prosodic subcategorization also allows subcategory-specific MATCH constraints that demand mismatches (Van Handel et al., Chapter 5). Van Handel et al. identify two classes of subcategory-sensitive

MATCH constraints that drive non-isomorphisms: those in which the second argument, but not the first, is subcategorized, such as MATCH(XP, $\varphi^{[+max]}$); and those in which the two arguments have conflicting specifications, such as MATCH(XP$^{[+max]}$, $\varphi^{[-max]}$). They introduce the term "Anti-Match effects" to refer to configurations where a subcategorized MATCH constraint conflicts with general MATCH(XP), rather than functioning as a special case of general MATCH. This chapter adds another configuration in which subcategory-sensitive MATCH leads to Anti-Match effects, of a sort: when the candidate set is restricted to structures that conform to Strict Layering, the general MATCH(XP, $\varphi$) itself favors strong mismatches, with the result that a constraint like MATCH(XP$^{[-min]}$, $\varphi$) conflicts with MATCH(XP, $\varphi$), although it does not directly favor strong mismatches. MATCH(XP$^{[-min]}$, $\varphi$) does not conflict with general MATCH(XP, $\varphi$) when recursive structures were included in the candidate set, as in Chapter 5.

For the sake of theory comparison, we also present an ALIGN/WRAP analysis of the same data, with the same non-recursive candidate set. We find that ALIGN constraints, like MATCH constraints, cannot capture the Xiamen Chinese pattern unless combined with prosodic subcategorization. Subcategorizing ALIGN to the non-minimal XP allows it to favor the same non-isomorphic parses that MATCH(XP$^{[-min]}$, $\varphi$) does, although with a larger typology.

The structure of this chapter is as follows: §9.2 introduces the general pattern of tone sandhi in Xiamen Chinese. Section 9.3 presents the specific sentences that are included in the analysis here, along with some generalizations about the syntax–prosody mapping involved. Section 9.4 presents the OT analysis, consisting of two systems sharing the same candidate set but differing in their constraints (MATCH vs. ALIGN/WRAP). Section 9.5 discusses and concludes.


## 9.2    Xiamen Chinese tone sandhi

Xiamen is a coastline city in Fujian Province which is the main base for the Min Dialect, and Xiamen Chinese is one of the widely studied Chinese dialects. It has a population of around 3.5 million among which 1.5 million are proficient speakers. The rest are speakers of other Chinese dialects like standard Mandarin and Hakka. Like most of the dialects in China, Xiamen has a restricted syllable structure, namely, [consonant [onglide [nucleus + coda]]] (Chen 1987). The only permissible codas in Xiamen are nasals, glides, and voiceless stops. Like most Chinese dialects, Xiamen Chinese is also a tonal language that has seven citation tones, presented in (2). The tones are represented using Chao numeric letters, where the highest number 5 is the highest pitch and 1 represents the lowest pitch (Chao 1930). Some examples of minimal pairs are shown in (3). Like other dialects in China, Xiamen Chinese has a distinction between checked syllables and free or smooth syllables. Checked syllables are those that end in stops, whereas free syllables end with either nasals or glides. The distinction between free and checked syllables is important because they are subject to different tone sandhi rules. Whereas free syllables form a tone sandhi circle as in (4a), checked syllables have their own distinctive sandhi rules as in (4b). For instance, a free syllable with a 22 base tone will surface as a 21 tone, whereas a syllable with a 21 tone will surface as 53, etc. If a syllable is checked, it will surface as 21 if the base tone is 4 and as 4 if its base tone is 32 and the syllable ends in a voiceless oral stop /p, t, k/.

(2)     The citation tones (in Chao (1930) tone letters)
        a. 44   b. 24   c. 53   d. 21   e. 22   f. 32   g. 4

(3)     Minimal pairs of Xiamen citation tones

| | | |
|---|---|---|
| po 44 褒 'praise' | si 44 诗 'poetry' |
| po 24 婆 'old woman' | si 24 时 'time" |
| po 53 宝 'precious' | si 53 死 'die' |
| po 21 报 'report' | si 21 四 'four' |
| po 22 暴 'violence' | si 22 寺 'temple' |
| poʔ 32 博 'extensive' | siʔ 32 薛 'Xue' (a Chinese family name) |
| poʔ 4 薄 'thin' | siʔ 4 蚀 'erosion' |

(4)     The mode of tone sandhi in Xiamen Chinese
    a.  Free syllables:

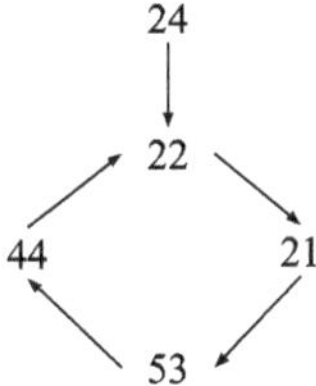

    b.  Checked syllables:
        i.    4    → 21  (-p, -t, -k, -ʔ)
        ii.   32   → 4   (-p, -t, -k)
                     53  (-ʔ)

(Chen 1987)

The basic tone sandhi rule in Xiamen Chinese is that base tones are preserved at the right edge of a tone group (TG) and undergo sandhi elsewhere—that is, a base tone changes to its sandhi equivalent when it is followed by any other tone within a tone group. This rule is formalized in (5). An example of tone sandhi is in (6) where *p'ang* 'fragrant' surfaces with its base tone 44 in *tsin-p'ang* 'very fragrant' whereas it emerges as 22 in *p'ang-tsui* 'fragrant water'. The difference between the two surface tones is explained by the location of the syllable: if it is located at the right edge of a TG, it preserves its underlying tone; if it is elsewhere, it undergoes tone sandhi. In other words, the faithful surfacing of a base tone marks the right edge of a tone group. Throughout the chapter we will follow the convention of using # to mark the right edge of a tone group.

(5)      Tone sandhi rule
         T →T′/ _____ T within a tone group
         (T=base tone; T′= sandhi tone)

(Chen 1987)

In (6), tone sandhi applies to the first word in an adjective phrase (AP), suggesting that the XP could be the domain of tone sandhi. However, examples (7) and (8) show that other syntactic units like words and utterances can also correspond to independent tone sandhi domains. In the idiom in (7), tone sandhi does not apply; each word in this complex NP forms its own tone group. For instance, *hong* 'wind' and *ts'e* 'blow' are independent from each other, though there seems to be a subject-verb relation between them. In contrast, in the sentence in (8), the whole utterance together comprises one tone group that crosses XP boundaries, as evidenced by the fact that only the utterance-final word surfaces with its underlying tone.

(6)          a. tsin-p'ang # 'very fragrant'    b. p'ang-tsui # 'fragrant water'
   Underlying: 44  44                  44      53
   Surface:     22  44                  22      53

(Chen 1987)

(7)          hong # ts'e #   hoo #   ak
   Underlying:   44        44      22       32
   Surface:       44        44      22       32
              wind     blow    rain    pour
              'stormy weather'

(8)              yi kiong-kiong kio gua ke k'uah puah tiam-tsing ku ts'eq #
   Underlying:    44 24    24    21 53  44 21    21    53      44  53 32
   Surface:       22 22    22    53 44  22 53    53    44      22  44 32
                  He by    -force cause I more read  half  hour          long book
                  'He insisted that I read for another half an hour.'

                                                                    (Chen 1987)

The examples in (6)–(8) suggest that a TG can correspond to a wide variety of syntactic units (words, syntactic phrases, and utterances). It seems a daunting task for a pure syntactic approach to explain tone sandhi's variable sensitivity to syntax. We therefore adopt a syntax-prosody approach instead, and assume that TGs in Xiamen Chinese are determined by the interaction between syntax and prosody, as previously argued by Zhang (2019). Here we adopt the assumption in Truckenbrodt (1999) and Zhang (2019) that TGs in Xiamen Chinese correspond to prosodic units φ, as stated in (9); specifically, the absence of tone sandhi signals the right boundary of a phonological phrase.

(9)      *TG formation in Xiamen*
         The domain of tone sandhi in Xiamen Chinese corresponds to the
         minimal φ.

There are other pieces of evidence which suggest that the phrase (syntactic or prosodic) is the domain of tone sandhi. Chen (1992) argues that the right edge of every XP corresponds to the right edge of a TG except when XP is an adjunct c-commanding its lexical head. Lin (1994) argues that the maximal projection of a lexical head is the TG. A more recent proposal by Zhang (2019) also argues that the right edge of every XP is the one that matters for tone group formation in Xiamen Chinese. The consensus among the above approaches suggests that XP, or its prosodic correspondent φ, is the relevant domain for tone sandhi.

We will foreground here our decision to assume a preference towards non-recursive phonological parsing in Xiamen Chinese. In an OT analysis, these non-recursive structures can emerge as optima through two routes. First, recursive structures can be included in the candidate set, dramatically expanding the number of candidates (see Shingler and Bellik, Chapter 2, for specifics), and the constraint set can include a violable constraint called NONRECURSIVITY, which penalizes recursive prosodic structures. Second, NONRECURSIVITY can be imposed on GEN, rather than CON, as an inviolable constraint, which greatly simplifies the candidate set, while potentially complicating the constraint interactions. For expository ease, we employ the second option in this chapter. This simplifies the presentation of the analysis, while essentially 'ruling out" the same structures that would be penalized by NONRECURSIVITY. Notably our analysis is relatively agnostic towards recursivity at the level of the phonological phrase for Xiamen Chinese, as there is currently no strong evidence that either supports or undermines recursive prosodic structure in this language. Our primary aim here is a theoretical one: to study the consequences of a non-recursive candidate set for the behavior of MATCH constraints, especially their subcategorized versions. It is in service to this aim that we adopt the assumption, already present in previous work (Truckenbrodt 1999, Zhang 2019), that TGs represent non-recursive, minimal φs.

The general pattern of TG boundaries, as summarized by Truckenbrodt (1999), is represented in (10). TG boundaries roughly correspond to the right edges of XP, especially when XP is the complement of another lexical head. Notably, $[_{VP}$ V NP$]$# forms a single TG, as the right edges of NP and VP coincide. However, Chen (1987) makes the generalization that arguments such as complements usually form their own TG, while adjuncts do not. This is schematized in (11), where the adjunct $XP_1$ and the non-maximal projection $YP_1$ form a single TG.

(10)     Generalizations from Truckenbrodt (1999) about Xiamen Chinese
         TGs
   a.    $[_{CP}$ YP$_1$#...YP$_n$ # VP #$]$
         where one of $YP_1$, ... , $YP_n$ is the subject, and the others may be
         sentential adverbs or preposed objects
   b.    $[_{NP1}$ NP$_2$ # N$_1]$ #
         where $NP_2$ is the complement of $N_1$
   c.    $[_{VP}$ V NP # YP$]$ #
         where NP and YP are complements of the verb

(11)     Generalizations from Chen (1987) about TGs for adjunction
         structures in Xiamen Chinese
   a.    $[_{YP2}$ XP$_1$ YP$_1]$ #
         Where XP1 is the adjunct of YP1, and appears to its left.
   b.    $[_{YP2}$ YP$_1$ XP$_1]$ #
         Where XP1 is the adjunct of YP1, and appears to its right.

Standard implementations of MATCH and ALIGN are not sensitive to the status of an XP as an argument vs. as an adjunct, so this invisibility of adjunct XPs to φ-formation in Xiamen Chinese, in contrast to the visibility of argument XPs, is potentially problematic. One possible solution, which we ultimately reject, is to make reference to the visibility of the different segments of an adjunction structure to phonology. In an adjunction structure of the form [$_{XP}$ XP YP], there are two distinct segments of XP. Bellik and Kalivoda (2016) identify three possible visibility settings for these segments, illustrated in (12): only the higher segment is visible to phonology (12a); only the lower segment is visible (12b); or both the low and high segments are visible (12c).

(12)     Adjunction visibility settings (Bellik and Kalivoda 2016)

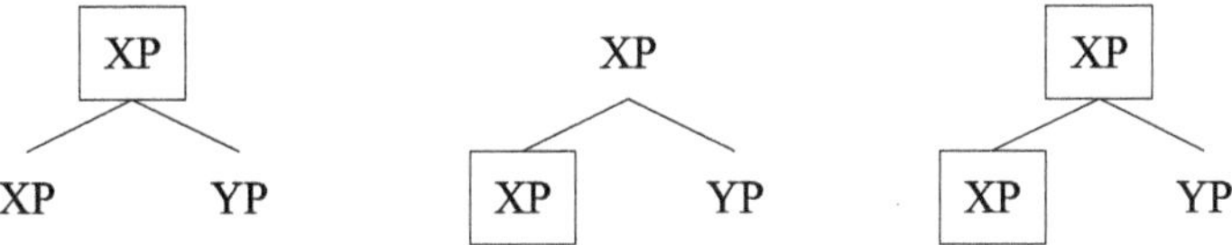


Truckenbrodt (1995, 1999) and Selkirk (2011) have argued that only the lower head projection should be visible to prosodic phrasing, as in (12b). In contrast, Bellik and Kalivoda (2016) establish that at least the high segment of the adjunction structure must be visible to MATCH constraints, as in (12a) or (12c), in order to capture the phrasing patterns of Kinyambo. For Xiamen Chinese, the lack of TG boundaries between the lower XP segment and YP in adjunction structures can be interpreted in two different ways. On the first interpretation, only the high XP segment is visible to phonology in this language, as in (12a), and the flat prosody for adjunction structures is thus maximally faithful to the syntactic information available to phonology. On the second interpretation, both segments of the adjunction structure are visible to phonology, as in (12c), and the flat prosody is a weak mismatch, which simply indicates that NONRECURSIVITY or other constraints on prosodic structure overcome the pressure to match the lower segment of the adjunction structure (on either interpretation, the high segment of the adjunction structure must be visible to the mapping constraints in Xiamen Chinese, given that the adjunction structure is mapped to a flat prosody that matches the high segment but not the low segment; (12b) is implausible for this language). We adopt the second interpretation, and assume going forward that both segments of the adjunction structure are visible to the mapping constraints, as in (12c).

Instead of deriving the distinction between adjuncts and arguments by treating the low segment of the adjunction structure specifically as invisible, our solution derives this distinction from the interaction of two factors: the invisibility of functional projections, and subcategorized mapping constraints that specifically target non-minimal XPs. To preview the results of §9.4, we find that in a system with strictly layered candidate sets, MATCH can indeed derive this flat prosody even when both segments of the adjunction structure are visible to phonology. Before turning to the OT analysis, however, we present the specific language data that we will try to account for, which both supports and complicates the argument-adjunct distinction claimed by Truckenbrodt (1999).

## 9.3    Tone group data and the Lexical Category Condition

The current section presents the language data that this analysis will account for. Section 9.3.1 fleshes out the argument-adjunct distinction with an example where TGs disambiguate the syntax, and introduces the Lexical Category Condition, which will prove crucial for our analysis. Later subsections examine TG placement in three other pairs of constructions: adverbs adjoined to the TP vs. VP level (9.3.2), the double object construction with two different word orders (9.3.3), and sentences with and without topic movement (9.3.4). We will see that arguments that occur to the right of the head (e.g., the complement of the verb) and adjuncts adjoined to a lexical XP are phrased with the syntactic head in the prosody, whereas arguments that occur to the left of the syntactic head phrase separately from the head in the prosody, as do adjuncts adjoined to a functional projection.

All data and syntactic structures come from Chen (1987) unless otherwise noted. Syntactic trees have been adapted to fit modern labeling conventions (e.g., TP replaces S, and CP replaces S′).

### 9.3.1    *Sesame seed big: adjunct vs. argument readings*

The difference between the prosody of arguments and adjuncts can be illustrated by an ambiguous complex NP whose two interpretations are represented in (13) and (14). The same sequence of words can be understood as a complex NP containing either a relative clause with a complement structure (Interpretation 1, in (13)), or an equative clause with an adjunction structure (Interpretation 2, in (14)). Our focus will be on the first two words, *mua-a tua* 'sesame-seed big.'

(13)   Interpretation 1: Relative clause with predicative adjective (*sesame seed* = argument)

|  | [$_{\text{TP}}$ [$_{\text{NP}}$ mua-a] | [$_{\text{AP}}$ tua]] | e | sio-piã |
|---|---|---|---|---|
| Underlying: | 44 **53** | 21 35 | | 35 53 |
| Surface: | 22 **53** | 21 42 | | 42 53 |
| TG: | [mua-a] # | [tua] # [e | | sio-piã]# |
| | Sesame-seed | big | COMP | bun |

'buns on which the sesame seeds are big"

(14)   Interpretation 2: Equative clause with adjunction structure (*sesame seed* = adjunct)

|  | [$_{\text{AP}}$ [$_{\text{NP}}$ mua-a] | [$_{\text{AP}}$ tua]] | e | sio-piã |
|---|---|---|---|---|
| Underlying: | 44 **53** | 21 | 35 | 35 53 |
| Surface: | 22 **44** | 21 | 42 | 42 53 |
| TG: | [mua-a | tua]# | [e | sio-piã]# |
| | Sesame-seed | big | COMP | bun |

'buns as big as sesame-seed"

(Chen 1987 (12d))

In Interpretation 1 (13), the subsequence *sesame-seed big* is interpreted as a relative clause that modifies the head noun *bun*. The adjective *big* is an argument, describing the size of the sesame seeds. The syntax for this interpretation is shown in (15a), where functional elements are shown in grey. Prosodically, each minimal XP, *sesame-seed* and *big,* is mapped to a separate φ, as indicated by the TG boundaries (#) between *mua-a* 'sesame seed' and *tua* 'big,' and the faithful surfacing of the underlying tones on both words. The subsequence *sesame-seed big* is phrased into two TGS, each of which corresponds to a minimal φ (15b). Under the assumption that TGs/ φs are not recursive in Xiamen Chinese, the TP containing both words is not mapped to a φ.

(15)   Trees for Interpretation 1 (argument) of *sesame-seed big*. Adapted from Chen (1987), (29b)

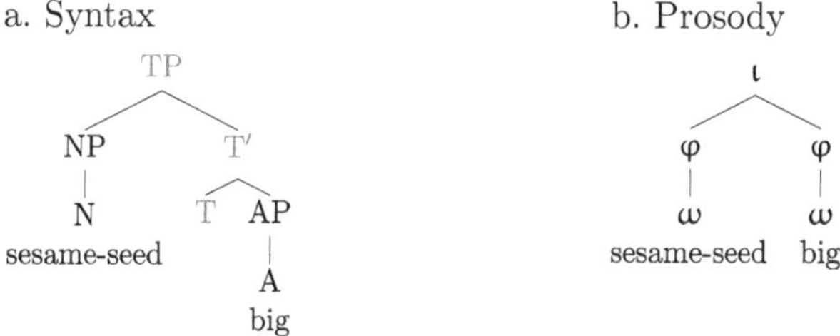

In this predicative structure, Xiamen Chinese phonology prioritizes matching the minimal, lexical XPs *sesame seed* and *big* over matching the non-minimal, functional TP. We therefore adopt the Lexical Category Condition (LCC) as formulated in (16). Various versions of the LCC have been proposed, and it is commonly employed in previous work (Selkirk 1995; Selkirk and Shen 1990; Elordieta and Selkirk 2022).

(16)   Lexical Category Condition
       Constraints relating syntactic and prosodic categories apply to lexical syntactic elements and their projections, but not to functional elements and their projections (Truckenbrodt 1999).

Due to the LCC, there is no pressure from the mapping constraints to match the TP, which is not headed by a lexical element. Throughout this chapter, we assume that the LCC holds, and therefore omit functional elements from the prosodic representations, or depict them as cliticized onto the adjacent lexical material, in keeping with previous descriptions of the prosody of this language (e.g., Chen 1987).

A second available reading of this complex NP is shown in Interpretation 2 in (14). Here, the NP *sesame-seed* is interpreted as being adjoined to the adjective *big* to create a larger equative AP, and the two words together form a single TG. This is shown by the surfacing of the sandhi tone in *sesame-seed,* in contrast to the underlying tone on *sesame-seed* in Interpretation 1 (13). That is, for this reading, the prosody prioritizes mapping the non-minimal AP, that is, the high segment of the adjunction structure, over mapping the two minimal XPs. The two words are parsed into a single minimal $\varphi$ ($_\varphi$ *sesame-seed big)*, as diagrammed in (17).

(17)   Trees for Interpretation 2 (adjunct) of *sesame-seed big.* Adapted from Chen (1987), (29a).

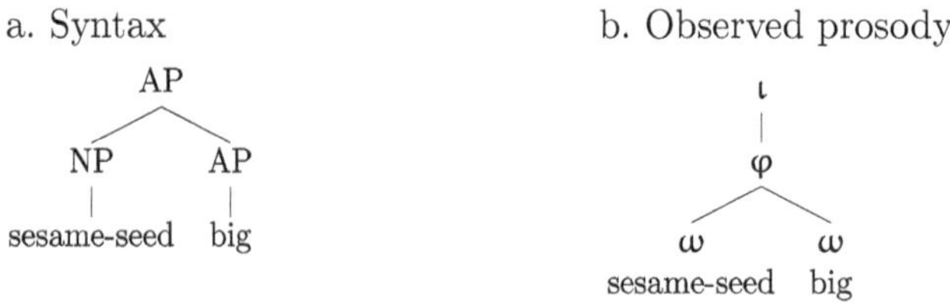


These two readings have the same syntactic constituency structure, but different prosodic constituencies. For us, the crucial difference between the two input structures is the status of the non-minimal syntactic phrase as a functional projection (TP in Interpretation 1), or a lexical projection (AP in Interpretation 2). The lexical projection is matched by the prosody, while the functional projection is ignored, due to the LCC.

### 9.3.2   Sentential adjuncts vs. VP adjuncts

The distinction between lexical and functional projections also accounts for the difference in the phrasing of adverbs adjoined at different heights. Adverbs adjoined to the VP are phrased into the same TG as the verb (18), while those adjoined to the TP are phrased into a separate TG (19).

The key prosodic difference between the two is that *probably*, as an adjunct to the entire sentence, forms a separate TG from the VP, whereas *already* does not. Their syntactic and prosodic structures are depicted in (20) and (21), respectively.

(18)    yi    yi-king       tsu     a
        [He   already       go    ASP] #
        'He has already gone.'                          (Zhang 2019, (10))


(19)    yi    tai-k'ai       tsu    a
        [He   probably] # [go    ASP]#
        'He probably has gone.'                         (Zhang 2019, (11))


Since *already* is adjoined to the VP, it is part of a non-minimal LexP (lexical XP) with the verb—the high segment of the VP adjunction structure. Prosody sees the high VP segment as well as the two minimal LexPs, the AdvP *already* and the minimal VP *go*. The high VP segment is prioritized for mapping, yielding the prosody in (20c) (We omit *he* and *ASP* from the prosodic representation due to the LCC, and root all prosodic structures in ɩ for the sake of ensuring that they are all valid trees).

(20)    Syntax and prosody of a verbal adjunction structure

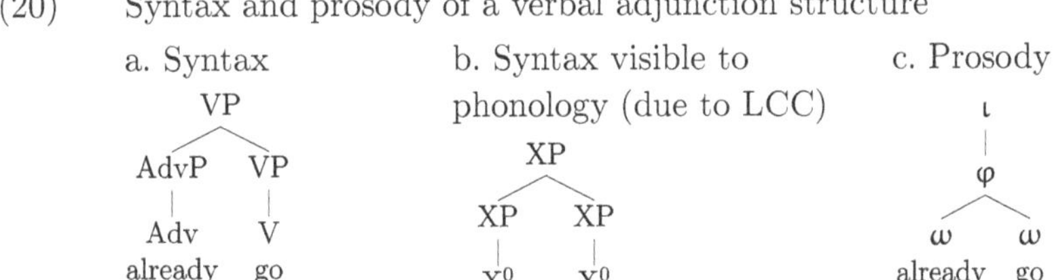


In contrast, with *probably*, the adverb is adjoined to the TP, which (as a functional projection) is invisible to the prosody, due to the LCC. For the sake of ensuring that the syntax visible to the prosody remains a properly

rooted tree, we depict the prosody's view of the syntax here as rooted in a
CP in (21b). Since the TP is invisible to prosody, there is no pressure from
the mapping constraints to map it to a φ, and instead, the two minimal
LexPs (AdvP and VP) are mapped to φs (21c).

(21)     Syntax and prosody of a sentential adjunction structure

         a. Syntax                    b. Syntax visible to        c. Prosody
               TP                     phonology (due to LCC)           ι

         AdvP      TP                        CP                    φ       φ

         Adv    T  VP                  XP       XP                ω       ω
       probably                        X⁰       X⁰          probably   go
                   V                probably    go
                   go

### 9.3.3  Double object constructions

Further insight into the syntactic structures that must be visible to the
syntax–prosody mapping in Xiamen Chinese comes from the prosody of
the double object construction. Like other argument structures, both direct
and indirect objects of ditransitive verbs form their own TGs in Xiamen
Chinese, as illustrated in (22) and (23) (example (16) in Chen 1987; Cl
stands for classifier). In both sentences, a TG boundary appears after each
of the objects of the verbs *give* and *introduce*, regardless of whether the
direct object (DO) or indirect object (IO) precedes the verb (In (22), the
direct object *hit pun ts'eq* 'that book" is shifted to the specifier position of
VP because of the object marker *tsiong*).

(22)     yi      tsiong         hit   pun ts'eq      sang   hoo    tang-oq
         [he     obj-marker  that Cl   book] # [give    to     schoolmate] #
         'He gave that book to his schoolmate.'

(23)     yi    kap    tang-oq          kai-siao    tsit   e   lu-ping-yu
         [He to      schoolmate] # [introduce   one   Cl  girlfriend] #
         'He introduced a girlfriend to his schoolmate.'

                                                              (Chen 1987, (16))

Based on the distribution of tone sandhi, we infer that a φ-boundary occurs after each object (i.e., after *to-schoolmate* and after *that-book*). On the
interpretation that every TG boundary only corresponds to the right edge
of a single, minimal φ, we instead interpret the TG boundaries as indicating that there is a φ extending from the left edge of the sentence until after

the first object (*that-book* in (22) and *to-schoolmate* in (23)), and a second φ that spans the remainder of the sentence, yielding parses like $\{_\iota \ (_\varphi \ that\text{-}book)$ $(_\varphi \ give \ to\text{-}schoolmate)\}$. This is the only available interpretation of the TG data that conforms to both NonRecursivity and Exhaustivity, although other non-exhaustive and/or recursive parses would become available under other interpretations of the TG phrasing diagnostic.

The syntactic structures and prosodic structures for (22) and (23) are shown in (24) and (25), respectively. For simplicity, we assume a Chomsky (1981)-style syntax for the double object construction, where one object appears in the specifier of VP and the other appears in complement position; however, this is not crucial for our purposes. Similar results obtain with a Larsonian vP shell analysis (Larson 1988), as long as V moves to v and thereby renders vP a lexical projection. What is crucial for our purposes, however, is that the constituents *give to schoolmate* in (24a) and *introduce a girlfriend* in (25a) are recognized by the prosody, since they are mapped to φs at the expense of failing to map the NPs *schoolmate* and *girlfriend*. These V+Obj constituents are intermediate projections in our syntax. Although intermediate projections are not canonically considered targets for syntax–prosody mapping, it appears that in Xiamen Chinese, at least, both intermediate and maximal projections of lexical heads count as phrasal for phonology.

(24)    Syntax and prosody of (22)

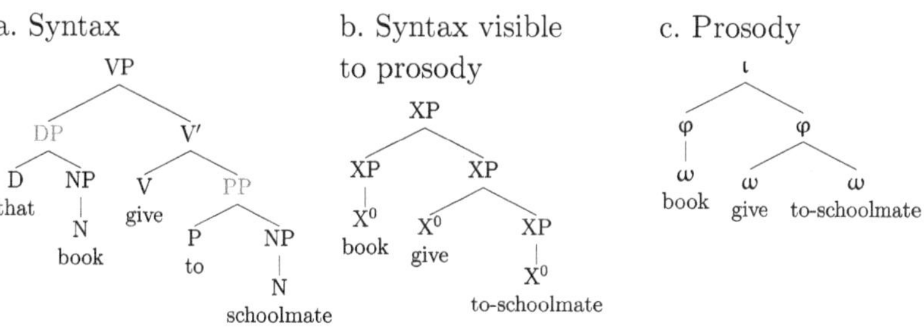

(25)    Syntax and prosody of (23)

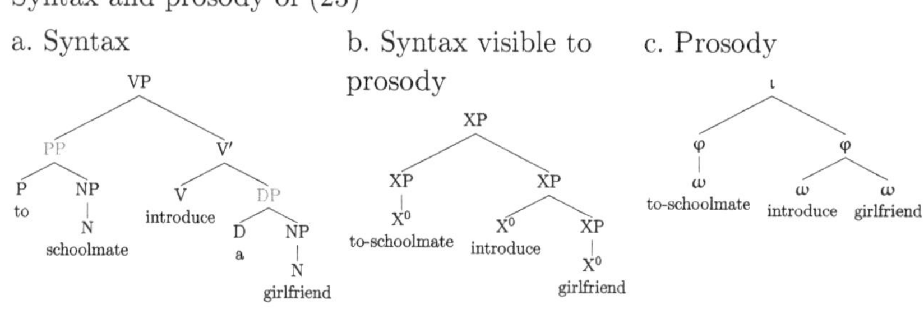

(26)      Syntactic and prosodic structures for the double object construction

      a.    $[\text{Subj} [_{\text{VP}} \text{DO} [_{\text{V}'} \text{V IO}]]] \rightarrow \{(\text{Subj-DO}) (\text{V IO})\}$

      b.    $[\text{Subj} [_{\text{VP}} \text{IO} [_{\text{V}'} \text{V DP}]]] \rightarrow \{(\text{Subj-IO}) (\text{V DO})\}$

This mapping again prioritizes the mapping of non-minimal LexPs over minimal LexPs. With the visibility of the V′ here, though, for the first time we have a syntactic input to phonology that contains three levels of nested LexPs: VP, V′, and NP. That is, the conflict is not only between mapping the minimal vs. non-minimal LexPs, but also between mapping maximal (VP) vs. non-maximal (V′) LexPs. The [–maximal, –minimal] V′ wins out here; the observed prosody fails to match both the maximal LexP (the VP) and a minimal LexP (the NP to the right of V).

### 9.3.4    *Topic movement*

The visibility of intermediate syntactic projections is also relevant to other expressions in Xiamen Chinese that contain three levels of LexPs, such as the transitive sentences with adjuncts and their topicalized equivalents in (27) and (28). In both base sentences, the expression *tso tsit ts'ut liok-yah-p'ih* 'rent one video movie' forms a TG/φ. This expression is the verb plus its direct object *video-movie*. In (28a), this is the entire VP, since the AP *very expensive* describes the whole VP and sits outside of it. But in (27a), the specifier *to watch* is situated inside the VP, since it describes the purpose of renting the video game. V+DO in (27a), then, is not a maximal projection, but an intermediate projection, V′. The fact that it is still mapped to a distinct tone group from *to watch* is further evidence that intermediate projections must be visible to the prosody here.

(27) a.    *Base sentence*

         tso    tsit   ts'ut   liok-yah-p'ih      lai   k'uah

         [rent   one   Cl     video-movie]#    [to    watch] #

         'rent one video-movie to watch'

     b.    *With topic movement*

         liok-yah-p'ih      tso tsit    ts'ut   lai   k'uah

         [video-movie ]#   [rent one   Cl      to     watch]#

         'rent one video-movie to watch'

                                  (Zhang 2019, (25); Chen 1987, (66))

(28) a.  *Base sentence*
      tso    tsit  ts'ut  liok-yah-p'ih        tsin  kui
      [rent  one  Cl    video-movie]#    [very expensive] #
      'it is very expensive to rent one video-movie.'
   b.  *With topic movement*
      liok-yah-p'ih        tso  tsit  ts'ut #   tsin  kui
      [video-movie]#    [rent  one  Cl]#    [very  expensive]#
      'it is very expensive to rent one video-movie.'

(Zhang 2019, (27))

It is also instructive to examine the prosody of the topicalized version of the sentences in (27b) and (28b). The basic pattern is that when a NP is topicalized by leftward movement, it is followed by a TG boundary at its right edge, separating it from the remaining material. Whether the remaining material from the V′ forms one TG with the following adjunct, or forms a distinct TG, depends on the height at which the following adjunct adjoins. The two examples here differ in whether the expression following *video-movie* in the base sentence is an adjunct to the VP or to the TP. In (27), the TP *to watch* is part of the VP remnant, and so when the NP *video-movie* moves out of the VP, there is no longer an XP edge between the verb *rent* and the TP *to watch*. Instead, they form a non-minimal LexP (LexP$^{[+min]}$ = VP *watch*), which is reflected in the prosody by the lack of TG boundary before *to watch* in the topicalized sentence (27b).

In (28b), by contrast, only *rent one* is left in the VP, since the adjunct AP *very expensive* is attached outside the VP, at the TP level. There is no LexP constituent that contains both the VP and the AP, and therefore no mapping pressure to create a TG/φ containing them both. Instead, (28b) emerges in the prosody with three separate φs, each corresponding to a minimal LexP. In fact, there is no recursion of LexPs in this sentence, so under the LCC, perfect mapping to a non-recursive prosody is possible.

Our interpretation of the syntax and prosody of (27) and (28) are shown in (29) and (30), respectively. The syntax in (29a) is minimally adapted from Chen (1987)'s (67b), where *to watch* is marked as an S′ in a rightward specifier to VP.

(29)  Syntax and prosody of a sentence with topic movement, no TG boundary after verb (27a).

a. Base syntax

b. Base syntax visible to prosody

c. Base prosody

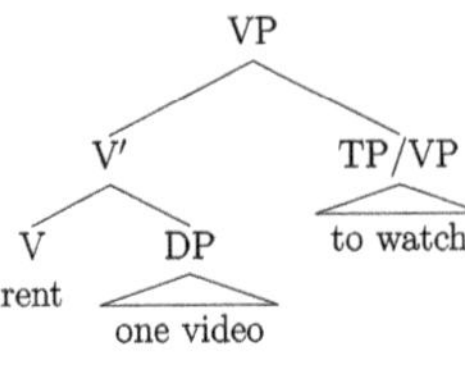
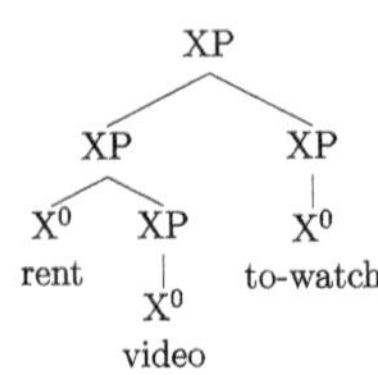
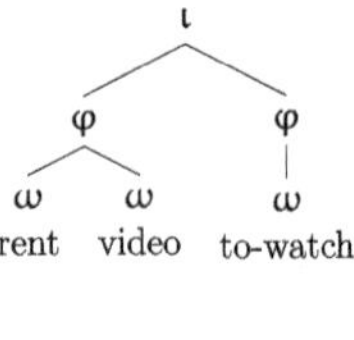

d. Topicalized syntax

e. Topicalized syntax visible to prosody

f. Topicalized prosody

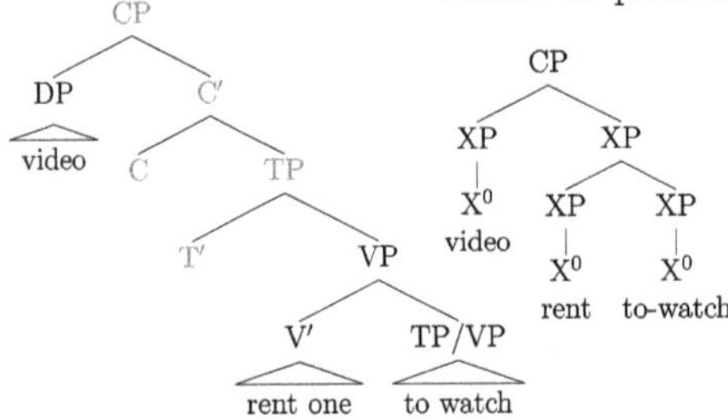
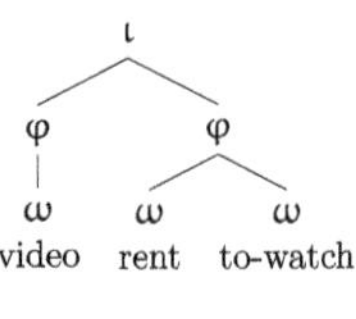

(30)  Syntax and prosody of a sentence with topic movement, with a TG boundary after verb (28)

a. Base syntax

b. Base syntax visible to prosody

c. Base prosody

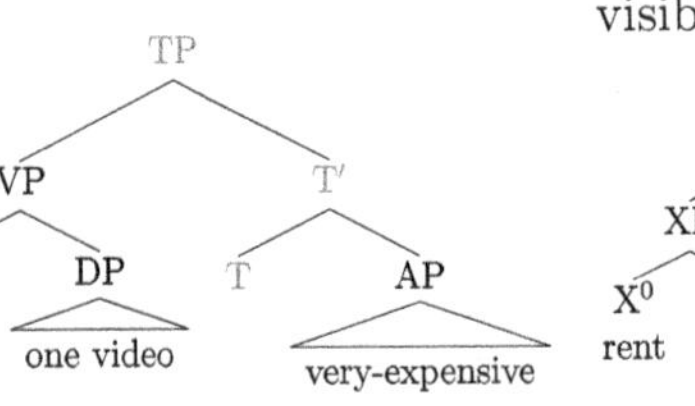
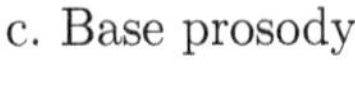
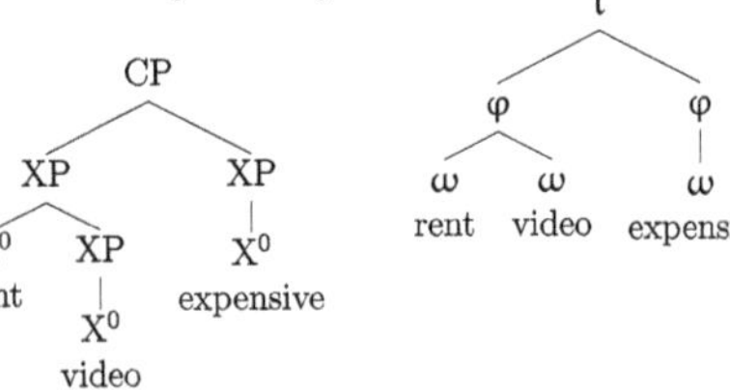

d. Topicalized syntax

e. Topicalized syntax visible to prosody

f. Topicalized prosody

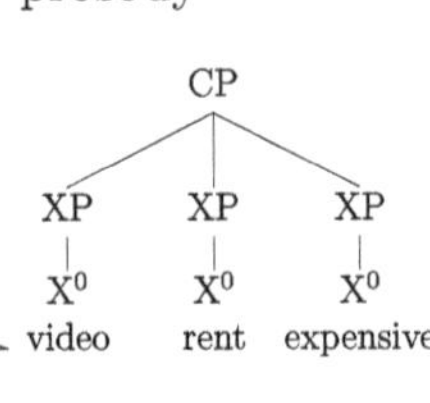
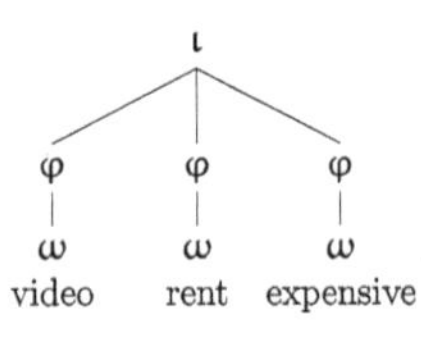

### 9.3.5   Summary of the data

Given our interpretation of each TG in Xiamen Chinese as a minimal $\varphi$, we can sum up with several observations about the syntax–prosody mappings described in this section. First, functional projections are never matched. We attribute this to the LCC being active in this language. Second, intermediate projections (bar levels) are sometimes matched; Xiamen Chinese phonology appears to treat them as phrasal. For example, in the double object construction, the V′ comprised of the verb and the following object is mapped to a TG/$\varphi$, indicating that it qualifies as a lexical phrase for the syntax–prosody mapping. Thirdly, non-minimal lexical XPs in Xiamen Chinese are prioritized over minimal LexPs in mapping to TGs (that is, $\varphi$s). For instance, in adjunction structures, the higher, non-minimal XP that incorporates the adjunct forms a TG/$\varphi$, and the lower XP surfaces with the sandhi tone, indicating that this lower, minimal XP does not map to a $\varphi$. The failure to match the minimal XPs constitutes a mismatch. Finally, where three levels of nested lexical XPs occur, the intermediate LexP (non-minimal and non-maximal) is prioritized for mapping over the maximal and the minimal LexPs.

The data is summarized in (31). The representations in the syntax column omit the CP level unless it introduces new phonologically overt material, as in sentences with topicalization. For simplicity, we omit most functional terminals from the prosodic representation, except where they are necessary to convey the meaning of the sentence. As summarized in the final column of the table, we can see that minimal LexPs are not matched unless they are simultaneously maximal—i.e., there is no recursion of lexical phrases in the input (a, c). Non-minimal LexPs are matched unless they contain another non-minimal LexP, as in (e, f, g), in which case the [–max, –min] LexP is matched instead.

Note that the AP with an argument substructure (31a) is structurally identical to the TP with an adverbial adjunct (31c) when we abstract away from lower functional projections and specific category labels. The LCC and the assumption that phonology does not see individual syntactic category labels combine to make these two structures, which from a syntactic standpoint appear totally unrelated, identical from the perspective of the syntax–prosody mapping constraints. The two ditransitive sentences (31e, f) are also identical to each other syntactically, differing only in their lexical items.

(31)    Data summary table

| | Syntax (abstracting away from categories) | Prosody as diagnosed by TGs | Are all LexPs matched? |
|---|---|---|---|
| a. AP w Arg. | $[_{FP} [_{LexP}$ sesame-seed$]$ $[_{LexP}$ big$]]$ | (sesame-seed) (big) | Yes |
| b. AP w Adj. | $[_{LexP} [_{LexP}$ sesame-seed$]$ $[_{LexP}$ big$]]$ | (sesame-seed big) | No, MinLexPs are not matched |
| c. TP adj. | $[_{FP} [_{LexP}$ probably$]$ $[_{LexP}$ go$]]$ | ( probably) (go) | Yes |
| d. VP adj. | $[_{LexP} [_{LexP}$ already$][_{LexP}$ go$]]$ | (already go) | No, MinLexPs are not matched |
| e. Ditrans. 1 | $[_{LexP} [_{LexP}$ he-that-book$]$ $[_{LexP}$ give $[_{LexP}$ to-schoolmate$]]]$ | ( book) (give to-schoolmate) | No, MinLexP and MaxLexP are not matched |
| f. Ditrans. 2 | $[_{LexP} [_{LexP}$ he-to-schoolmate$]$ $[_{LexP}$ introduce $[_{LexP}$ a-girlfriend$]]]$ | ( to-schoolmate) (introduce girlfriend) | No, MinLexP and MaxLexP are not matched |
| g. Base 1 | $[_{LexP} [_{LexP}$ rent-one $[_{LexP}$ video-game$]]$ $[_{LexP}$ to-watch$]]$ | (rent video) (to-watch) | No, Max and Min LexPs not matched |
| h. Topic 1 | $[_{CP} [_{LexP}$ video-game$]$ $[_{LexP} [_{LexP}$ rent-one$]$ $[_{LexP}$ to-watch$]]$ $]$ | (video) (rent to-watch) | No, 2 MinLexPs are not matched |
| i. Base 2 | $[_{FP} [_{LexP}$ rent-one $[_{LexP}$ video-game$]]$ $[_{LexP}$ very-expensive$]]$ | (rent video)(very expensive) | No, a MinLexP is not matched |
| j. Topic 2 | $[_{CP} [_{LexP}$ video-game$]$ $[_{FP} [_{LexP}$ rent-one$]$ $[_{LexP}$ very-expensive$]]]$ | (video) (rent) (very expensive) | Yes |

## 9.4    OT analysis

Now that we have examined a representative set of prosodic output forms in Xiamen Chinese, we attempt to derive these prosodic output structures using two types of mapping constraints, with and without subcategorization, by defining two OT systems (one using MATCH, the other using ALIGN/ WRAP). The OT analysis is conducted using SPOT (Bellik et al., 2015–2021) and OTWorkplace (Prince et al. 2007–2020). SPOT allows for automatic candidate generation, thus considering all the possible prosodic parses of each node in syntactic trees, including terminal lexical items and non-terminal syntactic phrases. SPOT assists in the definition of GEN and CON. GEN specifies parameters for the generation of input syntactic trees, and defines output parameters to constrain the set of prosodic output forms. Input syntactic trees for each structure (32) were built using SPOT's manual tree builder. Output parameters constrain the possible outputs of GEN to non-recursive, exhaustively parsed prosodic structures. This is an assumption of expository ease, capturing the same functional behavior as having a high-ranking NONRECURSIVITY constraint; for the purpose of studying the interaction of MATCH with Strict Layering, and of subcategorized mapping constraints with non-recursive structures, we follow previous analyses (summarized in Zhang 2019) in assuming non-recursive prosodic structure in Xiamen Chinese.

After SPOT produces a violation tableau, we feed it into OTWorkplace to calculate a factorial typology which predicts all the possible languages generated by the different rankings of constraints for the system under consideration. OTWorkplace provides a useful tool for constraint rankings and factorial typology. This way, a complete factorial typology and constraint rankings on all the possible candidates can be obtained, thus providing a comprehensive and rigorous OT investigation of the syntax–prosody mapping in Xiamen Chinese.

Since the purpose of this chapter is to compare the predictive powers of Match Theory and Align/Wrap Theory, and their interactions with strictly layered structures, we run two SPOT analyses separately: one analysis only using Match Theory and one only Align/Wrap Theory. To preview our results, we find that either theory of mapping can explain the distribution of TGs in Xiamen Chinese—if a mapping constraint subcategorized to the non-minimal LexP is included in CON. Omitting the subcategorized mapping constraint eliminates the Xiamen Chinese pattern from the typology. In these strictly layered systems, the general MATCH constraint favors prosodic structures that completely fail to reflect the syntactic constituency of the input; we find that subcategorizing MATCH to the non-minimal phrase improves the correspondence of syntactic and prosodic constituency despite the strictly layered candidate set.

We first present the GEN specifications shared by both systems, then the results of the MATCH and ALIGN systems.


### 9.4.1   GEN inputs (both systems)

The following specifications for GEN will be shared by both the MATCH system and the ALIGN/WRAP systems. The syntactic inputs for each system are a representative set of the structures demonstrating different TG patterns in Xiamen Chinese, as seen in §9.3. The syntactic inputs for both systems are provided in (32). We include the CP layer only where necessary to ensure that the syntactic tree is properly rooted (a, c, i), or where additional phonologically overt material is added at the CP level (h, j). In the *Input to SPOT* column, all square brackets [ ] represent lexical XP boundaries, and curly braces { } represent CP boundaries. Recall that we assume the LCC constrains the prosody's view of the syntax, such that functional projections are invisible to the mapping constraints. For this reason, the remainder of the chapter does not represent any FP boundaries at all, and the term XP will be used to refer exclusively to the XPs that are visible to prosody under the LCC, that is, lexical XPs.

(32)    Syntactic inputs for both systems

|  | **Syntax with FPs** | **Input to SPOT (omitting all FPs)** |
|---|---|---|
| a. AP w Arg. | $[_{FP} [_{LexP}$ sesame-seed] $[_{LexP}$ big]] | {[sesame-seed][big]} |
| b. AP w Adj. | $[_{LexP} [_{LexP}$ sesame-seed] $[_{LexP}$ big]] | [[sesame-seed][big]] |
| c. TP adj. | $[_{FP} [_{LexP}$ probably] $[_{LexP}$ go]] | {[probably][go]} |
| d. VP adj. | $[_{LexP} [_{LexP}$ already][$_{LexP}$ go]] | [[already][go]] |
| e. Ditrans. 1 | $[_{LexP} [_{LexP}$ he-that-book] $[_{LexP}$ give $[_{LexP}$ to-schoolmate]]] | [[book][give [to-schoolmate]]] |
| f. Ditrans. 2 | $[_{LexP} [_{LexP}$ he-to-schoolmate] $[_{LexP}$ introduce $[_{LexP}$ a-girlfriend]]] | [[to-schoolmate][introduce [girlfriend]]] |
| g. Base 1 | $[_{LexP} [_{LexP}$ rent-one $[_{LexP}$ video-game]] $[_{LexP}$ to-watch]] | [[rent [video]][to-watch]] |
| h. Topic 1 | $[_{CP} [_{LexP}$ video-game] $[_{LexP} [_{LexP}$ rent-one] $[_{LexP}$ to-watch]] ] | { [video][[rent][to-watch]]} |
| i. Base 2 | $[_{FP} [_{LexP}$ rent-one $[_{LexP}$ video-game]] $[_{LexP}$ very-expensive]] | {[rent [video]] [expensive]} |
| j. Topic 2 | $[_{CP} [_{LexP}$ video-game] $[_{FP} [_{LexP}$ rent-one] $[_{LexP}$ very-expensive]]] | {[video] [rent][expensive]} |

### 9.4.2   GEN *outputs (both systems)*

The set of prosodic output candidates for both systems is defined in (33). All prosodic output structures are required to be rooted in $\iota$, for the sake of ensuring that they are all valid trees, and are non-recursive. As discussed above, we enforce Strict Layering on GEN (33), in order to investigate the predictions of MATCH when all candidates are non-recursive.

(33)   $\textsc{Gen}(s) =$ all prosodic trees $p$ such that
   a.   $p$ is rooted in an intonational phrase ($\iota$).
   b.   $p$'s terminals are all prosodic words.
   c.   Every terminal $X^0$ in $s$ is mapped to a prosodic word $\omega$ in $p$, preserving linear order.
   d.   All non-root, non-terminals in $p$ are phonological phrases $\varphi$.
   e.   EXHAUSTIVITY and NONRECURSIVITY:
        Every child of $\iota$ is a $\varphi$, and every child of a $\varphi$ is an $\omega$

The results here concerning the behavior of MATCH when recursive candidates are excluded from GEN ($=$ a non-recursive system) can be extended to a similar system where GEN includes recursive structures ($=$ A RECURSIVE SYSTEM), while NONRECURSIVITY and EXHAUSTIVITY (or EQUALSISTERS; Myrberg 2013) are included in CON as violable constraints. In the languages of a recursive system where the constraints NONRECURSIVITY and EXHAUSTIVITY are undominated, MATCH will have the same effects as it does in this non-recursive system. For presentational simplicity, however, we exclude recursive candidates altogether here.

### 9.4.3   MATCH analysis

We define a system XC.Match in (34). In addition to MATCH(XP), we also include MATCHNONMIN(XP), because, as noted above, Xiamen Chinese prioritizes the matching of non-minimal XPs over the matching of minimal XPs where conflicts arise. No prosodic well-formedness constraints are included, because the principles of Non-Recursivity and Exhaustivity are already enforced on GEN. For the sake of creating a maximally simple system, we did not include any prosody-to-syntax mapping constraints; in any case, none of the desired optima in Xiamen Chinese violate MATCH($\varphi$, LexP).

(34)   XC.Match
   a.   GEN: All syntactic trees listed in (32) and all prosodic trees as defined in (33)
   b.   CON:
        i.   MATCH(XP) $=$ MATCH: Assign one violation for every lexical XP in the syntactic tree such that there is no node of the corresponding prosodic category $\varphi$ in the prosodic tree that dominates the same set of terminals. (Adapted from Selkirk 2011 and Elfner 2012)
        ii.  MATCH(XP$^{[\text{-min}]}$) $=$ MATCHNONMIN: Assign one violation for every non-minimal lexical XP in the syntactic tree for which there is

no φ in the prosodic tree that dominates all and only the same terminals. A lexical XP is non-minimal iff it dominates at least one lexical XP.

(Adapted from Ito and Mester 2009)

The typology for XC.Match, shown in (35), contains two languages. Grey backgrounds indicate phrasings that are incompatible with Xiamen Chinese. In Language 1, MATCHNONMIN outranks MATCH, and all optima are compatible with the observed TGs in Xiamen Chinese. In Language 2, the general MATCH constraint outranks MATCHNONMIN, and some optima are incompatible with Xiamen Chinese.

(35)     Typology of XC.Match.

| Inputs | L.1 | L.2 |
|---|---|---|
| [[already] [go]] | {(already go)} | {(already) (go)} |
| {[probably] [go]} | {(probably) (go)} | {(probably) (go)} |
| [[book] [give [to-schoolmate]]] | {(book) (give to-schoolmate)} | {(book) (give to-schoolmate)} |
| [[to-schoolmate] [introduce [girlfriend]]] | {(to-schoolmate) (introduce girlfriend)} | {(to-schoolmate) (introduce girlfriend)} |
| {[[rent [video]] [to-watch]]} | {(rent video) (to-watch)} | {(rent video) (to-watch)} |
| {[video] [[rent] [to-watch]]} | {(video) (rent to-watch)} | {(video) (rent) (to-watch)} |
| {[sesame] [big]} | {(sesame) (big)} | {(sesame) (big)} |
| [[sesame] [big]] | {(sesame big)} | {(sesame) (big)} |
| {[rent [video]] [expensive]} | {(rent video) (expensive)} | {(rent video) (expensive)} |
| {[video] [rent] [expensive]} | {(video) (rent) (expensive)} | {(video) (rent) (expensive)} |

(36)     Constraint rankings in XC.Match
     a.    L.1: MATCHNONMIN ≫ MATCH
     b.    L.2: MATCH ≫ MATCHNONMIN

For both languages of XC.Match, syntactic inputs like *{[probably][go]}* that do not contain any recursive LexP structure are perfectly matched in the output with prosodic structures like *{(probably)(go)}*. In addition, both languages map head-complement substructures like *[rent [video]]* to a flattened prosody of the form *(rent video)*. This is because the general MATCH cannot distinguish between the two possible phrasings—*(rent video)* and *(rent) (video)*—because each of them fails to map a single XP, and therefore tie on MATCH (see Tarlov, Chapter 3, for discussion of this pattern in another non-recursive MATCH system). Meanwhile, MATCHNONMIN prefers to match the higher, non-minimal XP, and makes the decision in both languages (37).

(37)     Parsing of head-complement structures (both L.1 and L.2 in
         XC.Match)

| $[_{-min}$ rent $[_{+min}$ video]] | Match | MatchNonMin |
|---|---|---|
| $\rightarrow$  i. (rent video) | 1 | 0 |
| ii. (rent)(video) | 1 | 1 |

The crucial difference between the two languages is their treatment of adjunction substructures of the form $[[X^0][X^0]]$. In L.2, these are always mapped to $(\omega)(\omega)$, contrary to the actual pattern in Xiamen Chinese, where the high segment of a lexical adjunction structure is always matched. This is because matching the two minimal XPs but not the maximal XP violates Match only once, whereas matching the higher XP but not the two lower XPs violates Match twice, as shown in (38) (See the discussion of the system Match.NR in Tarlov, Chapter 3). All prosodic trees are rooted in an $\iota$, but $\{$ $\}$ are omitted from the bracketed representations in (38) and the following tableaux for visual simplicity. Throughout this chapter, harmonically bounded outputs are omitted from tableaux unless specifically noted; OTWorkplace was used to determine which candidates are possible optima under some ranking, and which are harmonically bounded and never win under any ranking. Shading in a cell indicates that the winner has already been decided by higher-ranked constraints (shown to the left of lower-ranked constraints), so that the violations in that cell are not irrelevant to the selection of the optimum.

(38)     Match prefers to map minimal XPs (L.2 in XC.Match)

a.

| $[_{-min} [_{+min}$ already]$[_{+min}$ go]] | Match | MatchNonMin |
|---|---|---|
| i. (already go) | 2 | 0 |
| $\rightarrow$  ii. (already)(go) | 1 | 1 |

b.

| $[_{+min}$ video] $[_{-min} [_{+min}$ rent] $[_{+min}$ to-watch]] | Match | MatchNonMin |
|---|---|---|
| i. (video)(rent to-watch) | 2 | 0 |
| $\rightarrow$  ii. (video)(rent)(to-watch) | 1 | 1 |

In L.1, by contrast, the higher ranking of MatchNonMin allows the intended mapping $[[X^0][X^0]] \rightarrow (\omega\ \omega)$, combining adjuncts with their hosts into a single TG/$\varphi$, as shown in (39). This derives the observed prosodic distinction between adjuncts (flattened into one TG) and arguments (separated from the head by a TG boundary) in Xiamen Chinese, as well as the distinctions between adjuncts adjoined to a lexical phrase (flattened into one TG) and those adjoined to a functional phrase (separated from their host by a TG boundary).

(39)      MATCHNONMIN does not map minimal XPs (L.1 in XC.Match)

a.

| $[_{-min} [_{+min}$ already$][_{+min}$ go$]]$ | MATCHNONMIN | MATCH |
|---|---|---|
| → i. (already go) | 0 | 2 |
| ii. (already)(go) | 1 | 1 |

b.

| $[_{+min}$ video$] [_{-min} [_{+min}$ rent$] [_{+min}$ to-watch$]]$ | MATCHNONMIN | MATCH |
|---|---|---|
| → i. (video)(rent to-watch) | 0 | 2 |
| ii. (video)(rent)(to-watch) | 1 | 1 |

The reason that MATCH drives non-isomorphisms in Strict Layering systems like this one is that when recursive candidates are unavailable, MATCH favors matching the more numerous minimal XPs over matching non-minimal XPs, which are necessarily outnumbered. When the input contains a non-minimal XP that is not co-extensive with the entire expression, such as the VP *[[rent][to-watch]]* in (38b), then mapping the minimal XPs to φs (candidate ii) produces a prosody that contains no constituent of any category that has the same terminal string as the non-minimal XP in the syntax. The alternative parse (candidate i), which maps the non-minimal XP (but not the minimal XPs) to a φ, contains a prosodic constituent of some category that corresponds to every syntactic constituent. This is because the minimal XPs here are also syntactic / prosodic words ($X^0$s/ωs), so they do have ω correspondents even when they lack φ correspondents. In this sense, MATCH prefers a worse mismatch than MATCHNONMIN, when recursive structures are excluded from the candidate set.

While MATCHNONMIN would operate as a special case of the general MATCH in a system where recursive prosodic candidates were included, in this strictly layered system, the two constraints conflict with each other. By that definition, MATCHNONMIN is driving Anti-Match effects here, in contrast to its behavior in Van Handel et al. (Chapter 5), where recursion is permitted. Were MATCHNONMIN operating as a special case of MATCH in this system as it does in Chapter 5, this typology would contain only one language, rather than two, since there would be no conflict between the two constraints in the system.

### 9.4.3.1  Xiamen Chinese in XC.Match

Language 1 of XC.Match is compatible with Xiamen Chinese, as already noted. In this language, MATCHNONMIN outranks MATCH, with the result that the matching of non-minimal XPs is prioritized over matching of minimal XPs. The tableau in (40) gives the crucial winner-loser pairs for all inputs where the two languages differ (a-c) and two where both languages have the same winner (d, e).

(40)    Winner-Loser pairs in XC.Match

| Input | Winner | Loser | MATCH NONMIN | MATCH |
|---|---|---|---|---|
| a. [[already] [go]] | {(already go)} | {(already) (go)} | W | L |
| b. {[video] [[rent] [to-watch]]} | {(video) (rent to-watch)} | {(video) (rent) (to-watch)} | W | L |
| c. [[sesame] [big]] | {(sesame big)} | {(sesame) (big)} | W | L |
| d. {[[book] [gave [to-schoolmate]]]} | {(book) (gave to-schoolmate)} | {(book gave to-schoolmate)} |  | W |
| e. {[[rent [video]] [to-watch]]} | {(rent video) (to-watch)} | {(rent video to-watch)} |  | W |

For *[[book] [gave [schoolmate]]]* (d), the desired optimum is one that maps the XP containing *book* and the XP containing *gave schoolmate* to separate phonological phrases. This mapping correctly captures the TGs for this structure. This desired optimum violates MATCHNONMIN once, because the maximal XP that incorporates *book* and *gave to schoolmate* is not mapped to a φ; however, the loser also violates MATCHNONMIN, because it fails to match the maximal XP containing all three words. The winner and loser therefore tie on MATCHNONMIN, and the general MATCH decides between them instead. The winning output has only one violation of MATCH compared to the loser *(book gave schoolmate)* which violates MATCH twice. Similar reasoning obtains for *[[rent [video]][to-watch]]* in (e), which is the mirror image of (d).

### 9.4.4  ALIGN/WRAP analysis

We now turn to the Align Theory analysis, defining the system XC.Align in (41). This system has the same candidate set as XC.Match in the previous subsection, but employs ALIGN and WRAP constraints instead of MATCH constraints.

(41)    XP.Align
  a.    GEN: All syntactic trees listed in (32) and all prosodic trees as
        defined in (33)
  b.    CON:
        i.    WRAP(XP) = WRAP:
              Assign one violation for every XP in the syntactic tree
              that does not have a corresponding $\varphi$ in the prosodic tree,
              where $\varphi$ contains all the terminals dominated by XP.
              (Truckenbrodt 1995, 1999)
        ii.   ALIGN-LEFT(XP) = ALIGN-L:
              Assign one violation for every XP in the syntactic tree whose
              left edge is not aligned with the left edge of $\varphi$ in the prosodic
              tree.
              (Selkirk 1986, 1996; McCarthy and Prince 1993; Truckenbrodt
                                                                      1995, 1999)
        iii.  ALIGN-RIGHT(XP) = ALIGN-R:
              Assign one violation for every XP in the syntactic tree whose
              right edge is not aligned with the right edge of $\varphi$ in the
              prosodic tree.
              (Selkirk 1986, 1996; McCarthy and Prince 1993; Truckenbrodt
                                                                      1995, 1999)
        iv.   ALIGN-LEFT(XP$^{[-min]}$) = ALIGN-L$^{[-min]}$:
              Assign one violation for every XP[–min] in the syntactic tree
              whose left edge is not aligned with the left edge of $\varphi$ in the
              prosodic tree.
        v.    ALIGN-RIGHT(XP[–min]) = ALIGN-R$^{[-min]}$:
              Assign one violation for every XP[–min] in the syntactic tree
              whose right edge is not aligned with the right edge of $\varphi$ in the
              prosodic tree.

The typology for XC.Align contains six languages, shown in (42). The corresponding Hasse diagrams are given in (43). L.4 is compatible with Xiamen
Chinese. In this language, both ALIGNNONMIN constraints are ranked over
WRAP, which is ranked over the two general ALIGN constraints. Among the
other five languages, L.1–3 have too little structure in one or more outputs,
because WRAP dominates one or both of the ALIGNNONMIN constraints.
WRAP always prefers to match the maximal XP if there is one, at the expense of matching the more numerous non-maximal XPs. For example,
WRAP prefers to map ditransitives such as *[[book] [give [to-schoolmate]]]* to
a flat structure *(book give to-schoolmate)*, which wraps every XP in a $\varphi$ at
the expense of failing to align the right edge of *[book]* and the left edges of
*[give...]* and *[to-schoolmate]* to $\varphi$ edges.

In contrast to L.1–3, L.5–6 have too much structure compared to Xiamen Chinese. Whenever an adjunction substructure *[[a][b]]* occurs, L.5–6 both consistently map it to *(a)(b)*, because ALIGN-L or ALIGN-R dominates WRAP. Like MATCHNONMIN, WRAP would be satisfied by the parse *[[a][b]] → (a b)*. This parse fails to align the internal XP edges between $a$ and $b$ to φ edges, however, so it violates both ALIGN-L and ALIGN-R. The difference between L.5 and L.6 is that L.5 handles head-complement structures like *[rent [video]]* by flattening to, e.g., *(rent video)* (schematically: *[a [b]] → (a b)*), because WRAP ≫ ALIGN-L in L.5. Since complements occur to the right of the head in XC, the flattened structure matches all right edges but fails to match the left edge of the complement. In L.6, meanwhile, ALIGN-L dominates WRAP, so that [a [b]] cannot be flattened and instead is hyperarticulated like an adjunction substructure: *[rent [video]] → (rent)(video)*.

(42)    Typology of XC.Align

| Inputs | L.1 | L.2 | L.3 | L.4 | L.5 | L.6 |
|---|---|---|---|---|---|---|
| [[already] [go]] | {(already go)} | {(already go)} | {(already go)} | {(already go)} | {(already) (go)} | {(already) (go)} |
| {[probably] [go]} | {(probably) (go)} | {(probably) (go)} | {(probably) (go)} | {(probably) (go)} | {(probably) (go)} | {(probably) (go)} |
| [[book] [give [to-schoolmate]]] | {(book give to-schoolmate)} | {(book give to-schoolmate)} | {(book) (give to-schoolmate)} | {(book) (give to-schoolmate)} | {(book) (give to-schoolmate)} | {(book) (give) (to-schoolmate)} |
| [[to-schoolmate] [introduce [girlfriend]]] | {(to-schoolmate introduce girlfriend)} | {(to-schoolmate introduce girlfriend)} | {(to-schoolmate) (introduce girlfriend)} | {(to-schoolmate) (introduce girlfriend)} | {(to-schoolmate) (introduce girlfriend)} | {(to-schoolmate) (introduce) (girlfriend)} |
| {[[rent [video]] [to-watch]]} | {(rent video to-watch)} | {(rent video) (to-watch)} | {(rent video to-watch)} | {(rent video) (to-watch)} | {(rent video) (to-watch)} | {(rent) (video) (to-watch)} |
| {[video] [[rent] [to-watch]]} | {(video) (rent to-watch)} | {(video) (rent to-watch)} | {(video) (rent to-watch)} | {(video) (rent to-watch)} | {(video) (rent) (to-watch)} | {(video) (rent) (to-watch)} |
| {[sesame] [big]} | {(sesame) (big)} | {(sesame) (big)} | {(sesame) (big)} | {(sesame) (big)} | {(sesame) (big)} | {(sesame) (big)} |
| [[sesame] [big]] | {(sesame big)} | {(sesame big)} | {(sesame big)} | {(sesame big)} | {(sesame) (big)} | {(sesame) (big)} |
| {[rent [video]] [expensive]} | {(rent video) (expensive)} | {(rent video) (expensive)} | {(rent video) (expensive)} | {(rent video) (expensive)} | {(rent video) (expensive)} | {(rent) (video) (expensive)} |
| {[video] [rent] [expensive]} | {(video) (rent) (expensive)} | {(video) (rent) (expensive)} | {(video) (rent) (expensive)} | {(video) (rent) (expensive)} | {(video) (rent) (expensive)} | {(video) (rent) (expensive)} |

(43)      Grammars of XC.Align

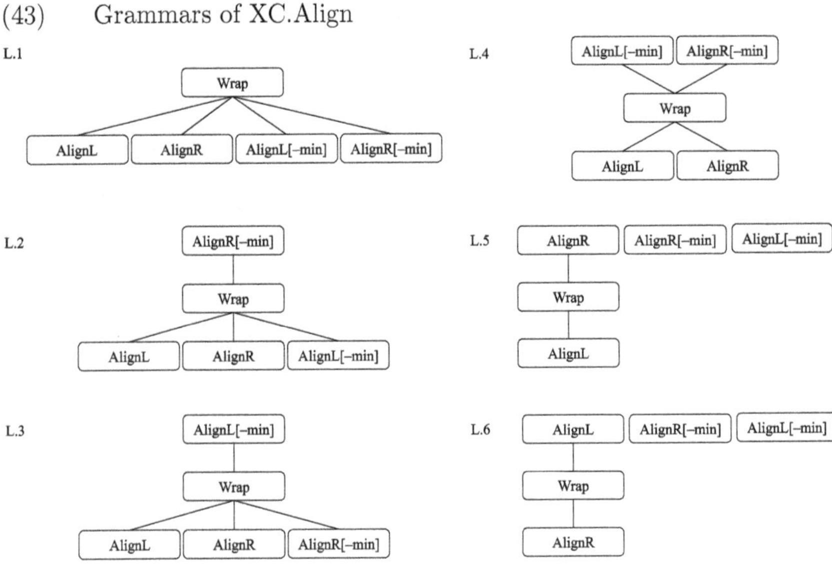

L.4 is the happy medium between excessive flattening (L.1–L.3) and excessive structure building (L.5–L.6). Its support is shown in (44). In this language, minimal XPs can be flattened, as in the mapping *[[already][go]]* → *(already go)*, due to WRAP's dominance over ALIGN-L and ALIGN-R. Our winner *(already go)* violates ALIGN-R once because *already]* in the input syntactic tree is not aligned with the right edge of a φ. But it satisfies WRAP because both *already* and *go* are enclosed within a bigger φ. So, WRAP should dominate ALIGN-R in order to give us the correct optimal output form for *[[already] [go]]*. Meanwhile, non-minimal XPs are protected by ALIGN-L[−min] and ALIGN-R[−min]. For *[[book] [gave [to-schoolmate]]]*, the optimal output *(book)(gave to-schoolmate)* violates WRAP but satisfies ALIGN-R and ALIGN-R[−min]. This mapping violates WRAP because the highest XP that contains both *book* and *gave schoolmate* is not encapsulated in any φ. It satisfies ALIGN-R and ALIGN-R[−min] because both *book* and *gave schoolmate* are each aligned to the right edge of a φ. So, for the correct output form *(book) (gave to-schoolmate)* to win, we need ALIGN-R or ALIGN-R[−min] to dominate WRAP. We have already established that WRAP dominates ALIGN-R, thus the more specific ALIGN-R[−min] must be the constraint to dominate WRAP, and cause the completely flat *(book give to-schoolmate)* to lose to the partially flat *(book)(give to-schoolmate)*.

(44)     Support for L.4 of XC.Align

| Input | Winner | Loser | ALIGN-L$^{[-min]}$ | ALIGN-R$^{[-min]}$ | WRAP | ALIGN-L | ALIGN-R |
|---|---|---|---|---|---|---|---|
| [[book] [give [to-schoolmate]]] | {(book) (give to-schoolmate)} | {(book give to-schoolmate)} | W | | L | W | W |
| {[[rent [video]] [to-watch]]} | {(rent video) (to-watch)} | {(rent video to-watch)} | | W | L | W | W |
| [[already] [go]] | {(already go)} | {(already) (go)} | | | W | L | L |

## 9.5   Discussion

In this chapter, we interpreted the tone group (TG) in Xiamen Chinese as corresponding to a minimal φ. According to this phrasing diagnostic, adjunction structures in Xiamen Chinese typically behave differently from arguments; adjuncts usually cannot form their own independent TGs apart from their hosts, whereas arguments, particularly subjects, often occur in a separate TG from the syntactic head, as noted in previous analyses (Truckenbrodt 1995, 1999; Selkirk 2011). This suggests that the highest segment of the adjunction structure must be visible to the prosodic phrasing rules, *contra* previous suggestions by Selkirk (2011) following Truckenbrodt (1995, 1999), but in accordance with Bellik and Kalivoda (2016)'s findings for Kinyambo. It is possible that the visibility of the highest segment of an adjunction structure is a language-specific parameter. More research is needed to determine whether apparent variation on this point can be fully attributed to differences in constraint ranking.

While adjuncts in the expressions $[_{AP} [_{NP}$ *sesame-seed*$] [_{AP}$ *big*$]]$ and $[_{VP} [_{AdvP}$ *already*$][_{VP}$ *go*$]]$ phrase with their hosts in a minimal TG, the adverb *probably* phrases separately from its host in $[_{TP} [_{AdvP}$ *probably*$][_{VP}$ *go*$]]$. We account for this distinction by following previous analysts in adopting the Lexical Category Condition. Under the LCC, syntax–prosody mapping constraints do not see the TP and other functional projections, so that there is no pressure to phrase *probably* and *go* together. The mapping constraints do see the higher segments of the VP and AP, creating pressure to match those in the phrasing.

In addition to lexical projections being more likely to be mapped to prosodic constituents than functional projections in Xiamen Chinese, non-minimal LexPs were more likely to be matched than minimal LexPs. This observation motivated the inclusion of mapping constraints subcategorized to the non-minimal level in our OT systems. Furthermore, where three levels of nested LexPs occurred, the intermediate level [–min, –max] was mapped in preference to the maximal or minimal levels. This was found to fall out from the behavior of general, un-subcategorized MATCH in a strictly layered system; no constraint specifically targeted this pattern.

A major contribution of this chapter is to provide a systematic OT analysis of the Xiamen Chinese TG data. Several syntactic accounts using c-command/m-command or even lexical government have been proposed to account for this old question of tone group formation in Xiamen Chinese (Lin 1994; Zhang 2019; Chen 1987, 1992). But they all explain the adjunct-argument distinction using an elsewhere condition. For instance, Zhang proposes that every right edge of every XP is marked with #, except where XP is an adjunct m-commanding either its head or the head of XP on the right except Infl (Zhang 2019). Non-OT analyses not only refer to the syntactic category XP, but also refer to syntactic relations like c-command or lexical government. In comparison, an OT analysis only needs MATCH or ALIGN/WRAP to ensure the correspondence between syntactic phrases and $\varphi$s, and the Lexical Category Condition.

We took a representative set of syntactic structures (adjuncts to the VP, TP, and AP; arguments in the TP, VP and AP; and topicalized sentences), that demonstrated different TG possibilities, and used these patterns to test the typological predictions of two OT systems: a MATCH system, and an ALIGN/WRAP system. The definition and analysis of each system was carried out using SPOT and OTWorkplace. The MATCH system demonstrated that MATCH constraints (general MATCH and non-minimal MATCH) can, in conjunction with a strictly layered candidate set, derive the desired optima for these constructions, as shown in (35). The Xiamen Chinese pattern appears in the language where the highest ranked constraint is the subcategory-sensitive constraint MATCHNONMIN, which penalizes prosodic outputs that have not mapped syntactic XPs that dominate some other XP to a $\varphi$. Similarly, in the ALIGN system, the Xiamen Chinese phrasing pattern appeared in the language where both ALIGNLEFTNONMIN and ALIGNRIGHTNONMIN dominated WRAP, which in turn dominated the general ALIGN constraints, as shown in (42) and (43).

Subcategorized mapping constraints were crucial in both the ALIGN and MATCH analyses. Subcategorization creates a large family of MATCH or ALIGN constraints, which demand matches on different prosodic levels. For Xiamen Chinese, MATCH(XP[–min]) only demands that non-minimal XPs be mapped to a $\varphi$, and ignores mismatches of minimal XPs. The possibility of having crucially ranked mapping constraints for different levels of phrasing greatly expands the number of structures that the mapping constraints can derive without the intervention of prosodic well-formedness constraints. However, as discussed in Van Handel et al. (Chapter 5), it may be theoretically desirable to restrict this range of (anti-)match effects. The contribution of this chapter to this discussion is to show that subcategorized mapping constraints can still be useful in a system where prosody is non-recursive. In fact, they were found to be more useful than the general mapping constraints, which by themselves favor only mapping minimal XPs to φs, just as they did in the non-recursive systems in Chapter 3.

While subcategorized MATCH constraints have been employed in several previous analyses (Ishihara 2014; Ito and Mester 2013, 2020; Kalivoda 2018; Bellik et al. 2022), subcategorization is not part of standard Align/Wrap Theory. One interesting finding about the subcategorized ALIGN constraints is that, unlike the subcategorized MATCHNONMIN which conflicted with general MATCH in the non-recursive system here, ALIGNLEFTNONMIN functioned as a special case of ALIGN-LEFT, and ALIGNRIGHTNONMIN likewise functioned as a special case of ALIGN-RIGHT. How generalizable this finding is to other systems is left for future research.

If subcategorized ALIGN constraints are found to be theoretically undesirable in later work, an alternative OT analysis of Xiamen Chinese could be to introduce another constraint that dominates WRAP, such as BINMAX, defined in (45).

(45)    BINMAX(branches): Assign one violation for every φ in the prosodic tree that has more than two children.

For our two-word inputs, no parse can violate BINMAX because no parse in our candidate set can contain a node with more than two children. BINMAX has no power to decide between the winning and losing parses of these two-word inputs. However, for a three-word input *[[book] [gave [schoolmate]]]*, BINMAX penalizes the flat candidate *(book gave schoolmate)* because the one and only φ in the prosodic output has three ωs as its immediate descendants. Though WRAP favors the loser for the three-word input, when it is dominated by a higher constraint BINMAX, we achieve the correct winner which contains two φs.

(46)     Winner-Loser pairs using Wrap/Align theory with BinMax.

| Input | Winner | Loser | Bin Max | Wrap | Align-R | Align-L |
|---|---|---|---|---|---|---|
| [[already] [go]] | {(already go)} | {(already) (go)} | | W | L | L |
| [[book] [gave [to-schoolmate]]] | {(book) (gave to-schoolmate)} | {(book gave schoolmate)} | W | L | W | L |
| [[to-schoolmate] [introduce [girlfriend]]] | {(to-schoolmate) (introduce girlfriend)} | {(schoolmate introduce girlfriend)} | W | L | W | L |
| {[[rent [videogame]] [to-watch]]} | {(rent videogame) (to-watch)} | {(rent videogame watch)} | W | L | W | L |

Examples like (8), however, in which an entire sentence containing at least
six lexical terminals is flattened into a single tone group, may pose a problem
for the binarity-based analysis.[1] Furthermore, Chen (1987, 140–141) states
that 'in normal everyday speech in Xiamen Chinese, TS [tone sandhi] is
largely independent of such phonological conditions as syllable count," which
seems to indicate that length considerations do not play an important role
in this language. We leave for future work the calculation and analysis of the
typology for this alternative length-sensitive system, as well as a comparison
of the relative merits of introducing subcategorized mapping constraints
compared to relying on standard prosodic well-formedness constraints.

Another possible direction for future work on Xiamen Chinese prosody is
a reanalysis of the TG as a possibly recursive $\varphi$. If the preservation of the
base tone at the right edge of the TG signals the right edge of any $\varphi$, not
necessarily a minimal $\varphi$, then the word following the end of a TG might
not stand at the left edge of a new TG at all, and we have no diagnostic for
the left edge of the $\varphi$. That is, *book # gave schoolmate #* could represent
a recursive phrasing like *((book) gave (schoolmate))* or even the isomorphic
*((book) (gave (schoolmate)))*. This reinterpreted phrasing diagnostic would
drastically alter the possible $\varphi$ structures that the empirical TG evidence
represents. Of course, in this chapter, we have assumed that the TG does
represent a minimal $\varphi$, and therefore enforced Strict Layering on the
candidate sets, for the theoretical purpose of examining the functioning
of Match, Align, and their subcategorized versions in two strictly layered

---

[1] Thanks to Nick Kalivoda for this point.

systems. This is a theoretical choice, rather than an empirically motivated one. Future work might look for other parameters, such as the interval time between $\varphi$s, to empirically pinpoint the $\varphi$'s left edge.

## References

Bellik, Jennifer, Bellik, Ozan, and Kalivoda, Nick (2015–2021). Syntax-Prosody in Optimality Theory (SPOT). Javascript application. http://spot.sites.ucsc.edu. Codebase at https://github.com/syntax-prosody-ot.

Bellik, Jennifer, Ito, Junko, Kalivoda, Nick and Mester, Armin (2022). Matching and alignment. In Haruo Kubozono, Junko Ito, and Armin Mester (eds.) *Prosody and Prosodic Interfaces* 457–481. Oxford University Press.

Bellik, Jennifer and Kalivoda, Nick (2016). Adjunction and branchingness effects in syntax-prosody mapping. In Gunnar Ólafur Hansson, Ashley Farris-Trimble, Kevin McMullin, and Douglas Pulleyblank (eds.) *Supplemental Proceedings of the 2015 Annual Meeting on Phonology*, Linguistic Society of America. http://doi.org/10.3765/amp.v3i0.3690

Chao, Yuen Ren (1930). A system of tone-letters. *Le Maître Phonétique* 45: 24–27.

Chen, Matthew (1987). The syntax of Xiamen tone sandhi. *Phonology Yearbook* 4: 109–149.

Chen, Matthew (1992). *Argument vs. adjunct: Xiamen tone sandhi revisited.* Ms., University of California, San Diego.

Chomsky, Noam (1981). *Lectures on Government and Binding.* Dodrecht: Foris Publications.

Elfner, Emily (2012). *Syntax-prosody interactions in Irish.* PhD dissertation, University of Massachusetts Amherst.

Elfner, Emily (2015). Recursion in prosodic phrasing: evidence from Connemara Irish. *Natural Language and Linguistic Theory* 33: 1169–1208.

Elordieta, Gorka and Selkirk, Elisabeth (2022). Unaccentedness and the formation of prosodic structure in Leikeitio Basque. In Haruo Kubozono, Junko Ito, and Armin Mester (eds.) *Prosody and Prosodic Interfaces* 374–420. Oxford University Press.

Ishihara, Shinichiro (2014). Match Theory and the recursivity problem. In *Proceedings of FAJL 7: Formal Approaches to Japanese Linguistics*, ed. Shigeto Kawahara and Mika Igarashi, 69–88.

Ito, Junko and Mester, Armin (1992/2003). Weak layering and word binarity. In Tekeru Honma, Masao Okazaki, Toshiyuki Tabata, Shin-ichi Tanaka (eds.) *A New Century of Phonology and Phonological Theory: A Festschrift for Professor Shosuke Haraguchi on the Occasion of His Sixtieth Birthday* 26–65. Tokyo: Kaitakusha.

Ito, Junko and Mester, Armin (2007). Prosodic adjunction in Japanese compounds. Prosodic adjunction in Japanese compounds. In Yoichi Miyamoto and Masao Ochi (eds.) *MIT Working Papers in Linguistics*

*55: Proceedings of Formal Approaches to Japanese Linguistics 4* 97–111. Cambridge, MA.

Ito, Junko and Mester, Armin (2009a). The extended prosodic word. In Janet Grijzenhout and Barış Kabak (eds.), *Phonological Domains: Universals and Deviations* 135–194. Berlin: Mouton de Gruyter.

Ito, Junko and Mester, Armin (2009b). The onset of the prosodic word. In Steve Parker (ed.), *Phonological Argumentation: Essays on Evidence and Motivation* 227–260. London: Equinox.

Ito, Junko and Mester, Armin (2013). Prosodic subcategories in Japanese. *Lingua* 124: 20–40.

Ito, Junko and Mester, Armin (2020). Match theory and prosodic wellformedness constraints. In Hongming Zhang and Youyong Qian (eds.) *Prosodic Studies: Challenges and Prospects*. London and New York: Routledge, 252–274.

Kalivoda, Nick (2018). *Syntax-Prosody Mismatches in Optimality Theory*. PhD dissertation, University of California, Santa Cruz.

Larson, Richard K. (1988). On the double object construction. *Linguistic Inquiry* 19(3): 335–391.

Lin, Jo-wang (1994). Lexical government and tone group formation in Xiamen Chinese. *Phonology* 11(2): 237–275.

McCarthy, John J. and Prince, Alan (1993). Generalized alignment. In Geert Booij and Jaap van Marle (eds.) *Yearbook of Morphology* 79–153. Dordrecht: Kluwer.

Myrberg, Sara (2013). Sisterhood in prosodic branching. *Phonology* 30: 73–124.

Prince, Alan and Smolensky, Paul (1993/2004). *Optimality Theory: Constraint Interaction in Generative Grammar*. Malden, MA: Blackwell Publishing.

Prince, Alan, Merchant, Nazarré, and Tesar, Bruce (2007–2020). OTWorkplace. https://sites.google.com/site/otworkplace/

Selkirk, Elisabeth (1984). *Phonology and Syntax: the Relation between Sound and Structure*. Cambridge, MA: MIT Press.

Selkirk, Elisabeth (1986). On Derived Domains in Sentence Phonology. *Phonology Yearbook* 3: 371–405.

Selkirk, Elisabeth (1996). The prosodic structure of function words. In James L. Morgan and Katherine Demuth (eds.), *Signal to Syntax: Bootstrapping from speech to grammar in early acquisition*, 187– 213. Mahwah, NJ: Erlbaum.

Selkirk, Elisabeth (2000). The interaction of constraints on prosodic phrasing. In Merle Horne (ed.) *Prosody: Theory and Experiment. Studies Presented to Gösta Bruce* 231–261. Dordrecht: Kluwer.

Selkirk, Elisabeth (2011). The syntax-phonology interface. In John Goldsmith, Jason Riggle, and Alan C. L. Yu (eds.) *The handbook of phonological theory* 435–484. Blackwell Publishing.

Selkirk, Elisabeth and Lee, Seunghun (2017). Syntactic constituency spell-out through Match constraints. Presentation at SPOT1 Workshop, University of California, Santa Cruz. Available at https://thi.ucsc.edu/wp-content/uploads/2017/10/Selkirk_SPOT_11_18_2017.pdf

Selkirk, Elisabeth and Shen, Tong (1990). Prosodic domains in Shanghai Chinese. In Sharon Inkelas and Draga Zec (eds.) *The Phonology-Syntax Connection* 313–337. Chicago: University of Chicago Press.

Truckenbrodt, Hubert (1995). *Phonological Phrases: Their Relation to Syntax, Focus, and Prominence.* PhD dissertation, Massachusetts Institute of Technology.

Truckenbrodt, Hubert. (1999). On the relation between syntactic phrases and phonological phrases. *Linguistic inquiry*, 30(2), 219–255.

Zhang, Hongming (2019). Prosodic studies of two Chinese dialects. In Hongming Zhang and Youyong Qian (eds.), *Prosodic Studies: Challenges and Prospects* 275–313. New York: Routledge.

## About the authors

*Yaqing Cao*

Ph.D. student, Department of Linguistics, UC Santa Cruz. Research interests: tone sandhi patterns in Chinese dialects including Xiamenese and Wenzhounese; wh-in-situ interrogatives, islands, and more general intervention structures in Mandarin. Recent presentations: 'Revisiting tone sandhi domain in Xiamen Chinese" *Annual Meeting on Phonology (AMP)*, Toronto, October 2021.

*Richard Bibbs*

Graduate research assistant for the SPOT project, Ph.D. student, Department of Linguistics, UC Santa Cruz. Research interests: phonetics, phonology, perception, and (sentence) processing, focusing on the behavior of laryngeals, especially in Chamorro (Austronesian, ISO: cha). Recent presentations: 'Perceptual factors license vocalic contrasts in Chamorro", *Annual Meeting on Phonology (AMP)*, Stony Brook, New York, October 2019.

*Jennifer Bellik*

Postdoctoral researcher and lecturer, Department of Linguistics, UC Santa Cruz. Research interests: syntax-prosody interface, Optimality Theory, Articulatory Phonology, and Turkish phonology. Recent publications: "An acoustic study of vowel intrusion in Turkish onset clusters", *Laboratory Phonology* 2018; "Automated tableau generation with SPOT" with N. Kalivoda, *Linguistics Vanguard* 2019; and 'The effect of speech style and deaccentuation on vowel intrusion in Turkish complex onsets", *Proceedings of ICPhS* 2019.

# Part IV

# Prosodic well-formedness constraints

# Chapter 10

# Size effects in prosody: Branch-counting, leaf-counting, and Uniformity

Jennifer Bellik and Nicholas Van Handel[*]

## 10.1 Introduction

In prosody, longer strings tend to be parsed into more constituents. For example, *abracadabra* is parsed into two feet *(abra)ca(dabra)*, but the shorter *shazam* only receives one foot, *sha(zam)*. Relatedly, longer or heavier elements may be parsed into a higher prosodic category than shorter or lighter ones. An example is the determiner *these* receiving a word stress, while the shorter determiner *a* remains unstressed. We refer to these phenomena as SIZE EFFECTS. Size effects are commonly captured using BINARITY constraints, which require a node to contain exactly two elements. The most well-known constraint on binarity is FOOTBIN (Prince 1980), which requires a foot to contain two syllables or moras. Other well-established constraints also address the binarity of prosodic words (Ito and Mester 1992/2003) and phonological phrases (Inkelas and Zec 1990, Elfner 2012). These constraints are some of the most commonly used prosodic well-formedness constraints in the study of syntax–prosody mapping.

Previous work (Mester 1994, Selkirk 2000, Ito and Mester 2007) has established the necessity of distinguishing two distinct kinds of BINARITY:

[*] Our thanks to Nick Kalivoda, a collaborator on earlier versions of this work, as well as to audiences at the 2019 International Conference on Phonetics and Phonology in Tokyo, the 2020 meeting of the Society for Typological Analysis, and season 4 of the Keio x ICU colloquium series. Thanks also to Junko Ito and Armin Mester for many helpful suggestions, and to reviewers Tor Håvard and Dan Brodkin whose comments also improved the clarity of the chapter.

minimal and maximal. MINIMAL BINARITY penalizes structures containing less than two elements. MAXIMAL BINARITY penalizes structures containing more than two elements. For example, the $\varphi$ in (1a) has a single word as its only daughter and violates minimal binarity, but satisfies maximal binarity because it does not have more than two words. The $\varphi$ in (1b) on the other hand, has three words as its children, so it violates maximal binarity but not minimal binarity. Finally, the $\varphi$ in (1c) has exactly two children, and so satisfies both maximal and minimal binarity.

(1)       Minimal and maximal binarity

    a.     $(_\varphi \; \omega)$            Violates minimal binarity, satisfies maximal binarity

    b.     $(_\varphi \; \omega \; \omega \; \omega)$    Satisfies minimal binarity, violates maximal binarity

    c.     $(_\varphi \; \omega \; \omega)$      Satisfies both minimal and maximal binarity

The primary topic of this chapter is an important distinction within maximal binarity, concerning a basic question: What counts as two elements? Consider the structure in (2). The highest phonological phrase, $\varphi_1$, has two daughters, $\varphi_2$ and $\varphi_3$. Each of those daughters has two words as its children. Does $\varphi_1$ satisfy maximal binarity because it has two daughters, or violate maximal binarity because it contains four (= more than two) phonological words? Each answer reflects a different interpretation of binarity.

(2)       $(_{\varphi 1} \; (_{\varphi 2} \; \omega \; \omega) \; (_{\varphi 3} \; \omega \; \omega))$

These two interpretations of binarity are informally stated in (3) for the phrase level. If phrasal binarity counts branches, then $\varphi_1$ satisfies maximal binarity. But if phrasal binarity counts the words contained in a $\varphi$, then $\varphi_1$ violates maximal binarity. We refer to the former conception of binarity as BRANCH-COUNTING, and the latter as LEAF-COUNTING. The term BRANCH refers to immediate descendants of a node—those that branch directly from it in a tree representation. The term LEAVES refers to the outermost nodes in the tree structure, the tree's terminal nodes. We refer to words as leaves here because we focus on prosodic trees in which an intonational phrase $\iota$ is the root node, additional non-terminal nodes are phonological phrases $\varphi$, and terminal nodes are prosodic words $\omega$. Since we abstract away from the sub-word constituents of syllable and foot, prosodic words are the 'leaves' of the trees. However, what matters when assessing BINMAXLEAVES violations for a subtree of category $\varkappa_i$ is the number of nodes of category $\varkappa_{i-1}$ dominated by $\varkappa$, not the number of terminal nodes dominated by $\varkappa$. In the cases we consider here, it so happens that $\varkappa_i = \varphi$ and $\varkappa_{i-1} = \omega$, in trees where every leaf is of category $\varkappa_{i-1}$ and every non-leaf is of category $\varkappa_{\geq i}$.

(3)      Two interpretations of phrasal binarity, informally
    a.   "A φ must have two daughters" = Branch-counting binarity
    b.   "A φ must contain two words" = Leaf-counting binarity

Both branch-counting and leaf-counting definitions of BINARITY are well-attested in phonological literature (see survey in §10.2 for references), but are rarely used together in the same analysis. The only exception we know of is Ito and Mester's (2020) analysis of Japanese phrasing, which is followed by Kalivoda (2018) and Bellik et al. (2022).

The two versions of BINARITY can be restated formally in a category-general fashion as in (4). These are the definitions that will be employed throughout the chapter.

(4)      Two notions of binarity, formally
    a.   BRANCH-COUNTING MAXIMAL BINARITY(K) = BINBR(K): Assign a violation for every node of category K with more than two branches (immediate children, of any category).
    b.   LEAF-COUNTING MAXIMAL BINARITY(K, L) = BINLV(K, L): Assign a violation for every node of category K that dominates more than two nodes of category L at any level, where L< K. If L is not explicitly specified, L = K − 1.

Branch-counting only counts immediate descendants. It is a structural constraint, similar to the definition of binarity employed in syntax, which also refers only to immediate children. Branch-counting binarity can be evaluated locally, as depicted by the dotted rectangle in (5). In principle, branch-counting can also be made sensitive to the category of the children,[1] although we are not aware of any analyses that employ category-sensitive branch-counting binarity. In contrast, leaf-counting binarity counts descendants of some particular lower category(s) (e.g., ω) *at any depth* in the tree. When unbounded recursion is allowed, leaf-counting binarity requires a global search through multiple layers of prosodic structure, depicted by the solid line in (5). As such, evaluation of leaf-counting binarity is much more algorithmically complex than branch-counting binarity. If $\varphi_3$ in (5) were changed to a recursive phonological word, a question arises as to whether every word in the tree would count as a leaf, or perhaps only the maximal words, or

---

[1] This suggestion is due to Nick Kalivoda (personal communication).

only the minimal ones. Standard word-counting definitions of binarity are ambiguous.

(5)      Search scope in evaluation of binarity for $\varphi_1$

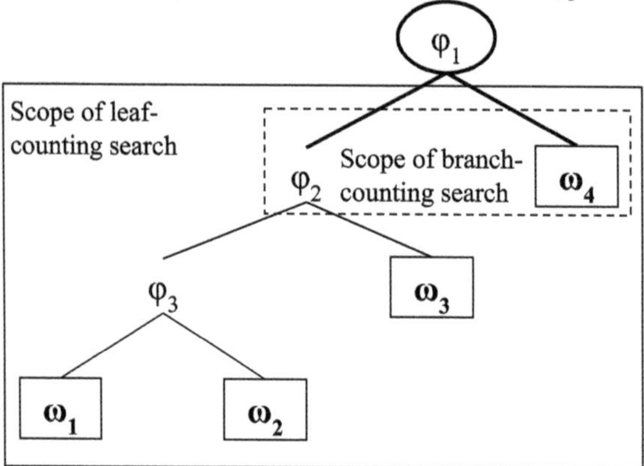


This chapter asks whether it is really necessary to have different versions of maximal binarity, and what the consequences of each version are for the predicted optima as well as the size and complexity of the typology. We find that each type of binarity favors a different kind of size effect. Branch-counting favors the building of recursive structure, and the matching of larger syntactic constituents. Leaf-counting favors the promotion of large prosodic constituents to a higher category and prefers to match only small syntactic constituents.

The chapter is organized as follows. First, we survey existing literature in §10.2, finding some analyses that require each version of binarity. Section 10.3 shows how branch-counting binarity, but not leaf-counting binarity, derives the building of additional recursive structure for longer strings, with a case study of Irish phrasing. Section 10.4, conversely, shows that leaf-counting binarity, but not branch-counting binarity, derives the promotion of long constituents to a higher prosodic category, with case studies of Italian phrasing and Japanese compound words. Section 10.5 contrasts the effect of each version of binarity on the typology, with a particular focus on the binarity constraints' interactions with syntax-prosody MATCH constraints. We find that leaf-counting binarity complicates the typology because it conflicts with sp.MATCH. Section 10.6 presents a constraint on Uniformity as an alternative to leaf-counting binarity. Section 10.7 discusses and concludes.

## 10.2   Cross-linguistic survey

To determine the need for both branch- and leaf-counting, we conducted
a cross-linguistic survey of syntax-prosody analyses that employ BINARITY
constraints. Of the sixteen analyses, nine define binarity in leaf-counting
terms, five define it in branch-counting terms, and two employ both versions.
Results from the full survey are presented in three separate tables: (8),
(11), and (12). Because the presence of recursive or non-exhaustive parsing
turns out to be necessary to distinguish the effects of branch-counting and
word-counting, we organize the results of the survey grouped by whether
the analysis assumes Strict Layering or Weak Layering, as well as by the
type of binarity that each analysis requires. The Strict Layering analyses
are presented first.

### 10.2.1   Strict Layering analyses

Many analyses of the syntax–prosody mapping, including seven of the
binarity analyses surveyed, adopt the Strict Layer Hypothesis (Selkirk 1984).
Under Strict Layering, prosodic structures conform to the principles in (6).

(6)      Requirements for prosodic trees under Strict Layering (Selkirk 1984)
   a.      Layering: Every child of a node of category $k$ in the prosodic hier-
        archy has category $\leq k$.
   b.      Non-Recursivity: No node of category $k$ has a child of category $k$.
   c.      Exhaustivity: Every child of a node of category $k$ has category $\geq k-1$.

Taken together, these three properties ensure that every child of a node of
category $k$ will be of category $k-1$, since no level-skipping (non-exhaustive
parsing) or level-doubling (recursion) is permitted. Every branch in a strictly
layered tree is a child of the next lower prosodic category (a leaf). Therefore, every violation of branch-counting binarity is also a violation of leaf-
counting binarity, and vice versa. This is illustrated by candidates (7a, b).
Candidate (a) contains two binary-branching φs whose daughters are words,
so it satisfies both branch-counting BINBR(φ) and leaf-counting BINLV(φ, ω).
Candidate (7b) consists of one quaternary-branching φ whose daughters are
all words, which violates both branch- and leaf-counting binarity. This ex-
emplifes how, in analyses that assume Strict Layering, leaf-counting binarity
can be replaced by branch-counting, or vice versa, with no consequences to
the predicted optima.

(7)       Strict Layering and binarity tableau

| $[[[X_1\ X_2]\ X_3]\ X_4]$ | $\textsc{BinBr}(\varphi)$ | $\textsc{BinLv}(\varphi,\ \omega)$ | *Layering* |
|---|---|---|---|
| a. | 0 | 0 | |
| b. | 1 | 1 | Strict |

The analyses in (8) assume Strict Layering, and consequently the size effects they report can be explained with either branch-counting or leaf-counting binarity; the two are equivalent. As it happens, they all define binarity in leaf-counting terms ("A $\varphi$ should contain two $\omega$s") in the original accounts. In (8) and subsequent tables reporting survey results in (11) and (12), a checkmark (✓) in the $\textsc{BinBr}$ column indicates that branch-counting binarity can account for the observed pattern, and a checkmark in the $\textsc{BinLv}$ column indicates that leaf-counting binarity can account for it. A checkmark with an asterisk (✓*) means both versions of binarity are needed.

(8)    Cross-linguistic survey, part 1: Binarity analyses with Strict Layering.

| Language | BinBr | BinLv | Source binarity | Desired effect of binarity |
|---|---|---|---|---|
| a. Brazilian Portuguese (Sandalo and Truckenbrodt 2002) | ✓ | ✓ | BinMaxLv($\varphi$) | Size effects (maximality) with Strict Layering |
| b. Catalan (Prieto 2005) | ✓ | ✓ | BinMaxLv($\varphi$), BinMaxLv(Rightmost-$\varphi$) | Size effects (maximality) with Strict Layering |
| c. English (Selkirk 2000) | ✓ | ✓ | BinMaxLv(MajorPhrase), BinMinLv(MajorPhrase), BinLv(MajorPhrase) | Size effects with Strict Layering |
| d. Taiwan Mandarin (Shih 2017) | ✓ | ✓ | BinMaxLv(MajorPhrase), BinMinLv(MajorPhrase), BinMaxLv(MinorPhrase), BinMinLv(MinorPhrase) | Size effects with Strict Layering |
| e. Serbo-Croatian (Zec and Inkelas 1990) | ✓ | ✓ | BinMinBr($\varphi$) | Size effects (minimality) with Strict Layering |
| f. Spanish (Prieto 2006) | ✓ | ✓ | BinMaxLv($\varphi$), BinMinLv($\varphi$), BinMaxLv(Rightmost-$\varphi$) | Size effects (maximality) with Strict Layering |
| g. Italian (Ghini 1993) | ✓ | ✓ | BinLv($\varphi$) | Size effects (maximality) with Strict Layering |

Some of the analyses in this survey predate Optimality Theory (Prince and Smolensky 1993/2004) and do not actually employ constraints per se. Zec and Inkelas (1990; row e) discuss binarity in terms of branches, and we therefore identify their use of binarity as BinMinBr($\varphi$). Similarly, Ghini (1993; row g) appeals to a principle of average weight, which claims that $\varphi$ contain two words at an average rate of speech. We have classified this principle as BinLv($\varphi$). In addition, in some of the sources that use Optimality Theory, it is not clear from tableaux whether leaves or branches are being counted. We have therefore relied on the wording of the constraint definitions to classify the binarity constraints as leaf-counting or branch-counting. For example, in

Prieto (2005, row b; 2007, row f), constraint definitions refer to the number of words, and we have therefore classified these constraints as leaf-counting, although the prose discussion also makes reference to branches. Similarly, we have classified the constraints in Shih (2017, row d) as leaf-counting based on the terms used in the constraint definitions, although a footnote in this chapter makes reference to branches. These chapters assume Strict Layering, however, and so the two types of binarity are indistinguishable.

Several analyses employ specialized binarity constraints that place restrictions on only a subset of members of a particular category. Again, we have adapted the names of these constraints to reflect the distinction between branch-counting and leaf-counting in order to facilitate comparison across analyses. For instance, Prieto (2005, 2006) introduces the constraints MAX-BIN-END and MAX-BIN-IP-HEAD, both of which require the last phonological phrase of the utterance (i.e., the head of the intonational phrase) to be maximally binary. We have called these constraints BINMAXLV(RIGHTMOST-$\varphi$).

### 10.2.2  Weak Layering

Subsequent work on the prosodic hierarchy (Ito and Mester 1992/2003, 2007, Selkirk 2011, Elfner 2012) established that many languages allow recursive and non-exhaustive parsing. With recursive parsing, a prosodic node may contain other nodes of the same category. For example, a phonological phrase may contain other phonological phrases. With non-exhaustive parsing, a prosodic node may be parsed directly into a parent that is two or more categories higher, such as when a free clitic (a foot or syllable) is parsed directly into $\varphi$, skipping the $\omega$ level. Weak Layering treats Non-Recursivity (6b) and Exhaustivity (6c) as violable, while retaining Layering (6a) as an inviolable constraint on GEN.

When the set of prosodic candidates includes candidates with recursion and level-skipping, not every branch is a "leaf." Branch-counting and leaf-counting are no longer equivalent. This is illustrated in (9). Candidates (9a–b) contain recursive $\varphi$s. The parent $\varphi_1$, being binary-branching, escapes a violation of BINBR($\varphi$). But the additional substructure does not prevent the parent from containing too many words at a lower level: it still violates BINLV($\varphi$, $\omega$). Level-skipping parses like (9c) can violate BINBR($\varphi$) without violating BINLV($\varphi$, $\omega$), or vice versa. In (9c), BINLV($\varphi$, $\omega$) is not violated because it does not count the syllables toward the maximum permitted length of $\varphi$. BINBR($\varphi$) does count all branches, and is violated.

(9) Layering and binarity tableau

| $[[[X_1 X_2] X_3] X_4]$ | BinBr($\varphi$) | BinLv($\varphi$, $\omega$) | *Layering* |
|---|---|---|---|
| a. 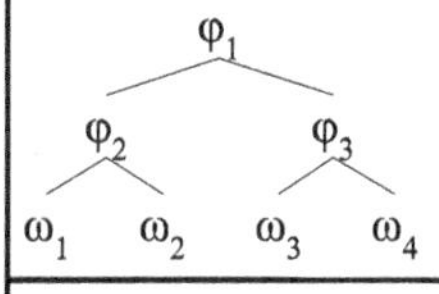 | 0 | 1<br>$\varphi_1$ | Recursive |
| b. 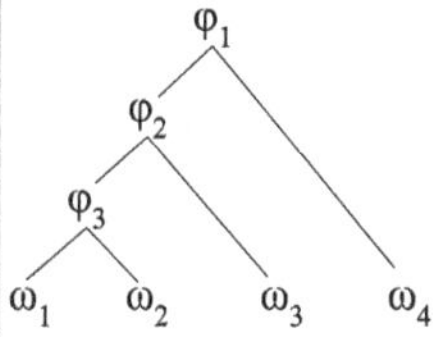 | 0 | 2<br>$\varphi_{1,}\ \varphi_2$ | |
| c. 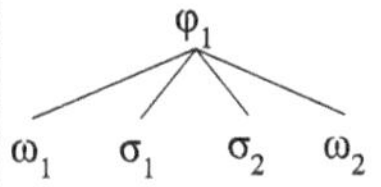 | 1<br>$\varphi_1$ | 0 | Non-exhaustive |

*10.2.2.1 The need for branch-counting*

In Weak Layering analyses, then, often only one of branch-counting and leaf-counting can account for the phenomenon of interest. The table in (11) shows the five Weak Layering analyses surveyed that could be described with branch-counting binarity. Size effects in the first language, Kinyambo (row h), could additionally be described with leaf-counting binarity. We will discuss this analysis more in §10.5.1. In the remaining four analyses (rows i – l), replacing branch-counting binarity with leaf-counting binarity failed to distinguish appropriately among candidates. The role of branch-counting in these analyses is not easily subsumed by other prosodic well-formedness constraints, either.

The basic size effect that binarity motivates in these five analyses is that larger or longer inputs are parsed with more recursive structure. We refer to this as SIZE-DRIVEN RECURSION (10). In most cases, this recursive structure provides a closer syntax-prosody match, with larger XPs being more likely to be matched in the prosody (SIZE-DRIVEN RECURSION WITH MATCHING, (10a)). The mechanisms for this will be detailed in in §10.3, a case study of Irish phrasing (row l in (11)).

Size-driven recursion does not always create a better syntax-prosody match, however. For instance, in Japanese phrasing (row p in (12), next table), parsing *[a [b [c d]]]* as *((a b)(c d))* involves creating a mismatched phrase *(a b)*, which is partly motivated by BINMAXBR. We refer to this type of interaction as SIZE-DRIVEN RECURSION WITH MISMATCH (10b), and it occurs in Kimatuumbi[2] as well as Japanese. Similarly, in Xitsonga, minimal binarity prevents matching of non-branching XPs, which are flattened to ωs instead, while maximal binarity contributes to the insertion of a correspondentless φ in the double object construction.

(10)       SIZE-DRIVEN RECURSION is present in a language if there exists at least one pair of candidates $<s_1, p_1>$ and $<s_2, p_2>$ such that $s_1$ has fewer terminal nodes than $s_2$, and $p_1$ has less prosodic recursion than $p_2$.

     a.     SIZE-DRIVEN RECURSION WITH MATCHING occurs when the additional recursive prosodic structure in $p_2$ has a syntactic correspondent in $s_2$, such that $<s_2, p_2>$ satisfies MATCH better than $<s_1, p_1>$ does.

     b.     SIZE-DRIVEN RECURSION WITH MISMATCH occurs when the additional recursive prosodic structure in $p_2$ lacks a syntactic correspondent in $s_2$, such that $<s_2, p_2>$ violates MATCH more than $<s_1, p_1>$ does.

---

[2]   Kalivoda (2018, Ch. 3) provides two distinct analyses of Kimatuumbi, one using Match Theory and the other using Command Theory. In the Match Theoretic analysis, the winning parse [V [N N]] → ((V N) N) involves a violation of ps.MATCH(φ), and the recursive structure (V N) is positioned at the left edge in order to satisfy STRONGSTART rather than any MATCH constraint. For this reason, we have categorized the analysis as involving a mismatch in the table. In the Command Theory analysis, 'matching" and 'mismatching" are irrelevant, and the Kimatuumbi surface form reflects the ranking C-COMMAND(φ) ≫ ANTI-C-COMMAND(φ).

(11)   Survey, part 2: Weak Layering with branch-counting binarity. Continued from (8).

| Language | BinBr | BinLv | Source binarity | Size effect |
|---|---|---|---|---|
| h. Kinyambo (Bickmore 1990, Bellik and Kalivoda 2016) | ✓ | ✓ | BinMaxBr($\varphi$), BinMaxLv($\varphi$) | Size-driven recursion (with matching) |
| i. Danish compounds (Kalivoda and Bellik 2018) | ✓ | — | BinMaxBr($\omega$) | Size-driven recursion (with matching) |
| j. Kimatuumbi (Kalivoda 2018, Ch. 3) | ✓ | — | BinMaxBr($\varphi$) | Size-driven recursion (with mismatch) |
| k. Xitsonga (Selkirk and Lee 2017) | ✓ | — | BinBr($\varphi$) (combined Max and Min) | Size-affected recursion (with mismatch) |
| l. Irish (Elfner 2012) | ✓ | — | BinMaxBr($\varphi$) | Size-driven recursion (with matching) |

### 10.2.2.2 The need for leaf-counting binarity

In the remaining four analyses in the survey (12), leaf-counting binarity is required. Instead of the increased matching of larger syntactic constituents under branch-counting binarity, only matching of smaller syntactic constituents (no more than two terminals) is permitted under leaf-counting maximal binarity. Smaller XPs (or words) are more likely to be matched in the prosody than large ones.

(12)    Survey, part 3: Weak Layering with leaf-counting binarity. Continued
        from (8) and (11).

| Language | BinBr | BinLv | Source binarity | Size effect |
|---|---|---|---|---|
| m. Italian (Van Handel 2021) | - | ✓ | BinMinLv($\varphi$), BinMaxLv($\iota$), BinMaxLv($\varphi$) | Size-driven category promotion (maximality) |
| n. Japanese, compound words (Ito and Mester 2007) | - | ✓ | BinMaxLv($\omega_{hd}$) | Size-driven category promotion (maximality) |
| o. Irish, focused constituents (Bennett et al. 2019) | - | ✓ Can be re-placed by EqSisters | BinMinLeaves($\omega_{foc}$, $\omega$) Counts words within a focused word | Size-driven category promotion (minimality) |
| p. Japanese, phrasing (Ito and Mester 2020; Bellik et al. 2022) | ✓* | ✓* Can be re-placed by Balanced Sisters | BinMinBr($\varphi$), BinMaxBr($\varphi$), BinMaxLv($\varphi$) | Size-driven recursion (with mismatch) |

In Japanese compound words and Italian phonological phrasing (rows m
and n), we found no possible replacement for leaf-counting binarity. In both
of these analyses, sufficiently long syntactic constituents are mapped to
prosodic constituents of a higher prosodic category than what would satisfy
sp.Match. We refer to this as SIZE-DRIVEN CATEGORY PROMOTION, and discuss
the mechanisms for it in detail in §10.4, using these two analyses as case
studies. To account for the prosody of focus in Irish, Bennett et al. (2019;
row o) have proposed the constraint BINARY-FOCUS (BIN-FOC), which assigns a violation to focalized constituents that do not contain at least two
prosodic words. Because this constraint counts words, we have called this
BinMinLv($\omega_{foc}$, $\omega$). In this case, EqualSisters was able to take the place of
leaf-counting in motivating the category promotion. The last leaf-counting
analysis (Japanese phrasing, row p) needs both branch-counting and leaf-
counting binarity, in order to derive size-driven recursion accompanied by
mismatching. Section 10.6 covers this analysis in more detail, and presents
an alternative analysis using a constraint on Uniformity (Ghini 1993) in
place of leaf-counting binarity.

## 10.3   Branch-counting and size-driven recursion

As noted above, it is often the case that longer strings are parsed into more prosodic constituents. Within Match Theory, this is modeled by building recursive substructure in longer strings, and building less (or none) in shorter strings where a flat parse does not create a suprabinary constituent. As will be seen in the following case study of Irish, branch-counting binarity achieves this size-driven recursion, but leaf-counting does not.

According to Elfner (2012, 2015), in Connemara Irish, a rising tone shows the left boundary of the non-minimal phonological phrase, a phrase that contains another phrase ($\varphi_{\text{NonMin}}$). A falling tone shows the right boundary of any phonological phrase $\varphi$. These diagnostics indicate that a transitive sentence with a branching object and non-branching subject is parsed into a symmetrically binary-branching phonological phrasing (13).

(13)    Rebracketing with non-branching subject in Irish (Elfner 2012, 2015)

    a.

| V | $N_s$ | $N_o$ | $N_o$ |
|---|---|---|---|
| *cheannaigh*[LH] | *múinteoirí*[HL] | *málaí* | *bána*[HL] |
| bought | teachers | bags | white |

    b.    Abstracted syntax–prosody mapping:

$$[\text{V} \; [_{\text{TP}} \; [_{\text{DP}} \, N_s] \; [_{\text{DP}} \, N_o \; A_o]] \;] \rightarrow ((\text{V} \; N_s)(N_o \; A_o))$$

This rebracketing is motivated by STRONGSTART (Selkirk 2011, Elfner 2012) (14), which penalizes the isomorphic parse in (15). The winning, rebracketed output (15) satisfies STRONGSTART, but violates ps.MATCH($\varphi$), because V and $N_s$ are in a $\varphi$ together in the output that lacks a correspondent XP in the input. It also violates sp.MATCH(XP), because the subject NP is not mapped to a corresponding $\varphi$ in the output. This establishes that STRONGSTART outranks sp.MATCH(XP) in Irish.

(14)    STRONGSTART (paraphrased from Elfner 2012): Assign a violation for every phonological word that is leftmost in the phonological phrase or intonational phrase, and is sister to a phonological phrase.

(15)    STRONGSTART and sp.MATCH(XP) in Irish (adapted from Elfner 2012)

| [V [[N] [N A]] ] | STRONGSTART | sp.MATCH(XP) |
|---|---|---|
| → a. ((V N) (N A)) | 0 | 2 |
| b. (V ((N) (N A))) | W$_1$ | L$_0$ |

A branching subject blocks this rebracketing, in an interaction with maximal Binarity. Irish phrasing tolerates STRONGSTART violations for the sake of avoiding BINBR violations, indicating that BINBR outranks STRONGSTART.

(16)    No rebracketing with branching subject in Irish (Elfner 2012, pp. 56, 160)

a.   V                $N_s$              $A_s$              $N_o$              $A_o$
     *díolfaidh*[LH]   *leabharlannaí*[LH]   *dathúil*[HL]    *blathanna*    *áille*[HL]
     sell.fut          librarian            handsome         flowers        beautiful

b.   Abstracted syntax–prosody mapping:
     $[V \,[_{TP} \,[_{DP} \,N_s \,A_s] \,[_{DP} \,N_o \,A_o]] \,] \rightarrow (V \,(N_s \,A_s)(N_o \,A_o))$

(17)    Binarity in Irish (adapted from Elfner 2012, p. 161)

| $[V \,[[N \,A] \,[N \,A]] \,]$ | BINBR($\varphi$) | STRONGST | sp.MATCH(XP) | BINLV($\varphi$) |
|---|---|---|---|---|
| → a. $(_1 \,V \,(_2 \,(_3 N \,A)(_4 N \,A)))$ | 0 | 1 | 0 | 2 |
| b. $(_1 \,(_2 V \,N \,A)(_3 \,N \,A)))$ | $W_1$ | $L_0$ | $W_2$ | $e_2$ |

If branching subjects were phrased according to the same pattern as non-branching subjects, the verb would be phrased with the subject in a minimal $\varphi$, as in the losing (17b). This rebracketed candidate satisfies STRONGSTART, but contains a ternary-branching $\varphi$. This violates BINBR and fails to match the four-word TP and the subject DP. This phrasing incorrectly predicts no tonal rise on the first N.

The observed tonal contour for this sentence is compatible with the perfectly matching phrasing in (17a). Candidate (a) does not phrase the verb inside the same minimal $\varphi$ as the subject. Instead, the phrasing of the optimum perfectly matches the constituency of the syntactic input, in which the verb occurs as sister to the TP. Winner (a) violates STRONGSTART, but this violation is offset by its better performance on BINMAXBR, compared to (b). The fact that (a) is more harmonic than (b) demonstrates that BINARITY outranks STRONGSTART.

Crucially, the binarity of $\varphi_{1,2}$ must be assessed by counting branches for (17a) to outperform (17b). Leaf-counting binarity does not distinguish these candidates. (17a)'s $\varphi_1$ dominates five $\omega$s, and its $\varphi_2$ dominates three words, so it violates leaf-counting BINLV($\varphi, \omega$) twice, just like (17b). If leaf-counting binarity were used instead of branch-counting, (17b) would be selected as optimal, since it does not violate STRONGSTART. Only branch-counting binarity correctly selects the real winner, (17a).

To summarize, in Irish, the verb is rebracketed into a minimal $\varphi$ with the subject to satisfy STRONGSTART, *unless* this strategy would create a ternary-branching φ. In that case, rebracketing is blocked by BɪɴMᴀxBʀ(φ), and matching occurs instead. BɪɴMᴀxBʀ(φ) functions as a special case of sp.Mᴀᴛᴄʜ(XP) here, and whenever the syntax visible to the mapping constraints is binary-branching, because every suprabinary φ results from at least one XP not being mapped to a φ. In this analysis of Irish, the special constraint BɪɴMᴀxBʀ and the general constraint sp.Mᴀᴛᴄʜ(XP) are both antagonized against SᴛʀᴏɴɢSᴛᴀʀᴛ, with the result that matching is prioritized for branching subjects. This is an instance of subject-branching sensitivity (Tarlov, Chapter 3), motivated by BɪɴMᴀxBʀ. Comparable results can be seen in Kinyambo, where branching subjects are matched but non-branching subjects are phrased with the verb (Bellik and Kalivoda 2016; Tarlov, Chapter 3).

A very similar phenomenon occurs in the prosody of Danish compound words. There, morphological words containing more than one foot are mapped to phonological words through the intervention of BɪɴMᴀxBʀ, while non-branching morphological words are flattened by NᴏɴRᴇᴄᴜʀsɪᴠɪᴛʏ (Kalivoda and Bellik 2018). Just as in Irish and Kinyambo phrasing, branching inputs are preferentially matched due to BɪɴMᴀxBʀᴀɴᴄʜᴇs, while non-branching inputs are subject to various mismatches due to the higher ranking of a markedness constraint over sp.Mᴀᴛᴄʜ. These languages exemplify size-driven recursion.

## 10.4   Leaf-counting and category change

Leaf-counting binarity does not favor building recursive substructure. Instead, it prefers candidates in which the root node is a higher category than the one targeted by the binarity constraint. This favors level-skipping under Weak Layering.

Both leaf-counting and branch-counting binarity are usually parameterized to penalize non-binary nodes of a particular prosodic category. Consequently, both types can favor changing the category of a node that has too many daughters or contains too many leaves. Leaf-counting binarity favors category promotion in more circumstances than branch-counting binarity does. We can see this by comparing the violations assigned by each constraint to the candidates in (18). (18a) satisfies BɪɴLᴇᴀᴠᴇs(φ, ω) but fails to wrap all of the words in a φ. The only phonological constituent that contains the same terminals as the root XP in the input is an intonational phrase. This mapping promotes the category of the prosodic node that corresponds to the syntactic root, at a cost to the candidate's performance on sp.Mᴀᴛᴄʜ(XP, φ), which is violated because of the mismatch in categories. The fact that this category promotion improves performance on BɪɴLᴇᴀᴠᴇs demonstrates that BINLEAVES conflicts with sp.MATCH in a way that BINBRANCHES does not.

BINBRANCHES($\varphi$) is satisfied by both (18a) and (18b), where no category promotion has occurred. Hence, branch-counting binarity does not favor the category-promoting parse (18a) over the category-matching parse (18b). Building recursive structure ameliorates performance on branch-counting, but not on leaf-counting, so leaf-counting favors the candidates with category promotion over all non-promoted candidates.

(18)    Tableau of category promotion

| $[_{\mathrm{XP1}}\,[_{\mathrm{XP2}}\,[_{\mathrm{XP3}}\,X_1\,X_2]\,X_3]\,X_4]$ | sp.MATCH(XP, $\varphi$) | BINBR($\varphi$) | BINLV($\varphi$, $\omega$) |
|---|---|---|---|
| a. 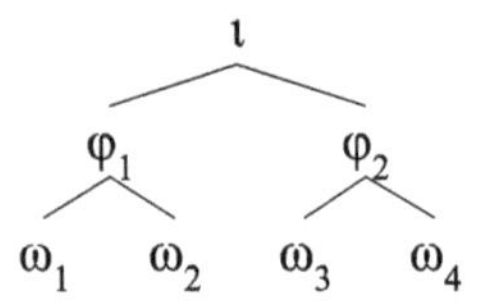  $\iota$ branching into $\varphi_1$ ($\omega_1\,\omega_2$) and $\varphi_2$ ($\omega_3\,\omega_4$) | 2 <br> ($\mathrm{XP}_1$, $\mathrm{XP}_2$) | 0 | 0 |
| b. 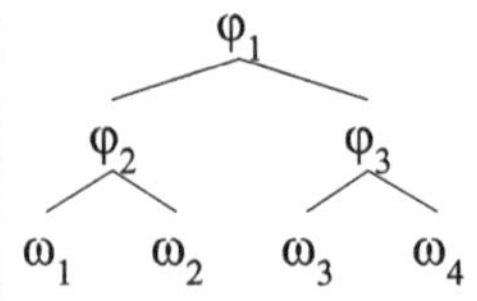  $\varphi_1$ branching into $\varphi_2$ ($\omega_1\,\omega_2$) and $\varphi_3$ ($\omega_3\,\omega_4$) | 1 <br> ($\mathrm{XP}_3$) | 0 | 1 <br> ($\varphi_1$) |

### 10.4.1 Leaf-counting for phrases in Italian

Phonological phrasing in Italian exemplifies category promotion of the kind schematized in (18), in which a $\varphi$ is promoted to an $\iota$ because it contains too many words. In Italian, final lengthening diagnoses the right edge of maximal $\varphi$ phrases: the stressed vowel of the final word in a maximal $\varphi$ undergoes lengthening (Ghini 1993, Van Handel 2021). This diagnostic shows that $\varphi$s in Italian consist of at most two $\omega$s at an average speech rate (Ghini 1993). For example, a right-branching structure consisting of three $\omega$ is split up into two separate maximal $\varphi$, as in (19).

(19)    $[_{\mathrm{TP}}$ vaccinerò $[_{\mathrm{QP}}$ tutte $[_{\mathrm{DP}}$ le scimmie $]]]$ $\rightarrow$ { (vaccine<u>ròo</u>) (tutte (le sc<u>ii</u>mmie)) }
        'I will vaccinate all the monkeys'

As shown in (20), this phrasing is derived when $\textsc{BinMaxLv}(\varphi, \omega)$ is ranked over sp.$\textsc{Match}$(XP): the root TP fails to map to a $\varphi$ because it contains three $\omega$s (Van Handel 2021). Instead, the only phonological constituent containing all three $\omega$ corresponding to the three $X^0$s within TP is an intonational phrase. $\textsc{BinMaxBr}(\varphi)$ cannot replace $\textsc{BinMaxLv}(\varphi, \omega)$ because it fails to distinguish (20a) and (20b), as both structures are maximally binary-branching. Leaf-counting is necessary in order to derive size effects in Italian.

(20)　　　Category promotion in Italian (adapted from Van Handel 2021)

| | $[_{\text{TP}}$ V $[_{\text{QP}}$ Q $[_{\text{NP}}$ N $]]]$ | $\textsc{BinLv}(\varphi, \omega)$ | sp.$\textsc{Match}$(XP) | $\textsc{BinBr}(\varphi)$ |
|---|---|---|---|---|
| → a. | { (V) (Q (N)) } | 0 | 1 | 0 |
| b. | { (V (Q (N))) } | $W_1$ | $L_0$ | $e_0$ |

The tableau in (21) further demonstrates that $\textsc{BinMaxLv}(\varphi,\omega)$ is a crucial ingredient of the analysis. Like $\textsc{BinMaxLv}(\varphi, \omega)$, the constraints $\textsc{Strong-Start}$ (SS), $\textsc{EqualSisters}$ (ES), and $\textsc{NonRecursivity}$ ($\textsc{NonRec}$) all favor the winner (21a) over isomorphic (21c). However, these three constraints also favor the loser (b) over (a). If any of these constraints were to replace $\textsc{BinMaxLv}(\varphi, \omega)$ and be ranked above sp.$\textsc{Match}$(XP), (21b) would incorrectly emerge as the winner.

(21)　　　Alternative markedness constraints

| | $[_{\text{TP}}$ V $[_{\text{QP}}$ Q $[_{\text{NP}}$ N $]]]$ | $\textsc{BinLv}(\varphi)$ | sp.M(XP) | SS | ES | $\textsc{NonRec}$ |
|---|---|---|---|---|---|---|
| → a. | { (V) (Q (N)) } | 0 | 1 | 1 | 1 | 1 |
| b. | {( V Q) (N)} | $e_0$ | $W_2$ | $L_0$ | $L_0$ | $L_0$ |
| c. | { (V (Q (N)))} | $W_1$ | $L_0$ | $W_2$ | $W_2$ | $W_2$ |

### 10.4.2 Leaf-counting for words in Japanese

Size-driven promotion of $\omega$ to $\varphi$ occurs in the prosodification of Japanese compound words (Ito and Mester 2007, 2021). In Japanese, the second member of a compound is normally its head. Compounds whose second member (head) consists of no more than two feet are parsed into a structure rooted in an $\omega$, as diagnosed by $\omega$-internal rendaku voicing and compound accent. When the length of the righthand member of the compound exceeds two feet, however, compounds are no longer parsed into a single phonological word. Instead, the root word's corresponding prosodic constituent is promoted to a phonological phrase, in order to avoid having a word whose head is suprabinary. Compare the longer $\varphi$-rooted compounds in (22a) to shorter, $\omega$-rooted compounds in (22b).

(22)    Japanese compound words (Ito and Mester 2007, 2021)
    a. head $>$ 2ft: $\varphi$-compound
        $(_\varphi$ chihoo $[_{ft}$ ken$][_{ft}$ satsu'$][_{ft}$ choo$]$ )       'local prosecutor's office'
        $(_\varphi$ chiho'o $[_{ft}$ kin$][_{ft}$ yuu$]$ ki' $[_{ft}$ kou$]$ )       'local financial institutions'
        $(_\varphi$ chiho'o $[_{ft}$ koo$][_{ft}$ kyoo$][_{ft}$ da'n$][_{ft}$ tai$]$ ) 'local public organization'
    b. head $\leq$ 2ft: $\omega$-compound
        $[_\omega$ chihoo $[_{ft}$ gi'n$][_{ft}$ koo$]$ $]$       'local bank'
        $[_\omega$ chihoo $[_{ft}$ ke'i$]$ba $]$       'local horse racing'
        $[_\omega$ chiho'o $[_{ft}$ ma'wa$]$ri $]$       'local rounds

This category change is driven by a restriction on the number of feet or syllables (leaves) in the head of $\omega$: $\text{BinLv}(\omega_{hd}, [ft, \sigma])$. Changing the root node to be a $\varphi$ exempts it from this binarity constraint, which only evaluates the heads of prosodic words. To take an example, in compounds whose head is of the form $[_{x0} [_{x0} ft][_{x0} ft \sigma]]$, the root node changes from $\omega$ to $\varphi$ (23), in violation of sp.$\text{Match}(X^0)$. The largest $\omega_{hd}$ in the $\varphi$-rooted structure (23a) is $\omega_4$, which consists of only one foot and one syllable—two leaves. This satisfies $\text{BinLv}(\omega_{hd}, [ft, \sigma])$. But the largest $\omega_{hd}$ in the $\omega$-rooted structure (23b) is $\omega_3$, which consists of two feet and a syllable—three leaves, violating $\text{BinLv}(\omega_{hd}, [ft, \sigma])$. Thus, leaf-counting drives the promotion of the largest $X^0$ to a $\varphi$ in the prosody, at the expense of sp.$\text{Match}(X^0)$. Branch-counting cannot drive this category promotion—both candidates (a) and (b) satisfy $\text{BinBr}(\omega_{hd})$, since the heads of all words are maximally binary-branching.

(23)    Japanese compound words (adapted from Ito and Mester 2007, (19)[3]). Word heads are bold.

| $[_{x0} [_{x0}$ hatsu$_{Ft}] [_{x0} [_{x0}$ kao$_{Ft}] [_{x0}$ awa$_{Ft}$ se$_\sigma]] ]$ | $\text{BinLv}(\omega_{hd}, [ft, \sigma])$ | sp.$\text{Match}(X^0)$ | $\text{BinBr}(\omega_{hd})$ |
|---|---|---|---|
| a.  $(_\varphi [_{\omega1}$ ft$] [_{\omega2} [_{\omega3}$ ft$] [_{\omega4}$ **ft** $\sigma)]]$ ) | 0 | 1 | e$_0$ |
| b.  $[_{\omega1} [_{\omega2}$ ft$] [_{\omega3} [_{\omega4}$ **ft** $] [_{\omega5}$ ft $\sigma)]] ]$ | W$_1$ | L$_0$ | e$_0$ |

---

[3]   The foot placement in (23) has been changed from that in Ito and Mester (2007) to reflect more recent understandings of footing in Japanese, conveyed by Ito and Mester (p.c.).

Ito and Mester's (2007) definition of $\text{BiNLv}(\omega_{hd}, [ft, \sigma])$ evaluates a node's complexity 'in terms of immediate daughters below the level where adjunction takes place." When $\omega_1$ dominates $\omega_2$, $\omega_2$ is not counted in evaluating the binarity of $\omega_1$. Instead, $\omega_2$'s children are counted. For example, in (24), the complexity of $\omega_1$ is assessed based on all the children of $\omega_2$ and $\omega_3$: $ft_1$, $ft_2$, and $\sigma_5$ (boxed).

(24)   Leaf-counting in Ito and Mester (2007), adapted from Ito and Mester's (2007) (17a).

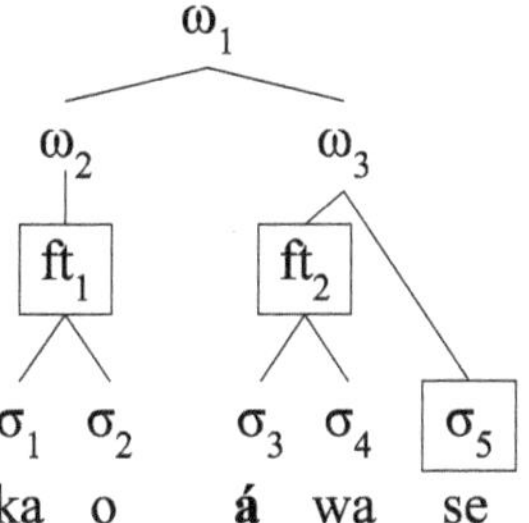

This is a form of leaf-counting binarity, in that it counts descendants (not branches) and is sensitive to the category of the dominated node. However, this version of binarity suggests a refinement to our notion of leaf. Here, both feet and syllables that are directly dominated by a prosodic word are also counted. We can redefine *leaf* accordingly in (25) so as to specify what happens when recursion and non-exhaustive parsing are combined. We believe this definition is compatible with previous work that employs leaf-counting binarity, while simultaneously allowing us to count $\omega_1$ in (24) as 'ternary" despite its consisting of exactly two embedded $\omega$s and two feet.

(25)   Leaf (relativized definition): The leaves of a node $p$ of category $c$ are all the nodes dominated by $p$ that are <u>not</u> of category c, and whose parent <u>is</u> of category $c$.

By restricting the count of leaves to those whose parents are of category $c$, (25) restricts leaves to being maximal as well. That is, were (24) to contain recursive feet, feet that are dominated by other feet would not qualify as leaves. Since recursive feet are not widely accepted, this problem is more likely to arise for a structure that includes both recursive phonological words and phrases and assesses the binarity of a phrase in terms of the number of words it contains.

Although in many cases, the leaves of a node $p$ are its grandchildren, the definition in (25) is more general, in order to account for multiple layers of recursive structure. This is shown in the following tree (26). Since $\omega_1$ is a prosodic word, none of the prosodic word nodes that it dominates ($\omega_2$, $\omega_3$...) is a leaf under (25). Syllables and feet immediately dominated by $\omega$-nodes, as in the case of $\sigma_1$ and $\mathrm{Ft}_1$, are leaves of $\omega_1$, because they are among the largest non-$\omega$ units contained within $\omega_1$. Other material that is equally deeply embedded, however, does not count as leaf-material, showing again that the definition is based on category status and not simple distance; in (26), $\sigma_2$ and $\sigma_3$ are not leaves, since they are contained within the leaf $\mathrm{Ft}_5$.

(26)     Relativized leaves of $\omega_1$ in boxes

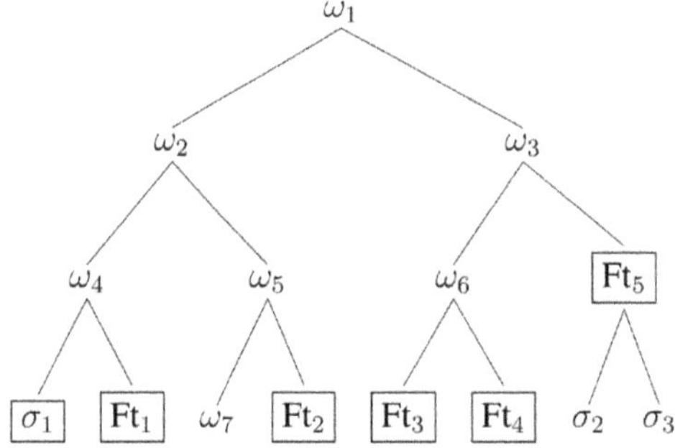

## 10.5    Consequences for typology size and complexity

Leaf-counting and branch-counting assign different violations, and therefore predict significantly different typologies. This section compares typologies generated by systems with BinBranches vs. BinLeaves, by comparing the size of typologies in a previous study of twelve systems that model Kinyambo phrasing (§10.5.1), and then by examining the constraint interactions in two very simple systems (§10.5.2).

### 10.5.1    Typology sizes in Bellik and Kalivoda (2016)

Bellik and Kalivoda (2016) draws on data and insights from Bickmore (1989, 1990) to use phonological phrasing in Kinyambo as a test case for several different theoretical issues. The study includes twelve different typologies which varied along three dimensions, one of which was whether binarity was assessed by counting branches or leaves (in this case, the leaves were phonological words). The other two dimensions, less relevant here but shown in (27), were: the choice of mapping constraints (Match vs. Align), and the visibility of high vs. low segments of adjunction structures. High segment visibility means that the highest NP in a structure like [$_{NP}$ [$_{NP}$ Noun][$_{AP}$ Adjective]] is required to be matched by the mapping constraints, but not the lower NP; low segment visibility means only the lower NP, but not the higher one, is counted for mapping constraints.

These parameters yielded six pairs of typologies that differed only in which type of binarity was employed (27). Either branch- or word-counting binarity systems could capture the Kinyambo phrasing pattern; all four systems in rows a and b predicted the Kinyambo pattern of phrasing. However, there were significant differences in typology size, based on the definition of binarity. In five out of six system-pairs (all but row b), the word-counting typology contained more languages than the branch-counting typology. In systems that employed ALIGN rather than MATCH constraints, the difference in typology sizes was dramatic, with the word-counting typologies being two to three times the size of the branch-counting typologies. The inflated size of leaf-counting typologies indicates that BINLEAVES conflicts with other constraints more often than BINBRANCHES does. The following subsection develops two simplified systems to illuminate Binarity's potential to conflict with sp.MATCH.

(27)    Impact of Binarity definitions on typology sizes (based on Bellik and Kalivoda 2016)

|  | Typology size with | | \|BINLV\| − \|BINBR\| | \|BINLV\| / \|BINBR\| |
|---|---|---|---|---|
|  | BINBR | BINLV |  |  |
| a. Only high XP segment visible, MATCH | 11 | 15 | 4 | 136% |
| b. Both XP segments visible, MATCH | 18 | 17 | −1 | 94% |
| c. Only low XP segment visible, MATCH | 17 | 19 | 2 | 112% |
| d. Only high XP segment visible, ALIGN | 12 | 28 | 16 | 233% |
| e. Both XP segments visible, ALIGN | 12 | 30 | 18 | 250% |
| f. Only low XP segments visible, ALIGN | 15 | 45 | 30 | 300% |
| Average | 14.2 | 25.7 | 11.5 | 188% |

### 10.5.2 Binarity's interactions with MATCH

In the case study of Irish phrasing above (§10.3), we saw that BINBRANCHES($\varphi$) acts as a special case of sp.MATCH(XP), but that BINLEAVES($\varphi$) does not. We now develop two systems, S.Branches and S.Leaves, to explore this interaction in greater depth. Outputs in both systems are trees that conform to Weak Layering; that is, recursion and level-skipping are permitted.

(28)    System S.Branches
   a.   GEN:
        i.   Inputs: All syntactic trees $s$ where $s$ has $n$ $X^0$ terminals, $3 \leq n$ $\leq 5$, consisting of head-complement structures.
        ii.  Outputs: $\mathrm{GEN}(s)$ = all $<s, p>$ pairs, where $p$ is a prosodic tree rooted in an intonational phrase, with words as its terminals, and with all non-root, non-terminals being φs. Every $X^0$ in $s$ is mapped to a prosodic word in $p$, and linear order is preserved.
   b.   CON:
        i.   sp.MATCH(XP): Assign a violation for every XP with no corresponding φ.
        ii.  ps.MATCH(φ): Assign a violation for every φ with no corresponding XP.
        iii. BINMIN(φ): Assign a violation for every φ that has only one child.
        iv.  BINMAXBRANCHES(φ): Assign a violation for every φ that has more than two children.

(29)    System S.Leaves
   a.   GEN: Same as GEN for S.Branches
   b.   CON: Same as CON for S.Branches, except that BINMAXBRANCHES(φ) is replaced by BINMAXBRANCHES(φ)
        i.   BINMAXBRANCHES(φ): Assign a violation for every φ that contains more than two prosodic words.

Using SPOT (Bellik et al. 2015–2021) and OTWorkplace (Prince et al. 2007–2020), we calculated the typologies for S.Branches and S.Leaves.

### 10.5.2.1 S.Branches

The typology for S.Branches contained two languages (30), whose grammars (31) are distinguished only by their relative rankings of sp.MATCH and BINMIN(φ). The other two constraints, ps.MATCH(φ) and BINMAXBR(φ), are freely rankable, and therefore have only es in their columns of the ERCs. The sole distinction between L.1 and L.2 is expressed as the property p.min in (32). (See Chapter 1 for a brief introduction to Property Theory, or Alber, DelBusso and Prince 2016 for more details.) In L.1, BINMIN(φ) dominates sp.MATCH(XP), so there are no unary φs, and non-branching XPs are not matched in the output. In L.2, all prosodic parses are perfectly isomorphic to the syntactic input, because sp.MATCH(XP) dominates BINMIN(φ).

(30)    Typology for S.Branches

|  | 3 terminals | | 4 terminals | | 5 terminals | |
|---|---|---|---|---|---|---|
|  | [a [b [c]]] | [[[a] b] c] | [a [b [c [d]]]] | [[[[a] b] c] d] | [a [b [c [d [e]]]]] | [[[[[a] b] c] d] e] |
| L.1 | {(a (b c))} | {((a b) c)} | {(a (b (c d))))} | {(((a b) c) d)} | {(a (b (c (d e)))))} | {((((a b) c) d) e)} |
| L.2 | {(a (b (c))))} | {(((a) b) c)} | {(a (b (c (d)))))} | {((((a) b) c) d)} | {(a (b (c (d (e))))))} | {(((((a) b) c) d) e)} |

(31)    Grammars of S.Branches

|  | sp.MATCH(XP) | ps.MATCH($\varphi$) | BINMIN($\varphi$) | BINMAXBR($\varphi$) |
|---|---|---|---|---|
| L.1 | L | e | W | e |
| L.2 | W | e | L | e |

(32)    Property analysis of S.Branches

|  | $\alpha <> \beta$ |
|---|---|
| p.min | sp.MATCH(XP)    $<>$ BINMIN($\varphi$) |

|  | p.min |
|---|---|
| L.1 | $\alpha$ |
| L.2 | $\beta$ |

The fact that BINMAXBR($\varphi$) is freely rankable in both languages demonstrates that branch-counting binarity does not conflict with sp.MATCH(XP). In fact, violations of branch-counting binarity only occur when sp.MATCH(XP) is also violated. Every violation of branch-counting maximal binarity entails a violation of sp.MATCH(XP). This is because ternary-branching phonological phrases only arise when smaller $\varphi$s that would have corresponded to binary or unary XPs in the input are missing from the output. BINMAXBR($\varphi$) and sp.MATCH(XP) are in a special-general relationship, where BINMAXBR($\varphi$) functions as a specialized version of sp.MATCH(XP). This is illustrated in (33) for a small sample of candidates, although the result holds true across the entire candidate set. When BINMAXBRANCHES is violated, as in (a) and (b), one or more XPs have not been matched. There are always at least as many sp.MATCH violations as BINMAXBR violations, and a perfectly matching prosody never violates BINMAXBR.[4]

---



[4]    It is not the case, though, that a sp.MATCH violation always leads to a BINMAXBR($\varphi$) violation, since failing to match a unary XP does not create a ternary $\varphi$, and also because BINARITY violations can be avoided by inserting additional $\varphi$s that lack XP correspondents (although this violates ps.MATCH($\varphi$)).

(33)  Special-general relationship between sp.MATCH(XP) and BINMAXBR($\varphi$)

| Input | Winner | Loser | sp.MATCH(XP) | BINMAXBR($\varphi$) |
|---|---|---|---|---|
| [a [b [c d]]] | (a (b (c d))) | ((a) (b) (c d)) | W | W |
| | (a (b (c d))) | (a b (c d)) | W | W |

### 10.5.2.2 S.Leaves

The leaf-counting system, S.Leaves, has a typology with four languages, rather than just two. The optima in L.1 and L.2 in S.Leaves are identical to those in L.1 and L.2 of S.Branches. The grammars differ, however, in having an additional crucial ranking, that of sp.MATCH(XP) against BINMAXLEAVES($\varphi$). This can be seen in the ERCs in (35), where the column for BINMAXLEAVES($\varphi$) is populated with *W*s and *L*s, rather than ambivalent *e*s. In S.Leaves, the optima of L.1 and L.2 appear when sp.MATCH(XP) dominates BINMAXLEAVES($\varphi$).

In L.3 and L.4, BINMAXLEAVES($\varphi$) dominates sp.MATCH(XP) instead. In both these languages, $\varphi$s can only contain a maximum of two prosodic words, because BINMAXLEAVES($\varphi$) is undominated. As a result, XPs containing one or two $X^0$s are matched, but larger XPs are not. This has the result of selecting mostly flattened optima like {(a b) c d e} (L.3), in which the prosodic words *c*, *d*, and *e* are parsed directly into the intonational phrase, flagrantly violating the parsing principle of Exhaustivity. This holds in both languages; they differ only in their treatment of unary $\varphi$s, which are permitted in L.4 but prohibited in L.3. The four languages of the typology can be distinguished by the two properties in (36): p.min describes the opposition of sp.MATCH(XP) to minimal binarity, and p.max describes its opposition to maximal leaf-counting binarity. Both are wide-scope.

(34)  Typology for S.Leaves

| | 3 terminals | | 4 terminals | | 5 terminals | |
|---|---|---|---|---|---|---|
| | [a [b [c]]] | [[[a] b] c] | [a [b [c d]]]] | [[[[a] b] c] d] | [a [b [c [d e]]]]] | [[[[[a] b] c] d] e] |
| **L.1** | {(a (b c))} | {((a b) c)} | {(a (b (c d)))} | {(((a b) c) d)} | {(a (b (c (d e))))} | {(((((a b) c) d) e)} |
| **L.2** | {(a (b (c)))} | {(((a) b) c)} | {(a (b (c (d))))} | {(((((a) b) c) d)} | {(a (b (c (d (e)))))} | {((((((a) b) c) d) e)} |
| **L.3** | {a (b c)} | {(a b) c} | {a b (c d)} | {(a b) c d} | {a b c (d e)} | {(a b) c d e} |
| **L.4** | {a (b (c))} | {((a) b) c} | {a b (c (d))} | {((a) b) c d} | {a b c (d (e))} | {((a) b) c d e} |

(35)     Grammars of S.Leaves

|      | sp.MATCH(XP) | ps.MATCH($\varphi$) | BINMIN($\varphi$) | BINMAXLEAVES($\varphi$) |
|------|--------------|---------------------|-------------------|--------------------------|
| L.1  | L            | e                   | W                 | L                        |
| L.2  | W            | e                   | L                 | L                        |
| L.3  | L            | e                   | W                 | W                        |
| L.4  | W            | e                   | L                 | W                        |

(36)     Property analysis of S.Leaves

|        | $\alpha <> \beta$ |
|--------|-------------------|
| p.min  | sp.MATCH(XP)  $<>$ BINMIN($\varphi$) |
| p.max  | sp.MATCH(XP)  $<>$ BINMAXLV($\varphi$) |

|      | p.min    | p.max    |
|------|----------|----------|
| L.1  | $\alpha$ | $\alpha$ |
| L.2  | $\beta$  | $\alpha$ |
| L.3  | $\alpha$ | $\beta$  |
| L.4  | $\beta$  | $\beta$  |

S.Leaves shows that BINMAXLEAVES($\varphi$) conflicts with sp.MATCH(XP) regularly. We can see from the optima in L.3 and L.4, where BINMAXLV($\varphi$) outranks sp.MATCH(XP), that leaf-counting binarity favors a range of optima that violate sp.MATCH(XP). The level-skipping optima in L.3 and L.4 of S.Leaves are harmonically bounded in S.Branches, because they do not improve performance on BINMAXBRANCHES($\varphi$), but do detract from performance on sp.MATCH(XP).

Prosodic parses that satisfy sp.MATCH(XP), such as those in (37), violate BINMAXLEAVES($\varphi$) if the input contains one or more XPs that contain more than two terminals. The input in (37) contains an XP with terminals {a, b, c, d}, and another with terminals {a, b, c}. So (a-d), which match those longer XPs, all violate BINMAXLEAVES twice. Because BINMAXLEAVES and sp.MATCH do not function in a special-general relationship, typologies that combine Match Theory with BINMAXLEAVES tend to be larger and are always more complex than those with BINMAXBRANCHES.

(37)     Parses satisfying sp.MATCH but violating BINMAXLEAVES

| [a [b [c [d]]]]       | sp.MATCH(xp) | BINMAXLEAVES($\varphi$) |
|-----------------------|--------------|--------------------------|
| a. (a (b (c (d))))    | 0            | 2                        |
| b. ((a) ((b) ((c) (d)))) | 0         | 2                        |
| c. ((a) ((b) (c (d)))) | 0           | 2                        |
| d. ((a) (b ((c) (d)))) | 0           | 2.                       |

### 10.5.3 Interim summary

To sum up the conclusions thus far, we have established that branch-counting binarity and leaf-counting binarity predict different types of size effects when recursion is permitted by GEN. Both kinds are empirically attested (§10.2). Branch-counting can drive size-driven recursion, as seen in the case study of Irish phrasing (§10.3). Leaf-counting binarity instead favors size-driven category promotion (§10.4). Such promotion occurs in Japanese prosodic words, where prosodic words are promoted to phrases when they would otherwise contain too many feet or syllables. It also occurs in Italian phrasing, where phonological phrases are promoted to intonational phrases when they contain too many words. Size-driven recursion is also attested both at the phrase level and at the word level (38).

(38)    Attested size effects with representative examples

| Size-limited category | Size-driven recursion (requires BINBRANCHES) | Size-driven category promotion (requires BINLEAVES) |
|---|---|---|
| ω | Danish | Japanese |
| φ | Irish | Italian |

Leaf-counting binarity creates larger, more complex typologies than branch-counting binarity, because it conflicts directly with sp.MATCH, whereas branch-counting binarity functions as a special case of sp.MATCH whenever the input syntax is binary-branching. (The comparison of typology sizes in Bellik and Kalivoda (2016) shows that systems with sp.ALIGN are also larger with BINLEAVES($\varphi$) than with BINBRANCHES($\varphi$), although the reasons for this are not directly investigated here.) Leaf-counting also favors level-skipping structures that linguists are unlikely to propose as optima. Therefore, it may be wise to avoid BINLEAVES unless the goal is to model category promotion.

## 10.6    Uniformity as an alternative to leaf-counting

One analysis that uses leaf-counting binarity without the aim of deriving category promotion is Ito and Mester's analysis of Japanese phrasing, previously listed in the table in (12). This analysis uses both branch-counting and leaf-counting binarity, and both are crucial to selecting the correct optima. In this section, we introduce a new constraint on Uniformity that can replace leaf-counting binarity in explaining Japanese phrasing, without having the same adverse effects on the size of the typology.

Like Connemara Irish, Tokyo Japanese phonological phrasing exhibits size-driven rebracketing (39). Unlike in Irish, the mismatching $\varphi$ is inserted on the right. Therefore, STRONGSTART, which drives the insertion in Irish, has nothing to say about the Japanese case; another prosodic well-formedness constraint must favor the rebracketing. This pattern can be captured by combining BINMAXBRANCHES($\varphi$) with BINMAXLEAVES($\varphi,\omega$), as in Ito and Mester (2020), Kalivoda (2018), and Kalivoda (Chapter 7). Leaf-counting binarity is needed to prevent matching (39b) Branch-counting binarity has no objection to this isomorphic candidate, but leaf-counting binarity disfavors it because of the two $\varphi$s that contain more than two words ($\varphi_{abc}$ and $\varphi_{abcd}$). As noted by Ishihara (2014), the use of BINMAXLEAVES($\varphi$) in this system favors a category-promoting parse (39c) which predicts the wrong tonal contour for this output. Phonological downstep applies throughout the maximal $\varphi$ in Tokyo Japanese, and is observed at the left edge of the second minimal $\varphi$, *(c d)*, meaning that there must be a $\varphi$ spanning all four terminals, not merely an intonational phrase. Ishihara (2014) proposes the constraint MATCHMAX(XP) (40) to avoid this category promotion.

(39)    Rebracketing in Tokyo Japanese

| | | | |
|---|---|---|---|
| a. | Observed: | [[[a b] c] d]] $\rightarrow$ ((a b)(c d)) | *Rebracketing* |
| b. | Not observed: | [[[a b] c] d]] $\nrightarrow$ {((a b) c) d} | *Matching* |
| c. | Not observed: | [[[a b] c] d]] $\nrightarrow$ {(a b)(c d)} | *Rebracketing +* |
| | | | *category promotion* |
| d. | Not observed: | [[[a b] c] d]] $\nrightarrow$ ((a b) c d) | *Squishing* |

(40)    MATCHMAX(XP$_{lex}$): Assign a violation for every lexical XP in the input syntactic tree that is not dominated by another lexical XP, and that lacks a $\varphi$ correspondent in the output prosodic tree (Ishihara 2014).

Kalivoda further observes that branch-counting binarity is needed to avoid squishing, as in (39d.) which produces a ternary-branching parse but avoids violating ps.MATCH($\varphi$), since it does not insert the correspondentless $\varphi_{ab}$. Hence the use of both leaf-counting and branch-counting in the same analysis.

The system definition in (41) represents Ito and Mester's (2020) OT description of Japanese rebracketing, with the distinction between accented and unaccented words. It generates a huge typology of 552 languages, one of which is compatible with the data from Japanese.

(41)    System BinLeaves-Japanese-Accent = Leaves.J.Acc

    a.    *Inputs*: All uniformly left-branching, binary-branching two-, three-, and four-word inputs, where each word is either accented (a) or unaccented (u) ([uu], [au], [ua], [aa], [[uu] u], [[uu] a], ...), for a total of $2^2 + 2^3 + 2^4 = 28$ inputs

    b.    *Outputs*: GEN *(s)* = all pairs $<s, p>$ such that $p$ that fulfills (i)–(iii)

        i.    $p$ is rooted in φ (That is, MATCHMAX is enforced as a condition on GEN)

        ii.    All syntactic words in $s$ are mapped to prosodic words in $p$

        iii.    Recursion (at the phonological phrase level) is allowed

    c.    CON: Replicates the constraint set in Ito and Mester 2020.

        i.    sp.MATCH(XP): Assign a violation for every XP in the syntactic tree that lacks a corresponding φ in the prosodic tree.

        ii.    ps.MATCH(φ): Assign a violation for every φ in the prosodic tree that lacks a corresponding XP in the syntactic tree.

        iii.    ACCENTASHEAD: Assign a violation for every lexically accented word that is not the head of a minimal φ.

        iv.    NOLAPSE: Assign a violation for every fully low-toned word, i.e., an unaccented word that follows an accented word without an intervening φ-left edge.

        v.    EQUALSISTERS1: Assign a violation for every pair of adjacent sisters that differ in prosodic category.

        vi.    EQUALSISTERS2: Assign a violation for every pair of adjacent sisters that differ in prosodic category and in which the higher-category sister is non-minimal.

        vii.    BINMIN(φ): Assign a violation for every φ that has less than two children.

        viii.    BINMAXBRANCHES(φ): Assign a violation for every φ that has more than two immediate children.

        ix.    BINMAXLEAVES(φ, ω): Assign a violation for every φ that contains (at any level) more than two prosodic words.


## 10.6.1 BALANCEDSISTERS

The observed phrasing involves size-driven recursion rather than size-driven category promotion, leading us to wonder whether another constraint could replace BINMAXLEAVES while reducing the size of the predicted typology. EQUALSISTERS does favor the rebracketed parse, but it cannot work in the Japanese system, because it needs to be ranked low to account for other input/output pairs (see Ito and Mester 2020, Kalivoda 2018). We propose an alternative constraint that demands that sisters be equal in length, rather than equal in prosodic category (42).

(42)      BALANCEDSISTERS($\pi$): Sisters under a parent node of category $\pi$
          should have the same number of children.
          *Formally:* Assign a violation for every node of category $\pi \in \{\iota, \varphi, \omega\}$
          whose children are not all of the same size. The size of a child is the
          number of interface nodes it branches into ($\iota$s, $\varphi$s, or $\omega$s; syllables
          and feet are not counted, by default).

This constraint definition avoids the computational complexity of BINLEAVES,
since it is restricted to local searches, and enforces the parsing principle Uniformity (43) proposed in Ghini (1993) for Italian $\varphi$-formation, and taken up
by Sandalo and Truckenbrodt's (2003) analysis of phonological phrasing in
Brazilian Portuguese.

(43)      *Uniformity and average weight (Ghini 1993)*
          A string is ideally parsed into same length units; the average
          weight of the $\varphi$s depends on tempo: at an average rate of speech
          (moderato), a $\varphi$ contains two phonological words; the number of $\omega$s
          within a $\varphi$ increases or decreases by one by speeding up or slowing
          down the rate of speech.

As illustrated in (44), both BALSIS and BINLEAVES favor the rebracketed candidate (a). The constraints differ, however, in that BALSIS assigns no violations at all to the rebracketed candidate, because each pair of sisters has the
same number of children: $\varphi_2$ and $\varphi_3$ each have two children; all $\omega$s have zero
children. BINLEAVES assigns (a) one violation. Both constraints assign two
violations to the matching candidate, BINLEAVES for the two phrases that
contain more than two words, and BALSIS to the two phrases whose children
are not of the same size.

(44) BINLEAVES and BALSIS

| | BINLEAVES($\varphi$) | BALSIS($\varphi$) |
|---|---|---|
| a. 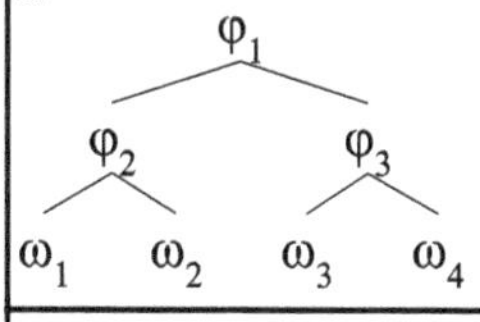 <br><br> $\varphi_1$ branches into $\varphi_2$ and $\varphi_3$; $\varphi_2$ branches into $\omega_1$, $\omega_2$; $\varphi_3$ branches into $\omega_3$, $\omega_4$ | 1 | 0 |
| b. 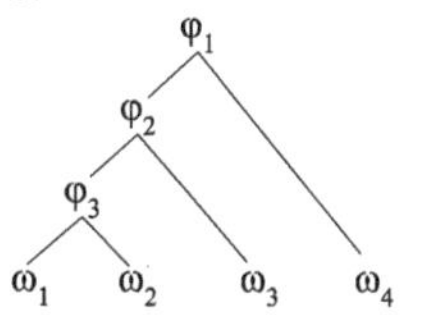 <br><br> $\varphi_1$ branches into $\varphi_2$ and $\omega_4$; $\varphi_2$ branches into $\varphi_3$ and $\omega_3$; $\varphi_3$ branches into $\omega_1$, $\omega_2$ | 2 <br><br> $\varphi_1, \varphi_2$ | 2 <br><br> $\varphi_2$'s children, <br> $\varphi_1$'s children |

To get a sense of the structures that satisfy BALANCEDSISTERS($\varphi$), consider the list of all the trees with two-, three-, or four-terminal $\omega$s, rooted in a phonological phrase that perfectly satisfy BALANCEDSISTERS($\varphi$) (45). For two words, there are two possible phrasings: one flat phrasing with no internal structure, which fulfills BALSIS because both of the $\varphi$'s children have no children; and one phrasing in which each word is parsed into a unary $\varphi$, which fulfills BALSIS because both of the root $\varphi$'s children have one child each. For an input of three words, there are likewise two structures, which can be characterized in the same fashion. Longer inputs, such as those four words long, can be parsed in more ways. For example, in addition to being parsed into a flat structure or a series of unary $\varphi$s, four words could also be parsed into two $\varphi$s that each contain two words—this is the desired rebracketed optimum for the input [a [b [c d]]] in Japanese. Such a parse satisfies BALSIS because each of the root $\varphi$'s children has two children of its own, and each of those children (the phonological words) is a terminal node. Each of those two-word phrases can also contain additional substructure, thus multiplying the total number of possible parses that satisfy BALANCEDSISTERS($\varphi$). For example, the root node in (vii.) satisfies BALSIS because it has two children that each have two daughters. In the left half of the tree *(a b)*, those daughters are both terminals with zero children, so this $\varphi$ also satisfies BALSIS. In the right half, *((c)(d))*, both daughters are unary $\varphi$s, so this also satisfies BALSIS, for zero violations for the tree as a whole.

(45)    Trees rooted in $\varphi$ that *satisfy* BALSIS($\varphi$)

| $2\omega$ | i.  ((a) (b)) |
|---|---|
|  | ii. (a b) |
| $3\omega$ | iii.((a) (b) (c)) |
|  | iv.(a b c) |
| $4\omega$ | v.  ((a) (b) (c) (d)) |
|  | vi.(((a) (b)) ((c) (d))) |
|  | vii.     (((a) (b)) (c d)) |
|  | viii.     ((a b) ((c) (d))) |
|  | ix.((a b) (c d))          ← Japanese rebracketing |
|  | x. (a b c d) |

A few of the many structures that violate BALANCEDSISTERS($\varphi$) are shown in (46), where "–" indicates sisterhood.

(46)   Some ways to violate BALANCEDSISTERS($\varphi$)

   a.   (a (b) (c))   1 violation for $\omega_a$–$\varphi_b$ under $\varphi_{abc}$: $\omega_a$ has 0 children, $\varphi_b$ has 1 child

   b.   (a (b c))   1 violation for $\omega_a$–$\varphi_{bc}$ under $\varphi_{abc}$: $\omega_a$ has 0 children, $\varphi_{bc}$ has 2 children

   c.   ((a) (b c))   1 violation for $\varphi_a$–$\varphi_{bc}$ under $\varphi_{abc}$: $\varphi_a$ has 1 child, $\varphi_{bc}$ has 2 children

   d.   (((a b) c) d)   2 violations: 1 for $\varphi_{ab}$–$\omega_c$ (2 children, 0 ch.), 1 for $\varphi_{abc}$–$\omega_d$ (2 ch., 0 ch.)

   e.   (a b (c d))   1 violation for $\varphi_a$–$\omega_b$–$\omega_{cd}$ (0 children, 0 children, 2 children)

### 10.6.2 BalSis.J.Acc

With these demonstrations that BALANCEDSISTERS can favor the desired optimum and disfavor undesirable parses for Japanese, we now compare the known leaf-counting solution of Leaves.J.Acc (41) to a minimally different possible solution that uses BALANCEDSISTERS instead of leaf-counting binarity (47).

(47)   System BalancedSisters-Japanese-Accent = BalSis.J.Acc

   a.   GEN: Same as GEN in Leaves.J.Acc (41a, b)

   b.   CON: Same as CON in Leaves.J.Acc (41c) but replace BINMAXLEAVES($\varphi$) with BALANCEDSISTERS($\varphi$)

      (i)   BALANCEDSISTERS($\varphi$) = BALSIS($\varphi$): Assign a violation for every $\varphi$ whose children are not all the same length.

The BalSis.J.Acc typology contains 283 languages, one of which is compatible with the facts about Japanese tones. This means that BALANCEDSISTERS is able to successfully replace BINMAXLEAVES in selecting rebracketed parses for four-word inputs. The constraint rankings for Japanese in Leaves.J.Acc and BalSis.J.Acc were very similar; their differences are highlighted in the table in (48).

(48)   Comparing Leaves.J.Acc and BalSis.J.Acc (partial constraint ranking only)

|  | Leaves.J.Acc | BalSis.J.Acc |
|---|---|---|
| Japanese | BINBRANCHES, BINLEAVES $\gg$ ps.MATCH($\varphi$) | BINBRANCHES $\gg$ BALSIS $\gg$ ps.MATCH($\varphi$) |
| # languages | 552 | 283 |

Two parses of the four-word input are optima in both BalSis.J.Acc and Leaves.J.Acc: the rebracketing parse and the isomorphic parse. Each system also has an additional possible optimum that is harmonically bounded (HB) in the other system. The tableaux in (49) and (50) shows these four candidates, along with the partial constraint rankings that derives the Japanese pattern in BalSis.J.Acc and Leaves.J.Acc, respectively. In BalSis.J.Acc, BINMAXBR outranks BALSIS, which in turn outranks ps.MATCH($\varphi$). The flat candidate (c) satisfies BALSIS, but violates BINMAXBR($\varphi$) since it consists of a $\varphi$ with four daughters. To rule this out, BINMAXBR must crucially dominate BALSIS($\varphi$), as well. In Leaves.J.Acc, no such crucial ranking can be established between BINMAXBR($\varphi$) and BINMAXLV($\varphi$). There are no candidates penalized by BINMAXBR($\varphi$) that are not also penalized by BINMAXLV($\varphi$), which objects to the root $\varphi$ in all candidates (50).

(49)      Japanese in BalSis.J.Acc (partial constraint ranking; candidates that are optima in BalSis.J.Acc or Leaves.J.Acc)

| [[[u u] u] u] | BINMAXBR($\varphi$) | BALSIS($\varphi$) | ps.MATCH($\varphi$) | sp.MATCH(XP) |
|---|---|---|---|---|
| →   a. ((u u) (u u)) | 0 | 0 | 1 | 1 |
| b. (((u u) u) u) | $e_0$ | $W_2$ | $L_0$ | $L_0$ |
| c. (u u u u) | $W_1$ | $e_0$ | $L_0$ | $W_2$ |
| HB   d. ((u u) u u) | $W_1$ | $W_1$ | $L_0$ | $e_1$ |

(50)      Japanese in Leaves.J.Acc (partial constraint ranking only; candidates that are optima in BalSis.J.Acc or Leaves.J.Acc)

| [[[u u] u] u] | BINMAXBR($\varphi$) | BINMAXLV($\varphi$) | ps.MATCH($\varphi$) | sp.MATCH(XP) |
|---|---|---|---|---|
| →   a. ((u u) (u u)) | 0 | 1 | 1 | 1 |
| b. (((u u) u) u) | $e_0$ | $W_2$ | $L_0$ | $L_0$ |
| HB   c. (u u u u) | $W_1$ | $e_1$ | $L_0$ | $W_2$ |
| d. ((u u) u u) | $W_1$ | $e_1$ | $L_0$ | $e_1$ |

The most striking difference between the two systems is in the size of their typologies. At 552 languages, Leaves.J.Acc's typology contains nearly twice as many languages as BalSis.J.Acc's typology (283 languages). This echoes the finding that BINLEAVES creates larger, more complex typologies than BINBRANCHES (§10.5), but with a constraint on uniformity of parsing, rather than on branchingness. So although BALSIS is able to motivate rebracketing in the same way that BINLEAVES does, it does not have the same explosive effects on the typology's size. BALSIS resembles BINBRANCHES both in its local evaluation and in its more limited effect on typology size, at least in this example.

If we compare the optima in Leaves.J.Acc to those in BalSis.J.Acc, we can see one reason why the BalSis.J.Acc typology is so much smaller: Leaves.J.Acc allows more optima than BalSis.J.Acc. The table in (51) shows, for a selection of inputs, all the optima that only occur in one system but not the other. In each case, BalSis.J.Acc contains only one optimum that Leaves.J.Acc excludes, and it is the structure in which every word is parsed into a unary φ. Leaves.J.Acc, on the other hand, includes multiple imbalanced optima— six of them in the case of input [[[u u] a] u]. None of them, strictly speaking, violate Exhaustivity, since all are rooted in φ, as per the requirements of Gen for these systems. The optima that are unique to Leaves.J.Acc violate BinLeaves(φ) all violate BalancedSisters and the principle of uniform parsing. Many also violate EqualSisters or EqualSisters2, because they contain sister nodes of uneven length, and often depth.

(51)    Parses that are optima in one system only (selected inputs)

| Input | Optimal in Leaves.J.Acc only | Optimal in BalSis.J.Acc only |
|---|---|---|
| uuuu | 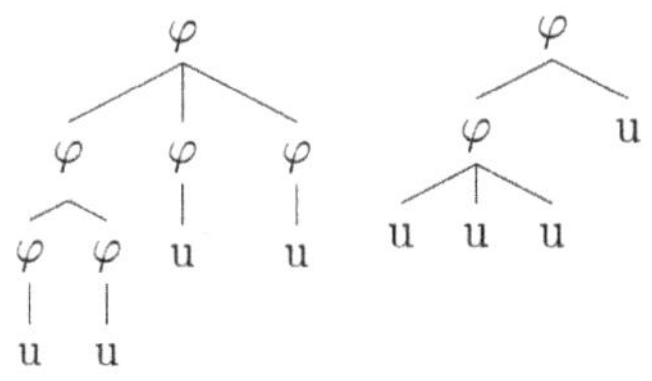 φ[ φ[ φ[u] φ[u] ] φ[u] φ[u] ] ; φ[ φ[u u u] u ] | 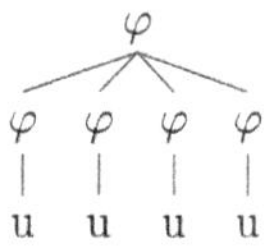 φ[ φ[u] φ[u] φ[u] φ[u] ] |
| uuua | 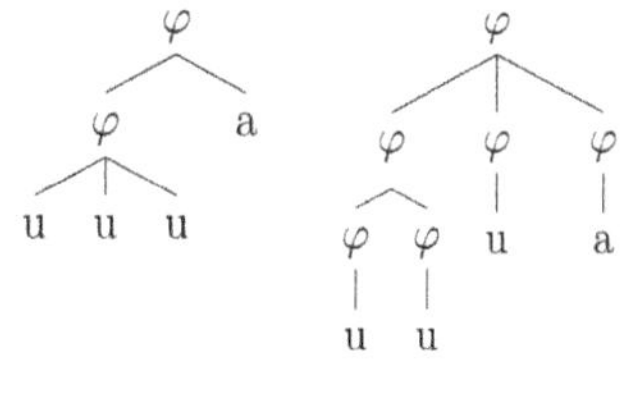 φ[ φ[u u u] a ] ; φ[ φ[ φ[u] φ[u] ] φ[u] φ[a] ] | 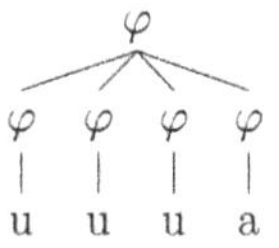 φ[ φ[u] φ[u] φ[u] φ[a] ] |
| uuau | 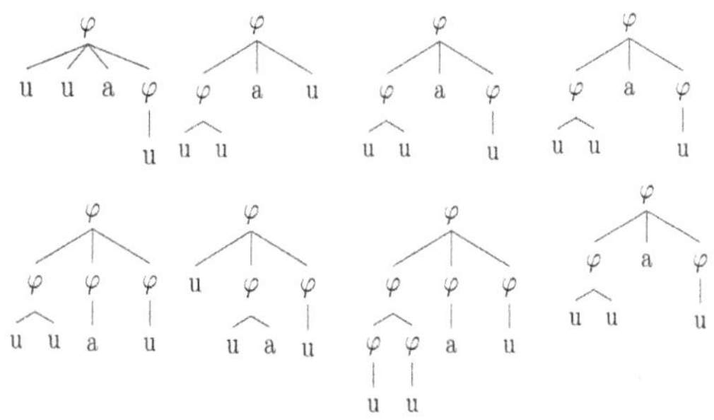 φ[ u u a φ[u] ] ; φ[ φ[u u] a u ] ; φ[ φ[u u] a φ[u] ] ; φ[ φ[u u] a φ[u] ] ; φ[ φ[u u] φ[a] φ[u] ] ; φ[ u φ[u a] φ[u] ] ; φ[ φ[ φ[u] φ[u] ] φ[a] φ[u] ] ; φ[ φ[u u] a φ[u] ] | 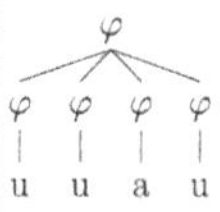 φ[ φ[u] φ[u] φ[a] φ[u] ] |

The few optima that are present in BalSis.J.Acc but not in Leaves.J.Acc both satisfy BALSIS and also violate BINLEAVES minimally,[5] while faring worse on sp.MATCH(XP) and/or BINMIN than the optima that are unique to the leaf-counting system. This is illustrated for inputs *uuuu* and *uuua* in (52), with the outputs shown above in (51). Meanwhile, the optima that are present in Leaves.J.Acc but not BalSis.J.Acc violate BINLEAVES minimally, but violate BALSIS.

(52)    BalSis.J.Acc optima (white background) vs. Leaves.J.Acc optima (grey background)

| Input | Output | BALSIS($\varphi$) | BINLV($\varphi$) | sp.MATCH(XP) | BINMIN($\varphi$) |
|---|---|---|---|---|---|
| [[[u u] u] u] | a. ((u) (u) (u) (u)) | 0 | 1 | 2 | 4 |
| | b. (((u) (u)) (u) (u)) | 1 | 1 | 1 | 4 |
| | c.    ((u u u) u) | 1 | 2 | 1 | 0 |
| [[[u u] u] a] | d.    ((u) (u) (u) (a)) | 0 | 1 | 2 | 4 |
| | e.    ((u u u) a) | 1 | 2 | 1 | 0 |
| | f.    (((u) (u)) (u) (a)) | 1 | 1 | 1 | 4 |

This comparison of optima that are unique to each system reveals that BINLEAVES filters out fewer candidates than BALANCEDSISTERS does. As a result, BINLEAVES leaves more candidates in the running for other constraints (sp. MATCH, ps.MATCH, ACCENTASHEAD, NOLAPSE) to select among. This appears to be the reason BINLEAVES results in a larger typology than BALSIS. BALSIS is not as easily satisfied as BINLEAVES, and filters out so many candidates that its typology here (BalSis.J.Acc) is nearly half the size of the equivalent BINLEAVES system (Leaves.J.Acc).

This finding that typology sizes are larger with BINLEAVES than with BALSIS complements our previous study of typology sizes with Kinyambo phrasing (§10.5.1). The upshot is that BINLEAVES accepts many prosodic structures that linguists are unlikely to think of as possible optima, and consequently interacts in complex ways with other constraints to yield typologies full of unexpected, and possibly undesirable, predictions. BALSIS, on the other hand, is able to do the same work that BINLEAVES does in selecting a rebracketed parse, without unnecessarily exploding the typology of predicted parses.

---

[5]   A minimal violation of BINLEAVES($\varphi$) with this candidate set is one violation; the root $\varphi$ in all outputs in this system violates BINLEAVES($\varphi$).

### 10.6.3  Filtering by BinBranches vs. BinLeaves vs. BalSis

We can further establish the differences in the filtering by each of these constraints on Binarity and Uniformity by examining a simplified system (53) and comparing the number of candidates that violate each constraint minimally, rather than calculating a typology. For this purpose, we consider two inputs, of three and four terminals. Their specific syntax is irrelevant, because we omit all syntax–prosody mapping constraints from the system. We include branch-counting binarity as well as leaf-counting binarity and BALANCEDSISTERS for the sake of comparing all three of the constraints on size side by side.

(53)　System BinUni
- a.　*Inputs*: [[[a] b] c], [[[[a] b] c] d]
- b.　*Outputs*: GEN*(s)* = all pairs $<s, p>$ such that $p$ that fulfills (i)–(iii)
  - i.　$p$ is rooted in ι.
  - ii.　All syntactic words in $s$ are mapped to prosodic words ω in $p$.
  - iii.　All non-root, non-terminals are φs. Recursion (at the phonological phrase level) is allowed.
  - iv.　$p$ contains at least one φ (HEADEDNESS).
- c.　CON
  - i.　BINMAXBRANCHES(φ): Assign a violation for every φ that has more than two immediate children.
  - ii.　BINMAXLEAVES(φ): Assign a violation for every φ that contains (at any level) more than two prosodic words.
  - iii.　BALANCEDSISTERS(φ): Assign a violation for every φ whose children are not all the same length.

This candidate set contains 47 parses of three words, and 351 parses of four words. The table in (54) shows how many of these parses minimally violate the three constraints of CON. The differences are substantial. Branch-counting binarity is satisfied by the greatest number of parses (39 for *a b c*, and 223 for *a b c d*). Next is leaf-counting binarity, which is satisfied by 23 parses of *a b c* and only 79 of *a b c d*. Finally, BALANCEDSISTERS is satisfied by fewer still: 17 parses of *a b c* and 57 of *a b c d*. Judging by raw numbers alone, then, we might expect that branch-counting would result in the largest typologies.

(54)   Number of candidates in BinUni that minimally violate each constraint

| Terminals | $\textsc{BinBr}(\varphi)$ | $\textsc{BinLv}(\varphi)$ | $\textsc{BalSis}(\varphi)$ | Total candidates |
|---|---|---|---|---|
| a b c | 39 | 23 | 17 | 47 |
| a b c d | 223 | 79 | 57 | 351 |
|  | 262 | 102 | 74 | 398 |

However, as we saw above (§10.3, §10.5.2), branch-counting binarity acts as a special case of syntax-prosody matching, and never conflicts with sp.$\textsc{Match}$(XP) when the syntax is binary-branching. It is due to this stringency interaction that $\textsc{BinMaxBranches}(\varphi)$ produces smaller typologies with sp.$\textsc{Match}$(XP) than $\textsc{BinMaxLeaves}(\varphi, \omega)$ does. Both $\textsc{BinLeaves}$ and $\textsc{BalSis}$ conflict with sp.$\textsc{Match}$(XP)—$\textsc{BinLeaves}(\varphi)$ for XPs that contain three or more terminals, and $\textsc{BalSis}(\varphi)$ for head-complement structures and any other structure in which syntactic sisters do not have the same length. $\textsc{BinLeaves}(\varphi)$ is satisfied by about one and a half times as many candidates as $\textsc{BalSis}(\varphi)$.

Since all the constraints here are indexed to the $\varphi$ level, the $\iota$ root is exempt from consideration, and does not violate $\textsc{BinBr}(\varphi)$, $\textsc{BinLeaves}(\varphi)$, or $\textsc{BalSis}(\varphi)$, no matter how suprabinary or non-uniform it is. Half of the candidate set contains a $\varphi$ that spans all the terminals (a $\varphi$ stem, if you will). The difference in the number of $\varphi$-stemmed candidates admitted by each constraint is more dramatic. $\textsc{BinBr}(\varphi)$ is minimally violated by 96 candidates, and $\textsc{BinLv}(\varphi)$ by 104, but $\textsc{BalSis}(\varphi)$ by only eight. It is possible to fully satisfy $\textsc{BalSis}(\varphi)$ even with a $\varphi$ stem that contains three or four words (i.e., the minimum violation of $\textsc{BalSis}(\varphi)$ is zero), as in the parses in (56). But it is not possible to fully satisfy $\textsc{BinLv}(\varphi)$ with these structures, because the stem $\varphi$ always violates it once. Thus, the minimum violation of $\textsc{BinLv}(\varphi)$ is one for this candidate subset, and there are even more $\varphi$-stemmed outputs that violate $\textsc{BinLv}(\varphi)$ minimally (once; 104 candidates) than non-$\varphi$-stemmed candidates that violate it minimally (zero times; 102 candidates).

(55)   Number of $\varphi$-stemmed candidates that minimally violate each constraint

| Terminals | $\textsc{BinBr}(\varphi)$ | $\textsc{BinLv}(\varphi)$ | $\textsc{BalSis}(\varphi)$ | Total $\varphi$-stem candidates |
|---|---|---|---|---|
| a b c | 16 | 24 | 2 | 24 |
| a b c d | 80 | 80 | 6 | 176 |
|  | 96 | 104 | 8 | 200 |

(56)    φ-stemmed candidates that satisfy BALSIS(φ)

|              | *a b c*      | *a b c d*           |
|--------------|--------------|---------------------|
| Flat         | (a b c)      | (a b c d)           |
| Rebracketed  |              | ((a b) (c d))       |
|              |              | ((a b) ((c) (d)))   |
|              |              | (((a) (b)) (c d))   |
|              |              | (((a) (b)) ((c) (d)))|
| Unary        | ((a)(b)(c))  | ((a) (b) (c) (d))   |

BINLV(φ) is minimally violated by many more structures than BALSIS(φ). Therefore, in a system with more constraints that conflict with each other, such as Leaves.J.Acc, those additional constraints would have half again as many candidates to choose from. This larger number of possible parses creates the potential for more linear extension grammars (legs, that is, constraint rankings; Alber et al. 2016, Alber and Prince 2021, Merchant and Prince 2021) to produce unique languages. The more unique languages are generated by legs, the larger the typology. The less strict filtering by BINLV(φ) compared to BALSIS(φ) is a factor in Leaves.J.Acc's typology being so much larger than BalSis.J.Acc's typology.

It is not the case, however, that every typology using BINLV(φ) is larger than a corresponding typology using BALSIS(φ). The table in (57) shows how typology size increases as more constraints are added, for systems using the inputs [[[a] b] c] and [[[[a] b] c] d], with leaf-counting or Uniformity, where all output trees are rooted in φ. The last row also shows another system with more inputs and a different constraint set, based on the sp.MATCH + ps.ALIGN system from Bellik et al. (2022). For all systems in (57), the typology sizes do not differ dramatically, and in fact BINLEAVES(φ) results in smaller typologies in most of these systems. The enormous difference in typology sizes between Leaves.J.Acc and BalSis.J.Acc is not manifested in these smaller systems. While we have identified some of the factors that contribute to increased typology size in systems that use BINMAXLEAVES, other factors clearly remain. A full understanding of the conditions under which BINLEAVES(φ) results in a dramatically larger typology than BALSIS(φ), however, is left for future research.

(57)    Typology sizes with BinLeaves($\varphi$) vs. BalSis($\varphi$)

| Inputs | | Constraints | | BinLv($\varphi$) | BalSis($\varphi$) |
|---|---|---|---|---|---|
| [[[a] b] c],<br>[[[[a] b] c] d] | a. | sp.Match(XP), ps.Match($\varphi$) | | 2 | 4 |
| | b. | a.Con + BinMaxBr($\varphi$) | | 3 | 8 |
| | c. | b.Con + EqualSisters1 | | 10 | 11 |
| | d. | c.Con + BinMin($\varphi$) | | 12 | 11 |
| | e. | d.Con + EqualSisters2 | | 15 | 15 |
| [a [b c]], [[a b] c],<br>[a [b [c d]]], [a [[b c] d]],<br>[[a b] [c d]], [[a [b c]] d],<br>[[[a b] c] d] | f. | sp.Match(XP), ps.AlignL($\varphi$),<br>ps.AlignR($\varphi$), BinMin($\varphi$),<br>BinMaxBr($\varphi$) | | 8 | 9 |

### 10.6.4 Squishing and flattening

The types of optima that emerge in leaf-counting systems and Uniformity systems differ. This is most apparent for systems that do not include EqualSisters as part of Con, such as rows a., b., and f. in (57). Among those systems, all permit isomorphic parses (when sp.Match is undominated) and symmetrically branching parses (which maximally satisfy all markedness constraints), only the leaf-counting systems admit squishing parses, and only the BalSis systems admit completely flattened parses. As previously shown in (49) and (50), this pattern also sometimes occurs in systems that include EqualSisters (Leaves.J.Acc vs. BalSis.J.Acc).

A squished candidate (Kalivoda 2018), as in (58), is one where small XPs containing one or two words are matched, but words outside of small XPs are parsed directly up into a higher node.

(58)    *Squishing*: [[[a b] c] d] → ((a b) c d)

Squishing candidates appear as optima in leaf-counting systems because they fare better on prosody-to-syntax mapping constraints than rebracketed optima like *((a b)(c d))*; equally well on syntax–prosody mapping constraints like sp.Match; and equally well on BinLeaves, though less well on BinBranches. The squishing candidate always harmonically bounds a completely flattened parse like *(a b c d)* in leaf-counting systems without EqualSisters, e.g., (57a, b, f), since the flattened parse incurs an additional sp.Match violation. These interactions are shown in (59).

(59)     Squishing tableau: $[[[a\ b]\ c]\ d] \rightarrow ((a\ b)\ c\ d)$ for (57f) with BinLeaves

|  | $[[[a\ b]\ c]\ d]$ | $\text{BinLv}(\varphi)$ | ps.$\text{AlignL}(\varphi)$ | sp.$\text{Match}(XP)$ | $\text{BinBr}(\varphi)$ |
|---|---|---|---|---|---|
| Matching | $(((a\ b)\ c)\ d)$ | $W_2$ | $e_0$ | $L_0$ | $L_0$ |
| $\rightarrow$ Squishing | $((a\ b)\ c\ d)$ | $1$ | $0$ | $1$ | $1$ |
| Rebracketing | $((a\ b)(c\ d))$ | $e_1$ | $W_1$ | $e_1$ | $L_0$ |
| HB Flattening | $(a\ b\ c\ d)$ | $e_1$ | $e_0$ | $W_2$ | $e_1$ |

In contrast, squishing candidates like *((a b) c d)* are harmonically bounded in BalSis systems, because BalSis does not penalize the rebracketed or the flattened candidates at all. As a consequence, the squishing candidate is collectively harmonically bounded by the other three candidates shown in (60). Flattening replaces squishing as the parse with the least structure. Unlike the squishing or rebracketed parses, which match one two-word XP for uniformly branching inputs, the flat parse only matches the maximal XP, so it incurs more sp.Match violations than the rebracketed parse for all inputs, whereas the squishing parse performs better than the rebracketed parse for mixed-branching inputs like [[a [b c]] d].

(60)     Flattening tableau: $[[[a\ b]\ c]\ d] \rightarrow (a\ b\ c\ d)$ for (57f) with BalSis

|  | $[[[a\ b]\ c]\ d]$ | $\text{BalSis}(\varphi)$ | ps.$\text{AlignL}(\varphi)$ | sp.$\text{Match}(XP)$ | $\text{BinBr}(\varphi)$ |
|---|---|---|---|---|---|
| Matching | $(((a\ b)\ c)\ d)$ | $W_2$ | $e_0$ | $L_0$ | $L_0$ |
| HB Squishing | $((a\ b)\ c\ d)$ | $W_1$ | $e_0$ | $L_1$ | $e_1$ |
| Rebracketing | $((a\ b)(c\ d))$ | $e_0$ | $W_1$ | $L_1$ | $L_0$ |
| $\rightarrow$ Flattening | $(a\ b\ c\ d)$ | $0$ | $0$ | $2$ | $1$ |

The flat prosodies favored by Uniformity have been proposed in many analyses: unaccented words in Basque (Hualde et al. 2002, Gussenhoven 2004); Kinyambo (Bickmore 1990); Chicheŵa (Truckenbrodt 1999); compounds in Greek (Nespor and Vogel 1986). The squishing prosodies favored by leaf-counting have been proposed much less frequently. Whether the preponderance of flat parses in existing analyses actually reflects their empirical frequency is not entirely obvious, since there is not always empirical evidence to distinguish between flat and squished parses, and some proposals of flat parses may have been partially motivated by the assumption of Strict Layering. We may conservatively conclude, however, that in any analysis that needs to model flattening (particularly in combination with rebracketing), BalancedSisters has an advantage over BinLeaves, since it can motivate both of these phrasing patterns. Employing BalancedSisters can yield the desired predictions with a smaller typology than what would result from using BINLEAVES to motivate rebracketing of some inputs, while using other constraints like EQUALSISTERS to motivate flattening of other inputs.

## 10.7    Discussion

Two different conceptions of binarity are represented in current syntax-prosody literature. The first is branch-counting binarity. Branch-counting binarity is structural and requires a strictly local evaluation, counting immediate children only. Branch-counting binarity plays a crucial role in several analyses of phonological phrasing, including Irish (Elfner 2012), Kimatuumbi (Kalivoda 2018), and Xitsonga (Selkirk and Lee 2017). It motivates size-driven recursion. Branch-counting binarity prioritizes matching branching syntactic constituents over non-branching syntactic constituents—a pattern is empirically attested at both the phrase level (Irish phonological phrasing) and word level (Danish compound words).

The second version of binarity counts leaves, descendants of a lower category. Leaf-counting binarity requires an unbounded, global search to evaluate how many children of some lower category are contained within a node. Leaf-counting binarity motivates a size-driven change of prosodic category for nodes high in the prosodic tree. Such category promotion is attested for phonological words (promoted to phonological phrases) in Japanese compound parsing, and for phonological phrases (promoted to intonational phrases) in Italian phonological phrasing. In languages where such category promotion is not observed or not desirable from an analytical standpoint, we put forth that leaf-counting binarity should be replaced with branch-counting binarity or by constraints on sisterhood, which can promote balanced, size-sensitive parsing without unintentionally inducing a category promotion.

We compared systems that used leaf-counting binarity to minimally different systems that replaced BINMAXLEAVES with BINMAXBRANCHES. BINLEAVES results in a larger and more complex typology than BINMAXBRANCHES. Comparing typologies that employ leaf-counting binarity to those that use branch-counting binarity, we find that leaf-counting tends to inflate the size of the typology, sometimes dramatically. This occurs because, where a maximally binary-branching input syntax is assumed, branch-counting binarity operates as a special case of sp.MATCH,[6] resulting in

---

[6]    Changing the visibility settings of MATCH to only see lexical XPs or only see overtly headed XPs, or to ignore bar levels, can have the effect of making some syntactic structures appear

smaller typology sizes in systems that employ Match Theory in conjunction with branch-counting binarity, than in equivalent systems that use leaf-counting binarity instead. Leaf-counting binarity does not operate as a special case of sp.MATCH; in fact, it conflicts with sp.MATCH(XP) whenever inputs contain syntactic phrases of more than two words. Thus, leaf-counting binarity conflicts with sp.MATCH in a way that branch-counting binarity does not. Leaf-counting binarity, when high-ranked, allows matching of one- and two-word syntactic phrases, but not longer ones. It therefore favors level-skipping, uneven squishing candidates.

### 10.7.1   Category promotion and constraint indexation

All the markedness constraints in this chapter were indexed to the φ. Such indexation to a particular prosodic category is common practice for prosodic well-formedness constraints. This is almost universal for BINARITY, and has been also proposed for STRONGSTART (STRONGSTART(ω) in Elfner 2012; STRONGSTART(χ, π) in Hsu 2016) and EQUALSISTERS (EQUALSISTERS(ι), Hsu 2016). The intended effect of this form of constraint is typically to exempt higher categories from the structural requirement imposed by the prosodic constraint. For instance, in Hsu (2016), unequal daughters of φ are tolerated, but unequal daughters of ι are not. Parameterizing EQUALSISTERS to the ι level ensures that unequal φ daughters will not be incorrectly penalized.

As discussed in §10.4 on category promotion with BINMAXLEAVES(φ), indexing a constraint to the φ level causes it to prefer structures where the higher levels of the prosodic structure are ιs, rather than φs. In the case of BINARITY, category promotion of φs to ιs is well motivated. The conceptual foundation for BINARITY is that there is some kind of upper-bound on the size of φs and ωs. A φ that is too large may be deleted in favor of an ι, which does not suffer from the same kinds of size limitations. The notion of category promotion does raise the question of what the effect of a leaf-counting binarity constraint on intonational phrases, however. In the standard Match Theoretic prosodic hierarchy, the intonational phrase is the highest category, and there is no higher category to which it might be promoted. BINMAXLEAVES(ι, φ) could motivate squishing (e.g., {$_{CP}$ {$_{CP}$ {$_{CP}$ XP XP} XP} XP} → {$_\iota$ {$_\iota$ XP XP} XP XP}), but not category promotion. Only one analysis in our survey (Van Handel 2021) uses a binarity constraint indexed to ι, and for that analysis, the distinction between leaf-counting and branch-counting at the ι level was not crucial. We tentatively suggest that

---

suprabinary to the phonology, in which case BINMAXBRANCHES would no longer act as a special case of sp.MATCH.

leaf-counting binarity may not be a desirable constraint for the intonational phrase level, since category promotion is not available there. Exploring the consequences of leaf- vs. branch-counting definitions of binarity at the $\iota$-level is an important area for future work. We also highlight the need for more empirical work on size effects at the intonational level, which are relatively understudied.

The finding that indexation to the $\varphi$ motivates a change of prosodic category to the $\iota$ or even $\omega$ extends to other constraints besides BINARITY. In the case of some, such as STRONGSTART, category promotion for the parent might be a problematic prediction. The goal of STRONGSTART is for a node's first child to be of a category at least as high as its following sister(s). If SS is indexed to the $\varphi$ level (61b), it would instead motivate promoting weakly starting $\varphi$s to $\iota$s, creating a level-skipping weak start, rather than the desired strong start. This is illustrated in (62), where the isomorphic candidate (a) is ruled out by SS($\varphi$), and the rebracketed, strongly starting candidate (b) is ruled out by ps.MATCH($\varphi$), while the level-skipping weak start in (c) violates only sp.MATCH(XP) and wins. This seems problematic from a conceptual standpoint.

(61)　　STRONGSTART
    a.　　STRONGSTART(any category): Assign a violation for every node whose initial child is of a lower category than some non-initial child.
    b.　　STRONGSTART($\varphi$ parent): Assign a violation for every $\varphi$ whose initial child is of a lower category than some non-initial child. (*Hypothetical*)
    c.　　STRONGSTART($\omega$ child): Assign a violation for every node whose initial child is a word and has a non-initial child of a higher category (cf. Elfner 2012).

(62)　　Category promotion with STRONGSTART($\varphi$)

| [V [S O]] | | SS($\varphi$) | ps.MATCH($\varphi$) | sp.MATCH(XP) |
|---|---|---|---|---|
| a. Isomorphic | (V (S O)) | $W_1$ | $e_0$ | $L_0$ |
| b. Strong start | ((V S) O) | $e_0$ | $W_1$ | $e_1$ |
| → c. Level-skipping weak start | {V (S O)} | 0 | 0 | 1 |

Versions of STRONGSTART indexation currently attested in the syntax-prosody literature do not fall prey to this particular problem, since they are either indexed to the $\iota$ parent, where no category promotion is possible (Hsu 2016), or to the category of the child (Elfner 2012)—although unintended category *demotion* might be favored by STRONGSTART($\omega$ child): converting faithful ($\omega$ $\varphi$) not to strongly starting ($\varphi$ $\varphi$) but to demoted ($\sigma$ $\varphi$).

The promotion of parent $\varphi$s to $\iota$s in order to avoid a violation of EQUALSISTERS($\varphi$ parent) may also be undesirable, if less obviously so. Like STRONGSTART, EQUALSISTERS has been used to motivate the promotion of children to a higher prosodic category. If the promotion of children is avoided by promoting the parent instead, unintended winners surface. The tableau in (63) illustrates this with an example parallel to the one discussed above for STRONGSTART($\varphi$). Indexing a constraint to a particular prosodic category always motivates either promotion or demotion of the categories of the nodes being evaluated. Care should be exercised in ensuring that the constraint as formulated does not motivate promotion of the wrong node (e.g., parent rather than child, as in (62)), or demotion rather than promotion (as risked by STRONGSTART($\omega$)).

(63)    Category promotion with EQUALSISTERS($\varphi$)

| [[a] b] | EqSis($\varphi$) | ps.MATCH($\varphi$) | sp.MATCH(XP) |
|---|---|---|---|
| a. Isomorphic    ((a) b) | W$_1$ | e$_0$ | L$_0$ |
| b. Child promo.  ((a)(b)) | e$_0$ | W$_1$ | e$_1$ |
| → c. Parent promo. {(a) b} | 0 | 0 | 1 |

A further complication of indexing constraints to particular categories is that, in restricting the scope of the indexed constraint, category indexation can disrupt normal stringency interactions between constraints. EQUALSISTERS often functions as a more stringent version of STRONGSTART (Bellik, Chapter 11). But if EQUALSISTERS is indexed to the $\varphi$ level and STRONGSTART is not, structures rooted in $\iota$ can violate STRONGSTART without violating EQUALSISTERS($\varphi$). For example, the output in (64) would violate STRONGSTART but not EQUALSISTERS($\varphi$), because the unequal sisters are daughters of $\iota$.

(64)    $\{_{\mathrm{CP}}$ a [b]$\} \rightarrow \{_\iota$ a (b)$\}$

One way to avoid unintended category promotion/demotion, as well as preserve stringency interactions among indexed constraints, is to refine the notion of how the categories function when constraints are indexed to them, by indexing constraints not to a specific category, but to that category and all categories above it (to avoid category promotion), or that category and all categories below it (to avoid category demotion) (65). This would create a stringency hierarchy within each constraint family.

(65)     Indexing to a range of categories

    a.    EQUALSISTERS(parent $\geq \varphi$): Assign a violation for every node of category $\varphi$ and above (i.e., $\varphi$ or $\iota$) whose children are not all of the same category.

    b.    STRONGSTART(child $\leq \omega$): Assign a violation for every node whose initial child is of category $\leq \omega$, and that has a non-initial child of a higher category.

If EQUALSISTERS is only parameterized to categories greater than or equal to (e.g.) $\varphi$, rather than to $\varphi$ specifically, then the typology will not contain languages in which an EQUALSISTERS violation at the $\varphi$ level is avoided by punting the violation up to the next higher category, because violations of ES($\geq\varphi$) will always be a superset of violations of EQUALSISTERS($\geq\iota$) (66). This strategy would ensure that all versions of EQUALSISTERS assign more violations than any of the versions of STRONGSTART in (61), because promoting the root node to a higher category would no longer be a means to escape a violation of the indexed EQUALSISTERS constraint. (Demotion of the parent to the $\omega$ level is harmonically bounded here and in general, because it incurs egregious sp.MATCH violations, or violates Layering.) It would also be compatible with ES($\iota$) in Hsu (2016)'s analysis of Bangla weak pronoun parsing, in which a $\varphi$ can have unequal daughters but an intonational phrase cannot.

(66)     Stringency between SS(any) and ES($\geq\varphi$) vs. ES($\varphi$)

| [a [b [c]]] | ES($\geq\varphi$) | SS(any) | sp.ps.MATCH | ES($\varphi$) |
|---|---|---|---|---|
| a. $\{a\ b\ (c)\}$ | 1 | 1 | 2<br>$XP_{abc}, XP_{bc}$ | |
| b. $\{a\ (b\ c)\}$ | 1 | 1 | 2<br>$XP_{abc}, XP_{c},$ | |
| c. $\{a\ ((b)\ (c))\}$ | 1 | 1 | 2<br>$XP_{abc}, \varphi_{b}$ | |
| d. $\{((a)(b\ c))\}$ | | | 2<br>$XP_{c}, \varphi_{a}$ | |

### 10.7.2 Leaf-counting vs. Uniformity

This chapter introduced a constraint on Uniformity, called BALANCEDSISTERS. BALANCEDSISTERS compares the length (the number of children of an interface category) of sister nodes. This constraint can replace leaf-counting binarity in an analysis of rebracketing in Japanese phrasing. Comparing systems that replaced BINLEAVES with BALSIS, while including BINBRANCHES in both constraint sets, we observed that leaf-counting binarity conflicts with EQUALSISTERS in a way that the alternative Uniformity-promoting BALANCEDSISTERS does not. This conflict is due to the success of "squishing" candidates like *(a b (c d))* in leaf-counting systems. Linguists generally do not interpret phonological data as pointing to a squishing parse; in fact, we currently do not know of any analyses where squishing parses are the desired optima. BINLEAVES's preference for squishing parses may be a problematic prediction.

BALANCEDSISTERS produces a much smaller typology than BINLEAVES in a pair of systems sensitive to accentedness and including two other constraints on sisterhood, EQUALSISTERS and EQUALSISTERS2 (Leaves.J.Acc and BalSis.J.Acc). This difference in typology sizes went away in subsequent comparisons of typologies with BINLEAVES and BALSIS, however. Teasing out all the details of the constraint conflicts that lead Leaves.J.Acc to have hundreds more languages than BalSis.J.Acc is left for future research, but surely an important factor is that BALSIS rejects the majority of the candidates that minimally violate BINLEAVES. In systems without EQUALSISTERS, both BINLEAVES and BALSIS can motivate matching and rebracketing, while squishing only occurs with BINLEAVES, and flattening only occurs with BALSIS. Flattening can be induced in leaf-counting systems if EQUALSISTERS is also included. It is also possible, but more complicated, to induce squishing co-optima in BALANCEDSISTERS systems without BINLEAVES: the parses *((a b) c d) ~ ((a b c) d)* are co-optimal in (57e), which includes EQUALSISTERS2 as well as EQUALSISTERS1 (see (41) for definitions), but no such parses appear in any of the other BALSIS systems examined here.

Squishing parses seem undesirable due to other principles, as well as being penalized by other constraints on prosodic well-formedness. They violate the principles of parsing prosodic words into phrases of uniform size (Exhaustivity and Uniformity). In systems where all candidates are rooted in a phonological phrase, and all non-flat parses involve recursive structure, these principles could be reframed in a way that takes recursive subcategories into account (67).

(67)    Parsing principles reframed for recursive parsing
   a.    Reframed EXHAUSTIVITY: Every node of category $k$ should be parsed into a *minimal* node of category $k + 1$. E.g., ω should be parsed into a minimal φ.
   b.    Reframed UNIFORMITY: Every node of category $k$ whose children are of (sub)category $j$ should be of uniform size, i.e., have the same number of children. E.g., φs whose children are ωs should be of uniform size.

In squishing candidates like *(a b (c d))*, some words are parsed into a φ, but are not in a minimal φ. Exhaustivity as reframed above objects to this structure. Both EQUALSISTERS and BALANCEDSISTERS disfavor it; as such, these constraints enforce Exhaustivity in an indirect way. This broader Exhaustivity is also violated by structures like *(a (b c))*, although *(a (b c))* is less objectionable as a prosodic output because it perfectly matches the syntactic input *[a [b c]]*, whereas *(a b (c d))* violates both sp.MATCH(XP) and these principles of markedness.

### 10.7.3   *Uniformity and prime numbers*

Where category promotion is not the desired outcome, but branch-counting binarity cannot replace leaf-counting binarity, BALANCEDSISTERS is a possible alternative constraint. However, BALSIS makes a surprising prediction. A preliminary investigation with inputs of length three to nine words revealed that BALSIS predicts the existence of languages in which inputs with a prime number of words are parsed as a flat structure, since this is the only structure that does not violate BALSIS. That is, three-, five-, and seven-word inputs are flattened, but not nine-word inputs. Inputs with a non-prime number of words are rebracketed into structures that also perfectly satisfy BALSIS, but which perform better on sp.MATCH(XP) and/or BINBRANCHES: *((a b)(c d))* for a four-word input, or *((a b c)((a b)(c d)(e f)))* for a nine-word input. Although computational limits currently prevent us from testing longer non-prime odd numbers, such as strings of 15, 21, or 25 terminals, we can reason out that such strings can also be divided into non-flat structures that satisfy BALSIS, as in (68). A string of fifteen terminals can be split into a flat five-terminal φ that is sister to a two-layered φ containing ten terminals, parsed into five two-terminal φs, for instance. The example of (68c) demonstrates that the number of terminals need not be divisible by three for this type of division to work; a string of 25 terminals can be split into a five-terminal φ and a twenty-terminal φ, which is divided up into five four-terminal φs (each of which can also be split up into two two-terminal φs).

(68)      Some parses of long strings that satisfy BALSIS

    a.    (1 2 3 4 5)((6 7) (8 9) (10 11) (12 13) (14 15))

    b.    (1 2 3 4 5 6 7) ((8 9) (10 11) (12 13) (14 15) (16 17) (18 19) (20 21))

    c.    (1 2 3 4 5) (((6 7) (8 9)) ((10 11) (12 13)) ((14 15) (16 17)) ((18 19) (20 21)) ((22 23) (24 25))

It seems implausible that such prime-recognizing languages exist—a point against the use of BALSIS as a constraint. If prime-sensitive languages do exist, on the other hand, they would provide evidence in favor of BALSIS as a constraint (at least for this particular implementation[7]). BINLEAVES does not predict such languages that distinguish between strings containing a prime (indivisible) and composite (divisible) number of words—only languages that distinguish between strings of length up to two, and those of length greater than two.

Under certain conditions, BALSIS may also predict the existence of languages in which only strings of a prime number of terminals are divided up into a series of unary φs, which also seems strange. Yet it might have some support from Brazilian Portuguese: Sandalo and Truckenbrodt (2002) report that three-word N A V is phrased (N)(A)(V) and N V N is phrased (N)(V)(N). Similarly, five-word [[N A] & [N N]] V is phrased (N)(A)(N) (N)(V)[8]. Meanwhile, two-word V N is (V N) and four-word N A V N is phrased (N A) (V N). If nine-word strings can be subdivided differently from three- and five-word sentences, more like even numbers of words, this would suggest that the language is sensitive to prime numbers in a way predicted by BALSIS. Further investigation of the conditions under which BALANCEDSISTERS predicts prime-sensitivity, and of whether prime-sensitivity has empirical support, is left for future research.

### 10.7.4  Conclusion

To sum up, branch-counting binarity and leaf-counting binarity predict different optima under Weak Layering, and must be distinguished. Branch-counting is useful for modeling size-driven recursion. It prioritizes the matching of larger XPs. Leaf-counting binarity is useful for modeling size-driven category promotion. It permits the matching of small (one or two element) syntactic constituents only.

Leaf-counting binarity enlarges and complicates the typology, due to its unintuitive interactions with both mapping constraints like sp.MATCH and markedness constraints like EQUALSISTERS. In many cases, the empirical coverage it provides can be provided by BINBRANCHES, EQUALSISTERS,

---

[7] Some other possible definitions of BALANCEDSISTERS are:
- BALANCEDSISTERSADJACENT-$k$: Assign a violation for every pair of adjacent sisters $s_1$ and $s_2$, such that $s_1$ and $s_2$'s mother is of category $k$, and $s_1$ and $s_2$ do not dominate the same number of children.
- BALANCEDSISTERSPAIRWISE-$k$: Assign a violation for every pair of sisters $s_1$ and $s_2$ dominated by a mother of category $k$, such that $s_1$ and $s_2$ have different numbers of children
We have not tested the typological consequences of either of these alternate implementations.

[8] Although not every five-word case is phrased this way: N A V N Adv is phrased (N A) (V N) (Adv), which Sandalo and Truckenbrodt relate to the XP status of the Adv.

or BALANCEDSISTERS instead, with a simplifying effect on the predicted typology. Although leaf-counting binarity remains useful in explaining size-driven category promotion, it is not useful in deriving flat structures, since it prefers uneven, squished candidates. How cross-linguistically prevalent such squished prosodic structures are is a question that deserves further investigation. We also leave for future investigation the question of whether any languages treat sentences with a prime number of words differently from those with a composite number of words—or failing that, treat sentences with an odd number of words differently from those than contain an even number—as BALANCEDSISTERS predicts.


## References


Alber, Birgit, Delbusso, Natalie, and Prince, Alan (2016). From intensional properties to universal support. *Language* 92: e88–e116.

Alber, Birgit and Prince, Alan (2021). *The Structure of OT Typologies.* Chapter 1: Introduction to Property Theory. Unpublished manuscript. ROA 1381, Rutgers Optimality Archive, http://roa.rutgers.edu.

Bellik, Jennifer, Bellik, Ozan, and Kalivoda, Nick (2015–2021). Syntax-Prosody in Optimality Theory (SPOT). Javascript application. http://spot.sites.ucsc.edu. Codebase at https://github.com/syntax-prosody-ot.

Bellik, Jennifer, Ito, Junko, Kalivoda, Nick and Mester, Armin (2022). Matching and alignment. In Haruo Kubozono, Junko Ito, and Armin Mester (eds.) *Prosody and Prosodic Interfaces* 457–481. Oxford University Press.

Bellik, Jennifer and Kalivoda, Nick (2016). Adjunction and branchingness effects in syntax-prosody mapping. In Gunnar Ólafur Hansson, Ashley Farris-Trimble, Kevin McMullin, and Douglas Pulleyblank (eds.) *Supplemental Proceedings of the 2015 Annual Meeting on Phonology,* Linguistic Society of America. http://doi.org/10.3765/amp.v3i0.3690

Bennett, Ryan, Elfner, Emily, and McCloskey, James (2019). Prosody, focus, and ellipsis in Irish. *Language* 95(1): 66–106.

Bickmore, Lee (1990). Branching nodes and prosodic categories: evidence from Kinyambo. In Sharon Inkelas and Draga Zec (eds.) *The Phonology-Syntax Connection* 1–18. Chicago: University of Chicago Press.

Elfner, Emily (2012). *Syntax-Prosody Interactions in Irish.* PhD dissertation, University of Massachusetts Amherst.

Elfner, Emily (2015). Recursion in prosodic phrasing: evidence from Connemara Irish. *Natural Language and Linguistic Theory* 33: 1169–1208.

Ghini, Mirco (1993). Φ-formation in Italian: a new proposal. In Carrie Dyck (ed.) *Toronto Working Papers in Linguistics* 12: 41–78.

Gussenhoven, Carlos (2004). *The Phonology of Tone and Intonation.* Cambridge: Cambridge University Press.

Hsu, Brian (2016). Syntax-Prosody Interactions in the Clausal Domain: Head Movement and Coalescence. PhD dissertation, University of Southern California.

Hualde, José, Elordieta, Gorka, Gaminde, Iñaki, and Smiljanic, Rajka (2002). From pitch-accent to stress-accent in Basque. *Laboratory Phonology* 7: 547–584.

Inkelas, Sharon and Zec, Draga (eds.) (1990). *The Phonology-Syntax Connection.* Chicago: University of Chicago Press.

Ishihara, Shinichiro (2014). Match theory and the recursivity problem. In Shigeto Kawahara and Mika Igarashi (eds.) *MIT Working Papers in Linguistics 73: Proceedings of Formal Approaches to Japanese Linguistics 7* 69–88. Cambridge, MA.

Ito, Junko and Mester, Armin (1992/2003). Weak layering and word binarity. In Takeru Honma, Masao Okazaki, Toshiyuki Tabata and Shin-ichi Tanaka (eds.) *A New Century of Phonology and Phonological Theory: A Festschrift for Professor Shosuke Haraguchi on the Occasion of His Sixtieth Birthday* 26–65. Tokyo: Kaitakusha.

Ito, Junko and Mester, Armin (2007). Prosodic adjunction in Japanese compounds. In Yoichi Miyamoto and Masao Ochi (eds.) *MIT Working Papers in Linguistics 55: Proceedings of Formal Approaches to Japanese Linguistics 4* 97–111. Cambridge, MA.

Ito, Junko, and Mester, Armin (2020). Match theory and prosodic wellformedness constraints. In Hongming Zhang and Youyong Qian (eds.) *Prosodic Studies. Challenges and Prospects* 252–274. London and New York: Routledge.

Ito, Junko and Mester, Armin (2021). Recursive prosody and the prosodic form of compounds. *Languages* 6: 65.

Kalivoda, Nick (2018). *Syntax-Prosody Mismatches in Optimality Theory.* PhD dissertation, University of California, Santa Cruz.

Kalivoda, Nick, and Bellik, Jennifer (2018). Prosodic recursion and pseudo-cyclicity in Danish compound stød. In Ryan Bennett, Andrew Angeles, Adrian Brasoveanu, Dhyana Buckley, Nick Kalivoda, Shigeto Kawahara, Grant McGuire and Jaye Padgett (eds.) *Hana-bana (花々): A Festschrift for Junko Ito and Armin Mester.* Santa Cruz: Linguistics Research Center.

Merchant, Nazarré and Prince, Alan (2021). *The Mother of All Tableaux: Order, Equivalence, and Geometry in the Large-scale Structure of Optimality Theory.* Equinox Press (to appear).

Mester, Armin (1994). The quantitative trochee in Latin. *Natural Language and Linguistic Theory* 12: 1–61.

Myrberg, Sara (2013). Sisterhood in prosodic branching. *Phonology* 30: 73–124.

Nespor, Marina and Vogel, Irene (1986). *Prosodic Phonology.* Dordrecht: Foris.

Prieto, Pilar (2005). Syntactic and eurhythmic constraints on phrasing decisions in Catalan. *Studia Linguistica* 59: 194–222.

Prieto, Pilar (2006). Phonological phrasing in Spanish. In Fernando Martínez-Gil and Sonia Colina (eds.) *Optimality-Theoretic Studies in Spanish Phonology* 39–61. Amsterdam: John Benjamins.

Prince, Alan (1980). A metrical theory for Estonian quantity. *Linguistic Inquiry* 11: 511–62.

Prince, Alan and Smolensky, Paul (1993/2004). *Optimality Theory: Constraint Interaction in Generative Grammar.* Malden, MA: Blackwell Publishing.

Prince, Alan, Merchant, Nazarré, and Tesar, Bruce (2007–2020). OTWorkplace. http://sites.google.com/site/otworkplace

Sandalo, Filomena and Truckenbrodt, Hubert (2002). Some notes on phonological phrasing in Brazilian Portuguese. In Anikó Csirmaz, Zhiqiang Li, Andrew Nevins, Olga Vaysman, and Michael Wagner (eds.) *MIT Working Papers in Linguistics* 42: 285–310.

Selkirk, Elisabeth (1984). Phonology and Syntax: the Relation between Sound and Structure. Cambridge, MA: MIT Press.

Selkirk, Elisabeth (2000). The interaction of constraints on prosodic phrasing. In Merle Horne (ed.) *Prosody: Theory and Experiment. Studies Presented to Gösta Bruce* 231–261. Dordrecht: Kluwer.

Selkirk, Elisabeth (2011). The syntax–phonology interface. In John A. Goldsmith, Jason Riggle, and Alan C. L. Yu (eds.) *The Handbook of Phonological Theory* 435–484. Blackwell Publishing.

Selkirk, Elisabeth and Lee, Seunghun (2017). Syntactic constituency spell-out through Match constraints. Presentation at SPOT1 Workshop, University of California, Santa Cruz. Available at https://thi.ucsc.edu/wp-content/uploads/2017/10/Selkirk_SPOT_11_18_2017.pdf

Shih, Shu-hao (2017). Major phrases are binary: Evidence from Taiwan Mandarin flat structure. In Aaron Kaplan, Abby Kaplan, Miranda McCarvel, and Edward Rubin (eds.) *Proceedings of the 34th West Coast Conference on Formal Linguistics* 454–461. Somerville, MA: Cascadilla Proceedings Project.

Truckenbrodt, Hubert (1999). On the relation between syntactic phrases and phonological phrases. *Linguistic Inquiry* 30: 219–255.

Van Handel, Nicholas (2021). Matching overtly headed syntactic phrases in Italian. *Phonology* 38: 317–356.

Zec, Draga and Inkelas, Sharon (1990). Prosodically constrained syntax. In Sharon Inkelas and Draga Zec (eds.) *The Phonology-Syntax Connection* 365–378. Chicago: University of Chicago Press.

## About the authors

*Jennifer Bellik*

Postdoctoral researcher and lecturer, Department of Linguistics, UC Santa Cruz. Research interests: syntax-prosody interface, Optimality Theory, Articulatory Phonology, and Turkish phonology. Recent publications: "An acoustic study of vowel intrusion in Turkish onset clusters", *Laboratory Phonology* 2018; "Automated tableau generation with SPOT" with N. Kalivoda, *Linguistics Vanguard* 2019; and 'The effect of speech style and deaccentuation on vowel intrusion in Turkish complex onsets", *Proceedings of ICPhS* 2019.

*Nicholas Van Handel*

Graduate research assistant for the SPOT project, Ph.D. student, Department of Linguistics, UC Santa Cruz. Research interests: Psycholinguistics and phonology, with a focus on implicit prosody, sentence processing, and the syntax-prosody interface. Recent publications: 'Matching overtly headed syntactic phrases in Italian" 2021, *Phonology*.

# Chapter 11

# Stringency hierarchies in prosodic sisterhood: STRONGSTART and EQUALSISTERS

Jennifer Bellik[*]

## 11.1 Introduction

Under Strict Layering (Selkirk 1984), the parsing principles of Exhaustivity and Non-Recursivity were requirements for possible candidates, and ensured that all prosodic nodes that share a parent (i.e., prosodic sisters) would be of the same category. Assuming the prosodic hierarchy in (1), Strict Layering requires that all daughters of an intonational phrase ($\iota$) are phonological phrases ($\varphi$), and all daughters of a $\varphi$ are prosodic words ($\omega$). Hence, all sisters of a $\varphi$ would also be $\varphi$s, and all sisters of a $\omega$ would also be $\omega$s.

(1)     Prosodic hierarchy: $\iota > \varphi > \omega > \mathrm{Ft} > \sigma$

With the advent of Weak Layering, these inviolable restrictions on GEN were reconceived as violable constraints in CON (Ito and Mester 1992/2003). MATCH constraints (Selkirk 2011) sometimes demand that an $\iota$ be sister to a $\varphi$, and vice versa (e.g., for input syntax $[_{\mathrm{CP}}$ DP $[_{\mathrm{CP}}$ RelClause]]), or that a $\varphi$ be sister to a $\omega$ (e.g., for input syntax $[_{\mathrm{VP}}$ V DP]). When clitics are present, a $\varphi$ may even be sister to a $\sigma$ (Selkirk 1996). Ensuring that prosodic sisters are equal in category became the province of the constraint EQUALSISTERS (Myrberg 2010, 2013) (2).

---

[*] I would like to thank Nick Kalivoda for many helpful discussions throughout the development of this chapter. My thanks also to Natalie Delbusso for an insightful review that greatly improved the analyses here. All errors and shortcomings remain my own.

(2)       Myrberg (2013)'s definition of EQUALSISTERS:
          "Sister nodes in prosodic structure are instantiations of the same prosodic category."

From the beginning of Match Theory, Selkirk (2011) also recognized a pressure toward exhaustive parsing at the left edge of the phonological or intonational phrase, which was codified as the constraint STRONGSTART (3).

(3)       STRONGSTART in Selkirk (2011):
          "A prosodic constituent optimally begins with a leftmost daughter constituent which is not lower in the prosodic hierarchy than the constituent that immediately follows: *( $\pi_n$ $\pi_{n+1}$ ... "

Since this proposal, STRONGSTART has been widely adopted, under at least three different implementations (e.g., Kalivoda and Bellik 2021, Bennett, Elfner, and McCloskey 2016, Elfner 2012). Like EQUALSISTERS, STRONGSTART is satisfied by a set of sisters that are all of the same prosodic category. But STRONGSTART is less particular than EQUALSISTERS; it is also satisfied by a set of sisters in which the leftmost is of a higher category than the following sisters. STRONGSTART, then, can be thought of as a less stringent version of EQUALSISTERS. This relationship has been noted in passing before (Bennett et al. 2016, footnote 28, p. 198), but not thoroughly investigated or connected to existing literature on stringency in Optimality Theory. This chapter aims to remedy this situation, as well as to define both STRONGSTART and EQUALSISTERS more precisely. The original formulations of both EQUALSISTERS and STRONGSTART, quoted above, are phrased positively, with the result that they are ambiguous. There are several different ways to reframe them as negative statements ("Assign a violation for every..."), as is arguably necessary (de Lacy 2002, McCarthy 2003). I identify multiple implementations of EQUALSISTERS and STRONGSTART in existing syntax-prosody literature, and examine their interactions and consequences.

The notion of stringency between constraints in Optimality Theory is well-established (Prince 2000; de Lacy 2002, 2004, et seq.), and its effect on typologies and property analyses (PAs) is well-studied as well (Alderete 2009; Alber, DelBusso, and Prince 2016; DelBusso 2018, 2020; Merchant and Krämer 2018). A more stringent constraint rules out all of the candidates that a less stringent constraint rules out, and more (Prince 2000). This is formally stated in (4).

(4)      Definition: Stringency
         A constraint X is more stringent than a constraint Y if the set of
         candidates that survive X is a subset of the set of candidates that
         survive Y (DelBusso 2020).

Stringency relations are best demonstrated in the context of the typology of
a formal OT system. Suppose a system contains three constraints, Special
(S), General (G), and Antagonist (A), where G and S form a two-step stringency hierarchy, and G is more stringent than S. There are 3! = 6 possible
total rankings of the constraints (5).

(5)      Possible orderings of three constraints
    a.   Antagonist on top: A–S–G, A–G–S
    b.   Special on top: S–A–G, S–G–A
    c.   General on top: G–S–A, G–A–S

However, since G is more stringent than S, S and G cannot conflict (Pāṇini's
Theorem on Constraint Ranking in Prince and Smolensky (1993/2004)). A
violation of S entails a violation of G, so it will never be the case that S
must be violated for the sake of satisfying G better, and S and G cannot be
crucially ranked against each other, as they are in (5a). Furthermore, when
G is satisfied, S will always be satisfied. As a result, G will never be crucially
ranked above S. Therefore, the ranking G–A–S is incoherent, because if G
is undominated, S will never be violated and therefore is also undominated.
Any pair of total orderings in which G and A have the same ranking relative
to each other will produce identical languages. Thus, the six legs collapse
into three distinct grammars (6).

(6)      Possible grammars for constraints Special, General, Antagonist
    a.   A ≫ {S,G}
    b.   S ≫ A ≫ G
    c.   G ≫ A (S is freely rankable anywhere)

In contrast, if the three constraints are all completely independent, they can
all be freely ranked against each other so that all six total orders may yield
distinct languages. The typology can be twice as large.

   This chapter examines STRONGSTART (SS; Selkirk 2011, Elfner 2012, Bennett, Elfner, and McCloskey 2016) and EQUALSISTERS (ES; Myrberg 2013)
with the goals of arriving at precise, unambiguous definitions of both constraints, and understanding the possible stringency relations between them.
It finds that treating phonological Headedness as inviolable simplifies the

interaction of three versions of SS with each other and with ES. Adopting a categorical implementation of ES (ES-parent) and the most stringent version of SS (SS-global) is argued to be theoretically beneficial. Property Theory (Alber and Prince 2021) is used as a lens for comparing the relative complexities of a series of typologies that differ in their candidate sets and in their implementations of EQUALSISTERS and STRONGSTART.

The chapter is organized as follows. Section 11.2 examines the various implementations that STRONGSTART and EQUALSISTERS have received, finding (1) that SS has been defined with three different scopes (called here global, local, and hyperlocal), and (2) that both categorical and gradient definitions of ES appear in existing literature, although empirical evidence for one implementation over the other is lacking. Section 11.3 investigates stringency relations among existing STRONGSTART definitions; when proper Headedness is enforced, SS-global is more stringent than SS-local and SS-hyperlocal, and is arguably the most useful version of STRONGSTART. Section 11.4 tests the interaction between SS-global and a categorical implementation of EQUALSISTERS, in systems with and without free clitics. Section 11.5 investigates the impact of using a gradient version of EQUALSISTERS. Section 11.6 discusses and concludes with recommendations for adopting unambiguous definitions of STRONGSTART (namely, SS-global) and EQUALSISTERS (categorical ES-parent).

## 11.2  Existing constraint definitions

### 11.2.1  Defining STRONGSTART

STRONGSTART (Selkirk 2011, Elfner 2012) is widely used in Match Theoretic analyses. This original definition of STRONGSTART evaluates only the first two daughters (7). We will refer to this as LOCAL scope.

(7)       STRONGSTART-LOCAL = SS-LOCAL: Assign a violation for every node
          that is leftmost in its set of sisters and is lower in category than the
          sister immediately to its right.
          Paraphrased from Selkirk (2011) and Elfner (2012).

Selkirk (2011) describes the purpose of STRONGSTART as left-edge strengthening; it is intended to ensure 'avoidance of 'stray' syllables or feet at the left edge of phonological phrases, an avoidance seen for example in the promotion of initial weak pronouns to ω status or in their obligatory rightward displacement (Werle 2009, Elfner 2011)" (Selkirk 2011, p. 37). That is, according to both the prose and desired optima in Selkirk (2011) and Elfner

(2012), SS-local is intended to favor PROSODIC CATEGORY PROMOTION (8) for the first daughter.

(8)      PROSODIC CATEGORY PROMOTION: A prosodic node $\pi$ has undergone category promotion if it corresponds to a syntactic node $\xi$ (i.e., $\pi$ and $\xi$ dominate all and only the same terminals), but is of a higher prosodic category than MATCH demands. That is, if $\xi$ is an $X^0$, then $\pi$ is a $\varphi$ or $\iota$, rather than a matching $\omega$; or if $\xi$ is an XP, then $\pi$ is a $\iota$, rather than a matching $\varphi$.

However, STRONGSTART-local is also satisfied by DOUBLY WEAK STARTS (9) like $(_\varphi\ \omega_1\ \omega_2\ (\omega_3))$. This structure does not violate (7) because the first daughter $\omega_1$ is not adjacent to a $\varphi$, while the daughter $\omega_2$ that is adjacent to a $\varphi$ is not first in the phrase.

(9)      DOUBLY WEAK START: A structure of the form $(\ \pi_n\ \pi_{\leq n}\ ...\ \pi_{n+1}\ ...)$, where the first daughter is not lower in the prosodic hierarchy than the constituent that immediately follows it, but is lower than some later sister constituent.

We will see that SS-local consistently predicts the existence of languages in which all right-branching input syntactic structures with three or more terminals are parsed prosodically with doubly weak starts. The fact that SS-local favors doubly weak starts suggests that it is not a desirable implementation of STRONGSTART; a better implementation will only be satisfied by category promotion at the left edge, not by a doubly weak start.

To achieve category promotion in this situation, the scope of SS can expanded to consider the categories of all daughters of the prosodic constituent: GLOBAL scope (10). This has been proposed by Kalivoda and Bellik (2021) and as STRONGSTRONGSTART by Chen (2021).

(10)     STRONGSTART-GLOBAL = SS-GLOBAL: Assign a violation for every node whose leftmost daughter is of a lower prosodic category than any sister to its right (Kalivoda and Bellik 2021).

STRONGSTART-global does penalize $(\omega_1\ \omega_2\ (\omega_3))$, because $\omega_1$ is lower in category than its sister $(\omega_3)$, even though they are not adjacent. This chapter advocates for SS-global as the best implementation of STRONGSTART. For binary-branching structures, a node can only have two daughters, and so STRONGSTART-global and STRONGSTART-local are identical. The first two daughters are all the daughters that exist. But when three or more daughters are present, the choice of scope (local vs. global) becomes crucial.

A third possible scope for STRONGSTART is employed in Bennett et al. (2016, (55), p. 198). Their STRONGSTART (11) penalizes phonological and intonational phrases whose first daughter is lower than the word, and assigns a violation even if the prosodically deficient daughter has no sister of a higher category. Since it only evaluates the first child and disregards any sisters, we refer to this implementation of STRONGSTART as having HYPERLOCAL scope. This constraint does not penalize $(\omega_1\ \omega_2\ (\omega_3))$, since $\omega_1$ is not prosodically deficient.

(11)   STRONGSTART-HYPERLOCAL$(Ft/\sigma)$ = SS-HYPLOC$(\sigma)$: Assign a violation for every node of a category higher than the word whose leftmost daughter is prosodically deficient (lower than the word) [paraphrased from Bennett, Elfner, and McCloskey 2016].

This definition's restrictions specifically to parent categories above the word level, and child categories below the word level, are not inherent components of a hyperlocally scoped SS constraint. A generalized version could be reconceived as a constraint on Exhaustivity specifically at the left edge, as in (12).

(12)   STRONGSTART-HYPERLOCAL (generalized) = SS-HYPLOC: Assign a violation for every node of category $x$ whose leftmost daughter is of category $< x - 1$.

In other words, although presented as a STRONGSTART constraint, SS-hypLoc is defined by Bennett, Elfner and McCloskey (2016) in terms of vertical relationships (parent-child) in a way that fundamentally differs from the horizontal relationships (sisters) referred to in the definitions of SS-global and SS-local. Different systems in this chapter employ both the generalized (SS-hypLoc) and the original definitions of SS-hypLoc (SS-hypLoc$(\sigma)$).

Although SS-hypLoc$(\sigma)$ is unique among STRONGSTART constraints in referring exclusively to vertical relationships, the fact that the 'weak' node is the leftmost child of a parent is crucial in all STRONGSTART definitions and other implementations of STRONGSTART also make reference to the category of the parent. For instance, Elfner (2012) keeps the basic conception of SS-local from (7), but expands SS into a constraint family that is parameterized to the weak category $x$, using both SS-local$(\omega)$ and SS-local$(\sigma)$ (13).

(13)   Elfner's STRONGSTART$(x)$: "Assign one violation mark for every prosodic constituent whose leftmost daughter constituent is of type $x$ and is lower in the prosodic hierarchy than its sister constituent immediately to its right: $*(x_n\ x_{n+1}\ ...$"

Furthermore, Hsu (2016) and Kalivoda and Bellik (2020), as well as Kalivoda (Chapter 4), propose category-sensitive versions of SS that consider not only immediate children, but descendants at any depth that are at the left edge.

(14)    Hsu (2016)'s STRONGSTART($\varkappa$, $\pi$): Assign a violation for every prosodic constituent whose leftmost daughter constituent is of category $\varkappa$ and is lower in the prosodic hierarchy than its sister constituent immediately to the right, where $\varkappa$ is at the left edge of a prosodic constituent of category $\pi$.
    A prosodic constituent $\varkappa$ is at the left edge of prosodic constituent $\pi$ iff
   a.    $\pi$ dominates $\varkappa$, and
   b.    no prosodic constituent that both dominates $\varkappa$ and is dominated by $\pi$ has a leftmost daughter constituent that does not contain $\varkappa$ (slightly paraphrased from Hsu 2016, pp. 94–95).

(15)    Kalivoda and Bellik (2020)'s STRONGSTARTINIT($\varkappa$): Assign a violation for every prosodic constituent of category $k$ whose leftmost daughter $p$ is of category $< k - 1$, and is lower in the prosodic hierarchy than its sister constituent immediately to the right, where $p$ is at the left edge of a node of category $k$.

These deep implementations of STRONGSTART have a different vertical scope from the other, "shallow" implementations.

### 11.2.2   Defining EQUALSISTERS

The constraint EQUALSISTERS was originally proposed as the motivation for why, when prosodic recursion is admitted to the candidate set, flat structures can still surface despite their deviation from syntactic structure (Myrberg 2010, 2013). Its original formulation is phrased positively (16).

(16)    Myrberg (2013)'s definition of EQUALSISTERS:
    "Sister nodes in prosodic structure are instantiations of the same prosodic category."

This positive definition is ambiguous as to how many violations should be assigned to a structure in which three (or more) sisters of unequal category are present. Several more precise definitions are possible; some examples are provided in (17). One is a categorical, parent-oriented version of EQUALSISTERS, in which parents of unequal sisters are counted (as in (17a)), rather than the unequal sisters themselves. EQUALSISTERS-parent, or any other implementation of ES, could be parameterized to a specific category—this is represented in (17) by the contrast between EQUALSISTERS($\varphi$ parent) in (17.a.i) and EQUALSISTERS(any parent) (17.a.ii), which is blind to the category of the parents. In principle, it is equally possible to parameterize ES to the category of the sisters. Such parameterization was not part of Myrberg's original constraint definition, but has been proposed for the intonational phrase parent (Hsu 2016, (41), p. 89), in order to permit unequal daughters of the $\varphi$ but exclude unequal daughters of the $\iota$.

Several gradient versions of ES are also possible. These definitions vary in the specific configurations that they penalize, such as penalizing only unequal sisters that are adjacent (17.b.i), as compared to penalizing any pair of sisters (17.b.ii), or penalizing sisters that do not share the same category as the leftmost sister (17.b.iii). This last implementation, ES-1st, is similar to SS-global in comparing all following sisters to the first sister, though they differ in their requirements for the relative categories. SS-global requires only that the later sisters not have a higher category than the first sister, while ES-1st requires that their categories be identical. They also differ in that SS-global assigns only one violation per set of sisters, while ES-1st assigns a violation for every non-initial unequal sister.[1]

(17)    Definitions of EQUALSISTERS
   a.    Categorical (assessed by parent)
         i.   EQUALSISTERS-parent($\iota$): Assign a violation for every node of
              category $\iota$ whose children do not all have the same category
              (Hsu 2016).
         ii.  EQUALSISTERS-parent(any category): Assign a violation for every
              node whose children do not all have the same category.
   b.    Gradient (assessed by pairs of children):
         i.   EQUALSISTERS -adjacent = ES-adj: Assign a violation for every
              pair of adjacent sisters that do not have the same category (cf.
              Myrberg 2013).
         ii.  EQUALSISTERS-pairwise = ES-pairs: Assign a violation for every
              pair of sisters (not necessarily adjacent) that do not have the
              same category.

---

[1] Thanks to Natalie Delbusso for this observation.

    iii. EQUALSISTERS-firstPrivilege = ES-1st: Assign a violation for every sister that does not have the same category as the first (that is, leftmost) sister.

Any of these ES implementations can account for the patterns in Stockholm Swedish intonation that motivated the original constraint, since they all assign the same violations when only two sisters are present. The child-oriented definitions assign more violations when more sisters of unequal category are present under the same parent. The tableau in (18) provides some examples of prosodic trees for which each of the gradient versions of EQUALSISTERS assesses a different number of violations. Here and throughout the chapter, curly braces { } denote CP boundaries in a syntactic input and intonational phrase boundaries in a prosodic output; parentheses ( ) denote phonological phrase boundaries. The candidates in (18) are prosodic trees containing four non-branching sisters of two different categories ($\omega$ and $\varphi$). ES-adjacent favors (18a, b) over all the other candidates, since these parses group all the sisters of the same category next to each other, meaning that there is only one transition between categories. It disfavors (18f) most of all, since the alternation between $\omega$ and $\varphi$ results in three sets of adjacent sisters that differ in category. ES-pairs prefers (18c, d, e), in which three sisters have the same category and only one differs, to (a, b, f), which involve two $\varphi$-sisters and two $\omega$-sisters. ES-1st has the same preferences as ES-pairs but assigns fewer violations. The parent-counting ES, meanwhile, assigns each of these structures only one violation, not differentiating between them.

(18)    Variable violation counts from different versions of EQUALSISTERS

|  | Gradient | | | Categorical |
|---|---|---|---|---|
|  | ES-Pairs | ES-Adj | ES-1st | ES-parent |
| a. { $\varphi\,\varphi\,\omega\,\omega$} | 4 | 1 | 2 | 1 |
| b. {$\omega\,\omega\,\varphi\,\varphi$ } | 4 | 1 | 2 | 1 |
| c. { $\varphi\,\omega\,\varphi\,\varphi$ } | 3 | 2 | 1 | 1 |
| d. {$\omega\,\omega\,\varphi\,\omega$} | 3 | 2 | 1 | 1 |
| e. { $\varphi\,\varphi\,\omega\,\varphi$ } | 3 | 2 | 1 | 1 |
| f. { $\varphi\,\omega\,\varphi\,\omega$} | 4 | 3 | 2 | 1 |
| g. { $\varphi\,\varphi\,\varphi\,\varphi$ } | 0 | 0 | 0 | 0 |

We can already see that ES-parent does not provide the degree of differentiation between candidates that other versions do; therefore, all other things being equal, systems using ES-parent will have more co-optimality than those using ES-adj, ES-first, or ES-pairs. (Of course, the addition of

enough other disambiguating constraints can eliminate co-optimality even
with ES-parent.) Also, for some sets of candidates, ES-adj and ES-1st can
prefer opposite optima—although they would both agree that ((a)(b)(c)(d))
would be best. Since ES-1st is not actually attested in existing literature,
however, the latter issue is left for future research. We take up the former
prediction in §11.5.

When EQUALSISTERS is applied to structures with only two children, all
the definitions of ES outlined above assign the same number of violations.
The majority of the papers that employ ES only include binary-branching
structures, and therefore are equally compatible with any interpretation
of ES. However, a few authors do disambiguate their definitions of EQUAL-
SISTERS or include ternary structures that reveal which implementation of
ES they were operating from. These disambiguations are in favor of either
EQUALSISTERS-adjacent or EQUALSISTERS-parent. The remainder of this section elaborates on these previous uses of disambiguated EQUALSISTERS with
two goals: first, to shed light on the field's conception of the role of EQUAL-
SISTERS; and second, to demonstrate that existing literature does not provide
any arguments, either empirical or conceptual, in support of any particular
implementation of EQUALSISTERS.

### 11.2.2.1 *EQUALSISTERS-adjacent in previous literature*

In an account of prosodically motivated extraposition of embedded clauses in
German, as in (19), Féry (2015) quotes Myrberg (2013) without amendment
for the definition of EQUALSISTERS. This leaves the constraint definition
ambiguous. However, Féry subsequently clarifies that the constraint assigns
a violation for every pair of adjacent sisters that differ in prosodic category.
That is, EQUALSISTERS in Féry (2015) is implemented as ES-adjacent. This
clarification occurs in a discussion of Féry (2015)'s Tableau 1, reproduced
and adapted here as (20): 'Each adjacent pair of [unequal] constituents
constitutes a violation of EQUALSISTERS" (p. 31). Candidates (b) and (c) each
receive two violations of ES-adjacent, since each contains ternary-branching
φ whose middle child is an intonational phrase, while its other two children
are either φs or words.[2] Both of these candidates are harmonically bounded
by candidate (a).

---

[2]   Féry (2015) says that ES 'is violated twice in each candidate [i.e., in (20b) and (20c)],
because the top φ-phrase dominates a φ-phrase, an ι-phrase and a ω-word," but based on the
bracketing in T1 as well as the diagrams in Féry's Figure 1, it does not appear that there is
a φ child in (20b), only in (20c).

(19)   DP + V + [$_{CP}$ dass-Compl] (Féry (2015)'s (1), amended with information from Figure 1)

   a.   Sie hat niemandem erzählt, [$_{CP}$ dass sie an dem Tag spät nach Hause kam].
      she has nobody told that she on that day late to home came
      'She didn't tell anybody that she came home late on that day."

   b.   *?Sie hat niemandem, [$_{CP}$ dass sie spät nach Hause kam], erzählt.

(20)   EQUALSISTERS-adjacent in German (adapted from T1 in Féry (2015), p. 31)

| DP + V + dass-Compl | LAYEREDNESS | ES-adj | ADJACENCY | MINBIN |
|---|---|---|---|---|
| → a. { $_\iota$ ($_\varphi$...DP V) }  { $_\iota$ dass-Compl } | | | | |
| b. { $_\iota$ ($_\varphi$...DP { $_\iota$ dass-Compl} V$_\omega$ ) } | *! | ** | | |
| c. { $_\iota$ ($_\varphi$...DP { $_\iota$ dass-Compl}($_\varphi$V$_\omega$) ) } | *! | ** | | * |

Other tableaux (T7, T8) in the paper also confirm that ES is being assessed based on pairs of adjacent sisters, since ternary structures are assigned two violations of ES. However, no tableau in the paper includes a candidate that violates ES-adjacent only once alongside the candidates that violate it twice, so it is impossible to tell whether the gradient violation counting is actually crucial here. None of the structures that violate ES-adjacent are optimal in any case, and they could be ruled out just as well by a single violation of ES-parent as by their double violations of ES-adj. Thus, Féry (2015) provides a useful insight into one analyst's interpretation of EQUALSISTERS as ES-adjacent, but does not provide clear empirical evidence for this particular formulation of the constraint.

EQUALSISTERS-adjacent was explicitly used in Bellik and Kalivoda (2016) in an analysis of phonological phrasing in Kinyambo. The intended optima in this study all satisfy all versions of EQUALSISTERS, however, and therefore Bellik and Kalivoda (2016) also does not provide empirical evidence for ES-adjacent.

### 11.2.2.2 *ES-parent in previous literature*

EQUALSISTERS-parent is used in multiple papers. Kim (2015) resembles Féry (2015) in quoting the original definition of EQUALSISTERS (Myrberg 2013) without modification. Based on the violation counts in tableaux, however, it is apparent that the operational definition of EQUALSISTERS in Kim (2015) is ES-parent: "Assign a violation for every node whose daughters are not all of the same prosodic category." This is clear from the paper's (17), reproduced below as (21). Columns in grey are my additions. Candidate (c) contains two phonological phrases that are sister to a medial, embedded intonational phrase. In Kim (2015), it incurs only a single violation of EqualSisters for this whole configuration, as shown in the column EqualSisters-parent. This single violation is also compatible with EqualSisters-firstPrivilege, since the second sister's category differs from the category of the first. It is not compatible with EqualSisters-adjacent, which would assign two violations, penalizing every change in prosodic category between adjacent sisters.

(21)    EqualSisters-parent, not ES-adjacent (adapted from (17) in Kim (2015))
[CP [NP kayka] [CP asitasiphi] [VP salamɨl ttalɨko]]
'Dogs, as you know, follow man and'
[HH] [HHLLL] [HHL LLL] → [HHL̲%] [HHLLL̲L̲%] [HHL LLL̲L̲%]

| {   {   }   } | EqualSisters | | | sp.Match(CP) | ps.Match(ɩ) |
|---|---|---|---|---|---|
| | parent | adj. | 1st | | |
| → a. {φ}{φ}{φ} | | | | | * |
| b. {φ   φ   φ} | | | | *! | |
| c. {φ {φ} φ} | *! | ** | * | | |

Kim (2015)'s (18), reproduced below as (22) (grey columns are my addition), further disambiguates between ES-parent and ES-1st. Here, ES-parent and ES-adjacent would each assign one violation to candidate (c), whereas ES-1st would assign two violations since the first sister in this structure is an intonational phrase while the second and third sisters are phonological phrases.

(22)    EqualSisters-parent, not ES-1st (adapted from (18) in Kim (2015))
[CP [CP asitasiphi] [[NP kayka] [[VP salamɨl ttalɨko] ]
"As you know, dogs follow man and"
[HHLLL] [HH] [HHL LLL] → [HHLLL̲L̲%] [HH] [HHL LLL̲L̲%]

| {{   } {   }} | EqualSisters | | | sp.Match(CP) | ps.Match(ɩ) |
|---|---|---|---|---|---|
| | parent | adj | 1st | | |
| → a. {{ φ }{ φ   φ}} | | | | | * |
| b. { φ   φ   φ } | | | | *! | |
| c. {{ φ } φ   φ } | *! | * | ** | * | |

Combining the information from those two tableaux, it is clear that Kim (2015) conceives of EqualSisters as EqualSisters-parent. However, the winning candidates in all tableaux in Kim (2015) never violate EQUALSISTERS, which is undominated. Therefore, the exact number of ES violations does not impact the predicted optima; changing to a different implementation of ES would not affect the analysis.

Hsu (2016) also uses EQUALSISTERS-parent. The location and prosodification of the clitic *je* in Bangla (Bengali) is partially determined by the undominated constraint EQUALSISTERS($\iota$). Hsu (2016) introduces an unambiguous definition of EQUALSISTERS, which assigns a violation for each parent whose children are not all of the same category (23). Alongside ES-parent($\iota$), Hsu employs STRONGSTART($\sigma$), using the local, indexed version of STRONGSTART introduced by Elfner (2012), as shown in (24). In Hsu (2016)'s analysis, (24b, c) are better than (24a) because they avoid (24a)'s violation of ES-parent($\iota$) by parsing the clitic *je* into a phonological phrase (The lack of closing parenthesis in (24c) and (25c) is replicated from Hsu 2016). Since ES is indexed to the intonational phrase, and SS is violated in structures where the syllable is daughter to a phonological phrase instead, SS-local in Hsu (2016) does not function as a special case of ES-parent here.

(23)    EQUALSISTERS($\iota$): Assign a violation mark if the immediate daughter nodes of an intonational phrase are not instances of the same prosodic category (Hsu 2016, p. 89).

(24)    ES-parent($\iota$) in Hsu (2016)'s (48), p. 91

| [XP [$_{\text{FinP}}$ [XP ...]]] V | ES-parent($\iota$) | ps.MATCH($\varphi$, LexP) | SS($\sigma$) |
|---|---|---|---|
| a. { (XP)  (XP) ...} | *! | | |
| b. { ((XP) ) (XP) ...} | | * | |
| c. { (XP) ( (XP) ...} | | * | * |

Despite Hsu (2016)'s unambiguous definition of EQUALSISTERS-parent($\iota$), the data presented do not argue decisively for this particular implementation. If ES is indexed to the intonational phrase, then only one of the candidates considered violates ES($\iota$) at all, and a change from ES-parent($\iota$) to ES-adjacent($\iota$) would only mean assigning an extra violation to a candidate that already loses with only one violation. Like ES-parent($\iota$), ES-1st($\iota$) would also assign one violation to the structure in (24a).

Furthermore, if the candidate set is restricted to the structures in (24), then an unindexed ES-adj can make the same cut between the marked (25a) and the less marked (25b) and (25c). Placing the syllable *je* between two $\varphi$s as in (25a) incurs two violations of ES-adjacent, one for each $\varphi$ that *je* is sister to. Parsing *je* into the edge of a φ as in (25b, c) means that it has only one sister, and ES-adjacent is violated only once.

(25)      ES-adj as an alternative to ES(ι)

| [XP [$_{\text{FinP}}$ [XP ...]]] V | ES-adj(any) | ps.MATCH(φ, LexP) | SS(σ) |
|---|---|---|---|
| a. { (XP) (XP) ...} | **! | | |
| b. { ((XP) ) (XP) ...} | * | * | |
| c. { (XP) ( (XP) ...} | * | * | * |

Subsequently, Hsu (2016) modifies SS to be an indexed, "deep" (my term) version of STRONGSTART that refers to syllables at the left edge of the φ (STRONGSTART(syll/φ)) or intonational phrase (STRONGSTART(σ/ι)), as described above in (14) and reproduced in (26).

(26)      STRONGSTART-deep(χ/π): Assign a violation mark for every prosodic constituent whose leftmost daughter constituent is of type χ and is lower in the prosodic hierarchy than its sister constituent immediately to the right, where χ is at the left edge of a prosodic constituent π. (Hsu 2016, p. 95, (56))
          A prosodic constituent χ is at the left edge of prosodic constituent π iff
     a.   π dominates χ, and
     b.   no prosodic constituent that both dominates χ and is dominated by π has a leftmost daughter constituent that does not contain χ (Hsu 2016, p. 95, (57)).

Later tableaux in Hsu (2016) that employ SS-deep do not include EQUALSISTERS or ps.MATCH(φ, LexP), so it is not immediately clear how the full constraint set interacts. However, it seems that all intended optima parse *je* into a binary-branching φ where it would receive one violation of any ES constraint.

A formal definition of EQUALSISTERS-parent is also given in Kusmer (2020) (27). This definition and the surrounding discussion make clear that Kusmer, like Hsu, conceives of EQUALSISTERS as counting parents with unequal daughters, rather than counting the sisters themselves. However, the actual structures being compared in the one tableau that explicitly uses this constraint do not crucially make use of this particular formalization; the substructures being compared are binary-branching and therefore do not distinguish between ES-parent and ES-adjacent.

(27)    EQUALSISTERS: Assign one violation to each prosodic constituent with daughters $\pi_i$, $\pi_j$, where $\pi_i$ & $\pi_j$ are at different levels on the prosodic hierarchy (e.g. ω & φ, or φ & ι) (Kusmer 2020, 143).

### 11.2.2.3 Summarizing the uses of EQUALSISTERS in previous literature

Other papers use EQUALSISTERS, but do not specify a more precise constraint definition than the original positive definition provided by Myrberg (2013), and also do not include any ternary-branching candidates that would disambiguate between the different possible implementations of EQUALSISTERS laid out in (17). These include the original analysis of Swedish (Myrberg 2013), as well as analyses of Japanese (Ito and Mester 2020), Korean (Baek 2017), and Irish (Bennett, Elfner, and McCloskey 2016).

Among the authors that do clarify their definition of EQUALSISTERS, at least one (Féry 2015) employs EQUALSISTERS-adjacent, explicitly stating that adjacent unequal sisters are being counted. Three authors (Hsu 2016, Kusmer 2020, Kim 2015) use a categorical, parent-counting implementation, termed here EQUALSISTERS-parent. EQUALSISTERS-firstPrivilege and EQUALSISTERS-pairwise are unattested in the literature, and will therefore be set aside. Despite the fact that these authors, laudably, make their violation-counting mechanism clear, the tableaux featuring EQUALSISTERS do not provide evidence that would differentiate between the sister-counting EQUALSISTERS-adjacent and parent-counting EQUALSISTERS-parent. Empirically, there does not seem to be evidence in favor of one definition or the other. This chapter therefore seeks out the formal typological implications of the different definitions.

### 11.2.3   Basic EQUALSISTERS-STRONGSTART interactions

For many definitions of EQUALSISTERS and STRONGSTART, the violations of SS are a subset of the violations of ES; every SS-global or SS-local violation is an ES violation, since the first sister in an SS-violating structure is of a different (lower) category from one or more non-initial sisters. In other words, STRONGSTART can function as a special, position-sensitive case of EQUALSISTERS (as noted by Bennett et al. 2016 in a footnote). Many ES-violating structures do not violate SS (28c), but every SS-violating structure also violates ES (28a, b). ES and SS can function in a stringency relationship.

(28)    SS as a special case of ES[3]

|  | ES | SS |
|---|---|---|
| a. $\{_{\iota}\ \omega_{a}\ (_{\varphi}\ \omega_{b})\ \}$ | * | * |
| b. $\{_{\iota}\ \sigma_{a}\ (_{\varphi}\ \omega_{b})\ \}$ | * | * |
| c. $\{_{\iota}\ (_{\varphi}\ (_{\varphi}\ \omega_{a})\ \omega_{b}\ )\ \}$ | * | |

The majority of this chapter examines the stringency relationships between ES and SS, and among SS constraints, in systems containing one ES constraint (ES-parent or ES-adjacent) and three SS constraints (SS-global, -local, and -hyperlocal). First, however, we present a very simple stringency system: ES.SS, defined in (30).

ES.SS and all other systems in this chapter employ a symmetric mapping constraint, MATCH-SP/PS, or simply MATCH, which combines MATCH(Syntax, Prosody) with MATCH(Prosody, Syntax) (29), rather than including the two MATCH constraints separately.[4] This is equivalent to using a symmetric Faithfulness constraint that combines MAX with DEP, or one like IDENT(F) that assigns a violation whether the mapping is [+F] → [–F] or [–F] → [+F]. Combining the two MATCH constraints into one has the effect of eliminating a distinction between languages that favor inserting φs (MATCHSP ≫ MATCHPS) and languages that make repairs through deletion instead (MATCHPS ≫ MATCHSP), which is not relevant to the present investigation.

(29)    MATCH(SYNTAX↔PROSODY) = sp.ps.MATCH = MATCH: Assign a
        violation for every violation of MATCH(SYNTAX→PROSODY) and for
        every violation of MATCH(PROSODY→SYNTAX).

That is: Assign a violation for every XP in the input that lacks a corresponding φ in the output. Also assign a violation for every φ in the output that lacks a corresponding XP in the input. Correspondence is established when two nodes dominate all and only the same phonological exponents.

------

[3]    For the structures in this tableau, all definitions of EQUALSISTERS that are not parameterized to a particular category agree, as do all definitions of STRONGSTART that are not parameterized to a particular category.

[4]    All systems in this chapter necessarily include both syntax-to-prosody mapping (MATCHSP) and prosody-to-syntax mapping (MATCHPS), because systems that include sp.MATCH as the sole antagonist to ES and SS, omitting ps.MATCH, generate typologies of only one language. Without ps.MATCH, there is always an output that perfectly satisfies all of sp.MATCH, ES, and SS, by inserting correspondent-less φs until the prosodic well-formedness constraints are satisfied.

(30)   System ES.SS

   a.   GEN = All $<s, p>$ pairs such that $s$ belongs to (31) and $p$ is a prosodic tree such that

      i.   $p$ is rooted in an intonational phrase.

      ii.   $X^0$s in $s$ are mapped to prosodic words in $p$.

      iii.   All non-root, non-terminal nodes in $p$ are phonological phrases.

      iv.   Linear order of terminals in $s$ is preserved in $p$.

      v.   Every node of category $k$ in $p$ contains at least one child of category $k - 1$.

   b.   CON

      i.   MATCH(XP↔φ) = MATCH: Defined in (29).

      ii.   STRONGSTART-global = SS-global: *( $\pi_n$ ... $\pi_{n+1}$ ...). Defined in (10).

      iii.   EQUALSISTERS-parent = ES: Assign a violation for every node whose children are not all of the same category. *(... $\pi_n$ ... $\pi_m$ ...), where $n \mathrel{!=} m$.

(31)   GEN Inputs: All syntactic trees $s$ such that

   a.   $s$ is generated by the phrase structure grammar in i.-iii.:

      i.   $s \rightarrow$ XP

      ii.   XP $\rightarrow \{X^0$ XP, XP $X^0\}$

      iii.   $X^0 \rightarrow \{$a, b, c, d$\}$

   b.   $s$ has two, three, or four terminals.

   c.   GEN Inputs =

| 2 terminals: | [[a] b] | | [a [b]] | |
|---|---|---|---|---|
| 3 terminals: | [a [b [c]]] | [a [[b] c]] | [[a [b]] c] | [[[a] b] c] |
| 4 terminals: | [a [b [c [d]]]] | [a [b [[c] d]]] | [a [[b [c]] d]] | [a [[[b] c] d]] |
| | [[a [b [c]]] d] | [[a [[b] c]] d] | [[[a [b]] c] d] | [[[[a] b] c] d] |

*11.2.3.1 Typology and grammars of ES.SS*

The typology for ES.SS was calculated using SPOT (Bellik, Bellik, and Kalivoda 2015–2021) and OTWorkplace (Prince, Merchant, and Tesar 2007–2021). It contains three languages (32), which can be informally characterized as in (33). Their grammars are depicted in (34).

(32)      Typology of ES.SS. Dark grey cells are unfaithful. White are faithful.

|        | [a [b]]              | [[a] b]              |
|--------|---------------------|----------------------|
| **L.1**| {(a b)}             | {(a b)}              |
|        | {((a) (b))}         | {((a) (b))}          |
| **L.2**| {(a b)}             | {((a) b)}            |
|        | {((a) (b))}         |                      |
| **L.3**| {(a (b))}           | {((a) b)}            |

(33)      Languages of ES.SS
   a.   L1: Always satisfy ES at the expense of MATCH. (Insert or delete
      φs.[5])
   b.   L2: Always satisfy SS at the expense of MATCH. (Insert or delete
      φs.)
   c.   L3: Always satisfy MATCH. (Don't insert or delete φs.)

(34)      Grammars of the languages of ES.SS

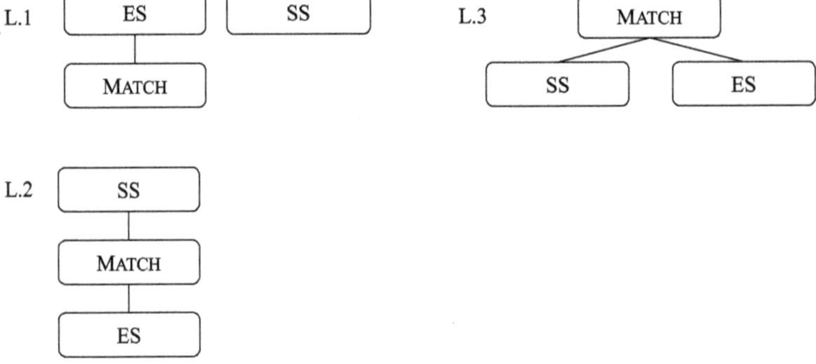


This pattern replicates the canonical typology for a system in which one
constraint functions as the antagonist to two other constraints that are in
a special-general relationship, as schematized above in (6). The typology
contains no language in which ES is ranked above SS, even with an antagonizing MATCH constraint in between them—an analogue to L.2, but with the
positions of ES and SS reversed. Instead, in L.1 where ES is undominated,
SS is not crucially ranked at all; since ES is undominated, so is SS. SS-global
functions as a special case of ES-parent.

---

[5]   'Insertion" and 'deletion" of φs are relative to the isomorphic parse that perfectly satisfies
MATCH.

*11.2.3.2 Property analysis of ES.SS*

The stringency relationship between ES-parent and SS-global is confirmed by the property analysis (PA) for ES.SS in (35) and (36). The first property is p.es, which determines whether violations of ES are tolerated (β value, L.2, L.3), or repaired (α value, L.1). The second property, p.ss, determines whether SS violations are tolerated (β value, L.3) or repaired (α value, L.2). The α value of p.es entails that all SS violations will be repaired, so p.ss scopes under the β value of p.es, and is moot for L.1. No property establishes a ranking between SS and ES, further demonstrating that they are never crucially ranked in this system, since SS is a special case of ES.

(35)    Properties of ES.SS
   a.    p.es: EqualSisters <> MATCH. Wide scope.
   b.    p.ss: StrongStart <> MATCH. Scopes under the β value of p.es.

(36)    Property table for ES.SS

| PA table | p.es | p.ss |
|----------|------|------|
| L.1 | α | moot |
| L.2 | β | α |
| L.3 | β | β |

We can compare the other systems in this chapter to this system, where EQUALSISTERS is more stringent than STRONGSTART. We will explore a number of factors that can break this basic stringency hierarchy. These factors include changes to the constraint implementations, such as: the scope of STRONGSTART (global / local / hyperlocal); the gradience of EQUALSISTERS; and changes to the set of input structures (e.g., including clitics in the dataset, or restricting syntactic head directionality). First, however, we take up the stringency hierarchy within STRONGSTART implementations.

## 11.3   STRONGSTART scope and prosodic Headedness

The scope of SS as local, hyperlocal, or global has consequences for which candidates are favored, particularly when non-binary structures are considered. SS-global assigns violations to more suprabinary structures than SS-local does; SS-hypLoc assigns violations to non-branching structures that SS-global and SS-local do not. This is illustrated in (37). The suffix $.\sigma$ indicates that a terminal is a syllable; unsuffixed terminals are prosodic words. Parentheses indicate φ boundaries.

(37)      Comparing STRONGSTART implementations

| [a [b [c]]] | | | SS-global | SS-local | SS-hypLoc |
|---|---|---|---|---|---|
| a. | ( (a) (b (c)) ) | *Category promotion* | 0 | 0 | 0 |
| b. | ( a (b (c))) | *Weak start* | 1 | 1 | 0 |
| c. | ( a b (c) ) | *Doubly weak start* | 1 | 0 | 0 |
| d. | ( a.σ (b (c))) | *Clitic start* | 1 | 1 | 1 |
| e. | ( a.σ b.σ (c)) | *Clitic doubly weak start* | 1 | 0 | 1 |
| f. | ( (a.σ) (b.σ) (c)) | *Clitic promotion* | 0 | 0 | 2 |

The types of parses preferred by SS can be broken down in two basic types:
category promotion (37a, f) and doubly weak starts (37c, e). SS-global is
satisfied only by category promotion. SS-local is satisfied by either category
promotion or by doubly weak starts. This indicates that SS-global is more
stringent than SS-local.

SS-hypLoc may or may not be satisfied by either category promotion or
by a doubly weak start, depending on whether level-skipping is involved.
SS-hyperlocal is satisfied by any structure where all φs begin with a word,
meaning that it is violated by (37d, e), but not by the word-initial weak
starts in (37b, c).[6] It is not the case that SS-hypLoc is simply less stringent
than SS-local, since SS-hyperlocal assigns a violation to the clitic doubly
weak start (37e) while SS-local does not. Structures like (37e) that violate
SS-hyperlocal without violating SS-local can be characterized as LEVEL-SKIP-
PING DOUBLY WEAK STARTS, defined in (38). SS-hyperlocal penalizes any level-
skipping at the left edge of a prosodic node. In (37), this level-skipping takes
the form of syllables parsed directly up to the left edge of the phonological
phrase, skipping the foot and word levels of parsing. Whether level-skipping
violates SS-local as well depends on whether the peninitial daughter is of
the same (or lower) category as the initial daughter—e.g., (σ σ...)—, or is a
higher category—e.g., (σ ω...). When both the initial and peninitial daughters are two or more levels lower than the parent node, the structure is a
doubly weak start, as defined above in (9), as well as a level-skipping structure: a level-skipping doubly weak start (38).

---

[6] SS-hypLoc is violated, however, by structures in which an intonational phrase has a word
as its first child, i.e., ɩ-rooted equivalents of candidates (b) and (c).

(38)    LEVEL-SKIPPING DOUBLY WEAK START: A structure of the form $(_k\ \pi_n$
        $\pi_{\leq n}\ ...\ \pi_{n+1}\ ...$, where $k \geq n + 2$. That is, a structure where the
        first daughter is at least two levels lower in the prosodic hierarchy
        than the parent, and the first daughter is not lower in the prosodic
        hierarchy than the constituent that immediately follows it, but is
        lower than some later sister constituent.

If level-skipping doubly weak starts ($\varphi$s beginning with multiple clitics, or
$\iota$s beginning with two consecutive words) are admitted to the candidate set,
SS-local is not more stringent than SS-hyperlocal; but if no more than one
clitic is included in each candidate, and all candidates are properly headed,
then SS-local will be more stringent than SS-hyperlocal as well.

Furthermore, wrapping weak terminals in non-branching prosodic nodes,
as in (37f), does not satisfy SS-hypLoc, but does eliminate violations of SS-
loc and SS-glob, since those constraints cannot be violated when sisters are
not present. (37f), and in fact all structures that violate SS-hyperlocal without violating SS-global, violate the principle of PROPER HEADEDNESS (39).

(39)    PROPER HEADEDNESS: Every (non-terminal) prosodic category of
        level $i$ must have a head, that is, it must immediately dominate a
        category of level $i - 1$ (Ito and Mester 1992/2003).

Candidate (37f) contains two $\varphi$s that contain no words and are therefore
headless (A headless $\iota$ that contains no $\varphi$ would be equally problematic).
Unlike Exhaustivity, Headedness is typically regarded as inviolable (Ito and
Mester 1992/2003, Selkirk 1996, McCarthy 2008, Bennett 2012). For instance, Ito and Mester (1992/2003)'s proposal of Weak Layering differenti-
ates between proper Headedness as an 'absolute and inviolable requirement,"
and Maximal Parsing (whose effects are similar to those of EQUALSISTERS)
as an 'optimization target" (p. 40). If Headedness is inviolable, it should be
considered a property of the candidate set, rather than a violable constraint
like Non-Recursivity or Exhaustivity. This underscores the importance of the
candidate generator function GEN. If GEN excludes headless candidates, then
SS-hyperlocal will be in a stringency hierarchy with SS-global. A violation of
SS-hypLoc will also entail a violation of SS-global. But if GEN admits headless candidates, then SS-hyperlocal pulls apart from the others, breaking
the stringency relationship between the different versions of STRONGSTART.

These claims about stringency relations among STRONGSTART constraints
are summarized in (40). They are tested by the systems in the remainder
of this section. In §11.3.1, we examine a system with level-skipping doubly
weak starts, breaking the stringency between SS-local and SS-hyperlocal,

and in §11.3.2 and §11.3.3, we compare a pair of systems with clitics, with and without headless candidates.

(40)    STRONGSTART stringency hypotheses
 a.     SS-global $>_s$ SS-local
        *SS-global is a more stringent version of SS-local, regardless of Headedness.*
 b.     SS-local $>_s$ SS-hyperlocal if and only if all candidates are headed and there are no level-skipping doubly weak starts. Otherwise, SS-local $\not>$s SS-hyperlocal.
        *SS-local is a more stringent version of SS-hyperlocal, if GEN excludes candidates that violate Headedness and also excludes level-skipping doubly weak starts.*
 c.     SS-global $>_s$ SS-hyperlocal, when all candidates are headed.
        *SS-global is a more stringent version of SS-hyperlocal, if and only if GEN excludes candidates that violate Headedness.*

### 11.3.1  SS3[–clitic]

We define a system SS3[–clitic] with the inputs in (41): two-, three-, or four-terminal syntactic trees rooted in the complementizer phrase (CP), in which all terminals are of category $X^0$ and all non-root, non-terminals are syntactic phrases (XPs). The remainder of the system definition appears in (42). This system does contain level-skipping doubly weak starts, but does not contain any prosodically headless optima. Admitting prosodically headless structures to the candidate set does not affect the typology, however.

(41)    GEN INPUTS:  All syntactic trees $s$ such that
 a.     $s$ is generated by the phrase structure grammar in i–iv:
        i.    $s \rightarrow$ CP
        ii.   CP $\rightarrow \{X^0\ XP,\ XP\ X^0,\ XP\ XP\}$
        iii.  XP $\rightarrow \{X^0\ XP,\ XP\ X^0,\ XP\ XP\}$
        iv.   $X^0 \rightarrow \{a,\ b,\ c,\ d\}$
 b.     $s$ has two, three, or four terminals.
 c.     GEN INPUTS (excluding those with adjunction substructures, [XP XP])

| 2 X⁰s | { [[a] b] } | | { [a [b]] } | |
|---|---|---|---|---|
| 3 X⁰s | { [a [b [c]]] } | { [a [[b] c]] } | { [[a [b]] c] } | { [[[a] b] c] } |
| 4 X⁰s | { [a [b [c [d]]]] } | { [a [b [[c] d]]] } | { [a [[b [c]] d]] } | { [a [[[b] c] d]] } |
|  | { [[a [b [c]]] d] } | { [[a [[b] c]] d] } | { [[[a [b]] c] d] } | { [[[[a] b] c] d] } |

(42)    SS3[–clitic]

    a.    GEN = All pairs $<s, p>$ pairs such that $s$ belongs to (41) and $p$ is a prosodic tree such that

        i.    $p$ is rooted in an intonational phrase.

        ii.    $X^0$s in $s$ are mapped to prosodic words in $p$.

        iii.    All non-root, non-terminal nodes in $p$ are phonological phrases.

        iv.    Linear order of terminals in $s$ is preserved in $p$.

        v.    Every node of category $k$ in $p$ contains at least one child of category $k$–1 (HEADEDNESS).[7]

    b.    CON

        i.    MATCH(XP$\leftrightarrow\varphi$) = MATCH: Defined in (29).

        ii.    STRONGSTART-global = SS-global: *( $\pi_n$ ... $\pi_{n+1}$ ...). Defined in (10).

        iii.    STRONGSTART-local = SS-local: *( $\pi_n$ $\pi_{n+1}$ ...). Defined in (7).

        iv.    STRONGSTART-hyperlocal = SS-hypLoc: *($_n$ $\pi_m$ ...), where $m < n - 1$. Defined in (12).

SS-hyperlocal in this system is not indexed to any specific category, and thereby differs from the version employed in Bennett, Elfner and McCloskey (2016). The structures in the candidate set that violate SS-hypLoc are all intonational phrases whose leftmost daughter is a prosodic word.

### 11.3.1.1 Typology and languages of SS3[–clitic]

Three inputs form a support for SS3[–clitic]. The possible optima and violation profiles for them are shown in (43). Multiple parses of each of these inputs perfectly satisfy the three SS constraints, and satisfy MATCH equally well. These are shown with white backgrounds in (43). Grey backgrounds indicate possible optima that violate SS-global.

---

[7] Removing the requirement of Headedness adds one more prosodic parse to each c-set: the structure in which all terminal words are parsed directly into the intonational phrase. This parse is always harmonically bounded, however, by a properly headed parse that outperforms it on MATCH. Removing the requirement of Headedness does not alter the predicted typology in any way in [–clitic] systems.

(43)  Violation tableaux of possible optima for a support of SS3[–clitic]

| input | output | SS-global | SS-local | SS-hypLoc | Match |
|---|---|---|---|---|---|
| {a [b]} | {(a) (b)} | 0 | 0 | 0 | 1 |
| | {a (b)} | 1 | 1 | 1 | 0 |
| {[a [b]]} | {(a b)} | 0 | 0 | 0 | 1 |
| | {((a) (b))} | 0 | 0 | 0 | 1 |
| | {(a (b))} | 1 | 1 | 0 | 0 |
| {a [b [c]]} | {(a b) (c)} | 0 | 0 | 0 | 2 |
| | {a b (c)} | 1 | 0 | 1 | 1 |
| | {(a) (b c)} | 0 | 0 | 0 | 2 |
| | {(a) ((b) (c))} | 0 | 0 | 0 | 2 |
| | {(a) (b (c))} | 1 | 1 | 0 | 1 |
| | {(a) b (c)} | 0 | 0 | 0 | 2 |
| | {a (b (c))} | 2 | 2 | 1 | 0 |
| {[a [b [c]]]} | {(a b c)} | 0 | 0 | 0 | 2 |
| | {((a b) (c))} | 0 | 0 | 0 | 2 |
| | {(a b (c))} | 1 | 0 | 0 | 1 |
| | {((a) (b c))} | 0 | 0 | 0 | 2 |
| | {((a) ((b) (c)))} | 0 | 0 | 0 | 2 |
| | {((a) b (c))} | 0 | 0 | 0 | 2 |
| | {(a (b (c)))} | 2 | 2 | 0 | 0 |

The typology for SS3[–clitic] contains five languages (44). Their grammars
appear in (45). In (44) and throughout the chapter, dark grey marks unfaithful optima that occur in L.1 (here, these satisfy SS-global). Medium grey
marks unfaithful parses that occur in L.3 but not L.1; here, these satisfy SS-
local but not SS-global. Lightest grey (L.4, second column) marks unfaithful
optima that appear in L.4 but not L.2 or L.1; here, those satisfy SS-hypLoc
but not SS-global or SS-local.

(44)   Typology for SS3[–clitic]

|  | {[a [b]]} | {a [b [c]]} | {[a [b [c]]]} |
|---|---|---|---|
| L.1 | {(a b)} <br> {((a) (b))} | {(a b) (c)} <br> {(a) (b c)} <br> {(a) ((b) (c))} <br> {(a) b (c)} | {(a b c)} <br> {((a b) (c))} <br> {((a) (b c))} <br> {((a) ((b) (c)))} <br> {((a) b (c))} |
| L.2 | {(a b)} <br> {((a) (b))} | {(a b) (c)} <br> {(a) (b c)} <br> {(a) ((b) (c))} <br> {(a) b (c)} | {(a b (c))} |
| L.3 | {(a b)} <br> {((a) (b))} | {a b (c)} | {(a b (c))} |
| L.4 | {(a (b))} | {(a) (b (c))} | {(a (b (c)))} |
| L.5 | {(a (b))} | {a (b (c))} | {(a (b (c)))} |

(45)    Grammars of SS3[–clitic]

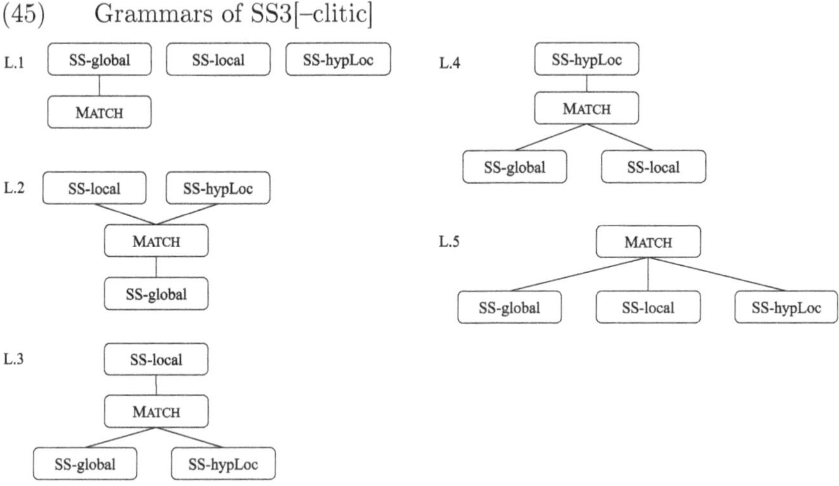


In the first language (L.1), there are no rises in prosodic category across sets of sisters. SS-global dominates MATCH, with the result that SS-local and SS-hypLoc are freely rankable. This supports the expectation established above that SS-global is more stringent than SS-local and SS-hypLoc. A striking feature of L.1 is its pervasive co-optimality; as noted above, there are often several distinct structures that satisfy SS-global perfectly while tying on MATCH.

In L.2, SS-global is dominated by MATCH, but both SS-local and SS-hypLoc dominate MATCH. The fact that both SS-local and SS-hypLoc must be separately ranked above MATCH demonstrates that they are not in a stringency relationship. In L.2, intonational phrases are parsed with category promotion. Undominated SS-hypLoc demands that the first daughter of an intonational phrase be a $\varphi$. As a result, every intonational phrase begins with a $\varphi$ and does not contain any rises in prosodic category among its daughters:[8] {a [b [c]]} → {(a b) (c)} and co-optima. SS-hypLoc does not distinguish among substructures rooted in $\varphi$s; although it requires that a $\varphi$'s first daughter be a $\omega$ or higher, all output candidates in GEN satisfy this requirement. Meanwhile, SS-local is satisfied by doubly weak starts: [a [b [c]]] → (a b (c)). Rises in prosodic category are possible within the $\varphi$, as long as the second daughter is not a higher category than the first. SS-local is satisfied in L.2 not by promoting the category of the first child, but by keeping its next sister weak as well: (a b (c)) does not violate SS-local since this constraint only compares the categories of the first two sisters. These structures avoid the SS-local violation only by spreading the first sister's weakness rightward in a doubly weak start to the $\varphi$. This seems like an unnatural and undesirable result—as discussed above, analysts use STRONGSTART-local to motivate $\varphi$-insertion at the left edge, rather than $\varphi$-deletion in the middle of the structure. In L.2, SS-local instead demotes peninitial material for the sake of avoiding a rise in category from first to second child. Of the three SS variants considered here, only SS-global prevents rises in category across the entire set of sisters, or promotes the category of weak initial elements.

In L.3, only SS-local dominates MATCH, so doubly weak starts are permitted for both the $\iota$ and the $\varphi$ level. This ranking further confirms that SS-local is not a more general version of SS-hypLoc. If SS-local were more stringent than SS-hypLoc, it would not be able to dominate SS-hypLoc, since a more stringent constraint is never ranked over a less stringent constraint from the same stringency hierarchy.

In L.4, only SS-hypLoc dominates MATCH, with the result that weak starts to the intonational phrase are ruled out, but isomorphic weak starts to the phonological phrase are unproblematic. For example, the $X^0$ $a$ in the CP {a [b [c]]} is promoted to a $\varphi$ in the output: {(a) (b (c))}. The isomorphic parse of this input would put a prosodic word at the left edge of the intonational phrase, violating SS-hypLoc since the $\varphi$-level would be skipped at the left edge. Other head-initial CPs also undergo category promotion at the left edge.

---

[8] It is impossible to have a rise in prosodic category after a $\varphi$ in this system, since $\varphi$ is the highest possible non-root category.

Finally, in L.5, MATCH is undominated, and all parses are isomorphic to syntax. In this language, all parses of inputs with left-aligned syntactic heads violate one or more SS constraints.

### 11.3.1.2 Property analysis for SS3[–clitic]

We can gain further insights into the structure of this typology by applying Property Theory (Alber and Prince 2021; Alber, DelBusso, and Prince 2016; DelBusso 2018, 2020), identifying the rankings that unite or divide the languages.[9] The typology can be described with three properties (47); each property consists of an opposition between one SS constraint and MATCH. The property analysis here verifies that SS-global is more stringent than both SS-local and SS-hypLoc, but that no other stringency relationships hold in this system.

(46)    Constraint order for property values expressed as ERCs:
        SS-global → SS-local → SS-hypLoc → MATCH

(47)    Property table for SS3[–clitic]

| Props | | α | β | Scope |
|---|---|---|---|---|
| p.glob | SS-global <> MATCH | WeeL | LeeW | Wide |
| p.loc | SS-loc <> MATCH | eWeL | eLeW | p.glob = β |
| p.hyp | SS-hypLoc <> MATCH | eeWL | eeLW | p.glob = β |

(48)    PA table for SS3[–clitic]

| | p.glob | p.loc | p.hyp |
|---|---|---|---|
| L.1 | α | moot | moot |
| L.2 | β | α | α |
| L.3 | β | α | β |
| L.4 | β | β | α |
| L.5 | β | β | β |

The first property, p.glob, opposes SS-global and MATCH, and takes wide scope (47). MATCH and SS-global must be ranked against each other in all four languages. Only in L.1 is SS-global ranked above MATCH (the α value of p.glob). In all other languages, MATCH outranks SS-global (the β value of the property). L.2–5 are united by sharing the subranking MATCH ≫ SS-global.

---



[9] See Introduction (Chapter 1) for more background on Property Theory and how to understand a property analysis.

Non-isomorphism in these languages occurs only to improve the prosodic well-formedness of the first two sisters in a set of sisters. In L.1, by contrast, φs may be added or removed to ensure that there are no rises in prosodic category across the entire set of sisters.

The second property, p.loc, opposes SS-local to MATCH, and scopes under the β value of p.glob. That is, p.loc is only relevant when MATCH outranks SS-global. When SS-global outranks MATCH (in L.1), then SS-local is not crucially ranked against MATCH. This confirms that SS-global is indeed more stringent than SS-local. L.2 and L.3 have the α value of this property, with SS-local outranking MATCH. In the remaining languages, L.4 and L.5, MATCH outranks SS-local instead (the β value of p.loc).

The third property is p.hyp, which opposes SS-hypLoc to MATCH. Like p.loc, p.hyp scopes under the β value of p.glob. When SS-global outranks MATCH, then SS-hypLoc is not ranked against MATCH and p.hyp is not active. The property p.hyp distinguishes L.2 from L.3, and L.4 from L.5.

The scopal relations in this PA demonstrate that SS-global is more stringent than SS-local and SS-hypLoc, as hypothesized in (40a, c). Consistent with the stringency interaction posited in (40b), SS-local was not more stringent than SS-hypLoc, because level-skipping doubly weak starts are present in the candidate set, and are not harmonically bounded.

### 11.3.2  SS3[+clitic, +Hd]

SS is often employed in analyses of datasets where certain lexical items must be parsed as clitics, rather than prosodic words. SS-hypLoc(σ) (Bennett, Elfner, and McCloskey 2016) is an example of an implementation designed specifically for this purpose. To explore the interaction of SS-hypLoc with SS-global and SS-local in structures where one terminal must be parsed as a free clitic, we construct a pair of systems SS3[+clitic, +Hd] and SS3[+clitic, −Hd]. These combine the three versions of STRONGSTART under discussion with MATCH. As before, all three versions of STRONGSTART are not indexed to any category; thus, SS-hypLoc differs from the indexed version in Bennett, Elfner, and McCloskey (2016).

Both systems in this section use the same set of syntactic inputs, defined in (49). Both left-headed and right-headed syntactic structures are included. They vary in the set of output candidates, however, with SS3[+clitic, +Hd] banning structures that violate proper Headedness, and SS3[+clitic, −Hd] allowing them. Since no input structure contains more than one clitic, no output structure will contain more than one syllable terminal.

(49)    GEN INPUTS:  All branching syntactic trees $s$ such that
    a.    $s$ is generated by the phrase structure grammar in (i-iv):
       i.    $s \rightarrow CP$
       ii.   $CP \rightarrow \{X^0\ XP,\ XP\ X^0,\ XP\ XP\}$
       iii.  $XP \rightarrow \{X^0\ XP,\ XP\ X^0,\ XP\ XP\}$
       iv.   $X^0 \rightarrow \{$a, b, c, a.clitic, b.clitic, c.clitic$\}$
    b.    $s$ has two or three terminals.
    c.    $s$ contains at most one clitic.

(50)    SS3[+clitic, +Hd]
    a.    GEN = All $<s,\ p>$ pairs such that s belongs to (49) and $p$ is a prosodic tree such that
       i.    $p$ is rooted in an intonational phrase.
       ii.   Clitics in $s$ are mapped to syllables in $p$.
       iii.  Non-clitic $X^0$s in $s$ are mapped to prosodic words in $p$.
       iv.   All non-root, non-terminal nodes in $p$ are phonological phrases $(\varphi)$.
       v.    Linear order of terminals in $s$ is preserved in $p$.
       vi.   HEADEDNESS: Every node of category $k$ contains a node of category $k - 1$.
    b.    CON
       i.    MATCH($XP \leftrightarrow \varphi$): Defined in (29).
       ii.   STRONGSTART-global = SS-global: $*(\ \pi_n\ ...\ \pi_{n+1}\ ...)$. Defined in (10).
       iii.  STRONGSTART-local = SS-local: $*(\ \pi_n\ \pi_{n+1}\ ...)$. Defined in (7).
       iv.   STRONGSTART-hyperlocal = SS-hypLoc: $*(_n\ \pi_m\ ...)$, where $m < n - 1$. Defined in (12)

*11.3.2.1 Typology and grammars of SS3[+clitic, +Hd]*

Four inputs form a support for the languages of SS3[+clitic, +Hd]. The typology contains five languages (51), whose grammars, shown in (52), are identical to the grammars of SS3[–clitic] above (45). As in SS3[–clitic], the languages exhibit varying degrees of unfaithfulness to satisfy the three SS constraints, and when SS-global outranks MATCH, SS-local and SS-hypLoc are unranked. Adding clitics to the system did not alter the typology in any meaningful way.

(51)     Typology for SS3[+clitic, +Hd], support columns and {a [b.clitic]}

| | {a [b]} | {[a [b]]} | {a [b.clitic]} | {a [b [c]]} | {[a [b [c]]]} |
|---|---|---|---|---|---|
| L.1 | {(a) (b)} | {(a b)} <br> {((a) (b))} | | {(a b) (c)} <br> {(a) (b c)} <br> {(a) ((b) (c))} <br> {(a) b (c)} | {(a b c)} <br> {((a b) (c))} <br> {((a) (b c))} <br> {((a) ((b) (c)))} <br> {((a) b (c))} |
| | | | {(a b.syll)} <br> {(a) b.syll} | | |
| L.2 | {(a) (b)} | {(a b)} <br> {((a) (b))} | {(a b.syll)} <br> {(a) b.syll} | {(a b) (c)} <br> {(a) (b c)} <br> {(a) ((b) (c))} <br> {(a) b (c)} | {(a b (c))} |
| L.3 | {(a) (b)} | {(a b)} <br> {((a) (b))} | {(a b.syll)} <br> {(a) b.syll} | {a b (c)} | {(a b (c))} |
| L.4 | {(a) (b)} | {(a (b))} | {(a b.syll)} <br> {(a) b.syll} | {(a) (b (c))} | {(a (b (c)))} |
| L.5 | {a (b)} | {(a (b))} | {(a b.syll)} <br> {(a) b.syll} | {a (b (c))} | {(a (b (c)))} |

(52)     Grammars of SS3[+clitic, +Hd]

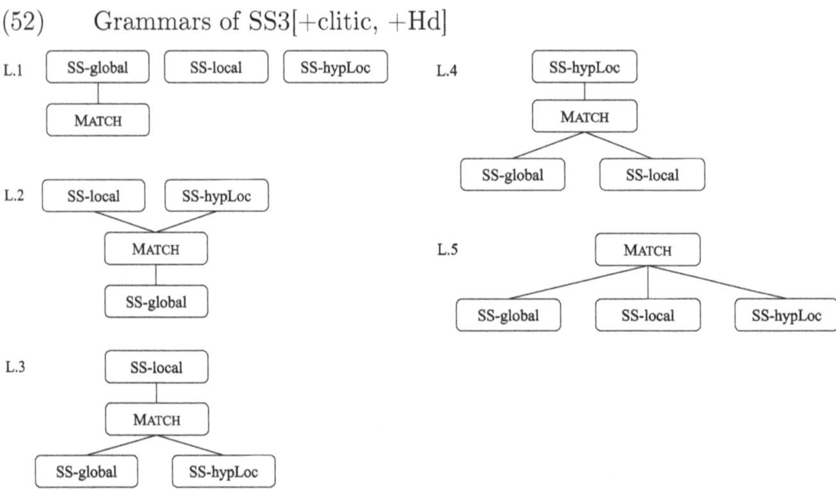



### 11.3.2.2 Property analysis of SS3[+clitic, +Hd]

The same properties that describe the typology of SS3[−clitic] also provide a full property analysis of SS3[+clitic, +Hd], confirming that the addition of clitics did not impact the interaction of the constraints. For a discussion of the properties, see §11.3.1.2.

(53)   Property table for SS3[+clitic, +Hd]

| Props | | α | β | Scope |
|---|---|---|---|---|
| p.glob | SS-global <> Match | WeeL | LeeW | Wide |
| p.loc | SS-loc <> Match | eWeL | eLeW | p.glob = β |
| p.hyp | SS-hypLoc <> Match | eeWL | eeLW | p.glob = β |

(54)   PA table for SS3[+clitic, +Hd]

| | p.glob | p.loc | p.hyp |
|---|---|---|---|
| L.1 | α | moot | moot |
| L.2 | β | α | α |
| L.3 | β | α | β |
| L.4 | β | β | α |
| L.5 | β | β | β |

### 11.3.3  SS3[+clitic, –Hd]

In SS3[–clitic], adding headless candidates did not affect the structure of the typology or interaction of the constraints. This is not the case when clitics are included, as will be seen in the present system SS3[+clitic, –Hd], which allows clitics to be directly parsed into a non-branching, headless φ.

(55) SS3[+clitic, –Hd]
   a.   Gen:
      i.   Inputs: Same as SS3[+clitic, +Hd]. See (49).
      ii.   Outputs: Same as SS3[+clitic, +Hd].Gen, but without the requirement of Headedness.
   b.   Con: Same as SS3[+clitic, +Hd].Con

### 11.3.3.1  Typology and grammars of SS3[+clitic, –Hd]

When headless candidates are admitted to the system, the typology contains six languages (56), one more than the previous system where Headedness was enforced. Some optima for structures containing clitics include headless φs or ιs, which are bolded in the typology table. Three languages in this system (L.1, L.2, L.5) have identical optima to languages in SS3[+clitic, +Hd] (51), and four languages (L.2, L.4, L.5, L.6) have grammars that are identical to grammars in SS3[+clitic, +Hd] (52). The unique language is L.3, which will be discussed last.

(56)    Typology for SS3[+clitic, −Hd]. Bolding marks headless φs and ιs.

|  | {a [b]} | {[a [b]]} | {a [b.clitic]} | {a [b [c]]} | {[a [b [c]]]} |
|---|---|---|---|---|---|
| L.1 | {(a) (b)} | {(a b)}<br>{((a) (b))} | {(a b.σ)}<br>{(a) b.σ} | {(a b) (c)}<br>{(a) (b c)}<br>{(a) ((b) (c))}<br>{(a) b (c)} | {(a b c)}<br>{((a b) (c))}<br>{((a) (b c))}<br>{((a) ((b) (c)))}<br>{((a) b (c))} |
| L.2 | {(a) (b)} | {(a b)}<br>{((a) (b))} | {(a b.σ)}<br>{(a) b.σ} | {(a b) (c)}<br>{(a) (b c)}<br>{(a) ((b) (c))}<br>{(a) b (c)} | {(a b (c))} |
| L.3 | {(a) (b)} | {(a b)}<br>{((a) (b))} | {a b.σ}<br>{(a) (b.σ)} | {(a b) (c)}<br>{(a) (b c)}<br>{(a) ((b) (c))}<br>{(a) b (c)} | {(a b c)}<br>{((a b) (c))}<br>{((a) (b c))}<br>{((a) ((b) (c)))}<br>{((a) b (c))} |
| L.4 | {(a) (b)} | {(a b)}<br>{((a) (b))} | {a b.σ}<br>{(a) (b.σ)} | {a b (c)} | {(a b (c))} |
| L.5 | {(a) (b)} | {(a (b))} | {(a b.σ)}<br>{(a) b.σ } | {(a) (b (c))} | {(a (b (c)))} |
| L.6 | {a (b)} | {(a (b))} | {a (b.σ)} | {a (b (c))} | {(a (b (c)))} |

(57)    Grammars of SS3[+clitic, −Hd]

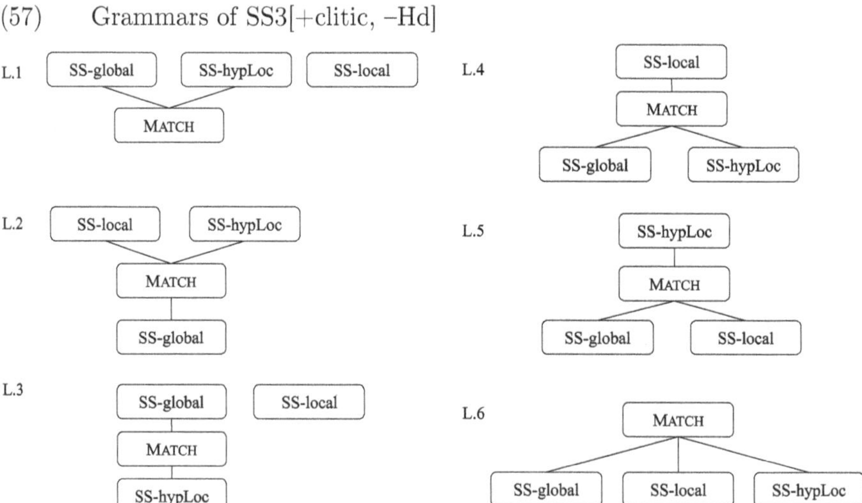

In L.1, both SS-global and SS-hypLoc outrank MATCH, and SS-local is un-ranked, which produces a set of optima that are identical to the optima in L.1 of the previous systems SS3[–clitic] and SS3[+clitic, +Hd], although the grammars that produce these optima differ across systems. All versions of SS are violated minimally in this language. The next language is L.2, where SS-local and SS-hypLoc dominate MATCH, which in turn dominates SS-global. It is identical to L.2 in SS3[–clitic] and of SS3[+clitic, +Hd]. Skipping L.3 for the moment, L.4 has SS-local over MATCH, which in turn dominates SS-global and SS-hypLoc; this is the same grammar as L.3 in SS3[+clitic, +Hd], although the optima differ in that they include headless structures (e.g., {a b.σ}, which contains no φ). L.5 in SS3[+clitic, –Hd] is the same as L.4 in the [+Hd] system, and L.6, where MATCH is undominated, has the same grammar as L.5 of the [+Hd] system. Its optima differ from those of the headed system, however, in that they are perfectly isomorphic to the input syntax, including mapping XPs whose only terminal is a clitic to non-branching, headless φs that contain only a syllable.

In the novel language L.3, SS-global dominates MATCH, as it does in L.1. Unlike in L.1, MATCH in L.3 dominates SS-hypLoc in turn. This ranking does not occur in the headed system SS3[+clitic, +Hd], or in the clitic-free system SS3[–clitic], because in those systems, SS-global is more stringent than SS-hypLoc, and the two do not come into conflict. With the admission of headless φs to the candidate set, however, conflict emerges. For the input {a [b.clitic]}, SS-global does not distinguish between optima that are not properly headed and violate SS-hypLoc, and other losing parses (58). The decision is left up to MATCH, which dominates SS-hypLoc and selects the improperly headed, SS-hypLoc-violating candidates. This exemplifies the conflict between SS-global and SS-hypLoc.

(58)   Support for L.3 of SS3[+clitic, –Hd], headless φ bolded

| Input | Winner | Loser | SS-global | SS-local | MATCH | SS-hypLoc |
|---|---|---|---|---|---|---|
| {a [b [c]} | {(a b) (c)}<br>{(a) (b c)}<br>{(a) ((b)<br>(c))}<br>{(a) b (c)} | {a b (c)} | W | | L | W |
| {a [b.clitic]} | {a **(b.σ)**)}<br>{(a) **(b.σ)**)} | {(a b.σ)}<br>{(a) b.σ} | | | W | L |

### 11.3.3.2 Property analysis of SS3[+clitic, −Hd]

The broken stringency relationship between SS-global and SS-hypLoc is on display in the PA for this system. The typology can be described with the same properties as SS3[+clitic, +Hd], but the scope relationships change to reflect the lack of stringency between SS-hypLoc and SS-global (59)–(60): while p.loc still scopes under the β value of p.glob, p.hyp is now wide scope. This supports hypothesis (40c): SS-global is not more stringent than SS-hyperlocal when headless candidates are present in GEN.

(59)     Properties of SS3[+clitic, −Hd]

|  |  | α | β | Scope |
|---|---|---|---|---|
| p.glob | SS-global <> MATCH | WeeL | LeeW | Wide |
| p.loc | SS-loc <> MATCH | eWeL | eLeW | p.glob = β |
| p.hyp | SS-hypLoc <> MATCH | eeWL | eeLW | Wide |

(60)     PA table for SS3[+clitic, −Hd]

|  | p.glob | p.loc | p.hyp |
|---|---|---|---|
| L.1 | α | moot | α |
| L.2 | β | α | α |
| L.3 | α | moot | β |
| L.4 | β | α | β |
| L.5 | β | β | α |
| L.6 | β | β | β |

### 11.3.4 Removing level-skipping doubly weak starts

Thus far, we have seen evidence of SS-global's greater stringency over SS-local and SS-hyperlocal, under the correct conditions. We now turn to a demonstration that SS-local can be more stringent than SS-hyperlocal with the correct candidate set, one in which no level-skipping doubly weak start is a possible optimum. This is ensured by requiring all input candidates to be rooted in XP, so that MATCH demands that all outputs contain a φ that dominates all terminals.

(61)     System SS3[XP root, +clitic, +Hd]: Same as SS3[+clitic, +Hd] (50), except that all input syntactic trees are rooted in XP, rather than CP.

### 11.3.4.1 Typology and languages of SS3[XP root, +clitic, +Hd]

The typology for this system contains four languages (62). In L.1, SS-global outranks MATCH, and SS-local and SS-hyperlocal are freely rankable. In L.2, SS-local dominates MATCH, and SS-hyperlocal is freely rankable, indicating that, unlike in the previous systems, SS-local is more stringent than SS-hyperlocal. In L.3, only SS-hyperlocal dominates MATCH, which in turn dominates the other two SS constraints. In L.4, MATCH dominates all three SS constraints.

(62)    Typology for SS3[XP root, +clitic, +Hd]

|       | [a [b]] | [a [b [c]]] | [a [b.clitic [c]]] |
|-------|---------|-------------|--------------------|
| L.1   | {(a b)} <br> {((a) (b))} | {(a b c)} <br> {((a b) (c))} <br> {((a) (b c))} <br> {((a) ((b) (c)))} <br> {((a) b (c))} | {(a b.σ c)} <br> {((a b.σ) (c))} <br> {((a) b.σ (c))} |
| L.2   | {(a b)} <br> {((a) (b))} | {(a b (c))} | {(a b.σ (c))} |
| L.3   | {(a (b))} | {(a (b (c)))} | {(a b.σ (c))} |
| L.4   | {(a (b))} | {(a (b (c)))} | {(a (b.σ (c)))} |

(63)    Grammars for SS3[XP root, +clitic, +Hd]

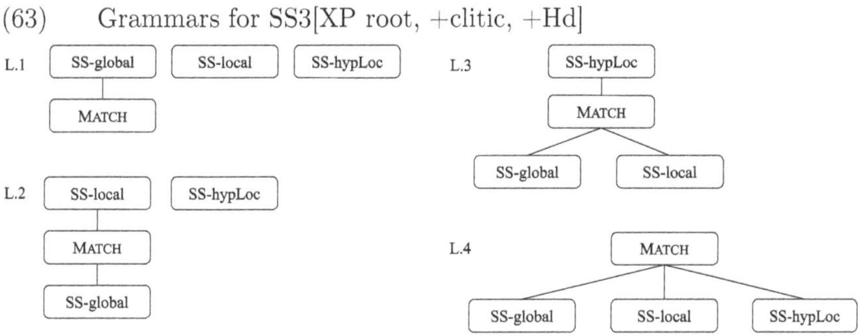


In no language does any optimum lack a φ wrapping all candidates; all parses which lack a φ-wrapper are harmonically bounded by equivalent φ-wrapped parses that perform better on MATCH by matching the root XP, as in (64). This means there are no level-skipping doubly weak starts to ιs, since every ι begins with a φ. Moreover, since each candidate contains no more than one clitic, there are no level-skipping doubly weak starts to φs. Hence, there are no optima that satisfy SS-local while violating SS-hyperlocal, and SS-local functions as more stringent than SS-hyperlocal.

(64)      Harmonic bounding of a level-skipping doubly weak start

| [a [b [c]]] | SS-global | SS-local | SS-hypLoc | MATCH |
|---|---|---|---|---|
| a. {(a b (c))} | 1 | 0 | 0 | 1 |
| b. {a b (c)} | 1 | 0 | 1 | 2 |

### 11.3.4.2 Property analysis of SS3[XP root, +clitic, +Hd]

The same properties as in the preceding systems account neatly for the four
languages here, but with a new scopal restriction. As before, p.loc is active only
when MATCH dominates SS-global (the β value of p.glob), showing that SS-
global is more stringent than SS-local. However, the scope of p.hyp is restricted
to the β value of p.loc, indicating that SS-local $>_s$ SS-hyperlocal. Excluding
level-skipping doubly weak starts from the set of optima (by changing the
inputs, in this case), while maintaining the requirement of proper Headedness,
establishes a three-step stringency hierarchy among SS constraints (67).

(65)      Property table for SS3[XP root, +clitic, +Hd]

| Properties | | α | β | Scope |
|---|---|---|---|---|
| p.glob | SS-global <> MATCH | WeeL | LeeW | Wide |
| p.loc | SS-loc <> MATCH | eWeL | eLeW | p.glob = β |
| p.hyp | SS-hypLoc <> MATCH | eeWL | eeLW | p.loc = β |

(66)      PA table for SS3[XP root, +clitic, +Hd]

| | glob | loc | hyp |
|---|---|---|---|
| L.1 | α | moot | moot |
| L.2 | β | α | moot |
| L.4 | β | β | α |
| L.5 | β | β | β |

(67)      Stringency among SS constraints in SS3[XP root, +clitic, +Hd]:
          SS-global $>_s$ SS-local $>_s$ SS-hyperlocal

### 11.3.5 Interim summary

A comparison of three systems that employ SS-global, -local, and -hyperlo-
cal, combined with MATCH, supports the hypotheses of (40). SS-local remains
a special case of SS-global regardless of whether all candidates conform to
Headedness (all systems), and SS-hypLoc functions as a special case of SS-
global when Headedness is enforced ([+Hd] systems), but ceases to be in a

stringency relationship with SS-global when headless candidates are admitted ([–Hd] systems). When level-skipping doubly weak starts are included in the candidate set (in SS3[±Hd, ±clitic], where inputs are rooted in the CP), SS-local never functions as a more stringent version of SS-hypLoc. But in SS3[XP root, +clitic, +Hd], which exclusively employs inputs rooted in XP so that level-skipping doubly weak starts are harmonically bounded, SS-local does act as a more stringent version of SS-hypLoc, as does SS-global.

The current systems are necessarily restricted in their set of inputs (two or three terminals, with zero or one clitic). Including multiple clitics in the same tree is unlikely to alter stringency relationships between SS-global and SS-local, and between SS-local and SS-hyperlocal, since level-skipping doubly weak starts are already present in the form of words at the left edge of the intonational phrase. Allowing longer inputs is unlikely to alter the interactions seen here, although confirmation of this is left to future research.

Overall, this investigation demonstrates the value of retaining Headedness as an inviolable condition on prosodic structures, as proposed by Ito and Mester (1992/2003). STRONGSTART-global is more stringent than its local and hyperlocal counterparts when all candidates are properly headed; SS-local also has a better chance of being more stringent than SS-hypLoc when all candidates are properly headed (although level-skipping doubly weak starts still break their stringency interaction). Since SS-global is, as expected, the most stringent version of STRONGSTART, it is possible that SS-global is the only version that is actually necessary; whether the doubly weak optima like (a b (c)) that occur in languages like L.2 of SS3[+clitic, +Hd] are actually attested in natural language is an open question. If such doubly weak structures are not more prosodically well-formed than singly weak starts like (a (b c)), then these systems show us that SS-global can replace SS-local entirely. Furthermore, if Headedness is taken as universally inviolable, and SS-hypLoc is a less stringent version of SS-global, then SS-hypLoc could be reframed as a category-sensitive version of SS, rather than one that differs in its scope.

## 11.4   ES-parent and STRONGSTART

In the system ES.SS (§11.2.3), SS-global functions as a special, less stringent case of ES-parent. SS-local and SS-hypLoc were seen in §11.3 to function as more specialized, less stringent versions of SS-global as long as Headedness is enforced. Do these other versions of STRONGSTART also function as successively more specialized cases of ES-parent? When all candidates are properly headed and when ES-parent is not parameterized to any particular category, then all versions of SS should belong to a three- or four-level[10] stringency hierarchy with EqualSisters. Among properly headed candidates, every violation of SS-hyperlocal entails a violation of ES: A node that violates SS-hyperlocal begins with a prosodically deficient child (e.g., a $\sigma$ at the left edge of a $\varphi$, or a $\omega$ at the left edge of an $\iota$), but must include at least one other child that is of a higher category (such as an $\omega$ in $\varphi$, or a $\varphi$ in an $\iota$) as its proper head. When headless candidates are allowed, however, then SS-hypLoc can conflict with ES-parent (as well as the other SS constraints), and is not part of a stringency hierarchy with ES or the other SS implementations. These hypotheses are laid out in (68). The systems ES.SS3[±clitic, ±Hd] test these claims. They are identical to SS3[±clitic, ±Hd], except that ES-parent has been added to the constraint sets.

(68)    ES-SS stringency hypotheses
    a.    All versions of ES that are not indexed to a specific category[11] are more stringent than SS-global. ES $>_s$ SS-global
    b.    All versions of ES that are not indexed to a specific category are more stringent than SS-local. ES $>_s$ SS-local
    c.    If and only if the candidate set is restricted to properly headed candidates, non-indexed ES is also more stringent than SS-hyperlocal. ES $>_s$ SS-hyperlocal $\forall$S: $\forall$c : c $\in$ S.Gen $\to$ $\forall\pi$ : $\pi$ $\in$ c $\wedge$ $\pi$ is of category n $\to$ $\exists\kappa \in \pi$: $\kappa$ is of category $\geq$ (n − 1)

### 11.4.1  *ES.SS3[–clitic]: A three-level stringency hierarchy*

We begin by defining a system ES.SS3[–clitic] (70) that extends SS3[–clitic] by adding a categorical implementation of EqualSisters. Bidirectional Match, as defined in (29), functions as the antagonist to ES and SS. All terminals are the same category in this system. All output candidates are properly headed, although admitting headless candidates does not alter the outcome here.

---

[10] When level-skipping doubly weak starts are excluded, SS-local is more stringent than SS-hypLoc, resulting in a four-level stringency hierarchy: ES $>_s$ SS-global $>_s$ SS-local $>_s$ SS-hypLoc. But if level-skipping doubly weak starts are included, SS-local is not more stringent than SS-hypLoc, and the stringency hierarchy has only three levels: ES $>_s$ SS-global $>_s$ {SS-local, SS-hypLoc}.

[11] Indexation to prosodic categories is discussed more in Bellik and Van Handel (Chapter 10).

(69)   GEN INPUTS:  All syntactic trees $s$ such that
   a.   $s$ is generated by the phrase structure grammar in i-iv:
      i.   $s \rightarrow \text{CP}$
      ii.   $\text{CP} \rightarrow \{X^0\ XP,\ XP\ X^0,\ XP\}$
      iii.   $XP \rightarrow \{X^0\ XP,\ XP\ X^0,\ XP\ XP\}$
      iv.   $X^0 \rightarrow \{a,\ b,\ c\}$
   b.   $s$ has two or three terminals.
   c.   Gen Inputs =

|   | Heads on right | | Heads on left | | Adjunction |
|---|---|---|---|---|---|
| 2 | {[a] b}, {[[a] b]} | | {a [b]}, {[a [b]]} | | {[a][b]}, {[[a][b]]} |
| 3 | {a [b [c]]} | {a [[b] c]} | {[a [b]] c} | {[[a] b] c} | ... |
|   | {[a [b [c]]]} | {[a [[b] c]]} | {[[a [b]] c]} | {[[[a] b] c]} |   |

(70)   SYSTEM ES.SS3[–clitic]
   a.   GEN = All $<s,\ p>$ pairs such that $s$ belongs to (69) and $p$ is a prosodic tree such that
      i.   $p$ is rooted in an intonational phrase.
      ii.   $X^0$s in $s$ are mapped to prosodic words in $p$.
      iii.   All non-root, non-terminal nodes in $p$ are phonological phrases.
      iv.   Linear order of terminals in $s$ is preserved in $p$.
      v.   Every node of category $k$ in $p$ contains at least one child of category $k - 1$ (HEADEDNESS).
   b.   CON
      i.   MATCH(XP$\leftrightarrow$φ) = MATCH: A bidirectional mapping constraint. Defined in (29).
      ii.   EQUALSISTERS-parent = ES: Assign a violation for every node whose children are not all of the same category. $*(... \pi_n ... \pi_m ...)$, where $n\ != m$.
      iii.   STRONGSTART-global = SS-global: $*(\ \pi_n ... \pi_{n+1} ...)$. Defined in (10).
      iv.   STRONGSTART-local = SS-local: $*(\ \pi_n\ \pi_{n+1} ...)$. Defined in (7).
      v.   STRONGSTART-hyperlocal = SS-hypLoc: $*(_n\ \pi_m ...)$, where $m < n - 1$. Defined in (11).

### 11.4.1.1 Typology and grammars of ES.SS3[–clitic]

The typology for ES.SS3[–clitic] contains six languages (71), one more than SS3[–clitic]. The grammars of these languages are depicted in (72). This typology extends the pattern in the system ES.SS (§11.2.3), in which ES is more stringent than SS, and both ES and SS were antagonized to MATCH. In ES.SS3, L.2–L.6 are identical to the languages of the previous typology for SS3[–clitic]: In L.2, SS-global is top-ranked, and SS-local and SS-hypLoc are freely rankable; in L.3, SS-local and SS-hypLoc both dominate MATCH; in L.4 and L.5, SS-local and then SS-hypLoc, respectively, dominate MATCH, which dominates all other constraints; and in L.6, MATCH dominates all other constraints. The new language in ES.SS3 is L.1, in which ES dominates MATCH, with the result that all SS constraints are freely rankable, indicating that ES is indeed more stringent than all SS constraints.

(71)　　　Typology of ES.SS[–clitic]

| Inputs | {[[a] b]} | {a [b [c]]} | {[a [b [c]]]} |
|---|---|---|---|
| L.1 | {(a b)}<br>{((a) (b))} | {(a b) (c)}<br>{(a) (b c)}<br>{(a) ((b) (c))} | {(a b c)}<br>{((a b) (c))}<br>{((a) (b c))}<br>{((a) ((b) (c)))} |
| L.2 | {((a) b)} | {(a b) (c)}<br>{(a) (b c)}<br>{(a) ((b) (c))} | {(a b c)}<br>{((a b) (c))}<br>{((a) (b c))}<br>{((a) ((b) (c)))} |
| L.3 | {((a) b)} | {(a b) (c)}<br>{(a) (b c)}<br>{(a) ((b) (c))} | {(a b (c))} |
| L.4 | {((a) b)} | {a b (c)} | {(a b (c))} |
| L.5 | {((a) b)} | {(a) (b (c))} | {(a (b (c)))} |
| L.6 | {((a) b)} | {a (b (c))} | {(a (b (c)))} |

(72)　　　Grammars of the languages of ES.SS3[–clitic]

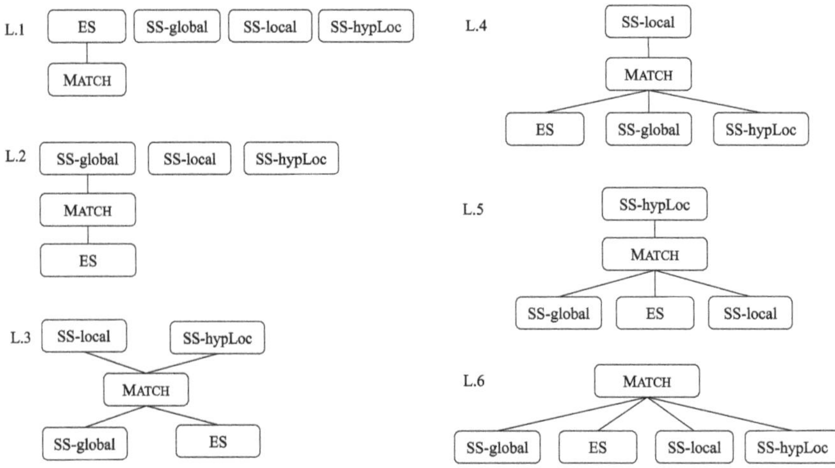

*11.4.1.2 Property analysis of ES.SS3[–clitic]*

The stringency relationship between ES-parent and SS-global here is confirmed by the property analysis for ES.SS3[–clitic] in (73) and (74). The first property is p.es, which determines whether violations of ES will be tolerated ($\beta$ value, L.2–6), or repaired ($\alpha$ value, L.1). The second property, p.ss, determines whether SS-global violations are tolerated ($\beta$ value, L.3–6) or repaired ($\alpha$ value, L.2). The $\alpha$ value of p.es entails that all SS violations will be repaired, so p.ss scopes under the $\beta$ value of p.es, and is moot for L.1. No property establishes a ranking between SS-global and ES, further demonstrating that they are never crucially ranked in this system, since SS is a special case of ES.

As in all previous systems, p.loc and p.hyp scope under the $\beta$ value of p.glob, indicating that SS-global is more stringent than SS-local and SS-hypLoc. Since ES-parent is in turn more stringent than SS-global, we have two three-tier stringency hierarchies (75).

(73)    Properties of ES.SS3[–clitic]
   a.    p.es: EQUALSISTERS <> MATCH. Wide scope.
   b.    p.glob: STRONGSTART <> MATCH. Scopes under the $\beta$ value of p.es.
   c.    p.loc: SS-local <> MATCH. Scopes under the $\beta$ value of p.glob.
   d.    p.hyp: SS-hypLoc <> MATCH. Scopes under the $\beta$ value of p.glob.

(74)    Property table for ES.SS3

|      | p.es      | p.glob | p.loc    | p.hyp    |
|------|-----------|--------|----------|----------|
| L.1  | $\alpha$  | moot   | moot     | moot     |
| L.2  | $\beta$   | $\alpha$ | moot   | moot     |
| L.3  | $\beta$   | $\beta$ | $\alpha$ | $\alpha$ |
| L.4  | $\beta$   | $\beta$ | $\beta$  | $\beta$  |
| L.5  | $\beta$   | $\beta$ | $\beta$  | $\alpha$ |
| L.6  | $\beta$   | $\beta$ | $\beta$  | $\beta$  |

(75)    Stringency hierarchies of ES.SS3[–clitic]
   a.    ES-parent $>_s$ SS-global $>_s$ SS-local
   b.    ES-parent $>_s$ SS-global $>_s$ SS-hypLoc

ES.SS3[–clitic] shows that ES-parent is more stringent than all versions of SS, when all terminal nodes are the same prosodic category ($\omega$) and all non-root, non-terminal nodes are the same prosodic category ($\varphi$). Admitting headless structures (in which the intonational phrase's children can all be phonological words) to the candidate set does not alter the stringency relationships.

### 11.4.2 System ES.SS3[+clitic, +Hd]

When some structures contain a free clitic, the interactions become significantly more complex. We begin with the system in which all candidates are properly headed, ES.SS3[+clitic, +Hd] (76). This system has the same candidate set as SS3[+clitic, +Hd] in §11.3.2, and the same constraint set as ES.SS3[−clitic] in the preceding subsection.

(76)      GEN INPUTS for ES.SS3[+clitic, +Hd]: All branching syntactic trees $s$ such that

     a.    $s$ is generated by the phrase structure grammar in (i-iv):

         i.    $s \to$ CP

         ii.    CP $\to$ {$X^0$ XP, XP $X^0$, XP}

         iii.    XP $\to$ {$X^0$ XP, XP $X^0$, XP XP}

         iv.    $X^0 \to$ a, b, c, a.clitic, b.clitic, c.clitic

     b.    $s$ has two or three terminals.

     c.    $s$ contains at most one clitic.

(77)      ES.SS3[+clitic, +Hd]

     a.    GEN: All pairs $<s, p>$ such that $s$ belongs to (76) and $p$ is a prosodic tree such that

         i.    $p$ is rooted in an intonational phrase.

         ii.    Clitics in $s$ are mapped to syllables in $p$.

         iii.    Non-clitic $X^0$s in $s$ are mapped to prosodic words in $p$.

         iv.    All non-root, non-terminal nodes in $p$ are phonological phrases.

         v.    Every phonological phrase in $p$ contains at least one phonological word (HEADEDNESS).

     b.    Linear order of terminals in $s$ is preserved in $p$.

     c.    CON:

         i.    MATCH(XP↔φ): Defined in (29)

         ii.    EQUALSISTERS-parent = ES: $*( \pi_n \ ... \ \pi_m ...)$, where n != m. Defined in (70b.ii).

         iii.    STRONGSTART-global = SS-global: $*( \pi_n \ ... \ \pi_{n+1} \ ...)$. Defined in (10).

         iv.    STRONGSTART-local = SS-LOCAL: $*( \pi_n \ \pi_{n+1} \ ...)$. Defined in (7).

         v.    STRONGSTART-hyperlocal = SS-HYPLOC: $*(_n \ \pi_m \ ...)$, where $m < n - 1$. Defined in (11).

### 11.4.2.1 Languages of ES.SS3[+clitic, +Hd]

This system's typology has nine languages (78), three more than the clitic-free system's six. This is because ES is not more stringent than SS-global in ES.SS3[+clitic, +Hd]; rather, ES conflicts with all three versions of SS, for reasons explained below. As in previous headed systems, SS-global is more stringent than SS-local and SS-hypLoc, but SS-local and SS-hypLoc conflict with each other. These relationships are apparent from the grammars (79).

(78)   Typology with left- and right-headed inputs: 9 languages. Dark grey = unfaithful + maximally satisfies ES. Light grey = unfaithful + satisfies SS-local. White = faithful.

| | {[a] b} | {[a [b]]} | {a [b [c]]} | {[a [b [c]]]} | {a [b.clitic [c]]} | {[a [b.clitic [c]]]} | {a [[b.clitic] c]} |
|---|---|---|---|---|---|---|---|
| L.1 | {(a) (b)} | {(a b)}<br>{((a) (b))} | {(a b) (c)}<br>{(a) (b c)}<br>{(a) ((b) (c))} | {(a b c)}<br>{((a b) (c))}<br>{((a) (b c))}<br>{((a) ((b) (c)))} | {(a b.σ) (c)}<br>{(a) b.σ (c)} | {(a b.σ c)}<br>{((a b.σ) (c))}<br>{((a) b.σ (c))} | {(a b.σ c)}<br>{(a) b.σ c} |
| L.2 | {(a) (b)} | {(a b)}<br>{((a) (b))} | {(a b) (c)}<br>{(a) (b c)}<br>{(a) ((b) (c))} | {(a b c)}<br>{((a b) (c))}<br>{((a) (b c))}<br>{((a) ((b) (c)))} | {(a b.σ) (c)}<br>{(a) b.σ (c)} | {(a b.σ (c))} | {(a b.σ c)}<br>{(a) b.σ c} |
| L.3 | {(a) (b)} | {(a b)}<br>{((a) (b))} | {(a b) (c)}<br>{(a) (b c)}<br>{(a) ((b) (c))} | {(a b c)}<br>{((a b) (c))}<br>{((a) (b c))}<br>{((a) ((b) (c)))} | {a b.σ (c)} | {(a b.σ (c))} | {(a b.σ c)}<br>{(a) b.σ c} |
| L.4 | {(a) (b)} | {(a b)}<br>{((a) (b))} | {(a b) (c)}<br>{(a) (b c)}<br>{(a) ((b) (c))} | {(a b c)}<br>{((a b) (c))}<br>{((a) (b c))}<br>{((a) ((b) (c)))} | {a b.σ (c)} | {(a b.σ (c))} | {a b.σ (c)} |
| L.5 | {(a) b} | {(a b)}<br>{((a) (b))} | {(a b) (c)}<br>{(a) (b c)}<br>{(a) ((b) (c))} | {(a b c)}<br>{((a b) (c))}<br>{((a) (b c))}<br>{((a) ((b) (c)))} | {(a b.σ) (c)}<br>{(a) b.σ (c)} | {(a b.σ c)}<br>{((a b.σ) (c))}<br>{((a) b.σ (c))} | {(a b.σ c)}<br>{(a) b.σ c} |
| L.6 | {(a) b} | {(a b)}<br>{((a) (b))} | {(a b) (c)}<br>{(a) (b c)}<br>{(a) ((b) (c))} | {(a b (c))} | {(a b.σ) (c)}<br>{(a) b.σ (c)} | {(a b.σ (c))} | {(a b.σ c)}<br>{(a) b.σ c} |
| L.7 | {(a) b} | {(a b)}<br>{((a) (b))} | {a b (c)} | {(a b (c))} | {a b.σ (c)} | {(a b.σ (c))} | {(a b.σ c)}<br>{(a) b.σ c} |
| L.8 | {(a) b} | {(a (b))} | {(a) (b (c))} | {(a (b (c)))} | {(a b.σ) (c)}<br>{(a) b.σ (c)} | {(a b.σ (c))} | {(a b.σ c)}<br>{(a) b.σ c} |
| L.9 | {(a) b} | {(a (b))} | {a (b (c))} | {(a (b (c)))} | {a (b.σ (c))} | {(a (b.σ (c)))} | {a (b.σ (c))} |

(79)    Grammars for ES.SS3[+clitic, +Hd]

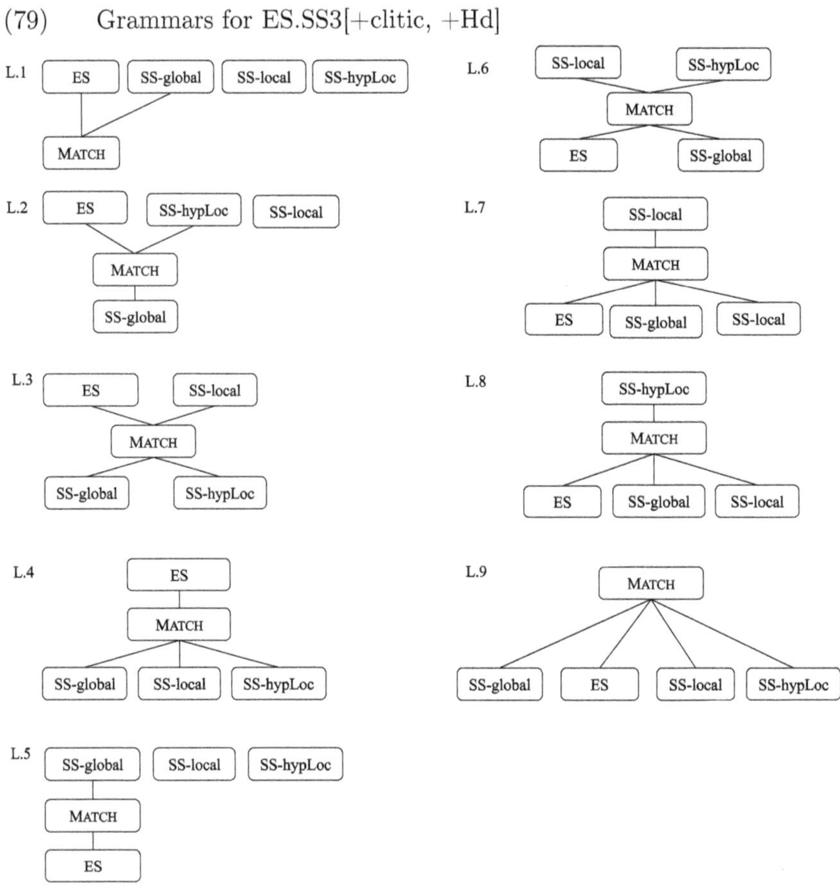

Five of these grammars are identical to grammars of languages in the previous clitic-free system ES.SS3[–clitic, +Hd]. As shown in (80), L.2–6 in ES.SS3[–clitic, +Hd] map to L.5–9 in ES.SS3[+clitic, +Hd]. But L.1 in the [–clitic] system becomes four languages (L.1–4) in the [+clitic] system. With no clitics in the candidate set, ES is more stringent than all SS constraints, and ranking ES over MATCH renders the three SS constraints freely rankable (L.1, ES.SS3[–clitic, +Hd]). But with the inclusion of clitics, ES comes into conflict with all three SS constraints, and therefore ranking ES over MATCH guarantees nothing about the ranking of the SS constraints. Each of them can be ranked over MATCH alongside ES (L.1–3, ES.SS3[–clitic, +Hd]), or all can be ranked below MATCH while ES dominates the other four constraints (L.4).

(80)     Comparing grammars of ES.SS3[+Hd, ±clitics]

| Constraints crucially ranked over MATCH | Lg. in [−clitic] | Lg. in [+clitic] | also ranked over MATCH |
|---|---|---|---|
| {ES} | L.1 | L.1 | {SS-glob} |
|  | All SS constraints | L.2 | {SS-hyp} |
|  | freely rankable | L.3 | {SS-loc} |
|  |  | L.4 | {} |
| {SS-glob} | L.2 | L.5 |  |
| {SS-loc, SS-hyp} | L.3 | L.6 |  |
| {SS-loc} | L.4 | L.7 |  |
| {SS-hyp} | L.5 | L.8 |  |
| {} | L.6 | L.9 |  |

### 11.4.2.2 Property analysis of ES.SS3[+clitic, +Hd]

The same properties that accounted for ES.SS3[−clitic] can capture the typology of the present system (81), although the scopal relationships differ. As noted above, all of the SS constraints conflict with ES, with the result that both p.es and p.global are wide-scope properties in (81). The properties p.loc and p.hyp scope under the $\beta$ value of SS-global, since SS-global remains more stringent than SS-local and SS-hypLoc; their scope is not restricted by the value of p.es. One surprise, however, is that p.loc is moot in L.2: When SS-hypLoc and ES are both ranked over MATCH, then SS-local is freely rankable.

(81)     Properties of ES.SS3[+clitic, +Hd]

| Property name | Value | Scope |
|---|---|---|
| p.es | ES-parent <> MATCH | Wide |
| p.glob | SS-global <> MATCH | Wide |
| p.loc | SS-local <> MATCH | $p.glob = \beta \lor (p.es = \beta \land p.hyp = \beta)$ |
| p.hypLoc | SS-hypLoc <> MATCH | $p.glob = \beta$ |

(82)    PA table for ES.SS3[+clitic, +Hd]

|      | p.es | p.glob | p.loc | p.hyp |
|------|------|--------|-------|-------|
| L.1  | α    | α      | moot  | moot  |
| L.2  | α    | β      | moot  | α     |
| L.3  | α    | β      | α     | β     |
| L.4  | α    | β      | β     | β     |
| L.5  | β    | α      | moot  | moot  |
| L.6  | β    | β      | α     | α     |
| L.7  | β    | β      | α     | β     |
| L.8  | β    | β      | β     | α     |
| L.9  | β    | β      | β     | β     |

Why does ES conflict with SS-global, -local, and -hyperLocal in this system with clitics, when it was more stringent than all SS constraints in the minimally different system without clitics? The answer is that ES-parent often cannot distinguish among candidates with a clitic in them. Every candidate with a clitic in it in this GEN violates ES-parent, because it necessarily contains a syllable that is sister to a ω or φ, regardless of whether the clitic is initial or non-initial. For right-branching syntaxes with a medial clitic, as in (83), the isomorphic prosody violates ES twice (rows with grey backgrounds), while all non-isomorphic possible optima (rows with white background) violate ES once, which is the minimum number of ES violations possible here. Thus, ES fails to distinguish among the non-isomorphic optima. The SS constraints do distinguish among them, however, since some optima receive zero violations, while others receive one. Thus, incurring the minimum ES violation does not guarantee the minimum violation of SS-global, SS-local, or SS-hypLoc. ES is not more stringent than SS in this system.

(83)   Violation tableau for right-branching, clitic-medial inputs in ES.SS3[+clitic, +Hd]

|  | | ES | SS-global | SS-local | SS-hypLoc | Match |
|---|---|---|---|---|---|---|
| {a [b.clitic [c]]} | {(a b.σ) (c)} | 1 | 0 | 0 | 0 | 2 |
| | {a b.σ (c)} | 1 | 1 | 0 | 1 | 1 |
| | {(a) b.σ (c)} | 1 | 0 | 0 | 0 | 2 |
| | {a (b.σ (c))} | 2 | 2 | 2 | 2 | 0 |
| {[a [b.clitic [c]]]} | {(a b.σ c)} | 1 | 0 | 0 | 0 | 2 |
| | {((a b.σ) (c))} | 1 | 0 | 0 | 0 | 2 |
| | {(a b.σ (c))} | 1 | 1 | 0 | 0 | 1 |
| | {((a) b.σ (c))} | 1 | 0 | 0 | 0 | 2 |
| | {(a (b.σ (c)))} | 2 | 2 | 2 | 1 | 0 |

While ES cannot distinguish among these right-branching candidates, the SS constraints cannot distinguish among the left-branching ones (84). These left-branching prosodic structures are possible optima when syntactic complements occur to the left of their heads (i.e., when syntactic heads are right-aligned). All possible optima for right-headed inputs perfectly satisfy all SS constraints,[12] since all constraints agree in favoring parses where the first daughter is a φ, corresponding to the most deeply embedded complement XP in the input. Thus, no SS constraint can distinguish among them. Were any SS constraint to be more stringent than ES, satisfying SS with the minimum violation would entail also satisfying ES with the minimum violation. This never occurs in this system. We conclude that SS constraints are not more stringent than ES, nor is ES more stringent than any SS constraint. The two constraints are independent.

(84)   VT for a left-branching, clitic-medial inputs in ES.SS3[+clitic, +Hd]

| Input | Output | ES | SS-global | SS-local | SS-hypLoc | Match |
|---|---|---|---|---|---|---|
| {[[[a] b.clitic] c]} | {(((a) b.σ) (c))} | 1 | 0 | 0 | 0 | 1 |
| | {(((a) b.σ) c)} | 2 | 0 | 0 | 0 | 0 |
| | {((a) b.σ c)} | 1 | 0 | 0 | 0 | 1 |

---

[12] When the first terminal is not a clitic, that is. In inputs like {[[[a.clitic] b] c]}, the initial clitic is the most deeply embedded complement, and it is not parsed as a phonological phrase because this Gen excludes headless φs. If φs containing only a syllable are admitted to the candidate set, then initial clitics in these inputs are also parsed as φs. These satisfy ES, SS-global, and SS-local, but violate SS-hypLoc, again demonstrating that prosodic Headedness promotes enhanced stringency relations among these prosodic well-formedness constraints.

The support for L.4 (85), in which ES is top-ranked but MATCH dominates all SS constraints, shows how it is possible for ES to indirectly dominate the three SS constraints. In the first row of (85), the parse {(a)(b)}, which includes a φ at the left edge that has no syntactic correspondent, triumphs over the isomorphic parse {a (b)}, which violates ES and all the SS constraints. This illustrates MATCH's usual opposition to all the prosodic well-formedness constraints. The second row demonstrates that ES crucially does not distinguish between the winning candidate, which contains a syllable-initial φ, and the losing parses, which sacrifice a closer syntax–prosody mapping for the sake of avoiding SS violations. All three of the SS constraints are violated by the winner: SS-global and -local because of the initial syllable $b$ that is sister to the word $c$, and SS-hypLoc because of the level-skipping at the edge of the φ. Violation counts for these structures can be seen above in (84).

(85)      Support for L.4 in ES.SS3[+clitic, +Hd]

| Input | Winner | Loser | ES | MATCH | SS-glob | SS-loc | SS-hyp |
|---|---|---|---|---|---|---|---|
| {a [b]} | {(a) (b)} | {a (b)} | W | L | W | W | W |
| {a [[b.clitic] c]} | {(a) (b.σ c)} | {(a b.σ c)}<br>{(a) b.σ c} | | W | L | L | L |

### 11.4.3 ES.SS3[+clitic, –Hd]

As seen in the system SS3[+clitic, –Hd] (§11.3.3), including headless structures breaks the stringency relationship between SS-global and SS-hyperlocal. Headlessness can also introduce a direct conflict between ES-parent and SS-hyperlocal. To show this, we define a system ES.SS3[+clitic, –Hd], calculated by removing the requirement of Headedness from the output GEN in the system definition for ES.SS3[+clitic, +Hd] (77).

### 11.4.3.1 Typology and languages of ES.SS3[+clitic, –Hd]

The typology of ES.SS3[+clitic, –Hd] has eleven languages (86) and is significantly more complex than that of the equivalent properly headed system—its PA requires a property directly opposing ES-parent to SS-hyp.

(86)    Typology of ES.SS3[+clitic, −Hd]

| | {[a] b} | {[a [b]]} | {a [b.cl]} | {[a [b.cl]]} | {[a [b [c]]]} | {[a [b.cl [c]]]} |
|---|---|---|---|---|---|---|
| L.1 | {(a) (b)} | {(a b)}<br>{((a) (b))} | {(a b.σ)}<br>{(a) b.σ} | {(a b.σ)} | {(a b c)}<br>{((a b) (c))}<br>{((a) (b c))}<br>{((a) ((b)<br>(c)))} | {(a b.σ c)}<br>{((a b.σ) (c))}<br>{((a) b.σ (c))} |
| L.2 | {(a) (b)} | {(a b)}<br>{((a) (b))} | {(a b.σ)}<br>{(a) b.σ} | {(a b.σ)} | {(a b c)}<br>{((a b) (c))}<br>{((a) (b c))}<br>{((a) ((b)<br>(c)))} | {(a b.σ (c))} |
| L.3 | {(a) (b)} | {(a b)}<br>{((a) (b))} | {(a) (b.σ)} | {((a) (b.σ))} | {(a b c)}<br>{((a b) (c))}<br>{((a) (b c))}<br>{((a) ((b)<br>(c)))} | {((a) ((b.σ)<br>(c)))} |
| L.4 | {(a) b} | {(a b)}<br>{((a) (b))} | {(a b.σ)}<br>{(a) b.σ} | {(a b.σ)} | {(a b c)}<br>{((a b) (c))}<br>{((a) (b c))}<br>{((a) ((b)<br>(c)))} | {(a b.σ c)}<br>{((a b.σ) (c))}<br>{((a) b.σ (c))} |
| L.5 | {(a) b} | {(a b)}<br>{((a) (b))} | {(a b.σ)}<br>{(a) b.σ} | {(a b.σ)} | {(a b (c))} | {(a b.σ (c))} |
| L.6 | {(a) b} | {(a b)}<br>{((a) (b))} | {(a) (b.σ)} | {(a b.σ)} | {(a b c)}<br>{((a b) (c))}<br>{((a) (b c))}<br>{((a) ((b)<br>(c)))} | {(a b.σ c)}<br>{((a b.σ) (c))}<br>{((a) b.σ (c))} |
| L.7 | {(a) b} | {(a b)}<br>{((a) (b))} | {(a) (b.σ)} | {(a b.σ)} | {(a b (c))} | {(a b.σ (c))} |
| L.8 | {(a) b} | {(a b)}<br>{((a) (b))} | {(a) (b.σ)} | {((a) (b.σ))} | {(a b c)}<br>{((a b) (c))}<br>{((a) (b c))}<br>{((a) ((b)<br>(c)))} | {((a) ((b.σ)<br>(c)))} |
| L.9 | {(a) b} | {(a b)}<br>{((a) (b))} | {(a) (b.σ)} | {((a) (b.σ))} | {(a b (c))} | {(a b.σ (c))} |
| L.10 | {(a) b} | {(a (b))} | {(a b.σ)}<br>{(a) b.σ} | {(a b.σ)} | {(a (b (c)))} | {(a b.σ (c))} |
| L.11 | {(a) b} | {(a (b))} | {a (b.σ)} | {(a (b.σ))} | {(a (b (c)))} | {(a (b.σ (c)))} |

(87)      Grammars of ES.SS3[+clitic, −Hd]

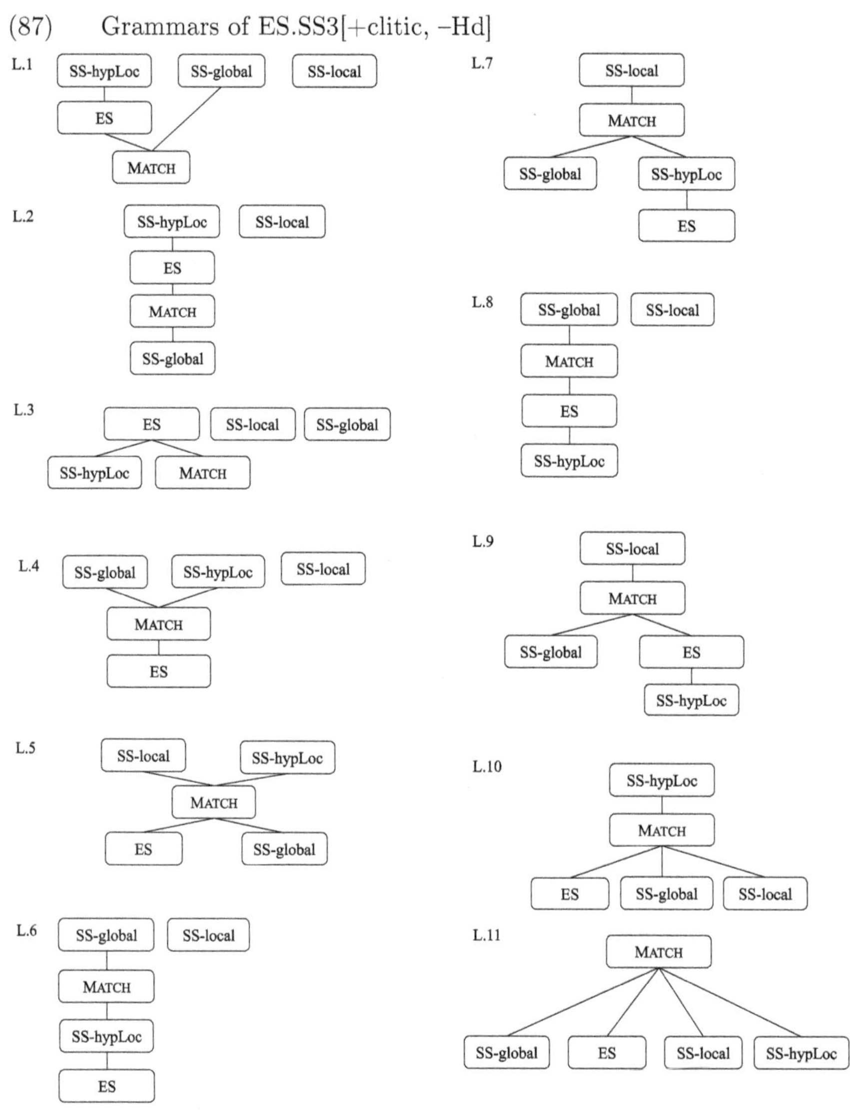

In this system, ES and SS-hyp are crucially ranked against each other in
all but the maximally matching language (L.11), where MATCH dominates
all other constraints. L.1 demonstrates the conflict between ES and SS-hyp.
The second row of its support (88) shows the direct conflict between SS-hyp
and ES: ES favors wrapping the clitic into a headless φ, which is the only
way to completely avoid violating ES-parent for inputs with clitics; SS-hyp,
however, objects to such parses because they put a free clitic at the left edge
of a φ. In this language, SS-hyp outranks ES, and the headless candidate

loses; in others (L.3, L.8, L.9), however, ES wins, and headless φs surface for some or all candidates with clitics. The support for one of these, L.3, is shown in (89).

(88)    Support for L.1 in ES.SS3[+clitic, −Hd]

| Input | Winner | Loser | SS-glob | SS-loc | SS-hyp | ES | MATCH |
|---|---|---|---|---|---|---|---|
| {[a [b.clitic [c]]]} | {(a b.σ c)} {((a b.σ) (c))} {((a) b.σ (c))} | {(a b.σ (c))} | W | | | | L |
| {a [b.clitic]} | {(a b.σ)} {(a) b.σ} | {(a) (b.σ)} | | | W | L | L |
| {[a] b} | {(a) (b)} | {(a) b} | | | | W | L |

(89)    Support for L.3 in ES.SS3[+clitic, −Hd]

| Input | Winner | Loser | ES | SS-glob | SS-loc | SS-hypLoc | MATCH |
|---|---|---|---|---|---|---|---|
| {[a] b} | {(a) (b)} | {(a) b} | W | | | | L |
| {a [b.clitic]} | {(a) (b.σ)} | {(a b.σ)} {(a) b.σ} | W | | | L | W |

SS-local is freely rankable in six languages (L.1–4, L.6, L.8). The ranking of SS-local only matters when MATCH dominates both SS-global and ES, as will be seen in the PA in (90). An examination of the Mother Of All Tableaux (MOAT) for this system verifies that ES and SS-global both meet DelBusso (2018)'s MOAT-based criteria for being more stringent than SS-local (these criteria are discussed further in §11.5.3). Both ES and SS-global filter out more candidates than SS-local does.

In L.3, not only SS-local but also SS-global is freely rankable, apparently as a consequence of the fact that ES is undominated. When ES is perfectly satisfied, SS-global and SS-local are, too. This follows from the inclusion of headless φs, which make it possible for ES to be perfectly satisfied in spite of the presence of clitics in the candidate set. It is not the case, however, that ES is more stringent than SS-global. This is evidenced in L.2, for instance, which has the subranking ES ≫ MATCH ≫ SS-global (90). Where ES fails to distinguish between candidates (as in the third row of the support), MATCH chooses a candidate over SS-global's objections.

(90)    Support for L.2 in ES.SS3[+clitic, –Hd]

| Input | Winner | Loser | SS-loc | SS-hyp | ES | Match | SS-glob |
|---|---|---|---|---|---|---|---|
| {a [b.cl]} | {(a b.σ)} {(a) b.σ} | {(a) (b.σ)} | | W | L | L | |
| {[a] b} | {(a) (b)} | {(a) b} | | | W | L | |
| {[a [b.cl [c]]]} | {(a b.σ (c))} | {(a b.σ c)} {((a b.σ) (c))} {((a) b.σ (c))} | | | | W | L |

*11.4.3.2 Property analysis of ES.SS3[+clitic, –Hd]*

The PA for this system reflects both the conflict between ES and SS-hypLoc, and the stringency of ES and SS-global over SS-local. The familiar properties p.glob, p.loc, and p.hyp oppose each SS constraint to Match in turn. Two additional properties pertain to ES. The properties p.esM and p.esCl oppose ES to Match and SS-hypLoc individually, since ES conflicts directly with each of those constraints in this system. Both of these properties have the $\alpha$ value in L.3, where ES is undominated and SS-global and SS-local are freely rankable. The property p.glob is active in all languages but L.3 (i.e., where ES is not undominated), while p.loc is active when both ES and SS-global are dominated by Match (i.e., p.glob $= \beta \wedge$ p.esM $= \beta$): ES $>_s$ SS-local and SS-global $>_s$ SS-local. Note that p.hyp is not restricted in scope by p.glob; as expected, SS-global is not more stringent than SS-hypLoc, since headless candidates are present.

This system shows that introducing headless candidates affects the stringency interactions of ES with the SS constraints in divergent ways, depending on their scope. The headless candidates make possible a direct conflict between ES and SS-hypLoc, complicating and enlarging the typology. At the same time, they reduce the minimum violations of ES to zero, restoring the stringency relationship between ES and SS-local.

(91)     Properties of ES.SS3[+clitic, –Hd]

| Props | $\alpha$ | $\beta$ | Scope |
|---|---|---|---|
| p.esM | ES-par | MATCH | Wide |
| p.esCl | ES-par | SS-hypLoc | Wide |
| p.hyp | SS-hypLoc | MATCH | p.esM $= \beta$ $\vee$ p.esCl $= \beta$ |
| p.glob | SS-global | MATCH | p.esM $= \beta$ $\vee$ p.esCl $= \beta$ |
| p.loc | SS-local | MATCH | p.esM $= \beta$ $\wedge$ p.glob $= \beta$ |

(92)     PA table ES.SS3[+clitic, –Hd]

| | p.esM | p.esCl | p.hyp | p.glob | p.loc |
|---|---|---|---|---|---|
| L.01 | $\alpha$ | $\beta$ | $\alpha$ | $\alpha$ | moot |
| L.02 | $\alpha$ | $\beta$ | $\alpha$ | $\beta$ | moot |
| L.03 | $\alpha$ | $\alpha$ | moot | moot | moot |
| L.04 | $\beta$ | $\beta$ | $\alpha$ | $\alpha$ | moot |
| L.05 | $\beta$ | $\beta$ | $\alpha$ | $\beta$ | $\alpha$ |
| L.06 | $\beta$ | $\beta$ | $\beta$ | $\alpha$ | moot |
| L.07 | $\beta$ | $\beta$ | $\beta$ | $\beta$ | $\alpha$ |
| L.08 | $\beta$ | $\alpha$ | $\beta$ | $\alpha$ | moot |
| L.09 | $\beta$ | $\alpha$ | $\beta$ | $\beta$ | $\alpha$ |
| L.10 | $\beta$ | $\beta$ | $\alpha$ | $\beta$ | $\beta$ |
| L.11 | $\beta$ | moot | $\beta$ | $\beta$ | $\beta$ |

*11.4.4 Summary of stringency relations between ES and SS*

This section explored the interaction between ES and the three SS constraints in three systems: one without clitics, and two with clitics. Both systems include both left- and right-headed syntactic inputs, rooted in either the CP or XP. All prosodic outputs in the first two systems were headed, which maintained SS-global's stringency over SS-local and -hyperlocal (as established in §11.3). In the last system, headless outputs were included, breaking SS-global's stringency over SS-hyperlocal.

In the system without clitics, ES.SS3[–clitic], every input can be parsed in a manner that completely satisfies ES (i.e., the minimum violation of ES is always zero). Satisfying ES also entails satisfying the three SS constraints: ES is more stringent than SS-global, which is in turn more stringent than SS-local and SS-hypLoc (93).

(93)     Stringency hierarchies of ES.SS3[–clitic] (repeated from (75))
   a.    ES $>_s$ SS-global $>_s$ SS-local
   b.    ES $>_s$ SS-global $>_s$ SS-hypLoc

In the headed system with clitics, ES.SS3[+clitic, +Hd], inputs that contain a clitic always violate ES in the output (i.e., the minimum violation of ES is 1), because GEN always parses the clitic, a syllable, directly into a φ or ι, as a free clitic. As a result, SS-global is able to make distinctions that ES cannot. The stringency relationship between SS-global and ES was therefore eliminated in this system. When the minimum violation of ES is one, while the minimum violation of SS-global is zero, SS-global does not function as a position-sensitive version of EQUALSISTERS.

The relationship between SS-global and ES is crucially affected by head directionality in the language or dataset of interest. In a mixed-headed language like German or Chamorro (see Bibbs, Chapter 8), if the dataset includes clitics, then SS-global and ES can be independent constraints with no stringency relationship between them (as in ES.SS3[+clitic, +Hd]). But STRONGSTART can sometimes do more than EQUALSISTERS in a head-initial language. In fact, if all head-final syntactic inputs are removed from ES.SS3[+clitic, +Hd] to create a minimally different system ES.SS3[+clitic, +Hd, L] where heads only appear to the left of their complements, SS-global becomes more stringent than ES, because SS-global can distinguish among possible optima that ES cannot, while there are no possible optima that ES distinguishes, but SS-global does not, due to the exclusion of head-final inputs from the candidate set (the Appendix presents the details of this system). This independence or reversed stringency is made possible when the candidate set (GEN) excludes the option of promoting a clitic to a prosodic word. It underscores the crucial importance of the candidate set.

The importance of the candidate set is further demonstrated by the headless system with clitics. In ES.SS3[+clitic, −Hd], ES is more stringent than SS-local, though not more stringent than SS-global. SS-hyperlocal, however, conflicts with both ES and SS-global. Admitting headless candidates complicates the interaction of SS-hyperlocal not only with SS-global, but also with ES.

Having examined the interaction of the three scopes of STRONGSTART with a categorical implementation of EQUALSISTERS, we now turn to gradient implementations of EQUALSISTERS.

## 11.5  Gradience in EQUALSISTERS

The preceding studies of the relationship between STRONGSTART and EQUALSISTERS were restricted to a single implementation of EQUALSISTERS, categorical ES-parent. This section investigates the effect of using gradient ES-adjacent in place of ES-parent. ES-adjacent has the potential to be more stringent than ES-parent, since it assigns multiple violations to a ternary-branching structure when the middle sister is of a different category than the sisters on the edges, rather than only one violation. This is illustrated in (94), where the input is a simple SVO sentence, with the subject in the specifier position of the VP, and the object in the complement position. If we interpret MATCH-Phrase as ignoring bar levels and only 'seeing" maximal projections as phrasal, then the matching candidate (94a) will receive two violations of ES-adjacent, but only one of ES-parent, whereas the mismatched (94b) receives the same number of violations from both versions of ES (adjacent and parent).

(94)    ES-adjacent vs. ES-parent: $[_{VP}$ $[_{DP}$ subject] $[_{V'}$ verb $[_{DP}$ object]]]

| [[subject] verb [object]] | ES-adjacent | ES-parent | sp.MATCH(XP) | ps.MATCH($\varphi$) |
|---|---|---|---|---|
| a.  ((subj) verb (obj)) | ** | * | | |
| b.  ((subj) verb obj) | * | * | * | |
| c.  ((subj)(verb)(obj)) | | | | * |

To determine how this gradience affects EQUALSISTERS' interaction with STRONGSTART, we examine two more pairs of systems, one with clitics in the candidate set (ESadj.SS3[+clitic, ±Hd]) and one without (ESadj.SS3[−clitic, ±Hd]).

### 11.5.1   No effect without clitics: ESadj.SS3[−clitic]

The system without any clitics, ESadj.SS3[−clitic], is identical to ES.SS3[−clitic] (§11.4.1), except that ES-parent is replaced by ES-adjacent. This substitution does not affect the typology's contents or structure in any way. Enforcing proper Headedness also does not affect the results at all, just as in the equivalent systems with ES-parent. Improperly headed candidates were all harmonically bounded because of their excessive violations of MATCH, and never surfaced to alter the interaction of the other constraints. This suggests that ES-parent and ES-adjacent are equivalent when it is possible to satisfy ES perfectly (i.e., the minimum violation of ES in the system is zero). This is the case when all terminals are the same category, or when there is no penalty for promoting a lower-category terminal, such as a syllable, to a higher category like ω or φ.

### 11.5.2  Complications to constraint interactions with clitics: ESadj.SS3[+clitic, +Hd]

When clitics enter the system, there is a pressure to avoid promoting them to the same prosodic level as other terminals, whether due to some form of lexical subcategorization ("Parse Clitic X as a syllable"), a word minimality constraint ("Words must be prosodically binary"), or a requirement that prosodic words have lexical correspondents in the syntax ($\text{MATCH}(\omega, X^0_{Lex})$). This complicates matters even more with ES-adjacent than it does with ES-parent, as will be demonstrated.

We define a system with clitics and gradient ES-adjacent: ESadj. SS3[+clitic, +Hd], which differs from ES.SS3[+clitic, +Hd] only in using ES-adjacent instead of ES-parent.

(95)　　System definition for ESadj.SS3[+clitic, +Hd]: Same as SS3[+clitic, +Hd] in (50), but add ES-adjacent to CON

　　a.　GEN (repeated from (50a)) = All pairs $<s, p>$ such that
　　　i.　$s$ is a two- or three-word syntactic tree rooted in CP or XP, i.e., $s$ belongs to (49).
　　　ii.　$p$ is a prosodic tree such that
　　　　A.　$p$ is rooted in an intonational phrase.
　　　　B.　Clitics in s are mapped to syllables in $p$.
　　　　C.　Non-clitic $X^0$s in $s$ are mapped to prosodic words in $p$.
　　　　D.　All non-root, non-terminal nodes in $p$ are phonological phrases.
　　　　E.　Every $\varphi$ in $p$ contains at least one $\omega$ .
　　　　F.　Linear order of terminals in $s$ is preserved in $p$.

　　b.　CON
　　　i.　$\text{MATCH}(\text{XP}\leftrightarrow\varphi)$: Defined in (29).
　　　ii.　STRONGSTART-global = SS-global: $*(\ \pi_n\ ...\ \pi_{n+1}\ ...)$. Defined in (10).
　　　iii.　STRONGSTART-local = SS-local: $*(\ \pi_n\ \pi_{n+1}\ ...)$. Defined in (7).
　　　iv.　STRONGSTART-hyperlocal = SS-hypLoc: $*(_n\ \pi_m\ ...)$, where $m < n-1$. Defined in (12).
　　　v.　EQUALSISTERS-adjacent = ES-adj: $*(...\ \pi_n\ \pi_m...)$. Defined in (17.b.i).

### 11.5.2.1  Typology and languages of ESadj.SS3[+clitic, +Hd]

Replacing ES-parent with ES-adjacent results in a typology of seven languages (96), whose grammars are shown in (97). This is two fewer languages than the nine in ES.SS3[+clitic, +Hd] (78). Languages (L.2–7) here have exactly the same grammars as L.4–9 in the ES-parent system ES.SS3[+clitic, +Hd], while L.1 here has three possible Hasse diagrams, each of which approximately corresponds to L.1–3 of the equivalent ES-parent system. L.1 is better expressed as an ERC with multiple Ws, as in (98). Essentially, changing the implementation of EQUALSISTERS from ES-parent to ES-adjacent has the effect of collapsing L.1–L.3 in the ES-parent system into a single language. Ranking the gradient ES-adjacent over MATCH, alongside any of the SS constraints, derives the same language, L.1, whereas ranking the categorical ES-parent over MATCH alongside a SS constraint derives a distinct language for each of the SS constraints in the minimally different system above. In L.1, MATCH is outranked by ES-adjacent in combination with any one of the SS constraints. The other two SS constraints are unranked. That is, ES-adjacent can act in conjunction with SS-local or SS-hypLoc to have the same effect as SS-global in this system.

(96)   Typology for ESadj.SS3[+clitic, +Hd] (Support columns only)

| | {a [b]} | {[a] b} | {[a [b]]} | {a [b [c]]} | {a [b.clitic [c]]} |
|---|---|---|---|---|---|
| L.1 | {(a) (b)} | {(a) (b)} | {(a b)} {((a) (b))} | {(a b) (c)} {(a) (b c)} {(a) ((b) (c))} | {(a b.σ) (c)} |
| L.2 | {(a) (b)} | {(a) (b)} | {(a b)} {((a) (b))} | {(a b) (c)} {(a) (b c)} {(a) ((b) (c))} | {(a) (b.σ (c))} |
| L.3 | {(a) (b)} | {(a) b} | {(a b)} {((a) (b))} | {(a b) (c)} {(a) (b c)} {(a) ((b) (c))} | {(a b.σ) (c)} |
| L.4 | {(a) (b)} | {(a) b} | {(a b)} {((a) (b))} | {(a b) (c)} {(a) (b c)} {(a) ((b) (c))} | {(a b.σ) (c)} |
| L.5 | {(a) (b)} | {(a) b} | {(a b)} {((a) (b))} | {a b (c)} | {a b.σ (c)} |
| L.6 | {(a) (b)} | {(a) b} | {(a (b))} | {(a) (b (c))} | {(a b.σ) (c)} |
| L.7 | {a (b)} | {(a) b} | {(a (b))} | {a (b (c))} | {a (b.σ (c))} |

(97)    Grammars for ESadj.SS3[+clitic, +Hd]

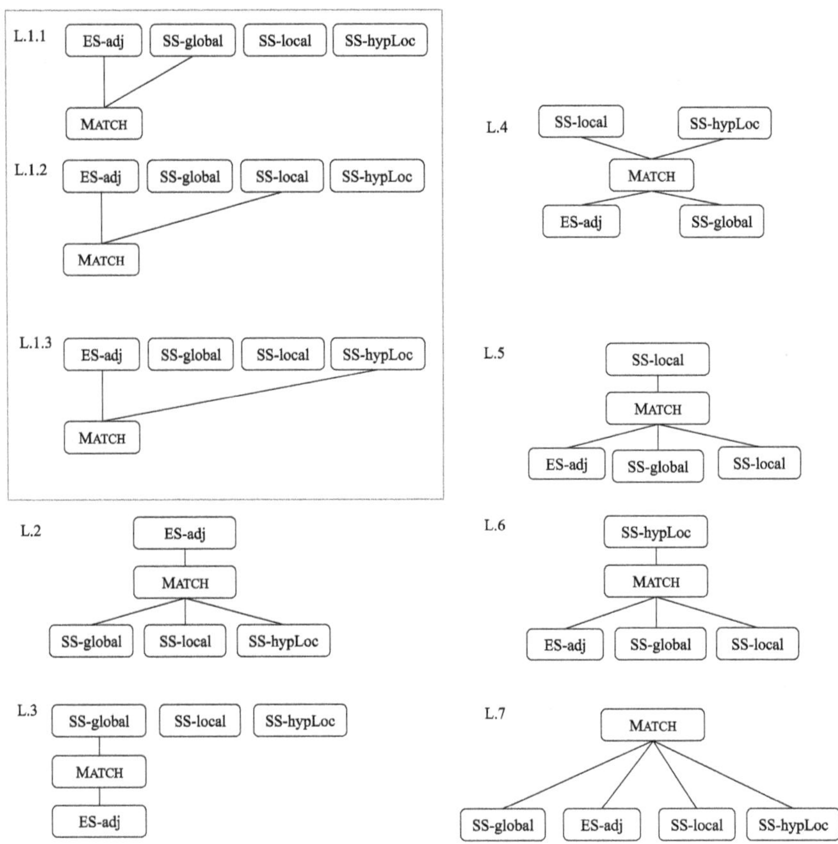

(98)    ERC for L.1 in ESadj.SS3[+clitic, +Hd]

| ES-adj | SS-glob | SS-loc | SS-hyp | MATCH |
|--------|---------|--------|--------|-------|
| W      |         |        |        | L     |
|        | W       | W      | W      | L     |

Why does ranking SS-local or SS-hyp over MATCH along with ES-adjacent
have the same effect as ranking SS-global over MATCH with ES-adjacent?
This equivalence does not hold with ES-parent in ES.SS3[+clitic, +Hd]. The
answer has to do with a candidate that ES-adjacent filters out, but that ES-
parent does not. With a right-branching, three-terminal input, in which the
middle terminal is a clitic, there is one structure that is a possible optimum
under ES-parent, but is not under ES-adjacent (99b). This structure is a
level-skipping doubly weak start that violates SS-global and SS-hypLocal,

but not SS-local. It incurs only one violation of ES-parent (which is the minimum possible violation count for this candidate set), but two violations of ES-adjacent (which is not minimal). ES-adjacent is violated twice because this ternary-branching structure has the clitic, a syllable, adjacent to both an ω and a φ, one on each side. Consequently, (99b) is filtered out by ES-adjacent, but not by ES-parent. Doubly weak starts like candidate (b) are the only structures for which SS-local conflicts with SS-global; level-skipping doubly weak starts are the only structures for which SS-local conflicts with SS-hyperlocal. Suprabinary-branching parses in which the middle daughter is a different category from the sisters on either side are the only structures for which ES-adjacent and ES-parent assign different numbers of violations. In filtering out (99b) and other structures like it, ES-adjacent ensures that the three SS constraints always agree, and therefore any one of them can be ranked alongside ES-adjacent, over MATCH, to derive L.1 of ESadj.SS3[+clitic, +Hd]. ES-parent, on the other hand, admits (99b) as a possible optimum, with the result that SS-glob, SS-loc, and SS-hyp are free to disagree about which of (99a–c) is preferable, deriving L.1–L.3 of ES.SS3[+clitic, +Hd].

(99)    ES-parent vs. ES-adjacent with a medial clitic

| {a [b.clitic [c]]} | ES-par | ES-adj | SS-glob | SS-loc | SS-hyp | MATCH |
|---|---|---|---|---|---|---|
| a. {(a b.σ) (c)} | 1 | 1 | 0 | 0 | 0 | 2 |
| b. {a b.σ (c)} | 1 | 2 | 1 | 0 | 1 | 1 |
| c. {(a) (b.σ (c))} | 1 | 1 | 1 | 1 | 1 | 1 |
| d. {a (b.σ (c))} | 2 | 2 | 2 | 2 | 2 | 0 |

Like ES-parent in ES.SS3[+clitic, +Hd], ES-adjacent here is not more stringent than SS-global or any of the SS constraints. This is clear from the grammar of L.2, where ES-adjacent is ranked over MATCH, which in turn is ranked above all three versions of SS. Optima in this language insert or delete φs to satisfy ES-adjacent wherever possible. As shown in the second row of the comparative tableau in (100), ES-adjacent, like ES-parent, sometimes does not distinguish between parses. The result is that, for this input, MATCH selects the winner. All three SS constraints favor the losing candidate, and ES-adjacent cannot make the cut between winner and loser. The choice is left to MATCH, which, in this case, favors a parse that puts a clitic initial to a phonological phrase.

(100)　　Conflict between ES-adj and SS-local and SS-hypLoc for input
　　　　　[a [b.clitic [c]]]

| Input | Winner | Loser | ES-adj | Match | SS-glob | SS-loc | SS-hyp |
|---|---|---|---|---|---|---|---|
| {a [b]} | {(a) (b)} | {a (b)} | W | L | W | W | W |
| {a [b.clitic [c]]} | {(a) (b.σ (c))} | {(a b.σ) (c)} | | W | L | L | L |

*11.5.2.2 Property analysis for ESadj.SS3[+clitic, +Hd]*

In ES.SS3[+clitic, +Hd], opposing each markedness constraint to Match in
turn yielded a simple property analysis with four properties (81). With ES-
adjacent instead of ES-parent in the present system, this property analysis
does not work. Because there are three possible grammars that yield L.1,
the properties p.glob, p.loc, and p.hyp (SS-hypLoc <> Match) are moot for
L.1. Applying the old PA to ESadj.SS3[+clitic, +Hd] fails to distinguish L.1
from L.2. These are the two languages in which ES-adjacent outranks Match
(i.e., they both have the α value of the first property, p.es, in (101)). What
distinguishes them is that in L.1, some SS constraint (it does not matter
which) must dominate Match, whereas in L.2, Match dominates all three
SS constraints. Thus, to distinguish L.1 from L.2, a property that opposes
the dominant one of the three SS constraints against Match is needed: this
is the second property in (101), p.ss. It is wide scope, but is only needed
under the α value of p.es.

The remaining languages, L.3–7, have the β value of p.es. They are distinguished by their values for p.glob, p.loc, and p.hyp, which oppose SS-global,
SS-local, and SS-hypLoc, respectively, to Match (as in the previously examined systems). As usual, p.loc and p.hyp scope under the β value of p.glob.

(101)　　Properties of ESadj.SS3[+clitic, +Hd]

| | Values | α | β | Scope |
|---|---|---|---|---|
| p.es | ES-adj <> Match | WeeeL | LeeeW | Wide |
| p.ss | {SS-global, SS-loc, SS-hyp}.dom <> Match | eWWWL | eLLLW | Wide<br>Or: p.es = α |
| p.glob | SS-global <> Match | eWeeL | eLeeW | p.es = β ∧ p.ss = β |
| p.loc | SS-local <> Match | eeWeL | eeLeW | p.glob = β |
| p.hyp | SS-hyp <> Match | eeeWL | eeeLW | p.glob = β |

(102)    PA table for ESadj.SS3[+clitic, +Hd]

|       | p.es | p.ss | p.glob | p.loc | p.hyp |
|-------|------|------|--------|-------|-------|
| L.1   | α    | α    | moot   | moot  | moot  |
| L.2   | α    | β    | β      | β     | β     |
| L.3   | β    | α    | α      | moot  | moot  |
| L.4   | β    | α    | β      | β     | α     |
| L.5   | β    | α    | β      | β     | β     |
| L.6   | β    | α    | β      | β     | α     |
| L.7   | β    | β    | β      | β     | β     |

This property analysis requires five properties, rather than the four that sufficed in previous systems, despite the reduced number of languages relative to the system with ES-parent (ES.SS3[+clitic, +Hd]). The interaction between ES-adjacent and the SS constraints, in which ranking any of the three over MATCH alongside ES-adjacent results in the other two being freely rankable, complicates the structure of the typology.

### 11.5.3 ES gradience and headlessness

Finally, we briefly consider the system ESadj.SS3[+clitic, −Hd], which is identical to the previous headed system except that headless candidates are admitted to GEN. The typology of this system is nearly identical to that of ES.SS3[+clitic, −Hd], examined in §11.4.3, except that the first two languages of the ES-parent typology collapse into a single language in the ES-adjacent typology, similar to the relationship between typologies in the headed systems with clitics. Where the ES-parent system requires a separate ranking of SS-global against MATCH when ES-parent is dominated by SS-hyperlocal, the ES-adjacent system has SS-global freely rankable whenever ES-adjacent dominates MATCH. As in the categorical system, SS-local is freely rankable whenever ES-adjacent or SS-global dominates MATCH. Superficially, then, there appears to be a stringency hierarchy of the form ES-adjacent $>_s$ SS-global $>_s$ SS-local. However, none of these apparent stringency relationships are upheld by the MOAT, which fails DelBusso (2018)'s MOAT-based stringency diagnostics (103). Neither SS-global nor SS-local preserves the seemingly more stringent ES-adjacent's equivalence of L.1 and L.2 (blue double line), violating Equivalence Maintenance in (103a), while SS-local shares SS-global's ordering of L.1 over L.2, violating No Sharing in (103d). A more in-depth analysis of why admitting headless candidates affects these stringency relations in this manner is left for future research, however, since it has already been argued above that Headedness is a desirable property of the candidate set.

(103)   MOAT-based stringency diagnostics (paraphrased from Delbusso (2018), (16), p. 75)

a.   EQUIVALENCE MAINTENANCE: For all pairs of grammars <A, B>, if A and B are equivalent for C2 (the more stringent constraint), then A and B are equivalent for C1 (the less stringent constraint).

b.   INCREASED ORDERING: For some pair of grammars <A, B>, A and B are equivalent for C1, but ordered for C2.

c.   NO CONFLICT: For all grammars A and B, if C2 orders A over B, then C1 does not order B over A.

d.   NO SHARING: For all grammars A and B, if C2 orders A over B, then C1 does not order A over B (instead, A will be equivalent to A', and A' will be over B).

(104)   MOAT for ESadj.SS3[+clitic, –Hd]

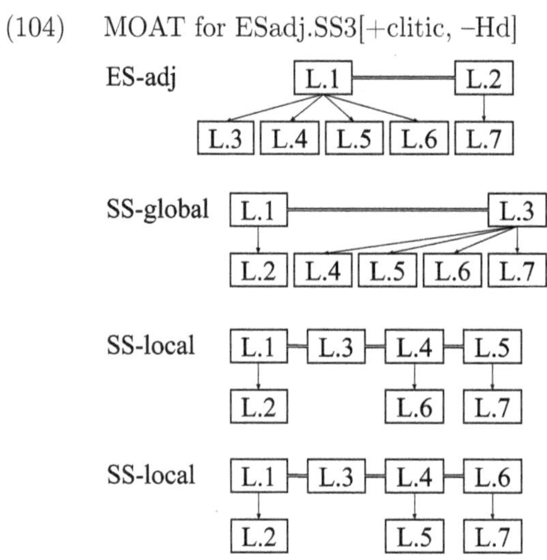


### 11.5.4   *Impact of ES gradience on stringency*

To understand the effect of making EQUALSISTERS gradient, we can compare three pairs of systems. First, the systems without clitics, ESadj.SS3[–clitic, ±Hd] vs. ES.SS3[–clitic, ±Hd], had typologies of the exact same size (six languages) and structure. ES is more stringent than SS-global in both systems; the gradience of ES has no effect in the [–clitic] systems. Second, the headed systems with clitics are the gradient system ESadj.SS3[+clitic, +Hd] and its categorical counterpart ES.SS3[+clitic, +Hd]. The ES-parent system generates a nine-language typology, which can be completely analyzed with four properties, opposing each markedness constraint to MATCH in turn.

Meanwhile, ES-adjacent generates a seven-language typology, which requires a fifth property, because ES-adjacent rules out some candidates for which the SS constraints conflict with the result that ranking any SS constraint over MATCH with ES-adjacent produces the same language in this system. In these systems with clitics, neither ES-adjacent nor ES-parent is more stringent than SS-global, nor is either ES constraint more stringent than either of the other SS constraints.

Thirdly, we can compare the [–Hd] systems, gradient ESadj.SS3[+clitic, –Hd] vs. categorical ES.SS3[+clitic, –Hd]. The relationship between their two typologies is similar to that between the headed systems. ES-adjacent produces a smaller but more complex typology, with no true stringency relationships, compared to ES-parent's. Both systems without Headedness are more complex than their properly headed counterparts.

The choice between gradient and categorical ES makes no difference in the [–clitic] systems, but when free clitics are added to the system, gradient ES-adjacent shrinks the typology, while simultaneously complicating its structure. This is true both when Headedness is enforced, and when it is not. The complexity of ES-adjacent's interaction with the three SS constraints suggests that ES-parent may be a better implementation of EQUALSISTERS, since it results in a more interpretable typology under a larger range of inputs.


## 11.6    Discussion

This chapter compared twelve systems, each including three implementations of STRONGSTART with three different scopes of evaluation, in order to gain an understanding of the stringency relationships that hold among STRONGSTART implementations. The systems also varied their candidate sets (whether Headedness is enforced as a condition on GEN, and whether free clitics were included), and what version of EQUALSISTERS, if any, was included in CON. Both the categorical and gradient versions of EQUALSISTERS were found to be more stringent than all STRONGSTART constraints in the clitic-free systems, and STRONGSTART-global was found to be more stringent than both STRONGSTART-local and STRONGSTART-hyperlocal when Headedness was enforced. The constraints were evaluated according to two metrics: the particular optima that they favor, and the complexity of the typologies they predict, with a focus on stringency hierarchies. The table in (105) summarizes the systems examined in this chapter. The stringency relationships discovered in each of them are summarized in (106).

(105)    Systems in this chapter

|              | SS only | ES-parent | ES-adjacent |
|--------------|---------|-----------|-------------|
| Without clitics | SS3[−clitic, ±Hd] | ES.SS3[−clitic, ±Hd] | ESadj.SS3[−clitic, ±Hd] |
| With clitics | SS3[+clitic, ±Hd]<br>SS3[XP, +clitic, +Hd] | ES.SS3[+clitic, ±Hd] | ESadj.SS3[+clitic, ±Hd] |

(106)    Stringency in this chapter
    a.    Systems with SS only: SS-internal stringency

| System | SS-global $>_s$ SS-local | SS-global $>_s$ SS-hyp | SS-local $>_s$ SS-hyp |
|--------|--------------------------|------------------------|-----------------------|
| SS3[−clitic, ±Hd] | yes | yes | no |
| SS3[+clitic, +Hd] | yes | yes | no |
| SS3[+clitic, −Hd] | yes | no | no |
| SS3[XP, +clitic, +Hd] | yes | yes | yes |

    b.    Systems with ES: ES-SS stringency

| System | ES $>_s$ SS-global | ES $>_s$ SS-local | ES $>_s$ SS-hyp |
|--------|--------------------|-------------------|-----------------|
| ES.SS3[−clitic, ±Hd] | yes | yes | yes |
| ES.SS3[+clitic, +Hd] | no | no | no |
| ES.SS3[+clitic, −Hd] | no | yes | no |
| ESadj.SS3[−clitic, ±Hd] | yes | yes | yes |
| ESadj.SS3[+clitic, +Hd] | no | no | no |
| ESadj.SS3[+clitic, −Hd] | no | no | no |

## 11.6.1 Headedness, free clitics, and stringency

Three possible stringency relationships among SS constraints were investigated in this chapter: (1) SS-global $>_s$ SS-local, (2) SS-global $>_s$ SS-hyperlocal, and (3) SS-local $>_s$ SS-hyperlocal. The first held in all but one system in this chapter. Almost regardless of variations in GEN or CON, SS-global was more stringent than SS-local. Only combining a gradient implementation of EQUALSISTERS with a candidate set that allowed headless φs in possible optima disrupted the SS-global / SS-local stringency. The stability of this stringency relationship makes sense, since SS-global evaluates a larger scope than SS-local using the same metric (the category of a non-initial sister being higher than that of an initial sister).

The second stringency relationship, between SS-global and SS-hyperlocal, holds when Headedness is enforced on GEN ([+Hd] systems), or when all improperly headed candidates are harmonically bounded ([–clitic] systems). If improperly headed candidates are possible optima, however, SS-hypLoc conflicts with SS-global, as in all [+clitic, –Hd] systems.

The third stringency relationship, between SS-local and SS-hyperlocal, is upheld only in SS3[XP root, +clitic, +Hd]. All other candidate sets include level-skipping doubly weak starts as possible optima, which violate SS-hyperlocal but not SS-local. But in SS3[XP root, +clitic, +Hd], all level-skipping doubly weak starts were harmonically bounded, with the result that SS-local was more stringent than SS-hyperlocal. The set of candidates filtered out by SS-hyperlocal was a subset of those filtered out by SS-local. If Headedness is enforced, SS-global is also more stringent than both SS-local and SS-hyperlocal, so that the three SS constraints function in a three-step stringency hierarchy: SS-global $>_s$ SS-local $>_s$ SS-hypLoc.

In addition to stringency relations among SS constraints, this chapter also tested stringency between EQUALSISTERS and STRONGSTART. STRONGSTART can be interpreted as a position-sensitive version of EQUALSISTERS, making it STRONGSTART less stringent than EQUALSISTERS. SS is also less stringent than ES because SS does not demand strict equality between sisters' categories as ES does, but merely prohibits a rise in prosodic category. A fall in prosodic category between the first sister and second is a problem for EQUALSISTERS but not for STRONGSTART. The expectation, then, was that ES would be more stringent than SS, except where headless candidates create a conflict between ES and SS-hyperlocal. This was borne out in systems without clitics, where the minimum violation of ES was zero. In [–clitic] systems, ES-parent and ES-adjacent are both more stringent than SS-global, -local, and -hyperlocal. Enforcing Headedness did not affect this interaction, because all headless candidates in the [–clitic] systems were harmonically bounded by MATCH.

However, when the minimum violation of ES for some inputs is one, rather than zero, as in [+clitic, +Hd] systems, ES-parent is not more stringent than SS-global. Instead, the two constraints are independent. In these systems, clitics are parsed as stray syllables, directly into the φ. When some input syntaxes are head-initial (X⁰-XP), then, SS-global can distinguish candidates that ES cannot, because ES (categorical or gradient) is always violated at least once when the input structure contains a clitic. Since any sisters to the σ are ωs or φs, the clitic is necessarily unequal to its sister(s) in the output, violating ES. SS-global, ignoring falls in prosodic category and only comparing the first sister to the following sisters, is able to make distinctions that ES cannot, thus breaking the ES-SS stringency relationship. Restricting the inputs to head-final structures eliminates any role for SS, which is not violated by any of the possible optima in the system. The basic stringency relationship between ES and SS, seen clearly in ES.SS3[–clitic], is vulnerable to disruption when clitics are included in the candidate set, depending on the set of input syntactic structures that are considered.

Lastly, in systems where Headedness was not enforced and clitics were included ([+clitic, –Hd]), clitics can be promoted into headless φs to satisfy ES, with the result that ES-parent and ES-adjacent both come into direct conflict with SS-hyperlocal. In ES.SS3[+clitic, –Hd], ES-parent remained more stringent than SS-local, as did SS-global. This was not the case in ESadj.SS3[+clitic, –Hd], where no true stringency relationships existed at all.

Restrictions on the candidate set can alter the expected stringency relationships. This goes for both input and output candidates. Restricting input candidates to head-initial syntactic structures and including clitics has the surprising effect of making SS-global more stringent than ES-parent and ES-adjacent (see Appendix for details). But including both head-final and head-initial syntactic structures, while retaining clitics, eliminates the stringency relationship between ES and SS-global altogether. They become entirely independent, freely rerankable constraints.

### 11.6.2 STRONGSTART conclusions

This chapter's comparison of three definitions of STRONGSTART, varying in their scope, offers two conclusions. The first conclusion is that SS-local can, and almost certainly should, be abandoned. SS-local is the original definition of STRONGSTART (Selkirk 2011, Elfner 2012), and only compares the first two children in a set of sisters. SS-local favors doubly weak structures of the form $(\pi_{n-1}\ \pi_{\leq n-1}\ ...\ \pi_n\ ...)$ over strongly starting structures of the form $(\pi_n\ \pi_n\ ...\ \pi_n)$. These doubly weak starts emerge as optimal parses of right-branching input syntaxes when SS-local dominates MATCH and SS-global is inactive or is dominated by MATCH. Doubly weak optima appear in at least one language in every system in this chapter that has SS-local in its CON. By postponing the rise in prosodic category demanded by MATCH to the third daughter, it is pushed outside the scope of SS-local's evaluation, thereby satisfying SS-local. This effect is contrary to the purpose stated by Selkirk (2011) and Elfner (2012) for STRONGSTART, which is to favor category promotion at the left edge.

Doubly weak starts are avoided by STRONGSTART-global, which evaluates the category of all sisters against the first sister, rather than only comparing the first two sisters. When SS-global is top-ranked, category promotion at the left edge does occur, as intended. SS-global is a more stringent version of SS-local in all but one system examined in this chapter (with or without clitics, with or without Headedness),[13] and better achieves the stated purposes of SS-local. When SS-global replaces SS-local, doubly weak starts are no longer predicted, and category promotion is predicted instead. Therefore, unless doubly weak starts are empirically attested, SS-local is not useful. The findings of this chapter suggest that SS-local does not need to be part of universal CON and should be replaced by SS-global.

(107)   *SS-local recommendation*: Avoid using SS-local unless doubly weak starts are a desired outcome. If doubly weak starts are unattested cross-linguistically (as they seem to be, based on the current literature), then SS-local should be eliminated from the universal constraint set. SS-global can be adopted without any negative consequences, since it is more stringent than SS-local and will therefore penalize all the structures that SS-local penalizes.

The second conclusion concerning STRONGSTART is that STRONGSTART-hyperlocal, an implementation originally proposed by Bennett, Elfner, and McCloskey (2016), is fundamentally different from previously proposed STRONGSTART implementations (SS-local and -global). It has the capacity to conflict with all the other prosodic markedness constraints on sisterhood considered here. SS-hyperlocal conflicts with SS-local in all systems with level-skipping doubly weak starts (108b), although this is not necessarily a problem, if SS-local is to be avoided anyway. SS-hyperlocal additionally conflicts with SS-global and with ES-parent and -adjacent when Headedness is not enforced (108a). Again, this is not necessarily a problem, since one of this chapter's arguments is that Headedness *should* be enforced. The brittleness of SS-hyperlocal's stringency relationships with other SS constraints reflects the different foci of their definitions. SS-hyperlocal avoids the problems of SS-local by restricting its scope to the very first daughter and comparing its category to that of the parent, disregarding the other sisters entirely. That is, it is vertically oriented. SS-global and SS-local, on the other hand, are horizontally oriented. They are defined in terms of comparisons across sisters, not from parent to child.

(108)   Structures that violate SS-hypLoc but not SS-local or SS-global
    a.   Headless: $(_\varphi\ \sigma)$, $(_\varphi\ \sigma_1\ \sigma_2\ ...\ \sigma_n)$, $\{_\iota\ \omega\}$, $\{_\iota\ \omega_1\ \omega_2\ ...\ \omega_n\}$
    b.   Level-skipping doubly weak start: $(_\varphi\ \sigma_1\ \sigma_2\ ...\ \omega)$, $(_\varphi\ \sigma_1\ \sigma_2\ ...\ \varphi)$, $\{_\iota\ \omega_1\ \omega_2\ ...\ \varphi\}$

---

[13] The exception is ESadj.SS3[+clitic, −Hd] (§5.3), in which SS-global superficially appears to be more stringent than SS-local, but is not more stringent according to the MOAT diagnostics.

As long as all candidates are properly headed, SS-hypLoc can be interpreted as a category-specific version of SS-global. The presence of additional sisters of a higher prosodic category is assumed implicitly, and is enforced by the requirement of proper Headedness for all prosodic structures as a condition on GEN. Where SS-global is violated by a $\varphi$-initial word that is sister to a $\varphi$, SS-hypLoc is only violated by a $\varphi$-initial foot or syllable; it could be restated as SS-global(child = ft or $\sigma$). Under this interpretation, all valid versions of STRONGSTART are evaluated globally, and SS-global can be indexed to particular prosodic categories, exactly as Elfner (2012) indexes STRONGSTART to the word level.

On the other hand, if the precise definition of SS-hypLoc in Bennett et al. (2016) is taken literally, then the scope of SS-hypLoc truly differs from SS-global, since it does not even consider sisters. SS-hypLoc can then be interpreted as a position-sensitive Exhaustivity constraint, prohibiting level-skipping at the left edge only.

(109)    *SS-hyperlocal recommendation*: Treat SS-hyperlocal as a less stringent version of SS-global. This is guaranteed if proper Headedness is enforced on the candidate set.

SS-hyperlocal might be reimagined as a category-specific version of STRONG-START-global, parameterized to the category of the child, as suggested above. Alternatively, we could expand STRONGSTART-global into a different kind of stringency hierarchy based not on horizontal scope, but on the number of prosodic levels of difference between the first sister and the highest later sister.

(110)    SS constraint scale based on vertical prosodic distance
   a.    SS-1: Assign a violation for every node whose first daughter is of category $k$ that has a non-initial daughter of category $> k$. *Schematically:* $*(\pi_k \ldots \pi_{>k})$.
         Violated by $\{\varphi \iota\}$, $(\omega \varphi)$, $\{\omega \iota\}$, $\{\sigma \iota\}$, ...
   b.    SS-2: Assign a violation for every node whose first daughter is of category $k$ that has a non-initial daughter of category $> k + 1$. *Schematically:* $*(\pi_k \ldots \pi_{>k+1})$.
         Violated by $\{\omega \iota\}$, $(\sigma \varphi)$, and $\{\sigma \iota\}$, but not violated by $\{\varphi \iota\}$ or $(\omega \varphi)$.
   c.    SS-3: Assign a violation for every node whose first daughter is of category $k$ that has a non-initial daughter of category $> k + 2$. *Schematically:* $*(\pi_k \ldots \pi_{>k+2})$.
         Violated by $\{\sigma \iota\}$, but not violated by $\{\varphi \iota\}$, $(\omega \varphi)$, or $\{\omega \iota\}$.

It would be conceptually more economical to have one definition of SS that varies in its distance requirements and/or its category indexation (two parameters), rather than having two versions that differ in scope *and* can each vary in distance requirements *and* can each be parameterized to particular categories (three parameters).

I leave for future research an examination of the consequences of the deep evaluation of StrongStart($\varkappa$, $\pi$) proposed by Hsu (2016) and Kalivoda and Bellik (2021) for the interaction of SS with ES and for the predicted typology. Deep versions of SS cannot be evaluated locally by looking only at a parent and its immediate children the way that the other implementations of SS can, since deep SS requires an unbounded search down the left edge of each constituent of the specified parent category. For that reason, it runs afoul of the principle that OT constraints should be local (in, e.g., McCarthy 2003). This is not necessarily a decisive mark against deep SS, though, since leaf-counting Binarity (see Bellik and Van Handel, Chapter 10) also requires a global search. It remains to be seen whether locality can be reconceptualized in a way that renders deep SS-local.

### 11.6.3 *EQUALSISTERS conclusions*

As with STRONGSTART, multiple implementations of EQUALSISTERS are possible. The original and widely-cited definition of ES (Myrberg 2013) is ambiguous as to the number of violations it assigns to suprabinary structures. Several reasonable implementations of ES are available, and they differ in the number of violations they assign. These various implementations therefore predict different optima, but they do not directly conflict with each other—a violation of one entails a violation of the others, even though the number of violations varies. Conflicts might be induced in a sufficiently complex system, though this point was not explored here. Two implementations of EQUALSISTERS have been explicitly used in the literature: EQUALSISTERS-parent (categorical evaluation) and EQUALSISTERS-adjacent (gradient evaluation).[14]

In systems without free clitics, both ES-parent and ES-adjacent are more stringent than all versions of SS, and replacing ES-parent with ES-adjacent does not alter the size or structure of the typology. In systems with free clitics, neither ES-parent nor ES-adjacent is more stringent than any of the SS constraints. Replacing ES-parent with ES-adjacent actually reduces the

---

[14] Another attested variation on ES is restricting it to a particular prosodic category (Hsu 2016), as is widely done for Binarity. The consequences of each of these versions for the typology, and for the stringency relationship of ES with SS, are briefly discussed in Bellik and Van Handel (Chapter 10).

size of the typology, while simultaneously complicating its structure. The additional complexity is due to the fact that ES-adjacent filters out ternary-branching candidates with medial clitics, for which the SS constraints conflict. As a result, ranking ES-adjacent and any one of the three SS constraints over MATCH produces the same language in ESadj.SS3[+clitic, +Hd], whereas ranking ES-parent over MATCH with each of the three SS constraints produces three distinct languages in ES.SS3[+clitic, +Hd]. When the minimum violation of ES is zero for all inputs, both ES-parent and ES-adjacent participate in a stringency hierarchy with the three SS implementations and produce a very clear typology structure; when the minimum violation of ES is one for some inputs, neither does.

The typological comparisons in this chapter do not provide a decisive argument in favor of one implementation over the other, but they do show that the constraint interactions are clearer with ES-parent than ES-adjacent. ES-parent is also explicitly employed by more previous analyses than ES-adjacent, and is sufficient for the data in the one paper employing ES-adjacent as well (Féry 2015). Finally, ES-parent is categorical while ES-adjacent is gradient. ES-parent assigns at most one violation per parent, while ES-adjacent can assign up to $n - 1$ violations for a parent that has $n$ children. McCarthy (2003) has argued previously that gradient OT constraints are problematic for theoretical reasons. These factors argue, albeit inconclusively, in favor of adopting ES-parent as the standard implementation of EQUALSISTERS.

### 11.6.4 A categorical constraint schema for trees

One problem for the claim that ES-parent is categorical while ES-adjacent is gradient is that no formal schema for categorical constrains on tree structures exists. The issue of gradience in constraint definitions has previously been addressed and formally defined in McCarthy (2003), but the categorical constraint schema in that paper (111) was designed for linear structures. I conclude with a proposal to extend the categorical constraint schema in (111) to better constrain prosodic well-formedness constraints.

All constraints employed in this chapter have been stated in terms that conform to McCarthy (2003)'s proposed schema for categorical OT constraints. However, I have argued that not all of the constraints in this chapter are equally good. Furthermore, even though ES-adjacent as defined above does conform to (111) (see (17) in §11.2, and system definitions in §11.5), it is not a categorical constraint in the same way that ES-parent is. My proposal, which further research may or may not validate, is that the schema for categorical constraints pertaining to tree structures should be amended as in (112).

(111)   Schema for categorical markedness constraint
*λ / C = For any λ satisfying condition C, assign a violation mark (McCarthy 2003).

(112)   Schema for categorical tree constraint
*λ / C = For any λ satisfying condition C, assign a violation mark. C may make reference to the children (or other descendants) of λ, but not to its sisters or parents.

In other words, λ (the locus of violation) in the definitions of prosodic well-formedness constraints should always be the *highest* node that is referred to in the condition C. Evaluation of constraints that adhere to this will only require traversing a node's children (and potentially their descendants)— traveling down the tree only, not up the tree. This will permit constraint formulations like EQUALSISTERS-parent, as well as other common prosodic well-formedness constraints (113). It will rule out constraints like EQUAL-SISTERS-adjacent (114). If we further state that constraints cannot refer to specific positions other than the first and last (i.e., C could make references to the first child or last child, but not to the second child or penultimate child), as an extension of the principle that phonology does not "count," and by analogy with the nature of constraints on foot structure (i.e., ALL-FEET-LEFT interacts with NONFINALITY, rather than having a constraint saying ALL-FEET-LEFT-BUT-ONE), then this schema can also rule out SS-local. SS-global, meanwhile, can be stated in a manner that conforms to (112), as in (113b), or restated in a manner that refers to sisters and therefore violates (112), as in (114d). The definition of ES-adjacent necessarily refers to sisterhood, which is prohibited in (112).

(113)   Examples of constraints that satisfy (112)
a.   ES-parent: For any λ whose children are not all of the same category, assign a violation mark.
b.   SS-global, v.1: For any λ whose first child is of a lower category than some later child, assign a violation mark.
c.   BINMAXLEAVES(φ): For every φ that contains more than two prosodic words at any level, assign a violation mark.

(114)     Examples of constraints that do not satisfy (112).

      a.     ES-adj: For any $\lambda$ whose <u>sister</u> to its right is not the same category as $\lambda$, assign a violation mark.

      b.     SS-local, v.1: For any $\lambda$ that has no <u>sister</u> to its left, and whose <u>sister</u> to its right is a higher category than $\lambda$, assign a violation mark.

      c.     SS-local, v.2: For any $\lambda$ whose first daughter's category is lower than its <u>second</u> daughter's category, assign a violation mark.

      d.     SS-global, v.2: For any $\lambda$ that has no <u>sisters</u> to its left and has a <u>sister</u> to its right that is of a higher prosodic category than $\lambda$, assign a violation mark.

      e.     EXHAUSTIVITY(child): For every $\lambda$ with category $k$ whose <u>parent</u> is of category $> k + 1$, assign a violation mark.

These restatements correspond to different algorithms for traversing and evaluating trees, even if they ultimately derive the same violation counts. The algorithms for (114) require either a more complex tree traversal, or an enriched tree representation, compared to those of (113). To assess a sister requires traveling up to a parent node and then back down to the sister, since sister nodes are not directly connected in the prosodic tree. This is illustrated below for $\omega_1$: To determine whether its sister is also a prosodic word by traversing the tree, one must travel up to the parent $\varphi_1$, and then back down to $\varphi_2$. Similarly, EXHAUSTIVITY(child) in (114e) necessarily refers to parents, and evaluating it requires traversing up the tree, as shown in (115b).

(115)     Improper tree traversal for gradient constraints

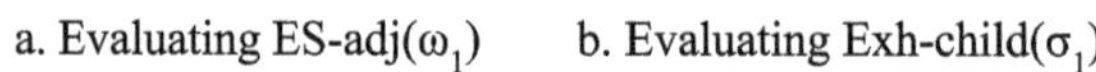


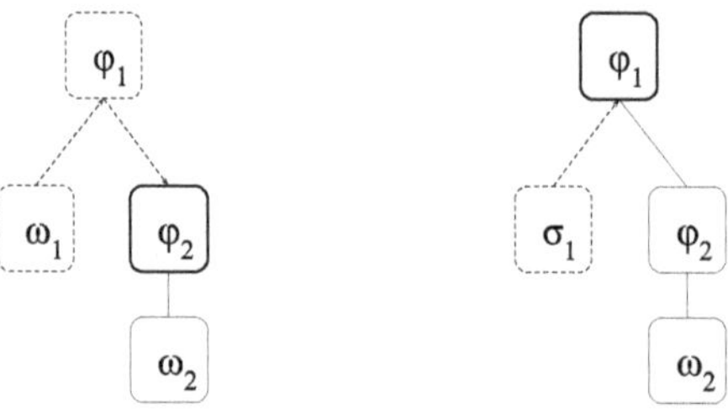


It is my hope that this proposal helps guide the phrasing and conception of future prosodic well-formedness constraints, the refinement of existing constraints, and perhaps the formulation of a stricter schema for constraints that refer to tree structures.

## References

Alber, Birgit, Delbusso, Natalie, and Prince, Alan (2016). From intensional properties to universal support. *Language* 92: e88–e116.

Alber, Birgit and Prince, Alan (2021). *The Structure of OT Typologies.* Chapter 1: Introduction to Property Theory. Unpublished manuscript. ROA 1381, Rutgers Optimality Archive, http://roa.rutgers.edu.

Alderete, John (2009). Exploring recursivity, stringency, and gradience in the Pama-Nyungan stress continuum. In Steve Parker (ed.) *Phonological Argumentation: Essays on Evidence and Motivation* 181–202. London: Equinox Publishing.

Baek, Hyunah (2017). A Match-theoretic approach to Korean intonational phonology. In Jessica Kantarovich, Tran Truong, and Orest Xherija (eds.) *Proceedings of the 52nd Annual Meeting of the Chicago Linguistic Society* 39–51.Chicago: Chicago Linguistic Society.

Bellik, Jennifer and Kalivoda, Nick (2016). Adjunction and branchingness effects in syntax-prosody mapping. In Gunnar Ólafur Hansson, Ashley Farris-Trimble, Kevin McMullin, and Douglas Pulleyblank (eds.) *Supplemental Proceedings of the 2015 Annual Meeting on Phonology*, Linguistic Society of America. http://doi.org/10.3765/amp.v3i0.3690

Bellik, Jennifer, Bellik, Ozan, and Kalivoda, Nick (2015–2021). Syntax-Prosody in Optimality Theory (SPOT). Javascript application. http:// spot.sites.ucsc.edu. Codebase at https://github.com/syntax-prosody-ot.

Bellik, Jennifer, Ito, Junko, Kalivoda, Nick and Mester, Armin (2022). Matching and alignment. In Haruo Kubozono, Junko Ito, and Armin Mester (eds.) *Prosody and Prosodic Interfaces* 457–481. Oxford University Press.

Bennett, Ryan (2012). Foot-conditioned Phonotactics and Prosodic Constituency. PhD dissertation, University of California, Santa Cruz.

Bennett, Ryan, Elfner, Emily, and McCloskey, James (2016). Lightest to the right: An apparently anomalous displacement in Irish. *Linguistic Inquiry* 47: 169–234.

Chen, Fulang (2021). On the left-/right-branching asymmetry in Mandarin tone 3 sandhi. In Ryan Bennett, Richard Bibbs, Mykel L. Brinkerhoff, Max J. Kaplan, Stephanie Rich, Amanda Rysling, Nicholas Van Handel, and Maya Wax Cavallero (eds.) *Proceedings of the 2020 Annual Meeting on Phonology*, Washington, DC: Linguistic Society of America. https:// doi.org/10.3765/amp.v9i0.4881

de Lacy, Paul (2002). *The Formal Expression of Markedness.* PhD dissertation, University of Massachusetts Amherst.

de Lacy, Paul (2004). Markedness conflation in optimality theory. *Phonology* 21: 145–199.

DelBusso, Natalie R. (2018). Typological Structure and Properties of Property Theory. PhD dissertation, Rutgers University.

Delbusso, Natalie (2020). The final-over-final condition, stringency, and typological structure. *Linguistic Inquiry* 51: 765–784.

Elfner, Emily (2011). The interaction of linearization and prosody: evidence from pronoun postposing in Irish. In Andrew Carnie (ed.) *Formal Approaches to Celtic Linguistics* 17–40. Cambridge: Cambridge Scholars Publishing.

Elfner, Emily (2012). *Syntax-Prosody Interactions in Irish.* PhD dissertation, University of Massachusetts Amherst.

Féry, Caroline (2015). Extraposition and prosodic monsters in German. In Lyn Frazier and Ted Gibson (eds.) *Explicit and Implicit Prosody in Sentence Processing* 11–37. New York: Springer.

Hsu, Brian (2016). Syntax-Prosody Interactions in the Clausal Domain: Head Movement and *Coalescence*. PhD dissertation, University of Southern California.

Ito, Junko and Mester, Armin (1992/2003). Weak layering and word binarity. In Takeru Honma, Masao Okazaki, Toshiyuki Tabata and Shin-ichi Tanaka (eds.) *A New Century of Phonology and Phonological Theory: A Festschrift for Professor Shosuke Haraguchi on the Occasion of His Sixtieth Birthday* 26–65. Tokyo: Kaitakusha.

Ito, Junko, and Mester, Armin (2020). Match theory and prosodic wellformedness constraints. In Hongming Zhang and Youyong Qian (eds.) *Prosodic Studies. Challenges and Prospects* 252–274. London and New York: Routledge.

Kalivoda, Nick and Bellik, Jennifer (2021). Overtly headed XPs and Irish syntax–prosody mapping. In Ryan Bennett, Richard Bibbs, Mykel L. Brinkerhoff, Max J. Kaplan, Stephanie Rich, Amanda Rysling, Nicholas Van Handel, and Maya Wax Cavallero (eds.) *Proceedings of the 2020 Annual Meeting on Phonology*, Washington, DC: Linguistic Society of America. https://doi.org/10.3765/amp.v9i0.4906

Kim, Gyung-Ran (2015). Recursive ɩ-phrasing: evidence from a boundary low tone in North Kyungsang Korean. *Studies in Modern Grammar*: 179–201.

Kusmer, Leland (2020). *Optimal Linearization: Prosodic Displacement in Khoekhoegowab and Beyond.* PhD dissertation, University of Massachusetts Amherst.

McCarthy, John J. (2003). OT constraints are categorical. *Phonology* 20: 75–138.

McCarthy, John J. (2008). The serial interactions of stress and syncope. *Natural Language and Linguistic Theory* 26: 499–546.

Merchant, Nazarré and Krämer, Martin (2018). The holographic principle: typological analysis using lower dimensions. In Gillian Gallagher, Maria Gouskova and Sora Yin (eds.) *Supplemental Proceedings of the 2017 Annual Meeting on Phonology.* Washington, DC: Linguistic Society of America.

Myrberg, Sara (2010). *The Intonational Phonology of Stockholm Swedish.* PhD dissertation, Stockholm University.

Myrberg, Sara (2013). Sisterhood in prosodic branching. *Phonology* 30: 73–124.

Prince, Alan (2000). The special and the general. Presentation at the 24th Penn Linguistics Colloquium, University of Pennsylvania. Available at https://ruccs.rutgers.edu/images/personal-alan-prince/gamma/talks/plc-hdt.pdf

Prince, Alan and Smolensky, Paul (1993/2004). *Optimality Theory: Constraint Interaction in Generative Grammar*. Malden, MA: Blackwell Publishing.

Prince, Alan, Merchant, Nazarré, and Tesar, Bruce (2007–2021). OTWorkplace. http://sites.google.com/site/otworkplace

Selkirk, Elisabeth (1984). *Phonology and Syntax: the Relation between Sound and Structure*. Cambridge, MA: MIT Press.

Selkirk, Elisabeth (1996). The prosodic structure of function words. In James L. Morgan and Katherine Demuth (eds.) *Signal to Syntax: Bootstrapping from Speech to Grammar in Early Acquisition* 187–213. Mahwah, NJ: Erlbaum.

Selkirk, Elisabeth (2011). The syntax–phonology interface. In John A. Goldsmith, Jason Riggle, and Alan C. L. Yu (eds.) *The Handbook of Phonological Theory* 435–484. Blackwell Publishing.

Werle, Adam (2009). Word, Phrase and Clitic prosody in Bosnian, Serbian and Croatian. PhD dissertation, University of Massachusetts Amherst.

## About the author

*Jennifer Bellik*

Postdoctoral researcher and lecturer, Department of Linguistics, UC Santa Cruz. Research interests: syntax-prosody interface, Optimality Theory, Articulatory Phonology, and Turkish phonology. Recent publications: "An acoustic study of vowel intrusion in Turkish onset clusters", *Laboratory Phonology* 2018; "Automated tableau generation with SPOT" with N. Kalivoda, *Linguistics Vanguard* 2019; and "The effect of speech style and deaccentuation on vowel intrusion in Turkish complex onsets", *Proceedings of ICPhS* 2019.

## Appendix: The effect of syntactic head alignment

The system ES.SS3[+clitic] above includes syntactic structures in which heads both precede and follow their complements. I also computed typologies for two similar systems in which inputs were restricted to a single head directionality: system ES.SS3[+clitic, L], in which all heads occurred to the left of their complements; and system ES.SS3[+clitic, R], in which all heads occurred to the right of their complements. This Appendix will refer to ES.SS3[+clitic] with the suffix L/R, to indicate that it contains both left- and right-headed syntactic inputs and differentiate it from the strictly left-headed and strictly right-headed systems.

*Strictly left-headed system*

In the left-headed typology, SS-global superficially appears to be more stringent than ES-parent. The typology contains five languages, rather than the six languages of left- and right-headed ES.SS3[+clitic, L/R], because in this system, SS-global makes more distinctions among candidates than ES-parent does. When SS-global is top-ranked (L.1), then ES-parent is freely rankable. This contrasts with ES.SS3[+clitic, L/R], where SS-global and ES-parent must be separately ranked against MATCH, and either one can dominate the other. In the strictly left-headed system here, ES-parent can be ranked over SS-global (L.2), but SS-global is never ranked over ES-parent (i.e., no equivalent of ES.SS3[+clitic's L.3 exists). This is because the right-headed input candidates for which ES-parent demands a mismatching parse, but SS-global does not, are missing from this strictly left-headed candidate set.

(116)    Grammars of ES.SS3[+clitic, +Hd, L]

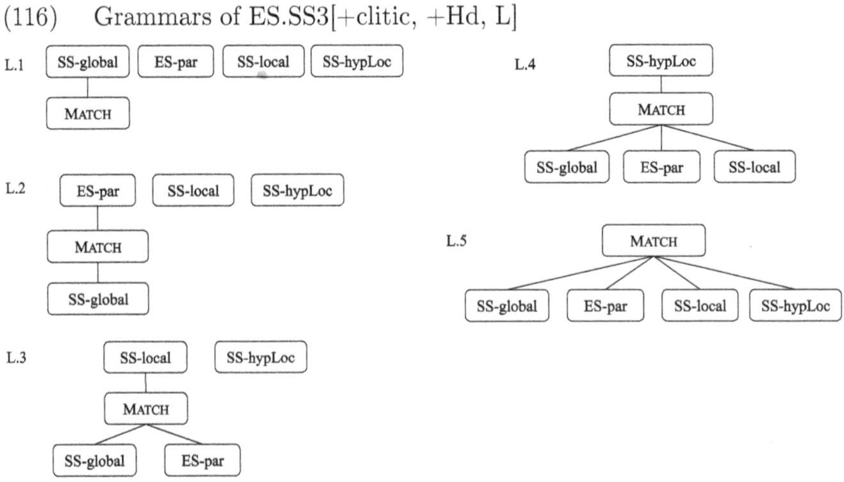

In all [+clitic] systems in this chapter, when a given input contains a clitic, the minimum violation of ES-parent for that input is 1. The candidate set does not contain any structures that avoid violating ES-parent at all for clitic-containing inputs, because GEN does not provide any options for parsing the clitic into a structure where it does not have any sisters of different categories (e.g., by wrapping it in a word). As a result, ES-parent cannot distinguish well between the candidates with clitics, since every such candidate violates it at least once, and no matter how many categories the different sisters belong to, ES-parent is violated only once. SS-global, on the other hand, can make more fine-grained distinctions, because some candidates do not violate it at all. This is illustrated in the comparative tableau in (117),[15] which shows all optima for input [a [b.clitic [c]]] in this system. L.2's winner is favored over the L.1 co-optima (first three rows) by MATCH, rather than by ES-parent. Both the L.2 winner and the three L.1 winners violate ES-parent once, so ES-parent fails to distinguish among them. Since MATCH is ranked above SS-global in L.2, it chooses the winning candidate, even though SS-global would prefer the losers in the first three rows, which do not include a rise in category. ES-parent is confined to ruling out the isomorphic parse in the last row.

(117)   L2 in ES.SS3[+clitic, +Hd, L]: ES-parent fails to distinguish some candidates. SS-local and SS-hypLoc are excluded from this tableau; neither candidate violates them.

| Input | W | L | ES-parent | MATCH | SS-global |
|---|---|---|---|---|---|
| [a [b.clitic [c]]] | {(a b.σ (c))} | {(a b.σ c)} | e | W | L |
| | | {((a b.σ) (c))} | e | W | L |
| | | {((a) b.σ (c))} | e | W | L |
| | | {(a (b.σ (c)))} | W | L | W |

---

[15] This is not the case for gradient versions of EQUALSISTERS, such as ES-adjacent and ES-1st. ES-1st would assign one violation to {(a b.σ c)} for the pair <a, b.σ> (categories: word, syllable), but two violations to {(a b.σ (c))} for the pairs <a, b.σ> and <a, (c)> (categories: word, φ). ES-1st, then, would favor the same candidate as SS-global, unlike ES-parent which could not distinguish between the two structures. ES-adjacent, however, would assign two violations to both, for the pairs of adjacent sisters <a, b.σ> and <b.σ, c> or <b.σ, (c)>, and therefore like ES-parent would be unable to distinguish between those particular candidates.

*Strictly right-headed system*

In the right-headed typology, there are only two languages: L.1 where MATCH outranks EQUALSISTERS-parent, and L.2 where EQUALSISTERS outranks MATCH. No version of STRONGSTART is ranked in either language, since the structures favored by ES and MATCH all satisfy all versions of SS. This small experiment confirms what may have already been obvious—that STRONGSTART only has a visible effect on the typology when isomorphic prosodic parses of the syntactic structures under consideration would violate it, and that isomorphic prosodic parses of strictly right-headed syntactic structures will always satisfy STRONGSTART. Replacing STRONGSTART with a mirrored constraint STRONGEND (considered and rejected in Bellik, Ito, Kalivoda, and Mester 2022) that penalizes a fall in prosodic category at the right edge of a constituent, could replicate the interaction of SS and ES seen in the left-headed system above (ES.SS3[+clitic, +Hd, L]).

*Summary*

To sum up, when output structures include free clitics, syllables that are parsed directly into the φ, then ES-parent is no longer more stringent than SS-global, because SS-global is able to make finer grained distinctions than ES-parent (117). In fact, when only left-headed syntactic structures are taken as inputs, then ES-parent's opposition to MATCH ends up being moot whenever SS-global is ranked over MATCH. But when right-headed syntactic structures are included in the set of inputs as well, then ES-parent and SS-global are no longer in any stringency relationship with each other. Each is able to make distinctions that the other cannot.

# Tutorial

# Chapter 12

# How to use SPOT: A tutorial

Jennifer Bellik and Nick Kalivoda[*]

## 12.1   Introduction

In order to create a valid analysis in Optimality Theory (OT), we must formally define the OT system that we are studying (Alber et al. 2016, Prince 2017a, b). A system S consists of two components: S.GEN and S.CON. S.GEN is the set of input and output candidates (algorithmically defined) in S, while S.CON is the set of constraints in S.

Under the widely assumed Prosodic Hierarchy Theory (Selkirk 1980, 1981, 1984; Nespor and Vogel 1986; adopted by many others), inputs to phrasal phonology are syntactic trees, while outputs are prosodic trees. Syntactic trees consist of heads ($X^0$), phrases (XP), and clauses (CP). Assuming the minimal prosodic hierarchy employed in Selkirk (2011), Ito and Mester (2013), and other works of Match Theory, prosodic trees consist of prosodic words ($\omega$), phonological phrases ($\varphi$), and intonational phrases ($\iota$). Because candidates are pairs of trees, even the strictest GEN function yields an exponential increase in the number of output structures as the number of words in the sentence grows, as discussed extensively in Shingler and

[*] We would like to thank SPOT co-creator Ozan Bellik for architecting the SPOT application, as well as RAs Colin Chen, Timothy Gee, Iva Petkov, Edward Shingler, Max Tarlov, and Su Zin, who were instrumental in developing the SPOT interface and many of the features demonstrated in this tutorial. Thanks also to participants at the 2020 meeting of the Society for Typological Analysis for helpful comments on an earlier version of this tutorial. This chapter is adapted from a 2021 Linguistic Society of America Proceedings paper, 'Syntax Prosody in Optimality Theory (SPOT) app tutorial," by the same authors.

Bellik (Chapter 2). This is illustrated graphically in (1), for four different
GEN functions.

Under Strict Layering (Selkirk 1984, Nespor and Vogel 1986), when level-
skipping and level-repeating are banned, the number of prosodic trees rooted in an intonational phrase and with prosodic words for terminals is $2^{(n-1)}$,
where $n$ is the number of terminals in the tree (dashed grey line in (1)). This
exponential function grows relatively slowly, such that six terminals can be
parsed into 32 strictly layered trees—a candidate set that would be tedious,
but possible, to generate and evaluate by hand.

With the inclusion of non-exhaustive parses (Weak Layering, Ito and
Mester 1992/2003), words can be parsed directly into the intonational
phrase, skipping the phonological phrase level.[1] This increases the number
of possible parses (compare [–Exhaustivity] black lines to [+Exhaustivity]
grey lines). When prosodic recursion is also allowed (Ito and Mester 2013),
the number of trees increases even faster (compare [–Non-Recursivity] solid
lines to [+Non-Recursivity] dashed lines of the same color).

(1)       Number of prosodic trees rooted in ɩ with $n$ words as terminals

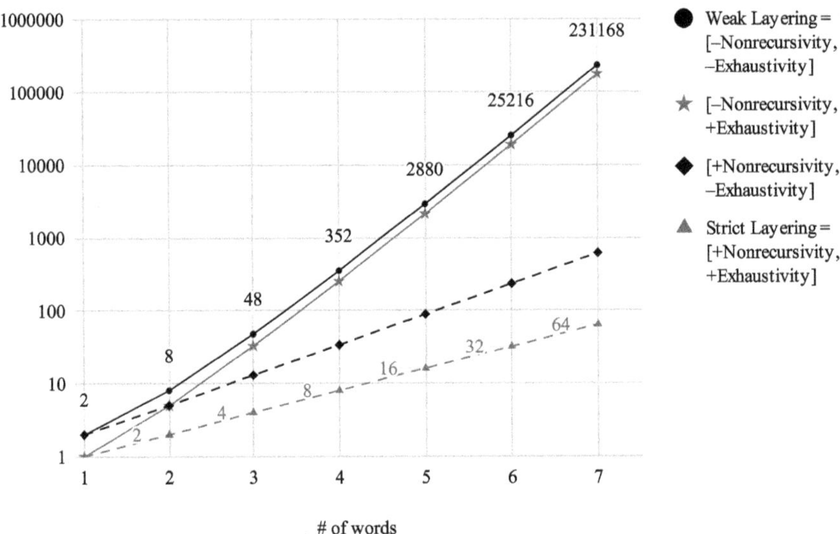


---

[1] SPOT has a distinct GEN parameter to enforce Headedness (proposed as an inviolable
requirement by Ito and Mester 2013), ensuring that every node of category $K$ has at least
one child of category $K$–1. The numbers for [–Exhaustive] black lines in (1) diminish by one
if Headedness is enforced on GEN, which excludes the single candidate in each set in which all
words are parsed directly into the intonational phrase. See Shingler and Bellik (Chapter 2)
for a discussion of the interaction of Headedness and Exhaustivity.

(2)      Eight parses of two words with Weakest Layering

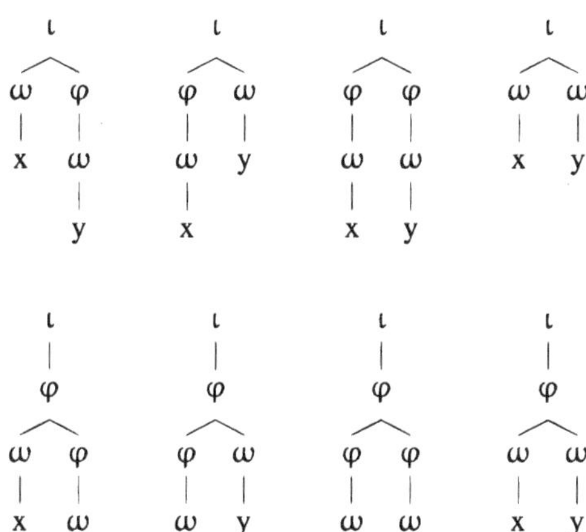

When both level-skipping and level-repeating are allowed, there are already eight possible parses of two words, depicted in (2) (or seven parses, if the headless candidate in the upper righthand corner is excluded). With six terminals, over 25,000 weakly layered parses become possible (1). Most of these candidates will ultimately be harmonically bounded, yet all must be considered lest an omitted candidate invalidate the final analysis (Bane and Riggle 2012, Karttunen 2006).

These huge numbers of candidates demand an automated tool for candidate generation and evaluation in syntax-prosody analyses. Obviously it is impractical to build and evaluate thousands of prosodic trees by hand. It is also impossible to do this automatically using OTWorkplace (Prince et al. 2007–2020) or other existing OT software, because their GEN capacity is limited to regular expressions, which cannot handle recursion.

This is where the Syntax-Prosody in Optimality Theory app (SPOT) comes in. It is a JavaScript application under development since 2015 (Bellik, Bellik, and Kalivoda 2015–2021) that automates candidate generation (GEN) and constraint evaluation (CON) for work on the syntax-prosody interface. SPOT news and information are available at the SPOT website (http://spot.sites.ucsc.edu), which links to the web application and codebase. SPOT was designed specifically to handle tree structures. It produces violation tableaux which can be viewed in the browser, or imported into the OT tool of your choice for further analysis.

This chapter explains, step by step, how to use SPOT to build a simplified version of a system that analyzes syntax-prosody matches and mismatches, inspired by data from Japanese. We will call this system Msp.Asp, which stands for MATCH(Syntax→Prosody), ALIGN(Syntax→Prosody). It is one of the systems in Bellik et al. (2022), and is closely related to the systems in Kalivoda (Chapter 7). After the instructions on setting up this system in SPOT, this chapter also briefly explains how to begin analyzing SPOT's violation tableaux in OTWorkplace.

## 12.2    Getting to the SPOT interface

To use SPOT online, navigate to the SPOT web interface by opening the SPOT website, preferably in Chrome or Firefox: spot.sites.ucsc.edu. At the top of the page, click 'SPOT Webapp." There is also a link at the bottom of all pages on the website. This will take you to the SPOT web interface.

It is also possible to install SPOT locally so that it can be used without an internet connection later. To take this route, click 'SPOT codebase" on the website to navigate to the Github repository, where you can follow the instructions in README.md to download the codebase from Github, build locally, and access the app in your browser from your local copy of the SPOT interface.

## 12.3    Defining inputs

The inputs to Msp.Asp are abstracted from data on Japanese phrasing in Kubozono (1989) (3). Of the five possible binary-branching syntactic trees with four words, four are mapped to matching prosodic structures in Japanese, while one, the fully left-branching input, is rebracketed into a balanced prosodic structure. These structures are diagnosed by %LH rises in pitch at the left edge of the φ, and by downstep that applies to non-initial rises throughout the maximal φ. In the mismatching prosody in (3b), an unexpected rise appears on the third word, indicating that it is at the left edge of a φ that does not correspond to any XP in the input. No such rebracketing occurs in its mirror image, the fully right-branching syntax in (3a), which features rises on the first three words. If (3a) were also rebracketed, it would have the same pitch contour as the left-branching input (3b) and the symmetrically-branching input (3e).

(3)      Schematization of Japanese phrasing patterns (abstracted from Kubozono 1989)

| | Syntax | Prosody | Match/ Mismatch |
|---|---|---|---|
| a. | Right branching | Right-branching | Match |
| b. | Left branching | Symmetric | Mismatch! (Unexpected %LH rise on c) |
| c. | Mixed branching (R + L) | Mixed branching | Match |
| d. | Mixed branching (L + R) | Mixed branching | Match |
| e. | Symmetric | Symmetric | Match |

The system Msp.Asp is designed to account for the observed asymmetry in the Japanese phrasing of four-word inputs, where the uniformly left-branching input is rebracketed into a symmetric prosodic phrasing, while the uniformly right-branching input is matched in the prosody. Therefore, the five four-word syntactic trees from (3) are the primary input syntactic trees to Msp.Asp (4). When the system has been fully defined and its violation tableau and typology are calculated, we will be looking for the output prosodic trees from the Prosody column of (3) in the typology, to see whether the system predicts a language with the Japanese phrasing pattern. In addition to the five four-word inputs, Msp.Asp.GEN also includes two three-word syntactic trees for completeness. The full set of inputs is shown in the Appendix.

(4)        Msp.Asp.GEN Inputs = All strictly binary-branching syntactic trees $s$ such that

      a.     $s$ contains 3–4 $X^0$s.

      b.     All terminal nodes are syntactic words $X^0$ and all non-terminal nodes are syntactic phrases XP.

      c.     The orthographic representation of the bracketing structure imposes a linear order on the leaves.

Input trees in SPOT can be constructed in two different ways. Section 12.3.1 explains the manual approach, which allows the analyst to decide exactly what trees to include, and provides a graphical tree depiction, rather than only a bracketed representation of the trees. Input syntactic trees can also be created algorithmically, as explained in §12.3.2.

### 12.3.1   *Building syntactic trees manually in SPOT*

To begin building the trees of Msp.Asp manually, find the heading **GEN: Input parameters**. By default, SPOT shows the Manual tab for this section, which is the portion needed for building trees by hand. Type the tree's terminal string, "a b c d," into "String of terminals." Click on the button "Build syntax" to open the tree builder, which will contain the seed of a four-terminal syntactic tree, as shown in (5).

(5)      Seed of a four-terminal tree

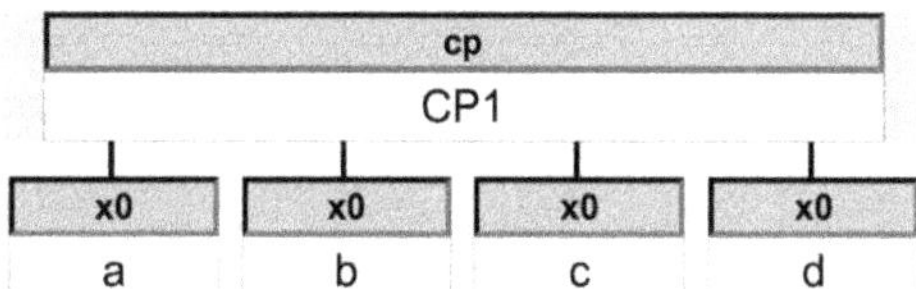

In SPOT's graphical tree representation, every node has two attributes: a category and an identifier. If the node is to be visible to the syntax–prosody mapping constraints, its category, shown with a grey background, must be 'cp' (complementizer phrase), 'xp' (syntactic phrase), or 'x0' (syntactic head). The identifier can be any alphanumeric string (no spaces or hyphens, please), and must be unique. (We give unique identifiers to the XPs as well, for ease of reference.) We use the notational convention *cat–id* to refer to specific nodes.

Our goal is to add structure to convert the seed in (5) into one of the binary-branching inputs to Msp.Asp. When building trees manually, it takes time to build each tree. To foreshadow the results of the investigation, it turns out that it is not necessary to build all seven of the inputs to Msp.Asp. When a factorial typology for Msp.Asp is calculated using the seven inputs defined in (4), it contains fourteen languages. Four of the inputs do not contribute to distinguishing between languages, however; if these redundant trees are omitted, the typology still contains the same fourteen languages. (See the Appendix for a discussion of why these trees are not informative.) The remaining three trees, shown in (6), suffice as inputs for calculating the full typology of Msp.Asp. In other words, they form a universal support for this system. Thus, to analyze this system, we only need to build the trees 4wR, 4wM, and 4wL in (6), although we can optionally also build the other trees specified by (4). The table in (7) shows traditional tree depictions of 4wR, 4wM, and 4wL, as well as the graphical depictions that SPOT's tree builder uses.

(6)      A universal support for the system Msp.Asp
   a.    [a [b [c d]]]        Four words, right-branching      = 4wR
   b.    [a [[b c] d]]        Four words, mixed-branching      = 4wM
   c.    [[[a b] c] d]        Four words, left-branching       = 4wL

(7)        Tree diagrams of the universal support for Msp.Asp

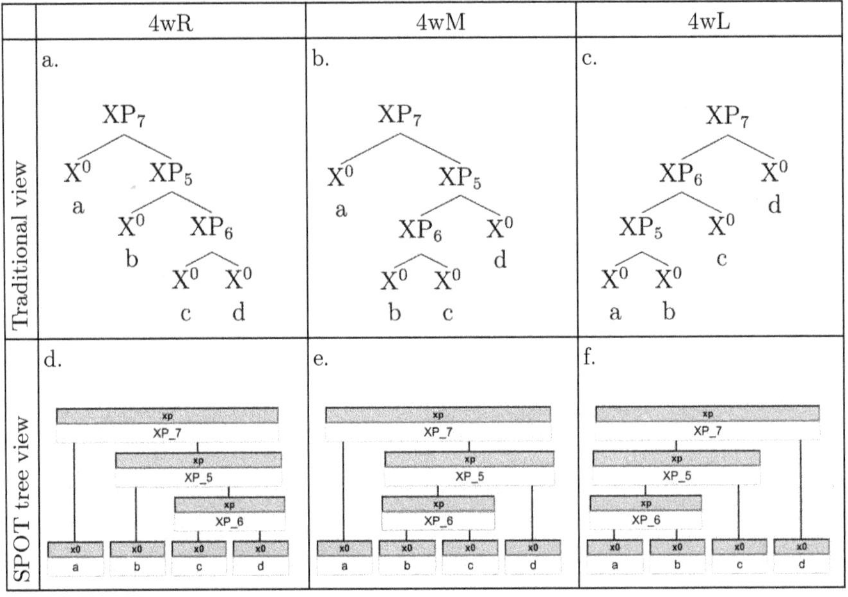

The remainder of this subsection details how to build 4wR in SPOT's manual tree builder. The root node of the tree initially has the category 'cp' and the identifier 'CP1.' Since all input syntactic trees to Msp.Asp are rooted in XPs, we need to change these labels to 'xp' and 'XP_7' (or some other identifier of your choosing), respectively. To do this, click in the text fields for *cat* and *id*, and change the text there. After relabeling the root node, the next step is to create the XP containing *x0–b, x0–c,* and *x0–d.* Hover over the space immediately surrounding node *x0–b,* and click on the grey area. This area will then turn light blue, indicating that you have selected that node. Now do the same to select *x0–c* and *x0–d.* Finally, click "Add Mother." This will create the node *xp–XP_ 5.* The tree should now look like (8).

(8)        With XP_5 containing *x0–b, x0–c,* and *x0–d*

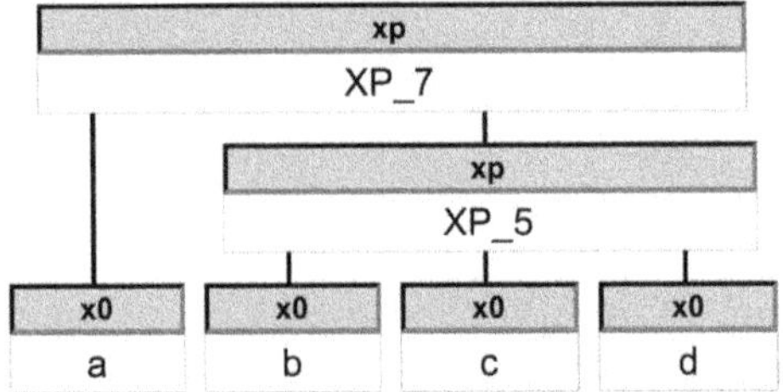

Next, create an XP above *x0–c* and *x0–d* by selecting those nodes and clicking "Add Mother" again. This XP will be labelled *XP_6*, and will complete the tree. It should look like 4wR in (7). When the tree is complete, click the button labeled "Done! Add trees to analysis" under the tree-builder. A message will appear next to it, saying, "The trees in the analysis are up-to-date." This means SPOT has translated that graphical tree representation into a JavaScript tree object. Its code can be viewed using the "Show code" toggle switch below the "Done!" button.

To create another tree, put the terminal string for your tree in the "String of terminals" box, and click on "Build syntax" again. The seed of a second tree will appear below the one you already built. Add additional structure using the same procedures as above, to create the other two trees of the universal support (4wM and 4wL).

Although not necessary for Msp.Asp, it is possible to add additional information to the trees, such as labeling some nodes as being functional projections, having silent heads, being accented, or bearing semantic focus. SPOT includes constraints that are sensitive to each of these features. For example, MATCH and ALIGN can be set to ignore nodes marked as functional to implement MATCH-LEXICALPHRASE. ALIGN-FOCUS (Truckenbrodt 1999), located in the "Show more" section of SPOT's Align/Wrap, is sensitive to focus marking in the syntactic inputs; ACCENTASHEAD and NOLAPSE (Ito and Mester 2013), under Pitch Accent, are sensitive to accent marking. Click on the info button immediately above the tree builder, next to the "Clear selection" button, to access information about how to add these features to a tree you have created.

Another feature available in the Manual tab of **GEN: Input parameters** is "Trim syntactic tree." If this is checked, SPOT prunes an elaborated syntactic tree down to only the structure that is visible to the mapping constraints in the version of MATCH proposed by Elfner (2012). Further details about this can be accessed on the SPOT interface using the information button next to "Trim syntactic tree" immediately above the tree-builder. Trimming will not alter the trees in Msp.Asp, however, since they do not contain any phonologically empty elements.

### 12.3.2 *Building syntactic trees automatically in SPOT*

The alternative to manual tree building is to use SPOT's syntactic tree generation algorithm. The primary theoretical advantage to building the trees algorithmically is that the analyst can be sure of having formally defined the space of inputs. However, algorithmically generating input trees offers less fine-grained control over input representations, since it is not possible to adjust individual trees, nor is it possible to label projections as functional or silent. An obvious practical advantage of automated tree generation is that it is much quicker than manual tree creation. This section, therefore, explains how to use SPOT's syntactic GEN algorithm to build all seven inputs to Msp.Asp, not only the three trees of the universal support.

To begin, click on the Automatic tab under **GEN: Input parameters**. Leave everything under **Syntax Parameters** on its default settings for this system. These parameters can be adjusted to exclude adjunction structures, root syntactic trees in the CP level rather than XP, restrict head alignment, and so on.

Click on **Visibility to phonology** to expand it, and check 'Treat non-branching XPs as X0s." This excludes non-branching XPs from the syntactic representation as an analytical simplification; it is not meant as a theoretical claim. It is equivalent to generating the subset of a system without this assumption in which BINMIN-$\varphi \gg$ MATCHXP.

Next, provide SPOT with the terminal strings for the input trees in Msp.Asp. The inputs have either three or four terminals, which we arbitrarily label 'a b c" and 'a b c d." To add the terminal strings, under **Specify terminals**, type 'a b c" in the box labeled 'String of terminals 1." Then click "Add terminal string" and type 'a b c d" in the box labeled 'String of terminals 2." SPOT now has all the necessary information to build the input trees. Click the orange button marked 'Generate trees." In the text area below, a table that looks like (9) should appear. These are bracket representations of the syntactic trees for Msp.Asp. Square brackets [ ] stand for XP boundaries, and the terminals a, b, c, d stand for $X^0$s. Since the input syntactic trees of Msp.Asp are rooted in XPs, there are no curly braces { }, which represent CP boundaries in SPOT's bracketed representations of syntactic trees; changing the root category under **Syntax parameters** from XP to CP would alter this.

(9)       Algorithmically generated inputs for Msp.Asp

| 1. | [a [b c]] |
|---|---|
| 2. | [[a b] c] |
| 1. | [a [b [c d]]] |

$= 4\text{wR}$

| 2. | [a [[b c] d]] |
|---|---|
| 3. | [[a b] [c d]] |
| 4. | [[a [b c]] d] |
| 5. | [[[a b] c] d] |

$= 4\text{wM}$ (row 2)

$= 4\text{wL}$ (row 5)

## 12.4  Defining outputs

Now that the syntactic tree inputs to GEN have been defined, we turn to defining the output structures, which are prosodic trees. We formally define the output structures of the system Msp.Asp in (10).

(10)    Msp.Asp.GEN Outputs = All possible phonological phrases $\varphi$ for which

    a.    Every syntactic word $X^0$ in the input is mapped to an output phonological word $\omega$. Linear order is preserved.

    b.    All non-terminal nodes are of category $\varphi$ (represented by parentheses).

    c.    Output representations are trees with ordered leaves.

    d.    The child of a unary-branching $\varphi$ must be an $\omega$.

This set of prosodic trees can be generated in SPOT by adjusting the settings in the next section, **GEN: Output parameters**. Leave the first checkbox for '‹No prosodic recursion" unchecked, to allow recursive prosodic structures. You can check '‹Enforce headedness" and/or '‹No level-skipping (Exhaustivity)" if you like, but these will be rendered redundant by the next step.

Next, click **Prosodic categories** to show additional GEN options. This allows the user to determine the prosodic category labels for the root, intermediate, and terminal nodes. For Msp.Asp, we select $\varphi$ in the first row, under '‹Root prosodic tree in." This ensures that all output prosodic trees are rooted in $\varphi$s (phonological phrases), rather than the default $\iota$ (intonational phrase). This halves the number of output candidates (since the first node to contain all the terminals in the tree can only be a $\varphi$, rather than either a $\varphi$ or an $\iota$), and is equivalent to examining the subset of the typology in which MATCH(XP$_{\text{Max}}$) (Ishihara 2014) is undominated. Leave '‹Intermediate nodes are" and '‹Prosodic terminals are" at their default values, which are $\varphi$ and $\omega$, respectively. With these settings, only two prosodic categories ($\varphi$ and $\omega$) are included in each tree, so all structures necessarily satisfy EXHAUSTIVITY, since every word is parsed into a phonological phrase. Likewise, all candidates will necessarily satisfy HEADEDNESS, because every $\varphi$ will certainly contain at least one $\omega$.

The prosodic trees whose characteristics can be determined in this section will not be viewable until the final violation tableaux are visible, unlike the syntactic trees produced in **GEN: Input Parameters**. That is because the prosodic trees are so numerous (see (1)).

## 12.5 Selecting constraints

To define a system and generate violation tableaux, we must also include a constraint set. We define CON in Msp.Asp as in (11). This CON includes both MATCH and ALIGN constraints, as well as three constraints on BINARITY, because of the asymmetries in Japanese phonological phrasing, which were noted in the discussion of (3) (see also: Kalivoda, Chapter 7; Bellik et al., 2022). The constraints are defined and motivated below, and the mechanisms for selecting them in SPOT are outlined in §12.5.1 and §12.5.2.

(11)  Msp.Asp.CON
   a.  Mapping constraints
      i.  MATCH(XP,$\varphi$) Assign one violation for every node of category XP in the syntactic tree such that there is no node of category $\varphi$ in the prosodic tree that dominates all and only the same terminal nodes.
      ii.  ALIGN(XP,L,$\varphi$,L) Assign a violation for every syntactic node of category XP whose left edge is not aligned with the left edge of a prosodic node of category $\varphi$.
      iii.  ALIGN(XP,R,$\varphi$,R) Assign a violation for every syntactic node of category XP whose right edge is not aligned with the right edge of a prosodic node of category $\varphi$.
   b.  Markedness constraints
      i.  BINMIN($\varphi$,branches) Assign one violation for every node of category $\varphi$ in the prosodic tree that has less than two children.
      ii.  BINMAX($\varphi$,branches) Assign one violation for every node of category $\varphi$ in the prosodic tree that has more than two children.
      iii.  BINMAX($\varphi$,$\omega$) Assign one violation for every node of category $\varphi$ in the prosodic tree that dominates more than two nodes of category $\omega$.

In the Japanese phrasing pattern that this constraint set is designed to account for, a uniformly left-branching input syntax is rebracketed into a balanced, symmetric prosody (12a). This rebracketing has previously been analyzed with combinations of MATCH and BINARITY constraints (Ishihara 2014, Ito and Mester 2013, Kalivoda 2018, Selkirk 2011). However, as detailed in Bellik et al. (2022), existing analyses fall short when other four-word syntactic structures are admitted to the candidate set. Both MATCH and BINARITY constraints are symmetric, so they cannot distinguish between the uniformly left-branching input that should be rebracketed, and the uniformly right-branching input that should be matched (12b).

(12)    Asymmetry in Japanese syntax–prosody mapping
   a.   Left-branching mismatch:  [[[a b] c] d] → ((a b)(c d))
   b.   Right-branching match:   [a [b [c d]]] → (a (b (c d))

Existing asymmetric markedness constraints such as STRONGSTART cannot solve this problem, so we introduce asymmetric mapping constraints in the form of Alignment to resolve the matter. We refer the reader to Bellik et al. (2022) for a full explanation of the typology and findings from this system.

### 12.5.1   Selecting mapping constraints

To add the mapping constraints to Msp.Asp on the SPOT interface, scroll down to **Mapping constraints**, then click **Match** to view the Match Theory constraints. All constraint definitions can be seen on the interface by clicking on the information buttons next to each constraint name. Mark the checkbox for "Match(Syntax→Prosody)" to add MATCH(XP, φ) to the analysis. We will keep the default category, "XP." Although we will not use them in Msp.Asp, other MATCH constraints are available in SPOT, and can be accessed by clicking "Show more" at the bottom of the **Match** section.

Next, click **Align/Wrap** to view alignment constraints. Select two constraints: "Align-Left(Syntax→Prosody)" and "Align-Right(Syntax→Prosody)." Keep the default category "XP" for these too. As with MATCH, other versions of ALIGN become available by clicking "Show more."

### 12.5.2   Selecting markedness constraints

Markedness constraints can be added in the same manner. Under **Markedness constraints**, click **Binarity** to view the binarity constraints. Under *...counting branches,* select "BinMin(branches)" and "BinMax(branches)." Under *...counting leaves,* select "BinMax(leaves)." Leave the default category settings at "φ."

Numerous other versions of both Binarity and other prosodic well-formedness constraints, such as EQUALSISTERS, STRONGSTART, and ACCENTASHEAD are available on SPOT as well, but do not feature in Msp.Asp.Con. To request a constraint or feature currently missing from SPOT, email the first author or submit an issue on Github (https://github.com/syntax-prosody-ot/main/issues).

## 12.6    Violation tableaux and typology

At this point, both GEN and CON are defined, so the system definition on
SPOT is complete. Scroll to the bottom of the interface and click the **Get
results** button to download and view the violation tableaux. If you have
followed the instructions in both §12.3.1 and 12.3.2, and therefore have
inputs in both the **Manual** and **Automatic** tabs, you will be prompted to choose
whether to use only the manually defined trees, only the algorithmically
defined trees, or both. After this, a dialog box will appear asking if you
want to save the violation tableau as a .csv file; save it for importing into
OTWorkplace or another OT tool of your choice.

Another option is to click on the **Save** button to download these settings
as a .spot file, in case you want to load them again later. (Since .spot files
are plain text, they can be viewed in any text editor.) You can use the **Load**
button on SPOT (also at the bottom of the page, next to **Save**) to upload
this analysis again at another time to regenerate the violation tableaux or
revise the analysis.

Once you have downloaded the violation tableaux, continue the investigation by opening OTWorkplace (Prince et al. 2007-2020; https://sites.google.
com/site/otworkplace/) and importing the .csv into Excel. (Alternatively,
open the .csv in Excel and then open OTWorkplace, or open the .csv in
another editor, select all, and copy-paste to add it to OTWorkplace.) Click
"**Add ins**" to display the OTWorkplace menu. Under **OTWorkplace**, click "**Project start...**" and name the new project. To calculate the factorial typology,
under OTWorkplace, click "**Factorial typology > FacTyp Calculate**." OTWorkplace will generate the typology predicted by Msp.Asp, which has fourteen
languages; one contains the Japanese phrasing pattern shown in (3).

For more on typologies and languages in OT, see Introduction (Chapter
1), as well as Prince (2017a, b) and Alber et al. (2016).


## 12.7    Conclusion

SPOT makes it easy to quickly create complete violation tableaux for an
OT analysis of syntax-prosody interactions. SPOT implements many of
the commonly used constraints in syntax–prosody mapping, including
constraints from both Match Theory and Align Theory, so that analyses
couched in both frameworks can be created and compared directly. In fact,
the system created here (Msp.Asp) is but one of several that we compared
in Bellik et al. (2022), a selection of which can be accessed via the **Built-in
systems** menu at the top of the SPOT interface. Msp.Asp is represented
there as "**Japanese ✓: MatchSP, AlignSP**" (Bellik, Ito, Kalivoda, and Mester,

2022); selecting that menu item is a shortcut to bringing up the entire system. Others can also be selected to view alternative analyses that do (✓) or do not (✗) capture the asymmetric Japanese phrasing pattern.

The violation tableaux created by SPOT can be analyzed by hand, but ideally, they should be imported into other software for Optimality Theory analyses, such as OTWorkplace or OTSoft, which can quickly generate the typologies that those systems predict. This is the method by which all the analyses in this volume were created. By combining SPOT with OT software, syntax-prosody analysts can create more theoretically rigorous analyses of phenomena at the syntax-prosody interface.

## References

Alber, Birgit, Delbusso, Natalie, and Prince, Alan (2016). From intensional properties to universal support. *Language* 92: e88–e116.

Bane, Max and Riggle, Jason (2012). Consequences of candidate omission. *Linguistic Inquiry* 43: 695–706.

Bellik, Jennifer, Bellik, Ozan, and Kalivoda, Nick (2015-2021). Syntax-Prosody in Optimality Theory (SPOT). Javascript application. http:// spot.sites.ucsc.edu. Codebase at https://github.com/syntax-prosody-ot.

Bellik, Jennifer, Ito, Junko, Kalivoda, Nick and Mester, Armin (2022). Matching and alignment. In Haruo Kubozono, Junko Ito, and Armin Mester (eds.) *Prosody and Prosodic Interfaces* 457–481. Oxford University Press.

Elfner, Emily (2012). *Syntax-Prosody Interactions in Irish*. PhD dissertation, University of Massachusetts Amherst.

Ishihara, Shinichiro (2014). Match theory and the recursivity problem. In Shigeto Kawahara and Mika Igarashi (eds.) *MIT Working Papers in Linguistics 73: Proceedings of Formal Approaches to Japanese linguistics 7* 69–88. Cambridge, MA.

Ito, Junko and Mester, Armin (1992/2003). Weak layering and word binarity. In Takeru Honma, Masao Okazaki, Toshiyuki Tabata and Shin-ichi Tanaka (eds.) *A New Century of Phonology and Phonological Theory: A Festschrift for Professor Shosuke Haraguchi on the Occasion of His Sixtieth Birthday* 26–65. Tokyo: Kaitakusha.

Ito, Junko and Mester, Armin (2013). Prosodic subcategories in Japanese. *Lingua* 124: 20–40.

Karttunen, Lauri (2006). The insufficiency of paper-and-pencil linguistics: the case of Finnish prosody. In Miriam Butt, Mary Dalrymple, and Tracy Holloway King (eds.) *Intelligent Linguistic Architectures: Variations on Themes by Ronald M. Kaplan* 287-300. Stanford: CSLI.

Kubozono, Haruo (1989). Syntactic and rhythmic effects on downstep in Japanese. *Phonology* 6: 39–67.

Nespor, Marina and Vogel, Irene (1986). *Prosodic Phonology*. Dordrecht: Foris.

Prince, Alan (2017a). What is OT? ROA 1271, Rutgers Optimality Archive, http://roa.rutgers.edu.

Prince, Alan (2017b). OT Checklist. ROA 1306, Rutgers Optimality Archive, http://roa.rutgers.edu.

Prince, Alan, Merchant, Nazarré, and Tesar, Bruce (2007–2020). OTWorkplace. http://sites.google.com/site/otworkplace

Selkirk, Elisabeth (1980). Prosodic domains in phonology: Sanskrit revisited. In Mark Aronoff and Mary-Louise Kean (eds.) *Juncture 7* 107–129. Saratoga, CA: Anma Libri.

Selkirk, Elisabeth (1981). On prosodic structure and its relation to syntactic structure. In Thorstein Fretheim (ed.) *Nordic Prosody* 111–140. Trondheim: TAPIR.

Selkirk, Elisabeth (1984). *Phonology and Syntax: the Relation between Sound and Structure.* Cambridge, MA: MIT Press.

Truckenbrodt, Hubert (1999). On the relation between syntactic phrases and phonological phrases. *Linguistic Inquiry* 30: 219–255.

## About the authors

*Jennifer Bellik*

Postdoctoral researcher and lecturer, Department of Linguistics, UC Santa Cruz. Research interests: syntax-prosody interface, Optimality Theory, Articulatory Phonology, and Turkish phonology. Recent publications: "An acoustic study of vowel intrusion in Turkish onset clusters", *Laboratory Phonology* 2018; "Automated tableau generation with SPOT" with N. Kalivoda, *Linguistics Vanguard* 2019; and "The effect of speech style and deaccentuation on vowel intrusion in Turkish complex onsets", *Proceedings of ICPhS* 2019.

*Nick Kalivoda*

Postdoctoral researcher, Centre for Languages and Literature, Lund University. Research interests: syntax–prosody interface, syntax, phonology, and Optimality Theory. Recent publications: "Automated tableau generation using SPOT (Syntax Prosody in Optimality Theory)", with J. Bellik, *Linguistics Vanguard* 2019, "XP- and X⁰-movement in the Latin verb: Evidence from mirroring and anti-mirroring" with E. Zyman, *Glossa* 2020, and "Match Theory: An overview", with S. Ishihara, *Language and Linguistics Compass* 2022.

**Appendix: Other inputs in Msp.Asp**

Msp.Asp as defined above has seven inputs, those in the 3w and 4w columns. Logically, we could also expand its input set to include analogous trees with one and two terminals, those in the 1w and 2w columns in (13). The number of inputs on $n$ words is Catalan number $n{-}1$. The $n$th Catalan number is $\frac{(2n)!}{(n+1)!\,n!}$ for $n{\geq}0$, and 1 for $n{=}0$.

(13)     All inputs of Msp.Asp

| 1w | 2w | 3w | 4w |
|---|---|---|---|
| [a] | [a b] | [a [b c]] | [a [b [c d]]] |
| | | [[a b] c] | [a [[b c] d]] |
| | | | [[a b] [c d]] |
| | | | [[a [b c]] d] |
| | | | [[[a b] c] d] |

We have calculated Msp.Asp with all of the inputs, and its factorial typology contains the 14 languages we just encountered with only three inputs (4wR, 4wM, 4wL). By removing inputs, we show that [a [b [c d]]], [[[a b] c] d], and one of either [a [[b c] d]] or [[a [b c]] d] are a universal support for Msp.Asp. As for the other inputs, the reasons they are redundant are explained in (14).

(14)     Redundant inputs

| Input | Comment |
|---|---|
| [a] | Msp.Asp.GEN admits only one candidate for this cset: [a]→(a) |
| [a b] | Only 1 candidate in the cset is an optimum: [a b]→(a b) |
| [a [b c]] | Only 1 candidate in the cset is an optimum: [a [b c]]→(a (b c)) |
| [[a b] c] | Only 1 candidate in the cset is an optimum: [[a b] c]→((a b) c) |
| [[a b] [c d]] | Only 1 candidate in the cset is an optimum: [[a b] [c d]]→((a b) (c d)) |
| [[a [b c]] d] | In every language, this input behaves the same way as [a [[b c] d]]. *Matching case:* If [a [[b c] d]]→(a ((b c) d)) is optimal, [[a [b c]] d]→((a (b c)) d) is optimal. *Squishing case:* If [a [[b c] d]]→(a (b c) d) is optimal, [[a [b c]] d]→(a (b c) d) is optimal. *Rebracketing case:* If [a [[b c] d]]→((a b) (c d)) is optimal, [[a [b c]] d]→((a b) (c d)) is optimal. |

# Index

www.ingramcontent.com/pod-product-compliance
Lightning Source LLC
Chambersburg PA
CBHW040215280725
30044CB00001B/3